THE LAST
BOURBONS OF NAPLES
(1825–1861)

Ferdinand II

[*Frontispiece*

THE
LAST BOURBONS
OF NAPLES

(1825–1861)

BY

HAROLD ACTON

METHUEN AND CO LTD

36 ESSEX STREET · STRAND · LONDON W.C.2

First published 1961
© 1961 by Harold Acton
Printed in Great Britain
by Hazell Watson & Viney Ltd
Aylesbury and Slough
Cat. No. 2/6463/1

CONTENTS

v

His recall from Sicily—Apotheosis of Bellini and Sicilian patriotism—The
Count of Syracuse marries—Birth of the Hereditary Prince Francis and
death of Maria Cristina—Miracles attributed to her.

CHAPTER V

CHAPTER VI

CHAPTER VII

CHAPTER VIII

ILLUSTRATIONS

xi

NOTE AND
ACKNOWLEDGEMENTS

AS in my former volume, *The Bourbons of Naples*, I have limited
footnotes to the bare minimum and provided a bibliography for
the benefit of students. In reply to several requests I have added
a brief genealogical table of Francis I's descendants without entering
into remote minutiae. Owing to the *Risorgimento* the wealth of literature dealing with this period is infinitely greater, more complex and
controversial. Many a volume deals with a single year, 1848, and even
with a single day, May 15. May the gentle reader bear in mind that my
subject is the ruling dynasty of Bourbons: if I have trespassed on
Trevelyan territory or into the intricate maze so brilliantly elucidated
by Mr Denis Mack Smith in *Cavour and Garibaldi 1860, A Study in
Political Conflict*, it has been with reluctance, for I am not concerned
with nationalism. The general tendency, as Mr Mack Smith has
suggested, is to justify the victors and to damn or forget the defeated.
I have tried to restore the balance.

I must again repeat grateful acknowledgements for the kind
assistance rendered in so many ways by Ferdinando Acton, Prince of
Leporano; the late Count Riccardo Filangieri, former director and
guiding spirit of the *Grande Archivio*, and to his courteous and helpful
successor, Dottoressa Iole Mazzoleni; Professor Ernesto Pontieri, the
director of the *Società Napoletana di Storia Patria*, that unique and
most hospitable institution for the study of Neapolitan history, and
his colleagues Professor Alfredo Parente and Signora Olga Quarta;
Letizia Carafa, Duchess of Andria, and her son Riccardo; Prince and
Princess d'Avalos, for the loan of the Prince of Capua's letters; Maria,
Duchess of San Cesario, who allowed me to reproduce the portrait
of Queen Maria Sophia recently in her possession and supplied me
with other rare photographs; Baroness Gabriella Barracco; Signora
Giulia Betocchi and her daughters Signora Clotilde Marghieri and

Signora Rosanna Parascandolo; Mme Grüber-Meuricoffre; the ever hospitable Count Paolo Gaetani; Doctor Gino Doria, director of the Museum of San Martino; Doctor Bruno Molajoli, the director, creator and impresario of the Museum of Capodimonte; Doctor Augusto Cesareo; Professor Mario Praz; Signor Salvatore Cafiero; and my good friends Professor and Madame Jean Pasquier, of the Institut Français de Naples. But I am doubtless indebted to more Neapolitans than I can mention here, and I must thank these en masse.

Among English friends I must again express my special gratitude to Mr Noel Blakiston, Head of the Research Department, Public Record Office, London, for his unfailing courtesy to a distant client; to Miss Margaret Franklin for her patient, skilful and sympathetic collaboration in transmitting valuable excerpts from F.O. 70/110–321; to Lady Berwick for permission to quote from the papers at Attingham Park; to Sir Osbert Sitwell for his constant encouragement; to Mr John Pope-Hennessy of the Victoria and Albert Museum; to Mr John Raymond and to Mr Reginald Colby for innumerable kindnesses. I must also thank Mr Robert D. Brewster, of New York, for trusting me with the letters of his ancestor Enos Throop, Governor of New York 1829–33, and chargé d'affaires at Naples 1838–42.

Florence, September 1960

INTRODUCTION

THE uncrowned Queen of Honolulu said to me: 'You have told us enough about the Bourbons to last a lifetime. Actually I don't think I should care to meet any of them. Why not turn to a more appetizing subject?' This gave me food for serious thought. In fact I was perturbed. For alas, she had spoken too late: the book was written. Another objection troubled me less: that for a professed aesthete I chose the most hideous people to write about, the big-nosed Bourbons and the heavy-jowled last Medici. So often the beautiful people are profoundly boring apart from the things that happen to them. Besides, they are too safe an investment from a literary point of view. Helen of Troy will ever find fresh devotees. And I sincerely believe that the Bourbons had a strange beauty of their own.

A writer becomes used to hearing compliments and reading complaints about his work. Without boasting, I may state that the majority of critics, including my kind publisher, persuaded me to continue the story of the Bourbons of Naples. It would have been churlish not to oblige them when the material was sitting in my cupboard. Moreover the story seemed worth telling for its own sake even if various episodes were familiar owing to their clinking connection with the Risorgimento.

King Ferdinand II, alias 'Bomba', has exerted a grudging fascination on students of royalty since Sir Osbert Sitwell introduced him with Hogarthian relish and much poetic licence into his delightful *Discursions*. Monsters can be fascinating, and during his heyday Ferdinand had been turned into a monster by the European press. He knew it; and he pretended not to care. '*L'avversione non pur d'Italia, ma di Europa*'—how often was this said of him! It is a pity to destroy a romantic myth, but on closer scrutiny Ferdinand becomes more prosaic. He had a coarse geniality quite *sui generis*, but he lacked the charm of his eccentric grandfather, who told petitioners pestering him for a Constitution: 'Yes, my children, I shall give you a Constitution, I shall even give you two. . . .'

When he succeeded his feeble father at the age of twenty Ferdinand II was mistaken for a liberal merely because he was progressive and familiar with the people. The decade of French occupation had improved bureaucratic administration but had left an aftermath of Carbonarism and conspiracy. The malcontents were mostly drawn from the middle class, civil servants who had been dismissed under the restoration and soldiers who had fought under the tricolour. Ferdinand reinstated the cleverest of these and rallied Murat's best officers round his banner; hence the army's loyalty during the twenty-nine years of his reign. A stringent economy was enforced in private and public. Although he suffered from epilepsy he was here, there and everywhere, energetic, frugal, yet popular with the masses. While sharing Metternich's ideas, he resented any form of foreign interference. He was never a satellite of Austria or of any other power. Independence was his watchword, and Naples remained independent during his lifetime.

Materially Naples contributed more than any other State towards the wealth of United Italy, and the facts and figures have all been published by Francesco Saverio Nitti in *Nord e Sud* (1900), as well as in other writings which have not been contradicted. In his *Scienza delle Finanze* Nitti gave the following summary of the wealth of the different States at the time of unification: Kingdom of the Two Sicilies: gold millions of *lire* 443,2; Lombardy: 8,1; Duchy of Modena: 0,4; Romagna, the Marches and Umbria: 55,3; Parma and Piacenza: 1,2; Rome: 35,3; Piedmont, Liguria and Sardinia: 27,0; Tuscany: 84,2; Venetia: 12,7. Thus in contrast with the 443 gold millions contributed towards the nuptials by the kingdom of the Two Sicilies, the rest of Italy—more than two-thirds of the peninsula—did not even supply half that dowry. On the whole the finances of Naples were ably administered, in spite of allegations to the contrary. And in spite of civil war, cholera, and the earthquake in Basilicata, the total population had been tripled since Charles III conquered the kingdom. The first railway in Italy, the first electric telegraph, the first lenticular lighthouse, and a number of other precursors in engineering and industry, were due to the 'retrograde' Ferdinand, and these have been fully described by Signor Michele Vocino in his recent *Primati del Regno di Napoli*.

That his schemes for developing the country were interrupted cannot be laid to Ferdinand's charge. He was conscientious, energetic and devoutly religious. It was only the intellectuals who had cause to complain of him. Reviewing his long reign in retrospect, one wonders what those intellectuals did for Naples in comparison with Ferdinand, for all his limitations. They had their chance and lost it in 1848. The barricades of May 15 were a foolish aping of the Parisians. Considering that the English Constitution had been the work of centuries, it is hardly surprising that Naples was unprepared for such a panacea. Dr Trevelyan, who abhorred the Bourbons, has admitted: 'There was a general want of experience, and, with honourable exceptions, a general want of public spirit.' In other words, after more than a century of Bourbon rule the masses were solidly behind the King. Their public spirit was Bourbonist. They had sufficient experience to realize that there was a worse tyranny than that of kings: the tyranny of demagogues and self-seeking petty politicians.

For an autocrat with an innate conviction of his divine right Ferdinand showed remarkable forbearance until he was actually threatened with civil war. May 15 gave him a lasting shock, and other shocks were to follow, not least of which was Agesilao Milano's attempt to murder him. He reacted ruthlessly, but the political trials for which he was held up to execration by Gladstone were less harsh than those which take place in several countries to-day, and the penalties were almost humane in comparison with the scientific horrors of modern concentration camps, not to speak of the inquisitions prolonged for whole nights with the assistance of nerve-racking drugs and electricity. Most of the Neapolitan prisoners survived to tell the tale of their martyrdom and win high honours and rewards after the annexation to Piedmont.

Ferdinand II was never forgiven for his victory over the liberal-radicals: he was accused of drowning the Constitution in their blood. When he, the chief target of their onslaughts, was dead and gone, they turned and clawed each other. This is amply proved by one of them, the brilliant Petrucelli della Gattina, in his Swiftian *I Moribondi del Palazzo Carignano*. Among other liberal heroes, for instance, Carlo Poerio is dismissed as a pure invention, the typical revolutionary of the Anglo-French and Italian press. The real Poerio, who 'had been created a great man by that jester Gladstone,' took the bogus Poerio in earnest, that personage fabricated by the journalists for twelve continuous years in penny-a-line newspaper articles. Such was the triumph of a press campaign that both readers and writers who did not know Poerio took him quite seriously; and what was even more surprising Cavour took him seriously too. Petrucelli might have added that the monster 'Bomba' was also a creation of the journalists and of the jester Gladstone. It was partly Ferdinand's fault for despising them. He considered them superfluous bores and mischief-makers. Accordingly he has been traduced by the historians, most of whom, like Oriani, portrayed him as nothing but 'an Austrian viceroy, protected by the Austrians and confiding only in them.' The truth was very different; and Ferdinand thought he was defending the truth. However much we admire the Risorgimento we must realize that he had nothing to gain and everything to lose by it. His experience of the Neapolitan liberals only strengthened his innate belief in his own infallibility. He was the extreme type of possessive Neapolitan paterfamilias, conscious of his power and virility—a type by no means extinct. As a literary person no doubt I should have suffered from his scorn and suspicion had I been his contemporary, but at this safe distance one can view him dispassionately and appreciate his good qualities. If not a great monarch he did more than merely occupy his throne: he filled it to bursting point. His massive body towers above the other Italian sovereigns of his age, from Charles Albert of Savoy to the Duke of Modena, and he compares favourably with Louis-Philippe and the Austrian Emperor. He knew his own people best, as he often remarked: did others know them better? But his was the age not only of industrial and scientific progress, but also of religious and political evangelism. The evangelists decided that his people ought to be 'converted' willy-nilly. They took their text from *Samson Agonistes*:

> '*But what more oft, in nations grown corrupt,*
> *And by their vices brought to servitude,*
> *Than to love bondage more than liberty,*
> *Bondage with ease than strenuous liberty.*'

They saw vices everywhere. Naples was a Paradise inhabited by devils, of course, with the King first and foremost. The law was a dead letter, justice unobtainable, judges were bought, witnesses bribed, juries intimidated. Mr Gladstone had positively said so. Lord Palmerston and his brother Sir William Temple, Lord Minto and Lord Napier, presumed that 'strenuous liberty' was the panacea when the Neapolitans were apparently satisfied with 'bondage with ease'. They deemed it their duty to remedy this.

Without foreign interference the kingdom might have been a contented and prosperous oasis. All Ferdinand asked was to be left alone—to be allowed to conduct his affairs in the manner he as a Neapolitan considered most advisable. The rebellious minority of native intellectuals, small but vociferous, attributed everything that irked them to the existing dispensation, while for the most part what they raged against was inherent in human weakness and the special nature of the country. Gladstone himself, in his famous diatribe, noted with creditable perspicacity that Neapolitans 'are perhaps most defective in practical energy and steady perseverance in giving effect to the ideas with which their high natural intelligence abundantly supplies them. But, while they seem to me most amiable for their gentleness of tone, and for their freedom from sullenness and pride, they are, I must say, admirable in their powers of patient endurance, and for the elasticity and buoyancy, with which in them the spirit lives under a weight that would crush minds of more masculine and tougher texture, but gifted with less power of reactive play.'

The climate was probably more responsible than the Bourbons for this lack of energy and perseverance, and Vesuvius rather than Ferdinand's despotism must have helped to teach patient endurance. But their weakness was also their strength. They would only strain themselves under dire necessity. They believed in conserving their elasticity and buoyancy for life and love.

In the 1860's W. D. Howells was struck by the languor of the Neapolitan ladies as they lolled on their carriage cushions, and by the 'gloomy rings about their fine eyes, like the dark-faced dandies who bow to them. This Neapolitan look is very curious, and I have not seen it elsewhere in Italy; it is a look of peculiar pensiveness, and comes, no doubt, from the peculiarly heavy growth of lashes which fringes the lower eyelid. Then there is the weariness in it of all peoples whose summers are fierce and long.' There is some truth in this generalization even now. Too many stress the vivacity of the Neapolitan expression, exaggerating the comical grimaces and gesticulations, without noticing the wistful pensiveness of their features in repose. But the weariness is not only due to fierce long summers and the sultry scirocco: it is also that of Pater's 'Lady Lisa' somewhat simplified, the result of reveries and passions, fantastic and exquisite perhaps, but certainly more Pagan than Christian, though saturated with the sense of tears in mortal things. It is older than the volcanic rocks among which they dwell. In a different climate or environment, in Milan, London or New York, it might vanish, but it is a recurrent motive of Neapolitan poetry and song.

Even under the bruited tyranny of Ferdinand II foreign tourists were struck by the pervading spirit of primitive independence. The populace resembled their King insofar as everybody seemed to do what he felt like doing without any morbid inhibitions. In many ways they were more free than their duty-shackled sovereign. Extremes met without collision. They do still, for the nature of Neapolitans has not changed. The flamboyant cavalcade of equipages—

> *'Each harness, in arch triumphal reared*
> *With festive ribbons fluttering gay'*—

rolling in the late afternoon over the lava pavement of the Chiaia, where most of the foreign embassies were, have been replaced by shabby automobiles whose klaxons are louder but less exhilarating than the cracking of whips; Vesuvius has ceased to smoke and the lazzaroni have disappeared—those three clerical musketeers Fathers Borrelli, Spada and Bruno Scott-James are looking after the last of the *scugnizzi* until they become absorbed into respectable professions—mediæval-looking friars and nuns are becoming almost as rare as elaborate military uniforms; but the traffic has a splendid vitality all its own, and there is a wondrous individual order amid the disorder. Life on and in the streets—and what a gallimaufry of *strade, vie, vichi, vicoletti, salite, rampe, calate, gradoni*, etc, with here and there a *rua* as a record of the Angevin dynasty!—is feverish, adventurous, tragic and gay. There is nothing of the bee-hive or ant-heap here, and pray Heaven there never will be. Humanity predominates. To those who are dulled by routine, by modern mechanization, fog, smog, cold murky climates, and the *fatigue du Nord*, Naples offers an invitation to join the tarantella of the living while there is time.

If, as Shakespeare said, 'All the world's a stage, And all the men and women merely players,' the men and women on this particular stage play their rôles with a zest that is a hymn to Life. Their exits and their entrances are equally dramatic. No danger of drab monotony in Naples! When asked why or how I came to be drawn to such a subject, my answer is that I was drawn to it by a profound sympathy and liking for Neapolitans in general, apart from the aesthetic fascination of their background and the symphonic prodigality of nature surrounding it. And for better for worse, the Bourbons have identified themselves with Naples more intimately than any other royal dynasty. As is often the case, their successors tried to reap the laurels which they had planted. Hundreds of statues of Bourbon kings were desecrated and destroyed, but their public works remain, more solid than the achievements of yester-year, and their interrupted projects were developed.

Compared with the eighteenth century the nineteenth was dull from an artistic point of view: except music, the fine arts suffered, as elsewhere, from the frequent political upheavals, especially from those of 1848. Literary romanticism had flowed into Rossini's *La Donna del Lago* (1819) and Donizetti's *Lucia di Lammermoor* (1835), both inspired by Sir Walter Scott, and it continued to flow with increasing fervour into the operas of the short-lived Bellini and the long-lived Verdi, whose whole career was a crescendo of masterpieces, the most popular of which, *Rigoletto*, *Il Trovatore* and *La Traviata*, were produced during Ferdinand II's reign. None of these composers were Neapolitans, but Bellini and Donizetti both studied and won their early plaudits in the capital. Giovanni Pacini, a Sicilian like Bellini, and the Calabrian Saverio Mercadante, were the best-known composers who settled at Naples and swayed the San Carlo audiences during Ferdinand's reign. But who now remembers *La Vestale*, once highly admired as Mercadante's masterpiece, or Pacini's *La Stella di Napoli*? Perhaps Glyndebourne will revive them in the right spirit. Enrico Petrella kept up the tradition of Paisiello and Cimarosa: he too has been forgotten, whereas *Santa Lucia* and other popular songs of the period are still universal favourites.

Neo-classicism persisted in architecture and sculpture under the influence of Herculaneum and Pompeii, but Neapolitans could not do without colour, and buildings were gaily stuccoed according to the taste of the proprietor. San Francesco di Paola is often called frigid, but it is an exuberant variation on the Pantheon theme, harmonizing

xxi

with the dove-greys and Pompeian tomatoes of adjacent structures. Antonio Niccolini, who restored the San Carlo theatre and built the Floridiana, was neo-classical with a Neapolitan difference. It was after the Bourbons that bad taste set in, with the disembowelling of the mediæval section, when the rigid Rettifilo was driven through the Porto district and the neo-Renaissance pastiche of the glass-domed Galleria was piled up opposite the San Carlo theatre. But even such bad taste becomes attractive in comparison with what has gone up since the last war, such as the immense slab which has dwarfed the graceful semi-circular Piazza del Mercato, and the similar slabs along the Via Foria just beyond the old Museum. Hereabouts good building ended with the Bourbons.

The rise of the School of Posillipo in painting—it rose but never soared high—was an agreeable flight from 'the cold performances of the classic easel'. Its origin is usually traced to the Dutch open-air painter Anthony Pitloo, who was appointed professor of landscape at the Neapolitan Academy in 1816 and worked on steadily until he died of cholera in 1837. Lord Napier's critical survey of this school has not been superseded, and most of us would agree with him that Pitloo's talent is more apparent in his studies than in his finished canvases: he was a romantic impressionist of delicate sensibility, and his influence on his pupils was considerable. Smargiassi, Giacinto Gigante, and the rest have perhaps been overpraised, but none have transferred the characteristic light and colour of Neapolitan scenery onto canvas with greater success.

Giacinto Gigante at his best may be said to stand somewhere between Guardi and Turner; at his worst he is photographic. Lord Napier wrote of him that 'for freedom of handling, fidelity of colour, transparency, perspective, and effect, his studies have no parallel on his own more ambitious canvas, or on the canvas of any living painter of his country.' Smargiassi was more absorbed in the emotion that the landscape conveys, and the result is apt to be sentimental. Giambattista Vianelli was the best illustrator of popular manners and religious scenes during Ferdinand's reign, while Salvatore Fergola was the pictorial annalist of palace life, 'reducing to canvas all the hunts, launches, reviews, processions, shows, and festivities which for a series of years assembled the courtiers and the multitude: such as the inauguration of the Neapolitan railroads, and of the tournament held at

Caserta in 1846.' The four Palizzi brothers are still extensively admired, especially Filippo, who has been compared with Courbet, but his rendering of texture, wool or hair, is more skilful than his sense of construction. 'His merit,' as Napier wrote, 'is particularly apparent in the portraiture of the domestic or servile animals, arranged in simple combination with popular figures, and accompanied by landscape selected from the inland vicinity of Naples.' His less ambitious studies of goats and donkeys are superior to his large pictures of stag-hunts which found eager purchasers among American and Russian tourists. As for his 'After the Flood' at Capodimonte, it is a sort of *presepio* with every species of beast and fowl from Noah's ark crammed onto the canvas, and would be far more appropriate in some natural history museum.

Luminosity and transparency are the chief virtues of the Posillipo School of painters, whose myriad gouaches, water-colours and sepias are the most accurate pictorial records of Naples under the last Bourbons. Ferdinand II could not, as Napier wrote, extemporize great artists, but he patronized the best that the age and the country afforded. 'On such occasions His Majesty displays none of the airs of a virtuoso, but shows a natural discrimination in the discovery of faults and merits; if the work be commendable, the painter obtains a commission for another; if defective, charity often accepts what criticism would be justified in rejecting. The evidence of this generous disposition, so worthy of royalty, is to be found in the Palace at Naples, the walls of which are covered with the productions of the contemporary pencil: the landscapes, genre pieces, and subjects of small figures being reserved for the private sitting rooms and cabinets, while those of larger dimensions and more ambitious design are distributed in the public apartments. . . . It is commonly believed at Naples that the King is indebted for his love of painting to the suggestions of his former minister, Niccola Santangelo; and undoubtedly the advice of that polite and accomplished councillor was not without its influence; yet it ought to be remembered that the Neapolitan Bourbons have never been altogether careless of the fine arts, and that the reigning sovereign might naturally succeed to an inclination which his predecessors certainly possessed, and which he shares with many of his living relatives. . . .'

Those productions of the contemporary pencil were too modest for their richly gilded setting—for apartments on a scale more suited to Solimena and Luca Giordano. In the same way the Victorian simplicity of Ferdinand's family life seemed incongruous amid the architectural splendours of Caserta. But even the King's enemies were impressed by it, for it was so thoroughly respectable. Queen Victoria would have admired his morals, if not his table manners. It is indeed a pity that they were never able to meet. The Queen, like Prince Albert, utterly disapproved of Palmerston's treatment of Ferdinand, and she had no sincere liking for Gladstone. Ferdinand's exuberant presence and sense of humour might have charmed the Queen out of her stiffness and cleared the air for happier relations. Balmoral and Caserta were poles apart, but their proprietors shared an addiction to informal family life in country surroundings and to simple substantial food: they shared, above all, a strong sense of royal dignity.

It is amazing to read Ferdinand's obituary notice in *The Times* of 1859, beginning: 'Ferdinand, King of the Two Sicilies, has at length been summoned from his earthly throne to a tribunal where he will be called upon to render a stern account of his stewardship . . .' and ending: 'He caused many tears to flow during his life; few will be shed for his death.' So many governments and régimes since then might with justice be described not only as the negation of God but as the negation of Everything that such rhetoric rings hollow. Tears for his death were shed in abundance during the chaos that followed it, when the *camorra* invaded the former capital and brigandage ran amok in the provinces.

Ferdinand II had been the keystone of an arch which collapsed soon after his demise. It had lasted 126 years. Maybe the moral is that individual men are not meant to be keystones. 'It is useless,' as Metternich wrote, 'to close the gates against ideas; they overleap them.' The ideas overleapt the gates closed by Ferdinand when Francis II succeeded him at the age of twenty-three. The brief disastrous reign of the too tolerant and gentle 'Son of the Saint' ended heroically with the long siege of Gaeta, which did not fall till February 13, 1861. The dignity of the defeated King and his brave and beautiful young Queen deserves a poetic treatment beyond my talents. I have to console myself with a quotation from Carlyle: 'History after all is the true Poetry; Reality, if rightly interpreted, is grander than Fiction; nay even, in the right interpretation of Reality and History, does genuine Poetry lie.' And I trust I may claim without arrogance that mine is the right interpretation of the history of the Bourbons of Naples.

I

THE brief reign of Francis I might best be described as an interregnum between the death of his fantastic old father and the accession of his dynamic son. Most of the time others ruled for him while he busied himself with trifling bureaucratic details. Luigi de' Medici governed the State and the King's valet Viglia governed the royal palace, while Francis fondly imagined that he controlled everything and everybody and wielded supreme authority.

Owing to the King's weakness of character and constitution his ministers became more powerful and the foreign ambassadors more domineering. In order to govern without interference Medici made a cynical compromise with the Court *camarilla*, as ignorant and as corrupt a set as ever surrounded any king, allowing them to glut their greed at the country's expense without a murmur. While he shut his eyes on their illicit gains he did succeed in getting rid of the Austrian troops. As Metternich was anxious for the latter to remain in the kingdom this was no mean achievement.

But a rot set in the body politic which was hard to extirpate. More than ever before gratuities—*regalie*—were typical of every government department, and the Neapolitan citizen became so inured to them that he regarded them as reasonable, fair and honest. Unfortunately this led to a popular conviction that everything could be bought and sold, from the favours of celestial saints to those of earthly sinners. As Mariano d'Ayala wrote,[1] the King and his ministers dispensed favours instead of administering justice. Officials all the way down the social scale, with few exceptions, did the citizens a favour in performing their ordinary duty, and they expected a corresponding reward. It was like the 'squeeze' of Chinese mandarins.

Gratuities were not necessarily paid in hard cash—often groceries, the products of the farm or market-garden, or the client's handiwork, the painter's picture, were equally acceptable. There was tolerance and understanding in these matters: each according to his capacity. Hence a certain venality became endemic. Employees with a monthly salary of six ducats (19/6d) managed to live quite comfortably and rear large families. Since salaries were low the office door was left open, as it were, for all sorts of contraband. 'One hand washes the other' became a respected maxim which nobody would venture to criticize, especially at Court, and the wheels of the government machine thus frequently oiled went smoothly round with an endless exchange of personal services big and small. Every other man had his price, but on lower levels he was ready to bargain and, at a pinch, be satisfied to ask less from those who could not afford it. This was anti-social behaviour perhaps, according to our purified standards, but it contributed towards much sociability. To guess, to calculate, to lay wagers on the other fellow's expectations and pretensions—all this could be very interesting and instructive and even fun of a kind. It added a pungent zest to daily life and turned nearly everyone into a student of psychology. And having experienced the joy or sadness of discovery—(So-and-so will be satisfied with such-and-such: who'd have imagined it! Or, he won't take a penny less than such-and-such, the cormorant!)—he went on his way a wiser if not a more cynical man, for he had also amassed more knowledge of human values.

Francis I was aged forty-seven when he succeeded to the throne of the Two Sicilies in January 1825, but he appeared more than a decade older. His astute father had often saddled him with his own responsibilities in a crisis and he had been a model son, conscientious to a morbid degree. Yet his filial devotion had endeared him to neither of his parents. His corpulent, genial and wildly extravagant younger brother Leopold, Prince of Salerno, had been their favourite, but he had never

[1] *Memorie di Mariano d'Ayala e del suo tempo, scritte del figlio Michelangelo.* Rome, 1886.

been put to any severe test beyond having to smile in public. Francis had had to bear the brunt of unpopular measures in Sicily and in Naples. He had started with liberal inclinations, but these had been slowly stifled by bitter experience.

An affectionate husband and father, all his virtues were domestic. Like his grandfather he was uxorious and humbly devout; if he had any temptations to philander he firmly resisted them. He had been deeply attached to his first wife but had remarried soon after her death because he could not endure celibacy. His second wife the Infanta Maria Isabella bore him twelve children but always remained somewhat infantile. A large, heavy man, shambling and stooping, with an assumed expression of benevolence, his bulging eyes were sad and suspicious and his flabby cheeks suggested a want of energy. He was more cultured but he had less character than his father; he loved the fine arts, or what passed as such in a tritely academic period; he cherished the classics he had been taught in early youth and often quoted their platitudes with unction, while agriculture was his special hobby. His tastes were simple. Usually he wore an ill-fitting colonel's uniform without epaulettes; for Court functions he donned the order of Saint Januarius; but whatever his garb he remained awkward and ungainly.

Lady Blessington, who had been taken by General Church to inspect the remains of the late King lying in state in the royal palace, remarked that 'the silver tears on the hangings were the only ones I witnessed in the chamber of death; and it struck me that they were a happy invention for such occasions. As dead kings are rarely wept for, their disappointed subjects (and how many of them, even under the sway of the best sovereigns, are to be found!) look to his successor for the fulfilment of their frustrated expectations, which the new one, in his turn, is probably destined to equally disappoint.' Many who had supported the 1820 revolution were feeling repentant. The expensive Austrian occupation was the deplorable result of their folly. Francis hoped to get rid of these troops as soon as possible, especially when he discovered that his father had had to pay for many more than had ever been in the country.

Opposition to the Bourbon dynasty in the capital was limited to a few exclusive coteries, which were apt to consume their ardour for a Constitution in idle chatter: they were not prepared for any drastic

3

effort. The majority desired a peaceful, paternal government, a return to the tolerant system which the Carbonari had wrecked. The frustrated Murattists hoped for a 'new deal'. The royal edict announcing the succession of Francis I contained no hint of administrative reform, but even the optimists realized that this would be premature with Austrian troops in the country.

After three days of lying in state on a catafalque of cloth of gold and silver with large plumes foaming at the four corners, surmounted by a royal crown, surrounded by officers and Court chamberlains in blackest mourning, the late King was buried in Santa Chiara.

As soon as Francis returned to the royal palace from Capodimonte he was busy with audiences, affable to all, quite needlessly so, it was thought, in his expressions of goodwill to the Austrians. Homage in verse and prose poured in from all quarters, especially from those who wished to ingratiate themselves with the new sovereign. The former ministry remained intact, presided over by Luigi de' Medici and Donato Tommasi, with Nicola Intonti as minister of police. Intonti had fallen ill just before the death of Ferdinand, who had sent him an image of the Madonna with a request to bring it back to him as soon as he recovered. The next council he attended was held by Francis, who had an exaggerated opinion of his merits.

The Austrian occupation absorbed nearly one-fifth of the national revenue, and Medici had a hard struggle to keep the country's finances afloat. Though indebted to Austrian sponsorship for his return to power, he never stopped protesting that their army was ruining the kingdom. Neapolitan officials whose salaries had been cut by ten per cent. were all the more bitter since it was an open secret that the Austrian government had saved over six million florins out of the sums extracted from Naples. Medici enforced retrenchment in every department. Carl Meyer Rothschild, who had established a branch of his family bank in Naples, contrived, as Count Corti wrote, 'to make himself indispensable to the Neapolitan Court in financial matters'.[1] If the national budget were wholly disorganized the loans handled and issued by his bank would decline seriously in value. He was therefore as anxious as Medici for a speedy evacuation.

The Emperor of Austria had awarded Francis the Grand Cross of Saint Stephen of Hungary as a public token of friendship and invited

[1] Count Corti, *The Rise of the House of Rothschild*. London, 1928.

4

him to a meeting in Milan. In his letter of acceptance, Francis said he intended to follow in his august father's footsteps, perfect his administration, and improve his army. His eldest son Ferdinand, the young Duke of Calabria, was to act as regent on ceremonial occasions during his absence, but all the protocols of the Council were to be sent to Milan for his approval.

Metternich maintained that the military occupation of Naples was the only guarantee for peace in Italy. 'The worst of evils,' he wrote,[1] 'which may be considered as incurable in the kingdom of the Two Sicilies, is the corruption and venality rife among nearly all members of the administration. Public opinion there is becoming increasingly vicious and depraved. The King vacillates without principles; his ministers do likewise; the immoral government inspires neither respect nor awe; the army seduced by sects affords no protection.' He felt certain that the Two Sicilies were drifting into a second revolution. But Austria could not stand aside and allow so great a calamity to be repeated. Unfortunately the Neapolitans were not in the least grateful for all the help he had given them.

To please Metternich, Francis should have asked for the foreign occupation to be prolonged. The spectre of revolution was always dangled before him as a scarecrow, but Medici was too exasperated by his financial problems to care.

His sister Marie Amélie was the first to disapprove of her brother's prospective visit to Milan: 'In the sincerity of my heart I must own that this journey at this particular moment displeases me because it seems a sort of summons to vassals. You might have explained that the enormous cost of foreign occupation forced you to economize. . . . But if you have decided to go you have done it for your good and that of your subjects, and perhaps you have better reason than I who only judge things by my own ideas and instincts, and I hope you will forgive my friendly motives for telling you all I think.' But Francis thought something might be achieved by personal negotiation.

He set out with the Queen and his one year old son, the Count of Aquila, accompanied by a small suite. The journey was leisurely and he was a methodical sightseer, but his diary is not very interesting. In Rome the Pope gave him a relic of the Cross; from there he went on

<hr />

[1] Bianchi, Nicomede, *Storia documentata della Diplomazia Europea in Italia dell'anno 1814 all'anno 1861*. Vol. II, p. 228.

to visit Assisi, the home of his Saint, whose greatness he never understood; in Arezzo he admired 'a perfect Gothic church' and 'a superb Vasari in the refectory of the Benedictine monastery' as well as a remarkable *trompe-l'œil* fresco by the Jesuit del Pozzo; outside Florence the luxuriant farms appealed to him, '*campagne stupende coltivate a meraviglia*', he noted, and the 'magnificent park in English style with a wall running round it' at Pratolino. Though the Queen suffered frequently from convulsions and leeches were applied to her gums for toothache she was able to nurse the baby. After two weeks in Milan a convention was signed by the Austrian ambassador Ficquelmont and Medici. The Austrian troops were to remain in the kingdom until March 1827, but they were to be reduced to 12,000 as soon as the Neapolitan forces could guarantee public order, and the first contingent was to leave before the end of 1825. When the royal party returned on July 18, William Noel Hill, the British minister, observed that their reception was even more lukewarm than he had expected. 'The city was illuminated by previous order from the police, and strictly enforced ... the great theatre of San Carlo was also illuminated, yet there was little or no applause on the appearance of the royal family, and all seemed heartless and cheerless.'

William Noel Hill, who eventually succeeded his brother as 3rd Lord Berwick, was a middle-aged sybarite who loved good cheer though some considered him heartless. His reputation for wit was not justified by his despatches. He was better known as one of the lovers of Lady Hester Stanhope. After many years as M.P. for Shrewsbury Town he was appointed envoy to Ratisbon in 1805. He never reached Ratisbon and he never married Lady Hester Stanhope, to whom he was said to have owed his advancement when she kept house for her uncle William Pitt. His engagement to her was announced: '*il est bien bon*,' was Lady Bessborough's comment. Evidently his intentions were not serious: as an *habitué* of Devonshire House he was often malicious at her expense—the flighty Lady Hester was an easy target. Appointed to Sardinia (Piedmont) in 1807, he resided in Turin after Napoleon's collapse. There Lady Bessborough stayed with him in 1821 and wrote: 'Mr Hill is very attentive to us, and makes us almost live with him, and is very amusing in his odd way.... You know his lisping, mumbling manner of speaking, which often gives more appearance of humour to what he says than it deserves.' Others, like

6

King Francis I

Lord Buckingham (a cousin of Lady Hester), called him a madman *tout court*. In 1824 he was transferred to Naples, where he collected many of the choice pieces of white and giltwood furniture which are still to be seen in the drawing-room of Attingham Park, near Shrewsbury. Most of these had been made for Caroline Murat when she was Queen of Naples—a fine day-bed was carved with her monogram—others had been brought with her from Paris. Noel Hill's collection reflects the sophistication of a luxurious bachelor of fifty-five.

Not only Lady Hester Stanhope was to complain of being jilted by the British envoy. A letter among the papers at Attingham inscribed by him 'Madness about Soirées'[1] betrays that he offended several of his countrymen then residing at Naples, where his lavish entertainments were much sought after. 'Dear Sir,' it runs, 'You will not, I am sure, suspect me of any wish to appear at your approaching soirées, when I declare that no consideration would now induce me to attend them and I trust to your liberality for putting the most favourable construction on the appeal which I feel it to be my duty to address to you on that subject. Several of my friends, travellers as well as resident, and who are well known to you, have inquired if I had received an invitation, and, while being rather mortified at being obliged to reply in the negative, I have found myself at a loss to explain upon what principle of consistency, good taste and good feeling I—your acknowledged "oldest acquaintance"—occasionally still further honoured by the appellation of your "old friend"—an *amicus curiæ*, etc.—should be excluded from a public assembly, while I am frequently admitted to your private society, your hospitality and your confidence! I shall very probably dine on the 5th of next month with a family who are going to you in the evening and from whom I must separate at 9 o'clock with feelings which, without being particularly sensitive I shall leave you to imagine. The fact is, that such exclusions appear to the world as a tacit stigma which no explanation can satisfactorily remove and they tend towards creating a coolness between the most intimate friends. In what light, too, do they place us with the Neapolitans?

'It has been said you had determined not to invite "settlers" as they are called and to make no exceptions. On the propriety of treating a respectable body of our countrymen in a foreign capital as a "caste" I

[1] For kind permission to print this I am indebted to my friend Lady Berwick.

shall offer no remark but, supposing some of the members of that body may not be deemed duly qualified, exceptions are everywhere constantly practised, as your own dinner parties prove, without occasioning either surprise or giving offence.

'With *Mr Hill's* domestic arrangements we by no means presume to interfere but when neglected by the *Minister*, our natural patron and protector, on whose conduct towards us *our consideration here so materially depends*, it is difficult to refrain from the language of complaint and remonstrance.

'I beg that this letter, of which I keep no copy, may (as marked) be confined to *your sole and exclusive perusal* and not to be mentioned *to anyone*. I trust that I shall not suffer in your estimation by the frank and candid exposure of my sentiments and when I can render you any service you will find me as willing as ever to do so. . . .'

Besides collecting exquisite commodes and sofas upholstered in pale blue satin damask, Noel Hill was anxious to improve the quality of Neapolitan pork: no doubt he hankered after good English bacon. Among his papers the following memorandum is indicative: 'To select a good Sow and Boar Pig, they should *not* be from the same stock as by having them distinct in the first instance the breed can be kept from degenerating much longer. The Pig's cheek should be *full* and *ample*, the coat *fine* and the bones *small*; it is desirable the animal should be shipped before the severe weather address to Lord Hill at the Horse Guards, etc. Query: What ship is on the point of sailing?' To which there is this dramatic sequel: '20 March, 1830. Brigantine *Sea Nymph*, Captain Robert Burroughs—4 pigs, viz, two Boars and two Sows, which the said Captain promise to maintain them during the passage. Not accountable for the pigs, dead or alive freight to be paid. Robt Burroughs.'

This particular *Sea Nymph* must have been awaited eagerly by H.M. envoy, since she was wafting such succulent mammals to Naples. It was a subject on which he could see eye to eye with King Francis, who retained a keen interest in animal husbandry. When politics became embarrassing they could always converse about farming with profit and pleasure.

'Mr Hill was our Minister at Naples, a *bon vivant* and very hospitable,' wrote Lord Malmesbury in 1829.[1] 'I dined there nearly every

[1] *Memoirs of an Ex-Minister.* London, 1885.

8

day, and remained at Naples in an hotel at Santa Lucia the whole summer. I never found the heat oppressive as exactly at 10 a.m. the sea-breeze entered my room, and the nights were delicious. Parties were made to sup by moonlight at the *trattorie* to eat the *frutti di mare*, which include all shellfish. . . . Mr Hill presented me at Court. . . . A circle was formed, the royal family going round and speaking to each person, which did not last long as there were not many present. The old King did not look like a tyrant, but rather the type of an English farmer. The Queen and the young and handsome Princess Christine, afterwards Queen of Spain, was present. The latter was said at the time to be the cause of more than one inflammable victim languishing in prison for having too openly admired this royal coquette, whose manners with men foretold her future life after her marriage to old Ferdinand. When she came up to me in the circle, walking behind her mother, she stopped and took hold of one of the buttons on my uniform, to see, as she said, the inscription upon it, the Queen indignantly calling to her to come on. From all I heard then, the King and royal family were not personally unpopular, and there was certainly more discontent in the Papal States than in the Neapolitan; but the revolutionists were working everywhere to upraise Italy, and the hatred of the Austrians, upon whom Bomba and the other princes of Italy were so imprudent as to depend for their power and policy, acted more against them than any local severities.'

On the King's birthday, August 14, an amnesty was proclaimed and many political exiles were allowed to return. Noel Hill reported: 'I have seldom witnessed such a change in popular feeling or popular opinion more marked. . . . From gloom and silence all became joy and cordiality, and the royal family at the theatres and whenever they have publicly appeared have been received by the whole population not only with applause but enthusiasm.'

Before the Austrian evacuation it was necessary to reform the army, which had been demoralized by Carbonaro infiltration. Francis had less to fear from foreign aggression than from native sectarians. The engagement of Swiss troops was galling to national pride, but those who inveighed most lustily against them had scarcely distinguished themselves for zeal or competence. As the Swiss had always proved reliable Francis began to negotiate with the Cantons for the enrolment of three more regiments. The negotiations were hampered by Carbonari sympathizers and Calvinists, who insisted on freedom of public worship, whereas Francis thought heretics should worship in private. In the meantime a scheme was launched to enrol two regiments of Sicilian volunteers. The ostensible purpose of this was to avoid a levy on the mainland and encourage the reluctant islanders to take up soldiering. But the covert aim of its promoters, as Ulloa[1] pointed out, was to secure good billets for their progeny. Some obtained commissions for three or four sons who were still at school or so young that they had to be escorted by their tutors. The veteran General Selvaggi objected that this would set a bad example and breed discontent among the regulars, but the Court *camarilla* had its way and the new law was passed. Its disadvantages were soon apparent. Volunteers were scarce in spite of rewards and blandishments, and after a while soldiers were recruited among prisoners with light sentences, since Murat had set such a precedent. Those who had won promotion after years of service were disgusted to see courtiers collect commissions as well as funds to enlist volunteers, and there was much sarcasm about little boys dressed up as officers. The situation was summarized by a cartoon of the King inspecting barracks where a tall grenadier was rocking his captain in a cradle.

'Since His Majesty's return from Milan,' wrote Noel Hill, 'he has been indefatigable in his attention to business. The Council at which His Majesty presides, sits regularly three and often four times a week from nine in the morning till four o'clock in the afternoon. The only apparent result of its labours appears as yet to be considerable reforms in the different Courts of Justice. Several judges have been superannuated and pensioned, and replaced by younger and abler men without attention to parties or politics. This measure seems to have given much satisfaction. . . . In the meantime the King's Ministers secretly deplore His Majesty's assiduous attention to business, as they confidentially declare that it is with much difficulty the current affairs of the country can be carried on, from their incessant and long attendance at the Council where His Majesty requires the most minute details to be submitted for his judgement.'

Worrying over minutiæ, the King's health suffered: it had never been strong. There was a yawning gulf between his excellent intentions and the tortuous practice of his ministers. He revived a number of

Pietro C. Ulloa, *Il regno di Francesco I*. Naples, 1933.

literary academies which had been closed in 1821. The quarrel between the linguistic purists and the neologists continued with a political undercurrent and merged into the larger quarrel between conservative classicists and liberal romantics. The purists dreamt of an independent Italy; the neologists defended the reforms introduced by the French; and political discussions were disguised as literary to elude the censorship. The Jesuits were allowed more influence over education; schools were to be inspected by bishops; and Latin authors were to be expurgated by a select committee. Priests tainted with liberalism were forbidden to teach or hear confessions. A public school of design was founded, and exhibitions of modern art were to be held every year with gold and silver medals for prizes. A heavy duty on foreign books in addition to a stricter censorship enabled the malcontents to complain that the government's policy was to encourage ignorance, but the duty was imposed to encourage local printers. Books which had only been available to a few were now translated and reached a larger public. Neapolitan printers and paper factories prospered in consequence.

Referring to the recall of political exiles, Noel Hill commented on December 20, 1825: 'I need not dwell on the increased and increasing popularity of the Court from these wise and beneficent measures, but simply add that we are looking forward to the great festival of the new year for further proofs of His Majesty's gracious intentions. If His Majesty continues thus employed we may indeed anticipate at no very distant period the return of comparative prosperity to this country, and the Austrians may be allowed to quit it without all those apprehensions of the public peace being again disturbed . . . whenever that event should finally occur.'

Those apprehensions were kept alive by Metternich, who sent the government frequent exhortations to deal more severely with sectarians. To avoid any pretext for prolonging the occupation Medici gave Intonti a free hand as police minister and Marchese Ugo more extensive powers as the King's Lieutenant in Sicily. The result of this was deplorable, for the police began to form a despotic Inquisition. Spies and informers accused loyal officials of belonging to secret sects. In spite of the King's efforts to restore order and alleviate poverty there was a recrudescence of political unrest in the provinces which occasionally led to crime. At Potenza some sectarians were accused of murdering the reactionary mayor of Montepeloso, but they were acquitted owing to their brilliant defence by the advocate Lauria. The verdict emboldened a few liberals to assault a hated reactionary in a crowded street and leave him hideously mangled. While the reactionaries disapproved of the King's amnesty, the liberals complained that his concessions were too limited. One government inspector proposed to ban the names Calderaro or Carbonaro, as the late King had banned those of Jacobin and Sanfedista in 1800. There was sporadic brigandage in out of the way places, but the worst bandits were suppressed in the beginning of Francis's reign.

The murder of a young English couple near Pæstum in 1825 was an exceptional case, as we may gather from the romantic Lady Blessington's account: 'All the inhabitants of Naples are in a state of excitement, caused by the murder of Mr and Mrs Hunt; which shocking event occurred close to Pæstum, on their return from that place. Murder, or indeed robberies, have been so unfrequent during the last few years, that this one has surprised, nearly as much as it has shocked, the Neapolitans. Mr and Mrs Hunt were both in the bloom of youth: newly married, they had set out for Italy immediately after their nuptials; little anticipating that in the beautiful land which they eagerly journeyed to see, they should so soon encounter a premature and violent death. I met them at Naples but three days previously to the fatal event: and was so struck with the beauty of this ill-fated young woman that I enquired her name; now that I hear it coupled with a horrible death, I can hardly bring myself to think that one I so lately saw full of life and health, is indeed her whose murder is the topic of every one I meet. The youth, personal attractions, and fond attachment of this young couple, have awakened a lively interest and regret in the minds of all who are acquainted with the sad tale of their deaths. They were on their return from Pæstum, attended only by a man-servant, who was on the box of their *calèche*, when three or four armed brigands stopped the carriage, and menaced them with death, unless they immediately delivered their money and baggage. Mr Hunt, a fine, spirited young man, was more disposed to offer resistance, than to comply with this demand; but Mrs Hunt, greatly alarmed, entreated him to give them the bag of dollars which was in the carriage, beneath their feet. His servant remonstrated with the brigands; who, incensed at his interference, violently struck him. Mr Hunt stooped down,

12

whether to seize the bag of dollars, or fire-arms, is not known; the brigands thought the latter was his intention, and they instantly fired at him. Mrs Hunt, seeing a robber take aim at her husband, threw herself between them, clasping him in her arms, and received two balls, which passed from her person to his, mortally wounding both. The brigands fled with their booty; and some peasants hearing the shot came to the spot, and found the young couple nearly insensible, and weltering in their blood. They removed the husband into the next hut on the road, where he soon expired; and took Mrs Hunt back to the wretched abode at Pæstum, which she had so lately quitted in the enjoyment of as much happiness as falls to the lot of mortals. The melancholy intelligence soon spread, and next day reached the residence of the worthy Miss White, an English maiden lady, of advanced years, who inhabits a house at La Cava, and she soon set out on horseback, to offer her services to her unhappy countrywoman. In the meanwhile, two young officers of the *Revenge*, who had gone to see Pæstum, arrived there within a short time of the fatal catastrophe, and undertook the care of Mrs Hunt; on whom they waited with all the tenderness and delicacy that could have been expected from the gentlest of her own sex. She, poor soul! kept enquiring continually for her husband, who she was told was doing well, in a house at a short distance, but whence it would be dangerous to remove him: she then entreated to be taken to him, making light of her own wound, which was so soon to consign her to the grave. She appeared to have no sense of her own danger; and preserved a degree of cheerfulness to the last, reverting to her distant home, and those dear relatives she was never more to behold; who would, as she asserted, be so grateful to her two kind young countrymen, who nursed her as though she were their sister. The wound produced fever and delirium, during the paroxysms of which, she raved of her husband; congratulated herself on having saved him at the expense of her own danger; addressed the most affectionate expressions to the far distant relatives, whom she believed to be close by her bed; and sang snatches of songs in a voice so harmonious, that those who heard it could hardly bring themselves to think, that it would soon be hushed for ever. She died the evening of the next day, unconscious of all that had occurred; and Miss White arrived only to see the corpse of her she would have so tenderly succoured.'

Most of these brigands happened to be Carbonari, and it suited Austrian policy to exaggerate their number. Mentioning the arrest of two officers at Bari on suspicion of belonging to the sect, the British minister wrote in January 1826: 'As this report proceeds through a channel from General Koller, the Austrian officer of all others most interested to remain at Naples from the nature of his different commissions and the large sums he consequently adds to his private fortune, I have little doubt that the affair has been in some measure magnified. . . . The Austrians have no time to lose in propagating disastrous intelligence.' As the interest on the public debt mounted and the greater part of Neapolitan public securities was held by foreigners, Medici became frantic. Growing taxation caused greater discontent, so that he could truthfully tell Metternich that the Carbonari were less noxious than the crippling cost of the occupation.

The Prince of Butera was sent to Vienna in September 1826, to solicit the refund of surplus payments to the army of occupation, but the Austrians would only agree to a small fraction of the Neapolitan claims after infinite haggling.

Butera also had a more intimate mission: he was to find out whether the Austrian Crown Prince was mentally deficient in case he should propose to Maria Cristina of Naples. Francis had twelve children, only two of whom were married, the Duchess of Berry, already widowed, and Luisa Carlotta, the wife of Don Francisco de Paula, King Ferdinand VII of Spain's youngest brother. He kept a dossier of eligible princes and princesses.

Luisa Carlotta was none too happy at the Spanish Court, partly owing to the jealousy of her sisters-in-law who dreaded her influence over the King, and partly to her meddlesome disposition. It was rumoured that she was scheming for a throne in Spanish America. When she wanted to go to Paris Ferdinand VII was persuaded to withdraw the permission he had granted for the journey. Marie Amélie's letters to Francis showed genuine concern about her. In February 1825, she wrote: 'All the French officers arriving from Spain agree that the position of the Infante Don Francisco is very painful, difficult and dangerous, surrounded by spies and persecuted. . . . I hope there is some exaggeration in this but there is certainly some truth. Cassaro had better look into this and send you an exact report. The King of Spain has been on the verge of death. Now he seems to have improved

14

but he has not quite recovered. If anything should happen to him Don Francisco's position would become even more terrible. He and Luisa think that the only remedy would be to travel abroad. The King (Charles X) does not want them here . . . for political reasons . . . but he has sent an officer to Madrid who is a personal friend of Don Francisco, to urge him to be patient, not to take any rash step, above all not to move without his brother the King's consent. . . . It would be most natural for him to visit Italy at this moment. I do not suggest Naples because I do not know your views on the subject, but either Lucca with his nephews or Rome for the Holy Year. . . . Carolina, my husband and I have all advised them to be patient and cautious, and to consider that in a large family one has to make sacrifices for the sake of peace.'

Francis appealed to Ferdinand VII in vain: Luisa Carlotta and her husband were not allowed to move. 'We too have preached patience,' he told Marie Amélie. 'In a large family one should be deaf, dumb and blind to live in harmony.' But it was owing to Luisa Carlotta's intrigues that her younger sister Maria Cristina eventually married Ferdinand VII.

Maria Cristina was the cynosure of the Neapolitan Court. Lady Blessington described her as: 'Slight and well-formed, with a countenance in which *finesse* and *esprit* are delineated, even as a grisette she would challenge admiration. Her features are small, and neatly finished; her eyes expressive, her teeth beautiful, and her smile full of fascination. Her complexion is of a pale clear olive, which, if less brilliant than the fresh roses and lilies of our English ladies, is not without its charm. . . . Having passed and re-passed the carriage in which she sat last evening, several times, I had good opportunities of examining her; and I must pronounce her to be worthy the admiration she excites in the combustible hearts of her countrymen, who view her less as a grand Princess than as a very bewitching woman.' In the royal box at the San Carlo, 'the Princess Christine looked exceedingly pretty . . . and many a furtive glance was cast towards her,—a homage that did not seem offensive to her feelings, if one might judge by her countenance, although it is strongly disapproved by the elders of the royal family. Curious stories are told on this subject at Naples; and it is asserted that more than one young noble has been advised to travel for his health, because detected in looking too often towards the pretty

Christine.' What a glamorous contrast with her parents! Lady Blessington remarked that the King's obesity 'indicates anything but health; and the stooping posture which he continually maintains, his head drooping over his chest, confirms the impression of helpless *embonpoint* which his countenance conveys. From this mode of holding his head, his glance has something disagreeable and sinister in it.' As for the Queen, 'her excessive *embonpoint* had destroyed every vestige of symmetry in form and face.'

The King suffered from what was then called 'the flying gout', but this seldom prevented him from transacting business with a scrupulous eye for detail. At the end of July 1825, Noel Hill wrote: 'The most extraordinary and exaggerated reports were circulated and believed by the middle and lower class at Naples, nor have these reports, now that His Majesty is recovered, totally subsided. It was positively declared that the King was insane, and a variety of acts of irritability, not to say violence, against some of the menial servants of the household and others, were related in corroboration of the fact. For these acts of irritability I fear there may be some foundation, but persons of less high rank than His Majesty, when tormented by such a trying disorder, have been often in a state of great excitement without provoking the report of insanity. Bulletins were at length regularly published of the King's health, and though each bulletin was more favourable than the preceding till His Majesty was convalescent, yet many of the same class of people still persisted in their belief in this insanity. I have dwelt long on these circumstances as they seem to convey a proof of the unpopularity of the King, and this appears to be the general opinion of the higher orders, and which is most unfortunate in the present situation of the country.

'The late King was at least popular with the lazzaroni, and attached to himself many warm personal friends, and unpleasant comparisons are continually made to this effect. In the intercourse I have had hitherto with His present Majesty I have not only found him affable and condescending, but though warm in temper, apparently endued with great good sense and right feeling.'

Affable though he appeared, those who knew him best could seldom fathom his thoughts. But he could not conceal his dread of revolution, and his choleric temper, provoked by gout, made him liable to frequent outbursts of violence. One morning he slapped

Cosimo de Horatiis, his private physician, because he had promised to cure a cold which was no better. These slappings were usually remunerative to the victim. In this case he said by way of apology: 'You may ask me a favour.' The doctor asked that one of his sons be appointed a judge, and the request was granted. Medici governed the State, but Michelangelo Viglia, the King's valet, and Caterina de Simone, the Queen's maid, had an extraordinary influence in the royal palace. It was said that the King could not sleep unless Viglia arranged his pillows, or rise in the morning unless Viglia pulled him out of bed. But the King's affection for this rascal was expressed in peculiar ways, such as letting hot candle wax drip on his nose. When somebody asked Viglia why his nose was so red, he replied: 'The master has been at his pranks again.' Once Medici met him on the palace stairs and remarked: 'Don Michelangelo, I'll warrant that the King has appointed a new archbishop of Capua.' He had observed that the valet's nose was redder than usual.

Viglia's artfulness under a simple exterior appealed to the King's odd sense of humour. Though he appreciated men of culture, he did not want them at close quarters. When his secretary Antonio Celebrano died it was suggested that a distinguished scholar should replace him. 'Never!' exclaimed the King, 'I prefer my ignoramuses.' Viglia was reputed to be illiterate, which was considered an insurance against indiscretion. The King was aware that he and Caterina de Simone collected bribes from office seekers but it did not perturb him. 'A man who has paid for his job will try hard not to lose it,' he said, 'and will therefore remain loyal.' Caterina fattened on tasting the dishes at the royal table before the King and Queen, who were both voracious eaters.

Nisco[1] relates a typical anecdote which he heard from Gennaro Fumo, a staunch monarchist. Having discovered that the administrator of Capitanata had left a deficit of 43,000 ducats (1 ducat—3/3d), a certain Carmine de Martino applied to Fumo for the post, offering to pay the deficit into the public treasury as well as a security of 105,000 ducats and a present of 12,000 ducats for Viglia. Fumo went straight to Viglia with this proposal, and the illiterate valet was astute enough to accept it on condition he produced the three vouchers before nine o'clock next morning. Fumo had to scatter more gratuities

[1] Niccola Nisco, *Storia del Reame di Napoli dal 1824 al 1860*. Naples, 1888.

to procure the vouchers in time. The King was already in council when he reached the palace. Viglia was waiting for him, however, and he conveyed the vouchers to the King. Interrupting the minister who was actually discussing the deficit, the King said: 'You create difficulties and I solve them. Here is a note for 43,000 ducats to pay the deficit, another for the security, and a third for Michelangelo who has saved the situation. You had better appoint de Martino who has incurred all this expense.' De Martino was duly appointed.

Viglia and Caterina de Simone ran an unofficial employment bureau for ecclesiastics and civil servants from which they reaped fat profits. According to Nisco they received 4000 ducats for bishoprics and the equivalent of eighteen months' salary for civil service jobs, while there was a sliding scale for tax collectors based on calculated gains. Substitutes for those eligible for military service were also provided on payment of 250 ducats. That hardened old cynic Medici winked at all this.

Only one person ventured to protest against Viglia. Monsignor Olivieri, the Duke of Calabria's tutor,[1] wrote to the King on February 9, 1827: 'I hear that Don Michelangelo Viglia has asked to resign because he has not been appointed administrator of Persano. Infamous and shameless man! This is the gratitude he shows a Sovereign who has loaded him with a thousand conspicuous and unheard of benefits even at the cost of injustice to others! He is not yet satisfied that in the last ten years he has risen from utter penury to a state of extraordinary opulence. Not content with having abused the name and authority of his Sovereign until it has become a fable in the kingdom and throughout Europe, he wished to expose it to further ridicule by procuring the post of administrator, though he has won general notoriety as the first of swindlers!

'Profit, Sire, from this Heaven-sent opportunity to get rid of a man who compromises your honour and conscience in every way; of a man who boasts: "I am the King of Naples"; of a man who does not serve you for love, but solely to rob you and take advantage of your royal name to succeed in all his fraudulent designs. . . . Dismiss this monster . . . and prove that you can be a King!'

So much water off a duck's back: the King considered his Michelangelo indispensable. He was impervious to the tutor's tirades.

[1] See Alfredo Zazo, *Ricerche e Studi Storici*, Vol. II, p. 46. Benevento, 1939.

Monsignor Olivieri had sent him an even more violent letter on February 6, 1826. As an attack on the first year of his reign it is probably unique. The priest castigated the King as if he, rather than the Duke of Calabria, were his pupil. He felt it his duty, he wrote, to inform him of the following truths, although he realized that no attention would be paid to his advice:

'1. All honest people, without exception, pity Your Majesty because in a single year you have lost the hearts of your subjects and have become the object of general hatred and public contempt. If any one tells you the contrary, he is a false flatterer who deceives in order to betray you.

2. Your subjects are divided into two classes, conspirators and neutrals. The former are working strenuously in all the provinces to foment a new revolution which is to be decisive, as they boast with impunity; and whose principal aim is to exterminate the royal family and its adherents. The latter are even prepared to accept the yoke of Mahomet ... hoping it may prove less baneful than Your Majesty's government.

3. The revolution is to begin all over Sicily as soon as the Austrian troops quit that island; and from thence break out in all the provinces of the kingdom of Naples.

4. The causes of the general discontent are many, but the chief ones are these. First, the despotism of the ministry, which has increased since the death of your father the late King, although Your Majesty may fancy you have curbed it. Second, the paralysis in all affairs. During the thirteen months since Your Majesty's accession nothing has been done, nothing is being done, and everything is put off to a vague, uncertain future. Third, the overweening power, corruption and venality of the magistrates, secretariats, and all provincial officials, who bring increasing odium on the royal authority. Fourth, Your Majesty's unhappy choice of servants, who are either sectarians, or scoundrels, or fools.

5. All favours are bestowed on the bad; none on the honest and deserving.

6. The lack of a council of state to examine the conduct of secretaries of state, who are detested by the whole nation.

7. The increase of customs duties and other public burdens, combined with Your Majesty's enormous waste of money on travels, hunting, fishing, luxurious buildings, and every kind of amusement.

8. The dismissal and pensioning off of the best magistrates in Naples and Sicily because they are opposed to the ruinous new systems.

9. Your Majesty's patronage of notorious reprobates and robbers, who, not content with robbing Your Majesty, embezzle even the alms of the poor to enrich themselves.

10. The neglect of the army which has become almost entirely hostile to you in consequence; and whoever tells you the contrary is either ill-informed or deceives you.

11. The chaos and anarchy that are the natural result of what is happening in all other administrative branches of the kingdom.

12. Finally, the bad odour surrounding the Queen (pardon this liberty, but I should betray you unless I spoke of it frankly), who is commonly said to be engrossed in coquetry, and the dishonour which this reflects on your daughter Donna Cristina, who will never find a husband, if she loses her reputation. . . .'

To summarize the rest of this philippic, the King led a life of selfish enjoyment and slept like another Jonah in the darkest tempest. Among other remedies Olivieri proposed that he should make a clean sweep of all the profligates, bigamists and thieves in the royal household; avoid all luxury and superfluous expense; encircle the Queen with carefully chosen guardians who would render it impossible for her to 'stray from her duties'; forbid the Queen and Princess Cristina to attend any theatre, which kindled passions, helped to foster scandal, and ruined virtue; lavish less money on street beggars and vagabonds, but reduce taxation; leave the petty details of public business to others and pay more attention to urgent affairs of State, simplify provincial administration, prevent abuses of authority, punish corrupt magistrates, and reform the present code of law, which was 'generally recognized as anti-monarchist and anti-Christian', etc.

The censorious tutor added that he had been prompted by foreign ambassadors, bishops, and impeccable officials to point out the abyss yawning under the King's feet. Let him not imagine that Sicily would repeat the welcome it had given his family on previous occasions! The island was seething with revolt, thirsting to avenge the myriad wrongs it had suffered.

There was some truth in these strictures, but it was not true that the King led a life of quiet enjoyment. He was seldom free from anxiety and physical pain. Olivieri's impressions were warped by his hatred of Medici. Distrusted by liberals and reactionaries, disliked by the King and Metternich, to whom he owed his return to power, it is remarkable that Medici stood his ground after so long and stormy a career. And in spite of the limitations forced upon him it is remarkable what he achieved. But he seemed devoid of sympathy or antipathy, both necessary ingredients of statesmanship: perhaps he had too low an opinion of mankind. His dealings with the Austrians were by no means irreproachable. Reporting General Koller's death in August 1826, the British minister observes: 'by his intimate connection with M. de Medici, who passed all his evenings in the General's society, he is said to have been a successful party in all the financial operations of this country from the commencement of the Austrian occupation.'

A more recent critic, Signor Ruggero Moscati,[1] has pointed out that Medici 'improved the administration of indirect customs, put some order into the pile of public debt, and tried to repair the enormous breach in the budget caused by the 1820 revolution. . . . While curbing expenditure, he stimulated the increase of public works, roads, bridges and highways, entrusting that department to the capable Afan de Rivera. He checked deforestation, regulated the water supply, encouraged local industries by a wholesome protectionism, recreated the merchant marine, and laid the foundations of economic, agricultural and industrial progress which was to bear its best fruit in the first fifteen years of Ferdinand II's reign.'

[1] Ruggero Moscati, *Ferdinando II di Borbone*. Naples, 1947.

II

Withdrawal of the Austrian troops—Arrival of the Swiss mercenaries—
The Hereditary Prince given command of the army—His education—
Rise of the secret societies—The Cilento revolt—Del Carretto—Capture
of the Capozzoli brothers—A futile expedition to Tripoli—Matrimonial
projects for Ferdinand—Maria Cristina's betrothal to Ferdinand VII of
Spain—Francis accompanies her to Madrid—Death of Medici—The
Hereditary Prince as Vicar General—'Dancing on a volcano'—The
King's return to Naples—The Orleans monarchy—Arrival of the Dey of
Algiers—The De Mattheis trial—Death of Francis I.

IN February 1827, the Austrian army withdrew from Naples.
'Unpopular as their long occupation of this country has been,'
wrote Noel Hill, 'it must be admitted that their discipline and conduct in general has been most exemplary.' The worst thing they left
behind them, as Ulloa[1] remarked, was the vast debt contracted for their
maintenance: they had relieved the treasury of at least two million
ducats.

The Prince of Cassaro, who had succeeded Prince Ruffo as ambassador in Vienna, wrote to Medici on March 30, 1827, 'His Majesty (the
Emperor) told me that he was satisfied to see that our Government
was now in a position to maintain itself and that he hoped there would
be no further trouble, as the help he had given our august Sovereign
had cost him immense sums and that if, unhappily, we had to sue for
his troops again, he would not be able to send them on such moderate
terms, which I confess surprised me exceedingly.'

After prolonged negotiations three Swiss regiments had been
enrolled. The liberals alleged that Francis was so terrified of his own
subjects that he could only trust foreigners, but the Neapolitan army

[1] Op. cit.

had been in a chaotic state since 1821. The Swiss deserved their reputation for loyalty and efficiency. The officers told their troops: 'We shall be the stout supporters of the throne of the Two Sicilies and when our service is over, we shall return to our Alpine hearths with a clear conscience and the means to enjoy a calm old age amid the snows of our fatherland.'

In May 1827, the King put his eldest son in command of the army. 'This event,' wrote Noel Hill, 'would give still more pleasure and satisfaction were it not accompanied by the reflection of an increased expenditure . . . and His Royal Highness has only just entered his eighteenth year. Many persons hoped the nomination might be deferred till a later period. There is also a report of some intention to allow the Prince a separate household and establishment.'

Ferdinand had been born in Palermo on January 12, 1810. He was shy and quiet, unlike his brothers, with a preference for sedentary amusements. Monsignor Olivieri, Bishop of Arethusa, was given charge of his education, and although he has been attacked as a pernicious influence by Nisco and his tribe, his letters show that he took his duties seriously and defended his convictions with amazing courage. Nobody else dared to address the King in such blunt language. He tried to model himself on Bossuet, and his aim was to mould a virtuous, enlightened sovereign.

In his educational programme he placed religion first: all the Prince's studies should tend to promote piety and good manners. Authors should be read in entirety and not in snippets, with a preference for Virgil, Terence, Sallust and Cæsar. While geography might be treated like a game or a journey, history should be taught with great precision, especially that of the Two Sicilies. 'We shall not enter into minute and petty details . . . but our thoughts will dwell on the good or evil customs of nations, ancient usages, fundamental laws, great changes and the causes which produced them, the secrets of councils and unforeseen events, to train the mind and prepare it for every predicament, the mistakes of monarchs and their disastrous effects. . . . We shall pay special attention to the life of Saint Louis as the example of a perfect king. . . .'

Important passages of history should be learnt by heart and translated into French and Latin. As regards philosophy, it was necessary to distinguish between doctrines of practical use, and those which gave rise to disputable opinions: the Prince should learn to judge rather than to dispute. Logic and ethics came next: Plato and Aristotle should help to form the judgement with solid reasoning. Holy Scripture and the Gospels should be the sole source of moral doctrine. Some notions of physics and natural science were also necessary, and a grounding in Roman law. Separate instruction was to be given in mathematics and military science.

When Ferdinand was six years old, Monsignor Olivieri reported that he had a good brain but a weak constitution. He recommended more exercise: he should be encouraged to walk, run and play with his younger brother Charles, who was more robust. Ferdinand soon benefited from this advice: he went for donkey rides, played bowls in the palace garden, and became more cheerful and expansive. Olivieri hoped that his father would notice an improvement.

Ferdinand expressed himself with energy and showed a capacity for 'judicious reflection in advance of his years', but he was also regrettably stubborn. Whether in town or country the princes led secluded lives. To acquire an ease of manner befitting their rank, they should get used to appearing in public. They were ill too often 'because their appetite exceeded the capacity of their digestions'. They were badly dressed, moreover, and their apartments lacked many essential commodities. When their old French teacher was pensioned off Olivieri had to nag for a whole year before another was engaged.

Captain Scarola, who taught Ferdinand 'the science of military principles', was able to report that he was making rapid progress: at the age of nine he was eager to take part in manœuvres. But Monsignor Olivieri protested vigorously against a proposed visit to Rome when Ferdinand was fourteen: if his studies were interrupted at this critical age he would be 'like an unripe fruit plucked off a tree'. Look at Francis's brother the Prince of Salerno, who had natural talents and a kind heart, but had never been properly educated owing to his early travels.

The tutor also inveighed against the game of *biribissi*, for which there seems to have been a hereditary weakness in the family. Let the princes play billiards, draughts, chess, anything but games of chance, 'whose nature is to corrupt the spirit of youth'. Evidently *biribissi* was not banned, as Olivieri wrote that Prince Charles always won at this game and suggested that at least his winnings should go to the poor.

He prophesied that at this rate Charles would turn into an inveterate gambler, useless to the State and destructive to his family, for he hated study and loved every kind of dissipation.

These 'dissipations' consisted of shooting practice, an occasional hunt, the visits of royal relations, 'very decent comedies' performed in the little Court theatre, and poetical improvisations on family birthdays. Whenever the princes picked flowers they sent them to the local churches. Ferdinand was devoutly religious, unlike his naughty brother Charles. *Non nobis, Domine, sed nomini tuo da gloriam!* exclaimed the tutor. And the King replied that this was a great consolation. But Olivieri was sixty-nine and felt even older. His pupils squabbled, made fun of their mathematical teacher, and became more unmanageable. He proposed two gentlemen-in-waiting under his supervision, and when the King failed to answer he appealed to the Queen 'to banish the King's habitual irresolution'. In the families of the nobility, he wrote significantly, the children were often left to grow up among servants, whose bad habits they were apt to copy. He felt most concerned about Prince Charles, who was indulging precociously in amorous escapades: it was essential 'to remove temptation from hot-blooded youths who were as combustible as gunpowder'.

In 1826 the old tutor himself exploded in another long letter to the King. He had striven to educate the four princes entrusted to him, at the cost of a thousand trials and tribulations, and serious detriment to his health. He had not done this for ambition or lucre, but only 'to benefit this poor kingdom by providing it with enlightened princes capable of healing its wounds'. But the King frustrated his efforts. 'Instead of giving them employment suited to their birth and the requirements of State; instead of putting them at the head of regiments to inspire loyalty and devotion, you only think of making hunters and farmers of them, thus provoking the contempt, hatred and ridicule of the entire nation. Sire, allow me to kneel at your feet, and with all the respect and zeal of a good subject declare openly that if you continue to spoil my Princes as you have done hitherto, their education will be wasted and the result will only be discreditable. Let me beseech you to grant my retirement, that I may abandon a task which I cannot fulfil except with disgrace and detriment to my conscience. Perhaps this language will offend you, but it is that of an honourable man, a minister of the Lord, and a faithful servant who cannot sacrifice his duties to human considerations and to the vile adulation of the Court.'

Far from taking umbrage the King replied: 'It always gives me the greatest pleasure to hear you express your opinions.' But another year was to elapse before he increased the tutor's salary and carried out some of his suggestions. Olivieri's persistence was admirable: he urged the King to 'raise the morale of the army and put his eldest son in command of it with the assistance of honest and respected persons'. This advice was accepted in May 1827, and it was a triumph for the tutor-bishop, who wanted Ferdinand to become a real king, not a dummy like his father. The young Prince had much to learn, but he took up his nominal command with an enthusiasm which endeared him to his officers and men.

In November urban guards were substituted for the civic guards to keep order and help the police, and they were carefully selected for their fidelity. Secret sects still pullulated in the provinces, such as the Filadelfi whose aim was to revive the Constitution of 1820; and the Edennisti who hoped to revive the bliss of the garden of Eden and wore glass beads of red, blue, black and yellow under their shirts ending in a triangle inscribed with the letters for Liberty, Equality and Justice. Many of the latter were denounced and prosecuted, including the ambitious lawyer-politician Liborio Romano, who was banished with some nineteen others.

A sect called the Central Tomb had been founded at Barletta 'to combine Carbonarism with Freemasonry and smother despotism in the common tomb'. This was merged with the reformed Carbonari, called The White Pilgrims. Other sects were called The French Reform and The Faithful Hermits with secret signs, symbols and passwords of their own. They flourished in Sicily too, and the King was kept on tenterhooks by reports inflated by the police with an eye to promotion and profit.

One case in particular alarmed the too credulous monarch. A Dominican novice called Calabrò alleged that two monks of the Soriano monastery had urged him with threats 'to follow the Law of Saint Theobald,[1] the only true law desired by God', that he had reported this to the Prior who told him to obey them, that he had been

[1] 1017–1066. Patron Saint and protector of the Carbonari or charcoal burners; canonized in the eleventh century.

forced to swear blind obedience to the sect of Freemasons before a Crucifix and dagger between three candles on a refectory table, surrounded by all the monks, that he had fled by night and denounced this to the Bishop of Melito, who told him it was his duty to obey the Prior and sent him back to the monastery, where he was called a spy and threatened with death. The sub-intendant of Monteleone had also called him a slanderer of good friars and ordered him to obey Father Procopio, the master of the novices who had given him the catechism of the sect. Whatever the truth, Intonti was embarrassed. When the subject was raised at the next Council he produced additional reports, including one from the Superior of the Dominicans on the Vomero, declaring that Calabrò was 'a fanatical dreamer of sects and a slanderer of the Dominicans of Soriano, religious and faithful subjects, in order to procure high patronage by his denunciations', and proposed that the King should banish him to Leghorn; and banished he was.

All these sects had been dormant under the Austrian occupation. The majority consisted of ex-Carbonari, small landowners, lawyers, doctors and provincial clergy who believed that the Constitution of 1820 had been broken against the King's wishes, and that he only needed their encouragement to restore it. Some were republicans, but they were ready to forget minor differences when the time was ripe for action, as it seemed to be in the spring of 1828. The Greeks had revolted against Turkish domination and the Egyptian-Turkish fleet had been destroyed at Navarino; in France the Villèle ministry, which had alienated extremists of right and left, had fallen, and the liberals were elated by the appointment of Martignac. Moreover the Holy Alliance had been dissolved.

In Naples the 'high chamber' of the secret Filadelfi sect decided to hoist the constitutional banner between May 25 and June 25. This was known to the police and the conspirators were watched. When a few were arrested owing to the indiscretion of one of their leaders, Antonio Galotti, who had mistaken a Carlo Iovane for a sectarian and been reported by him to the inspector of police at Salerno, Canon De Luca and the other leaders decided to start the insurrection in the hilly Cilento district south of Salerno. It was rumoured that the small fort of Palinuro contained 1500 guns, twelve cannon and plenty of ammunition, guarded by a mere handful of men. Galotti had enlisted the support of the three Capozzoli brothers, notorious brigands who had exterminated whole families and terrorized the countryside during the last decade. These helped to disarm the urban guards of Centola village who were forced to accompany them to Palinuro, in order to trick and overpower the customs officials and garrison in the fort. But instead of the copious arms and ammunition they had expected they found a few old muskets and flints; the gunpowder was mouldy. To make amends they broke up the semaphore station and read a proclamation to the people of Naples, demanding 'the good government of the French Constitution', promising to reduce the salt and land taxes and to abolish all other tolls and customs duties. This ended with the words: 'Long live God, our King, and the Constitution of France!' The same day they marched on to the small town of Forio, where they were joined by several sympathizers, and proceeded to the sea village of Camerota where they overpowered the local gendarmes and were joined by Father Carlo of Celle, a Capuchin with a considerable following. The friar shouted 'Long live Liberty and the French Constitution!' and harangued the population. A *Te Deum* was then sung in the church for the success of the rising. Next day the procession, which had gathered strength, went on to Licusati where the same ceremony was repeated amid joyful demonstrations.

The leaders intended to proclaim the rising in every district, collect more volunteers and march to Vallo, disarming the local troops, freeing political prisoners and seizing munitions. So far the rebels had prospered, but on June 30 the population of San Giovanni a Piro rang their church bells in alarm. The urban guards had fled, but the mayor and parish priest refused to celebrate a *Te Deum*. Several houses were sacked in retaliation, and a few loyalists were wounded. At Bosco the rebels met with a warm welcome, however. Domenico Capozzoli dined and spent the night with the family of a man he had murdered together with his servant about five months previously. The subject was discussed at dinner, and Capozzoli explained that his victims had been killed for maltreating his emissary: the rest of the family had been spared owing to his intercession. The panic-stricken survivors could only thank the assassin for being so merciful. At Montano the rebels had another festive reception and the news was spread through neighbouring villages: better times were nigh, and all taxes would be reduced! But on July 1 they heard that Marshal Del Carretto was coming with 8000 troops, contingents of which had landed along the coast.

They decided to set their prisoners free and occupy a strategic position on a hill between Montano and Cuccaro. Canon De Luca urged them to disband since the promised help had failed and they had insufficient arms to resist. They spent that night among the rocks; next day torrential rain added to their dejection. Cuccaro, Montano and Celle were already occupied by royal forces, and it was no use waiting for aid. The majority preferred to surrender at Vallo on July 7; the rest went into hiding. Galotti, the Capozzoli brothers and a few of their gang decided to live or die together.

The King feared this was a preliminary to a Murat restoration, engineered by exiles in Malta. Medici advised him to send Del Carretto as the man best qualified to deal with rebellion. Though born in Sicily he was of Piedmontese origin. After distinguishing himself in Spain, where he had fought against the French, he had joined the Carbonari in 1820 and become chief of General Pepe's staff. But when the Constitution was torn up he retained his rank in the army, having satisfied the investigating committee that he had only served the revolution in order to compromise it. As an ex-Carbonaro he was an expert on secret societies, and he had been appointed commander of the gendarmerie after destroying the robber bands of Puglia. His present plan of action, which he discussed in detail with the King, was to isolate the rebels and prevent the neighbouring districts from joining the revolt. Within a few days he telegraphed the King that the rebels had been reduced to twelve or fifteen including the Capozzoli brothers, who had fled to the hills and woods of Monteforte, pursued by two companies of infantry. But the provincial authorities, he added, had been more of a hindrance than a help. On July 7 he issued a vindictive manifesto: Bosco, which had supported the rebels, was to be razed to the ground. Other communes which did not 'promptly deliver any villain among them claimed by the sword of justice' were threatened with the same fate. As soon as this was reported to Intonti he sent word to Del Carretto that the King wished him to revoke his order to destroy Bosco. Too late: it had been reduced to rubble. In a letter more than patronizing Intonti asked him to abstain from publishing manifestoes in future. Del Carretto attributed this reprimand to jealousy. Controlling his anger he wrote to Intonti: 'An example was imperative and urgent in order to terrify and reform other evildoers. The burning of Bosco has produced a noticeable change in the savage and corrupt inhabitants of this district, transforming them into another species.'

Among the prisoners were several who denounced their accomplices to save their own skins. Galotti, the Capozzoli brothers and their gang were declared outlaws and a price was put on their heads. Del Carretto fired guns into the forest where they were said to be hiding and the thickets were set on fire. 'The sight was majestic and terrible,' he wrote, 'and the Capozzoli fled beyond the mountain.' Canon De Luca and his nephew had to be unfrocked before their trial, but it was hard to find a bishop who would perform this unpleasant office. The bishops of Capaccio, Policastro and Campagna either refused or made lame excuses. De Luca and his nephew were finally unfrocked by the Archbishop of Salerno in the sacristy of the cathedral. After the dismal ceremony they were led to a chapel where a monk recited prayers for them. Canon De Luca asked the monk not to weary them any longer, but to tell his old friend Ludovico Coscia that he was dying serenely for the commonweal and urged him to avenge both him and his companions. Both De Lucas were shot in the back. Altogether nineteen of the twenty-seven rebels sentenced to death were executed, and their heads were exhibited in iron cages in the villages near Palinuro.

After extraordinary adventures the Capozzoli brothers were captured almost a year later. They were betrayed by an old comrade while staying in his sister's house. A barking dog woke Domenico Capozzoli during the night of June 17. He noticed figures lurking in the shadows outside and fired. His hostess started screaming when he rushed downstairs and urged his brothers to resist. One of them wished to cut the woman's throat, but Domenico prevented him. All three fired lustily, and when they ran out of ammunition they hurled every available missile, even tiles from the roof. The church bells of Perito, the next village, had been tolled for the urban guards who besieged the house for four hours. Finally they decided to burn it. Barricaded on the upper floor, the brothers agreed to surrender when they saw the flames rising. After destroying all his papers Domenico shouted to the urban guards: 'Cowards, if we only had weapons we should put you to flight. You forget how often you have kissed our hands.' The Capozzoli were tried by court martial at Vallo on June 23 and condemned to death. After confessing and receiving Holy Communion they were shot at Palinuro, and their heads were exhibited in cages at Monteforte.

Referring to the executions of the Cilento rebels in 1828, Noel Hill reported: 'I have learnt from my Russian colleague that M. de Medici wholly disapproves of the extreme severity which has been exercised against these delinquents, and had declared to him confidentially that it had proceeded entirely from the commands of the King, whose feverish and extreme apprehensions could be not otherwise allayed. . . . The unpopularity of the King increases almost daily and the Liberal party associate with His Majesty the young Duke of Calabria, his eldest son, for participation in the acts of severity.' It was typical of Medici to feign disapproval after recommending Del Carretto to the King, certain that he would antagonize Intonti, his only potential rival. The King owed much of his unpopularity to Medici, who had become almost as powerful as Acton in the previous generation. Noel Hill had written: 'All the bright hopes which were raised upon the accession of the present Sovereign have long since been extinguished; and even if, as some continue to believe, the personal wishes of the King are still for the improvement and regeneration of his people, it is evident that the pernicious influence which surrounds him is too strong to admit of the smallest hope of his being able to assert them. His Government is become more hated than ever was that of his predecessor.'

An ill-fated expedition to Tripoli brought further discredit upon the government in 1828. The Two Sicilies had always been exposed to piratical incursions, but these had dwindled since a treaty had been signed with the Bey of Tripoli in Ferdinand's reign. After Ferdinand's death the Bey claimed that this treaty had lapsed: unless he were paid 100,000 ducats down, his pirates would return. Francis refused to be blackmailed and the corsairs infested Sicilian waters again. Remembering that Sardinia had repulsed the Bey by burning his little fleet, he sent a squadron to Tripoli on August 14, but its commander Sozi Carafa was warned not to risk his ships or the lives of his men. A week later he landed at Tripoli and tried to persuade the Bey to respect the treaty. The Bey was defiant, and neither the British nor the Tuscan consul, both of whom were present, spoke up for the Neapolitan.

The Bey's flotilla of light ships were lined up before the rocks protecting the harbour. Captain Roberti ordered the Neapolitan gunboats to fire at these but their powder, which had been dumped at Baia by the British in 1809, was completely innocuous, and their ill-directed

31

bombs fell into the sea. More noise than damage ensued, and the noise was mingled with laughter. Owing to adverse winds the Neapolitan squadron suspended hostilities, if such they could be called. They returned on August 26 and the next two days were filled with loud explosions. The Tripoli galliots attacked some crippled gunboats which would have been sunk had not Captain de Cosa, of the frigate *Isabella*, rushed to their rescue. After five days of futile combat, with a violent gale increasing, the whole squadron sailed back to Naples.

The failure of this expedition caused such an outcry that the ministry decided to prosecute its commander. Opponents of the régime declared that it was tyrannous at home and cowardly abroad, and that it had stained the national honour. When Sozi Carafa was exonerated by a naval tribunal the public applauded to show that they only blamed his superiors. It was known that the young Duke of Calabria sympathized with the scapegoat. He had inspected the powder store at Baia, and warned the King that it was useless. But the Minister of War, Scaletta, had contradicted him, and the veteran's opinion had prevailed. Knowing that Scaletta was duped by corrupt advisers—he was even said to have shared their ill-gotten gains—Ferdinand was extremely irritated. During the trial he had remarked that Sozi Carafa could not be held guilty—unless he was guilty of obedience. When Ferdinand succeeded to the throne Sozi was appointed governor of the royal arsenal.

The frequent capture of their xebecs and galliots damped the pirates' ardour and led to a suspension of hostilities. A treaty with Tripoli was announced on November 4, but as the terms were not published they were probably none too brilliant. This seemed an odd moment for founding new orders of chivalry: the Order of Francis I to reward civil merit and that of Saint George for the military. The King was Grand Master of these, as of the other three Neapolitan Orders of Saint Januarius, Saint Ferdinand, and Constantine. That of Saint Januarius was restricted to the aristocracy, but since that of Saint Ferdinand was rarely bestowed it was the most highly prized.

After the Tripoli fiasco there was growing indignation against Scaletta, the Minister of War. General Nunziante accused him of filling his office with Freemasons, and the young Duke of Calabria, disgusted by such niggardly economies as the reduction of officers' pay, threatened to resign his command. But the King loathed change and

Scaletta had powerful partisans at Court. Francis thought his son over-zealous, too young to be taken seriously. In spite of wretched health he said he hoped to live a few years longer so that Ferdinand might acquire more experience before succeeding him. He was also anxious to find him a suitable bride.

Of the three Princesses who had been proposed two were his nieces, Louise, daughter of the Duke of Orleans, and Maria Cristina, daughter of the late King Victor Emmanuel I of Sardinia; the other was the King of Bavaria's daughter Matilda. Francis had a preference for Louise, but Metternich disliked any connection with so liberal a family: he considered the Bavarian Princess more desirable. Tentative negotiations were pursued in each case: in that of Bavaria Francis wished to combine his son's engagement with that of his daughter Maria Cristina to the Crown Prince. Unfortunately the King of Bavaria had a lax reputation. Marchese Gagliati was sent to Munich to make private enquiries about the Crown Prince under the pretext of taking some salutary baths. His report was rosy. The King of Bavaria visited Naples in February 1829, but the negotiations were dropped because, while willing to give Ferdinand his daughter Matilda, he refused to commit himself further.

Ferdinand himself was prejudiced against his French cousin on account of her father Louis-Philippe. The idea of his Italian cousin appealed to him more, though her mother refused to send him her portrait. The widowed Queen of Sardinia maintained that princes should marry in obedience to their parents; a picture should have nothing to do with it. Supposing Ferdinand chose another bride after seeing her daughter's portrait? Royal marriages were made in Heaven.

Francis was even more anxious to find a husband for the vivacious Maria Cristina, who was now twenty-four. Since the Queen of Spain's health had deteriorated he had written to his ambassador Partanna to 'seize the chance should the King desire to remarry'. Negotiations were well advanced when the Queen of Spain expired. Ferdinand VII's first three marriages had been sterile, and it seemed likely that his brother, the Infante Don Carlos, should succeed him. Luisa Carlotta, who had married the King's youngest brother, the Infante Don Francisco de Paula, was determined to prevent this. She had long been scheming to marry her sister Maria Cristina to the King of Spain. The late Queen was hardly buried before Partanna presented the bereaved monarch with an alluring portrait of Maria Cristina. He was so dazzled that he hastened negotiations. On July 16, 1829, Noel Hill wrote: 'Her Majesty the Queen Dowager of Sardinia having arrived at Rome with the two Princesses her youngest daughters during this period, it was currently reported that a marriage was projected between H.R.H. the Duke of Calabria and one of these Princesses; the Chevalier de Medici has however confidentially assured me that should H.R.H. hereafter not make a decided objection, it has been settled by the illustrious parents of H.R.H. and of the Princess that he should marry the eldest daughter of H.R.H. the Duke of Orleans.

'It has already been anticipated in the public papers that H.M. the King of Spain would marry the Princess Christine, the eldest unmarried daughter of their Sicilian Majesties.

'My Spanish colleague General Toledo has constantly denied to me that any overtures for this purpose had yet been made, as the decease of the late Queen of Spain was too recent, but admitted that such a marriage was very probable.

'Monsieur de Medici nevertheless at once confessed to me that a correspondence had passed directly between the two sovereigns of Spain and Naples for this purpose, and that a person sent by the "Camarilla" had already been here. . . .

'The royal personages in question are unfortunately most nearly related on every side. The Kings of Spain and Naples are cousins german. The Queen of Naples is the King of Spain's sister, and the first wife of the King of Spain was sister to the King of Naples.

'The talents, accomplishments, and beauty of the Princess Christine are so well known that it is unnecessary to dwell upon them, but they are such, it is conjectured, as will ensure a more than ordinary influence in Spain.'

The latter conjecture was soon verified. Ferdinand VII invited the King and Queen to accompany their daughter to Madrid, and in spite of the King's gout, the Queen was so anxious to revisit her native land that she induced him to accept the invitation. In January 1829, Noel Hill had reported: 'I am sorry to observe that the state of M. de Medici's health is so indifferent, together with the constant fatigue to which he is exposed of attending the daily and protracted Councils, that the final completion of any business becomes proportionally more difficult.' Even so Medici was determined to join the party, though he disapproved of the expense involved. It was said that he bribed Mariella, a prophetess from the Vomero whom the King consulted occasionally, to warn him that he would encounter many dangers if he left. But the Queen's influence was decisive. Francis told the surprised seeress that Medici had advised him to go. Intonti supported Medici at the Council: he described the poverty of the country and the unrest of which the rising at Vallo was a symptom; taxation ought to be reduced, but this could only be done by cutting down expenditure. The King agreed, but nothing would prevent his journey.

The royal party left for Spain on September 28, travelling by land instead of by sea. Noel Hill noted that between £50,000 and £60,000 would be sufficient for all purposes if the King and Queen were only absent for six months, but that their departure for such a length of time and at such an expense in other countries, was attended with great unpopularity. The King entrusted the regency to his son Ferdinand with full powers of *alter ego*, and each minister was handed minute written instructions. In Rome he was much fêted by Pius VIII, whose election on March 31 he had helped to promote; in Florence he tried to be generous to the Neapolitan exiles whose dignified conduct had been praised by the Grand Duke, but most of them spurned his offers of financial assistance. Borrelli, though very poor, was harshly criticized for accepting 500 ducats from the King. An equal sum was offered to Gabriele Pepe, who replied that he was not yet reduced to beggary. This Pepe—not to be confused with Guglielmo—had won popularity for wounding Lamartine in a duel provoked by some offensive verses he had written about Italy. The royal party filled eleven carriages and five vans, followed by Medici and several secretaries. Michelangelo Viglia was in charge of the King's domestic arrangements and Caterina de Simone of the Queen's. The Court painter Salvatore Fergola had a carriage of his own with every facility to sketch historical and romantic scenes along the road, and the King took the keenest interest in his drawings. The entire journey was punctuated with pompous receptions. The Duchess of Berry seized this opportunity to embrace her father whom she had not seen since her marriage. Though she must have been struck by the change in him she said nothing of this in her diary. She met him outside Grenoble on October 31. 'Awakened at seven o'clock, I dressed and, after drinking a cup of chocolate, I left at eight o'clock. . . . The road along the valley is very pretty. . . . After several hours we met M. de Blacas who told us that Papa was following him. We got down and found ourselves in the arms of Papa, Mamma and Christine who is charming; I was extremely happy to see my parents again after thirteen years. . . .'

A triumphal arch had been raised with the arms of France, Naples and Spain before the château de Trouvet and the whole avenue was decked with garlands. Thirty little girls dressed in white came to offer the Princesses baskets of fruit and flowers, and the mayor of Grenoble welcomed the King with a speech. 'Sire, the city of Grenoble deems itself fortunate to be the first in France to pay Your Majesties the honour of its respects and thank you for your noble gift to our country in the person of your illustrious daughter, Madame, the Duchess of Berry. May the future Queen of Spain long adorn the throne she is going to occupy, and reign over the hearts of her subjects as her heroic sister reigns over ours.' The King and Queen, the Duchess of Berry and the future Queen of Spain travelled in an open carriage as far as Perthus on the frontier, where they were greeted by the guns of Bellegarde fort. Here two Spanish regiments and a squadron of body-guards awaited them with the governor of Catalonia, a Spanish bishop and a posse of magistrates in velvet and lace. 'All kissed the future Queen's hand,' wrote the Duchess, 'the ceremony was very imposing and the weather superb. There we took leave of my parents and Christine! God preserve her. . . .'

Ferdinand VII was so impatient for his bride that he ordered the postal relays to be doubled. The cold was intense, but the Spaniards gave their new Queen a rapturous reception. Her buxom beauty seemed to promise a brighter future. The marriage was celebrated in the Escurial on December 2, and early next year it was known that Maria Cristina was with child.

Winter in Madrid proved lethal to Medici, who was seventy and suffered from gall stones as well as asthma. He died on January 25, 1830. The Sicilians rejoiced, as they blamed him for abolishing their Constitution, but his death was considered a blow to the Neapolitan exchequer. His financial experience had been acquired in the period of transition from feudalism and the shackled economy of the eighteenth century, and he had invariably soared on the wings of a national crisis. He used to say that 'abuses should not be tackled outright but removed with subtle dexterity, especially when long continuance had grafted them on to habits and customs.' He has been aptly described as a better banker than financier, more capable of controlling wealth than creating it.

Noel Hill reflected the consensus of foreign opinion when he wrote in February: 'As the whole financial system of this country depended upon the late Minister, when the news of his death was promulgated the Neapolitan funds fell considerably, and it will be most difficult to supply his place in this respect, and indeed his loss will be long and severely felt in every department of the Government.

'The Prince of Cassaro, though not endued with the same abilities as the late Minister, was perhaps the best selection His Majesty could make, and on my own account I am particularly rejoiced at his nomination. He was, for many years, my colleague at Turin and I have always found him to be a plain, honest and unaffected person, and apparently much attached to England, which is a quality not uncommon in the natives of Sicily where the Prince was born and holds his entire property.' Camillo Caropreso became Minister of Finance, Tommasi President of the Council of Ministers, and Cassaro Minister for Foreign Affairs.

Even in Naples the winter was exceptionally cold. Among the veterans who succumbed was General Baron Joseph Acton, the great minister's brother. Born at Besançon in 1733, he had entered a French cavalry regiment at the age of fourteen: after being wounded in the battle of Rossbach he was promoted and decorated for valour; in 1784 he became a Chevalier de Saint Louis. When the French Revolution broke out he was commanding a regiment of Saxon hussars which he marched beyond the frontier with banners flying; in Holland he fought under the Duke of York; and he entered the Neapolitan service as a cavalry colonel in 1795. Since then he had commanded the Neapolitan cavalry in Tuscany and the Papal States, and had succeeded his brother-in-law, the Prince of Hesse-Philippsthal, as governor of Gaeta, a post which he retained until five years before his death. His large family were long identified with various branches of the Neapolitan service.

Francis, weary of festivities, and worried by reports from Intonti that France was on the verge of another revolution, was anxious to go home. Ferdinand as Vicar General was showing more energy than he had bargained for. Hampered in his desire to reform the army, he sent frequent complaints to his father. He had collected abundant proofs of corruption in the naval arsenal. But his father paid no attention to his letters. Suspecting that this was due to Medici, who wished to prevent any change before his return, Ferdinand wrote to his sister, sending his letters privately through the Spanish consul, urging her to plead for Scaletta's removal. Still the King was silent on the subject. Scaletta had a potent ally in the royal valet. The King's toleration of Viglia's misdemeanors was astonishing. Before leaving Madrid he distributed a glittering array of necklaces and snuff-boxes among the Spanish courtiers of both sexes, but the gems these contained were all discovered to be false; it was printed in the French newspapers that 'the King had sincerely wished to leave his portrait behind him'. The Queen's Spanish pride was offended, and she urged him to punish the culprits. But the King merely said: 'I would rather not have this matter discussed, as it would only upset Michelangelo. The best solution would be to distribute 70,000 *reals*[1] in compensation, and charge this sum to the ministries of Foreign Affairs and Finance.'

The Duchess of Berry had persuaded her father to stop in France on his way home, and he was welcomed by his old crony the Duke of Blacas on behalf of Charles X. At Pau he visited the room where his great ancestor Henri IV was born, and he appeared to be deeply affected. If only he had inherited a few sparks of his ancestor's pluck! The Duchess of Berry entertained him at Chambord and introduced him to his little grandson, the Duke of Bordeaux. Magnificent receptions followed in the Tuileries, at Saint-Cloud, and at Rosny. The choice of *La Muette de Portici* for a gala performance at the Paris Opera was not felicitous, with its evocation of Masaniello's revolt. But there was a shoot at Compiègne which the Queen enjoyed hugely, though she had to fire in a sitting posture owing to her corpulence. 'A little bell,' remarked the Maréchal de Castellane, 'gives an idea of the grace of her figure.' As for the King, he seemed a decrepit old man of seventy. His brother-in-law the Duke of Orleans gave a ball in his honour on May 31. So splendid were the apartments of the Palais-Royal that night that Charles X said to the Duke: 'Do you know, sir, that you are better lodged than I am?' Gazing into the starry night he remarked: 'This is perfect weather for my fleet at Algiers.' He could see victory in the distance, as it were, but not the near defeat of his

[1] A Spanish silver coin worth 6¼d.

government. While the guests were dancing there was a hubbub in the garden. An excited crowd had swept past the palace guards and set fire to some piles of chairs. The Duchess of Berry had just danced a tarantella with a bevy of beauties from the Faubourg Saint Germain, but remained as unruffled as Charles X himself and with exquisite composure soothed the frightened ladies. Her father, the guest of honour, she failed to soothe. He left the party in haste. The ball became famous for Salvandy's oft-quoted remark. Viennet has described it in his *Journal* without mentioning the mob episode. Under the heading of June 1, he writes: 'Yesterday I went to the ball given for the King of Naples and his family by the Duke of Orleans. It was the first time I set foot in the rooms of the Palais-Royal. . . . The ball was very beautiful. The whole of the royal family were present and Charles X did not appear to be amused. The sovereigns of Naples are nothing wonderful. The King has the features of a man of eighty and he is not even fifty-four. The dancing was solemn; and solemnity is always sad. There were many deputies in our midst, beset by grim anxieties like everybody else. M. de Salvandy, a wit who enjoys scintillating, has neatly summarized the situation. "We are dancing," he said, "on a volcano." He was quite right.'

The Duchess of Berry prevailed on her father to linger another month in spite of his misgivings. But when Intonti urged him to leave Paris immediately, he would brook no further delay. 'My Intonti makes no mistakes,' he muttered. On June 30 the King and Queen left for Genoa, where they met the widowed Queen of Sardinia and her daughter Maria Cristina whose future engagement to Ferdinand was vaguely discussed. They reached Naples on July 31. Noel Hill reported: 'Their Majesties with their suite disembarked immediately and were received with great acclamation by the people. In the evening there was a more general and brilliant illumination and a greater crowd in the streets than I have ever before witnessed at Naples. The illuminations, which are however strictly enforced by the police, are to continue for three nights.

'I lament to add that although the King appears in public, and has ordered a Court to be held, a visible alteration has taken place in his health and appearance. Being afflicted with gout and other infirmities His Majesty was not in the most perfect health when he ventured upon his long journey . . . Prince Cassaro . . . dates his present reduced state and alarming cough from a shooting party to which he was invited by H.M. the King of France at Compiègne where His Sicilian Majesty, already unwell, was long exposed to a severe rain.'

Ulloa[1] has recorded that the King had shrunk so that his uniform was too big for him; he stooped more than ever and seemed to be smiling and frowning at the same time. The smile was mechanical: he could hardly conceal his depression. He chatted amiably with his ministers about Paris and Madrid. 'Naples surpasses both those cities for the beauty of its climate,' he told them, 'but much will have to be done before it equals Paris in elegance.' The Prince of Cardito and Monsignor Rosini noticed that he often harped on 'the happy days of yore'. Speaking of his recent journey, he added: 'Spain is too antiquated and France is far too modern.' The guests left the palace with forebodings, for the King seemed a querulous old man. He spent the rest of the evening with his family. A member of the household asked little Prince Anthony: 'Did His Majesty enjoy himself in Paris with all the French festivities?' 'Yes, indeed he did,' the Prince replied, 'but those people are our enemies.'

Next day the King attended a thanksgiving service in the cathedral. After benediction, the Cardinal Archbishop assured him that the younger generation of Neapolitans was just as religious as the old. Francis gazed at him gloomily and said: 'The generation is young, Your Eminence, but the Kings are old.' The Cardinal looked bewildered.

On the very day of the King's return to Naples, Louis-Philippe, draped in the tricolour, was receiving the plaudits of the French populace. The news of Charles X's four ordinances had at first caused rejoicing at Court, and his firmness was praised by Francis. But a few days later it was known that the French government had fallen, and that 'the throne of Charles X had already passed from him in blood'. There was great excitement among the Neapolitan liberals—smiles, handshakes, eager whispers, exclamations of joy. At Court there was only despondency. Some realized that a monarchy based on insurrection would perish. Others said: 'Before next Easter 50,000 Frenchmen will be at our gates.'

Francis received tender letters from his sister Marie Amélie, assuring him that Louis-Philippe would never forget his hospitality at Palermo;

[1] *Op. cit.*

40

but he was not comforted. General Guglielmo Pepe had been trying to organize an Italian legion in France, and the Neapolitan consul at Marseilles had reported that he was preparing to sail with a shipload of arms to Calabria. Viscount La Passe had removed the French arms from the embassy in Naples and was nervously awaiting instructions from Paris. Francis was distressed about the fate of Charles X, so recently his host. At the end of August he received a letter from Louis-Philippe explaining that he had accepted the crown in order to save the nation and the monarchy. Francis was painfully perplexed. Soon after hearing from Louis-Philippe he heard of the outbreak in Brussels against the King of Holland and the Belgian declaration of independence on August 25. All this would add fuel to the unrest in Italy. It looked as if France would return to her previous rôle of world shaker and trouble-maker. But England recognized the sovereignty of Louis-Philippe on September 1, and Naples followed suit. Noel Hill asked Cassaro if it were true that His Sicilian Majesty had been advised by his sister the Queen of the French to adopt more liberal measures. 'Prince Cassaro replied that she certainly had advised affectionately, but only generally, some concessions. The Prince, however, added that His Majesty had no intention at present of following such advice. . . . The Austrians are now known to be in great force in Lombardy. This has produced a most salutary effect, but His Sicilian Majesty has not neglected to take some precautions for his safety or escape in case of necessity. The passages from the royal palace to the sea have been lately repaired. . . . The Duke de Blacas has written from Nice . . . to say he should come here for a few days, and then return to join the exiled Court in England. . . . His Sicilian Majesty remains in the same precarious state of health.'

At the same time (September 24, 1830), the Austrian ambassador informed Metternich that Marie Amélie had advised Francis to grant a Constitution rather than have it wrested from him. 'The King did not conceal how shocked and offended he was by so misplaced and improper a suggestion and confided this profession of faith to his minister (Cassaro): "There was a time when I thought that a partial sacrifice of the rights of the Crown in favour of national representation might have a beneficial influence on the development of our internal resources, efficient methods of administration, and the prosperity of the State in general, while diminishing the sovereign's burden of responsibility. In this illusion about the possibility of obtaining such desirable results I was completely sincere (*de la meilleure foi du monde*), but I was undeceived in 1820, when by my late father's wish I was placed at the head of the constitutional régime. I then became convinced that a Constitution . . . was only the first step towards democracy and anarchy, and I am firmly resolved not to take a road which must lead to the most fatal consequences." '

The King's health was deteriorating rapidly. Sometimes he talked so wildly that he seemed to be losing his wits. Even at Mass he was visibly distracted, and he had frequent fits of irritability followed by remorse. While walking in the palace with Micheroux he attacked a servant who was scrubbing the pavement and struck him with his cane. Later he handed Micheroux some gold coins for the victim of this assault, asking if these would suffice. Micheroux told him candidly that the remedy was scarcely more dignified than his behaviour. The King pressed his hand without a word, as if to confess that he had lost all self-control. Benevolence was not natural to him, says Ulloa,[1] but he now took pains to appear more benevolent than before.

A mild diversion had been created by the arrival of the dispossessed Dey of Algiers on board the French frigate *Jeanne d'Arc*. The sight of the tricoloured flag on the ship aroused enthusiasm among the liberals and Muratists, irritation among the royalists and troops who had returned from Sicily. But as Naples had often suffered from his pirates nobody felt much sympathy for the Dey's misfortune. Noel Hill reported on August 3: 'The Dey made immediate application to His Sicilian Majesty for permission to land and fix his residence here, with which request His Majesty has been graciously pleased to comply. . . . His Highness with a suite of one hundred and nine persons, of which the majority are women, will disembark from the frigate this evening and tomorrow. They will first be lodged in the suburb of Posillipo, and the Dey himself and some of his suite in the house which was formerly prepared for the ambassadors from the Levant. . . . The Dey is strongly recommended to my good offices and protection.'

According to Alexandre Dumas père he stayed at the smart Hotel Vittoria. Perhaps he spent a few days there, when some such incident occurred as that embellished in *Le Corricolo*[2] concerning a careless

[1] *Op cit.*   [2] *Osmin et Zaida*, pp. 4–13.

eunuch and a member of the harem whose execution was prevented in the nick of time by the hotel manager. The Duke of Serradifalco told Senior[1] that during the Dey's visit to Naples, 'one day Mustapha, his head servant, came into the kitchen and asked for a large knife. One was given to him, but it was too small; and another, but it was still too small. They asked what he could want with one. "I have to cut off," he said, "Ali's head." The cook went to the master, to whom Mustapha repeated his business, and begged not to be kept waiting. They kept him, however, till the master had seen Del Carretto, the Minister of Police, who thought the matter deserved his presence at the hotel. The Dey received his visitor with Oriental politeness, and told him that it was quite true that he had ordered Mustapha to cut off Ali's head, and that he was surprised to find that it was not yet done. He yielded, of course, to the representations of Del Carretto, but left Naples next day for some country of freedom where a man can do what he will with his own.' Del Carretto later confirmed the truth of this story, though he was not Police Minister at the time.

After a while the Dey moved into a villa at Portici. 'He seemed resigned to his fall,' wrote Ulloa, 'saying: Allah has willed it. But he became red with fury when England was discussed. He did not wish to see or to be seen, and took pleasure in the planetary system. Watching the stars revolve, he was like a child with toys. The government merely saw that his person was respected, from a duty of hospitality, not of sympathy.' In October he left for Leghorn, saying that he intended to visit Mecca.

As regent during the King's absence, the Duke of Calabria had at length succeeded in removing Scaletta, the Minister of War. General Fardella, who had won the Prince's confidence, was appointed in his stead. He was reputed to be honest and energetic, though he had an old-fashioned prejudice against engineers. 'A corporal,' he used to say, 'is more valuable in wartime than a hundred little sappers.' Perhaps he had Napoleon in mind. While Ferdinand had been allowed his own way with the army, the King had other plans for the navy. As soon as he returned, he appointed his favourite younger son Charles, Prince of Capua, Vice-Admiral and Commander General of the Marine, since he seemed to be interested in naval affairs. Charles had

[1] Nassau William Senior, *Journals kept in France and Italy from 1848 to 1852.* London, 1871.

43

studied English not only as the language of a great sea power but because he had a penchant for English girls. Caropreso succeeded Medici in the finance department, and it was rumoured that he had to bribe Viglia exorbitantly for this post. Ferdinand believed this, but as Caropreso had been Medici's protégé, the choice was natural. The department had run smoothly during Medici's absence and the King was wary of unknown quantities.

For the time being the verdict against De Mattheis and his accomplices after their seven-year trial put other topics in the shade. De Mattheis was a rabid partisan of the exiled Prince of Canosa, whose devotion to the Altar and the Throne had become so warped by fanaticism that it was akin to frenzy: as intendant of the province of Cosenza he and his vicious underlings had introduced a local reign of terror. But in spite of their influential connections and their protests of devotion to himself, the King was determined to have them tried 'with the most impartial justice'. He could have hushed up the scandal, but his conscience would not let him. The records of the trial filled 108 stout volumes. Though De Mattheis had been able to destroy many incriminating documents, there was enough evidence to prove that he had revived the sect of Calderari with appalling results: false accusations, illegal arrests, bribery, intimidation, torture, the complete subversion of justice. His private and political enemies had been persecuted with relentless brutality. From a distance Canosa did everything possible to save his creatures, 'martyrs in the good cause'. He wrote a virulent pamphlet in which De Mattheis was compared to Cicero against Catiline, and had it smuggled into Naples. The trial was intensely dramatic. De Mattheis played his Mephistophelian rôle to perfection, and the court shuddered when witnesses maimed with torture testified, while the judges remained impassive. Celentano, the Advocate General of the Supreme Court, accused De Mattheis, D'Alessandro and De Gattis of 'having conspired for criminal thirst of honour and selfish gain against citizens who were probably innocent'. They had grossly prostituted their powers and trampled on every vestige of humanity, government and religion. Celentano closed his harangue with an invocation to justice. He begged God to inspire him, purifying his soul from all dross of partisan hatred. Then, as if his prayer had been answered, he demanded the death penalty for the chief defendants. The court applauded. In this hostile atmosphere the

44

defence tried to prove that this accusation of 'conspiracy against a whole region' was absurd, but for all their dialectical skill they could not demolish the imputations of cruelty and abuse of authority. De Mattheis was condemned to ten years' imprisonment. The others were detained for further investigation or absolved. This mild sentence pleased nobody outside the government, which considered it 'not a party triumph, but a proof of justice'. But the case had revealed festering sores in the provincial administration.

Profoundly dejected and racked with gout, the King was advised by his doctors to stay at Castellammare. Many believed that his illness was the belated effect of poison administered by his mother eighteen years previously. He refused to be bedridden, and in spite of increasing fits of giddiness he was obsessed with State affairs. Early in September Cardinal Albani, on behalf of Pius VIII, sent warning that bands of Carbonari brigands were harrying the provinces of Frosinone and Pontecorvo and appealed for co-operation to suppress them. A 'little holy league' was formed with the Pope, and Del Carretto was sent to Frosinone to prevent any outbreak of disorder. The Pope's health was failing too, and many feared that Francis and Pius VIII would expire simultaneously with a fresh crop of disturbances as the result. Francis spent more and more time with his family and had many private talks with Ferdinand about the future of the dynasty. He expressed great concern lest his sons should quarrel after his death. 'To preserve the splendour of the Throne', he decreed that all members of the royal family were to submit to the sovereign in arranging marriage contracts and disposing of family property.

Ferdinand had already shown such intelligence and enterprise that the corrupt faction led by Scaletta and Marchese Ugo delle Favare made an attempt to postpone his succession. How could a callow youth of twenty be expected to rule when the whole of Europe was in turmoil? The question was merely rhetorical. To stave off the evil hour they plotted to make Queen Isabella regent after the King's death. But the Queen was totally devoid of political sense or ambition: it is doubtful whether she had an inkling of this plot, whose details have never come to light. The King knew even less. Ferdinand was informed, however, and a devoted band of young officers were prepared to act in case of emergency. The liberals were also ready to rouse the provinces in Ferdinand's name. It was rumoured that Intonti would support a regency as he had been at loggerheads with Del Carretto since the Vallo insurrection. Each had his own partisans among the police and gendarmerie. Intonti fulminated against the misdeeds of the gendarmerie in Council while Del Carretto complained about the police at command headquarters. Since nobody dared to propose a regency to the King, the plot flickered out. Yet it had brought the rival parties into the limelight and would influence subsequent events.

Noel Hill reported on November 6: 'The health of His Sicilian Majesty, which has been so long in a precarious state, has within the last two days declined so considerably that at length a bulletin has been issued. It is not supposed that His Majesty can survive many days or even hours.

'He had a convulsion fit the night before last and was with difficulty recovered from suffocation. His Majesty does not as yet appear perfectly aware of his situation, and observed this morning that he should keep his bed only a few days at the request of his physicians. He gave his orders with his usual clearness to Prince Cassaro, was equally interested about political events. . . .

'It has been for some time rumoured that disturbances might take place on the King's demise, and that evil-disposed persons were simply waiting for that event. The alarming situation of His Majesty now occupies all parties, and no other subject is considered.'

Noel Hill went on to reflect the opinions of the pro-regency party. While admitting that the Duke of Calabria was by no means without talents and resolution, 'it is feared, but I hope without reason, that he will not on his first assumption of the crown listen sufficiently to the advice of his ministers'.

The King received Extreme Unction on November 8 and took an affectionate leave of his sobbing family. 'I am detached from everything mundane,' he murmured. 'I do not wish my sufferings to cease, but to suffer more in order to atone for my sins.' Then he asked for some water, but he could not swallow and seemed about to suffocate. Fervently clutching a holy image given him by Pius VII, he said: 'I wish to join Jesus Christ with my heart and soul.' Beckoning to Ferdinand, he told him: 'I have come to the fatal moment when time ends and eternity begins. My power and glory on earth are finished; these honours, this Court will vanish like a dream. You will soon ascend the throne, my son: listen to your dying father. . . . Be good and just

46

before God; do not let yourself be seduced by power and pleasure. Bear these words in mind: all is vanity in this world, all is a dream, a passing shadow.' Dominicans, Theatines, and monks of other Orders came to bring him plenary indulgence, and he welcomed them all with a smile. Seeing that he was in pain while clasping a crucifix, Monsignor Giunta bent over to relieve him. As if he feared that the crucifix might be removed, he clutched it convulsively with both his withered hands. Then he made signs for a holy candle to be lighted beside his bed. His articulation became blurred as he tried to repeat the prayers of his confessor; then his voice was silent. These details are gleaned from an account published by a witness. Ulloa adds that the King made a gesture as if to bless his children, but his arm dropped languidly. 'Oh Naples!' he murmured with a sigh, and fell back dead.

None could deny that the King's death had been edifying. Indeed— 'Nothing in his life became him like the leaving it.' For all his religious zeal, his meticulous attention to State affairs, he had never endeared himself to the Neapolitan people. He might have been admired in the eighteenth century, but the times were against him and he was against the times. He left a large family: six sons and seven daughters; and Ferdinand, his heir, was a youth of unusual promise. The royal corpse was exposed for three days before the funeral in Santa Chiara. On the third night the two bodyguards on duty beside the elaborate catafalque were startled by a sinister thud. They scampered off in a panic. One of the dead King's arms had fallen on the floor because his corpse had been embalmed too hastily.

III

O N November 8, 1830, Ferdinand II announced his succession in a vigorous proclamation: 'God having summoned us to occupy the Throne of our August Ancestors, in consequence of the death of our beloved Father and King Francis I, of glorious memory; while our heart is pierced with the anguish of the severe loss we have sustained, we are conscious of the enormous burden which the Supreme Dispenser of Realms has wished to impose on our shoulders, in entrusting to us the government of this Kingdom. We are convinced that God, in investing us with His authority, does not intend it to remain idle in our hands, nor does He wish us to abuse it. He wishes our Kingdom to be a Kingdom of justice, vigilance, and wisdom. . . .' Ferdinand's first care would be to preserve the Catholic Religion; his second, to secure an impartial administration of justice. He would pay special attention to finance as he realized that there were 'deep wounds' to be healed in this department, and that his people hoped for a reduction of the taxes to which they had been subjected as a result of past upheavals.

On the same day he appointed his third brother, Leopold, Count of Syracuse, Lieutenant General in Sicily. Marchese Ugo delle Favare, who had made himself so unpopular and had plotted to install the King's mother as regent, was ordered to leave the island within twenty-four hours, and General Nunziante was sent to take charge until the Count of Syracuse arrived. General Saluzzo was given command of the army. Ferdinand rode into Naples on a magnificent bay horse, accompanied by his staff in brilliant uniforms. He was a dark plump youth with piercing round eyes and an upturned nose, but his dignified manner made up for a lack of physical distinction. Plumpness is commonly associated with good humour, and this hale and hearty looking monarch who could be jocular as well as pious made a pleasing impression on the masses. Cheers raucous and shrill; fluttering handkerchiefs of every hue; flowers falling through the air; windows, balconies, terraces, verandas packed with voluble excited citizens; Naples, which seemed a perpetual carnival to foreign visitors, at least became a carnival for the moment.

The young King immediately got rid of Viglia, Caterina de Simone, Colonel Carbone and others who had turned the palace into an employment bureau for their profit; and he dismissed the palace police which had done little but invent conspiracies to frighten his ailing father. The Prince of Scaletta, who had been responsible for so much extortion in the war ministry, would have been tried for peculation had he not produced documents proving the late King's connivance. Ferdinand gave up 180,000 ducats of his allowance, and abolished a number of royal game preserves including his grandfather's favourite haunts of Persano, Venafro and Mondragone, which were to be thrown open to the public to promote agriculture. 'As a great expense is saved by this act, this decree gave great satisfaction,' wrote the British minister. But the changes in the Cabinet, which included the discharge of the Finance Minister Caropreso, 'are rather unpopular, not so much perhaps from attachment to the former ministers, but . . . from some suspicions of the party of the exiled Prince Canosa being restored to favour. There has been some intrigue to displace Prince Cassaro, but for the present, at least, it has been defeated. The rumour generally afloat was that upon the death of the late King, a revolt was to have taken place in Sicily which was to have declared itself independent of Naples, the Prince of Salerno was to have been proclaimed King, and that the Marquis Ugo was supposed to be connected with this plot. These rumours seem almost incredible, yet the public have waited in vain for any explanation.' As the Prince of Salerno had only recently returned from Vienna, and evinced as little ambition as the Queen

Mother whose corpulence he rivalled, the rumour had little foundation. The Sicilians always wanted independence, but they hated Ugo delle Favare and were gratified by his disgrace.

There was no question of Canosa returning to power, though he had paid court to Monsignor Olivieri with that aim. Some colour might have been given to this suspicion by the King's pardon of Canosa's protégé, De Mattheis, who had been sentenced to ten years' imprisonment, but at the same time he proclaimed an amnesty for political offenders. The Minister of Police Intonti proposed in Council that two lists be compiled, the first of those who could return *ipso facto*, the second of those who could not return without a special application. In most cases the applications were granted. Guglielmo Pepe would not deign to send one in; and in spite of Del Carretto's championship, the King vetoed Carascosa. But General Filangieri, Prince Ischitella, Luigi Blanch, and many others who had served and won their spurs and rank under Murat were soon reinstated. Filangieri's full rank was restored, and the King himself gave him the Order of Saint Januarius, expressing regret that he had been excluded from the army so long. Filangieri's daughter wrote that her father never forgot this gracious act as long as he lived.[1] The generals of the pro-Austrian party could not conceal their resentment. In his unpublished *Memoirs* Filangieri wrote: 'A stranger to the ideas of faction and favouritism which had swayed the Court of Francis I, the young King had taken scrupulous care to investigate the true merit of his officers. He knew the name, the conduct, the record of each individual. He had already had a struggle with his father's ministry . . . which had constantly thwarted his proposals to rescue good officers suspected of being revolutionaries or Muratists from poverty and oblivion.'

Besides throwing open the royal hunting preserves, Ferdinand stopped most of the private allowances granted by his father and halved those granted by his grandfather. Instead of 8000 ducats a year the Prince of Canosa received 3500. He tried to parry this bitter blow, but 'the miserly lad', as he called Ferdinand, was deaf to his indignant protests. The corps of royal huntsmen, who had been chosen for their robust physique and loyalty, were all disbanded. The rare birds and exotic beasts his father had collected were also got rid of. When Ascoli

[1] Teresa Filangieri Fieschi Ravaschieri, *Il Generale Carlo Filangieri*. Milan 1902.

begged Ferdinand to spare his father's pet parrots, he said: 'We must show that the season of parrots is over.'

At the risk of his own popularity he was determined to balance the budget. Various taxes were reduced, but so were the salaries of officials. He held public audiences without intermediaries; he made lightning tours of the provinces without pomp or preparation, staying in monasteries, dining with local mayors and magistrates, to find out their requirements and see things for himself.

His edicts inspired confidence. His decree of January 11, 1831, is a good example: 'We have investigated the actual state of the public treasury. Bad as it is, we make no mystery about it. This honest candour will be worthy of Us, and worthy of the generous people whom Providence has entrusted to our government. In bare figures, the deficit for 1831 amounts to 1,128,167 ducats. We were deeply grieved but not discouraged by this. Faithful to our promise to make every personal sacrifice, We have already contributed a grant of 180,000 ducats from our privy purse, and another of 190,000 ducats from our household allowance. We have saved 350,000 ducats from various branches of the marine and war departments. Strict retrenchment in various ministries has produced a further economy of 351,667 ducats. Balancing current income with army expenses for 1831, the sum of 110,050 ducats remains at our disposal. We have proposed to use this for public relief by reducing the tax on flour. . . .' etc.

Hitherto copious alms and subsidies had been distributed from the King's privy purse with more munificence than discernment. Often able-bodied rascals reaped more benefit than the deserving poor. To remedy this the King founded a Royal Charity Commission before his twenty-first birthday. 'At the great theatre of San Carlo brilliantly illuminated upon the birth night,' wrote Noel Hill, 'His Majesty was enthusiastically received, but as the pit was chiefly crowded with officers a correct judgement could not be formed of the general feeling of the populace without. The next morning, however, there was a great review and fortunately one of the finest days ever known even in an Italian winter. The streets were overflowing with persons of all ranks and descriptions, and the acclamations which rent the air could not be mistaken.'

Thus Naples, in the dawn of Ferdinand's reign, was like a clear patch of sunlight surrounded by storms. The July Revolution in

France had tumultuous reactions on Central Italy, especially on Modena and the Papal States. Thanks to such conspirators as Guglielmo Pepe, who had cajoled General Lafayette into promising arms and money, the illusion was fostered that France would lend active support to revolution in Italy. While invoking French aid the revolutionists invoked that principle of non-intervention which Louis-Philippe had proclaimed on his accession—as if aid did not mean some sort of intervention. From Bologna a wave of insurrection spread through the Romagna, the Marches and Umbria. But French support failed: Louis-Philippe clung awkwardly to his principle. Austria, which had intervened in Modena and Parma, proceeded to intervene on the Pope's behalf.

Marchese Intonti, the Neapolitan Minister of Police, had a presentiment that constitutional governments were about to become general and wished to be in the vanguard of the movement. Perhaps he visualized himself as a liberal dictator. An ambitious opportunist, he thought he would alarm the young King into submission. In the meantime he hob-nobbed with the liberals. Cassaro, the Minister for Foreign Affairs, suspected that he was being lured by France. A letter from Latour-Maubourg (the new French ambassador who had been detained in Rome), advising changes in the ministry and timely concessions, and the acting chargé d'affaires' championship of local radicals, seemed more than a coincidence. He decided to air his impressions to the King. Ferdinand was unperturbed. 'Marchese Intonti is at the back of this,' he remarked, before Cassaro had even hinted at his suspicions. 'Intonti is eager to remain on good terms with all parties: he began his career as a liberal. Later, seeing that my father wished to follow a certain line of conduct—too exclusive in my opinion—he went too far in that direction and antagonized the liberal party. Now, since the events of last July, he wants to rejoin the liberals, and if the dynasty were to fall he would like to find himself on good terms with my successor! As I favoured a system of moderation he thought this an excellent chance, and as I am young he hoped to drag me as far as it suited him. That is why he and his fellows have besieged me ever since my succession; but to-day their manœuvres are clear to me. They will never be able to convince me. I would leave the crown and abandon Naples rather than subscribe to a constitution: in the backward state of civilization in this country its only result would be to encourage excesses and disorders, plunging us into a sea of woes.' The King went on to describe Intonti's plans.

Armed with this private information Cassaro attended the next Council of Ministers of February 11. When called upon to speak Intonti announced that there was fighting in the streets of Rome: he had had to warn the King that the situation was ominous and that it had become imperative to change the ministry. Bewilderment followed this statement and there were murmurs of mass resignation. Cassaro declared that such conduct would be cowardly: having served the King in prosperity, it was their duty not to desert him in time of danger, supposing any danger existed. If they were so weak as to resign, the liberals would merely step into their shoes and try to force obnoxious concessions on the King. All of them should stay at their posts.

This speech was a tonic to all the waverers save Intonti, who turned livid. In the absence of the president Tommasi, who was fatally ill, the Duke of Gualtieri was delegated to express these sentiments to the King, who praised their firmness. Posters demanding a national guard, the reinstatement of employees discharged in 1821, the dismissal of the ministry, etc., were set up in the streets; and no doubt Intonti was ready to create disturbances. Rumours were more fantastic than usual, and the Minister of Police did not scruple to exploit them.

But the King was ready too. On the night of February 16, he instructed Gualtieri, escorted by Colonel Martinez and a body of gendarmes, to order Intonti to embark within an hour on a brigantine sailing to Trieste. Intonti begged to be allowed to leave by land and his request was granted, thanks to Gualtieri's intercession. The King wished to camouflage Intonti's banishment as a mission to Vienna, but the Austrian minister Lebzeltern objected to this on the score that his government would be blamed by the liberals. 'The fact is,' wrote the British minister on February 19, 'that the Marquis is not only suspected of having fallen too much into the hands of the Liberal Party, but has been accused by his enemies of fabricating the very placards and reports which it was his duty as Minister of Police to prevent and suppress.' On March 1, he continued: 'The extraordinary circumstances under which the Marquis Intonti was sent from this country still excites considerable sensation . . . its precipitation being attributed to the youth and inexperience of His Sicilian Majesty. The time chosen was otherwise not ill selected, as it was the day following . . . Carnival, and the lower and middling classes after its fatigues as well as enjoyments had retired from the streets for quiet and repose. . . . The Marquis was not allowed to wait for his family, but was accompanied by a superior officer of the gendarmerie in his carriage and escorted by several soldiers of that corps to the frontier. I must not conceal that for many hours it was believed the Marquis was the victim of an intrigue carried on by my respectable colleagues of Russia and Austria, but . . . I can safely acquit them of any settled plan for this purpose, and entirely of any approbation of the manner of its execution.

'I have some reason to hope that in order to counteract the unpopularity of the transaction His Sicilian Majesty will permit a large proportion of exiles to return to this country, and believe the old royalists think it unfair that the liberal party should have the entire credit for every act of conciliation . . . the Marquis Intonti is now accused together with General Filangieri . . . of the intrigue against the Marquis Ugo, the former Viceroy of Sicily, not so much with a view of injury to the Viceroy as that of driving from his post here the General Nunziante. . . .

'Notwithstanding . . . the want of a master mind to direct, the discordance in the Cabinet, with an empty Exchequer and innumerable intrigues afloat, all is yet tranquil, and the King is still popular.' The ultra-liberal Nisco,[1] who gives a different version of the episode, says that even those who wanted a Constitution blessed Ferdinand for expelling Intonti.

Ferdinand's father and grandfather had been more or less at the mercy of their ministers, but Monsignor Olivieri had instilled a deep distrust of these domineering servant-masters into his young pupil. Intonti was the first of the old brigade to go; and Medici's old crony Tommasi died in April of the same year. Ferdinand even applied Olivieri's doctrine to his mentor, who vanished from the scene in clouds of incense. Over ten years later the Duke of Montebello wrote to Guizot that Ferdinand II had ever before his eyes as examples of warning 'the ghosts of Acton and Medici'. He was determined to rule without interference from any quarter. He was neither pro-French nor pro-Austrian: he was passionately pro-Neapolitan.

Unlike his father, who had been haunted by the Napoleonic night-

[1] *Op. cit.*

54

mare, Ferdinand was able to judge his subjects impartially according to their merits. Most of the officers who had served under Murat were more efficient than the faithful old royalists whose experience was limited to Sicily, but as the former were liberals, anti-Austrian if not pro-French, it was commonly assumed that Ferdinand had liberal sympathies when he reinstated them. His amnesty seemed to prove it. The Austrian ambassador was puzzled and suspicious. He knew that letters from all over the peninsula were begging the King 'to take advantage of actual circumstances and assume the brilliant rôle of King of Italy'. This would never suit Metternich. And the amnesty had been published soon after the revolt in Warsaw, which seemed a sinister coincidence. Cassaro told the ambassador that he tried to oppose it, and that the other ministers had backed him. But the King had made his decision without consulting them. 'What can a foreign diplomat do,' exclaimed Lebzeltern, 'against measures the King has taken on his own initiative and which he strenuously maintains without consulting his ministers, who dare not even venture to express their own opinion?'

Lebzeltern, who had been Medici's abomination, had left Vienna while King Francis was still alive. But instead of the sick and weary Francis, it was to a self-confident young man of twenty that he had to offer his credentials. This was a shock, but there were greater shocks in reserve. In spite of the King's assurances and his treatment of Intonti, Lebzeltern was disturbed by rumours of Ferdinand's marriage to a daughter of Louis-Philippe. It was also said that the Prince of Capua might accept the crown of Belgium. The French ambassador was equally worried, fearing that Naples would return under the Austrian yoke. Lebzeltern wrote to Metternich saying that if war broke out the King would sympathize with France, and the French Cabinet would do their utmost to decoy him. Cassaro was too much of a courtier to resist these tendencies, and the King seemed to take a perverse pleasure in alarming his ministers with oracular and contradictory statements. At one Council meeting he said that if he were not King of Naples he would be the greatest republican in the world; a few minutes later he declared that as far as he was concerned laws did not exist, that he only recognized his aim, which was a sound one. To achieve this he would set himself above the law. When French propaganda in Italy was discussed the King shouted: 'The French

55

have no common sense! By encouraging revolution among the Italians they are acting against their own interests because they are merely fetching in the Austrians; every partial revolution will be quelled and the whole peninsula will end in the hands of Austria. I have told the French that they would do better to support order in Italy so that the southern States, banded together, may be strong enough to drive the Austrians beyond the Po, which is what the French really want, in the event of war.'

Cassaro repeated all this to Lebzeltern, who concluded that the King lacked solid principles: when experience had taught him a few lessons he might show more wisdom. But the King cherished one solid principle: his personal independence, which he identified with that of his realm. By employing men like Filangieri he hoped to wean them from their Constitutional antecedents. The fallen police minister had been succeeded by Marchese Del Carretto, who was detested by the liberals as a renegade, and who has therefore gone down to history as a monster. But nobody holding his office at such a time could expect to be popular, and all parties had to admit that he performed his odious duties efficiently. He was a professional soldier, brisk and ener-getic, and he disliked subservience to Austria as much as Mazzini's 'Young Italy'. Nisco[1] described him as a liberal opposed to absolutism unless it was wielded by himself. Unlike Intonti, who had invented conspiracies to make himself indispensable, he tried to create an atmo-sphere of security. His reports were rosy; his eye was all-seeing. He had to make use of unscrupulous agents, but a private dossier proves that he was familiar with their qualities and defects. Thus he noted that Commissioner Morbillo 'must often be curbed; he has the ambition to be feared and is therefore no respecter of persons'. Campobasso was 'rapacious without betraying his duty; nobody knows better how to deal with the dregs of society; but we must shut our eyes on his dis-honesty'. Marchesi was most suitable for political investigations: 'sentiment does not affect his reason'. Another was a liar and a thief, 'but he might serve on some exceptional occasion'. Through such agents as these Del Carretto kept a finger in every pie, but he was convinced he was working for the best of causes and there is no longer any doubt about his personal integrity.

When the King visited Sicily on July 2, 1831, Palermo, Trapani,

[1] *Op. cit.*

Messina, Catania and Syracuse vied in giving him a tremendous ovation. Crowds wished to drag his carriage through the streets. At the same time a volcanic island suddenly rose from the sea near Sciacca. This was a mile and a quarter in circumference, but it entirely disappeared on August 3, the day before the King's return to Naples. Before Father Neptune reclaimed it, a British captain cruising in the vicinity had actually planted the Union Jack upon it, and taken formal possession in King William IV's name. For a time it was a dangerous obstacle to navigation, and even when it had sunk to the depth of eleven feet below the surface of the Mediterranean it was known to our Admiralty officials as Graham's shoal. It is interesting to speculate on what would have happened to the island had it remained an English dependency. In spite of all the enthusiasm and festivities recorded in the local press, there was an attempted revolt in Palermo on September 1. This had no connection with the contemporary rebellions in Modena and the Romagna, but it suited certain propagandists to pretend that it had wide significance. Some thirty-eight ruffians, led by a former Carbonaro, rushed through the Termini gate with cheers for Liberty, the King, and Saint Rosalia. After a skirmish with the police in which several were killed or wounded, most of them guzzled in a tavern to recruit their strength for an assault on a customs house. Thirty-three were arrested, and the Lieutenant-General expressed satisfaction for the calm behaviour of the population who were indignant about the whole affair. The serious liberals were afraid it might compromise their plans for the future.

The curious 'monk conspiracy' to proclaim a Constitution was disarmed in 1833. It was led by the magnetic monk Angelo Peluso, and the conspirators, including many ex-deputies of 1820 and other malcontents, held meetings by night in the Sanità monastery. Simultaneous risings were to break out at Ariano, in Calabria, and in the Abruzzi. Appropriately disguised as a Doctor Dulcamara dispensing quack medicines, Brother Angelo set off for Ariano with a quantity of printed proclamations, patents and diplomas, ammunition both material and spiritual, and a tricoloured flag. He succeeded in recruiting a stout band of peasants who hoisted the banner in a peaceful valley, where he preached a stirring sermon on all the potential benefits of a Constitution. But, as often happened, somebody betrayed the plot. The bayonets of Del Carretto's gendarmes broke up the happy meeting, and the whole affair ended before it had begun. Nearly three hundred insurgents were arrested, but only a few were sentenced to death and reprieved, while Brother Angelo vanished into limbo.

As cholera was rampant throughout Europe Ferdinand published sanitary regulations and sent commissioners to strategic points along the coast; as well as a circular to every bishop in the kingdom for special prayers to be invoked. He made a careful inspection of the lazaret at Nisida to ascertain that his orders had been obeyed. Next year he created a provisional sanitary council. Many volunteers, such as the hospital friars of San Giovanni di Dio, offered their services, and several doctors were sent to Paris to study the latest methods of dealing with the epidemic. The King was ubiquitous, inspecting orphanages, the madhouse at Aversa and the Albergo dei Poveri, but most of his time was taken up with military parades and manœuvres. 'Economy is professed to be the leading principle of the administration,' wrote the captious British minister, 'but a large and useless army is still supported at a great expense, not three fourths of which are effective. The full number, however, may exist on paper and is consequently paid for by His Sicilian Majesty.' The King's constant endeavour was to improve his army. Sir Walter Scott, who had attended evening classes in Italian in Edinburgh so as to read Boiardo and Ariosto in the original, did not come to Naples till 1831 when he was suffering from 'a total prostration of bodily strength,' yet he saw the young King and confided to his diary:[1] 'He has made efforts to lessen his expenses. But then he deals in military affairs, and that swallows up his savings, and Heaven only knows whether he will bring (his subjects?) to fight, which the Martinet system alone will never do. His health is undermined by epileptic fits which, with his great corpulence, makes men throw their thoughts on his brother Prince Charles. It is a pity.'

Amid Ferdinand's strenuous activity it was not generally realized that he suffered from epilepsy, but he had an acute attack on his return from Sicily. 'I have some reason to believe,' wrote Noel Hill, 'that delay in the long projected marriage has in some measure arisen from the repetition of this illness. I have also reason to believe that in consequence of these events the French ambassador has it in contemplation to promote a marriage between Prince Charles the King's next brother

[1] *The Journal of Sir Walter Scott 1829–32.* Edinburgh and London, 1946.

and a French Princess.' Reports of Ferdinand's ill health coupled with the cholera scare had prevented the widowed Queen Maria Theresa of Sardinia from accepting him for her daughter Maria Cristina. The reigning King of Sardinia, Charles Albert, made several efforts to obtain her consent, but Maria Theresa remained obdurate.

The youngest of King Victor Emmanuel I's four daughters, Maria Cristina, had been born at Cagliari in 1812 and brought up in an intensely religious atmosphere. One of her aunts was Maria Clotilde, the saintly sister of Louis XVI of France, whose husband Charles Emmanuel had left his throne of Savoy to become a Jesuit, another was her pious namesake, the widow of King Charles Felix, and she had always been surrounded by dames of irreproachable virtue. After her father's death she had lived with her mother in dignified seclusion at Genoa, occasionally visiting her sisters, the Duchesses of Modena and Lucca. She spent five months in Rome for the Jubilee of 1824, visiting holy shrines and relics, touring the basilicas on foot but heavily veiled, with a coronet in her hand, in order to acquire indulgences. Her existence was almost a series of religious functions, and when her mother died in 1832 her first and deepest impulse was to take the veil. King Charles Albert became her guardian, and for the next six months, aided by the Queen and Maria Cristina's sisters, he did everything possible to persuade her to marry Ferdinand. 'To those who warmly recommended to her the young monarch of the Two Sicilies, and everybody did so,' wrote her biographer the Abate De Cesare,[1] 'she answered modestly that she was not born for the joys of this world, and desired nothing better than peace of mind and the retirement of a cloister. Her devotion to her mother had long prevented this, but now that she was a free agent, annoyed by worldly pomp, she wished to find calm in a convent. To the Queen, to the ladies and maids who spoke of the rigours of the cloister which she would find hard to bear, she replied that she had put her trust in God and depended for strength on Him alone.'

Every argument was broached to melt her resistance: Ferdinand's kindness of heart, the beauty of his kingdom, the excellence of the climate, and, above all, the benefits she could confer on her subjects, who yearned for her and already considered her as their Queen. Her

[1] D. Guglielmo De Cesare, *Vita della Venerabile Serva di Dio Maria Cristina di Savoia Regina delle Due Sicilie.* Rome, 1863.

sister, the Duchess of Modena, pointed out that she could achieve perfection in a palace as well as in a cloister, and that the edifying conduct of a Christian Queen was more valuable than solitary prayer: it was more difficult to sanctify a royal Court than a convent; the greater the risk of danger, the greater the prize. Her spiritual director, Father Terzi, was a Neapolitan, and he told her he believed it to be the will of God that she should comfort Ferdinand II with her consent. After a long and silent struggle she accepted, but the prospect of matrimony continued to alarm her. Her sisters and her pious aunts rejoiced, and the King of Sardinia expressed his gratification. Messengers brought the glad news from Turin to Naples; portraits were exchanged; gifts and congratulations poured in; and both Charles Albert and Ferdinand decided to go to Genoa in the autumn of 1832. Amid all the nuptial preparations the bride remained dreamily detached. 'I cannot understand yet,' she wrote, 'how, with my character I could change my mind and say yes. It can only be explained by recognizing the very will of God, to Whom nothing is impossible.'

Ferdinand travelled north incognito, without pomp of any kind. When he reached Rome on November 10 he stayed in a hotel on the Piazza di Spagna instead of in his family residence, the vast Farnese Palace. In spite of his incognito he rushed to visit the recently elected Pope Gregory XVI. After being blessed he inspected a few of the chief sights and drove on to Florence, where he arrived on November 13, again staying at a hotel. That minute chronicler Mauro Musci[1] has naïvely recorded his meeting with the Grand Duke, who was soon to become his brother-in-law: 'It is a habit of the good Prince Leopold to wander through Florence nearly always on foot and move among the crowd without molestation. . . . On November 14 the Grand Duke, unaware of the illustrious guest visiting his capital, clad in black since he had recently lost his wife, was walking through the public galleries of the Pitti Palace rapt in thought, when King Ferdinand appeared. Leopold noticed the young incognito, whose quick, lively and speculative manner of examining the most famous pictures roused his interest and sympathy . . . so that he offered to guide him. . . . Ferdinand courteously assented and started an animated conversation with him under the impression that he was a curator of the museum.

[1] Mauro Musci, *Storia civile e militare del regno delle Due Sicilie sotto il governo di Ferdinando II dal 1830 al 1849.* Naples, 1855.

Leopold, noting the southern pronunciation, inquired politely, "Are you from Naples, sir?"—"From Naples, at your service." "Oh, what luck to meet so young a student of the Fine Arts who is a subject of Ferdinand II. What is your King doing? Is he well? When did you see him last? Have you just arrived?" "I have come from Naples; the King is well; and I thank you for your kindness to one of his subjects and for the esteem you express for him." "It is a duty to praise a sovereign who at a tender age and in times none too happy has succeeded in winning the most flattering opinion of himself throughout Europe, and in delighting his people with extraordinary acts of clemency. You are fortunate. Cherish your generous Prince with all your heart, for he deserves it. Your people's love for him will be a fertile portent of progress, civilization and peace for the beautiful country you inhabit."

'Touched by this eulogy, Ferdinand almost betrayed his identity. "You are also fortunate in your Prince," he said. "Leopold is good, the father of his States; his cultured manners and his existence dedicated to his people are a rich heritage for the government of gentle Tuscany. How is the Grand Duke? What is he doing at present?"

'The Grand Duke, equally touched, revealed himself unintentionally: "He is well. In fact he is here. Every day he takes an hour's relaxation after the cares of State, studying the national monuments, the ancient records of his people."

"Is Leopold here? Do I actually behold him?"

'"At your service."

'"Then I must inform you that I am Ferdinand of Naples."

'There were exclamations of mutual pleasure and surprise. The two sovereigns, who had admired each other from a distance, hugged each other and wept for joy at this unexpected meeting. The Grand Duke wished to give Ferdinand a more public reception but as he insisted on remaining incognito he gave him a quiet family dinner.'

The modern reader cannot help suspecting that this episode was not entirely spontaneous, as the Grand Duke's police must have informed him of Ferdinand's arrival. Ferdinand's large retinue joined him in Genoa where there were official festivities. We have no record of his emotions: he had set his heart on this marriage even if he was not in love. The Princess was tall, slim and delicate-looking, with a broad forehead, melting blue eyes under long lashes, and abundant

61

fair hair over a long neck; her bearing was modest but she had an innate dignity. 'You will have the best of Queens,' the widow of King Charles Felix told a Neapolitan lady, 'her only fault is that she is a little shy, but she is an absolute angel.' In fact she was almost too ethereal a mate for the practical, exuberant Ferdinand, whose piety was of a more earthly texture. After signing the marriage contract she confided to the Queen of Sardinia that only Christian obedience had overcome her sense of monastic vocation; yet she appeared to be painfully distracted. While being dressed for the ceremony she burst into tears, and her ladies-in-waiting did not know how to comfort her. One of these, Countess Piossasco, broke the sobbing silence by asking what had distressed her. She replied that she could not help dreading the prospect of matrimony, for which she had never felt the slightest inclination. 'I suffered from the same sensations myself,' said the Countess, 'but take courage, Your Highness, for these are things that pass.' The Princess clasped her hand and said with deep emotion: 'That is so, because if things do not pass, we do.' She made a supreme effort to control herself and walked calmly down the staircase to the great hall where her bridegroom and the sovereigns of Sardinia with their separate Courts were assembled. Though she kept her composure, it was noticed that she was extremely pale. As it was only eight months since her mother's death she had requested a quiet service in the sanctuary of Voltri, near Genoa, where there was an image of the Blessed Virgin for which she had a special veneration. The Bishop of Novara officiated, and only the royal family of Savoy and her own suite were present. Since the dawn of that day, November 21, 1832, she had prayed for the strength to smile: her pallor suddenly vanished and she smiled. After the rite the widow of Charles Felix took her hand and told the bridegroom, who was her own nephew: 'I am giving you a shy young maiden with little experience of this world. Cherish her, for she is worthy of you: you will have a young Saint for a companion.' There were tears of tenderness and joy in the eyes of all beholders. Later the Queen of Sardinia remarked to Countess Piossasco: 'Have you seen the Princess Cristina? Surely a miracle has happened since our last conversation. If you could have witnessed all the affection she showed her husband (on the way back from Voltri), with what courtesy she addressed him, to the extent of fearing that the cold draught and pelting rain might injure him. "My dear Ferdinand," she said, "I'm afraid this damp air may be bad for you," and she suggested closing the windows of the carriage. I could hardly believe my eyes. She spoke like a loving bride of three or four months. I did not recognize the Cristina I had known. There is something supernatural in this.'

King Charles Albert had prepared a grandiose apartment for the royal couple, but Ferdinand preferred to stay in the same rooms he had occupied since his arrival in Genoa with a minimum of pomp. Here the young Queen greeted her new suite from Naples and her graciousness captivated them. When Countess Piossasco came to take leave of her she said with a demure smile: 'Oh, if you knew how good my Ferdinand is!' These ingenuous words showed that she had conquered her prejudices. In spite of rainy weather there were public festivities for three consecutive days: the fortifications and the harbour were illuminated, and the Genoese merchants erected an elaborate 'machine' with allusive transparencies on the Piazza Banchi.

Ferdinand and Cristina sailed for Naples on November 25. The fame of the young Queen's piety preceded her, and the people were pleased that the King had chosen an Italian bride. They disembarked on November 30 amid the thunder of guns from the castles and the naval squadron in the bay. Though it was raining heavily they were cheered by enormous crowds, and all who could catch a glimpse of the Queen felt as if they had seen an angel. Some described her beauty as a ray from Heaven, a flower of holiness. This first impression remained and gathered intensity; and those who were privileged to approach her were in raptures. One of her chambermaids said: 'Everybody marvelled at the Queen's rare modesty. As for me, her face was a subject of spiritual meditation.' Others were struck by 'the dignified humility which surrounded her with an aureole of majesty, all the more splendid because it was quite unconscious.' Modesty and innocence of heart: such virtues were seldom seen in a royal palace. A fleeting glimpse of her was caught by a young American, N. P. Willis.[1] 'As we entered the Toledo,' he wrote, 'the cavalcade came to a halt, and with hats off and handkerchiefs flying in every direction about them, the young new-married Queen of Naples rode up the middle of the street, preceded and followed by outriders in the gayest livery. She has been married about a month; is but seventeen, and is

[1] N. P. Willis, *Pencillings by the Way*. London, 1835.

acknowledged to be the most beautiful woman in the kingdom. The description I had heard of her, though very extravagant, had hardly done her justice. She is little above the middle height, with a fine lift to her head and neck, and a countenance only less modest and maidenly than noble.'

The palace of Naples was a humming hive of young Princes and Princesses who were neither innocent nor modest. Most of them had inherited their mother's frivolity. The Prince of Capua, only one year younger than Ferdinand, of whom he was openly jealous, was already an accomplished rake; Leopold, Count of Syracuse, was also an unabashed Lothario; and Anthony, Count of Lecce, had the reputation of a budding satyr at sixteen, so that Lecce and lechery had more than a punning connection. The Princesses were more demure than their married sisters, thanks to the good example of Maria Antonia, who was engaged to the Grand Duke of Tuscany. But the Queen Mother was far from edifying. The flesh is weak and she was a mound of flesh, palpitating with the desire to be regarded as a sprightly nymph, and be treated as such by young stalwarts beneath her station. Her roving eye was a cause of frequent embarrassment to Ferdinand, who could not approve of his mother's foibles. Monsignor Olivieri had waged a steady campaign against her wanton behaviour, but the merry widow continued to have her way. Her zest for life, her beaming affability and her massive *embonpoint* combined to make her popular. With her other children she was on terms more sisterly than maternal: they too believed in enjoying themselves. But there was a coldness between her and Ferdinand. Whether Maria Cristina realized this or not she was resolved to treat the Queen Mother with conspicuous respect. Soon after her arrival she fell on her knees before Maria Isabella, who blessed her and hugged her to her capacious bosom, telling her that she felt sure of her wonderful influence over the King.

This influence was soon reflected in several decrees: Ferdinand increased the endowment of the military orphanage so that three hundred orphans received monthly subsidies in future; he condoned all fines of less than twenty ducats, and ordered the release of those who had been imprisoned for debts not exceeding two hundred ducats if they had not been guilty of peculation; and he abolished penalties for infringements of the law previous to this decree, unless with malice prepense. The *Monte di Pietà*, or municipal pawn-shop, was to restore all articles pawned up to the sum of six ducats apiece. When a courtier remarked to the Queen that such objects were often pledged for an immoral purpose or to squander the money in taverns, the Queen replied with a pitying smile that 'those who had pawned them could only be the poor.' The King also forbade communes and municipalities to waste money on public celebrations: they were to spend it on works of charity instead. It was known that the Queen had suggested this, and while it was impossible to prevent private festivities, vast sums were distributed among the needy. Everybody except the liberals blessed the young Queen: the political malcontents accused her of being bigoted, superstitious and under the control of the Jesuits. According to them this marriage was detrimental to popular liberty.

Of course Ferdinand was anxious to place his bride under the protection of the patron saint of Naples, and there was frantic rejoicing on December 1, when the royal pair with appropriate pomp set forth to venerate the blood of San Gennaro. The buildings along the way were festooned with silk hangings and flowers, and the Queen, who had led a secluded existence at the staid Court of Savoy, was pleasantly fluttered by the noise and picturesque variety of this spectacle. The King and Queen were escorted by the canons of the cathedral to the patron saint's chapel, where they were met by the mayor and a deputation of nobles in charge of the relics, which the Queen kissed with fervent prayers, and the saint's treasury was further enriched with precious gifts.

Maria Cristina felt that her mission was to purify the Court by her own example. She soon won the confidence and affection of her numerous in-laws, who went to her with their problems as to a youthful Mother Superior unscathed by their petty jealousy and wrangling. That she found inward peace where she least expected it is proved by her letters, in spite of rumours to the contrary spread by the liberals. To her former governess, Countess Piossasco, she wrote: 'I could not be happier, and I should never have believed that one could be so happy in this ugly world, especially with my character, which you know. Well, it is evident that this whole affair was directed by God, since human works could never succeed like this, and I cannot thank God sufficiently for favours past and present.' And speaking of the royal family, she added: 'Beginning with my mother-in-law who has been infinitely kind, all of them show me so much affection and cordiality. Antonietta is very dear too, and I am exceedingly fond of her.'

After a short stay in the capital the King brought her to Caserta, San Leucio and Quisisana, where she took a personal interest in the welfare of the local peasants, and spent much time in neighbouring churches and chapels, leading her little sisters-in-law by the hand and teaching them to sublimate their thoughts. She could not help noticing the regrettable breach between Ferdinand and his mother. Though she never mentioned it outright, she made a point of asking his leave to visit her every day, until he realized that she longed for a reconciliation. Admiring her delicate tact, he accompanied her to his mother's apartment when he was least expected, after which he treated Maria Isabella with more deference, even when he was exasperated by her flirtations.

Maria Cristina's life was full of such domestic triumphs. There was a vast difference between the Piedmontese and the Neapolitan temperament, and Ferdinand had assimilated the manners and customs of his people. Physically he bore no resemblance to his grandfather, but he took after him in other ways, above all in his exuberance and love of the dialect. Willis, who saw him at the races in March 1833, has left a lively description in *Pencillings by the Way*, which also shows how cosmopolitan the society of Naples was at this period. 'The King of Naples, who has a great admiration for everything English, has abandoned the Italian custom of running horses without riders through the crowded street, and has laid out a magnificent course on the summit of a broad hill overlooking the city on the east. Here he astonishes his subjects with *ridden* races; and it was to see one of the best of the season that the whole fashionable world of Naples poured out to the campo this morning. The show of equipages was very brilliant: the liveries of the various ambassadors, and the court and nobles of the kingdom, showing on the bright green sward to great effect. I never saw a more even piece of turf, and it was fresh in the just-born vegetation of spring. The carriages were drawn up in two lines nearly half round the course, and for an hour or two before the races the King and his brother, Prince Carlo, rode up and down between with the royal suite, splendidly mounted, the monarch himself upon a fiery grey blood horse, of uncommon power and beauty. The director was an Aragonese nobleman, cousin to the King, and as perfect a specimen of the Spanish cavalier as ever figured in the pages of romance. He was mounted on a Turkish horse, snow-white, and the finest animal I ever saw; and he carried all eyes with him, as he dashed up and down like a meteor. I like to see a fine specimen of a man, as I do a fine picture or an excellent horse, and I think I never saw a prettier spectacle of its kind, than this wild steed from the Balkans and his handsome rider.

'The King is tall, very fat, but very erect; of a light complexion, and a good horseman, riding always in the English style, trotting and rising in the stirrup. Prince Charles is smaller and less kingly in his appearance, dresses carelessly and ill, and is surrounded always in public with half a dozen young Englishmen.'

Having spent so much time with the army, the King's language was distinctly coarse—so coarse that it made the Queen shudder. She begged him not to use what she called 'those soldiers' words'. On the surface she seemed to have no will of her own. She made such a cult of being submissive to Ferdinand that she even handed him the letters she received from her sisters, which she would not open until he had returned them to her. She chose her maids for their respectability and gave them orders indiscriminately, so that none might have any cause for jealousy. The courtiers, more prone to discover the weaknesses than the virtues of their masters, were astonished by the strict routine of the Queen's private life: she devoted several hours a day to prayer and religious exercises, without letting these interfere with her domestic duties. She introduced the practice of attending two Masses every day, one to thank God for mercies received, the other to pray for a continuation of His benefits. Every day she visited the Sacrament with Ferdinand, and they would kneel together at the foot of the altar. At first she recited the rosary alone, but soon her husband joined her. Having acquired this habit he made it an inviolable rule for the rest of his life. The Queen lowered her eyes in the presence of men and would never let anyone help her into or out of a carriage; it was noticed that she held her arms close to her waist to make this evident.

All this had an effect on her environment: language was chastened; the ladies dressed more modestly, went to church more often, and gave more time to philanthropy. 'As the modest violet, hidden among leaves, becomes known by the scent it exhales,' wrote the Abate De Cesare, 'the noble qualities of this virtuous soul did not remain immured behind the walls of the palace, but were soon manifest to all. . . . Whenever the people caught sight of her in the streets, they rushed to meet the Saint, as they called the Queen; and the women pointed her out to their daughters and said she was a heavenly spirit. . . . It was enough to see her to realize her purity of heart.' Consequently rich and poor christened their daughters Maria Cristina, and those who congratulated them exclaimed: 'May she become as saintly as our *Reginella*!' Anecdotes of her piety were on every tongue. One day while driving through the city she heard the tinkling of bells announcing that the Blessed Sacrament was being conveyed to an invalid. Although it was pouring with rain she ordered the coachman to halt, whereupon she stepped out and knelt on the muddy pavement before the Host. The priest blessed her; and the public was awed by this 'humiliation of human majesty before the majesty of the Eternal.'

While she was watching some military manœuvres one of the soldiers fainted. At once the Queen rose and summoned the nearest officer, telling him to see that the poor man was properly looked after. When she heard that this often happened at parades under the scorching sun, she begged the King to lighten the equipment of his troops during the summer. Her request was granted, and it was remembered by the army with gratitude. On another occasion she was shocked to notice that the groom preceding her carriage dispersed the crowd with his whip. The horses were stopped, and she gave strict orders never to use the whip again for this purpose: in future her coachman was to drive more slowly through the populous parts of the city. Later, when the same groom applied to her for some special benefaction for his family, she replied: 'Those who show no mercy to others deserve none.' Since she could never refuse a charity she gave him all he asked for, on condition he promised to abstain from such brutal methods. She longed to nurse the poor in the hospitals, but the King would not let her. Though she pleaded the examples of Saints Elizabeth of Hungary and Portugal (both Queens who had devoted their lives to the poor), Ferdinand put his foot down. While he was no stickler for Court etiquette there were times when it seemed to be necessary. Much as he admired his wife's virtues, it was not easy for a young man of twenty-two to be pious all the time: it was not even natural.

And Maria Cristina was almost too good to be true. If Ferdinand had any temptation to glance at another woman he repressed it instantly.

'The Queen is a fine woman, but she is cold,' he is reputed to have said; and his own temperament was hot-blooded if not volcanic like his brother Charles. Considering his plump physique he was remarkably austere, but he could not repress a sense of fun too gross for so ethereal a mate. From Sardi's[1] authoritative biography of the Queen, a few details may be gleaned which are like whiffs of garlic in a sacristy. The Queen was indifferent to clothes and let her ladies choose them for her. One day she was wearing a new straw-coloured dress with a pattern of green flowers which was considered fashionable; as soon as the King saw it he burst out laughing. 'It's exactly like an omelette with parsley,' he exclaimed. Another time when he had ordered the carriage for a drive and the Queen had not finished dressing, he told her that the coachman was swearing on account of the delay. At this the Queen became flustered. She reached the carriage out of breath and asked the coachman if it was true that he swore when she kept him waiting. The poor fellow protested his innocence and added: 'I am Your Majesty's servant to wait as long as you please.' The Queen went on questioning him, not suspecting that her husband had invented it to make her hurry. She only saw the joke when Ferdinand burst into a guffaw. Her seriousness and lack of humour must have got on his nerves occasionally, and he reacted with schoolboy crudity.

Settembrini and other political opponents have made much ado about his pulling her chair away when she was about to sit down: to aggravate this episode they alleged that she was pregnant at the time. But as Croce[2] pointed out, a diplomatic despatch dated February 1833, long before the Queen had become an expectant mother, relates that this had happened at a ball, from which the Queen withdrew to show that she had been offended. If Ferdinand hoped to break down her solemnity with such antics, he failed. After a while he was forced to realize that she was on a higher plane, and he would listen respectfully to her reproaches and gentle advice. 'Cristina has educated me,' he confessed naïvely. One is reminded of his grandfather's education

[1] Sardi, *La venerabile Maria Cristina di Savoia, regina delle Due Sicilie*. Rome, 1895.
[2] Benedetto Croce, *Uomini e cose della vecchia Italia, Serie Seconda*. Bari, 1927.

under Maria Carolina—but the difference between the two Queens was considerable.

On one of the King's birthdays she presented him with a piece of her own embroidery, adding: 'But I have done something else for you. This morning I distributed four thousand ducats among the poor.' The large scale of her charities was not discovered till after her death, when she left a book with all the names of indigent families she had given support, requesting the King to continue the good work. Many were not aware that she had helped them; as she spent little on herself or on entertainment she was considered stingy. Croce has observed with acumen that the Neapolitans preferred ostentatious forms of charity. Ferdinand would hand the cigar he was smoking to the lazzarone who had begged for it—a royal gesture that would be magnified and 'remembered for years, remembered with tears.'

IV

FERDINAND II remained an enigma to foreign diplomatists. What would this boisterous young man do next? Lebzeltern was afraid he would turn liberal at any moment. Cassaro, the Minister for Foreign Affairs, had been kept utterly in the dark during his marriage negotiations. Smarting under a sense of injury, he would have resigned had not Metternich pleaded with him to persevere for the sake not only of Naples but of Europe. The King had got into the habit of dealing with State business as if the ministry were non-existent. Resolutions passed in Council were suddenly altered owing to the advice of the King's private secretary, Abate Caprioli. Cassaro thought it undignified as well as futile to remain in office. 'I have made and shall continue to make great sacrifices if I may still be of service to the good cause,' he wrote to Lebzeltern on November 5, 1832. 'but when treaties and negotiations are made through private secretaries, and ambassadors and their staffs are appointed independently of the Ministry of Foreign Affairs, I could not guarantee that tomorrow some alliance might not be settled to suit some venal intriguer, and that I should then be ordered to give full powers to the signatory without knowing its contents.'

Metternich suspected that Louis-Philippe was hovering in the background and Cassaro feared there might be a secret pact. Lord Ponsonby, the British chargé d'affaires, reported: 'The truth I fear is, the King listens to no one of his Ministers but is governed by a knot of persons who approach his person. His Ministers have not the courage to tell him their sentiments and the whole business of the government is conducted by a dark intrigue.

'The King has endeavoured to get rid of Prince Cassaro by naming him Minister at Paris, but the Prince has refused, and is still Secretary of State for Foreign Affairs. I am sorry to add that my information leads me to fear the King animated by boyish presumption and confidence in his own power, insomuch as to care little what may be the opinion of those who have the most indisputable power of knowing the facts and I do not imagine they speak sincerely.'

Signor Ruggero Moscati[1] has shown that soon after Ferdinand's marriage he wished to promote a league of Italian States. In December 1832, he invited Charles Albert to discuss an agreement, 'in order to nullify foreign influence on Italian affairs, and prevent the sovereigns of Italy from becoming involved in complications remote from their interest.' Lebzeltern felt sure that the King was referring to Austria; so did Metternich, who wrote: 'He is trying to form a confederation of which he hopes to become the leader, hence his anxiety to increase his army to 80,000 men, a figure too large for the means and requirements of his State not to doubt the purity of his intentions. . . . It is enough to know that France is not opposed to Ferdinand's ideas to conclude that these are not aimed against France but against Vienna.'

Both Charles Albert and the Pope replied evasively to Ferdinand's overtures, and a good opportunity was missed. The negative reaction of other Italian States and the indiscretion of the liberal press, which hastened to brand the league as anti-French, soon chilled the King's enthusiasm. As soon as Lebzeltern adopted the plan the King backed out of it, and the French were led to believe that Austria's desire for an Italian league had been frustrated by Ferdinand's opposition.

A revolt organized in the provinces of Terra di Lavoro, Avellino and Molise to restore the Constitution of 1820 had been discovered and prevented in 1832, and the King had been lenient with the ring-leaders, who accused each other to exculpate themselves. He lightened their sentences, although these were legally justified. As Ferdinand had forgiven the 1820 Constitutionalists this conspiracy was as ill-

[1] *Op. cit.*

King Francis I and his family returning from Palermo to Naples

timed as it was foolish. His moderation was not appreciated, for a more serious conspiracy followed. Several officers and non-commissioned officers of the royal horse guard were implicated: among these Lieutenant Angellotti and two corporals, Vito Romano and Cesare Rossaroll, were to assassinate the King. Discovering that their secret had leaked out, Romano and Rossaroll decided to shoot each other instead of their intended victim. Romano was killed on the spot; Rossaroll, though severely wounded, failed to die. In his delirium and despair he confessed the plot and the names of his accomplices. Their trial was held on December 13, 1833, and both Angellotti and Rossaroll were condemned to death by a majority of five votes to one; all the others were released. William Temple, Lord Palmerston's younger brother who had become British minister at Naples, reported on December 16: 'It would appear that Rossaroll and Romano being desirous of a change in the government and of establishing a republic, conceived the idea of murdering the King, which they hoped to be able to effect while His Majesty was engaged with the troops, and they trusted that the anarchy and confusion which would ensue might enable them to remodel the Government according to their wishes.

'It does not appear that they communicated their design to any other person but Angellotti, having only endeavoured to induce others to promise that in the event of a change in the government taking place they would be prepared to support the new order of things.

'Saturday last, the 14th instant, was the day fixed for the execution. . . . A detachment of a hundred men from every regiment quartered in the neighbourhood, and the regiment to which the prisoners belonged were drawn up to witness it. The prisoners having arrived, the previous preparations were gone through, when it was announced to them that the King had been graciously pleased to commute their punishment to perpetual imprisonment in one of the islands where the galley slaves are confined.

'This act of clemency produced the strongest sensation upon all present. His Majesty was loudly and heartily cheered by all descriptions of persons on his appearing in the evening at one of the theatres— adding if possible to the great popularity which His Sicilian Majesty so justly enjoys among all classes of his subjects.'

The Queen had begged Ferdinand to pardon his would-be murderers. From a balcony of the royal palace he stood peering through a telescope while General Saluzzo was sent to the place of execution with his pardon. 'It is done,' he exclaimed when he saw the General returning. The Queen, who had not been let into the secret, almost fainted at these words, but the cheers of the people were so loud that they reached the balcony, and a few minutes later she was delighted by Saluzzo's report. Ferdinand's act of mercy has been belittled, yet at the same period there were ruthless executions in the Romagna, in Modena and in Piedmont. In April 1833, Charles Albert had exacted a bloody revenge against the members of Mazzini's 'Young Italy' who had plotted an insurrection in Piedmont. Mazzini escaped—to plot and plot again. Another insurrection planned to break out in Capua, Salerno and Aquila simultaneously on August 10, in Puglia on the 11th and in Calabria on the 12th, was stopped by the arrest of Piersilvestro Leopardi and Marchese Luigi Dragonetti, who were merely sent into exile. It seemed as if the liberals were determined to antagonize the most tolerant of Italian princes except the Grand Duke Leopold of Tuscany, who had married Ferdinand's sister Maria Antonia in June, and whose rule was singularly benign.

In September, as if to prove his confidence in his subjects, Ferdinand issued a decree for the organization of a national guard to maintain internal security under the command of his uncle the Prince of Salerno. It was to consist of nobles and landed gentry, merchants, professors, leading artisans and shopkeepers between the ages of twenty-one and fifty. Other companies of guards to escort the King on his travels were organized in the provinces. The popular Prince of Sirignano was appointed first colonel of this citizen cavalry which assembled in Naples every year, bringing the scions of provincial families together and broadening their outlook.

The Duke of Roccaromana, that veteran of 1799 who had subsequently served under Murat and fought in the Russian campaign, was appointed to the command of the royal bodyguard—another proof of the King's independence of mind. 'His character stands high with the moderate party in this country,' wrote Temple, 'and though this appointment is not calculated to meet the approbation of the party who are desirous of inducing the King to adopt severe and rigorous measures against all whom they please to suppose to entertain opinions other than their own, it cannot fail to conciliate a numerous and influential part of the nation who apprehended that the continued efforts of the alarmists might at length produce some effect.' 'My life has nothing more to desire,' exclaimed the delighted veteran who had reminded Lady Blessington of the days of chivalry, but he did not live long to enjoy this belated honour. The Court must have seemed strangely dowdy and dull to this eighteenth-century gallant.

To gratify the Queen, who disapproved of bare arms and *décolleté* gowns, the ladies of the Court vied in modesty of costume. One of these had been taught a lesson which was not soon forgotten. Noticing that her gown was cut too low, the Queen hastily covered her bosom with a handkerchief, saying sweetly: 'Now you look better!' Such was her concern for decorum that she would not allow an engraved portrait of herself to be published because the artist had not observed 'the sacred laws of modesty'. Much as she disliked the theatre, the King obliged her to accompany him to the San Carlo now and then as her attendance gave pleasure to the public; besides it was a family tradition. To overcome her reluctance it was explained to her that in Naples 'music was the profession of many and the delight of all, and that this art, one of the finest glories of the country, would certainly languish for lack of royal protection.'

According to her biographer De Cesare, the Queen's influence on the theatre was beneficial. 'Observing the immorality of the verses, the quasi-nudity of the dancers, the lasciviousness of their movements, so dangerous to youth and scandalous to respectable people . . . she was grieved by those dramatists who strained themselves to leave the world more corrupt than they found it. Speaking to the King about these depraved tendencies of the age, she told him that while he reigned the theatre should not offend the holy laws of morality: that the immodesty of the male dancers and the fatal prestige of the ballet-girls might induce young women to mistrust those who spoke to them of morals; and she roundly declared that she would renounce the theatre for ever unless he put a prompt and vigorous stop to these serious inconveniences. The remonstrances of the august sovereign produced the desired effect, and the provisions made were so prompt and efficacious that they distinguished the long reign of Ferdinand II. . . .'

The length of the ballet-girls' skirts, which were to be green above the knee so as not to inflame young blood, the colour of their bodices and other details of their costume, were all prescribed by regulation. But it was owing to Monsignor Cocle, the King's confessor, that immodest statues from Herculaneum and Pompeii were relegated to remote rooms of the museum and kept under lock and key. Such survivors of Murat's régime as the Duke of Roccaromana must have smiled cynically at this Puritan invasion of the capital.

The Court resembled a monastery, it was said, since the arrival of Maria Cristina. She was constantly warning Ferdinand against excessive familiarity with his entourage: gradually he became less accessible. Many who had been privileged to enter the royal apartments at all times without ceremony were mortified to find themselves excluded. Ferdinand was expansive by nature, like his subjects. But if his wife had accepted her crown 'as a crown of thorns' in resignation to the Divine will, he had to accept the fact that he was married to an angel. Whenever he attended the Council of Ministers she knelt down and prayed God to enlighten him. Once when the Minister of the Interior was announced she was heard to say: 'Ferdinand, do be careful, as he may turn your people against you. Before listening to him recommend yourself to the Madonna.' When the Minister of Finance was announced, she prayed all the more fervently, dreading that he might advise the King to increase the municipal tolls, which would alienate his subjects. She would often exclaim: 'Oh, how much better to be in Heaven than on this earth!'

After two years of marriage there was no sign of a son and heir. 'The King and I are the only ones not to be afflicted by this,' she wrote, 'and we leave it entirely in the hands of God.' All the same it was a secret worry. The gossips discussed whether she or the King were to blame. According to Sardi,[1] the doctors told the King that his wife was consumptive and warned him to be careful. Perhaps he was too careful. The Bourbons had always been philoprogenitive. Perhaps, on the other hand, the Queen was too cold. No doubt the King's brothers bandied bawdy jokes at his expense. Prince Charles began to preen himself as successor to the throne and the malcontents rallied round him. Ferdinand's sister Maria Antonia, the Grand Duchess of Tuscany, was already expecting a child and the Queen Dowager was going to Florence for her confinement.

All the royal family went to Rome for the Holy Week of 1834. The

[1] *Op. cit.*

King and Queen travelled without pomp: it was a modest pilgrimage. They drove through the fertile province of Terra di Lavoro where the Queen saw the first iron suspension bridge in Italy crossing the Garigliano. This had been christened the 'Ferdinandeo'; that which crossed the Calore was called the 'Cristino'. Crowds came from afar for a glimpse of their sovereigns. Though they were offered a choice of regal mansions in Rome, they preferred to stay in a private hotel on the Piazza di Spagna like ordinary tourists. In the evening they had a private audience with Gregory XVI, who blessed them with singular unction. On Palm Sunday they attended High Mass in the tribune set apart for them in Saint Peter's; the Pope himself sent them a palm which he had blessed.

Witnesses of the Queen's piety were moved to tears. Accompanied by the King, without any suite, she visited the sepulchres on foot and climbed the Scala Santa on her knees. From shrine to shrine, lighting candle after candle, meditating in the church of the Jesuit novices on Monte Cavallo before the tomb of her pious uncle Charles Emmanuel IV and the statue of the eighteen-year-old Saint Stanislaus Kostka which had converted the Calvinist sculptor Le Gros who had made it— a Christian pendant to the pagan myth of Pygmalion—visiting the hostel of poor pilgrims, where she donned the apron of the sisters of mercy and waited on the paupers, to the amazement of all the foreign ladies present, the Queen was in her element, to all intents and purposes a nun.

But there was no escaping her royal duties for long, and she was obliged to hold a large reception in the Farnese palace, which was followed by a glut of entertainments given by Princes Borghese, Massimo, Torlonia, and the French and Austrian ambassadors. After taking leave of the Pope, the King and Queen returned to Naples on April 3. They did not stay long in the capital: the Queen went to San Leucio where the colony of silk manufacturers claimed her bountiful attention, while the King went to direct his army manœuvres near Capua.

On June 18 they sailed for Sicily on the steamer *Francesco I*, and with a speed then considered marvellous arrived in Palermo next day. The citizens had not had time to complete their festive preparations before the King and Queen went quietly to the Cathedral. In the meantime the news of their arrival spread like wildfire; the streets were strewn with flowers, windows were hung with damask, and all the dignitaries repaired to the palace to pay homage, while the people surged outside with incessant cheers and the Queen gazed down on them from a high balcony with tears in her eyes. Young though he was, the amiable Count of Syracuse had done much as Lieutenant-General to restore credit by promoting enlightened reforms. After a strenuous round of inspections of colleges, academies, convents and charitable establishments, such as the newly opened institute for the deaf and dumb, as well as local industries, the Queen lost no time in visiting the cave on Monte Pellegrino where Saint Rosalia had lived in solitary meditation amid the constant dripping of water so that when she died she was preserved in a layer of stalagmite, her head crowned with roses by ministering angels. When the Queen and her ladies returned from this shrine in the dusk, the steep path down the mountain was lit with the torches of hundreds of peasants. Seeing this flickering procession from a distance, the citizens set forth with lanterns to meet the royal carriage. Such frequent effusions of loyalty were as genuine as they were spontaneous, although 'patriots' nagged away to persuade them that the Bourbon monarchy was the cause of all their ills.

The festival of Saint Rosalia was delayed by an explosion in the factory where the fireworks were being prepared: at least ten men were killed and as many wounded. The accident had been due to a careless smoker, but the malcontents murmured about sabotage. In spite of the King's personal encouragement of public and private enterprise which resulted, last but not least, in the publication of a 'Practical Manual for the Succour of the Asphyxiated', compiled by the Royal Academy of Medical Science in Palermo, Temple wrote of their visit: 'Nothing has been done for Sicily excepting that the judges who are very numerous and very ill-paid have been made to remove from their former to other districts under the idea that they will act more impartially in their new situations where they have no connections or local ties to bias their judgements. Unfortunately the administration of justice is generally admitted to be so corrupt in Sicily that it is therefore doubtful whether this measure will be attended with any real advantages.' It never occurred to the Sicilians, especially those clamouring for autonomy, that they were more responsible for prevalent conditions than the well-intentioned young King and that reforms, like charity, should begin at home.

Nobody could deny that the Count of Syracuse was a man of good-will. He persuaded the King to revive the Ministry for Sicilian Affairs which had been founded in 1821 and suppressed in 1824, and for a while there was an end of political persecution. Everything seemed placid on the surface, but even in Sicily Mazzini's *Giovine Italia* was conspiring. The Count of Syracuse had received such ovations during his tour of the island that their echoes reached the mainland, where it was rumoured that he coveted the crown of an independent Sicily; and he was portrayed as a puppet of the autonomists. Unfortunately it was easy for trouble-makers to play upon the King's suspicions. Prince Leopold organized a masquerade for the carnival of 1835 representing the entry of the Norman King Roger into Palermo, but it was alto-gether too splendid; it reminded the Sicilians, moreover, of their bygone independence. Ferdinand was led to believe that this was symptomatic, and that the Sicilians wanted to crown his brother. Leopold was instantly recalled, and a war frigate was sent to fetch him. It was announced that he had been assigned to an important mission abroad. Temple reported on April 22, 1835: 'His Royal Highness Prince Leopold, Count of Syracuse, third brother of the King, left Naples on the evening of the 9th inst., intending to make a tour in the North of Europe. . . . He travels incognito under the name of the Count de Teramo, accompanied by General Saluzzo . . . and Marquis Forcella. The Minister of State Prince Campofranco will act for Prince Leopold as Lieutenant General of Sicily. . . . It is believed here that the journey to Paris may not be unconnected with a renewal of the negotiations of a marriage between His Royal Highness and Princess Marie of Orleans, which it is said he is very desirous should take place.'

After Leopold's departure the commander of the gendarmerie was ordered to send fortnightly reports on conditions in the island. All these betrayed anxiety about the Prince's absence and the date of his return. There was considerable discontent when his absence was indefinitely prolonged. The Prince of Campofranco who replaced him was a Sicilian, but two Neapolitans were substituted for the Sicilian Ministers of Finance and Justice. Giustino Fortunato and Carlo Vecchioni were liberals, and Vecchioni was noted for his honesty—when asked to attend a *Te Deum* after Murat's execution he replied it would be better to recite the *De Profundis*, and he stayed away. Both were Neapolitans, however, and that was enough to prejudice the islanders against them. Two political parties now sprang forward, one Sicilian and the other Italian. The former wanted independence and the old Constitution; the latter was inspired by the doctrines of Mazzini, disseminated by Giuseppe La Farina and other young collaborators.

Sicily had produced one musical genius who seemed to focus all the melancholy yearnings of the modern romantic spirit in a series of lyric operas. Vincenzo Bellini left his native Catania at the age of fifteen to study at the Naples Conservatory, and he was barely twenty-five when his opera *Bianca e Fernando* was performed with resounding success at the San Carlo in 1826. Within less than a decade he composed seven famous operas of which *Norma*, *I Puritani* and *La Sonnambula* are still performed when coloratura voices worthy of them, such as that of Maria Callas, can be found. Rossini, whose genius was so diverse, conceived an intense admiration for his achievement and was generous with practical advice when he went to Paris: their friendship was free from envy. As if to show that the title of 'Swan of Pesaro', which had been conferred upon him, was quite unsuitable, wrote Heine—since swans sing at the end of their lives—Rossini had left off singing in middle age. Bellini was the true swan, singing in a golden sunset. He remarked that *William Tell* made all contemporary music, including his own, seem like the work of pygmies. In his *Florentine Nights*, Heine contrasts the jovial Rossini, who had already accomplished his masterpieces, with the fragile Bellini who so dreaded an early death. Bellini died in September 1835, at the age of thirty-three, only a few months after the triumphant success of *I Puritani*.

The German poet's acid description of him is more poignant than the pæans of his compatriots, perhaps on account of a basic antipathy: 'He had a tall, slender figure which moved in an elegant, I might say a coquettish manner; always *à quatre épingles*; a long, regular face, with a pale rosy complexion; very fair, almost golden hair, twisted into small curls; high noble brows, a straight nose, pale blue eyes, a beautifully chiselled mouth, a round chin. His features had something vague and characterless; something like milk, and in this milk-face often mingled, half sweet, half bitter, an expression of sorrow. This expression compensated for the want of soul in Bellini's face, but it had a sorrow without depth; it glistened in the eyes without poetry, it played passionless about his lips. The young *Maestro* seemed anxious to make his flat, languid sorrow conspicuous in his whole person. His hair was curled in such a fanciful, melancholy style; his clothes sat so languidly about his frail body, he carried his little Spanish cane in so idyllic a way, that he always reminded me of the affected young shepherds with their beribboned sticks, and bright-coloured jackets, and pantaloons that we see in our pastorals. And his gait was so young-lady-like, so elegiac, so ethereal. The whole man looked like a sigh in dancing-pumps. He had received much applause among women, but I doubt if he anywhere awakened a strong passion.' After a comical discursion on Bellini's execrable French—'he spoke the language so badly that even in England it could scarcely be spoken worse'—Heine confessed that: 'Bellini's face, like his whole appearance, had that physical freshness, that bloom of flesh, that rosiness which makes a disagreeable impression on me—because I infinitely prefer what is death-like and marble. Later on, when I had known him a long time, I felt some liking for Bellini. This arose after I had observed that his character was thoroughly noble and good. His soul was certainly pure and unspotted by any hateful contagion. And he was not wanting in that good-natured, child-like quality which we never miss in men of genius, even if they do not wear it as an outward show.'

A Sicilian admirer has maintained that Bellini succeeded, as no other composer had done so often and to so high a degree, in proving 'the pleasure of weeping'. All over Sicily the news of his premature death excited frenzies of grief mingled with patriotism, and was exploited politically by foes of the government. The delicate Bellini became a battle-cry against the Bourbons, almost as if they had murdered him. Giuseppe La Farina's elegy was typical of those recited in innumerable academies. He described Bellini's *Pirata* as a moral lesson drawn from old chronicles of the fatherland, as a lament for the peoples oppressed by ruthless power, and as a message of divine vengeance. *Giulietta e Romeo* made all who had heard it curse Italian conflicts and civil war, which had not been extinguished in spite of the vaunted progress of civilization. Bellini's death should unite all Sicilians.

The government pricked up its ears and banned 'The Foreign Review', a pseudo-literary journal supposed to be the organ of *La Giovine Italia*. Michele Amari's 'Story of the Sicilian Vespers' was frowned upon as subversive, and its author was obliged to emigrate. In September, not long before Bellini's death, William Temple reported from Naples: 'Admiral de Rigny, who was lately sent on a special mission from the French Government to this Court, having been detained twenty days at Rome to perform quarantine . . . reached Naples on the evening of the 10th instant. . . . The object of his mission, which I understand related to the proposed marriage between Prince Leopold and Princess Marie of Orleans, appears to have failed of success, and the parties here who are adverse to a French alliance, and have been actively exerting themselves to prevent its taking place, are much elated by the result. Prince Leopold has been removed from the situation of Lieutenant-General of Sicily, and since his return from his northern tour has had apartments allotted to him in the royal palace where, at the King's desire, he now resides.

'This change appears to be far from agreeable to the Sicilians with whom Prince Leopold was extremely popular, and indeed, to this popularity his removal from office has been attributed by many persons who conceive that it gave umbrage to the Neapolitan Government. His successor (Prince Campofranco) is a Sicilian, and having been for some time chief minister at Palermo, is well known to his countrymen, who consider him more disposed to allow things to remain in their present state than to exert himself in removing the numerous evils of which the Sicilians so generally complain.'

Disappointed in love and never very ambitious, the Count of Syracuse became an amateur sculptor and settled down to an existence of sensuous pleasure, polite scepticism and patronage of the arts. He married the Princess of Savoy-Carignano in 1837, but owing to her frantic bigotry the marriage was not a success. They lived apart after she had given birth to a dead child, for which she blamed her husband's irreligion. Now and then the Prince visited his spouse in the nun-like seclusion of her palace on the Chiaia, after which she would call a priest to bless the room he had sat in and have his chair disinfected. When obliged by the King's orders to accompany her husband on a pilgrimage to Monte Vergine, she burned the dress she had worn and saw that the carriage cushions were aired in the sun for several days. But he consoled himself easily for this failure in domesticity: he had so many other interests.

For two years Ferdinand and Maria Cristina had been hoping for a child, and as time went by they became increasingly worried. The Queen suffered and prayed in silence, but everybody noticed her extraordinary pallor. At last these prayers were heard, but the Queen was too coy to mention the subject.

The King was exultant. The Queen wrote to a former lady-in-waiting: 'Does it not seem strange to you that I am about to become a mother? What pleasure it would give me to have you meet the little urchin!' In spite of this she betrayed a secret melancholy and spent more and more time in her oratory. As if inspired, her biographers relate that she spoke of God and His divine attributes, of the Virgin and Saints, with such mystical transport that her listeners were astounded. She distributed her articles of personal use among her maids with the indifference of one who was about to leave them for ever, and she only asked for prayers in exchange. The cloud that had darkened her usual serenity was attributed to her physical condition. Nobody had the courage to question her about it, and it would have remained a mystery had she not confided a presentiment of her death to her sisters and her confessor. On the other hand nobody dared to congratulate her for fear of offending her innate modesty. The King took her to Portici to escape the noise of the city and the fatigue of Court functions; even here she devoted much time to charity and noted the names of poor families who needed assistance. She sent a touching letter to her old maid Rosa Borsarelli whom she had known since childhood: 'I hasten to write to you once more before this great event to ask you to pray much to God and Our Lady for me, that they may help me and give me the grace to bear a strong and healthy child, who may grow up to be good and in time become a saint.'

Since there was a family tradition that the heir to the throne should draw his first breath in the capital, the Queen had to return to Naples. Before leaving the peace of Portici she wrote to her sister Maria Teresa, the Duchess of Lucca: 'This old crone is going to Naples to be delivered and to quit this life.' As if to bequeath a last pledge of affection to her other sister Maria Anna, now Empress of Austria, she wrote: 'I shall die, and wish to leave the dearest thing I possess to my Maria Anna.' This was an album of Victor Emmanuel's drawings, which she had always treasured in memory of her father.

On her drive to Naples, strikingly spiritualized by her pallor, she saw crowds who had come to wish her good luck and she bowed to them with languid grace before entering the royal palace. On January 16, 1836 the cannon of Sant' Elmo, followed by a burst of artillery from all the castles and the clangour of church bells, announced that Ferdinand II was a father, and that the Two Sicilies had an heir. Messengers flew in all directions bearing the glad tidings, and a steamer sailed for Genoa with a letter from Ferdinand to the King of Sardinia. William Temple reported: 'Immediate notice of this happy event having been given, the Diplomatic Body, the Ministers, the Great Officers of State and the Municipal Body of the town of Naples repaired to the palace, and were assembled in a room adjoining the Queen's apartment. Towards eleven o'clock His Majesty the King of Naples entered the room followed by the Princess Bisignano carrying the royal infant in her arms, which was shown to the circle assembled, and the act of the infant's birth which had been previously drawn up was read by the Chief Magistrate of the town of Naples and signed by the proper functionaries. The Court then proceeded to the chapel of the palace where the baptism took place. Her Majesty the Queen Dowager and H.R.H. the Prince of Salerno stood sponsors to the young Prince who was christened after his grandfather, the late King, Francesco d'Assisi. After the conclusion of the ceremony the King and the royal family held a Court to receive congratulations on this joyful occasion.'

Public and private buildings were gaily illuminated and adorned with flowers and auspicious emblems. For two years many had feared that the direct succession from Charles III might be interrupted: it was unusual to wait so long. Hence the people spontaneously shared the King's joy and relief. The Queen celebrated the birth of her son in a characteristic manner. Besides sending lavish gifts to many Neapolitan churches, she made arrangements for fifty orphan girls to be educated at her expense. The King distributed 12,000 ducats from his private purse among the poor of Naples, and 4,000 in Palermo. Many political exiles were amnestied, including Francesco Paolo Bozzelli, who returned after sixteen years' absence with an enhanced reputation as a political scientist and jurist; many criminals were pardoned and the sentences of others curtailed; many titles and rewards were bestowed.

But while congratulations were showered on the King and the people made merry, the Queen was wracked with puerperal fever. Her presentiment had materialized. On January 30 Ferdinand and Father Terzi, her confessor, making a supreme effort to restrain their tears, had to tell her that it was time for her to receive the last Sacraments. She had asked for them frequently during the previous days. In spite of intense suffering she removed her veil to receive them, repeating the priest's words with her lips. She alone seemed calm while those around her wept. After she had kissed the Crucifix and pressed it to her heart, Father Terzi said: 'Trust in God, Who may give you the grace of bodily health.' 'I have ceased to think of this world,' the Queen replied. 'Say rather: Lord, if You believe I am still needed here below, allow me to remain.' 'Oh, Father, let the Lord's will be done,' she said. Seeing tears in the old man's eyes, she gave him her handkerchief. 'Be comforted, Father, and dry your tears,' she continued, 'for God calls me above.' Then, after a short rest: 'You taught me resignation to the Divine Will: I am ready to obey.' Overcome though he was, the King exclaimed to his sobbing family: 'See, even as you live, so you will die!' Her patience throughout her agony was sublime. When one of her maids tried to lift her from the bed to make her more comfortable, she told her to spare herself the trouble. 'I would willingly give my blood to ease Your Majesty,' said the maid. 'Carolina,' the Queen replied, 'do not call me a Queen any longer, because I am now like you.'

All Naples was praying for her: the Cardinal Archbishop Caracciolo, surrounded by the metropolitan chapter, spent the whole night prostrate before the relics of San Gennaro, imploring his intercession. Though her strength was failing, the Queen asked to bless the child who was the innocent cause of her death. When her husband brought the infant to her she was speechless, but her eyes said clearly: 'Ferdinand, I trust him to you. You shall be responsible for him to God and your subjects.' Aware that her end was near, she took tender leave of the royal family, begging them to control their feelings and forgive her if she had ever upset them in any way. As this only made them weep more hysterically the King motioned them out of the room. Towards dawn he was still standing at the foot of the bed, haggard and over-wrought. Eventually his confessor, Monsignor Cocle, urged him to retire: as a King and as a father he should bow to the divine decree and consider his own health for the sake of his subjects and his infant son. Almost demented, the King gazed for the last time at his agonizing wife and looked up to Heaven; then he covered his eyes and staggered out of the death-chamber on the arm of his confessor.

Between fits of delirium the Queen could hear priests reciting the litany of the Virgin, and with the mere ghost of a voice she repeated: 'Pray for me, pray for me.' While she was struggling for breath her maids moistened her dry lips and wiped the sweat off her brow. On the morning of January 31 her motionless limbs were convulsed with a violent shudder: she was heard to whisper: 'Ferdinand!' One of the maids rushed to the King's apartment, but Monsignor Cocle barred the way: he forbade her to repeat the Queen's last message. She was to say that the King was in Council with his ministers. Wishing to comfort her *in extremis* the Congregation of the Oratory brought her the cap of Saint Philip Neri, who had summed up his doctrine in the maxim: 'Despise the world, despise yourself, and despise being despised.' The Queen kissed the relic and fell into a lethargy. While the priest was reciting the prayer for the dying, she opened her eyes and exclaimed: 'I believe in God, I hope in God, I love God,' and closed her eyes for ever.

Father Terzi's account of the Queen's death has been mangled by adverse historians, who asserted that the callous King was impervious to her last appeal. The truth is that he was urged to leave her room between two and three o'clock in the morning, and that the priests, doctors and courtiers, who knew that he was subject to epilepsy, wished to spare him needless anguish. Temple reported: 'His Majesty has been so deeply affected in consequence of the severe loss which he has sustained that it was feared his health might be impaired by his mental suffering. According to the accounts which I received yesterday from Portici he was stated to have passed a tolerable night and was free from fever, but he continued to be greatly agitated. . . . The young Prince is, I am happy to say, doing extremely well.' And on February 17: 'His Majesty the King of Naples still remains at Portici in great affliction, not seeing anybody but his family and those immediately about his person, with the exception of his ministers who occasionally visit him on business.' Two months later the Sardinian ambassador Di Breme reported: 'The fatal event of January 31 has dealt the King a physical and moral shock from which he is far from recovered: he is immersed in total inaction, consequently there is a deplorable stagnation in all affairs.' While the capital was in mourning the Sardinian fleet cast anchor in the bay with a message of congratulation from King Charles Albert. The festive volleys of guns from Piedmont resounded while the funeral bells were tolling. It seemed a tragic omen.

Maria Cristina was regarded as a saint during her lifetime, but the liberals resented her influence. Charles Albert, who had hoped that she would lend her support to his national policy, was disappointed. The Queen had abstained from politics; yet her piety had helped to increase the power of the Church. Even an impartial chronicler[1] has written that the headquarters of Monsignor Cocle, the King's confessor, in the convent of Sant' Antonio di Tarsia, resembled an annexe to the royal palace where he held court despotically. 'This had become a market, a factory, to which everybody crowded, where there was a busy traffic in favours and justice was distributed.'

Unfortunately there was a horde of hungry Tartuffes ready to exploit the spiritual zeal of their sovereigns, which was caricatured as in a distorting mirror. From Mazzini's correspondence it is evident that his adherents considered the Queen's death 'a benefit to Naples', because she had been opposed to liberalism and might have acquired greater influence after the birth of an heir. However, the Church has declared her 'Venerable', and her tomb in Santa Chiara soon became a popular shrine. Many miracles were attributed to her, and the Hereditary Prince became known as 'the son of the Saint'. Her virtues were commemorated in at least fifty panegyrics.

Besides the special graces she obtained after death for her former subjects, she procured several outside the kingdom and her picture was in great demand in other Italian cities. Her niece Beatrice, a daughter of Duke Francis IV of Modena, wrote to the Empress Mary Anne of Austria: 'I hasten to inform you of a wondrous grace which God has granted me owing to the intercession of your dear sister and my aunt Cristina. To-day I might have been the most unfortunate of mothers, instead of which I am so happy! My part in this incident is that of the careless fool I am, but God has brought good out of ill and has used my imprudence to glorify His faithful servant, my dear aunt Cristina. Yesterday at half past nine I was in the garden with my children and Elisa, the daughter of their governess, and seeing that the small canal was dry I thought I would amuse the boys by filling it with water. I went to set the pump in motion, about ten steps from where they were to stand and watch the water flow. This was my imprudence. I put all my strength into an effort to start the pump working.

[1] M. Farnerari, *Della Monarchia di Napoli*. Naples, 1876.

It was moving with full force when Alfonso escaped from Elisa and ran towards it. I happened to let go of it at the same time, and with incredible violence it struck the boy on his temple and knocked him senseless to the ground. I thought I had killed my son! Truly the place where he was struck, the way he fell, his age (only three years), the instrument, a very heavy iron lever with a knob also made of iron, the force of the current which the pump set in motion—everything contributed to make this a mortal blow.

'Until then, not only had I never invoked my aunt Cristina but I confess, to my shame, that I still had certain doubts about her great holiness, though I regarded her as an angel of goodness and virtue. When I heard of the miracles associated with her I feared there was some Neapolitan exaggeration about them, owing to the enthusiasm she had inspired during her lifetime. In spite of the little devotion I had shown for my saintly godmother, in that first moment of true despair I thought neither of invoking God nor the Blessed Virgin, which would have been more natural, but exclaimed: "Oh Aunt Cristina, help him, save him!" and threw myself beside my boy. I felt incapable of looking at him. Alfonso seemed senseless: I thought I would find his head broken. Elisa removed his hat, examined him and said: "I see nothing." Then I looked and examined him and became convinced that there was nothing. The boy cried a little, but only from shock, and in a few minutes he said it had stopped aching. "Mamma was frightened, not I!" he added, and ran through the garden more briskly and merrily than before. As a sign of this grace a slightly livid mark remains on his temple, which shows how fatal the blow might have been but nothing more. Our surgeon saw the pump and judged it capable of killing him; he saw the boy and found him quite unhurt. A bit later, while we were still dazed and nobody had mentioned thanking God and Aunt Cristina for the grace received, Alfonso said to his governess: "To-day let's go to San Cataldo to say a few Hail Maries, and then go on to the Four Towers,"—as if he meant we should thank God first of all. While we were on our way to San Cataldo, to grant the boy's pious wish, the same day after dinner, the horses of the carriage in which we were all sitting became unruly and frisked around us: I invoked Aunt Cristina and no accident occurred. Having put Alfonso to bed that night, I stood gazing at him in rapture as if he were a newly sent gift from God and he said: "Don't stay, Mamma, the Lord is here and that is enough: when I'm with Him there is no need for anything else." A wise priest tells me that these religious sentiments in a child incapable of realizing the grace received, imply the certainty of a divine miracle.'

The news of this spread to other countries. As time went on Ferdinand marvelled more and more at his marriage and read supernatural meanings into past episodes. For him, too, Maria Cristina became a spiritual cult, and his conscience smote him for not appreciating her sufficiently while she was alive. His constant reluctance to shed blood was said to be due to her memory.

V

Ferdinand's grief—The Prince of Capua—His elopement with Penelope
Smyth—Ferdinand refuses to recognize his marriage—A journey to
Austria—Carlist sympathies—Ferdinand's engagement to Archduchess
Maria Theresa—The Prince of Capua's problems—Outbreak of cholera
—The King's re-marriage—A fire in the royal palace—Cholera and riots
in Sicily—Del Carretto as alter ego—Disturbances in the Abruzzi.

FERDINAND II celebrated his twenty-sixth birthday on
January 12, 1836; his son was born on the 16th and his wife
died on the 31st of the same month. The gamut of so many
violent emotions in so short a time prostrated him. He had an epileptic
relapse; for a while he was unable to walk and he fell into the blackest
despondency. These facts should be considered in judging his harsh
treatment of his younger brother Charles.

The Prince of Capua had always been the spoiled darling of his
parents. Appointed a Vice-Admiral at the age of nineteen, he had won
an easy popularity with Ferdinand's political opponents who flattered
his youthful vanity. He was frivolous and gay, and he had a sympathetic weakness for pretty women. Some considered him handsome,
but there is little trace of this in his portraits. At the staid Court of
Ferdinand and Maria Cristina his amorous escapades provided some
comic relief. Until the Queen's child was born his sycophants assured
him that he had a good chance of inheriting the crown, since Ferdinand might be carried off by one of his convulsions. Those who wished
to divide the brothers for their own ends did much to widen the growing rift between them, and Charles went his way regardless of Ferdinand's disapproval.

During the winter of 1835 Charles fell in love with Penelope Smyth,
a beautiful Irish visitor to Naples, and he chose the King's birthday to

90

inform him that he intended to marry her. In spite of his *lazzarone* lapses Ferdinand's family pride was colossal: he was outraged by the very idea of such a *mésalliance*. As usual he did not mince his words. It was commonly reported that Charles became violent and drew his sword, and that the Queen, although in an advanced state of pregnancy, rushed forward to protect her husband, receiving a blow which knocked her down and endangered the life of her unborn infant. That there was an altercation between the brothers is certain: all their latent antagonism had come to the boil. Charles withdrew in a towering rage. After attending the King's birthday gala at the San Carlo that night, he secretly left the city with his beloved. Ferdinand's first impulse was to have him arrested at the frontier, but on second thoughts he sent him a letter by private messenger advising him to stay. Fearing arrest, Charles whipped out his pistols. Penelope tried to calm him while he read his brother's letter. Since love is deaf as well as blind, he said he would send an answer later and dashed across the frontier.

On January 16 William Temple reported to his brother Lord Palmerston: 'It is with great regret that I have to announce to Your Lordship that His Royal Highness Prince Charles, second brother of His Sicilian Majesty, has suddenly left Naples, having eloped, as there is every reason to believe, with Miss Penelope Smyth, a sister of Mr Smyth of Ballynatra in the county of Waterford.

'Miss Smyth and her sister, accompanied by a married lady Mrs Phaire, a friend of theirs, arrived at Naples some months ago, having passed the two previous winters in Paris and Rome. Prince Charles having made the acquaintance of the Misses Smyth, accompanied them frequently on riding excursions and was a constant visitor at their house, but as His Royal Highness had frequently shown a great preference towards English ladies, his attentions to the eldest Miss Smyth were not considered likely to lead to any more serious consequences than his former attachments of a similar nature.

'It appears, however, that this attachment was so strong as to induce him to ask permission of His Majesty the King and of the Queen Dowager of Naples to be allowed to marry the young lady, notwithstanding the disparity of their rank. His request being refused, as might have been expected, he seems to have persuaded Miss Smyth to elope with him. They disappeared from Naples on the night of the 12th of January after the opera, at which Prince Charles was present.

'The parties were assisted, as it would seem, in their escape by Mr Patrick O'Conor of the Navy, who with his family has been residing for some time at Naples. This gentleman called at the British Legation on the 7th instant, stating that he intended to go through Florence to Paris with his family, and requested a passport for that purpose. As he was well known, and nothing had arisen to create any suspicion, it was accordingly granted to him, and in it, at his desire, were inserted the names of five persons, three male and two female, being Mr Patrick O'Conor, Mrs O'Conor, Richard O'Conor, their son, Jane Lloyd and James Scot, servants, and this passport afterwards received the visa of the Nuncio and of the Missions of the other countries through which his route lay.

'Mr O'Conor, it now appears, as I understand from a report of the police, accompanied Miss Smyth and her maid to the barrier where they were joined by Prince Charles who took an English servant with him. They then all proceeded on their way to Rome and it is supposed made use of the passport which Mr O'Conor had obtained, as its contents agreed with the number and sex of the party. I have also been informed that Mr O'Conor has gone away from Naples, leaving his family behind him.

'Mrs Phaire and Miss Smyth's sister remain here, and disclaim any previous knowledge of the elopement. They went to the opera the same night leaving Miss Smyth at home, complaining of a sore throat, and believing that she was gone to bed, did not discover that she had left the house till late the following morning, when a letter was found from her to her sister requesting forgiveness for the step she had taken and for the secrecy she had observed, but she said she had not confided her plan to them in consequence of a promise made to Prince Charles, and from an unwillingness to implicate her in the business.

'There is a report that Prince Charles and his party were met by a traveller within the Roman frontier and I understand a messenger was sent off to Rome last night by this Government.'

Thus began a harassed life of exile for Prince Charles who, whatever his faults, remained steadfastly faithful to his Penelope. On March 12 the King issued a decree based on those of Francis I and Charles III: as sovereign and head of the family he ordained that no member of the royal family was to leave the kingdom without permission under penalty of forfeiting his revenue, which after six months' residence abroad would devolve to the Crown; that no marriage of a royal person without the King's consent was to be considered legitimate, as the King 'should exercise the necessary authority to preserve in its purity the splendour of the throne'. The Prince was notified of this, and all consular agents were warned in order to prevent the marriage.

On April 4 Temple wrote to his brother: 'My dear Palmerston, I received your letters of the 10th March on the 2nd of April, and I called the same morning on the Duke of Gualtieri to ascertain from him, in obedience to the King's commands, what the wishes of the King of Naples would be with regard to the manner in which Prince Charles and his wife should be received in the event of their visiting England. Having stated to him confidentially the substance of your letter, the Duke assured me that he considered this communication as a most courteous and kindly attention on the part of the King of England towards his Sovereign. . . . In the meantime, however, he could say that no information had been received of any marriage ceremony having taken place between Prince Charles and Miss Smyth since their departure from Naples, and indeed he did not believe that any valid marriage could have taken place ever according to the laws of the countries through which they had travelled, as they had not remained long enough resident in any town to justify a priest to consider them as domiciled there and marry them without ascertaining whether there was any legal impediment to this their union. . . . Even if a marriage has taken place which would be valid before the Catholic Church, it would be wholly invalid as far as related to civil and political rights, so that Miss Smyth would not be entitled to take either the title or the name of Prince Charles, neither would the children be considered as belonging to the royal family.'

A day after this letter was written Charles married Penelope Smyth at Gretna Green on the Scottish border, where it sufficed for couples merely to declare their wish to marry before witnesses: they were re-married at a religious ceremony in London. Ferdinand never forgave this public act of defiance. His mother pleaded with him in vain: he refused to recognize the marriage as legal. All Charles's estate was sequestrated except the county of Mascali in Sicily which had been left him as an entailed property by his father, but Mascali was badly administered and brought in little revenue. Charles soon found himself in financial straits, but he was equally stubborn in standing up for what he considered his rights.

Gradually Ferdinand's health improved but his spirits were at a low ebb: he was perhaps further embittered by comparing his brother's reckless rapture with his own desolation. In May he decided to travel, but he tried to keep his plans secret. His confessor Monsignor Cocle persuaded him that a journey would act as a tonic and enable him to seek another wife. This was an important duty: his people expected it of him. His ministers were merely informed of his imminent departure. Nothing was said about the extent of his journey or the period of his absence, but it was rumoured that he was going to Vienna. On May 19 Temple reported: 'The King travels under the name of Don Fernando di Napoli and intends preserving the strictest incognito. His suite is small, consisting only of General Saluzzo . . . the Duke of San Cesario, and a private secretary. . . . The Queen Dowager remains at Naples, the King having confided to her care his infant son, who is now become a strong and healthy child.

'The restoration of His Sicilian Majesty's health and spirits is the principal reason for his journey, but it is supposed that he will take advantage of the opportunity it affords of becoming acquainted with several princesses that he may be better able to choose a Queen should he be induced at a future time to contract another marriage. The daughter of the Duke of Modena, the daughter of the Viceroy of Lombardy and the daughter of the Archduke Charles have been mentioned as the princesses who have been particularly pointed out to His Majesty's attention.'

So far Ferdinand had not committed himself to any special plan of foreign policy. Having spent his early youth under the costly wing, rather than yoke, of Austrian occupation, he enjoyed tantalizing the officious Lebzeltern. As soon as his idea of an Italian league had been adopted by Metternich he would have no more to do with it. This snub to Austria was relished by England and France. Palmerston had sent his brother Temple to Naples to encourage Ferdinand's independence. It was hoped that he would recognize his niece Maria Isabella as heiress to the Spanish throne. But Ferdinand was equally touchy and suspicious in his relations with England and France. He had been the first to protest against Ferdinand VII's Pragmatic Sanction which permitted the succession of women, though his own sister had brought it about.

The question was complicated. The old laws of Spain had allowed women to succeed until Philip V was obliged to publish the so-called Salic Law of 1713, to prevent any union of the Spanish and French crowns in one person by giving preference to the male line. Charles IV had abrogated the Salic Law in 1789 but this return to the status quo was kept secret, although recorded in the State Archives. The astute Maria Cristina induced Ferdinand VII to publish it on May 19, 1830, before her child was born. The child proved to be a daughter, who was christened Maria Isabella and proclaimed Princess of Asturias. This began the struggle between Maria Cristina and the King's brother Don Carlos, the leader of the ultra-Royalists known as *apostolicos*, which caused a protracted civil war after the King's death in 1833. If Philip V had been entitled to change the law of succession in 1713, why should the same right be denied to Ferdinand VII in 1830? But Austria, Prussia and Russia regarded Don Carlos as the champion of their absolutist ideas, and Ferdinand II supported him on principle against his own sister, who was Queen Regent during her daughter's minority. Great Britain, Portugal and France, on the other hand, supported the *Cristinos*, who were composed of Radicals and Moderates. Louis-Philippe had at first been tolerant towards the Carlists, but dynastic ambition induced him to change his mind: he hoped to marry one of his sons to the Spanish heiress. He was therefore vexed by Ferdinand's pro-Carlist policy as well as by his opposition to the Count of Syracuse's marriage to his daughter Louise. He vented his displeasure on the Neapolitan ambassador, the Prince of Butera, after whose recall in October 1835, the French embassy at Naples and the Neapolitan in Paris remained vacant for four years.

At one moment, as frightened by the Constitutionalists as by the Carlist victories and general anarchy, the Queen Regent of Spain wrote to her brother that she was 'altogether alien to the atrocious acts of a Government in which she had only exercised a fictitious power, and that her ardent desire was to withdraw from such an odious tyranny, taking refuge with her children and dearest ones at the Court of Naples'. This was agreeable news to Ferdinand, who started secret negotiations with her and Don Carlos to end the civil war by a marriage which should unite the two dynastic branches. But they came to nothing. Maria Cristina, the most fickle of women, drew back when she was on the verge of a settlement, and the Carlist cause declined in consequence.

Lebzeltern's fears that Ferdinand intended to lead a national movement in Italy were groundless. In availing himself of the talent of Filangieri and others who had distinguished themselves under Murat he wished, as de Mazade[1] observed, 'to break the bond between the military spirit and constitutional tendencies, the two forces which together had given birth to the revolution of 1820'. He hoped to save the principle of legitimism, hence his championship of Don Carlos. Owing to a more adult appreciation of Metternich his relations with Lebzeltern became so cordial that the latter exclaimed: 'At last he has become a Royalist!'

Ferdinand's visit to Vienna in June and July 1836, convinced Metternich that he would support the conservative cause against that liberalism which he viewed as a disguised middle-class dictatorship. As if to cement his Austrian sympathies, he became engaged to the Archduchess Maria Theresa, a daughter of the Archduke Charles, the Emperor's militant uncle who had won Napoleon's respect. The engagement was kept so secret that his own government knew nothing about it will December, when it was published in the *Augsburg Gazette*. 'This reserve on the part of His Majesty,' wrote Temple on December 6, 'may have arisen in some measure from a feeling of delicacy towards the memory of his late Queen, as well as from the desire which he entertains of keeping his plans secret until the moment of putting them into execution, and which marked his conduct on the occasion of the journey . . . last summer.'

During Ferdinand's absence the Prince of Capua had attempted to return to Naples and been stopped at Pietrasanta on the Tuscan frontier, where he was informed that he might enter Tuscany but no foreign member of his suite was to accompany him. The same orders had been issued at Leghorn and Civitavecchia. Unwilling to be separated from his wife, he went to Genoa. According to Ferdinand's decree any member of the royal family who absented himself from the kingdom for more than six months without his permission should forfeit all his rights and property. The six months had elapsed. Prince

---

[1] Charles de Mazade, *Le roi Ferdinand II et le royaume des Deux-Siciles. Revue des Deux Mondes, Tome XXII.* Paris, 1859.

Charles had been advised to return to Naples alone and, while Ferdinand was in Vienna, endeavour to reconcile the rest of his family to his marriage. But he was afraid of falling into a trap: once he crossed the frontier he might never be allowed to leave the kingdom, or his wife to enter it. 'The Queen Dowager,' wrote Temple on July 13, 'is very fond of Prince Charles and is, I believe, anxious to bring about a reconciliation between him and the King, feeling that however much the marriage is to be regretted, as it has taken place the wisest course would be to make the best of it. . . . This Government has sent a messenger to Vienna to know what the King's intentions are respecting Prince Charles, but nothing is at present known upon the subject. The household establishment of Prince Charles has been kept up and paid for during his absence by order of the King . . . but no money has been transmitted to H.R.H. since his departure.'

In September Temple heard that Charles had succeeded in obtaining a brief interview with the King on his way to Toulon. Apparently the King had been curt. The Prince 'was referred by His Majesty to M. de Traetto the Neapolitan chargé d'affaires in Paris, who was instructed to repair to Marseilles and communicate to H.R.H. the King's orders and the conditions upon which he might be allowed to receive his income. The Prince was, I understand, led to expect that if he resigned all pretension on the part of his wife and children to be considered as part of the royal family, he would be allowed to return with her to Naples. M. de Traetto, however, presented to Prince Charles a letter for his signature in which the Prince was not only to give up all claim upon the part of his wife to rank and title and consider his marriage as one "*à la main gauche*", but to repair immediately to Brünn in Moravia where he was to take up his residence. With the latter condition the Prince declined to comply, as he considered it equivalent to banishment in a country where he should be kept a prisoner under the surveillance of Austria, and the immediate vicinity of Brünn to the State Prison of Spielberg tended much to increase the alarm felt by the Prince and his wife as to their future fate, and the intentions of those who sent him into that neighbourhood.

'I received a short time ago a letter from the Prince's wife requesting me to deliver a packet addressed to the Queen Mother and setting forth the melancholy situation in which she and the Prince were placed, expressing her willingness to comply with all the conditions required, and saying that she hoped to be permitted to enter Naples with the Prince as a private individual and under any name (even that of Signora Smyth) which the King might wish her to assume, but if that could not be granted, that they might at least be permitted to choose the place of their residence abroad.

'I called upon the Queen Dowager to deliver the letter for her which had been entrusted to my care. . . . I told her I had received a letter from the Prince's wife which, as it expressed a desire to conform in every way to the wishes of the King, I would, if Her Majesty pleased, read to her, which I did at her request.

'She expressed her satisfaction at its contents and said she would mention them to the King as they appeared likely to remove many difficulties which had risen from the Prince having at first refused to make the concessions required. I believe, however, that there are persons about the King who endeavour to prevent the return of Prince Charles to Naples and seek rather to widen the breach than to effect a reconciliation between the royal brothers.

'In the meantime the Prince of Capua has freighted a vessel for Malta, where he is probably by this time arrived. The motives for this step are not very apparent, but I understand the Prince wished to be nearer Naples to await the final decision of the King, and if he is forced to go to Brünn would there embark for Trieste without having to make a long journey through Italy. . . .

'The Government is said to feel, or pretend to feel, some alarm at this determination of the Prince and reports have been spread that he may intend to land in Sicily where his property lies which was left him by the late King, and excite troubles in that country. The Neapolitan Consul at Malta who is staying at Naples upon leave of absence has been suddenly ordered to return to his post, and I hear that the Sicilian Board of Health have just ordered a quarantine of observation against all foreign vessels sailing in the Mediterranean under the pretext that they may during their voyage have fallen in with vessels coming from infected places. I am inclined to think that this absurd regulation has been adopted to prevent the possibility of Prince Charles landing in Sicily unknown to the authorities there. I shall of course use my utmost endeavours to have this regulation rescinded if I find the report is true.'

It is clear that Temple sympathized with the reckless runaway, but his brother Palmerston took up the cudgels on the Prince's behalf for his own political ends. The King's attitude was stigmatized as cruel, petty and vindictive. Yet in England, too, there was a Royal Marriage Act, as George IV and his brothers who had contracted irregular unions had been forced to realize. For twenty years the reigning King William IV had lived with jolly Mrs Jordan before marrying the demure Princess Adelaide of Saxe-Coburg-Meiningen. But a Royal Marriage Act seemed to change its significance once it had crossed the channel: like certain kinds of Chianti it had turned sour. Ferdinand II was regarded as a tyrant for applying it to his younger brother, yet in his eyes Penelope Smyth was no more suitable a bride for a Bourbon than Mrs Fitzherbert had been for the Prince of Wales. And the Prince of Capua could hardly complain that he had not received due warning.

Ferdinand had more serious preoccupations. Since cholera had broken out at Ancona in August all communication with the Papal States was cut off for the time being, and the King was urged by his ministers to come home as soon as possible. He had issued two decrees from Vienna, to establish a sanitary cordon along the Adriatic coast of the kingdom and to stiffen penalties for transgressing the health regulations. He arrived in the bay of Naples on September 1, but he would not land until the 4th in spite of his ministers' entreaties, to show that he respected his own laws. At first he expressed annoyance for being hurried home so prematurely, as he had planned to extend his journey to France and England. Temple considered that their strongest motives for taking this step 'was their fear that during his residence in France and England he might imbibe more enlightened ideas, and be inclined to introduce alterations and reforms at home inconsistent with their interests and policy'. But the cholera had made ravages in the north of Italy, and already several cities in Puglia were infected.

In Naples special hospitals had been prepared in every commune, seven in various parts of the capital, and four first-aid stations in each quarter. The King inspected these and the city markets to ascertain that they were amply supplied with provisions at reasonable prices. Satisfied that every precaution then known to medicine had been taken, he turned his attention to the army. His energy was indomitable, but an incident during a field-day betrayed the state of his nerves. A mistake in the manœuvres so infuriated him that he struck Captain

99

Ascenza on the shako with his sword, slicing part of it clean off. The Captain was a proud Sicilian descended from the Dukes of Rosalia. 'The King feeling that he had gone too far in the heat of the moment, desired the Major in command of the Regiment to express to the officers his regret at what had happened, attributing it to forgetfulness in a moment of excitement. The officer who was struck, however, felt that as the attack had been directed personally against himself, this general expression of regret on the part of the King ... did not remove the stigma which had been cast upon him individually by the blow which he had received. He has therefore tendered his resignation to the King, stating his reasons ... being a person well known and very popular in the best society of Naples and Palermo, his case excited much interest. ... It is hoped that the King may decline accepting his resignation.' This public affront was neither forgiven nor forgotten.

On October 2 the cholera broke out in Naples. Opponents of the government took advantage of the epidemic to spread alarming reports and accuse the King of attempting to poison the people. But the King's courage and firmness were the best antidote to venomous propaganda. He visited the new hospitals to see that his orders had been carried out and went on foot through the most crowded districts where the cholera was raging. 'My children,' he said, 'I have come to see with my own eyes what can be done for you.' In the presence of his soldiers, he ate the bread which was supposed to be poisoned; he even went from house to house to make sure that the proper remedies were being applied. He distributed large sums from the royal treasury, and when public prayers were recited in the Cathedral he prayed long and fervently. Throughout the crisis he set a splendid example. More money and provisions were collected by private charity; a Neapolitan chemist offered to deal out free medicines to the needy, and Cavaliere Santoro, the first surgeon of the hospital of Santa Maria della Fede, devoted his whole salary to the indigent patients while the epidemic lasted; the clergy, from the Cardinal Archbishop Caracciolo down, went at all hours of the night and day to minister to the sufferers and distribute alms, and the Archbishop opened a hostel for poor girls who had been orphaned by the epidemic 'to provide them with board and lodging and protect them from the perils of seduction'. The police commissioner of Rodi in Puglia was discharged for deserting his post when the cholera broke out there, and a few doctors were disqualified for bolting, but these were exceptions. Many of the foreign diplomats considered the sanitary precautions excessive. Thus Temple complained on November 26: 'all the correspondence passing through the North of Italy and letters brought by courier or by post is still being subjected to fumigation. Strong remonstrances have been made to the Government upon the subject by all the Diplomatic Body, but hitherto without avail.' During the winter months the cholera subsided, and on March 7, 1837, it was announced officially to have ceased, having caused about 6200 deaths in the capital and its vicinity.

On January 2, 1837, the King left Naples for Trent, sailing by steamer up the Adriatic. He was accompanied by the Count of Syracuse and a small suite of four chamberlains and two ladies of the Court, the Princess of Bisignano and the Duchess of Ascoli. His marriage to the Archduchess Maria Theresa was celebrated quietly on the 9th, and he returned with his twenty-year-old bride to Naples by sea on the 26th. Three days of public festivity in Naples and Palermo ensued, and the King abolished a number of penalties for crimes, diminished others, and cancelled fines of under twenty ducats and debts of under ten ducats. According to Temple—no partisan of Austria—the Queen's affable and dignified manners made a favourable impression upon all classes. She suffered from two initial handicaps: she was more of a foreigner than her predecessor, and it was none too easy to succeed a popular saint. The King's enemies muttered that he had become an Austrian satellite, a mere tool in the hands of Metternich.

A fire which broke out in the royal palace soon after the Queen's arrival was generally regarded as a portent of future calamities. Had not a fire followed the nuptials of Louis XVI and Marie Antoinette, and had not the same sinister omen been repeated when Napoleon married the Austrian Marie Louise? On February 7 Temple reported: 'Their Sicilian Majesties and the Royal family were present on Sunday night at the masked ball at the theatre of San Carlo, and having supped in the Royal boxes did not return till near three o'clock yesterday morning. About two hours afterwards an alarm of fire was raised in the Royal palace and the flames were discovered issuing from a portion of the building which unites two parallel ranges of apartments which run back towards the Castel Nuovo at right angles to the centre of the palace. In this part of the palace are the apartments of Her Majesty the

Queen Mother and above them those of H.R.H. the Count of Syracuse. The flames had already reached Her Majesty's sleeping room when a sergeant of gendarmes forced his way into her chamber and carried Her Majesty to a place of safety. H.R.H. the Count of Syracuse had only time to save himself by a rapid flight, leaving every article of clothing, furniture and property in his apartments, which were completely destroyed, so that he was obliged to borrow some clothes from his brother Prince Anthony to appear in. . . . The damage done to the building is considerable, and the loss in furniture, pictures, and other objects of value which were either destroyed by the fire or injured from being thrown into the courtyard, is very extensive.

'His Majesty the King, assisted by his staff, was extremely active during the whole day in directing the operations of the persons employed in extinguishing the fire. . . . There are various rumours respecting the origin of the fire, but hitherto the real cause has not been discovered.'

This was probably accidental, but in March a plot to burn down the San Carlo theatre was frustrated. 'The person whose duty it was to go round the building in order to ascertain that all was safe, discovered at the back of the stage where old scenery was deposited, a light on the floor which he immediately extinguished. . . . Upon further investigation it was found that the light proceeded from a large piece of tinder communicating with a packet of gunpowder to which cotton wicks saturated with brimstone, turpentine and other inflammable substance were attached.' In the latter case it was suspected that 'the train was placed by the person who gave the alarm, in order to obtain a reward'.

On April 13 there was a devastating recrudescence of cholera. Again the King was tireless in visiting hospitals, comforting the sick, and encouraging the overworked doctors and their attendants; again he walked through the crowded Capuan Gate district and inspected the cemetery from which noxious exhalations were said to infect the neighbourhood; nor did he leave until he was satisfied that this was a malicious fabrication. In June the cholera invaded Palermo. The Sicilians promptly accused the Neapolitans of spreading the contagion; the old rumours of poison were revived. Auto-suggestion replaced reason to such an extent that Michele Muccio, a chemist, who was analysing a powder confiscated from an innocuous German named Schwentzer, dipped his finger into it, touched his tongue, and dropped dead. The Archbishop of Palermo refused all medical aid and expired, saying: 'There is no remedy against this poison.' Public fountains, the flour at the bakeries, the air itself, were said to be lethal. This dread was as contagious as the disease. Many harmless creatures were massacred as poisoners, often owing to some rumour started by a private enemy. Vendetta loomed large in these crimes.

At Messina cholera was the pretext for revolt. A *speronara* or small lateen-rigged craft from Palermo had been allowed to enter the port, and printed protests were scattered, calling for revenge 'against the oppressors of our fatherland and our lives'. To make matters worse, a steamer from Naples with a cargo of equipment for the garrison appeared in the harbour on July 12. Even if the government intended to relax the quarantine regulations the citizens were determined to apply them. When it was announced that the ship was going to unload, a large mob broke into the health office, destroying all the documents and burning the royal coat of arms. Fortunately the riots died down without military intervention, owing to the tact of General Carafa di Noja and local immunity from the epidemic. The revolt had been fomented by radical politicians who obtained passports from the intendant, Marchese della Cerda, and left the island with impunity. Ignorance and superstition were easy prey for those who wanted insurrection at all costs, intoxicated by the writings of Mazzini.

The worst excesses took place at Syracuse, where George Schwentzer, a German who earned a living by exhibiting a cosmorama, had been detained by the epidemic on his way to Malta. No doubt he seemed a magician, like Doctor Caligari in the film. He was soon suspected of being a poisoner. An excited mob arrested him and confiscated his paraphernalia. His wife and infant daughter, his servant, and two friends who had gone to rescue him were also seized, but the former managed to slip away through the crowd. Schwentzer was thrown into prison and the police commissioner who attempted to placate the mob was brutally murdered. A woman attacked him from behind with a bludgeon which she had concealed under a cloak. His hat fell off as he reeled under the blow, and in bending to pick it up the blood was seen streaming over his white trousers: this had the effect of a red rag on a herd of bulls. He was pierced with daggers, dragged and bound to a granite pillar where he was shot. Schwentzer's two friends, his servant, and another suspect were butchered.

In order to curb this violence the mayor created a committee of responsible citizens for defence against suspected poisoners. The interrogation of Schwentzer, whose replies were vague and ambiguous owing to fright, only provoked greater suspicion. His innocent wife was accused of being an accomplice. In the meantime others were massacred, including the intendant Andrea Vaccaro, who was dragged from the ancient stone-quarries where he had hidden, the police inspector Li Greci, and his son, a tax-collector.

One member of the mayor's committee, the elderly lawyer Mario Adorno, was convinced of the poison hypothesis. As his voice was weak he asked his secretary to read a long proclamation to the crowd assembled in the Cathedral square. This announced that the cradle of Archimedes would be the tomb of the Asiatic cholera morbus. 'As soon as the reputed plague broke out among us, it was discovered to be nothing but the result of poisonous powders and liquids which acted upon solid and liquid foods and even upon the respiratory organs, infecting the air with homicidal fetor. The cosmographer Schwentzer . . . during a preliminary investigation has declared one Bainard of German nationality to be the disseminator of lethal substances, adding that he recently left Syracuse to carry the infernal scourge to Messina and Catania. The various proofs which have shown us that nitrate of arsenic was among the noxious materials found in the house of the acting intendant, besides the specific, written and oral proof, give us grounds to hope for a successful trial. All these elements lead us to conclude that the acting intendant and the commissioner of police were guilty of this public crime, and in the heat of discovery they were victims of the people's righteous anger. However, we have been gratified to observe that owing to this timely discovery the victims of our fellow-citizens have been very few.

'To-day we are justified in believing that we may be tranquil in this respect, and we can afford to hope that this proclamation will prove beneficial to our dear Sicilian brothers and to humanity in general; but we desire for the common welfare to see free communications speedily restored, so that we may disclose the most interesting documents of the trial as they come to our knowledge, and encourage you to defend our national health.' Though written by Adorno, this was signed by the mayor Pancalì and dated July 21, 1837. Far from soothing the people, it had the reverse effect. Those who saw their loved

Queen Maria Isabella

ones die rushed to the prison to implore Schwentzer for an antidote. Hoping to save his skin, he prescribed whatever remedies he could think of.

On July 24 the sound of cannon increased the general panic. General Tanzi, the aged commander of the local garrison, had declared a state of siege. The mayor retired to his villa in the country; the acting intendant wished to wind up the criminal investigation; but as several chemical experts and other witnesses were cholera stricken, the judge Mistretta explained that the trial would have to be postponed. On hearing this the exasperated people forced their way into the prison and took the supposed poisoners to be judged. Schwentzer's young wife clung weeping to her husband, but she was dragged off to the Cathedral square with fourteen other suspects as innocent as herself, and done to death with barbarous cruelty. Schwentzer's baby was rescued by a merciful midwife. Next day a blind beggar was murdered. He had accused a corn-merchant of being a poisoner and confessed before dying that he had done this because the merchant had refused him alms.

Adorno's proclamation, approved by the mayor and his committee, had an even more disastrous effect on the people of Catania. United by the dread of poison, they were bent on massacre and destruction. The commander of the small garrison shut himself up in the fort. The intendant and other authorities were arrested, their houses were ransacked; the police were disarmed; and the people, encouraged by a group of liberals, elected a committee of so-called public safety. The radicals felt certain that the whole island was ripe for revolt. The scenes of terror, bloodshed and mourning seemed to them happy portents. Demagogues who did not really represent the people wished to transform the committee of public safety into a provisional government. There was a general outcry for Sicilian independence; a national flag was hoisted to the popping of petards; a statue of Francis I was destroyed; and a proclamation was circulated declaring that the cholera had been introduced intentionally by the Bourbons: in order not to lose Sicily Ferdinand had resolved to annihilate its population. But the news that Del Carretto was advancing at the head of an expedition put a sudden stop to these excesses. The radicals fled ignominiously and there was an outburst of loyalty to the King.

When the local authorities were unable to cope with the disorders in Catania and Syracuse the King decided to send Del Carretto, his energetic Minister of Police, with the full powers of an *alter ego* in Sicily. Since he had suppressed the Cilento revolt and levelled Bosco to the ground, a reputation for ruthlessness preceded him. He issued a reasonable appeal for law and order and set up military commissions to try the ringleaders of rebellion. Eighty were condemned to death, and several hundreds to various terms of imprisonment or exile. Mario Adorno, who had done more than anyone to whip up popular frenzy with his wild accusations, was among those condemned to death. He spoke for an hour and a half in his own defence, still protesting his belief in poison and in the guilt of the wretches whom the good people had slaughtered. The radical propagandists made a martyr of him; but even if he was more fool than knave he had unleashed the forces of evil. Noto became the provincial capital instead of Syracuse, 'because it would seem monstrous that a place where a bloody rebellion had occurred should continue to be the seat of local government'. Naturally the people of Noto were delighted and gave Del Carretto a warm welcome. The mayor of Acireale, which had resisted an invasion of rebels from Catania, described the general relief at the sight of the royal ships: the troops who had landed there were taken aback by their enthusiastic reception, and Del Carretto treated the authorities with extreme courtesy and consideration.

The ravages of the epidemic were far worse in Sicily than elsewhere: 65,256 persons perished, about ten per cent of the island's population. In and around Naples it had claimed 13,798 victims before it ceased in September. While the poison myth had soon been exploded in the capital, it had been cultivated elsewhere by radicals on the mainland. At Penne in the Abruzzi they had filled the public fountain with coloured hosts. The sight of these caused a riot, and the attempts of the Bishop and police officials to pacify the people only convinced them that their bread and water had been poisoned by orders from above. Led by Sigismondo de Santis and the three de Cesaris brothers, the local liberals fanned the flame. De Santis, a receiver in the district treasury, having heard from the inspector of police that the provincial commandant had sent for reinforcements, decided to act promptly. On the evening of July 23 the local garrison was disarmed, the barracks were seized, and the Constitution of 1820 was proclaimed amid public festivities. The leaders convoked an assembly in the town hall which elected a constitutional committee to administer the province and appointed commanders of the militia and national guard. A *Te Deum* was then sung for the success of the revolution.

As soon as the King heard of this, on July 25, he sent Field-Marshal Lucchesi-Palli to restore order. Of the hundred and two persons implicated eight were condemned to death and the others to various terms of imprisonment by a military commission, but the King suspended these sentences except in the case of three ringleaders who had fled. There were other symptoms of unrest in the provinces: a seditious faction was reported from Salerno; at Cosenza a jar of poisoned water was found in a shoemaker's shop; at Avellino a plot for another insurrection was discovered; a new sect called 'Italian Federation' was spreading in Lecce and Bari. Cholera, conspiracy and brigandage were the three musketeers of the season.

VI

THE cholera riots had shown that Sicily was the Achilles heel of Ferdinand's kingdom. Not long before that calamity, on April 14, 1837, William Temple had reported: 'The Austrian Minister at this Court has made urgent representations to the King of Naples upon the state of Sicily, and the necessity of taking measures for the improvement of the administration of that part of his dominions, but I fear there is much reason to doubt whether they will be productive of any useful result.

'The education of the King was unfortunately entirely neglected as to almost all the branches of knowledge which could be useful to him as a Sovereign, and the only principles which the late Monsignor Olivieri, his tutor, appears to have endeavoured to instil in his mind in addition to a blind reverence for the ceremonies and ordinances of the Roman Catholic religion, were a distrust of all persons who might surround him, and a narrow economy which has almost degenerated into avarice.

'These dispositions were probably much strengthened by a consideration of the evils entailed upon this country by the unlimited powers enjoyed by former Ministers, and by the profuse expenditure of the Court and the peculation which pervaded all departments of the

State during the reigns of his two predecessors. Unfortunately too, His Majesty has a great distaste for business, and with the exception of military details his Ministers can scarcely induce him to attend to the affairs of the State. As there is no minister who has any influence beyond his own immediate department, and each entertains a jealousy of his colleagues, consequently there is no directing mind to give influence or unity of action to the march of government, which indeed may be said to stand still.

'On the accession of His Majesty to the throne he certainly displayed much good sense and energy in recalling many of the persons who had been banished or who had quitted the country on account of political opinions, a measure which rendered him deservedly popular, and which has been of infinite service in maintaining tranquillity by allaying personal and political animosities. Great expectations were also raised of improvements in the administration of the country, and particularly in Sicily, where on his first visit to that island, he was received with the greatest enthusiasm. Unfortunately however these expectations have not been fulfilled, and on his second visit to Sicily in 1834 his reception was cold though respectful, and the Sicilians evidently wished to make him sensible of their feelings of disappointment.

'The recall of the Count of Syracuse was not a popular measure, and since that time the government of the island has been entrusted to Prince Campofranco, who is altogether null and inefficient and can do nothing without reference to Naples.

'The wisest plan certainly for the King to adopt, and which I believe has been proposed to him, would be to go over to Sicily and reside there some months with his Court in order to examine into the state of the country, listen to the complaints of his subjects, and remedy the evils of the administration; but he objects, I believe, to this plan from a feeling of his not being popular in that island, and certainly unless he went there with a well digested plan of reform and the determination to carry it into effect, his visit would be productive of more harm than good.

'It is to be feared therefore that although the King and his ministers are fully sensible of the evils which exist in Sicily they do not possess sufficient talent or energy to meet them, and will leave things to take their chance, trusting that as they have gone on so long, they may continue to do so in the same manner, and fearing that their interference would be more likely to lead, as in the case of a corrupt body, to complete dissolution than to a restoration of health and vigour.'

Temple seems to have expected too much of the young King in too short a space of time. Many of the problems that vexed Sicily then have not been solved to-day. In the past such enlightened viceroys as Marchese Caracciolo and the Prince of Caramanico had tried to introduce reforms but had only succeeded in stirring up hornets' nests.

Gradually the powers of the barons had been restricted, and their resentment against the Crown was natural. As prices rose their expenditure increased; the absentee landlords delegated their responsibilities to agents and the profits they had once enjoyed were reduced to such an extent that many did not mind renouncing their feudal privileges. The barons and their dependents, including agents, tenants, lawyers and clergy, remained the ruling class, rigidly opposed to the government's policy of centralization. Failing to appreciate the benefits of Bourbon rule, they exaggerated its defects.

Since 1735 the population of Sicily had increased from one million to one million eight hundred thousand, in spite of the disastrous Messina earthquake of 1783 and the cholera epidemic of 1837. As the British consul John Goodwin pointed out:[1] 'In both the Sicilies every branch of industry was in a decayed or drooping state at the era of the Spanish conquest. Husbandry was backward and trade was stagnant; manufactures were stationary; fisheries were neglected, and mines were abandoned. Improvement took place under the reigns of Charles III and Ferdinand his son. The plough, the loom and the anvil became busy throughout the land. Trade with foreign countries sprang up by degrees, and the coral fishery rose and prospered for a season. The mining industry of Sicily first became active under the reign of the present sovereign. In a word, all the useful arts have risen, slowly but steadily, from insignificance to importance during the past century.' Every branch of industry had improved, but the Bourbons were blamed for sacrificing Sicilian to Neapolitan interests and for keeping the people backward.

From 1806 until 1815, when the Court was at Palermo and the island was occupied by English troops, Sicily had benefited from Napoleon's blockade of the Continent. Unlike the Neapolitans, they

[1] Progress of the Two Sicilies under the Spanish Bourbons from the year 1734–5 to 1840. London Statistical Society, 1842.

had not been conscripted by foreigners and forced to fight their distant battles; they had not had to suffer exile, confiscation, arbitrary executions, the mass destruction of towns, villages and fields, and the ruin of their local industries. England had lavished money, troops and ships to keep Sicily in friendly hands. The barons grew louder in their clamour for autonomy and Lord William Bentinck, as Minister to the Sicilian Court and Commander-in-Chief in the Mediterranean, enabled their resistance to the Crown to bear fruit—if such apples of Sodom deserve that appellation—in the sterile Constitution of 1812. Far more was said than done by the Sicilian Parliament. The English officers who had been in favour of it were soon thinking that such 'miserable wretches' were only fit to be dealt with by martial law. Even Bentinck, the temporary dictator, confessed in a moment of disillusion that 'the Sicilians in general are bullies and are only to be managed by fear. They take advantage of the least concession and always construe conciliation into weakness.'

Since the Congress of Vienna the Two Sicilies had been technically united and the Constitution of 1812 had been annulled. Seven new provinces were set up under intendants, with new municipal councils appointed by the King. The Sicilians thus inherited the centralized system which had been imposed on Naples by the French, and their animosity against the Neapolitans became fiercer than ever. The nobility still hoped to recover their feudal power and shake off what they felt to be the stigma of Neapolitan domination. Vanity was the great defect of the country, as Bentinck had observed: only vanity could expect to gain from autonomy at this period. Ferdinand II had sent his younger brother Leopold to restore confidence in the throne, but when he saw that the Sicilians were exploiting his inexperience for their selfish ends he appointed their countryman Campofranco in his stead.

The collapse of local administration during the cholera epidemic forced the King to revise his policy. On October 31, 1837, he abolished the Ministry for Sicilian Affairs at Naples: the principle of 'separate rights' was replaced by the principle of 'common possession', and the subjects of both realms were equally eligible to all civil and ecclesiastical offices. The Sicilians might hold as many posts in Naples as the Neapolitans held in Sicily. The Neapolitan Onorato Gaetani, Duke of Laurenzana, replaced the inept Campofranco as Lieutenant-General.

According to partisan historians the King was so disgusted with the Sicilians that he made no further effort to conciliate them. On the contrary, he hoped that an interchange of Sicilians and Neapolitans might lead to a better understanding of their common interests, and to closer co-operation in trade. But while Sicilians did not mind giving orders on the mainland, they regarded it as slavery to obey a Neapolitan magistrate on their island. The barons played a double game to win lucrative posts at Naples and popularity at home. Regional sentiment was far stronger than common sense.

Early in 1838 the cultured Pietro Ulloa was sent to Sicily with Giuseppe Ferrigni to reform the corrupt magistrature. He reported to the Minister of Justice Parisi that 'there is scarcely an official who is not prostrate at the sign of a grandee, or who does not intend to reap profit from his post. This general corruption has driven the people to seek strange and dangerous remedies. There are secret brotherhoods in several districts, or a kind of sect without meetings or any token save dependence on a chief—here a landowner, there a parish priest. A communal cash reserve supplies their needs, now to exonerate an official, now to support or to suborn him, to protect a prisoner or incriminate an innocent man. The people have a convention with criminals. When robberies occur mediators offer to negotiate for the recovery of the stolen goods. Many high magistrates cover these brotherhoods with an impenetrable shield. . . . It is impossible to induce civic guards to patrol the streets, or find witnesses for crimes committed in broad daylight. At the centre of this state of dissolution there is a capital with its luxury and feudal pretensions in the midst of the nineteenth century, a city containing 40,000 proletarians whose lives depend on the luxury and caprices of the great. In this navel of Sicily public offices are sold, justice is perverted, and ignorance is encouraged. Since 1820 the popular revolts have been due to discontent, not to the visionary utopias of the period. When insurrection breaks out, as is bound to happen, it might well be compared with that of the Neapolitans under the Aragonese and Spaniards, when the people cried: "Death to bad government!" '

The King embarked for Sicily in September 1838, accompanied by the Queen, Santangelo the Minister of the Interior, Del Carretto the Minister of Police, General Filangieri, and a large suite. After visiting Messina, Milazzo, Trapani, and other cities, he entered Palermo on

October 25, where he met with such an ovation that nobody would suspect any discontent. The military commissions were dissolved and most of the political prisoners were amnestied. The King ordered a network of new roads to be built, especially round Noto, Caltanisetta and Girgenti: within the next few years 1305 miles of new roads were laid out, and another thousand miles had been planned and were under construction when the revolution of 1848 broke out. Orphanages, almshouses, asylums for the deaf and dumb, a *Monte di Pietà* or public pawn-shop at Trapani, a stock exchange and free port at Messina, hospitals and charities, the encouragement of agriculture and industry, rewards and diplomas for merit, severe laws against duelling, all sorts of reform claimed the King's attention during the three strenuous months he spent in Sicily.

The most valuable mineral of the island was sulphur, which furnished four-fifths of the world's supply. Many of the mines about six miles from Girgenti, in a burnt hilly landscape of the utmost desolation, were owned and managed by Englishmen against whom there was a certain amount of jealousy and ill feeling. As in other industries there were periods of depression when the English were blamed for faulty mining methods and for selfish profiteering. Irritated by constant complaints about excessive production and the fall of prices, Ferdinand granted a virtual monopoly of the sulphur trade to a French company, Taix, Aycard of Marseilles, which was to pay the government 400,000 ducats a year with the proviso that not more than 600,000 hundredweight a year were to be mined and that 20,000 hundredweight were to be delivered to the royal gunpowder store. The contract was signed in July 1838, although Kennedy, the British chargé d'affaires in Temple's absence, had protested against it as a violation of the treaty of 1816 between England and the Two Sicilies.

Cassaro, the Minister for Foreign Affairs, was aware of the King's right to do as he pleased, but he had advised him not to allow the contract to be signed as it would antagonize a potential ally. He had already assured Temple that British interests would not be damaged by the contract, but as on previous occasions he was kept in the dark, and the contract was signed without his knowledge. At an official dinner, Lord Palmerston vented his indignation on old Count Ludolf, the Neapolitan ambassador in London, and sent a threatening note to Naples. The latter reached Ferdinand while he was in Sicily. He was so enraged that he sent a violent reply through Cassaro, who was still trying to placate Kennedy. The horrified Minister for Foreign Affairs persuaded the King to soften his language. He withdrew the reply but gave orders that Ludolf was to repeat its contents to Palmerston. Ludolf died before this could be done.

Sir Frederick Lamb, the Prime Minister Lord Melbourne's brother and British ambassador in Vienna, happened to be in Naples to discuss a new commercial treaty on a basis of reciprocity. Thanks to Cassaro, who appreciated its advantages, the negotiations had gone so smoothly that the British government had sent a special envoy called Mac Gregor to conclude them. Cassaro thought this would be a fine opportunity to cancel the French contract spontaneously instead of under pressure, and the King appeared ready to consent. But he had been deeply offended by Palmerston's arrogance and he was torn by conflicting emotions. On the one side Santangelo and Filangieri, who supported the French company, maintained that the British pretensions were a gross interference with his rights as an independent sovereign; on the other Cassaro and Regina, his chargé d'affaires in London, urged him to satisfy the British demands before they gave rise to a diplomatic incident.

Cassaro sent the King a detailed memorial explaining all the disadvantages of prolonging the controversy, but the King turned a deaf ear. The English merchants, who complained of heavy financial losses, continued to press for energetic action. Kennedy had written privately to London on December 29, 1838: 'Prince Butera exerts himself to moderate the effects of the bad measures of the Government but with little success. He tries occasionally to persuade me that I must excuse their ignorance—but they are a *bad* set and Santangelo is assuring everybody that the answer to England is *very strong*. If he gives me a good opportunity I will expose him, for it makes my blood boil to hear him crow thus on his own dung-hill, and whisper so softly in London. Poor Prince Cassaro grows more inefficient every day. He is afraid of the King, afraid of losing his place, afraid of the effects of the King's measures on England, France and Austria . . . I cannot but think that firmness will bring them to a sense of justice, although the King is very positive and blind.'

Kennedy regarded Santangelo as the villain of the piece. Two months later he wrote of him: 'He is very deceitful and I think he now feels his favour precarious. He is generally detested throughout the country and only does good through fear.' On August 29, 1839, Kennedy wrote an elaborate letter to Lord Palmerston informing him that the King would cancel the French contract: 'The King assured the Prince (Cassaro) that the monopoly should be set aside, that he would support him in taking proper steps to that effect, and that he would no longer listen to M. Santangelo, adding with great feeling: "I really thought when I sanctioned the measure that I was doing a good thing for Sicily; hardly had I approved of it before I regretted it, but I shall never regret the first motives which induced me to sanction it."

'Prince Cassaro immediately sent to M. Taix desiring him to come to him on the following morning, when he communicated to him the determination of the King to get rid of the contract, and insisted upon his at once making his proposals. M. Taix asked leave to refer the question to Paris, but Prince Cassaro observed that the Neapolitan Government knew but him, with whom they had made the contract. That if the proposals were reasonable the King would take them into consideration, if not other means would be resorted to.

'M. Taix mentioned that the company had made immense purchases of sulphur in Sicily, and that there still remained six months consumption in France and England (over which I believe the company has got control). Prince Cassaro promised that a certain time should be allowed the company to get rid of their stock.

'M. Taix in the course of the day sent in a calculation of four millions of ducats, equal to about £666,000, as an evaluation of present loss and of the profit they would be deprived of. This calculation is grossly exaggerated . . . Prince Cassaro has written to the Neapolitan chargé d'affaires to induce the French capitalists . . . to be more reasonable than M. Taix, who has acted for them. He hopes the French Government may facilitate an amicable settlement of the question. . . .

'May I hope that if your Lordship has it in your power, you will kindly assist the King, who has listened to our representations.

'At any rate there will now remain but the delays incidental to a final arrangement of this troublesome question, and when I consider the embarrassment it has caused to the British merchants, and how prejudicial it has been to the trade between the two countries, I hope my incessant efforts to defeat it may meet with your Lordship's approbation.

'From this moment Prince Cassaro's influence will be greatly strengthened, and the commercial treaty with England be comparatively an easy question.

'It may perhaps be better that the intention of the King be not divulged until the company has taken steps to get rid of their sulphur, otherwise they will claim a larger amount of indemnity.'

Kennedy's optimism was premature. On January 4, 1840, he wrote: 'I am afraid that no personal exertions of mine can any longer hasten the termination of this question. . . . Unless Her Majesty's Government is determined that the question be finally decided within a reasonable time it may still be protracted indefinitely.' And on January 21: 'The associates and friends of M. Taix . . . are again full of hopes respecting the stability of their contract, and I cannot learn from Prince Cassaro that this Government has come to any serious determination for its abrogation.' On January 29 he reported: 'Yesterday in the Council of Ministers it was decided that the sulphur monopoly should be set aside. Prince Cassaro did not attend the Council and I am not able to give your Lordship any information of what steps will be taken next. I merely state this because up to the last moment I have doubted of any decision being come to, but now I hope in a few days to be able to state to your Lordship the intentions of the Neapolitan Government.'

In the meantime, on January 26, Palmerston sent Kennedy a blunt despatch for Cassaro demanding the immediate withdrawal of the sulphur monopoly and making the Neapolitan government responsible for the losses it had caused to British subjects. Cassaro then sent Kennedy a confidential letter on February 23 which had been authorized by the King, assuring him that 'in deference to England' the sulphur question had been settled, but that the King desired secrecy. 'I trust that your Lordship will take into consideration the personal position of Prince Cassaro and the character of the King, which has often puzzled the diplomacy of Austria and France,' wrote Kennedy to Palmerston. Cassaro had threatened to resign if the treaty with Great Britain and the annulment of the monopoly were not carried through. He had been hindered all along by the intrigues and opposition of Santangelo, the Minister of the Interior, whom he described as the author of the monopoly.

Palmerston was the last person to consider the susceptibilities of

Ferdinand II, and if it was his intention to goad him to exasperation he succeeded admirably. Besides his attitude in the sulphur question the King resented his championship of Prince Charles, his runaway brother. Although he had sent Palmerston polite messages thanking him for his efforts to hasten a *rapprochement*, he was inwardly boiling with rage at his presumption.

The correspondence about this family quarrel was almost as long and as complicated as that about the sulphur monopoly. The Prince of Capua steadily refused all his brother's proposals. He had appealed to his aunt Marie Amélie, the Queen of the French, but she too thought that his wife and her children should renounce all pretensions to be considered as part of the royal family and, of course, all right of succession to the throne. When he begged her for a large sum of money she rebuked him for leading an extravagant life in London. As the Prince's wife was a British subject Palmerston thought fit to interfere. Irritated by the sulphur monopoly, he criticized the King's neglect of his brother, who was living at the expense of his wife and her relatives. As an indispensable condition of further negotiations the King insisted that his brother should leave London. How could he leave London honourably, exclaimed Palmerston, without paying his creditors? His stay there was 'not due to choice but to sheer necessity'. Palmerston thought the King should settle his brother's debts, which amounted to 36,000 ducats, and provide him with sufficient means to depart with dignity.

Heckled alternately about sulphur and about his younger brother, the King became aware that Palmerston was making political capital out of the latter's indiscretions. Judging from Kennedy's correspondence he did not seem to realize that the King regarded him as an impudent busybody. On July 2, 1839, for instance, he wrote to Palmerston a letter worth quoting in full for its underlying irony: 'On receiving Your Lordship's despatch relative to Prince Charles of Capua, I requested an audience of the Queen Mother, who has always been the Prince's friend, and begged her to prepare the King to listen to Prince Cassaro. The Queen desired me to send Prince Cassaro to her to concert measures.

'I likewise communicated privately with the King and advanced such arguments as I thought calculated to remove irritation and to induce him to forgive.

'I then waited upon Prince Cassaro and communicated Your Lordship's despatch.

'Prince Cassaro saw the King and informed me that he had found H.M. much better disposed, adding that M. Regina had already written in the same sense. He thought the King would grant an income to Prince Charles equal to that of the Count of Syracuse and on the same terms . . . a title to his consort, and when the time should arrive, would do something for the children. Prince Cassaro showed to me the law of 1829 and said that Prince Charles had forfeited everything, and that if too much was attempted nothing would be obtained.

'I said that my wish was to do everything agreeable to the King but that circumstances were so altered that I thought everything might now be forgiven—and that clemency was better than too severe justice, that history would pronounce an opinion upon what was done to-day, and that it would redound much to his honour to have effected a reconciliation between the royal brothers.

'After the lapse of several days, finding that nothing was done, having consulted with those best able to give me advice I determined to draw the King's attention again to the subject and ventured to draw up a few "observations" which I sent to Prince Cassaro.

'I then again, after a few days, saw Prince Cassaro. He declared that for himself he agreed in what I said, but that the King was mistrustful, that he had spoken upon the subject of my private communication and said, "I am sure they want to get everything out of me." To that I said that since I had taken an unauthorized step I would withdraw my "observations" and not add anything to Your Lordship's despatch. I took back my "observations".

'I heard in the meantime that when the King received my request to listen to Prince Cassaro, he said nothing, but "bit his lip and turned pale" which he does when strongly excited. I contented myself with begging Prince Cassaro to do something out of consideration for Prince Charles's sad situation.

'Two days ago Prince Cassaro informed me that he had written to M. Regina and was authorized by the King to show me the despatch (I obtained leave to take a copy of it). He added confidentially that the King could not make up his mind to trust Prince Charles; that he felt really obliged to Your Lordship for the interest you had taken and even added: "*Il n'y a que Lord Palmerston qui pourra faire quelque chose avec lui.*" Prince Cassaro said: "*Je vous assure que c'est une chose fort désagréable.*"

'Your Lordship will see that Prince Cassaro is displeased with M. Regina for having communicated in writing what he was instructed to say verbally: the idea is that Prince Charles would "show it about and make a bad use of the communication"—the despatch where Regina then expresses pleasure at Your Lordship's interference and acquiescence in the non-necessity of a formal renunciation, quoting the law of 1829. It then (and such is the King's impression) shows distrust of Prince Charles and the necessity of his giving some pledge that he will observe the law and admit its validity respecting his wife and children, that the King will give him an allowance and a title to his wife.

'It allows M. Regina to present Prince Charles at Court and take leave, but not his wife, and to give them separate passports.

'I pointed out to Prince Cassaro how sorry I was to see this despatch sent, as it contained so little positive. That Prince Charles could not be expected to leave England without money, and the question being so little advanced, and my regret that he did not specify everything.

'It is evident that H.E. does not like having anything to do with it, unless Prince Charles gives an assurance of perfect submission to the law and the King's wishes. . . .'

Paolo Versace was sent to London as a special envoy with the King's latest proposals to his brother. These were briefly that the title of Duchess of Villalta should be conferred upon his consort; the Prince's sons were to receive six thousand ducats a year, and the daughters a dowry of thirty thousand ducats; a sum of forty thousand ducats would be advanced for the liquidation of the Prince's debts; the Prince might select any place in Italy for his residence except the kingdom of the Two Sicilies and the Papal States; the Prince was to write to the King expressing his grateful acceptance of these proposals, which Versace communicated to Palmerston.

'My conviction,' wrote Kennedy very sensibly, 'is that it is most desirable that the Prince of Capua should accede with gratitude to these offers, and thus gradually remove every feeling of displeasure on the part of the King. The law of Naples is plainly against the Prince and this change of sentiment towards him is owing entirely to Your

119

Lordship's intercession, whereas opposition would only irritate the King, and retard the moment of reconciliation.'

Palmerston answered Versace that the Prince first required a certain sum to enable him to move from the country to London, and that he wished to have all the relevant documents brought over by Versace in order to examine them. The King's decree stated: 'We confer upon Mrs Penelope Smyth the title of Duchess of Villalta, which may be transmitted to her sons and those of Prince Charles, who will bear their mother's surname.' If elder sons were to have the title of Villalta, what, enquired Palmerston, were the younger sons to be called, Villalta or Smyth? In the former case the Prince would consent, but in the second neither he nor his consort would agree to such a condition. Palmerston quoted the example of the Duke of Sussex, who had given his children the name of d'Este, which belonged to his own family. Cassaro sent word that the Prince's younger sons were to bear their mother's surname Smyth, as the title of Villalta could only be transmitted to the elder son, but that the King might even allow the title of Villalta to be inherited by all his offspring in token of his desire to remove all obstacles to their reconciliation. But the King would not grant any money unconditionally. The Prince wished to defer his journey till the spring. Versace was to persuade him to leave sooner, observing that he would be going to a better climate. If the Prince remained stubborn, he was not to be paid until the time of his departure.

The Prince of Capua replied through Palmerston that he claimed the title of Princess instead of Duchess of Villalta for his consort; and the surname of Bourbon for his children, whose allowance should be increased; and that he requested permission to remain in England. Palmerston supported all these claims in terms most offensive to the King, alleging that both Prince Charles and himself knew that the decree of April 7, 1829, did not exist; that the King had never published his father's will because he had appropriated eleven thousand ducats a month which had been bequeathed to Prince Charles.

Versace considered it futile to negotiate further with the Prince, who was being used as a pawn by Palmerston. He sent Palmerston a copy of the 1829 decree whose existence the Prince had denied, and took leave of him on January 28, 1840. Palmerston's parting tirade confirmed Versace's suspicions. He told him that Penelope Smyth claimed the title of Princess because she wanted to be 'the wife of her husband'; he hoped that Prince Charles would receive four thousand ducats a month besides his revenue from Mascalì. Versace's departure, he added, would wake up the Prince's creditors who had stopped dunning him because they had expected a settlement. Some of these threatened to have the Prince imprisoned for debt. In this humiliating situation the Prince was certain to pose as a victim before the whole of Europe: he might write or publish things which, even if untrue, would influence public opinion against King Ferdinand, and try every means of exciting sympathy. Turning from the particular to the general, Palmerston remarked that many complaints had reached the British Parliament about the sulphur monopoly, which he considered a manifest infraction of the treaty of 1816. These well-founded complaints would oblige his government to adopt more strenuous measures to obtain compensation for British subjects, and put an end to the monopoly. Palmerston also demanded a prompt decision with regard to the opening of a Protestant chapel in Naples. Since the Pope had allowed one in Rome, he saw no reason why Ferdinand should object.

The King had sent word that he would make every concession to Prince Charles providing that he and his consort both wrote him submissive letters, apparently on their own initiative, repenting of the past, expressing gratitude for favours received, and submission to the will of the august head of the royal family. But this they would not do. 'I understand that the King of Naples has been very much affected on hearing that H.R.H. the Prince of Capua has refused the terms offered through M. Versace,' wrote Kennedy on January 4, 1840. The Prince was to remain the loser. His dispute was suffocated, as it were, in the fumes of sulphur. Ferdinand wanted to repay in kind the exasperation which Palmerston had caused him.

Temple had returned to Naples in the meantime, expecting the sulphur contract to be cancelled from day to day. After waiting three weeks he sent Cassaro Palmerston's despatch which had previously been withdrawn. At a meeting of the State Council on March 16, Cassaro tried to urge the King to relent. But Ferdinand was convinced that he was in the right and now declared that he would resist to the death. 'Gentlemen,' he addressed his ministers, 'you have heard the British note, and to-day we must decide whether to yield or not to the claims and threats against us: it is a question of our honour and dignity. For my part I am ready to resist. There was a time when Naples made Europe tremble; I will not say she can do so now, but there is no reason why we should tremble. What can the English do to us with their ships? More than six ships will be needed to blockade our extensive coast! And supposing we were blockaded, it would be of greater advantage to ourselves than to the English, because it would help to stimulate our native industries. As for our vessels at sea, they will adapt themselves as best they can to circumstances and run the blockade. Moreover, if the English wanted to capture our ships . . . there are no sacrifices of which we should not be capable. Some would advise us to yield, but do they realize what we should gain thereby, apart from the loss of our dignity and the stain on our honour? We should have to submit to the relentless demands of England. Once the sulphur contract was broken, she would try to make us revive the tariff of 1816 and add other extravagant demands. . . . If we surrender to England now we should have to surrender to others as well in future. . . . They always dangle Sicily before me as a scarecrow. In '37 everybody in Sicily, except Campofranco, was crying for separation; but I was able to banish the thought of it from their minds and make them return to their allegiance. It will be the same to-day. I know what has to be done: keep quiet and fear nothing. In sanctioning the sulphur contract I stood within my rights; and it violates no treaty whatever. It is an undeniable sovereign right to consult the prosperity and the welfare of my subjects. The English earned so much in the sulphur trade at the expense of the natives, that they are unwilling to see their profits diminish, therefore they would dictate to us. I wanted to settle this affair of my accord and could have done so, but this has become impossible under intimidation: it would discredit me. . . . We should stand firm against unjust pretensions.'

Having given repeated assurances that the King would annul the contract, Cassaro resigned. The King was so furious that he exiled him to Foggia. 'The following morning,' Temple reported, 'he received orders to depart within two hours, and an officer of the police was sent to see these orders carried into execution. This arbitrary act has created a general feeling of surprise and dissatisfaction, as no specific charge has been brought against Prince Cassaro, whose high qualities and honourable conduct have obtained for him a general esteem. . . . I should not be surprised if the King were to do something ill-advised by seizing British property or firing upon our ships, but I do not think he will be quite so rash, though he is extremely irritable and obstinate.'

The King's private secretary, Monsignor Caprioli, whose influence over his master was only less than that of Monsignor Cocle, caused the Prince of Scilla to be appointed Foreign Minister in Cassaro's stead. At first the King thought that Palmerston was bluffing but Admiral Stopford, the commander of the Mediterranean fleet, was ordered to send two squadrons into Neapolitan and Sicilian waters and seize their ships, which were to be held at Malta until the sulphur contract had been cancelled. Early in April a British squadron performed various monitory manoeuvres in the bay of Naples and anchored in the Santa Lucia roads.

Rear-Admiral Winnington-Ingram related[1] that H.M.S. *Talbot* was ordered from her station at Corfu to capture Neapolitan vessels wherever met with on the high seas, and proceeded to cruise off Santa Maria in the Heel of Italy. 'To avoid being reported on the coast, and also to deceive unwary vessels, she sailed chiefly under Austrian and Neapolitan colours, only hoisting the English flag when a capture was being made. Another device from the scheming head of the clever Captain (the late Admiral of the Fleet, Sir Henry Codrington, K.C.B.) was to make use of the only two long guns in the ship's armament to the best advantage, for the purpose of bringing vessels to at their farthest possible range. . . . The surprise shown by some of the foreign ships at having a shot dropped close to them from a vessel two or three miles distant, was evident by their letting fly tacks and sheets and bearing up in confusion, like a wounded bird with feathers dishevelled by the sportsman's fire. Through this method many Neapolitan coasting vessels, called "trabaccolos", were captured, and sent with the brigs and schooners—also taken to Corfu, there to have their rudders unshipped and sails sent ashore, pending the settlement of the dispute.

'As a prize crew could not be spared for every capture, it was the practice to wait for the whole day's "bag", and then start them off under convoy of one of their smartest craft with an armed party of our blue-jackets and marines on board her. Perhaps a steersman was supplied to the other vessels to insure their following the convoy, but

[1] H. F. Winnington-Ingram, *Hearts of Oak*. London, 1889.

123

in time this precaution was dispensed with, as a warning shot from a musket occasionally was found sufficient to keep order in the sailing of the prizes . . . whilst we in the *Talbot* were arresting Neapolitan trade to the best of our power, the remainder of our squadron blockading Naples were enjoying the hospitality of that port, and giving return entertainments on board to both our countrymen and natives.'

The King made bellicose preparations on his side and sent twelve thousand troops to Sicily. There was also intense diplomatic activity. Circulars were sent to the Courts of Russia, Prussia and Austria, 'stating that Great Britain has made some extraordinary and unwarrantable demands upon the Neapolitan government; that the King of Naples had entered into the contract for the sulphur monopoly in Sicily at the request of his subjects, that it was a measure highly beneficial to his country, that no other government had remonstrated against it but that of Great Britain, which had used every unfair method to obtain abolition by bribing vile men and even a high personage (referring to Cassaro). . . . That His Majesty was resolved to maintain the contract, and he called upon these Powers to endeavour to prevent England from carrying these threats into execution. . . . The representations sent to Russia were the strongest, holding out the probability that the conduct of England might lead to an European war.'

But none of these powers showed any sympathy for Ferdinand II. As Metternich said, nobody wished the whole of Italy to be set on fire by the sulphur of Etna. Lebzeltern praised Cassaro's dignified behaviour. And when Ferdinand appealed to his father-in-law, the Archduke Charles, he received the following reply dated April 10: 'Dearest Son, after sending you a few lines in my last letter to Theresa I saw Marchese Gagliati whom you had ordered to enlighten me about your dispute with England. I am very sorry indeed that it has become so serious. . . . As a friend and an affectionate father I can only advise you to proffer your hand for a speedy and sincere reconciliation. I do not know the reasons which prompted you to demand the recall of Count Lebzeltern. But however just these may be, such a step at this moment might appear as if Lebzeltern or our Court had sown discord between you and the English, and even so two friendly Courts should avoid all public scandal. This becomes more than ever a political duty when the whole dispute arises from a resolution as harmful to Austria as to England and Sicily.'

Ferdinand was disgusted with Metternich, who had inspired this retort. 'There is nothing worse than selfish and calculating relatives,' said Monsignor Cocle. 'Since Austria will not help us, we will have to throw ourselves into the arms of France.' Ferdinand wrote to Louis-Philippe, who seemed eager to oblige him. While the Prince of Castelcicala went on a special mission to London and military preparations were continued on a spectacular scale, the Duke of Serracapriola went to Paris with the able Versace as his secretary.

Thiers had sent Guizot as French ambassador to London, whose offer to mediate was accepted by Palmerston on April 10. On April 19 Thiers telegraphed d'Haussonville, the French minister in Naples, to offer mediation on condition Serracapriola were given full powers to negotiate, not only to spare Ferdinand the humiliation of a treaty which appeared to be dictated by force, but to spare the negotiators from the continuous doubts and subterfuges which, as Guizot remarked, constituted the whole policy of the Neapolitan Court. French mediation was accepted on the 26th, but as Ferdinand had laid an embargo on the British ships in the bay at the same time, Temple was prevented from ordering the suspension of hostilities. Consequently seven Neapolitan ships were captured at the very moment when French mediation was announced. Twenty-four hours later the King realized the necessity of removing the embargo, and hostilities ceased.

There was many a hitch before the final settlement in July. First Serracapriola's instructions were incomplete, then Castelcicala raised difficulties to please the King, while Palmerston complained to Thiers through the ambassador Lord Granville and Thiers informed Palmerston through Guizot that since the documentary evidence relating to the claims of the British merchants had not been received nothing could be done. Palmerston would have preferred to deal directly with the Court of Naples, which could be bullied more easily.

'I have been informed,' reported Temple, 'that Monsignor Caprioli has fallen under the displeasure of the King. It is possible therefore that Monsignor Caprioli and the Prince of Scilla disguised or concealed some of the truth from the King in order to induce him to agree to more moderate counsels and now, to screen themselves, they pretend that other terms had been verbally offered to them by M. d'Haussonville than was really the case. Monsignor

Caprioli has had leave to retire for two months to Portici, and there are rumours that various changes will take place in the Ministry, but none which can as yet be depended upon.' 'I have been informed,' he wrote a week later on May 11, 'that the King of Naples was in a state of great excitement after having agreed to and signed the instructions and full powers which were sent off yesterday to Paris . . . and expressed himself with asperity against the Prince of Satriano, who had incited him to make extensive military preparations which have been going on throughout the Two Sicilies, and which no doubt were a source of considerable profit to the Prince under whose directions they were executed. His Majesty's determination to embark (for Sicily) appears to have been very sudden and the Queen made a point of accompanying him, although it had not been previously His Majesty's intention that she should do so. It is possible that the state of excitement in which His Majesty was said to be, made her the more anxious not to leave him. The passage must have been rough and long as the wind has been very high and contrary to their course.'

The King spent all his time in Sicily inspecting military establishments. Palmerston began to lose patience again: Guizot reported to Thiers on June 19 that he had limited the period of mediation to six weeks, but that he had agreed that a mixed commission should be held in Paris. Thiers drafted an agreement in which Ferdinand's rights over the management of Sicilian mines and the export duties on sulphur were recognized; simultaneously the monopoly conceded to the Taix company was abolished, and a fixed indemnity was settled for the English merchants. Palmerston said he was satisfied. The contract of 1838 was cancelled by a decree of July 11, 1840. But the King considered that his sacred rights had been trampled on by pragmatical Pharisees. The first ten years of his reign, so full of hope and confidence charged with a fresh vitality, ended on a note of bitterness and disillusion.

VII

THE sulphur dispute had a profound effect on Ferdinand's subsequent policy. Insofar as he had any foreign sympathies he had gravitated towards Austria, but now he felt that Austria had deserted him in time of crisis. Though he had a certain affection for his aunt Marie Amélie, with whom he corresponded regularly, he had never been on cordial terms with Louis-Philippe. The King of the French was disappointed because he had not married one of his daughters nor allowed his brother, the Count of Syracuse, to marry another; he was vexed by his Carlist bias; and he resented his hospitality to the Duchess of Berry, Ferdinand's widowed half-sister, and to her son the Duke of Bordeaux, whom far too many persisted in calling Henry V of France.

'As sister to the King,' wrote Faucigny-Lucinge,[1] 'the Duchess of Berry was received throughout the Two Sicilies with all the honours due to her. As soon as she arrived in a town all the civil and military authorities rushed up to her coach desirous of paying their homage. When she stopped at Capua she found herself in the presence of all the local functionaries, who had assembled at the door of the house where she was to spend the night. At their head stood the prefect or governor

[1] Prince de Faucigny-Lucinge, *Dans l'Ombre de l'Histoire*. Paris, 1951.

of the city in full uniform with a scroll in his hand, whose contents he was prepared to read aloud to her. But Madame did not give him time to do so for, great princess though she was, it was no less true that just like the humblest of mortals there were moments when . . . In short, she experienced the most pressing desire for privacy. Sweeping aside all personal vanity, she asked the astounded official to kindly pocket his compliments, which she would be delighted to hear later on, but she wished that without further delay they would lead her first to the apartment which had been reserved for her, and the high dignitary hastened to obey. After showing her into this apartment he stood discreetly outside the door, waiting for her to leave it. He did not have to wait long. Suddenly the door opened and the Princess indignantly summoned him, bidding him come and see for himself that the object which was most necessary to her at this moment had been forgotten, and that she had found the small piece of furniture which is placed beside all beds quite devoid of the utensil that usually adorns it. It was truly not worth the trouble of coming to Capua, whose pleasures had been so acclaimed! The poor prefect, blushing all over, was forced to admit the deficiency, but being a resourceful man he drew his sword from its sheath without further hesitation and proceeded to poke about under the bed with his weapon until he had the luck to strike the article required. This he hastened to offer the Princess in such a manner that she could conveniently seize its only handle. After which he vanished, blushing more and more furiously, to take up his sentry-duty by the door. Shortly afterwards the Duchess of Berry reappeared with a radiant smile and, relieved from all anxiety, received the civic authorities, listened to their compliments, and sent them off well satisfied with her amiable reception. The Princess used to laugh heartily when she told this story.'

The heroine of the Vendée had lost the sympathy of her French supporters since her secret marriage to Count Lucchesi-Palli. Released from her prison at Blaye when the French government ceased to consider her dangerous, she continued to conspire for her son's sake. Though her complexion remained fresh and youthful she was already too stout for her age. Enos Throop, the American envoy who saw her at this time, wrote: 'She has nothing left of the beauty which was once attributed to her, and which must have been partly fabulous. Nothing could be more unlike it than her face at rest, and her form has lost in grossness its delicacy and agility. Yet when she speaks her face lights up agreeably, and her manners are easy and graceful.'

'The partisans of the Duchess of Berry give often a Carlist tone to this Court and Government offensive to France, but the King takes no part in such absurdities,' wrote Kennedy in 1839. Casimir Périer, the French chargé d'affaires, was shocked by the prevalence of Carlists at Court balls: 'he dwelt much upon the forbearance of his Government, as caused by the affection of the Queen of the French for the family of Naples, but even Her Majesty must see the impossibility of going on in the same way.' The Duchess of Berry on her side 'found fault with M. Casimir Périer's dancing with the Princess of Salerno's daughter in her presence, and those around her have even criticized his sailing past the palace at which she resides with the tricoloured flag at the mast of his pleasure boat.' It was rumoured, moreover, that the Duke of Bordeaux was to marry Princess Carolina, the King's sixth sister, while Mademoiselle, the Duchess of Berry's daughter, was to marry the Count of Lecce, the King's third brother. Mademoiselle had a fortune of nearly 400,000 francs per annum, besides great expectations from the Duchess of Angoulême. The King was as anxious for these marriages as the Duchess of Berry, whose second husband, Count Lucchesi Palli, acted as go-between, but the negotiations broke down owing to the Duchess of Angoulême's opposition.

Kennedy reported that Casimir Périer 'represented strongly to this Government the impropriety of allowing the Duke of Bordeaux to come to Naples,' but the King took no notice of such impertinence. The Duke arrived in January 1840, and he received all the honours due to the King's nephew; the small palace on the Chiatamone was placed at his disposal, and he was welcomed by a military band. 'Certainly the Duke of Bordeaux is the nephew of the King of Naples,' wrote Kennedy, 'but it is impossible to divest him of his political character as regards the French Government after all that has passed. . . . I saw no necessity of my waiting upon the Duke to whom I am individually unknown at a moment when such a visit would be really offensive to the French Government.' Both the Austrian ambassador and the papal nuncio had tried to induce Kennedy to call on the Duke. Just before his arrival 'Count Lebzeltern drew up a code of regulations for the etiquette visits of the diplomatic body at Naples and even for their dress, and he slipped in an article that we should call upon the princes of the royal family after their arrival from foreign parts. This awoke the suspicions of the French embassy and M. Casimir Périer refused to accede to the regulations. I was unwilling to sign it because I thought it absurd, and Count Lebzeltern was much annoyed at what he was pleased to consider my conspiring with the French against a regulation acceded to by all the rest, though I suspect his vanity was a little hurt at our attacks upon his pet composition.'

The Duke stayed with the royal family but had a separate box at the opera, so that there was no cause for Louis-Philippe to take umbrage. Had not some members of the diplomatic body put themselves forward on this occasion, said Kennedy, the Duke's visit would have passed off without comment. The Carlists who surrounded him were very dissatisfied with their reception, and at variance among themselves. Yet Louis-Philippe was always querulous about the legitimate heir, having tried in vain to cast doubt on his legitimacy. In April 1839, he opened his heart to Versace. He had had reliable reports that the Duchess of Berry held receptions for all the Carlists in Naples twice a week, and feared that their influence—she was far too credulous—might lead to some reckless enterprise: would not the King do something to restrain her? As for Ferdinand, he was glad to improve relations with France at such little cost to himself. Before the Duchess of Berry sailed for Palermo he extracted a written declaration from her, promising not to plot against the French government. After some delay this document was signed and sent to Versace, who brought it to Louis-Philippe. Hence Louis-Philippe's readiness to oblige Ferdinand in the sulphur dispute.

So violent was Ferdinand's revulsion against Metternich and Lebzeltern that he changed his attitude towards France. In his secret instructions to the Duke of Serracapriola who was sent to Paris as ambassador in 1840, he wrote: 'Louis-Philippe undoubtedly deserves the gratitude of all good governments, as he should be considered the safeguard of European peace. . . . We are also grateful to him for his contributions to public order, to the stability of thrones, and to the tranquillity of Europe.'

The new French ambassador, the Duc de Montebello, had all the tact which Lebzeltern and Temple so sadly wanted, not that his task as *ambassadeur de famille* to the touchiest of the Bourbons was easier than theirs. Ferdinand regarded foreign diplomats as pests, hence his appointment of the Prince of Scilla, a genteel mediocrity, as Minister for Foreign Affairs. Scilla possessed the virtues of a wet blanket. Since the King had to bear with a diplomatic corps, as Montebello said, 'he has managed to raise a wall of incapacity in between.' The Neapolitan ministry's communications with foreign diplomats became almost farcical. Replies to official notes were limited to formal acknowledgements, and unofficial attempts to approach ministers were paralysed by Ferdinand's orders to avoid contact with the tiresome foreigners. When Scilla succeeded Cassaro he kept Temple waiting for weeks before answering an urgent note with the excuse that he was 'not yet acquainted with the sulphur question'. Ferdinand, having applied in vain for the recall of both Lebzeltern and Temple, paid little attention to either of them. His relations with France became increasingly cordial.

The historians for whom only Mazzini or Gioberti and their adherents mattered have depicted this phase of Ferdinand's reign as one of mere stagnation and oppression. In fact it was a period of bustling enterprise and commercial activity. Apart from an occasional flare-up, nearly always due to outsiders, aspirations towards a new order were either concealed or dormant. Mazzini's 'Young Italy' gained few recruits in the Two Sicilies until much later. A spirit of unrest might be detected in the new romantic literature, with its rebellious heroes, its rhetorical naturalism, and its vague yet expansive feeling for 'the folk'. But even in Naples the eighteen-forties were a bourgeois period and Ferdinand, for all his autocracy, was a bourgeois King. Even in his private life he had more in common with Louis-Philippe than with other reigning monarchs. His devoted Austrian spouse, who shared his love of simple domestic pleasures, presented him with eleven children, the first of whom, Luigi Maria, Count of Trani, was born in 1838. The short-lived Alberto Maria, Count of Castrogiovanni, was born in 1839, and in settling on him and his next heir male the estate of Carditello, the King's decree stated that he was to reside within the kingdom, and would forfeit his property if he married without the consent of his sovereign. After reporting the articles of this decree, Kennedy commented: 'This is an additional proof of the feelings which still animate His Sicilian Majesty respecting Prince Charles's marriage, and of his determination to prevent similar marriages in future. . . . It is not universally known that His Majesty forms establishments for the members of the royal family as much as possible out of the Crown revenues without burdening the State, and that the expenses at present being incurred at Capodimonte and the other palaces are defrayed from his private treasury.' The same article about marriage was repeated when the next Prince Alfonso Maria, Count of Caserta, was born in 1841. Though he was endowed with Crown lands near Caserta, he was not to enjoy the full control of his property until he entered his thirty-second year.

The King tried to manage his entire family, including his mother. The full-blooded Maria Isabella had inherited her own mother's weakness for men, preferably robust and younger than herself, irrespective of class. Widowed at forty, she required the constant attentions of a chamberlain to console her. Though past her prime, her dimples, her double chins, her capacious bosom radiated a warmth more than maternal and gave promise of 'pneumatic bliss' at a time when the fashion for pronounced feminine curves was rather Turkish. And she was known to be generous and tender-hearted, the most amiable of women, too amiable perhaps for a Queen Dowager. In many ways she remained a frivolous child, eager to be played with and petted. She loved theatres, balls and public festivities, and as an embodiment of good nature she was eminently popular. This made her an easy target for the revolutionary press, especially that of Malta, which flooded the kingdom with libels. She was described as 'an adulterous old Queen, still wallowing in vice, who hires foreign pimps and paramours.' Such gossip, like smoke, was not wholly without fire. Her connection with an Austrian officer called Baron von Schmuckher gave rise to some speculation in diplomatic circles when the King expelled him from Naples. Monsignor Fara, a representative of the Holy See, reported to Cardinal Lambruschini on January 6, 1838, that a police officer had requested him to endorse Schmuckher's passport for Rome. 'One hour after midnight the same officer was to escort him to Capua, and another from Capua to the frontier. At the time fixed for the Baron's departure the King, in order to prevent any access to his person, called for his carriage . . . and proceeded with only one servant to an unknown destination.' Three days later he reported that all the Baron's papers had been sealed. 'These severe measures seem to have been taken by the King in agreement with his august mother. Next day the Queen Mother's return was celebrated with a dinner for twenty-five at Fusaro. . . . The King has appointed the Princess of Paternò lady-in-waiting to the Queen Mother. Thus Heaven appears to have granted the wishes of his good and faithful subjects, who were anxious to see an end of what had given rise to scandalous gossip and compromised the decorum of the royal family. This event has caused general rejoicing in the capital.'

In a subsequent letter the Monsignor explained that the Queen Mother had grown tired of Baron von Schmuckher's behaviour during the last two years, and had even complained to the King about it. Sometimes she had decided to break with him, but he had only to appear slightly more respectful and submissive to make her change her mind. When his wife died of cholera in 1837 the Queen Mother might have married him if he had not made several preposterous claims, such as for the title and privileges of a Royal Highness. He became so insolent when these were rejected that she appealed to her son to get rid of him. He had amassed a fortune of 120,000 ducats from what the Monsignor described as 'the services he had rendered the Queen'. Next year there was talk of her marrying a son of the Prince of Sirignano, but she took offence because he had shown a want of alacrity. Then in January 1839, Monsignor Asquini, the Papal nuncio, informed Cardinal Lambruschini that the Queen Mother was privately married to Captain Del Balzo, the thirty-six-year-old brother of the Duke of Presenzano, and that the King had attended the ceremony incognito. The bridegroom was to be promoted to Lieutenant-Colonel of the Guards as well as majordomo to his august consort. The Monsignor continued: 'I saw the King after the marriage at the Academy ball, accompanied by his Queen, the Count of Syracuse, and the Prince and Princess of Salerno, and to tell the truth everybody was happy and their Majesties took part in the dances. . . .' Enos Throop, the American chargé d'affaires, wrote to his niece[1]: 'The town has been somewhat amused for a few days by a recent marriage of the Queen Mother. She has twelve children, and among them is the Queen Mother of Spain, the King of this kingdom, and the Duchess of Tuscany, and is between 49 and 50 years of age. She had expressed a determination to get married, and it is said that the King caused a list of all the young noblemen of the kingdom to be

[1] January 22, 1839. For the loan of his correspondence from Naples I am indebted to the kindness of his descendant, Mr Robert D. Brewster.

laid before her to choose from. It is said that the two first indicated by her manifested some hesitation which she considered incompatible with the ardent love which she exacted from her swain, and she immediately withdrew the proposal. She at length selected a young lieutenant of the army of fine personal appearance, about thirty years old, of a noble though decayed family, who consented to the union, and receives a palace, 6000 ducats in hand, and is to have 600 ducats a month.

'The happy pair have been seen riding together every day through the streets. This marriage, however, is not recognized as a legal one, and the husband takes no rank in consequence of it, and the King was the only member of the royal family who was present at the celebration of the nuptials. The King has raised him to the rank of Colonel in the army, and made him Chamberlain to the Queen Mother. The Queen Mother appears as usual at Court and public places where her husband has not the privilege of appearing, or if he does appear is not permitted to occupy the same elevated seat as his spouse.

'These little sketches of manners will make you somewhat acquainted with the notions of these people, and I am sure better satisfied with our own.'

Maria Isabella retired with her enterprising young husband to Capodimonte. Her favourite son Charles was still an exile unwilling to compromise about his wife's position. Her fourth son Anthony, Count of Lecce, came to a bad end at the age of twenty-seven. Temple reported in January, 1843, that he 'had been for some time in a precarious state of health, having had repeated attacks of paralysis, from the last of which he was recovering when he was seized by a typhus fever.' But it has since been proved that he acquired a small country house at Giugliano for his amorous assignations, and that he was repulsed in attempting to seduce a young matron. One morning he was found lying in a pool of blood with his head broken. Apparently the woman's husband had clubbed him to death in his rustic retreat, and the crime was hushed up to avoid scandal. The King's other brothers gave him less trouble. Though the Count of Syracuse had liberal tendencies these were not strong enough to divert him from his sculpture and patronage of the arts. The Count of Aquila had chosen a naval career.

The King's relations with his wife were all that could be desired.

She too preferred the delights of a well-filled nursery to the ceremonies of Court. Domestic life was simplified; on the other hand public festivities and military parades became more gorgeous: 20,000 infantry, 3500 cavalry and 112 pieces of cannon were assembled for the Piedigrotta festival of 1838. Since boyhood Ferdinand had been as interested in military costume as in drill and manœuvres, and his personal inspection was carried down to the minutest details: it was even said that he appointed one day for the examination of hats, another for boots, a third for coats, with never a button overlooked. His enthusiasm for military discipline, his relish for reviews and military pageants, contributed a great deal to his popularity, for the Neapolitans were ever ready to appreciate a royal impresario. On his return from France he was inspired to introduce new changes, as Kennedy noted: 'The guards who formerly wore red uniforms were dressed in blue coats, but still had their summer trousers. The cavalry wore blue jackets with garance trousers. Blue was originally the colour of the Bourbon troops. The whole Neapolitan squadron consisting of two frigates and a corvette, three sloops, a brig, a schooner and a steamer, were anchored in a line opposite the Chiaja, and added to the beauty of the scene.'

The façade of diplomatic life was as formal and pompous as in the reign of Ferdinand's grandfather. 'The amusements,' wrote Enos Throop, 'are attending at Court on gala days, the Monday evening dancing parties at the royal academy of balls and music, and dining and wining parties at the houses of the ministers and noble families. . . . The wealth of many of the noble families here consists in those things which enable them to make outward show . . . and on public occasions the display of jewelry and equipages is very splendid.

'On the 12th of this month the birthday of the King came round (29 years old) and there was a grand gala and *baciamano* at Court. On this occasion all the foreign ministers and great officers and lords and ladies of the Court put on their richest attire and made a magnificent display. The King and Queen stood upon the throne, he in a military uniform and hat and she in a splendid white garment and train covered with silver, and her head and bust covered with diamonds, and received the homage of their subjects. First the great officers of the household, followed by the train of pages in proper costume, singly in succession approached, kneeled at the foot of the throne first to the King and then to the Queen, and kissed their hands. After them the Council of State marched up in front in two lines with their President a little in advance, who made an address to the royal personages, to which the King made a very short reply, and then they advanced singly, knelt and performed the same ceremony. The City Council in the same manner. . . . After them the principal clergy from the Cardinal down, and the military officers performed in succession the *baciamano*. . . . The ladies here cannot be called handsome, but their complexion is generally good, and they have that fullness of face and bust and roundness of shoulders which presents great beauty in an assemblage seen at that distance which conceals all blemishes.'

The illuminations for the birth of the King's latest, Mr Throop described as: 'I doubt whether there is a place in the world elsewhere so susceptible of displaying to advantage a tasteful arrangement of lights as the approach to Capodimonte. The palace is situated upon a high hill of tufa and the ascent is by many detours yet it is always in view; it seems to come into position as you ascend, to all the points of the compass. As you approach the foot of the hill you pass through an avenue of trees. These were hung with little lamps of all-coloured lights, and from a small distance in front of the spectator to the remote end, the trees on both sides seemed to bear leaves of gems; nearer, the brilliants seemed fruit. At the end of the avenue, and the foot of the hill, there is a circular enclosure like the bowling green in New York, filled with trees and flowering shrubs. In the centre of the enclosure was a splendid Chinese temple, which seemed when lighted up to be built of precious stones. Farther up the hill was a high obelisk lighted in the same manner, and still higher up, on the top of a house was erected a large comet. These three erections were in a direct line, and the temple and obelisk seen through the avenue of trees appeared to be one structure, the temple forming a well-proportioned base to the obelisk, and the comet seemed to be directly over it high in the heavens. There was one design in the whole of it and it was all in good taste; and it is difficult to give any idea of the effect of it when seen together. The end of the avenue of trees which seemed to hang with brilliant fruit near you, diminished in size and clustered more in the distance . . . shed a radiance of intermingled coloured lights upon all the surrounding objects, while the huge comet radiated upon nothing but itself in the dark heavens above. There was an eastern magnificence

Ferdinand II as Duke of Calabria

in the show, which is improved by this climate, for the sky was clear and a brilliant moon was riding in the heavens.'

Throughout the long sulphur dispute Temple and Kennedy had to admit, in spite of frequent complaints about 'the arbitrary and vexatious system pursued by this Government, and arising partly from the personal character of the King', that Ferdinand was exceedingly courteous to English visitors. Thus in 1838 Captain Long of H.M.S. *Barham* and his officers were given permission to shoot in the preserves near Baia, 'a favour which is seldom granted, as these preserves are generally reserved for the royal family'. And when the Queen Dowager Adelaide of England arrived in November of the same year, 'the ceremony with which it had been intended to receive Her Majesty could hardly have been more flattering,' though she said she did not wish to be received with the honours due to her exalted rank. She landed under a royal salute from H.M.S. *Hastings* and the forts of the capital; Princess Colli received her in the name of the royal family, and the Marquis d'Avalos, master of ceremonies, and several officers of rank conducted her to the state royal carriages which were to take her to her residence, while a battalion of marines was drawn up in line by the landing place. 'Prince Pignatelli Ruffo had been most anxious that Her Majesty should stop at the palace of the Chiatamone for one night, and though aware that she preferred going to the hotel pressed his wish so much as to induce her to alight there for a moment, when, to the surprise of all, she was received by the Queen Dowager and by all the other members of the royal family who were most anxious to welcome her, and to testify their wishes to render her residence at Naples agreeable.' The King, who was in Sicily, offered her a palace in Palermo and sent a steamer from there on purpose to fetch her, but she was too exhausted with sight-seeing to accept. The Pope had sent her permission to visit the convents of Santa Chiara, San Martino and the Camaldoli; she had spent a day at Pompeii and ascended Vesuvius; and she had dined with the Queen Mother, so opulent a contrast with her plain evangelical self, and accompanied her to the royal box at San Carlo which was illuminated in her honour.

In February, 1840, when Palmerston was breathing fire and brimstone against Ferdinand in London, Kennedy reported: 'Many of the English at Naples having expressed their wish to give a ball as a token of their gratitude for the kind manner in which they had been received at the private Court balls of the King and at the Accademia balls, which were given by the Neapolitan nobility, and being doubtful whether they could expect the honour of His Sicilian Majesty's presence, the King on hearing of their intention went up to Lord de Tabley and in the most kind and gracious way assured him of the pleasure it would give him, and at once fixed a day, and the ball will take place this night at the Villa Acton. The King has, as a special mark of distinction, ordered the Court to appear in uniform.'

Apart from the official *Annali civili* and *Giornale del Commercio*, the copious literary annuals and keepsakes of this period with their sentimental sketches, gentle satires, parodies and light verse, illustrated by languid lithographs and vignettes, waft the modern reader into a placid world remote from revolutionary strife. The bourgeois tone of the Court pervaded society. Romanticism was in vogue, but it was more artificial than real, like the taste for the vaguely Oriental and Gothic which even affected crockery, cutlery and glassware. That sprightly new dance, the polka, seems to express the prevalent optimism which Luigi Settembrini described with such lofty scorn in his *Ricordanʒe*. The great majority of Neapolitans, who were not in the least concerned with a United Italy, had ample cause for optimism. Even if the middle class did not enjoy the same wealth and prestige as in England or France, they exerted a growing influence in the capital and provincial centres; all over the kingdom a growing number of small proprietors and tenants were beginning to supplant the ancient aristocracy. 'On my first excursion into Abruzzo,' wrote Keppel Craven,[1] 'I was received at Venafro in the house of a proprietor belonging to the middling class, whose territory in the environs placed him far above mediocrity, and enabled him to receive strangers with a degree of liberal hospitality which might have compensated for the overstrained display of this quality usually exhibited to guests, but which, in this instance, was exercised with such forbearance as to be principally limited to the luxuries of the table, composed of the best wine, fish, and vegetables I ever tasted: productions which indicated that Venafro had not lost, in modern days, that fertility of soil and excellence of vegetation for which it was noted in more remote times.

'The second time I visited the place, the master of the house was

[1] The Hon. Keppel Craven, *Excursions in the Abruʒʒi*. London, 1838.

138

absent the whole day, inspecting the work of his reapers; while his wife remained indoors, more busily employed in preparing the successive supplies of food and refreshment, which form a portion of their daily stipend. These consist of three substantial meals of meat, vegetable soup (or *minestra verde*), bread, and as much wine as they can consume. Each person receives, besides, two carlins (about ten-pence), which may, in this country, be considered as an equitable, if not liberal remuneration for labours, which, nevertheless, appear to an inhabitant of the north, from their nature, and the season in which they are performed, fearfully severe and oppressive.'

The old ornamental vanities fell out of fashion: a theatrical simplicity replaced the more natural baroque. Neo-classical architecture, lush parks in the English style, a self-conscious cult of the picturesque, went hand in hand with more sober pleasures. The *salons* of the aristocracy were opened to 'nature's aristocrats', who could truthfully assert that merit and ability were given their due. If an increase of population be an indication of progress, that of the kingdom of Naples had increased from 5,732,114 in 1830 to 6,177,598 in 1840 despite the ravages of cholera in 1837. A number of impartial witnesses and foreign observers noted the general improvement of living conditions, of cleanliness, culture and civility. Then as now the southern economy was mainly agricultural, though the fertility of the soil was greatly exaggerated. There was a constant menace of drought on the pastoral plateau of Puglia, and large tracts of land were marshy and malarial. Olive oil was one of the richest exports from Puglia and Calabria alternatively, as the product was biennial. Though wine abounded, scarcely any was sent abroad. A great deal of timber was exported from the forests of Calabria, and the raw silk competed with that of France and China in the distant markets of North and South America. During his travels in Calabria Edward Lear had to stay in a house which he called the Palace of Cocoons, and sleep among the silkworms. 'To the cultivation of this domestic creature all Staiti is devoted; yellow cocoons in immense heaps are piled up in every possible place, and the atmosphere may be conceived rather than described; for there is no more sickening odour than that of many thousand caterpillars confined in the closest of chambers. . . . So completely did silkworms seem the life and air, end and material, of all Staiti, that we felt more than half sure, on contemplating three or four suspicious-looking dishes, that these interesting lepidoptera formed a great part of the groundwork of our banquet—silkworms plain boiled, stewed chrysalis, and moth tarts.' Adjoining the royal palace of San Leucio, near Caserta, was a silk factory whose products were among the finest in Europe.

One of Ferdinand II's chief aims was to make his kingdom self-sufficient. He was the first Italian sovereign to take a serious interest in railways, and the line from Naples to Granatello (1839) was the first in Italy. On December 14, 1843, William Temple reported: 'A Railroad which has been undertaken under the direction of His Majesty the King of Naples and the expense of which is defrayed by the Government, has been sufficiently completed to allow trains to proceed upon it as far as Caserta. This Railroad is to be carried on to Capua in the course of the next year. . . . His Majesty proposes ultimately to continue this line . . . to the Roman frontier and it is hoped that the Papal Government will in the course of time be induced to overcome the prejudice it entertains against these modern improvements, and that ultimately a communication will be established through the Roman territory and the Tuscan States, between this country and the northern parts of Italy.

'The inauguration of the railroad took place on the 11th instant, on which occasion the Diplomatic Body, the Ministers of State and the principal persons belonging to the Court and to the Magistracy of the town of Naples were present.

'An Altar having been prepared for the occasion the ceremony of blessing the Railroad was performed, after which Their Majesties the King and Queen accompanied by the Royal Family entered the carriage destined for them, which had been made in England, and the rest of the party followed into the train and proceeded at about eleven o'clock to the station at Caserta where refreshments were served to them. . . . The Railroad is about eighteen Neapolitan, or nearly twenty English miles in length, and the journey both going and returning was performed within the hour.'

The capital was lit with gas in 1840, and the profusion of shops was another indication of increased prosperity. About two-thirds of the domestic produce were exported under the national flag. According to the British consul John Goodwin, the building of merchant ships, promoted by the abundance of materials and the cheapness of labour, and encouraged by the granting of bounties for Baltic and Indian voyages, had made great progress within the last twenty years. 'In 1824 the total capacity of the Neapolitan marine was about 8000 tons; in 1832 it had reached 99,800; and in 1837 it amounted to 150,634. In the latter year the number of vessels was 7800, the tonnage of which averaged somewhat less than twenty tons each. Naples can boast of only ten or twelve coppered ships of moderate burden. As the Abruzzi, Naples and Calabria produce timber, hemp and iron respectively, and as workmen's wages are unusually low, good strong vessels may be built and fitted out for about ten guineas a ton, or from twenty-five to thirty per cent. below the cost in the Thames. Manned with frugal Neapolitans, who are paid by the lay or shares of the freight, these vessels sail cheaper than British bottoms.'

More than ever Naples was the goal of sentimental pilgrims, who sought the pulsing picturesque rather than the rotting remains of classical antiquity. Poets and novelists in quest of inspiration found it here, or fancied they had, but they could not help repeating themselves and each other, and the fashionable rhetoric which infected their style makes most of them tedious reading. Sir Walter Scott went to Naples in search of health when his physical strength and mental powers were failing, and Sir William Gell, who had won an international reputation with such works as the *Topography of Troy* (1804), *Geography and Antiquities of Ithaca* (1807), *Itinerary of Greece* (1810) and *Itinerary of the Morea* (1817), became his guide and left a somewhat pathetic account of his visit.[1] 'It is probable,' he wrote, 'that our mutual infirmities, which made us suitable companions in excursions in the country, contributed in a great degree to the intimacy which immediately took place between us.' Though so crippled with gout that he had to be carried, Gell was an indefatigable cicerone. But the Wizard of the North had come to Italy too late: his thoughts invariably drifted home to Scotland. The Lago d'Agnano evoked a Scottish loch, and Gell found that 'his only pleasure in seeing new places arose from the poetical ideas they inspired, as applicable to other scenes with which his mind was more familiar.' He had been meditating a romance on the subject of Queen Joan of Naples who, as he observed, 'was to a certain degree in the predicament of Queen Mary of Scotland,

[1] *Reminiscences of Sir Walter Scott's Residence in Italy, 1832,* first published in Canada in 1953.

141

being held by one party as the model of female virtue, and by the other as a monster of atrocity.' Driving to the Benedictine monastery of La Trinità della Cava, the scenery again recalled his native land, so that he was inspired to recite the ballad of *Jock of Hazeldean* with great emphasis in a clear voice. It was here that the Neapolitan painter Morani made a sketch of Sir Walter which of all his portraits was considered the best likeness. During an excursion to Pozzuoli and to Cumae, Gell explained the history of the ruins they were passing. 'There is a point in going toward the Arco Felice whence at a turn of the road a very extensive and comprehensive view is obtained of the Lake of Avernus. The Temple of Apollo, the Lucrine Lake, the Monte Nuovo, Baiæ, Misenum and the sea are all seen at once, and here I considered it my duty in quality of cicerone to enforce the knowledge of the locality. I observed to Sir Walter that several of these places he would hear mentioned in society, and that I was therefore anxious that he should remember something of their respective situations. He submitted to my representations, and attended to the names I repeated to him, and when I asked whether he thought himself sure of remembering the spot, he replied that he had it perfectly in his mind. I found however that something in the place had inspired him with other recollections of his own beloved country and the Stuarts, for, on proceeding, he immediately repeated in a grave tone and with great emphasis

> '*Up the craggy mountain, and down the mossy glen,*
> *We canna gang a milking for Charlie and his men.*'

I could not help smiling at this strange commentary on my dissertation upon the Lake of Avernus, and I took the first opportunity of relating it to the gentlemen of the party, who were no less surprised than myself.'

Gell also showed Sir Walter the human sights and took him to dine with the venerable Archbishop of Taranto, then in his ninetieth year, 'but yet retaining his faculties unimpaired and the warmer feelings of youth, with well known hospitality. The two elders seemed mutually pleased with the interview, but the difficulties of language were opposed to any very agreeable conversation.'

According to Gell, Ferdinand II was another of Scott's admirers, so that he may not have been quite as impervious to literary merit as his enemies made out. 'On the occasion of a Circle at Court Sir Walter was presented to the King of Naples, who received him with marked attention and insisted on his being seated, on account of his infirmity. They both spoke, and the bystanders believed that His Majesty mentioned the pleasure he had received from reading the works of his visitor. Sir Walter answered in French, but not in a clear tone of voice, and he afterwards observed that he and "the King parted mutually pleased with the interview, considering that neither had heard or understood one word of what was uttered by the other."' An old English manuscript of the *Romance of Sir Bevis of Hampton* had attracted Sir Walter's attention in the royal library, and hearing that he wished to have it copied the King sent it to his house.

Gell published *Pompeiana*, the most popular of his books, in the same year, but his visit to Pompeii with Sir Walter was not an unqualified success: 'I did not go in the same carriage, but arriving at the Street of the Tombs, found him already almost tired, before he had advanced 100 yards. With great difficulty I forced him to accept the chair in which I was carried, supplying its place with another for myself, tied together with cords and handkerchiefs. He thus was enabled to pass through the city without more fatigue, and I was sometimes enabled to call his attention to such objects as were the most worthy of remark. To these observations, however, he seemed generally nearly insensible, viewing the whole and not the parts, with the eye not of an antiquary but a poet, and exclaiming frequently "The City of the Dead", without any other remark. An excavation had been ordered for him, but it produced nothing more than a few bells, hinges and other objects of brass which are found every day. Sir Walter seemed to view, however, the splendid mosaic representing a combat of the Greeks and Persians with more interest, and seated upon a table whence he could look upon it, he remained some time to examine it. We dined at a large table spread in the Forum, and Sir Walter seemed cheerful and pleased.' He died in September of the same year.

N. P. Willis's account of Sir Walter's visit to the Museo Borbonico seems to be based on a fuller account given by Gell to Lady Blessington: 'It happened that on the same day a large collection of students and Italian literati were assembled, in one of the rooms, to discuss some newly discovered manuscripts. It was soon known that the "Wizard of the North" was there, and a deputation was sent immediately to request him to honour them by presiding at their session. . . . He was dragging about among the relics of Pompeii, taking no interest in any thing he saw, when their request was made known to him through his physician. "No, no," said he, "I know nothing of their lingo. Tell them I am not well enough to come." He loitered on, and in about half an hour after, he turned to Dr. H. and said, "Who was that you said wanted to see me?" The Doctor explained. "I'll go," said he, "they shall see me if they wish it"; and against the advice of his friends, who feared it would be too much for his strength, he mounted the staircase, and made his appearance at the door. A burst of enthusiastic cheers welcomed him on the threshold, and forming in two lines, many of them on their knees, they seized his hands as he passed; kissed them, thanked him in their passionate language for the delight with which he had filled the world, and placed him in the chair with the most fervent expressions of gratitude for his condescension. The discussion went on; but not understanding a syllable of the language, Scott was soon wearied, and his friends, observing it, pleaded the state of his health as an apology, and he rose to take his leave. These enthusiastic children of the south crowded once more around him, and with exclamations of affection and even tears, kissed his hands once more, assisted his tottering steps, and sent after him a confused murmur of blessings as the door closed on his retiring form. It is described by the writer as the most affecting scene he had ever witnessed.'[1]

Impressions of Pompeii flowed thicker and faster. 'It is as if the inhabitants had just gone out,' wrote Mendelssohn in 1831, 'and yet almost every object tells of another religion and another life; in short, of seventeen hundred years ago; and the French and English ladies scramble about it as gaily as possible, and make their sketches. It is the old tragedy of the Past and the Present, a problem I never can solve.'

To reconstruct the past in the light of the present was what Bulwer set out to do in *The Last Days of Pompeii*, published in 1834. The first idea of the book may have come from his friend Lady Blessington. 'Glad as I was,' she had written, 'to profit by the *savoir* of Sir William Gell, whose acquaintance with Pompeii and its antiquities renders him the best cicerone in Italy, yet I could have wished to ramble alone through the City of the Dead, which appealed so forcibly to my

[1] Willis, *Pencillings by the Way*, Vol. III, pp. 97-9. London, 1835.

imagination, conjuring up its departed inhabitants, instead of listening to erudite details of their dwellings, and the uses of each article appertaining to them.' After attempting a description in prose she turned to verse:

> '*Lonely City of the Dead!*
> *Body, whence the Soul has fled,*'—

and returned to prose again to lament the vanity of all attempts at description—'save, indeed, by a master hand'. The master hand in this case was Edward Bulwer's. As soon as he reached Naples in 1833 he imbibed all the knowledge he could from Sir William Gell, listening to erudite details of custom and costume and conjuring up departed inhabitants under the guidance of that best of ciceroni, to whom he duly dedicated one of the most triumphantly successful of all historical novels. But *The Last Days of Pompeii* were not the last words on Pompeii. Before the era of tourist-agencies Bulwer-Lytton excited universal interest in the subject, which continued to tempt the amateur as well as the master hand for many a year to come.

Over seven thousand foreigners flocked to Naples in 1837. Many stayed for weeks, months and years, forming a large colony; others chose it as an annual health resort. None of them were pressed for time like the modern tourist; and they brought more money to squander on guides, coachmen, shop-keepers, artists, craftsmen, inn-keepers and their employees. The tourist industry began to swell. Hence the flood of travel books which devoted more chapters to Naples than to other Italian cities. As little remained to be said about the beauties of the bay, the life and manners of the population claimed closer attention. 'The place is inexhaustible in street amusements,' wrote Fenimore Cooper. 'The mole of Naples, and the entire strand from the Castel Nuovo, near it, to the eastern extremity of the town, offer extraordinary exhibitions. This was the region of the Lazzaroni; and finer-looking or merrier vagabonds than those who are now found in it, it is not easy to meet. The streets that they frequent, and in which they may be said to live, lie in this quarter, and are altogether unique. Brawling, laughing, cooking, flirting, eating, drinking, sleeping, together with most of the other concerns of life, are all transacted here beneath the canopy of heaven. . . .

'The veritable Lazzarone, however—the houseless fellow who

looks to Abraham's bosom as his first regular lodgings, has greatly diminished of late years, if he exists at all. Murat made soldiers of them, and otherwise gave them something to do, and they are now less averse to regular employment than formerly. I saw many at work, quite as near a state of nature as our Indians in a war dress, the paint and feathers being so much the more in favour of the latter.' After a summer at Sorrento, Fenimore Cooper concluded: 'I consider the common population of this country, by nature, one of the finest I know.'

From a critical American the tribute is refreshing. From a critical Englishman, no less than the great Macaulay, we have another tribute in January 1839. He had just arrived from India, and after four strenuous years on the Governor General's Council he was all the more able to appreciate the change. 'I must say that the accounts which I have heard of Naples are very incorrect. There is far less beggary than at Rome, and far more industry . . . as soon as you enter Naples, you notice a striking contrast. It is the difference between Sunday and Monday. Here the business of civil life is evidently the great thing, and religion is the accessory. A poet might introduce Naples as Martha, and Rome as Mary. A Catholic may think Mary's the better employment; but even a Catholic, much more a Protestant, would prefer the table of Martha. . . . At present my impressions are very favourable to Naples. It is the only place in Italy that has seemed to me to have the same sort of vitality which you find in all the great English ports and cities. Rome and Pisa are dead and gone; Florence is not dead, but sleepeth; while Naples overflows with life.'

Dickens, too, was attracted by the street-scenes: he kept a sharp eye on 'the real life of Naples', and his account of the public lottery is far more vivid than that of Pompeii. A performance in the splendid San Carlo disappointed him. 'But, for astonishing truth and spirit in seizing and embodying the real life about it, the shabby little San Carlino Theatre—the ricketty house one story high, with a staring picture outside; down among the drums, and trumpets, and the tumblers, and the lady conjuror—is without a rival anywhere.' Without understanding the dialect he could appreciate the ludicrous artistry of Pulcinella. While Dickens the observer made a rapid inventory of sights, smells and sounds, and evoked them with gusto, Dickens the moralist was forced to exclaim: 'Painting and poetizing for ever, if you will, the

146

beauties of this most beautiful and lovely spot on earth, let us, as our duty, try to associate a new picturesque with some faint recognition of man's destiny and capabilities; more hopeful, I believe, among the ice and snow of the North Pole, than in the sun and bloom of Naples.'

Henceforth evangelical denunciations of the fatal siren Parthenope were to become hackneyed. Thus Dr Arnold of Rugby wrote from Naples in July, 1840: 'Here we actually are, looking out upon what but presents images which, with a very little play of fancy, might all be shaped into a fearsome drama of Pleasure, Sin and Death. The Pleasure is everywhere—nowhere is nature more lovely, or man, as far as appears, more enjoying; the Sin is in the sty of Capreæ, in the dissoluteness of Baiæ and Pompeii—in the black treachery which, in this ill-omened country, stained the fame even of Nelson—in the unmatchable horrors of the White Jacobins of 1799—in the general absence of any recollections of piety, virtue or wisdom—for "he that is not with me is against me". And Death stands manifest in his awfulness in Vesuvius—in his loathsomeness in the abominable Campo Santo. Far be it from me, or for my friends, to sojourn long in such a place; the very contrary, as it seems to me, of the Hill Difficulty, and of the House Beautiful and of the Land of Beulah. . . .' It is a relief to know that Dr Arnold's son Matthew did not agree with these strictures, that he considered Naples 'the most brilliant and lively of places, brilliant and lively as Paris, only in a natural, popular sort of way'—but then Matthew was a poet.

Of all the accounts of Neapolitan life in the first decade of Ferdinand II's reign Carl August Mayer's *Neapel und die Neapolitaner oder Briefe aus Neapel in die Heimat* (Oldenburg, 1840) wins the prize for thoroughness. Signora Lidia Croce has chosen the quintessence of these two volumes for her delightful translation, *Vita popolare a Napoli nell'età romantica* (Bari, 1948). Dumas *père's Corricolo* is a more rollicking but less reliable series of fantasies about the same subject: his Neapolitan collaborator Pier Angelo Fiorentino contributed the grist to this whirling windmill.

Mayer confirms Fenimore Cooper's statement that the lazzaroni were rapidly diminishing and losing their original character. At first he was disappointed to find that those he had mistaken for lazzaroni were actually fishermen running round with their baskets or street pedlars of various kinds, porters or roadmenders, peasants or beggars, such as existed all over Italy then except in Lombardy and Venetia. 'Certainly they do not work as hard as a German woodcutter,' he wrote, 'but why should they? Their clothes are sufficient in such a climate; their bed—a bench or a doorstep—satisfies them; their scanty earnings not only suffice to nourish these moderate and sober men, but even provide them with amusements. . . . The lazzarone does not require a house, or firewood for cooking, because he eats fruit or buys ready cooked food in the street; he does not have to provide for the winter, because there is hardly any winter (compared with that of Germany); he scarcely needs any clothes, yet he is rebuked for not working. "I did not leave my mother's womb to wear myself out in toil. I'm not a hack, but a Christian, and I want to live," says he.'

Foreign travellers continued to be shocked and fascinated in turns by this teeming, primitive section of the population, and, as the age became more mechanical, to repeat mechanically with Dickens: 'But, lovers and hunters of the picturesque, let us not keep too studiously out of view the miserable depravity, degradation, and wretchedness with which this gay Neapolitan life is inseparably associated!' All this depravity, degradation, and wretchedness was a flea-bite to what Friedrich Engels, as thorough as his compatriot Mayer, described in *The Condition of the Working Class in England in 1844*. Perhaps the lazzaroni did not belong to the working class proper. Like King Ferdinand they loved their independence, and to a certain extent they were able to enjoy it. There is undoubtedly much truth in Mayer's account of an average lazzarone's working day: 'He wakes up on the pavement. His limbs are not stiff, as he has been accustomed to this rough bed since childhood. His first sensation is hunger. He searches his pocket: not even a farthing, and the chunk of bread he had put there the day before has vanished. By Bacchus, he says laughing, some dog must have run away with it, or that rascally peasant who laid himself down to sleep beside me last night.

'He goes to the nearest church and listens devoutly to Mass, then scurries up and down the streets, singing, whistling, chatting and joking with acquaintances, but keeping a weather eye open for foreigners. By chance he happens to meet a painter who asks him the way to a certain street. The lazzarone offers to accompany him and though the painter refuses he is so insistent that the latter cannot shake him off. "Your Excellency," says the lazzarone, "my name is Antonio and I'm a famous Neapolitan guide. May I take you to San Gennaro? It is the finest and richest church in the world, and possesses sixty saints of solid silver. Or to the Catacombs, where the bones of more than a hundred thousand Christians lie like orange peel along the mole? Or would you like to take a boat in the cool of this fine morning and be rowed towards the Villa?" The painter retorts crossly that he is in a hurry to keep an appointment, and the lazzarone can only draw his attention with florid speeches to the curiosities along the road. On arrival the lazzarone mops his dry forehead with his cap and fetches a deep sigh, as if all out of breath. The painter gives him a coin. It may be much or little, but the Neapolitan swears and declares that his service is worth more after having taken so much time, and gone so many miles, and that no foreigner had ever rewarded him so meanly.

'To get rid of him the painter hands him another couple of *grani* and goes off.[1] The lazzarone bursts into loud laughter at the expense of the stupid foreigner and leaps for joy. He has twenty *grani* to his credit, enough to last him easily for four or five days, but he wants to spend them all in a single day. First he buys an enormous slice of water-melon for two *grani* and fills his belly with it. For an extra *grano* he buys some garlic, which he chews with great relish as he wanders on his way. He stops at a tobacconist's—to-day he will act the gentleman—and buys himself a cigar for two *grani*, which he flaunts with a supercilious air before his comrades and the wenches of his set. When a regiment marches by to the strains of music, he is tempted to march behind it and watch its exercises for an hour. Meantime his cigar has dwindled to a stump no bigger than his thumb; a ragged urchin asks him for it and he bestows it with the gesture of an Englishman handing a gold coin to a pauper. On his return to the city he drinks two glasses of delicious snow-water for a *grano* from the water-seller's booth, goes to the nearest macaroni vendor and empties a bowl of his favourite food with his fingers, and then—determined to be luxurious to-day—he repairs to the fried fish man and chooses some fried fish with lemon, all of which costs him six *grani*.

'Abundantly sated, he lies down on a big stone bench in front of the royal palace and takes his siesta for a couple of hours. Upon rising he steers for the mole, singing lustily the song of Teresella who had to be a nun. In Castle Square he stops to play *mora* (guessing fingers)

[1] 1 *grano* = $\frac{1}{2}d.$

149

with two porters and wins two *grani*, one of which he drops into a mendicant lay-brother's bag as a contribution to the poor souls in Purgatory. On the mole some foreigners call to him, but he pays no heed; he has no more desire for work, because he still has nine *grani* in his pocket. He looks at the new ships in the port and the boats on the sea, gazes pensively at the grey cloud over the crater of Vesuvius, listens for an hour to Pulcinella, a Capuchin preacher, and a declaimer of Ariosto, and admires the art of a conjurer. Thus another couple of hours go by, and he still has nine *grani* in hand. He eats two strawberry ices, enters a church to say a long prayer to his patron saint, and then with five or six jolly fellows he drives in a one-horse gig along the Strada Nuova (now Via Posillipo). The carriages of dukes and princes roll before him; the most beautiful landscape in the world surrounds him. It is evening. Returning from his drive he loiters on the royal palace square, where a band plays overtures and marches for an hour, and he hums the tunes as he listens. He has two *grani* left. He spends the first at the marionette theatre, to see Metastasio's Dido or the duel between Charles XII and Peter the Great; the other pays for two more glasses of iced water. Now his pocket is empty and his daily task is done. He stands on the steps of a church, says a prayer to the Madonna, and falls into a deep delicious slumber. This is a crude sort of happiness, but how many of the poor in Germany have anything like it?' Those who could afford and appreciate such simple pleasures were surely better off than most of their descendants.

Mendelssohn only spent a couple of months in Naples, but his impressions are complementary to Mayer's. Though he completed his 'Walpurgis Night' there, he complained that he felt languid and lazy and out of humour, incapable of collecting his thoughts and ideas. As an incessant scirocco was blowing, he blamed the climate. 'As I lounged about the streets all day with a gloomy face, and would have preferred lying on the ground, without the trouble of thinking, or wishing, or doing anything, it suddenly occurred to me, that the principal classes in Naples live precisely in the same manner; that consequently the source of my depression did not spring from myself, as I had feared, but from the whole combination of air, climate, etc. The atmosphere is suitable for grandees who rise late, never require to go out on foot, never think (for this is heating), sleep away a couple of hours on a sofa in the afternoon, then eat ices, and drive to the theatre at night, where again they find no subject for thought, but simply make and receive visits. On the other hand, the climate is equally suitable for a fellow in a shirt, with naked legs and arms, who also has no occasion to exert himself—begging for a few *grani* when he has literally nothing left to live on—taking his afternoon's siesta stretched on the ground, or on the quay, or on the stone pavement (the pedestrians step over him, or shove him aside if he lies right in the middle). He fetches his *frutti di mare* himself out of the sea, sleeps wherever he may chance to find himself at night; in short, he employs every moment in doing exactly what he likes best, just as a brute does.

'These are the two principal classes of Naples. By far the largest portion of the population of the Toledo there, consists of gaily-dressed ladies and gentlemen, or husbands and wives driving together in handsome equipages, or of those olive *sans-culottes* who sometimes carry about fish for sale, crying in the most stentorian way, or bearing burdens when they have no longer any money left. I believe there are few indeed who have any settled occupation, or follow up any pursuit with zeal and perseverence, or who like work for work's sake. . . .

'Thence it is that there is so little industry or competition, and that Donizetti finishes an opera in ten days; to be sure, it may be hissed, but that does not matter, for it is paid for all the same, and he can then go about amusing himself. If at last however his reputation should become endangered, he would in that case be forced to work in real earnest which he would find by no means agreeable. Therefore he sometimes spends as much as three weeks on an opera, bestowing considerable pains on a couple of airs in it, so that they may please the public, and then he can afford once more to divert himself, and once more to write trash.'

Mendelssohn had a low opinion of music in Italy, but he was writing in 1831, four years before the first performance of Donizetti's *Lucia di Lammermoor*, which had a fabulous success at the San Carlo for twenty-two nights running. Great changes took place within the next decade, the first of Ferdinand II's reign. In his survey of the progress of the Two Sicilies under the Bourbons until 1840, the cautious British consul John Goodwin concluded that 'the condition of the people is materially improved, and that the improvement bids fair to proceed, if it be accompanied by an amendment in the executive power, according to which its progress will be faster or slower'.

VIII

IT soon became clear that France had won the first round in the struggle with Austria for influence in southern Italy. The Duc de Montebello eclipsed all his diplomatic and undiplomatic rivals in Naples. Even socially, he entertained with a difference. In a diary of events ranging from the serious to the comic during the year 1841 De Sterlich described a party he gave at the Acton palace where he resided. 'Four thousand glass lanterns of many colours scattered among the trees illuminated the garden; eighty lamps of bronze whose flames were protected by globes of opaque crystal and a thousand candles glittered in the many luxurious halls, dazzling the eyes of five hundred guests. When the King and Queen appeared, followed by all the princes and princesses of the royal family, a charming Bengal blaze lit the path for them which led from the garden entrance to the festive hall. This unexpected vision was accompanied by a burst of melody which seemed magical, not knowing whence it came: an orchestra hidden among the trees was playing the Bourbon anthem. The Duke and his pretty consort went instantly to meet the royal party, who opened the ball by dancing in the first quadrille. . . . As representative of the nation where personal merit is above aristocracy the Duc de Montebello had invited illustrious Neapolitans of all classes: among these were the encyclopedic Pasquale Borrelli, the botanist Antonio Tenore, the astronomer Ernesto Capocci, the painter Camillo Guerra, and others of equal renown, besides the Barons Poerio and Galluppi, the former famous at the bar, the latter as a philosopher, though both were entitled to be present only by right of birth. The King was pleased to meet so many learned men and deigned to converse at length with several of them. The splendour of this *fête* was all the more original insofar as it was not dominated by luxury and gallantry, as usual, but rather by science and intellect. The ball ended at seven o'clock on Sunday morning. The King and Queen withdrew towards four o'clock and the other royal princes at five-thirty. The host offered coffee and chocolate to the hundred guests who remained when day was bright.'

French comedies such as *La maîtresse du logis* and *Le cabinet de Lustucru* became popular at private theatricals. Louis-Philippe's name-day was celebrated with conspicuous pomp on May 1. When his third son, the Prince de Joinville, arrived with a French squadron in July 1843, Ferdinand sailed from Castellammare to meet him and Temple remarked that the senior officers of the squadron and the French chargé d'affaires were also invited to the royal banquet given in his honour: 'I mention this circumstance as it is, I believe, the first occasion upon which any member of the Diplomatic Body has been invited to dine with their Majesties, or indeed any persons but those of royal birth and the persons waiting upon them, the etiquette of that Court being much the same as that formerly followed in the Courts of France and Spain. . . . The present King, however, appears more disposed to dispense with etiquette than his predecessors, and the near relationship of the Prince de Joinville and the favour apparently enjoyed here at present by the French may have induced His Majesty on this occasion to adhere less rigidly to it by inviting the French chargé d'affaires and naval officers to his table. . . .'

Most disturbing to Metternich's peace of mind was Ferdinand's change of attitude towards the Spanish question. After the defection of General Maroto, Don Carlos had been compelled to cross the frontier into France in June 1840. Thus ended the first Carlist war, which had dragged on for seven years. As the pretender's chance of succession seemed hopeless, Ferdinand tried to induce him to renounce his claim in favour of his son, the Count of Montemolin, whose marriage to the Infanta Isabella, if it could be arranged, would solve the legitimist problem. But his candidature was vetoed by the Spanish government and other projects had been mooted in Paris, London and Madrid.

Louis-Philippe was proud of his physical resemblance to Louis XIV, and he endeavoured to emulate that monarch by placing one of his grandsons, if not one of his sons, on the throne of Spain. In exchange for his political support the Queen Mother Cristina was willing to marry both her daughters to his sons, the Duc d'Aumale and the Duc de Montpensier. This would never suit the English government, anxious to preserve the balance of power. According to the Treaty of Utrecht signed in 1713, the Crowns of France and Spain were never to be united. But as Guizot told Greville, great changes had taken place since that time. 'It was true France had acquired Algeria, and through it a certain power in the Mediterranean; but that we had acquired Gibraltar, Malta, and Corfu, which we had not been possessed of before, and which were quite sufficient to secure our power there.' The candidate favoured by England was Prince Leopold of Saxe-Coburg, a cousin of Queen Victoria and Prince Albert, and from Louis-Philippe's point of view a Coburg marriage involved an equal threat to the balance of power. 'There was already a Coburg in England, another in Portugal, and to have had a third at Madrid would have been to make Spain a part of Portugal and to have exhibited to all the world the triumph of English over French influence.' Both proposals were withdrawn; then Louis-Philippe suggested that while an eligible candidate was being sought for Isabella, Montpensier might marry her sister, the Infanta Maria Luisa Fernanda. Palmerston objected to this on the score that Montpensier would become King Consort of Spain if Isabella died without issue.

It occurred to Louis-Philippe that one of Ferdinand's II's brothers, the Count of Aquila or the Count of Trapani, might engage the young Queen's heart. This would not hinder Montpensier's marriage to her sister. The Duc de Montebello was instructed to start negotiations with Ferdinand. But in July 1843, Aquila accompanied his sister Teresa to Brazil where she married the Emperor, and he returned there in the following February to marry the Emperor's sister Princess Januaria. Trapani, the next choice, was being educated at the Jesuit college in Rome as he was destined for the Church. Latour-Maubourg, the French ambassador to the Holy See, described him as 'very ugly, small, of sickly appearance, without expression of intelligence; and when I remember in what conditions of health I saw Queen Isabella during my stay in Spain (she suffered from an acute form of eczema), I cannot help thinking that, at least from the physical point of view, they could choose better.' But the human aspects of the case were scarcely considered. Trapani was only three years older than Isabella, who was declared to be of age in November 1843, when she was thirteen. In addition, as Mr E. J. Parry observed, 'he would enjoy the doubtful advantage of being both cousin and uncle to his intended bride, as the son of the Queen Dowager of Naples, a sister of Ferdinand VII, father of Isabella, and as the brother of Queen Cristina, the mother of Isabella.[1]

Apparently his picture appealed to the juvenile Queen. Trapani was at first refractory, but he became amenable to priestly persuasion. Owing to his strong legitimist scruples Ferdinand himself was less enthusiastic than might have been expected. He said he would only recognize Isabella II officially after her marriage to his brother, but Louis-Philippe and Guizot put so much pressure on his ambassador Serracapriola that he was induced to yield on this important point. While delicate negotiations were in progress with the Tuileries, Antonini, his ambassador in Vienna, reported that Metternich roundly disapproved of such a match and would regard any Neapolitan prince-consort as an usurper. This was enough to encourage Ferdinand. He ordered Versace to write a memorandum on his reasons for recognizing Isabella and accepting her hand for one of his brothers. He blamed the Northern Powers for the failure of her engagement to the son of Don Carlos: they were more concerned with their selfish interests than with the defence of legitimism. The document ran as follows: 'The King profits by the declaration of Isabella's majority to recognize her as Queen of Spain. He wishes to be the first of Conservative Sovereigns to take this step, not only to give an example of noble independence, which will sooner or later be followed by the other Powers, but also because he is convinced that it is better to change policy, when it has failed to serve the cause which was to have been defended, than to have no policy at all, as the Conservative Cabinets have clearly demonstrated in the Spanish question.'

[1] E. Jones Parry, *The Spanish Marriages 1841—1846*. London, 1936.

Metternich was so upset that he reluctantly asked Lebzeltern to resign his embassy in December 1843. Queen Victoria and Prince Albert had already visited King Louis-Philippe at the Château d'Eu and come to a friendly agreement. The British government should not promote the candidature of the Prince of Saxe-Coburg, and no son of Louis-Philippe should marry Isabella, but Montpensier should be free to marry her sister as soon as the Queen was married and had issue.

Guizot urged Ferdinand to send a special envoy to Madrid to pave the way for Isabella's engagement to Trapani. Prince Carini was sent in November 1843, and this odd choice reflected the King's ambiguous attitude. Besides protesting against Ferdinand VII's Pragmatic Sanction, Carini had been a secret Carlist agent and still sympathized with the cause. Though nobody had confided in Temple, he was able to report Carini's departure on November 7 on board the *Nettuno*, a government steamer, the captain of which had sealed orders not to be opened until he had left the bay of Naples. In spite of all this secrecy, Temple had got wind of the plan. Carini was not to present his credentials to the Queen of Spain until she had chosen Trapani as her consort and the choice had been approved by her government. But the French ambassador Bresson insisted that the success of his mission depended on a preliminary recognition of the Queen, and he bullied Carini into presenting his credentials before he was authorized to do so. Weeks and months went by without any sign of an agreement. Carini's mission was to last for many years.

Other candidates for Isabella's hand were mentioned: the Austrian and Prussian governments supported the Count of Montemolin, the Spanish liberal party the Duke of Seville. Whom did the Queen Mother Cristina support? Over ten years' experience at the Spanish Court had converted her into an accomplished intriguer. As Mr E. J. Parry wrote, 'she would exploit every device for obtaining whatever marriage was most politically advantageous for her daughter, and at the same time most satisfactory to her own private interests'. And who could blame her? She was competing with foreign statesmen even more shrewd and slippery than herself.

One belated result of Carini's mission was that a Spanish minister was appointed to Naples, and the Duke de Rivas took up this post in March 1844. To neutralize the effect of this Prince Felix Schwarzenberg, the new Austrian ambassador, arrived in April, when relations with his government were at their lowest ebb. Metternich's instructions to him contained a character sketch of Ferdinand II for his guidance. The King had a keen intelligence and remarkable perspicacity, he explained, combined with irreproachable conduct and a lofty idea of his position, which should have enabled him to remedy the evils caused by previous revolutions. But while he had a laudable intention to reorganize the internal administration of the country, he attached a value to the word independence which it could not possess in a practical policy: independent as a person, he had no ministers; independent as a sovereign, he had no allies, and was consequently without counsellors at home and friends abroad. . . . He only trusted himself and feared, above all, to give an impression of yielding to any sort of influence. This was due to his strange notion of foreign politics. He imagined that the geographical position of his kingdom rendered relations with the rest of Europe almost superfluous. Schwarzenberg should avoid seeming to lecture him while conveying wholesome advice.

Still vexed with Austria, the King gave Lebzeltern's successor a lukewarm reception, but Schwarzenberg tactfully marked time 'until the wind should change'. He was genial, distinguished and self-confident, having gained much experience as minister at Turin. After the bustling officiousness of his predecessor his calm prudence was a relief. Gradually Ferdinand began to thaw towards him, whereas he was growing suspicious of the French ambassador. Surrounded by Carlists and legitimists, his former scruples were roused. Having been hustled into recognizing Isabella as Queen of Spain, he was annoyed by the procrastination of his brother's engagement. Guizot heard with dismay that the Count de Montbel, one of Charles X's ministers, had arrived in Naples to negotiate a marriage between the Duc de Bordeaux and Princess Carolina, one of Ferdinand's sisters. Temple reported in May 1844: 'The French Government, as might be supposed, exerted all their influence to prevent this marriage taking place, more especially after the endeavours made by the Duc de Bordeaux during his visit to England to organize a party in favour of his pretensions and adverse to the present French Dynasty. It is believed that to counteract this marriage more effectually a proposal was made by the French Government for a marriage between the Duc d'Aumale and the Princess Caroline, and also a marriage between the Duc de Montpensier and the daughter of the Prince of Salerno, and the visit of the Count of Syracuse

to Paris is believed to be connected with these intended alliances.'
Guizot also threatened to withdraw his support of Trapani's marriage.
The Duc d'Aumale married the Prince of Salerno's daughter in
December. As he had been Louis-Philippe's candidate for the hand of
Isabella of Spain, this also served as a guarantee for the Château d'Eu
agreement. The Count de Montbel's mission was therefore nipped in
the bud.

Conspirators had lain low since their abortive insurrection at Aquila
in 1841, when the local commandant Colonel Tanfani and a gendarme
had been murdered by an armed mob. The chief engineer of this rising,
the wealthy Marchese Luigi Dragonetti, had plotted with several
officers of the local garrison to make a pronunciamento at the Piedigrotta festival, but after Tanfani's murder the rebels were crushed.
Dragonetti escaped with some three hundred fellow-conspirators. The
riots kindled by Mazzini in the Romagna in 1843 had no repercussions
in Naples, in spite of the infiltration of skilled agitators.

A vaster conspiracy spread throughout Italy in 1844. In Calabria
Mazzini's followers endeavoured to organize guerrillas on a grand
scale and revolutionize the Two Sicilies. They succeeded in mustering
between fifty and a hundred armed men who marched into Cosenza
on March 15 shouting for Italy and a Constitution and hoisting a tricoloured flag. Five were killed and more were wounded in a skirmish
with the police; the rest took to flight. In the trial of those who were
caught twenty-one were sentenced to death on July 10, but all except
six were reprieved.

A few hours after the Cosenza rising Carlo Poerio and Mariano
d'Ayala were arrested with other prominent liberals. Although the
police could find no incriminating documents they were certainly on
the right track.

D'Ayala had been educated at the Nunziatella military college where
he became an instructor in geometry and the science of projectiles
after publishing a book in praise of the Neapolitan republicans of
1799—another proof of the King's tolerance. The book had appeared
before Colletta's history, which was widely read *sub rosa*, a strong
diatribe against the royal dynasty. On returning the latter to d'Ayala,
General Begani wrote in 1835: 'The style and many of its maxims have
enchanted me, and I should have enjoyed it more had I not been
poisoned by the well-founded suspicion that he has told many lies. . . .

It is not to speak ill of the dead but to honour the truth: I have concluded that he has invented in writing as he used to invent in conversation. He was born to produce delectable novels, but not histories.' The comment is valuable from a contemporary who knew the author well.

Thanks to d'Ayala's tuition the Nunziatella was soon crammed with budding rebels such as Carlo Pisacane, Enrico Cosenz and Giuseppe Virgili. Colonel Nocerino, the commandant in charge, complained to the King that d'Ayala was perverting the minds of his pupils, and the King told Filangieri to get rid of him. But Filangieri, who had been his sponsor, threatened to resign if d'Ayala was dismissed, and Colonel Nocerino was sent away for slandering him instead. Eventually the subversive instructor got into trouble for publishing a panegyric of Murat and a condemnation of his treatment by the people of Pizzo in a literary journal called *Iride*. The King came across it by chance. One of the princesses had been shocked by the sensuality of another contribution entitled 'Version from the Greek', signed by Basilio Puoti who also taught at the Nunziatella, and had shown it to Ferdinand, who was even more outraged by d'Ayala's article in the same number. He protested to Filangieri that he could not allow two teachers at the military college to offend his moral and political sense in such a brazen manner. Puoti was merely admonished, but d'Ayala was treated more severely. 'You see, Colonel Nocerino was right when he warned us four years ago, and we dismissed him on account of this snake. To-day I shall recall Nocerino and dismiss d'Ayala.' In defence of his protégé Filangieri pleaded that he had only recorded a historical event known to everybody. Though he had to leave the college he was given a post at the Mongiana arsenal in Calabria. Hoping the King's anger would die down, Filangieri urged d'Ayala to apply for an audience, but he retorted that he had done nothing for which he need beg the King's pardon and resigned from the army after twenty-four years of service: he was only thirty-three. He continued to write the lives of famous Neapolitan soldiers and hob-nob with the liberal set. It is obvious from his biography that he had been plotting when he was arrested.

Del Carretto gave orders that the political prisoners were to be treated with the greatest leniency. The rigid martinet was becoming an advocate of compromise, in order, as he said, 'to avoid a state of chronic unrest'. Seeing their chief so amiably disposed the police relaxed their vigilance. Sant' Elmo became, as d'Ayala wrote, the headquarters of the liberal party. General Roberti, the governor, sent them special dishes and often invited them to dine with him, and d'Ayala could work at his lives without interruption, visited almost every day by his wife and child and his best friend Alessandro Poerio.

Though the Cosenza rising had failed to stir public sympathy and had been easily repressed, the attempt was renewed by three idealists whose names were to become symbols of youthful heroism. The two Bandiera brothers, Attilio and Emilio, were both naval officers and sons of a Venetian admiral in Austrian service. Under the spell of Mazzini's writings they deserted their Austrian frigate and induced Domenico Moro, a fellow officer, to join them. Their first plan was to seize a ship, sail to Messina and launch a revolution there, but the news leaked out and they had to take refuge in Corfu. Exaggerated reports of the Cosenza rising encouraged them to rush to the aid of the rebels. They embarked, altogether a band of nineteen patriots, on the night of June 12. On the 16th they landed near Cotrone to start the liberation of Italy. Kissing the soil they exclaimed: 'You gave us life and we shall devote it to you!' Their fervour found no echo; no Calabrians came to join them. For three days they wandered through woods and hid behind rocks in the direction of Cosenza, where they intended to set all the political prisoners free. Betrayed by a Corsican companion, they were soon surrounded by hostile peasants and urban guards. During a ten minutes' struggle one of them was killed and the others were captured. The prison gates which they had ventured from afar to open closed upon them. Attilio Bandiera wrote a spirited letter to King Ferdinand expounding his ideals and promising to devote body and soul to him if he would become the constitutional sovereign of United Italy. The King, who was then in Sicily, felt inclined to pardon the knight-errants. Unfortunately the Marchese di Pietracatella, acting as Minister of Police in Del Carretto's absence, urged that since six Neapolitans had been executed in the Cosenza rising, the King should deal even more severely with foreigners. To liquidate them, he argued, would stop the revolutionary contagion; to pardon them would be an act of culpable weakness. Nine of the prisoners, including the Bandiera brothers, were sentenced to death by a court martial on July 23: next day they were shot, crying 'Long live Italy!' as they fell.

The King was blamed universally for not pardoning them, but from his point of view they were merely mischievous aliens trying to bring civil war into a peaceful country.

Guizot regarded the Bandiera expedition as an episode in the struggle with Austria for influence at Naples, but he felt sure that France would win. Having recognized the constitutional régime in Spain Ferdinand might go further when his brother had married the Queen. But the King's secretary Caprioli remarked: 'At last Austria has succeeded in her double game of setting the King at odds with the liberals, by using him to extirpate the Bandiera brothers.'

Owing to Schwarzenberg's unusual tact Austria had begun to recover lost ground at Naples. The insurrections of 1844 and the growing ascendancy of Pietracatella, the anti-French president of the council, helped to strengthen Austrian influence. To flaunt his independence and counteract adverse propaganda Ferdinand allowed the next scientific congress to be held at Naples in 1845. Science was a superficial pretext for these meetings, the first of which had opened at Pisa in 1839 under the auspices of Ferdinand's brother-in-law, the well-meaning Leopold II of Tuscany. Pope Gregory XVI and the Duke of Modena would have nothing to do with them but Ferdinand sympathised with their professed aim, 'the advancement of natural science', and Santangelo, his cultured Minister of the Interior, persuaded him that a congress in Naples would show that he was not so retrograde as he had been painted by the liberals.

The seventh of these congresses was welcomed by the King with princely hospitality on September 20 and Santangelo was duly appointed its president. Each member was offered a handsome illustrated guide to Naples in two stout volumes published for the occasion, and they were lavishly entertained during the next two weeks. Carriages were provided for them to visit the famous beauty spots; special arrangements were made for those who wished to climb Vesuvius; a splendid ball was given by Santangelo and another more splendid in the royal palace. Political exiles were allowed free entry and exit while the congress lasted. But all this hospitality was ill repaid by the guests who, as elsewhere, converted their meetings into arenas for political agitation. While in Naples they flattered the King—Orioli compared him to 'thundering Jupiter transformed into peaceful Jupiter'—but as soon as they left they reverted to their virulent campaign of calumny. The Neapolitans dubbed those *scienziati* (scientists) *scoscienziati* (men without conscience). The King shrugged his shoulders and became even more suspicious of the intelligentsia.

The Austrian ambassador could afford to bide his time: his adversaries were doing his work for him. Everything combined to propel Ferdinand into the absolutist camp. In October 1845, Czar Nicholas I arrived at Palermo with his wife and daughter, the Grand Duchess Olga, hoping that the milder climate would benefit the Czarina's health. Nicholas I was the extremest of living autocrats: he regarded himself as the only bulwark against revolution in continental Europe. Like Stalin, he dominated the lives and thoughts of his subjects. The Marquis de Custine's description of this tall, handsome despot who was so certain of being divinely inspired is convincing: 'He always expects to be looked at and does not forget for an instant that he is being looked at; you would even say that he wishes to be the cynosure of all eyes.' The Prussian-born Czarina already appeared to be dying in 1839: 'her eyes, sunken, blue, and gentle, betrayed profound suffering borne with angelic calm'. The Sicilians, ultra-sensitive to tyranny at home, gave the imperial visitors a rapturous reception, and poets of local renown greeted the persecutor of Poland with panegyrical odes. Even eagles have to relax. At Palermo the Czar won popularity by posing as a private gentleman of leisure, affable with all and so munificent that he made the King look mean. His cold severity thawed in the Sicilian sunshine, and under the gleam of the Byzantine mosaics of Monreale, where Christ's coronation of the Norman King William I is a graphic image of divine right in a style reminiscent of Russian churches. The imperial party chose to stay at the Villa Butera rather than in one of the royal palaces placed at their disposal. Military reviews and manœuvres were held in their honour, and the King did his best to amuse them in other effective ways.

Montebello wrote to Guizot that Ferdinand was irritated by the Czar's patronizing airs, but on one subject they were bound to agree. 'I can understand the republic,' the Czar had told Custine, 'it is an open and sincere government, or at least it could be; I can understand the absolute monarchy, since I am the head of such a government; but I cannot comprehend the representative monarchy—it is a government of lies, of fraud and corruption, and I would withdraw as far as China rather than ever adopt it'. Ferdinand had an instinctive horror of representative monarchy which the Czar intensified. Nicholas told him bluntly that he was considered a mere satellite of Louis-Philippe. While he could see the necessity of friendly relations with France, this did not justify his curious distrust of Austria, which had no desire to meddle in his affairs and was only concerned with the peace of the peninsula. Besides, his autonomy was guaranteed by treaties with Russia and other Powers. Ferdinand made no specific accusation against Austria, but he complained bitterly of the ex-ambassador Lebzeltern. All this was reported to Metternich by Schwarzenberg after a long conversation with the Czar. 'I am very satisfied,' said the Czar, 'with all I have heard from the King. His principles are as excellent as his intentions, and I think he does not lack energy.' Schwarzenberg said he doubted whether the Czar's good influence on him would last, but the Czar was optimistic. 'Your position here may not be easy,' he said, 'but I can assure you that the King, who could not abide your predecessor, is very pleased with you. I can only advise you to follow your present line of conduct. I cannot believe that a king who is so familiar with his own interests will be led astray.' Ferdinand took the Czar's advice to heart. Next year the Czar sent him a solid and symbolic souvenir of his visit in the form of two groups of prancing bronze horses restrained by muscular Muscovite grooms. These were modelled with creditable artistry by the Russian sculptor Baron Clodt and cast in St Petersburg. Ferdinand had them set up before the entrance to the small 'English garden' beside the San Carlo Theatre.

The Queen and Monsignor Cocle were also responsible for the King's friendlier attitude towards Austria, which resulted in the commercial treaty of 1846 and a mutual agreement for the extradition of criminals. Commercial treaties with England, France, Russia and America had been signed in 1845, but Lebzeltern's efforts to arrange one had invariably failed. The delay over the Spanish marriage filled Ferdinand with distrust of Louis-Philippe and his minister Guizot, though it has since been proved that they were sincere in their wish to promote it.

'A league of Bourbon States linked up by a series of royal marriage alliances': it looked impressive on paper. But it was the design of a doctrinaire. Guizot had cleared several high hurdles yet others continued to crop up. He confessed his bewilderment. 'I do not quite understand,' he wrote, 'it is a real Spanish comedy of sudden surprises, intersecting intrigues, reticences and enigmas.' The Spanish

Court contained such a variety of oddities, unlike that of Louis-Philippe and his virtuous consort. Maria Cristina was alternately swayed by maternal ambition and by her passion for the Duke of Rianzares. Her elder sister Carlotta hoped to marry one of her own sons to the girl-Queen. Neither of these had a savoury reputation. Though the girl-Queen had a precocious yearning for marriage, her retarded puberty had become a national obsession. Some were impatient and others relieved, depending on which candidates they favoured. General Narvaez, a vigorous soldier of fortune, was virtual dictator. He had revised the Constitution of 1837, and one of its new clauses authorized the Queen to marry without the assent of the Cortes. But even the tough Narvaez was eventually overridden by the temperamental Queen Mother. The atmosphere of Madrid was viscous with jealousy and suspicion, and the rival British and French ambassadors, Sir Henry Bulwer and the Comte de Bresson, vied with the Spaniards in arrogance and subtle intrigue.

Prince Carini, the Neapolitan ambassador, found himself at a disadvantage from every point of view. As Ferdinand had not given him an adequate salary he had to live modestly at his own expense: at a Court which revelled in ostentation he could not compete with his grand colleagues. The opponents of Trapani's marriage depicted him as the worthy representative of a penurious fortune-hunter. Carini's one doubtful advantage was that he had a winsome young wife whom Narvaez was anxious to seduce. Narvaez pretended to favour the Neapolitan match while his flirtation was in progress. But the Count of Trapani disliked the idea of it as much as his Spanish opponents.

On June 4, 1845, Temple reported: 'The negotiations for the marriage of H.R.H. the Count of Trapani with the Queen of Spain are not likely, for the present at least, to be brought to a successful termination. H.R.H. has, I have been informed, expressed his disinclination to the marriage in so decided a manner that the King of Naples, at a meeting of the royal family at which the Duc de Montebello was present, declared that he could not force his brother to marry against his will, and that for the present at least the marriage must be delayed.

'The repugnance of H.R.H. to the marriage arises, I understand, from the feeling that his youth and inexperience would make him unequal to meet the difficulties of the position in which he would be placed as Consort of the Queen of Spain.

'I have been told that the King of Naples a short time ago received a letter from H.R.H. the Count of Syracuse who is now in Paris, repeating a conversation with the King of the French who had expressed to H.R.H. his regret at finding that the King of Naples did not show the same desire to forward the wishes of the French Government as the latter had always shown towards His Majesty, which he feared might be attributed to the influence of Austria; upon which His Majesty observed that he did not desire to be under the influence either of Austria or France, and that both were equally disagreeable to him.'

Trapani's brother the Count of Aquila, as well as his confessor, and other pro-Austrians, encouraged him to resist. As Montebello wrote to Guizot: 'they have persuaded him that the King (Louis-Philippe) wanted to trick him; that the Queen of Spain could never bear children; and that the King wished to marry the Duke of Montpensier to the Infanta and then thrust him aside'. But Montebello was very determined, and he persevered until he had overcome Ferdinand's scruples. A family council was held on June 17: subjected to a battery of argument from Ferdinand, the Queen Dowager, and the French ambassador, the reluctant Prince burst into tears and consented to marry his niece.

Louis-Philippe began to crow somewhat prematurely. It was Spain's turn to make the next move: Trapani could not ask for the Queen's hand: she had to offer it. Maria Cristina suggested waiting till October when Isabella would turn fifteen. Narvaez, after positive assurances to Carini, began to temporize. There were copious excuses: the Queen was still under-developed whereas her younger sister had already reached puberty. In spite of a violent campaign against Trapani's candidature Maria Cristina invited Ferdinand to address formal overtures for Isabella's hand in November, and these were sent under French cover to Madrid. Narvaez was to announce the Queen's intention to marry Trapani, and dissolve the council before the opposition had time to raise objections. But the secret leaked out. The Paris correspondent of a Spanish newspaper revealed that the Neapolitan ambassador had been authorized to demand the Queen's hand for Trapani while the Cortes had been ignored. This caused a national crisis. Narvaez tried to hedge, but forty deputies signed a petition against this marriage, 'fatal to the country, to its institutions, and to the consolidation of the monarchy'. The press became obstreperous. Trapani was trepanned with insults. At one moment Narvaez thought of imposing the marriage by force and making himself dictator, but Louis-Philippe put his foot down as this would ruin his son's prospects. Narvaez was dismissed in February 1846, and recalled in March, when his successor the Marquis of Miraflores refused to support Trapani's candidature. Carini's hopes revived, but Narvaez was dismissed again in April, which dealt a final blow to Trapani's engagement.

Ferdinand was left in the lurch by his sister and Louis-Philippe. Montebello continued to pretend that the Trapani match was feasible when Isabella's engagement to the Duke of Cadiz and her sister's to Montpensier had already been settled in Paris. Bresson broke the news to the ever-hopeful Carini on August 28, 1846, by order of the Queen Mother 'who did not wish to suffer the displeasure of communicating it directly'. Carini described it as a bombshell. 'This solution,' he wrote, 'has convinced me forcibly that France has behaved with the same bad faith and lack of consideration as England. . . . I foresee that I am destined to be the victim of every side. I am ruined in reputation, in finances, and in health; my conscience tells me that I have not deserved so sad a fate; but I am resigned to everything save losing the regard of the King, and the sympathy of my friends and protectors.'

Palmerston's succession to Aberdeen had hastened this solution, which benefited nobody, least of all Louis-Philippe. Ferdinand had more personal reason to be mortified than Queen Victoria. The whole of Europe seemed to be mocking him. His resentment was none the less deep for being controlled. On January 21, 1847, Temple reported: 'I understand from Prince Scilla that this Government had no previous intimation which could lead them to anticipate the sudden arrangement for the marriages of the Queen and Infanta of Spain, and that the communication of them by the French Ambassador being quite unexpected, caused as much surprise at this as at the other Courts of Europe.

'The difficulties which opposed the marriage of the Count of Trapani with the Queen of Spain were of course known to this Court, but it was thought possible that they might be overcome in the course of time, and hopes were still entertained, particularly by the Queen Dowager, that the union might ultimately be effected. . . . I understand that the King did not express his dissatisfaction to the Duc de

Montebello on the communication of the Spanish marriages to him but he received it coldly. The Duc de Montebello left Naples on the 5th instant for Paris on leave of absence.'

Ferdinand blamed his sister Maria Cristina rather than Louis-Philippe, and when she returned to Naples he avoided her conspicuously. The whole incident was turned to Austria's advantage by Schwarzenberg, who told Metternich that it had produced 'a painful but salutary impression on the King'. 'The *Journal des Débats*,' he wrote, 'which had enjoyed the privilege of directing political opinion in Naples, now irritates it: the hymns of triumph to celebrate the successes of Louis-Philippe, seem especially contrived to wound everybody who is not wholly unconscious of the European position of Naples and its sovereign, and shows what we Austrians should not do.'

Ferdinand became morbidly suspicious of foreigners. Not only foreigners: how a gentle Jesuit could also fall under his suspicion has been related by Father Curci of that Order.[1] Father Manera, the provincial in Naples, had presented the King with an image of Saint Ignatius on the eve of July 30, the vigil of that saint's day, for whom as a soldier he professed a special devotion, conferring on him the rank of Field Marshal and regularly handing over his pay to the Society of Jesus. Grateful for his gift, Ferdinand himself lighted two candles before it. The Queen and his children were summoned, and all knelt down and recited a few prayers with Father Manera, who took leave of them with the kindest expressions of benevolence after some edifying conversation.

Within a short time Father Manera received a note informing him that His Majesty wished to see him at twelve o'clock next day, to discuss a very serious matter concerning the Society. The curt tone of this message—such a contrast with the King's previous affability—perplexed the good priest and kept him awake at night wondering what had happened. 'Punctual at the palace, he was introduced into a private room and Ferdinand soon appeared, but *quantum mutatus ab illo!* He seemed sulky and almost threatening. He cut his greetings short with a blunt: "Good morning, Father Provincial", made him sit beside him and asked: "Tell me, is there a Father Alfonso Maria Vinzi among the Jesuits at Naples?"—"Yes, Your Majesty."—"Did he preach the last Lenten sermons in the cathedral of Bari and spend his

[1] *Memorie del Padre Curci*. Florence, 1891.

167

evenings in conversation with that Archbishop?"—"Yes, Your
Majesty, he did preach in the cathedral. As he was staying with the
Archbishop it is quite probable that he conversed with him in the
evenings."—"We've got it!" said the King, squeezing Manera's arm
with so much vigour that he still felt the bruise in describing it to me.
After a short silence, as if to control his temper, he continued in a
quiet voice: "Listen, Father, I call upon God to witness that when I
ordered a little tournament at Caserta during the last Carnival, my
sole intention was to give a respectable entertainment to my family
and the good population who are fond of me, as well as to provide
my officers and men with some useful exercise. Now this Father
Vinzi of the Society of Jesus has dared to say in public conversation
with the Archbishop that I had ordered the tournament to pay court
to Countess Gaetani, who is my mistress!"—While uttering the
last words with rising excitement he gave Manera's arm a more
powerful squeeze. After a pause, during which Manera could find
nothing to say, he continued more calmly: "As a Christian I pardon,
but as a King I cannot permit so base a calumny to pass. If I loved the
Society less I should put this into the hands of the director of police
and the public prosecutor of the Grand Criminal Court, but because
I love the Society I put it into the hands of the Reverend Father Provincial, who will certainly do his duty." Having said this, without
waiting for an answer he rose abruptly and said: "Keep well, Father
Manera!"—(*Stia bene!*) and left him in a daze.

'On his return from the audience Father Manera soon sent for me
and confided all this to me with due reserve. . . . After some discussion
he said he thought Father Vinzi should leave Naples as soon as
possible to prevent the King from changing his mind, either owing to
resentment or to the malicious suggestions of others, adding that he
could explain to the King quite truthfully that he had submitted so
serious a case to the judgement of the Father General. However, I
thought that apart from this we should first find out from Father Vinzi
whether there was any truth in this accusation. . . . When summoned
he admitted that he had seen the Archbishop in the first evenings of
Lent, not in general company but alone, as he was indisposed. The
Monsignor having asked him, as is usual with newcomers, what was
being said and done in the capital, Father Vinzi replied that there had
been much talk about a tournament which the King had ordered for the

Queen Maria Cristina, first wife of Ferdinand II

Carnival at Caserta and that malicious gossips had said he had done it to flatter the Countess Gaetani, adding definitely that nobody believed this as the Christian behaviour of the King was known to all.

'Obviously the case had changed aspect and the whole thing was reduced to an innocuous word about which the malicious had built a castle. This should be explained to the King when the heat of his first impression had cooled off, but there was still a chance that under that first impression, from one moment to the next, he might take a sudden step, unpleasant for us and perhaps not creditable to himself. So Father Vinzi left for Rome. . . .

'After a few days the Provincial applied for an audience through the King's private secretary and obtained it immediately. Received with the King's usual benevolence, he eloquently craved pardon for the annoyance caused him by a member of the Society, on whose behalf he asked it, adding that Vinzi, as a good priest, had accepted without demur the punishment imposed on him by the General in Rome. "So he went to Rome?" asked Ferdinand with some embarrassment. "Yes, Your Majesty. It seemed to me that the gravity of the case demanded the intervention of the supreme chief of the Order, though I must conscientiously assure you that the case was very different from that reported to Your Majesty." At the King's request he repeated the true story and when he mentioned the King's Christian behaviour known to all, Ferdinand bowed and said thoughtfully: "It is all divine grace, not personal merit." And he continued: "In this case Father Vinzi should be recalled from Rome immediately. I am sorry to have caused him this undeserved trouble." "Forgive me, Your Majesty, this is beyond my faculty, having submitted his case to the supreme chief of the Society. Besides it was silly of him to repeat ill-natured gossip without sufficient reason."—"No, no, I shall write to my ambassador at Rome to ask the Father General on my behalf to send him back quickly."—"Pray allow me then to act as Your Majesty's envoy, and to inform the Father General of this generous indulgence. When Father Vinzi returns, let me have the honour of presenting him." —"Yes, yes, I'll be glad to see him." And talking of other topics, the King took leave of Manera with his usual courtesy.

'In due course the presentation took place. Father Vinzi said a few words of modest excuse which were benevolently accepted by the King, who deplored the distortion of other people's affairs and sayings at Court but finally added with deep earnestness: "From this incident we all have something to learn. You, reverend Fathers, may learn to be more careful in conversation; I shall learn to be less ready to believe what I am told."

'There was King Bomba, the tyrant, the new Tiberius!'

The swelling ambitions of the House of Savoy were becoming an active menace, and the death of Pope Gregory XVI on June 1, 1846, deprived him of his moral mentor. 'We were prepared for everything but a Liberal Pope,' said Metternich after the election of Pius IX, 'and now that we have one, who can tell what may happen?' The new Pope's amnesty of July 17, barely a month after his election, released over a thousand political prisoners and enabled hundreds of exiles to return. This meant that Rome was flooded with Mazzini's agents and other revolutionaries. The amnesty was interpreted as a tacit disapproval of the late Pope's policy. Gregory's Swiss Guard was dismissed; the civil and penal codes were revised; and the press was given so much freedom that nearly a hundred newspapers, many of them blatantly subversive, were allowed to flourish. After these reforms a State Council (*Consulta di Stato*) to which laymen were eligible, was appointed to advise the Pope and his ministers on questions of administration and finance. Rome was granted a municipal government with one hundred members only four of whom were clerics. Finally the Council of Ministers was reorganized so that all its members might be laymen except the Secretary of State. This spate of reforms strengthened the liberals all over Italy. A fiercer spirit of antagonism to Austria was aroused. After seventeen years of vacillation Charles Albert, nicknamed King Wobbler (*Re Tentenna*), became its leading spokesman.

Ferdinand took immediate precautions, as against an epidemic. He sent more troops to guard the frontier; he ordered the strictest vigilance to prevent the diffusion of Roman newspapers; and he tried to restrict the entrance of foreigners. But he saw Richard Cobden when he came to Naples in 1847, and the great champion of free trade wrote on March 6: 'At 11 o'clock to the palace to see the King by appointment; conversed for a short time with him upon Free Trade, about which he did not appear to be altogether ignorant or without some favourable sympathies. He questioned me about the future solution of the Irish difficulty, a question which seems to be uppermost in the minds of all statesmen and public men on the Continent. The King is a stout and tall man, heavy looking, and of restricted capacity. I am told he is amiable and correct in his domestic life, excessively devout and entirely in the hands of his confessor, of whom report does not speak favourably.' He preferred the Count of Syracuse whom he found, 'for a king's brother, a very clear-headed, well-informed man'.

Cobden's Neapolitan cicerone was Mariano d'Ayala, who showed him over the royal arsenal. 'In a few years' time this will be museum stuff,' said Cobden with a smile, but d'Ayala could not share his optimism. On leaving Naples he wrote to d'Ayala from Rome, April 12, 1847: 'I cannot resist the pleasure of telling you how much I have been gratified with the intelligence and activity of mind which I have met with in those Italians with whom I have been brought in contact. I only regret the more that you have not a freer and larger field for the exercise of those powers with which God has endowed the inhabitants of this peninsula. But I do not despair that better times are in store for you. It is difficult to be patient when there is so much to be done, and man's life is so short. Yet there is no other road for moral reforms but that which conducts us by slow stages of education. You will say that your government prevents education, and therefore there is no hope. But I do not believe in the power of any government to prevent the growth of intelligence, so long as the nations of the earth remain at peace, and the people are allowed to see, to hear and to talk. By talking I do not mean public speeches, but daily and hourly conversation. I wish I could persuade you to have my faith in the irresistible tendency of man to ascend in the scale of intelligence in spite of the repressive forces of arbitrary government. I should be glad to inspire you with better hopes, and make you more happy in your views of the future. You must not despair, for that is a state of mind which disqualifies us for all exertion even in the common private affairs of life; and after all, our chief happiness and main duty lie in the discharge of the every-day claims upon us as private citizens. Keep up your spirits then for the sake of your amiable wife and dear little one, to whom my wife begs to join me in kind remembrance.' The language of this letter may be Victorian but the tone is quite modern. D'Ayala and his associates had less faith in slow stages of education than in armed force. They believed in the *fait accompli*. Enthusiasm for the reforming Pontiff had already swept the kingdom, and the Roman amnesty was also placarded on the walls of Naples. Ferdinand saw no reason why another sovereign's decree should be circulated in his capital, and had it removed. Devout Catholic though he was, he shared Metternich's belief that any concession to liberalism would start an avalanche of revolution. The Pope's innovations seemed too sudden and far too drastic: he felt sure that the Holy Father had been led astray. But a clandestine liberal committee had been organized in the capital which corresponded with similar committees in Rome and Palermo and spread their propaganda. The Pope's amnesty was printed on handkerchiefs; his portrait on medals and silk scarves was so widely distributed that Ferdinand took umbrage.

One of the chief causes of distress throughout Europe which led to the upheavals of 1848 was the general grain shortage due to a succession of bad harvests. Ferdinand banned the export of cereals and travelled through the provinces to see that the hungry were fed, and to prevent hoarding and speculation. He lowered prices and had grain sold at a loss. 'His Majesty's object,' wrote Lord Napier, 'is to depress the market by artificial means for the contentment of the common orders, whose loyalty moves on a sliding scale in inverse ratio with the price of macaroni.'

The Hon. William Temple had decided to go home for a holiday, leaving behind him as chargé d'affaires the secretary of legation Lord Napier, who was only twenty-eight and looked even younger. Temple was much critized for playing truant at a moment of impending crisis. As Charles MacFarlane wrote: 'During the many years that Mr Temple had been envoy extraordinary at Naples, he certainly had had no extraordinary or hard work to complain of; he had led one of the easiest and pleasantest of diplomatic lives in the most beautiful country of Europe. Except in discussing that wearisome question about sulphur and brimstone, which after all was not settled by him, but by his brother Lord Palmerston, he had done very little, and had had but little to do. The first fresh hour after breakfast must have been more than enough for his usual daily work; and he had secretaries and attachés to help him, and a consul and vice-consul under him to attend to commercial business. He bore the character of an easy, self-indulging, somewhat indolent man, but amiable, accessible, prudent, and dispassionate. He was of mature age: an advantage in his favour, for youthful diplomatists do not generally inspire confidence or impose

respect. The King of Naples had at one time entertained a strong prejudice against him, believing that he had co-operated with Lady S——
in inveigling his brother, the Prince of Capua, into his *mésalliance* with Miss Penelope Smyth; but this had been cleared up, to the perfect exculpation of Mr Temple. . . .'

He was to remain absent for more than a year, postponing his return because his Neapolitan residence had to undergo repairs, and the smell of fresh paint and plaster was offensive to him. In the meantime the livelier quality of young Lord Napier's despatches afforded some compensation for Temple's departure. And he has left a precious little volume called *Notes on Modern Painting at Naples* as a record of his stay, which shows that he was a dilettante above the average. Though modest in appearance it was a pioneer work on the subject, the first to appreciate the School of Posillipo at a time when, as he wrote, 'the appropriate pastimes of that pleasant city were discarded for the illusions and regrets of political change. . . . The resources of society were limited by the suspicions and passions which altered and envenomed the conversation even of cultivated men; and the author was induced, alike by necessity and taste, to expend his relaxation and recover his serenity in the study of the local Arts'. The style is suavely florid, the humour urbane. For instance: 'A plate of sweetmeats by Recco, was honoured by the miscarriage of a lady, imprudently permitted to behold its unsubstantial temptations; and the same success ensued upon the exhibition of one of his baskets of fish.' His æsthetic excursions puzzled the police, 'who conceived that they were tracking a conspirator when they were only chasing a virtuoso'. Bored by the limitations of conservative society, young Napier sought the company of artists and littérateurs, and most artists are born rebels. His house became a social centre for the enemies of the sovereign to whom he was accredited, and from these he gathered most of his information. On June 27, 1847, he wrote: 'The journeys which H.M. has lately made in all directions with a celerity and mystery intended to baffle and surprise the provincial authorities, who are to remain till his arrival ignorant of his approach, have, no doubt, been prompted by an honourable desire to ascertain the condition of his dominions, unvarnished by the preparation for a Royal Progress, and to promote the public welfare by the direct interposition of the Royal Power. Yet there are many who assert that the stagnation of business at the capital consequent on the prolonged absence of the head of State is a serious evil, not counterbalanced by the King's exertions in the provinces which must unavoidably too often evaporate in blame without punishment, and excellent projects never realized.

'The King has distributed great sums in alleviation of the late distress, he has liberated an immense number of prisoners for petty offences, partly perhaps on account of the expense of maintaining them in gaol. . . . H.M. has also restored to liberty at least three persons long confined for political offences.' On July 7 he continued: 'During the absence of H.M. and the consequent disorder and stagnation of public business the secret press has been more than usually active in disseminating tracts and satires levelled against the alleged incapacity and corruption of the Ministers and the Royal Confessor (Monsignor Cocle) to whose secret and powerful inspirations the unpopular acts of H.M. are vulgarly ascribed.'

One of the disadvantages of a patriarchal State was that personal patronage played a preponderant rôle. Santangelo was euphemistically described by Lord Napier as 'a person of an accommodating character, not averse to use his influence in facilitating transactions for the convenience of those who invoke his assistance privately'. Ferdinando Ferri, the Minister of Finance, had once been the lover of Luisa Sanfelice, but that had been long forgotten: the republican of 1799 had become a loyal supporter of the dynasty. In 1847 Temple described him as 'old and infirm, (he) has been excused from attending the Councils and gives out that he is very anxious to retire from office, but the King will not accept his resignation. Upon this plea he does nothing. He gets hold, however, of all the money he can lay his hands upon for the Government, but takes special care to avoid refunding money or satisfying claims.'

The King had few illusions about his ministers, but for one reason or another they seemed adequate. Their deficiencies were human: he did not expect perfection. Loyalty to the throne came first in his estimation, and he considered all politicians more or less dishonest. Compared with those in other countries, with the Protestant Guizot in France who had bamboozled him over his brother's marriage, with the piratical Narvaez in Spain, with the bullying Palmerston in England, his own ministers were innocuous. Mediocrity had its merits. Compared with the other Italian States, his own was peaceful and orderly.

He held the reins, and his popularity had been tested on many occasions. But he was increasingly nervous about events in the rest of Italy. In Lombardy, Venetia, Tuscany and Piedmont, as well as in the States of the Church, the Pope's reforms had excited Italians of all classes to challenge Austrian domination. When the Austrians reinforced their garrison in Ferrara on the anniversary of the Pope's amnesty (July 1847)—an act which angered Pius IX and had deplorable repercussions—Castelcicala warned the King that Palmerston had threatened to send a British fleet to Sicily if the Austro-French should intervene on the peninsula.

It was while Ferdinand was touring Sicily and the provinces that Luigi Settembrini's anonymous *Protest of the People of the Two Sicilies* was published. The effect of this passionate diatribe was out of all proportion to the number of copies printed, one thousand one hundred, of which seven hundred were burnt in sudden panic. It contained enough truth to make the whole sound convincing, but it was obviously and intentionally a work of propaganda, and therefore not free from exaggeration. How it impressed foreign diplomats may be seen from their reports. Lord Napier wrote on July 25: 'The *Protest of the People* passed, it is said, to Sicily under the cloak of a friar and was presented to H.M. the King in the guise of a petition. It was tossed into Prince Scilla's carriage in the Toledo, and has reached the hands of all the Ministers and Magistrates at times and by devices worthy of a nation for which no business is sufficiently serious to exclude a stroke of wit. The authors and locality of the secret Press have remained undiscovered, notwithstanding a keen enquiry set on foot by the Minister of Police. . . . On the truth or merit of these compositions it would be difficult and unbecoming for me to pronounce a favourable judgement, but unquestionably no art and no veracity could better fulfil their object than they do, for the animus is strong, the aim clear, and the audience already convinced. They proceed, in general, by adducing a store of old acknowledged evils and abuses, and ransacking the past history and private life of every public man for matter of reproach, offering thus, by accumulation of assertion rather than by method of argument, a frightful picture of the dangers contingent on the duration of the present system of government. If on the one hand it be evident that no falsehood is too gross for the popular palate, it is yet confessed by impartial men, too experienced to mix in new troubles, that it would be difficult to invent an act of turpitude or of tyranny which has not been committed by one or other of the Ministers now or lately in high power, while their subordinates here and in the provinces make a practice of sordid venality and vexatious oppression.

'One of the pamphlets in question betrays such a nice acquaintance with the machinery of government, the animosities of the Council and the habits of the King as to cause a singular degree of surprise and amusement, and a persuasion that the Revolutionary Party have an accomplice within or near the precincts of the Court. The Council itself is bewildered by the double difficulty of the brigands and the books. . . .

'I hazard nothing in assuring your Lordship that the Government of Naples occupies an ignominious if not a perilous position, that the King, however estimable in his private character, has not a personal friend or faithful adviser.'

Monsignor Garibaldi, the Papal nuncio, wrote in similar vein about this *Protest* to Cardinal Ferretti, the Roman Secretary of State. 'The libel,' he wrote on August 4, 'has distressed those who are attached to the King because it attempts to make his character utterly odious, and responsible for all the evils of the public administration which are exposed and deplored, attributing to him greater faults than he has and concealing his merits. But it must be said that the substance of the abuses against which it inveighs happens to be true; I mean the lack of order and legality in the administration, of zeal and probity in public employees from top to bottom. . . . The facts were already familiar, and respectable people were hoping for their reform long before it was circulated. Hence there are several distinguished and honoured persons devoted to the King who are not unduly upset by the libel's appearance, as they think it may draw his attention to existing evils and prompt him to remedy them. . . .'

Settembrini has described the genesis of his sensational squib in his more famous *Memories* (*Ricordanze*). He tells us that he was inspired by d'Azeglio's *Casi di Romagna*: 'I wished to paint a general picture, as it were, of all the miseries our people had suffered for twenty-seven years, and offer it as a protest to the whole civilized world. . . . The first copies were brought to Palermo by Giuseppe del Re who went to the festival of Saint Rosalia and distributed them among his friends; the others were distributed in Naples.

' "Have you read the *Protest*?" a gentleman asked me.

' "No I haven't. What does it say?"

'And he repeated the whole thing to me, and the passages that had made the deepest impression on him, the judgements on men, even sentences and words.

' "Might I read it too?"

' "That seems difficult. I had it for six hours with the obligation to return it punctually."

' "Is it known who wrote it?"

' "Who can tell? It must have been someone with inside information about the royal family, as he has revealed many secrets."

'The gentleman, who had relations at Court and in the Government and was a person of consequence, had clean forgotten that he had told me many of those secrets himself. I had only gathered and jotted down all I had heard from him and from other trustworthy folk.

'Furthermore he told me that the King had read it, and that the passage which had given him most offence was that about the royal audiences, where he answered nothing but "All right, all right, in a raucous voice." And he asked someone near him: "Have I a raucous voice?"

'The book flew from hand to hand: it was read by small groups of friends, and everybody discussed it.'

It is still more spoken of than read, but the chapters about the King and his government were the source of all subsequent libels, and at least have the merit of being entertaining. The thesis is stated in the introduction: 'This government is an immense pyramid with priests and police-agents at the bottom and the King at the top: every employee, from the usher to the minister, from the common soldier to the general, from the gendarme to the chief of police, from the priest to the King's confessor, every petty scribe is a merciless mad despot over those beneath him, and the most abject of slaves towards his superiors. Whoever does not happen to be one of the oppressors feels crushed on every side by the tyranny of a thousand knaves; and peace, liberty, the lives and substance of honest men depend on the whim, not merely of the prince or of a minister but of every wretched clerk, strumpet, spy, police-agent, Jesuit, and priest.' There was no hope for the future, because the King got worse as he grew older, and his children, brought up by priests, would be even more pernicious. Armed revolt was the only solution. As head of the government, Ferdinand II was the cause of every evil. 'This prince is stupid, presumptuous, avaricious, superstitious, a typical Bourbon, foolishly cruel and arrogant. Unfit for anything, he wishes to do everything and revels in it; he scorns advice, is incapable of making a friend, and is even despised by the very few he benefits,' etc.

Ferdinand was shaken by the virulence of this attack. Not even his mother was spared. The presumed author or authors had fled. The printers, who were under arrest, attributed it to a certain Don Luigi whom they failed to identify. Ferdinand's decree of August 13, 1847, was generally interpreted as a retort. After describing the financial administration during the seventeen years of his reign, the payment of the heavy national debt and the reduction of taxes, he had abolished the duty on grinding corn (which brought in 625,946 ducats a year) and reduced a third of the salt tax and the duty on Sicilian wines. By diminishing taxes, which were trifling by modern standards, he hoped to keep down the cost of living, which was lower than elsewhere. But that was not what the liberals wanted. As Lord Napier wrote on August 17: 'This decree is marked by a singular peculiarity which gives it more than common significance at the present moment. It is prefaced by an apologetic enumeration of the different fiscal improvements embraced since the accession of the reigning sovereign, and accordingly passes for an answer by authority to the charges advanced by certain nameless authors. . . . Such a step on the part of a Power which is not in the habit of appealing to reason has caused much surprise and satisfaction, being regarded as a confession of weakness and an offer of conciliation; but it may be doubted whether the Neapolitan Government have acted wisely in entering the field of controversy . . . with all the disadvantages of decorum and publicity against the reckless and invisible champions of reform.'

According to Settembrini, Monsignor Cocle had persuaded Ferdinand that Pius IX was a Jacobin, so that when the King sent his children to bed he asked them to pray for the Pope, who did not know what he was doing. Undoubtedly he regarded the Pope as a holy man led astray by faction. Wherever there was a disturbance 'Pio Nono' was shouted as a slogan. Since the Cosenza rising of 1844 the liberals had been quiescent, but there had been an intensification of revolutionary propaganda, especially through the clandestine press.

178

Revolt was in the air: on September 2 Schwarzenberg wrote that something was bound to explode soon. Almost simultaneously, insurrections broke out at Reggio and Messina. Edward Lear, then travelling on foot with his sketch-book through Calabria, has described the gradual crescendo of nervousness created by his appearance, which puzzled him until he reached Reggio:

'At the hour of one in the night we reached Reggio, and here the secret divulged itself at once.

'How strange was that scene! All the quiet town was brilliantly lighted up, and every house illuminated; no women or children were visible, but troops of men, by twenties and thirties, all armed, and preceded by bands of music and banners inscribed, "Viva Pio IX", or "Viva la Costituzione", were parading the high street from end to end.

' "Cosa x'è stata, Ciccio?" said I.

' "O non vedete," said the unhappy muleteer, with a suppressed groan. "O non vedete? è una rivoluzione! Dighi, doghi, dà!"

'No one took the least notice of us as we passed along, and we soon arrived at Giordano's Hotel. The doors were barred, nor could I readily gain admittance; at length the waiter appeared, but he was uproariously drunk.

' "Is Signor P—— arrived by the boat from Messina?" said I.

' "O che barca! O che Messina! O che bella rivoluzione! Ai, ao! Orra birra burra—ba!" was the reply.

' "Fetch the keys of my room," said I; "I want to get at my roba"——

' "O che chiavi! O che camera! O che roba! ai, ai!"

' "But where are the keys?" I repeated.

' "Non ci sono più chiavi," screamed the excited cameriere; "non ci sono più passaporti, non ci sono più Ré—più legge—più giudici—più niente—non x'è altro che l'amore la libertà—l'amicizia, e la costituzione—eccovi le chiavi—ai! o-o-o-o-o-orra birri bà!!" (There are no more keys—there are no more passports, no more kings, no more laws, no more judges, no more nothing! Nothing but love and liberty, friendship and the constitution!)

'Without disputing the existence of love, liberty, friendship or the constitution, it was easy to see that matters were all out of order, so, taking Ciccio with me, I went hastily through the strangely-altered streets to Cavaliere da Nava's house. From him, whom with his family I found in serious distress, I heard that a concerted plot had broken out on the preceding day; that all the Government officials had been seized, and the Government suspended, he (da Nava), the Intendente, and others being all confined to their houses. That the telegraph and the castle still held out, but would be attacked in a day or two; that the insurgents, consisting mostly of young men from the neighbouring towns and villages, had already marched into Reggio, and were hourly increasing in number; that on the opposite shore, Messina was also in full revolt; and that the future arrangements of the Government could only be known after time had been allowed for telegraphic communication between Reggio and Naples. The Government impiegati are all naturally dejected, as nothing of their future fate is known, except so much as may be divined from the fact that no one has hitherto been maltreated. . . .

'All that long night the movement increased: large bodies from Santo Stefano, and other places—most of them apparently young mountaineers—thronged into Reggio, and paraded the streets, singing or shouting "Viva Pio Nono", with banners, guns, swords, and musical instruments.

'September 3.—No boat stirs from Messina. I watch on the beach in vain. I sit with Da Nava and his perplexed family. The telegraph works away incessantly; but there is no attempt to stop it, and no attack on the castle. If there is no movement in the northern provinces, troops will certainly march hither, and, in any case, steamers will come, and this wretched town will assuredly be bombarded into annihilation or repentance. On the other hand, Messina will as surely undergo the same fate, and the more probably, inasmuch as it is of more importance. Nevertheless, as P—— is detained there, and I cannot ascertain what extent of fighting therein prevails (owing to no boats having put off from the Messinese shore), it appears to me better to go over to him if possible.

'So, by hard work, I persuade some very reluctant boatmen to take me: and I quit the Da Nava family with regret, for a cloud of uncertainty seems to hang over all Southern Italy, and the foreshading gloom of it has earliest reached this remotest place.

'After intolerable waiting for five hours with a boat-load of depressed and anxious natives, we were towed by oxen as far as Villa San Giovanni, and thence (the sea was rough and the wind contrary) came over to a point about a mile from Messina, where we landed out of reach of the guns of the fort. Here I was glad at Nobile's Hotel to rejoin P——, whose suspense had been equal to mine. The revolt at Messina has occasioned the death of fourteen or fifteen men; but the Government has firm hold of the citadel. Distress and anxiety, stagnation and terror, have taken the place of activity, prosperity, security, and peace. . . .

'September 4.—Two war-steamers are at Reggio, and firing is heard, though the details of action are of course unknown to us. The poor town is undergoing evil I fear, nor will it be wonderful that it does so; for that 400 or 500 men should seize and hope to hold permanently a distant part of a large kingdom, unless assisted by a general rising, appears to be the extreme of folly, and can only, whatever the cause of complaint, meet with ultimate ill-success and probably with severe chastisement.'

The candid impressions of nice Mr Lear serve as a corrective to the blurred accounts of biased historians. The drunken waiter had echoed the parrot-cries of the irresponsible minority, who were trying to force modern middle-class 'French ideas' on a semi-mediæval agricultural community. The minority cared nothing for peace and prosperity under Ferdinand's rule. What they wanted was political power for themselves. The majority were as unhappy about the insurrection as the groaning muleteer.

The King had been swindled by Bonucci, a customs official, who had been ordered to sell government corn cheap to the victims of bad harvests in Calabria. Bonucci and his accomplice Domenico Romeo used the proceeds of this sale to organize an extensive revolt. None of the revolutionary committees were prepared, and that of Palermo decided to petition the King before resorting to violence. 'We shall have to manage it without Sicily and the aristocrats,' said Romeo in disgust. 'Against the Bourbons we need weapons, not words.' Before his malversation was discovered he returned to his native Santo Stefano, mustered a band of supporters, and marched to Reggio. Here they forced the whole garrison to surrender, hoisted the tricoloured flag, and set up a provisional government which proclaimed the Constitution of 1820: 'Reggio to the Provinces of Naples and Sicily.—Faithful to our promises, we have already raised the three colours of national Italian independence with loud cheers for the Constitutional King

Ferdinand II and liberty. The Constitution of 1820 so happily obtained, so spontaneously sworn, and violated since, was attacked and destroyed by foreign bayonets. How many have tried to revive its memory during the last twenty-six years? Brothers, to arms! The progress of civil and political liberty can be seen in several Italian States, and above all in the religious and evangelical State of the Vicar of Jesus Christ, where the glorious Pius IX confirms us in our sacred desire to be free. . . . Strong in numbers, union, will, and faithful to previous agreements, we shall hasten to the capital of the kingdom, where we are eagerly expected. . . .'

Some fifty Sicilians had also attempted a rising at Messina on September 1, and Gerace had followed suit, but the rebels were soon dispersed and chastised. These incidents were enormously inflated by Mazzinian propaganda abroad. The King, who seemed to have crushed a revolution, received fervent congratulations from Austria, Russia, and even from France. But this was only the prelude.

IX

FROM Ferdinand's point of view his administration was adequate. In spite of such unforeseen calamities as earthquakes, volcanic eruptions, epidemics, and bad harvests, the country was more prosperous and the population was rapidly increasing. Most of the Pope's reforms were provided for in the Neapolitan code. As the official press declared, the Neapolitan government acted 'according to its own lights, took its own counsel, and pursued its even course without fear or envy of other luminaries.' The King was indifferent to the theories of Gioberti, Balbo, and Mazzini. The only independence he could appreciate was that of his kingdom, and he thought he had achieved it. With his alert mind, practical sense and prodigious memory, Ferdinand had a high opinion of himself. He failed to understand his political foes, but he had the strength of his limitations and he was determined not to yield to pressure. That pressure was swelling and menacing him from every direction.

Lord Palmerston was stirring up hornets again. He had sent Lord Minto—'one of those geese of whom his friends continue to make swans,' as Greville wrote—on a roving commission to encourage the Pope and other Italian princes to promote substantial reforms, or teach politics to the country where Machiavelli was born, as Disraeli said. Though Minto was far from revolutionary, he roused ardent hopes among all the radicals. Apparently he was unable to distinguish between blatant demagogues like the Roman Ciceruacchio and respectable liberals of the English type. Though he could not grasp half of what was said to him at the numerous meetings he attended on his Grand Tour, he caught their general drift to such an extent that he shouted in Italian: '*Viva l'Indipendenza Italiana!*' While he was in Florence the streets were hung with placards inscribed 'Death to the King of Naples!' At Leghorn there were demonstrations against the Neapolitan consulate and the Bourbon coat of arms was destroyed: it was said that a large sum of money had been raised to assassinate Ferdinand as a result of slanderous articles published in *L'Alba*. Undoubtedly Minto was affected by this combustible atmosphere. He assured the Sicilian exiles that unless reforms were granted to their island within two months a revolution there was inevitable and England would support it.

All this was disconcerting to Ferdinand II, who regarded Minto as a dangerous firebrand. He had cause to be nervous of British aims in Sicily. Many of the islanders gazed towards England with nostalgic memories of the 1812 Constitution and their prosperity during the English occupation. While a Constitution was the first goal of liberals on the mainland, the Sicilians wanted a separate administration as well. If the island were to revolt now under the ægis of Great Britain, the mainland might easily follow her example.

Carlo Poerio, d'Ayala and their fraternity were again rounded up after the revolts at Reggio and Messina. Again their prison became the headquarters of the liberal party—for three hectic months. That they were fully in favour of armed insurrection has been admitted in Michelangelo d'Ayala's memoirs of his father. On this occasion an official called on Mariano d'Ayala's wife to enquire on Del Carretto's behalf if the police had been polite and if she had any complaints. He said the Minister wished to speak to her and would see her to-morrow at his house. 'She found the terror of Naples meek as a lamb, almost humble and penitent. He apologized for the precaution he had had to take in spite of himself, wished to know if the police had been as courteous as he had commanded, and expressed great esteem for the prisoner's virtue and intellect. "But what will you," he added, "the King no longer trusts me. I never stop assuring him that there are no conspiracies here. He does not believe me, and it was he that insisted on these arrests. I am truly very sorry, and I beg you to say so to Don Mariano. I have already given instructions that he is to have books, paper, everything he requires; and you may see him whenever you please, in the warder's house." ' The prisoners were not only allowed to receive numerous visitors who brought them all the newspapers not normally in circulation, such as *L'Alba*, *La Patria*, *Il Mondo Illustrato*, and *Il Contemporaneo*, which they read aloud 'with virginal enthusiasm', while Saverio Altamura drew their portraits; they discussed the latest news, the state of public opinion, the changes in the government barometer, and made plans for the future.

On October 29 Schwarzenberg informed Metternich that if there was a revolt in Sicily, which England was likely to aid and abet, Ferdinand was determined to defend his rights there, but that he counted on Austrian help in an emergency, as he was entitled to under a secret clause of the 1815 treaty. The ambassador proposed that 8–10,000 Austrian troops be sent to the Neapolitan shore of the Adriatic, whose mere presence would produce 'a moral effect so powerful as to save the threatened authority of the Sovereign and reduce all the revolutionaries in the Two Sicilies to impotence.' Should the King appeal to Austria in vain, he might grant the concessions demanded.

Metternich was cautious and non-committal. He had prophesied that the Pope would destroy his own temporal power, that the veil concealing reality would soon be lifted. 'The veil is liberalism;' he wrote, 'it will disappear in Italy, as in every other country, before radicalism in action.' He advised Ferdinand 'to remove the causes of discontent which were latent even in the sound and enlightened part of the population'. Perhaps a change of ministers would suffice. But the King was hard to convince while Monsignor Cocle stood at his elbow.

On October 31 there was a plot to murder Ferdinand on his way to Portici and start a revolution with the slogan 'Blood for Blood', but the police got wind of it. Ferdinand stayed at home that day and seven of the conspirators were arrested. Possibly this reinforced Schwarzenberg's arguments. On November 12 he reported that Corsi, the King's secretary, had asked his private opinion of the cabinet. His candid reply was that he thought it contained the King's worst enemies. 'When the Cavaliere (Corsi) asked if I might repeat this to his master, I answered that I authorized him once for all to repeat to the King every word I had uttered.'

The Austrian ambassador had at last won Ferdinand's confidence, and this must have tipped the balance. On November 11 the aged Minister of Finance Ferri was replaced by the liberally inclined Giustino Fortunato; on the 16th the detested Santangelo was allowed to resign and his department was divided between Parisi for the Interior, Spinelli for Agriculture, Commerce, Public Health, Education and the Fine Arts; and d'Urso for Public Works and Penal Establishments. There was general jubilation over the removal of Santangelo. Lord Napier wrote (November 21): 'The King thus discharged from his Councils a man who for many years has exhibited in his conduct the hateful combination of capacity for good and preference for evil, who has united elevated tastes with sordid propensities, and who being at once learned and depraved would grasp a bribe to buy a picture and filled his museum with the misery of his suitors. Under this Mæcenas of Thieves the contamination eat into all the ramifications of his department, and years of austerity on the part of his successor will scarcely suffice to restore the vitiated tone of official morals. . . .

'What the ultimate intentions of the King really may be is not easy to determine. My own impression is that His Majesty has been made aware by the explosion of discontent in Sicily and Calabria, by the diminution of commerce, revenue, and the alienation of the country in general from his Government, that it had become indispensable to introduce into the Cabinet a new expansion and some men of intelligence and vigour. His Majesty desires to facilitate and rectify the march of the present system; he does not meditate any important innovation, any change of policy. In what he has done, and means to do, he will deny that he is influenced by the example of his contemporaries, or the menaces of his people, but he is, perhaps, not the less in reality the victim of internal pressure. While he dreams of bestowing, he is in fact compelled to yield, and thus at first unconsciously, and subsequently against his will, he will shape his course in conformity with the wishes of his subjects and in harmony with the rest of the Italian States.'

As a postscript to the news that Santangelo had been made a marquis, Lord Napier added with ironic humour: 'I have been since assured that it formed no part of the King's first intention to confer any token of favour on His Excellency. His Majesty is said to have been prompted to this injudicious step by the suggestion of Monsignor Cocle the Confessor, who has received as the price of such good service from Mr Santangelo a rare tabernacle of vermeil, used for preserving in private chapels the consecrated wafer and the sacred vessels. This tabernacle was given by the Queen of the French to Monsignor Corbi, her Confessor at Naples, and after his death was purchased by Mr Santangelo, who by a pleasant inversion of his former habits, has been at last compelled to give, and in parting with his acquisition has doubtless been made to feel the pain he so often has inflicted.'

Later—too late—Lord Napier repented of his attacks on Santangelo and made *amende honorable* in his *Modern Painters of Naples*, published in 1855. It is interesting to compare this obituary with his previous despatches. 'During the period of his ascendancy,' he wrote, 'he manifested by the courtesy of his personal intercourse, by his sympathy for obscure merit, by his intercession at Court, by the example of his private acquisitions, by the promotion of public works, a praiseworthy desire to raise the artist in social estimation, and the arts to that development, which the political system of the country denied to the other branches of intellectual culture. He regulated the exhibitions; he multiplied the rewards of proficiency; and, what was of no slight utility, he facilitated the royal purchases by economizing on the budget of his department, and furnishing, in many cases, half the price for the works chosen for the collection of the sovereign; an arrangement of which we may admire the benevolence, and excuse the irregularity. . . . During the long ascendancy of Marquis Santangelo, he laboured under grievous imputations, engendered in the feverish fancy of a people, who thought virtue and merit impossible in the instrument of arbitrary power. It was rumoured and believed, that he made the authority of a minister instrumental in gratifying the passions of a virtuoso. He might be propitiated with a picture or a vase. Guilt, it was alleged, was secure in a suit of Roman armour. Poverty was fain to present a gem; and grief might expect redress if provided with a lacrymatory or an urn. His Excellency filled his museum with the misery of his suitors. Time has dispelled many delusions; the antagonists of the deceased statesman would probably now allow, that he directed the internal affairs of his country with systematic industry, and with an improving spirit; and that he would have operated greater reforms, had he not been crossed by the malevolence of his colleagues. After his return, in the year 1849, from an unmerited exile, the moderation and ability of his rule were heightened by the crimes and errors of his successors; and his death has cleared his fame by revealing the honourable mediocrity of his fortune.'

Though Schwarzenberg complained of the King's lack of firmness he was sufficiently firm to paralyse his ministers. De Mazade has related that 'one day the Cabinet, consisting of men who had no connection with liberalism, was dismayed by the growing agitation in the north and centre of Italy. Fearing a violent reaction at Naples, some thought of proposing a slight change in the government. But the difficulty was to broach the subject to the King. The boldest of them, Spinelli, took charge of this delicate mission, and his colleagues were to support him. When the Council met, Spinelli spoke up: "What does Your Majesty think of these clouds which are gathering round us?" The King glowered at him angrily without a word. The other ministers were not bold enough to utter, and the meeting closed.'

There were other meetings, however, where the liberals discussed their plans with buoyant optimism. Many of these took place in the prison of S. Maria Apparente, where Poerio was allowed to receive guests in the chief warder's room. The Calabrian revolts having failed, the liberals modified their tactics: they would stage a series of peaceful demonstrations. The first was arranged for November 22. While the military band was playing in the crowded square before the royal palace sudden cheers were raised for Italy, Pius IX and the King. 'At this the dilettanti who were present for their usual entertainment fled in all directions, leaving the liberals in presence of the guard. The latter ran to arms but were withdrawn when it became apparent that the demonstration was of a loyal character.' Two evenings later the scene was repeated by a larger chorus, which scattered coloured leaflets demanding an amnesty, political reforms, and a further change of ministry. The cheer-callers then marched up the Toledo urging everybody to join them. Seeing the advance of this boisterous throng without knowing the cause of the commotion, the shopkeepers began to bolt their doors and shutters. After prolonged cheers for Pio Nono before the nuncio's residence, the crowd dispersed.

As the King's name was invariably coupled with that of the liberal

Pope in these acclamations he realized that he was not being cheered for his own sake. He rebuked Del Carretto and ordered the band to stop playing outside the palace. Next day the police published a notice forbidding such outbursts as 'tending to disturb the public peace'. But the demonstrations went on. In a scuffle with the police many young dandies with flowing whiskers were arrested, including the son of the Prince of Torella, the witty Duchino Proto, the Duke Malvito, the painter Saverio Altamura, and others who had taken part in the fracas just for the devilry of it, though some perhaps fancied that a Constitution would solve their problems. Lord Napier reported that 'a thousand stories to the prejudice of the King are circulated with the effect, if not the intention, of rendering His Majesty odious and contemptible in the eyes of his people.' Apparently Lord Napier believed these stories, but he was not mistaken when he observed: 'The King desires to wrap this Government in obscurity, and maintain a state of unapproachable isolation.' Metternich having withdrawn the Austrian troops from Ferrara on December 16, Ferdinand could expect little help from that quarter.

Public demonstrations in Palermo resembled those in Naples except that loud cheers for independence were added. The first occurred during a performance of Donizetti's *Gemma di Vergy* at the Teatro Carolino. When the 'faithful slave' sang the moving aria:

> *Mi togliesti e core e mente,*
> *Patria, Numi, e libertà,*
> (You took away my heart and soul,
> Country, gods, and liberty,)

the whole audience rose automatically, waving handkerchiefs and shouting: 'Long live the Pope, the King, and the Italian league!' Again, when the prima donna Parodi appeared on the stage with a tricoloured flag to sing 'It is already the first dawn of the new year', a shower of leaflets fluttered over the pit and there were frantic cries of *Viva l'Italia!* 'Though universally and eagerly joined in by all classes from the highest to the lowest, they both quickly terminated without the slightest violation of order,' wrote Lord Mount-Edgcumbe[1] who was present—'unless indeed the act of pelting with cushions one

[1] Extracts from a Journal kept during the commencement of the Revolution at Palermo in the year 1848. London, 1850.

in authority at the theatre till he joined in the cry (having locked him up in his box), may be so termed; which it hardly can be, as immediately on his doing so, the greatest good humour was restored. A more violent spirit was undoubtedly displayed the following day at the theatre, and a paper was signed by many, demanding a national guard.' Hugs, kisses, hand-shakes, tears of emotion: the scene was repeated with variations here and in other cities. A tricoloured flag was thrust into the hands of Saint Rosalia's statue; at Trapani a bust of Pius IX was pompously crowned amid orations and the municipality formed a national guard. The appearance of English ships off the coast led to rumours that these were coming to restore the Constitution.

The discreet police seldom ventured to interfere with these effusions. As for that instrument of tyranny the Lieutenant-General, he assured the home government that there was no cause for alarm. De Majo, the Duke of S. Pietro, was in fact the mildest of men. So the demonstrations continued, and more and more appeals to revolt were printed anonymously and scattered through Palermo. General Vial, who was in command of the garrison and head of the police, warned de Majo several days in advance that an armed rising was likely to occur on January 12, the King's birthday, but de Majo refused to believe him. On January 9 the following proclamation was posted on the walls: 'Sicilians! The time of prayers has passed in vain. Protests, supplications, peaceful demonstrations have been useless. Ferdinand has spurned everything. And shall we, a people born free but now reduced to chains and penury, still delay to reconquer our legitimate rights? Sons of Sicily, to arms! The might of all is omnipotent: the union of peoples is the downfall of kings. At dawn on January 12, 1848, the glorious period of universal regeneration will commence. Palermo will welcome with rapture all armed Sicilians who volunteer to support the common cause, to establish reforms and institutions analagous to the progress of the century, desired by Europe, by Italy, and by Pius,' etc.

The author of this, Francesco Bagnasco, is supposed to have acted on his own initiative. Since many historians have denied the existence of an organizing committee in spite of the assertions of Giuseppe La Masa, the obscure Bagnasco was apparently the chief instigator of the Palermo rising. Beyond arresting a few moderate liberals, two of whom sought safety in the British consulate, the police took no serious precautions. Consequently the first revolution of the ultra-revolutionary year 1848 broke out punctually according to proclamation if not to plan.

Various and confusing are the accounts of the celebration of the King's thirty-eighth birthday in Palermo. Larger crowds than usual wandered through the streets and loitered in the squares listening to incendiary speeches: on the Toledo a priest called Ragona, crucifix in hand, exhorted the people to revolt in the name of God while the young lawyer Paternostro harangued a gathering on Piazza della Fieravecchia and La Masa led an armed band with a banner of red and white handkerchiefs tied to a stick with green ribbon. Then shots rang out, and the fighting began. The mounted patrols who attempted to restore order were fired at and overwhelmed by a discharge of furniture and hot water from the windows and balconies of narrow streets, suffering severe casualties. Since de Majo chose to adopt defensive instead of offensive measures, the rioters soon gained the upper hand. By nightfall the royal troops were shut up in their barracks while the insurgents were swaggering in the centre of the city. A provisional committee of government was formed with headquarters in Piazza della Fieravecchia. As soon as the news reached the neighbouring communes, they sent large contingents of armed men to join the rebels. More and more continued to arrive, and they were encouraged by the extreme prudence of the foe to attack the most important buildings and destroy the military stores, while de Majo and Vial held futile conferences.

It was not until the 15th, when he had lost all control of Palermo, that the Lieutenant-General ordered Colonel Gross, the Swiss governor of the Castellammare fort, to bombard the city. His plan, or eleventh hour inspiration, was evidently to attack without fighting, and to resist without self-defence. These belated and intermittent explosions only served to exasperate the populace and to call forth protests from all the foreign consuls, who appealed to the distraught de Majo in the name of Europe 'to stop this horror which deserved the execration of the civilized world'. According to some this incident gave rise to the nickname of *Bomba* which clung to Ferdinand II for the rest of his harassed life and became a byword.

Marshal De Sauget, who had been Florestano Pepe's chief of staff in 1820, was given command of the Neapolitan expedition of about 5000 men which landed in Palermo on the night of January 15. There was a wave of panic among the insurgents, several of whom took refuge on board H.M.S. *Bulldog*. Thanks to the Marshal's inertia their self-confidence soon returned. He remained at Quattroventi outside the city. Instead of reinforcing the strategic positions inside it, he gave his men a rest and wrote a series of plaintive letters to the King. The Marshal was a defeatist from the start. 'The inhabitants are much bolder than in 1820,' he wrote on the 16th. 'Since it has been forbidden to fire on the city after the protests of the British consul and commodore, the guns of the fortresses are useless: street-fighting is impossible unless we proceed to storm houses, churches, monasteries, and belfries one by one. . . . Surrounded by enemies, without provisions, wine, fuel, tobacco, water, or even hay to lie on, our troops will eventually become demoralized, however great their sense of duty.'

The Austrian, French and Sardinian consuls tried to mediate, but their good offices were repulsed. The insurgents had gathered strength and felt they could rely on the support of the whole island as well as on foreign, which meant British, protection. On the 18th the mild de Majo sent a note to Marchese Spedalotto, the mayor of Palermo, deploring the bloodshed and inviting him to a conference. Spedalotto replied that he should open negotiations with the newly formed General Committee, whose authority de Majo could not recognize. In spite of rebuffs de Majo persisted in trying to obtain an armistice. 'So far as I am concerned,' he wrote, 'I shall not fail to send a steamship to Naples, and I am ready to co-operate in expressing my own sentiments to H.M., should the demands be moderate. I beg you for a prompt reply: in the meantime I shall not fire a single shot, provided that the people do likewise, and I shall await H.M.'s answer, since I can make no decisions on my own responsibility and have no alternative but to sacrifice myself in H.M.'s service.' After all that had been said, done and repeated before and since January 12 this letter betrayed the Lieutenant-General's ineptitude. The mayor's retort was crushing: 'The people having courageously rebelled, will not lay down their arms or suspend hostilities until Sicily, reunited in General Parliament at Palermo, adapts to her present needs that Constitution which, sworn to by her kings, and recognized by all the Powers, has never been openly ravished from this island. Without this, any negotiation is useless.'

The Count of Aquila, who had commanded the flotilla for the transport of De Sauget's troops, returned to Naples on the 17th with a dismal account of the situation. A Council of State was hastily assembled, and the party in favour of concessions prevailed. The King issued four decrees appointing the Count of Aquila his Lieutenant in Sicily with a separate Council and administration: 'promiscuity' was abolished, and all official posts on the island were reserved for natives. The press was promised greater freedom, and when calm was restored the King would draw a veil over these deplorable events. But the General Committee in Palermo greeted these concessions with contempt and hostilities continued with ferocity on both sides. One after another the buildings held by the royal troops were evacuated. On the 24th de Majo decided to withdraw his garrison from the royal palace and join De Sauget's troops at Quattroventi. They had been cut off from provisions and suffered from a shortage of water. During this disastrous retreat, as they marched through the city at night encumbered with numerous women and children of all ages, they were fired upon from roofs, walls and hedges along the way. Some stopped to fire back, but the enemy was invisible. They reached Quattroventi more dead than alive. Here De Sauget told de Majo that he had been ordered to retire to Messina. Without more ado de Majo resigned and sailed to Naples with General Vial, leaving De Sauget to cope with the anarchy for which their folly was largely responsible.

As soon as the royal palace was evacuated the mob burst in like a destructive torrent, shattering the fine furniture, porcelain, mirrors and crystal chandeliers, and tearing the ancient carpets and tapestry: very little could be salvaged from the vindictive frenzy of these vandals. Less damage was done to the palace of finance as the governing committee was anxious to appropriate all the funds and securities in the bank. The four provisional committees were merged into a general committee on the 24th with the veteran Ruggero Settimo as president and Mariano Stabile as secretary general, both flaming patriots with British sympathies and a stubborn hatred of the Bourbons. Bentinck's esteem for Settimo had survived his disillusion with most Sicilians in 1815. Born in 1778, Settimo was still vigorous at the age of seventy, and braver than most of his colleagues. Stabile, his right-hand man, was forty-two; and his motto, *Tout ou rien*, expressed his intransigence. Lord Mount-Edgcumbe, who was in Palermo when the insurrection broke out and tried to act as an intermediary, was favourably impressed by his ability; so was Lord Minto. He was probably responsible for Settimo's proclamation urging all the rest of Sicily to follow Palermo's example 'to secure the triumph of the common cause'.

After the failure of another attempt to negotiate with the general committee De Sauget decided to withdraw to Messina by land instead of by sea, which meant marching across the island in the teeth of a violently hostile population, whereas it would have been easier to embark directly. He invariably chose the worst alternative. An eight hours' march to the village of Villa Abate was accomplished in twenty hours. The rugged winding road was full of ambushes; the troops were harried by bands of peasants, sniped at from hedges and rocks and clumps of trees. Thirsting for revenge, they fell upon the foe wherever visible, sweeping all obstacles until they climbed the craggy heights of Casteldaccia whence they saw the Neapolitan fleet which had been sent for them. On the shore near Solanto De Sauget received orders to return to Naples: he obeyed with unseemly haste. Before embarking he commanded his gunners to leave behind all the arms and equipment they could not take with them; the cavalry and artillery were to kill all their mules and horses—a command which few had the heart to obey. Several horses tried to follow their masters and leapt into the sea neighing pitifully, while their masters had to watch them drown. The beach was strewn with clothing, knapsacks, every sort of weapon, and horses dead and alive, an unexpected harvest for the local peasantry. Thus, within a fortnight, the expedition which was to have quelled the revolt returned to Naples in a miserable plight.

Towards the end of January Sicily was almost entirely evacuated by the royal troops. On February 2 the general committee announced: 'Our fatherland is free, and we are worthy of our fatherland.' The fort of Castellammare near Palermo still held firm, but its stalwart commandant Colonel Gross received orders from Naples to capitulate with the honours of war and three steamships were sent for the garrison. The first phase of the Sicilian revolution was over. On February 5 Ruggero Settimo announced 'that the evils of war had ceased, and that from this moment an era of happiness had begun for Sicily.' There was a thanksgiving ceremony in the cathedral, with a funeral oration for the fallen and the blessing of tricolour flags, attended by all the consuls of foreign powers except Austria. The stirring strains of 'Guerra Guerra' from the *Norma* of Bellini, the most famous of Sicilian composers, enlivened this picturesque ceremony. 'The scene both without and within was most curious,' wrote Lord Mount-Edgcumbe. 'The streets were thronged, firing off their muskets in token of joy, with vast crowds of wild armed men—and the great excitement displayed by all classes crowding the windows and balconies was extreme. The church was filled to excess, a passage from the great entrance to the altar being kept clear by lines of banditti-looking men, presenting a scene as little in accordance with our notions of solemnity as possible. At intervals, a wild-looking fellow who had distinguished himself in the combats would be brought up to the Cardinal, the church resounding with clapping of hands, *vivas*, and *benes*, and the ladies shaking hands which had apparently never touched water. This lasted a little too long, for the Committee, for whom places were reserved, arrived considerably after the time appointed. Their approach was announced by firing, so close to the door that it seemed to be actually within the church. They advanced up the aisle, preceded by a band of music playing the duet from the *Puritani*, after which the flags were carried up amidst clamour to the altar, and blessed. This was followed by a sermon, which was vehemently cheered. The people then joined for some time in a very discordant chorus, in which no leading voices were heard, and this, I afterwards discovered, was the *Te Deum*. . . .

'I drove about the town, and could but in a few places see any marks of injury to the buildings from the fire to which they had been exposed . . . upon the whole the injury was extremely trifling. If the orders given to ten steamers and the forts had been dictated by the cruel feelings attributed to the King of Naples, "*could this have been the case?*" Fear could not have prevented them from executing the most severe orders, for by so doing they would have been exposed to no more danger than they incurred when remaining inactive. . . .

'During the time that the ceremony was taking place in church the garrison, consisting of about 600, headed by Colonel Gross, marched out of Castellammare for embarkation; but even that gallant old man would not venture to do so without escort of the two British captains (Lushington of H.M.S. *Vengeance* and Key of H.M.S. *Bulldog*), who placed themselves at their head. The precaution, however, was unnecessary, for upon this occasion as upon all others (except where the *sbirri* were concerned), the people showed the best and kindest feeling towards the vanquished opponents, the gigantic Colonel Gross having to bring down his weather-beaten face to the level of ordinary men, that he might be kissed by dirty, whiskered mouths, much oftener than could, even here (where the practice of men slobbering each other's faces is common), be thought agreeable.'

The slaughter of captured *sbirri* or police was supposed to have been justified by the discovery of skeletons in the police offices and by their former harshness in carrying out the law. 'Had their lives only been taken, it would have created but little surprise,' wrote Mount-Edgcumbe, 'but that a people who, in other respects, had displayed so much good feeling, should take a pleasure in after death dragging about the bodies of their victims, and permit their children to join in the disgusting mutilation of them as in sport, would be past belief, had it not been witnessed by many, and at a distance by British officers. Captain Lushington saw from his ship one of these barbarous spectacles, and most properly made a most energetic remonstrance against such proceedings, after it was pretended that the power of law was enforced. The remonstrance at the moment seemed to have effect, but that very night so feeble a guard was placed over thirty-five who were in the hospital, that they were removed by a mob so quietly that a resident close by, whose attention had been called by some unusual sound, heard nothing like a contest, and they were all taken to a spot some distance from the town, and shot. These they were prevented from mutilating, and they were buried on the spot; but pools of blood were visible for days after.' Compensations were promised to those who deserved well of their country 'for the sacrifices they had made, the valour they had shown, the blood they had shed'. Sicilian heroism was lauded hyperbolically for all the world to admire. But the war was not over yet. Ruggero Settimo forgot to mention that the citadel of Messina, a bridgehead as it were uniting Sicily with the mainland, was still in enemy hands.

The apparent success of this revolution produced frenzied excitement among the radicals at Naples. Why shouldn't we imitate the Sicilians? they thought. Proclamations were printed for distribution in the provinces and emissaries were sent to Salerno where Costabile

Colonna, an innkeeper, was organizing an insurrection in the Cilento district, famed for its turbulence since the time of Murat. A curious adventurer called Leipnecher volunteered to support him. Born in Syracuse, he had been expelled from the royal military college, had fought in Algeria with the foreign legion and returned to Naples after marrying a Parisian with whom he opened a flower-shop: he also dabbled in painting. Leipnecher felt quite at home in the Cilento, which was almost as wild as Algeria, and he rallied hundreds of ruffians to the tricolour banner. After destroying the telegraph at Castellabate and a bridge over the Sele, they scoured the country helping themselves to public and private funds, attacking and disarming the local police, robbing and murdering loyal officials, in the name of liberty and a Constitution. But they were no match for the disciplined force that was sent against them under Colonel Lahalle, who routed them near Laurino on January 30 when a Constitution had been granted.

The Cilento rising was also inflated by liberal propaganda, which announced that ten thousand revolutionaries were on the march to Naples. Had other provinces caught the contagion it would have been serious, hence the recall of the troops from Palermo. After the King's fruitless concessions to Sicily, which had been followed by an amnesty, the agitators in the capital tested a new technique. Lord Napier reported on January 23: 'Yesterday there was a kind of sudden disorder and panic in Naples which spread all over the city and caused the shops to be shut. Confidence was restored in the afternoon, and it is difficult to ascertain the origin of such a general dismay. The guards stood to their arms, the artillery men to their pieces and the civic force ran to their quarters where they received a complimentary address from H.R.H. the Prince of Salerno.'

The students were enjoying themselves. Crowded in cabs and curricles they rattled through the city at a frantic speed. Pretending to be terrified—no doubt some of them were in earnest—they shouted at gaping bystanders: 'Run! Run for your lives!' or else: 'They're coming, they're coming! Look out for your goods!' Many shops were closed in a hurry. If anyone asked: 'Why run?' the students answered: 'They're coming!' 'Who's coming?'—'Woe betide us! Can't you hear them? It's going to be the end.' Nobody could make head or tail of what was happening, but many a simple citizen was alarmed. As a practical joke it was quite effective.

197

The disasters in Sicily had shaken the King's confidence in his army, but he did not appeal for Austrian aid. Although he realized that it was too late, Schwarzenberg made a last attempt to dissuade him from granting a Constitution. On January 27 he informed Metternich: 'Yesterday morning I wrote the brief memorial which I take the liberty of enclosing with the present respectful report. It does not contain a word which I do not consider wholly true, and I am absolutely convinced that if the King wished to follow the course I have indicated he would have several chances of honourable escape from the miserable situation in which he finds himself, and at least the certainty of delaying the ruin towards which his lack of firmness and the wretched counsels of his ministers, his family and court are all dragging him.

'As I know from experience that here one must formulate exactly whatever one requires, to make up for the ineptitude and indolence of those who should do the work, I have even drafted the minutes of the King's proclamation.

'Count Chreptovitch and the Prussian chargé d'affaires Schulenburg are associated with me in this step; they have approved my effort and have also signed the memorial which was submitted yesterday to the King.' Schwarzenberg added that he had little hope of success as the King was nervous and dejected: his health had been upset by recent events.

The memorandum stated that a Constitution under actual circumstances would ruin the kingdom and the whole of Italy. The minority clamouring for it did not exceed two thousand and consisted of hotheads and inflammable adolescents. The masses had no desire for it: their discontent was due to various abuses in the administration. By what means would the factious minority strive to effect its aim? The population of the capital was anything but aggressive, and armed resistance to the government was improbable. Moral aggression was organized because it had been given time to gather strength, and because the King, betrayed by disloyal servants and deserted by the cowardly, was defenceless against the steady onslaught of the revolutionary faction. The danger of this moral aggression was exaggerated. The turbulent minority could only expect to win if the government resigned through fear of a conflict while every chance of success was in its favour. The government could count on 9000 well equipped troops and a peace-loving population which realized that political agitation caused unemployment and poverty. The King should immediately proclaim his intentions, to encourage and enlighten the wiser part of the nation. It was possible, however, that the faction might try to intimidate the government with the forces it had been able to muster under the very eyes of the police. In that case the King should boldly adopt repressive measures.

The proclamation repeated that the organic laws of the country 'offered all the elements of material and moral progress', recapitulated the King's recent reforms and concessions, and promised to prevent abuses and guarantee the faithful execution of the laws. A Constitution would only create disorders and hinder administrative reform. The King would never allow a factious minority to impose concessions which must lead to anarchy all over the peninsula.

The King agreed with Schwarzenberg, but the pressure from the other side was overwhelming. Even Del Carretto was sliding towards the liberals. The Apostolic nuncio remarked to Lord Napier that he could not find a weak point in His Majesty's impenetrability. All his instincts were to resist: he hesitated until the revolts in Sicily and the Cilento wrung a decision from him. The mob had cheered Pio Nono. Very well, he would go farther than Pio Nono. He would be the first Italian sovereign to grant a Constitution. 'They push me, and I'll precipitate them,' he is said to have exclaimed. He must have smiled grimly through his exasperation. Once he had made up his mind he acted quickly. On January 26 Del Carretto and Monsignor Cocle were dismissed; on the 27th a new cabinet was formed: and on the 29th a royal edict announced the fundamentals of a Constitution.

Like his predecessor Intonti, Del Carretto wished to set up his sail to the prevailing wind. As Minister of Police he was well informed, and he thought his prestige would compensate for his lack of popularity. Perhaps he did not realize how unpopular he was. With some 12,000 police at his bidding, the renegade Carbonaro had begun to visualize himself as a dictator. Apparently his plan was to extort a Constitution from the King, and proclaim himself the saviour of his country. But the King had been warned in advance.

Del Carretto's disgrace was a repetition of Intonti's seventeen years ago. According to Nisco he was summoned to the palace during dinner and ordered by General Filangieri to leave the country. When Del

Carretto answered him defiantly Filangieri pointed his pistol at him with the single word: 'Obey!' Lord Napier wrote on January 27: 'When Marquis Del Carretto, Minister of Police, entered the Council yesterday forenoon the president read him a royal decree, by which His Excellency was summarily dismissed from his office. The Minister in vain protested against the injustice and ingratitude of such a measure, recapitulating the undeniable though disgraceful services which for a long course of years he had obediently rendered to the Neapolitan Crown; he was imperatively silenced, and General Filangieri and Major Steiger of the Swiss Guard took away his sword and led him out of the Council Chamber informing him that a ship was prepared to convey him from the country. And in fact, unless I be misinformed and the public deceived, Marquis Del Carretto was hurried on board a steam vessel without being allowed to take leave of his wife and family. His Excellency's destination is variously stated to be Leghorn or Trieste and a great uncertainty prevails as to the motives and manner of his removal from power.

'If the preceding version which is generally accredited, be substantially correct, the Neapolitan Government has been guilty of an odious violation of the law even in performing a popular act, for the fallen Minister has been condemned to banishment without legal trial or sentence for crimes unspecified, and by a wanton and unfeeling exercise of power. . . .

'Monsignor Cocle, the Royal Confessor, has for several days been absent from the usual scene of his activity. By some he is said to have retired to Benevento, by others to a convent of his order at Nocera. The former seems more probable.'

'The game is up', wrote Schwarzenberg to Metternich on the same day. 'The King and his ministers have completely lost their heads.' And Metternich scribbled characteristically on the margin: 'I defy the ministers to lose what they have never possessed.'

In the meantime several petitions with hundreds of signatures demanding representative government were addressed to the King. To intensify the effect of these, and to celebrate Del Carretto's expulsion, the Italian tricolour was unfurled at a mass meeting amid cries of *Viva la Costituzione*, and a cockaded and beribboned procession led by the bombastic Saverio Barberisi in a tricoloured sash marched down the Toledo towards the palace square. Although it was pouring with

Leopold, Prince of Salerno

rain groups of ladies applauded from balconies and windows, waving tricoloured scarves, handkerchiefs and bouquets. Quantities of cockades had been imported in spite of police regulations. A gun was fired from Sant' Elmo and the castles hoisted red flags, but the leaders of the demonstration imagined that these were Belgian, and so predicted a Belgian Constitution. The King sent General Statella, the governor of the city, to investigate. He rode from the palace with twelve mounted hussars and asked the people what they really wanted. Old Barberisi strode up to him and said: 'Tell the King what you see, and that his people are unanimous in demanding a Constitution.' The General promised to oblige.

That same evening the King convoked a Council of State, and another of generals. Anxious to avoid extremities, and aware that the army, though loyal, sympathized with the movement, all except General Saluzzo advised Ferdinand to gratify what they believed to be the universal craving. Harassed and exhausted by the conflict between his sense of Divine Right and the cumulative pressure of public opinion, the King said he was willing to try the experiment. It may have been a sop to his pride that in doing so he outstripped other Italian sovereigns. He was thoroughly Neapolitan in his love of generous gesture. Having assumed a liberal rôle he decided to play it with grandeur. He would concede more than anyone expected. A new ministry was formed at once under the Duke of Serracapriola, who became President of the Council and Minister for Foreign Affairs. He had been ambassador in Paris until recently, and considered the French Constitution an excellent model. Francesco Paolo Bozzelli, the new Minister of the Interior, agreed with him and was appointed to draft the document. A barrister with a solid reputation and a pillar of the liberal party who had suffered for the cause by a long period of exile and imprisonment, Bozzelli was the man of the moment, likely to predominate, as Lord Napier wrote, 'both in council and debate, by the force of his character and the extent of his knowledge'. Napier regarded the new administration as a respectable government of transition.

On January 29 the royal decree was published as follows: 'Having heard the general desire of our beloved subjects to have guarantees and institutions consistent with the present state of civilization, we declare it is our will to gratify this by granting a Constitution. We have therefore charged our Ministry of State to submit a plan to our approval within the next ten days on the following bases:

'The legislative power shall be exercised by us and by two Chambers, one of Peers and the other of Deputies; the first will be composed of individuals appointed by us, the second of Deputies chosen by electors on the basis of a census which will be fixed.

'The only religion recognized by the State will be the Catholic, Apostolic and Roman. Other cults will not be tolerated.

'The King's person will always be sacred and inviolable. The ministers will be responsible for all the acts of the Government. The forces of sea and land will be dependent on the King. The national guard will be organized throughout the whole kingdom in uniformity with that of the capital. The press will be free, subject only to a restrictive law in cases offending morality, public order, the King, the Royal Family, foreign Sovereigns and their families, as well as the honour and interests of private individuals.

'We make this our sovereign and free resolution known to the public, and we trust the loyalty and integrity of our peoples to see that order is maintained and the respect due to the laws and constituted authorities.'

X

THE leaders of an insurrection at St Petersburg once persuaded the troops that the word Constitution was the name of their supposed Empress, the wife of Constantine, whose brother Czar Nicholas I was said to have usurped the throne. Hence they shouted under the windows of the palace: 'Long live the Constitution!' In Naples there were close analogies. The average Neapolitan had as little knowledge of the meaning of the word as in 1820, which had left bitter memories of foreign occupation and increased taxation. But it had been dinned into their ears so often that even the ignorant assumed it was either a panacea or an entrance to Eldorado.

To some it seemed as if a golden age were dawning when the King's decree was published on January 29. At any rate it started an artificial carnival among most Neapolitans, delighted to avail themselves of any pretext for revelry. In this case amusement might masquerade as patriotism. Those who were taken by surprise, who feared it was a hoax of the secret societies, were soon reassured. The newspapers overflowed with raptures such as: 'The word has resounded. The word that redeems and regenerates a Nation has made itself heard! *Constitution!* Every eye is bathed in tears, every heart almost leaps from the breast! And to us this sublime word means love, brotherhood, fatherland, freedom! Naples and Sicily exchange the first embrace. Palermo and Naples have become the most illustrious capitals in Italy. Italy has recovered her pride among the nations. And the name of Ferdinand II who has been the first to pronounce the heavenly word will be blessed by all, the glory of our joys and destinies.

'We wept this morning when our Sovereign appeared in the midst of his people to gather the fruit of his magnanimous labour. Oh fortunate day! Oh day which enfolds a whole history in thyself!'

To show that his gesture had been voluntary the King rode through the city with a few officers. He kept his horse at a slow pace all along the Toledo with a dense crowd surging on either side of him, some kneeling, others trying to kiss his hands or feet or saddle-cloth, others weeping hysterically; and this time the cheers were evoked by the sight of their King, whose simple dignity and friendliness made up for his lack of glamour. Conscious royalty—and Ferdinand felt every inch a king though partly dispossessed—was still able to cast a spell. The windows and balconies on either side of the street were festive with flags and tapestry, but cheers also rang out for Gioberti and Mazzini in the general confusion. The carnival aspect was enhanced by the multi-coloured costumes worn by many liberals: some wrapped themselves in tricoloured flags from head to foot or stood in open carriages waving banners, posturing, bellowing slogans and bandying jokes with the passers-by. It was a harlequinade with an ominous undercurrent.

When the King drove into the heart of the old capital he was surrounded by a very different crowd—by petty merchants, hucksters, stall-keepers, market-gardeners, fishermen, sailors, and those who were roughly lumped together as lazzaroni rabble when they displayed their loyalty to the throne and their loathing of innovation. They had heard that the King had been forced to change the ancient laws, and they feared that his life was in danger. Their expressions of sympathy were almost menacing: 'Death to the Constitution! Long live the King! Down with the enemies of God! Never fear, Your Majesty, leave the traitors to us!' And they swore they would rend the *setiglie*—silk coats, an expression for gentry—to rags and tatters. To show that they meant it they tore up a mass of tricoloured ribbons in front of him. Deeply touched by the contrast between their language and that of the educated classes on the Toledo, he attempted to calm them with voice and gesture. 'Friends,' he said, 'I only want the welfare of my people. Everything will be settled, you will see. Patience,

let's trust in God!' Their protestations of affection became so obstreperous that he spurred his horse towards the palace. The Queen
Mother with his wife and children had been praying for him in the
royal chapel. When they saw him return safe and sound they were
intensely relieved. The King appeared to be placid. He had been
comforted by what he had seen during his ride through the city. He
had heard the true *vox populi*, and he felt that his people were with
him.

The next night the royal family attended a gala performance at the
San Carlo and the King was greeted with thunderous applause. A
hymn of gratitude from Verdi's *Proscritto* was sung in his honour.
There was a noticeable absence of tricoloured ribbons since it was
known that the King disliked them: the men wore white ties and the
ladies waved white handkerchiefs from their boxes.

Luigi Settembrini has described the euphoria of these days in his
Ricordanze. Thanks to Lord Napier's protection he had taken refuge
on H.M.S. *Odin* to avoid arrest as the author of the *Protesta del Popolo*.
He returned to Naples on February 7 to be met in the bay by a flotilla
with tricoloured flags. From one of these boats he could hear his
brother shouting: 'Constitution! Amnesty! Bozzelli is Minister of the
Interior and Carlo Poerio Director of Police. Everything has changed.
Come down, come down!' His brother soon told him all the details:
'And do you know what the King said when he signed the decree for
the Constitution? He said, "Don Pio Nono and Charles Albert wanted
to throw a stick between my legs. I'll fling this beam at them, and now
we'll all have fun together."' Though apocryphal this oft-repeated
remark had a plausible ring. But Ferdinand had really granted the
Constitution to save Sicily.

Upon landing Settembrini had to report to the police, which made
him nervous until he heard that the new prefect was an old acquaintance, the ultra-liberal Giacomo Tofano. The prefect shook his hand
and said: 'Welcome home. Let's hope that you will write no more
protests.' 'Why not, if they're necessary?' exclaimed Settembrini's
brother. Settembrini bowed and said nothing, but he noticed that
Tofano had already assumed all the airs of a conservative functionary.
Besides Bozzelli, Poerio and Tofano in the capital, Imbriani, d'Ayala,
de Tommasis, Aurelio Saliceti, and other extreme liberals were
appointed to important posts in the provinces. The amnesty of political

offenders brought hundreds back to Naples, and most of these had been warped by their self-styled martyrdom.

In the meantime Bozzelli retired into his shell to concoct a Constitution. He consulted nobody. 'If Solon had discussed his laws with his friends,' he told Poerio, 'he would not have left an immortal monument behind him.' The result was a close adaptation of the French Charter of 1830 with a slight admixture of the Belgian, but he was so pleased with what he came to consider his original invention that he quite forgot his indebtedness to the former. On February 8 he presented it to the King, who signed it on the 9th. On the 11th it was promulgated, and the next day sent to Palermo. In every parish there were services of thanksgiving, and in spite of heavy rain there were renewed processions and celebrations. The King bowed again and again from the grand balcony of the palace, surrounded by his family, his ministers and retainers in splendid liveries. Then he drove out with the Queen in a small open carriage, holding the reins himself and whipping up his horses. To Settembrini he seemed to be in a ferocious temper. There was the same dense flag-waving crowd along the Toledo. Among the many types of vehicle the most conspicuous was a chariot with Michele Viscusi dressed up as one of the populace (the term *lazzarone* was disappearing) with twelve picturesque companions representing the twelve sections of the capital, each holding a placard with the name and virtues of his parish. This Don Michele was a popular buffoon who preached to the illiterate in the tradition of Father Rocco, explaining the Constitution in vigorous vulgar terms. He compared it to a cart-wheel, for instance; the King was the hub, the ministers were the spokes, and the parliament was the iron axle; and so the wheel went round. 'And where is it going, Don Miché?' they would ask him. 'Bundle of balls! over our shoulders.' 'Well, what of it?' 'What of it? Now there is only a wheel, instead of the whole weight of the cart crushing our ribs.' *'Viva Don Michele!'*

All night the rejoicings continued. Utter strangers embraced each other; street urchins shouted *'Vivooo'*, without knowing why. There were torchlight processions and impromptu illuminations. The leading liberals offered their Roman comrades a banquet at the Hotel des Empéreurs on Santa Lucia with speeches and recitations in honour of the Roman civic guard. Princess Cristina of Belgiojoso arrived majestically in the middle waving a flag, and the enthusiasm became

frantic. Was she not a living legend, the Egeria of the Risorgimento?
The party broke up with more cheers for Italy, the Constitution and
the Roman civic guard, but not without blows since the inhabitants
of Santa Lucia were hostile 'reactionaries'.

The grand climax was the ceremony in San Francesco di Paola
on February 24 when the King took the oath. A salvo of artillery from
the four forts announced his departure for the basilica where he swore
to the Constitution with his hand on the Bible after Mass. Another
volley of guns punctuated this procedure. The royal Princes also took
the oath at the foot of the throne, followed by the ministers, courtiers,
and generals, who touched the Bible with their swords as they pronounced the formula. Then the King rode out in front of the troops
paraded on the square and ordered one of his generals to read it.
Officers repeated it to their respective units while the castles fired a
third salvo to announce that the ceremony was over. Several Sicilians
refused to take the oath, and the Sicilian General Statella, acting
governor of Naples, who was so loyal to the King that he incurred the
odium of many compatriots, took it under protest: 'But I formally
and devoutly protest that my present oath does not bind my natural
civil and indestructible obligations nor any rights of nationality
towards the kingdom of Sicily, my native country, and the Constitution of the said kingdom.' The ambassadors of Russia, Austria and
Prussia had abstained from the ceremony under the pretext of sudden
indisposition.

There were more illuminations and public concerts during the next
few nights. But a sombre note was struck by Mammone Capria, a
Calabrian chemist who had raised a subscription for a symbolical
chariot to celebrate the King's concession. This was a cardboard hearse
drawn by six white oxen with huge horns, preceded by doleful instruments droning a dirge and accompanied by about two hundred national guards and students holding torches. Very funereally the procession crawled down the Toledo and came to a halt before the royal
palace. Here the hearse was transformed into a pyramid suggesting
a mausoleum with pictures and epitaphs of the republicans who had
been executed in 1799, and loud cheers were called for Sicily. But this
ingenious device, intended to rouse revengeful spirits, only roused
indignation. And the King was shown what to expect from the radicals
in return for his concessions.

The prototype of Bozzelli's Constitution had been destroyed in the meantime. Settembrini relates that two days after Ferdinand had given his oath a messenger arrived at Court with urgent despatches. 'What news?' asked the majordomo on duty. 'Revolution in Paris, the flight of Louis-Philippe, and a Republic in France!' 'Holy Mother of God!' gasped the majordomo and fainted away. The so solid-seeming Citizen King had lost his throne on February 24, and the success of this revolution, far more than that of Sicily, started a landslide in the rest of Europe. In Italy it fanned the most fervent hopes of the ultra-radicals. Republicanism was once more in the ascendant. Ferdinand was allowed no credit for what he had done, and Bozzelli became a target of suspicion, as the designer of a Constitution like that which had been jettisoned by France. Leopold in Tuscany and Charles Albert in Piedmont soon had to follow Ferdinand's lead, and give their subjects Constitutions too. Revolution broke out in Vienna on March 13 and Metternich, who for three decades had been the dominant figure in Central Europe, fled into exile. This had lightning repercussions in Italy, where its first effects were the risings in Venice and Milan. Before the news from Austria reached Rome Pius IX, who had started the ball rolling with such innocent optimism, had also to grant a Constitution which was based on that of the fallen Louis-Philippe. '*Essi mi spingono, io li precipiterò:*' even if Ferdinand had not uttered these words he had precipitated the movement with a vengeance.

While the electoral law published on February 29 announced that 164 deputies were to be chosen by ballot, and that the two chambers, of peers and of deputies, were to assemble on May 1, the radicals chafed at this delay as if the complex machinery of parliament could be set in motion overnight. Political clubs of many hues which shared a common restlessness sprang up like poisonous mushrooms. 'What is called Constitution to-day,' wrote Metternich, 'is nothing but "get out so that I can get in!" ' The truth of this was soon apparent in Naples. Many who had recently been exiled or imprisoned now stepped into high government positions, and they were followed by a horde of hungry claimants to whom they made lavish promises. As manifestations had become a regular routine they gathered outside the residence of a minister they wished to replace and bellowed 'Down with him!' Such tactics resulted in a continuous shuffling of officials. There were four different ministries within the next three months.

The disgruntled accused their old comrades of ingratitude and vented their spleen in virulent satires and libels. Petitions were presented at the point of a dagger. Newspaper editors, café demagogues and presidents of clubs issued lists of their latest candidates. Nobody could feel sure of his job.

The King was most anxious to appease Sicily, which refused to be appeased. The Duke of Serracapriola, President of the Council, and the revolutionary committee of Palermo had both solicited French and English mediation. Bozzelli, the tutelary genius of the new ministry, was all in favour of concessions until he realized with a shock what they really implied. Lord Napier and Lord Minto were misled by his assurance that Sicily would be granted a separate Constitution, and became vexed when Serracapriola declared that this could not be done without violating article 104 of the Treaty of Vienna (June 9, 1815) whereby both parts of the kingdom—the Two Sicilies—were to be united in a single State. They suspected that Serracapriola wished to provoke, by delay, a general intervention of the great powers, and that the King had been 'inspired with a jealous dread of Great Britain'. Apart from unpleasant memories of Lord Bentinck, there was some reason for this dread. It was common hearsay that the British fleet had been giving active assistance to the Sicilians. 'I was for some time enabled to pass over such groundless aspersions in silence,' wrote Napier on February 23, 'but a strong feeling having arisen among English residents upon the subject, and a distinct assertion having been made to Mr Beck by Major Steiger of the Stipendiary Swiss Regiments to the effect that H.M.S. *Vengeance* acted in concert with the Sicilians, I have felt it my duty to bring the subject under the notice of the Duke of Serracapriola. (Major Steiger was on the King's staff and had just returned from Palermo.)

'I must also acquaint Your Lordship that in a private conversation with Mr Bozzelli, Minister of the Interior, some time ago, His Excellency, whose discretion is not equal to his learning, imprudently disclosed that official reports had reached the Neapolitan Government to the same effect. I recommended His Excellency to speak with caution on such a subject, and contented myself with denying any such accounts verbally to him and the Duke of Serracapriola.'

In spite of this denial Commander Lyon had supplied some of the rebels with fire-arms and ammunition, the consul Goodwin had hidden others from the police and had been the first to protest against Neapolitan bombardments, British warships had protected panicky members of the Palermo committee during negotiations for an armistice, the commander of the British squadron had saluted the Sicilian flag, and all the British colony had shown cordial sympathy for the Sicilian cause. Small wonder that the Sicilians put their trust in British support. Mariano Stabile was wont to say: 'Thanks to English influence, we will not have to fire a gun.' No doubt Napier was sincere and Commander Lyon had exceeded his instructions. That the King remained sceptical has been confirmed by Guglielmo Pepe and others. As Pepe wrote:[1] 'Both the King, his brother, and Ischitella affirmed that the English government had assisted the Sicilian rebels, and, among other acts, had sent them arms. I replied that this might have been done by private merchants, but not by the English government. Finding them obstinate in their opinion, I said, with a frankness which astonished myself, that before the King had promised the Constitution, I had written to London to three of my friends there, who were members of Parliament, to obtain information from the government as to what assistance I could hope to receive from them, if I landed in Sicily, in order to assist the revolution there. The answer was, that I might expect much sympathy, but not the smallest aid in arms, men, or money.'

Owing to its inability to solve the Sicilian question the ministry resigned on March 1, but as no substitute could be found it returned on March 6 under the same President, Serracapriola, with a larger infusion of liberals, such as Aurelio Saliceti (Grace and Justice), Carlo Poerio (Education), and the economist Giacomo Savarese (Public Works). Prince Cariati, who had been a devoted henchman of Murat, became Minister for Foreign Affairs. To propitiate the Sicilians an extraordinary Council was held in the presence of Lord Minto and several prominent islanders, and the decrees of March 6 were the outcome. The island was to have a separate Parliament 'to adapt the Constitution of 1812 to contemporary needs'; Ruggero Settimo, the hero of the recent revolt, was appointed Lieutenant-General to govern in the King's name; and a special office was created at Naples under the widely respected Scovazzo as Minister of Sicilian Affairs. Lord Minto

[1] Lieutenant-General Pepe, *Narrative of scenes and events in Italy from 1847 to 1849*. London, 1850.

consented to take these edicts to Palermo and negotiate peace. But the islanders, drunk with their easy victory and the latest news from Paris, were implacable. They insisted on becoming a separate kingdom with its own army and flag and the right of coining its own money. The Neapolitans were to evacuate the forts they still occupied within a definite period. Lord Minto returned to Naples with this ultimatum; both he and Lord Napier urged the Neapolitan government to accept it. There were limits, however, to the King's patience. He was being treated like a vanquished foe, whereas he still held the citadel of Messina and an army eager to redeem its lost reputation. The Sicilian ultimatum was rejected on March 22, and the King sent a written protest to Palermo, declaring 'null and void all the acts of the Sicilian government'. The Palermo committee thanked Lord Minto for his friendly efforts. He had set out as an appeaser but ended as an ardent champion of the Sicilians.

The Palermo Parliament assembled amid frantic enthusiasm on March 25. After a salvo of 101 guns Ruggero Settimo, the aged president of the general committee, read a long and lofty speech. The Almighty, he said, had blinded the government He had wished to confound, and the people, in admirable unison, had recovered their rights. Without the guarantee of a Sicilian army Ferdinand's decrees of March 6 were worthless. On March 27 Settimo was appointed regent.

While Palermo was jubilating the rest of the island was in a state of anarchy. As in Naples there was a plethora of newspapers to whip up excitement. Although Mazzini disapproved of Sicilian separatism, many of these echoed his republican slogans. The Jesuits were suppressed without mercy or justification. The guerrillas who had done most of the hard fighting, vocational brigands, now preyed upon the helpless suburbs, forcing their way into private houses under the pretext of searching for 'rats', as they called the Bourbon police, who were promptly butchered when found. It was less safe than ever for unprotected persons to venture out alone after nightfall. Lord Mount-Edgcumbe wrote that before he left Palermo in 1848 security had ceased even by day. 'One wealthy inhabitant had his carriage stopped in the main street, and one man getting on the box, and another inside, the coachman was obliged to drive into the mountains, the master was not allowed to return until he had sent for a large sum of money from his house. Such acts were several times repeated. Affrays arose from the most trivial causes between the patrols. One was thus described: —I heard a great number of shots, and was told, Oh! it was nothing, only a mistake in the Saint.—A Saint's name was always the watchword, and one party giving the wrong one, both immediately rushed behind the door-posts and began firing away, while people from the windows did the same till an explanation took place. No harm was done, and the affair was no more thought of.'

In distant communes there was no longer any semblance of administration, and of course no taxes were collected. Everybody claimed some tangible reward for his patriotism. The King realized that a policy of procrastination would serve him best in Sicily. Anarchy would help him to subdue the stubborn island.

In Naples too there was a drift towards anarchy. The King was accused of exploiting it in order to recover absolute power. But to a certain extent he shared the fatalism of his subjects. Having granted a Constitution, he stepped aside to watch developments. With hysteria on every side of him he kept his apparent calm. The ultra-liberal Francesco Pignatelli, Prince of Strongoli, took over the command of the national guard from the King's kindly old uncle, Prince Leopold of Salerno. This was reorganized with results fatal to discipline, since the men were allowed to choose their own officers. More momentous questions were shelved to discuss the new uniform, whether a cap or a crested helmet was to be worn, whether a sword or a dagger. As soon as this was settled everybody rushed to join the national guard. The new recruits, as De Sivo wrote, were a heterogeneous mixture of old and young, rich and poor, peasants, Sicilians, foreigners, reactionaries, liberals, Mazzinians, nobles, plebeians, householders, landowners, honest men, thieves and vagabonds. As everybody was eager to command rather than to obey—obedience seemed to clash with liberty—the spirit of jealous rivalry was intense. Many who got commissions considered themselves above the law and behaved accordingly. The King congratulated Pignatelli because 'the national guard had achieved wonders; those who had never done a stroke of work had suddenly become energetic'. Unfortunately this energy was sporadic and superficial.

The real weakness of the new ministry came to the fore when the Jesuits were illegally expelled. Since Gioberti had inveighed against them as the chief tools of tyranny, the Jesuits had been persecuted all over Italy: in February they had been expelled from Cagliari and Genoa, in March from Piedmont, Piacenza and Verona. Saliceti proposed their expulsion from Naples: they were incompatible, he alleged, with a constitutional State.

The radical students who had been surging into the capital from the provinces started a series of rowdy demonstrations, backed by the national guard. On March 10 a deputation of these agitators ordered the good fathers to leave their college. They replied that they would wait for an official warrant, but as none was forthcoming they were bullied into consent. Public proclamations warned the parents of children in Jesuit schools to remove them immediately, otherwise they might suffer 'from the righteous indignation of the people'. This added to the turmoil, as terrified parents hurried to fetch their offspring, some in carriages, others on foot; some of the boys had already been driven out, others had run away. Though the Jesuits had promised to leave, national guards occupied their church and adjacent buildings, posting sentinels at the doors, and proceeded to loot their kitchen and store-rooms after searching in vain for fabulous hidden treasure. While the mob shouted: 'Out with the Jesuits, death to the traitors!' all those who attempted to sneak out were driven back.

The chief of police explained to them apologetically that the government could do nothing: they had better leave the country and escape the fury of the population. The fathers replied that they had only promised to leave their college. Since they had not been condemned for any crime, why should they be banished? When this was reported to the Council of Ministers the latter sent word that every Jesuit was free to go where he pleased; the old and the sick might stay on, as well as four priests to look after their church. They could remove their private chattels, but their library and archives were to be sealed. As soon as this was known the demonstrators returned, shouting that they had been betrayed. All the Jesuits were to go, even the old and the sick. Pickets of national guards kept them prisoners all night; next day they were bundled into closed carriages and driven to the mole, whence they were to sail for Malta. The procession, which included a dying priest with two others reciting prayers for him on foot in the pouring rain, was escorted by national guards armed to the teeth. Spectators were appalled, but Saliceti and the demagogues had won. The

213

government had proved its impotence against a riotous minority.

When the same gangs of students started threatening the Carmelites, the sturdy population of the market and port attacked them with sticks and stones. This time the radicals got the worst of it, and the windows of the cafés they haunted were broken. The ministry, which had been so apathetic about the Jesuits, became more active in ordering the dispersal of the 'superstitious rabble'. A ban on street assemblies was proposed in Council, but this did not suit Saliceti. Lord Napier reported on March 19: 'Mr Saliceti was summoned with the rest, but excused himself on the plea of illness. The President of the Council then addressed His Excellency in a letter demanding his presence or his resignation. Mr Saliceti resigned. Mr Marcarelli was then sent for . . . and accepted the portfolio of Grace and Justice.

'The conduct of Mr Saliceti on this occasion though vaunted by the Radical Faction, has deserved the condemnation of judicious and temperate Liberals. His illness if not feigned was certainly never of so serious a character as to prevent him attending a debate (of the most serious interest). But it is believed, and I apprehend with good reason, that he feared becoming party to the Riot Act to compromise himself with the agitators and the clubs, and flinched at the moment of danger. In consequence of Mr Saliceti's resignation, Mr Savarese, Mr Poerio and Colonel degli Uberti also manifested a determination to retire, but not until they had sanctioned a measure so necessary. . . . These gentlemen were disgusted by the timidity of the President of the Council.'

The Riot Act was passed after being rendered innocuous, and the national guards were placed under the protection of the Madonna del Carmine, in whose honour a great *festa* was given to reconcile them with the populace. After the news of the rising in Vienna on March 13 and the flight of Metternich, followed by the famous Five Days in Milan (March 18–22), there was a violent demonstration in Naples before the Austrian embassy, whose coat of arms and flag were destroyed. Prince Schwarzenberg demanded immediate reparation. Prince Cariati, the Minister for Foreign Affairs, tried to temporize, while a manifesto signed by Tofano, the Minister of Police, officially encouraged the recruiting of volunteers for North Italy, and 'To Lombardy, to arms!' was shouted under the royal palace. Without more ado Schwarzenberg sailed for Trieste on March 28. At this juncture the veteran swashbuckler Guglielmo Pepe, one of the leaders of the ill-fated 1820 revolution, returned to Naples after an absence of twenty-eight years, as ebullient as ever.

Schwarzenberg's departure forced the cabinet to face another dilemma: whether to take part in the war of independence. The ultras were clamouring for troops to help Charles Albert. Bozzelli and the majority were against sending soldiers out of the kingdom when they might be needed in Sicily, or to prevent disturbances at home. Poerio, Savarese and the minority were eager to get rid of them, above all Saliceti, whose disruptive influence had increased since his resignation. These were well aware that the army would remain loyal to the King. Bozzelli was attacked for his narrow, municipal, exclusively Neapolitan outlook. To add to the general confusion Saliceti published a new political programme. He demanded sovereign power for the chamber of deputies to legislate on a broader basis, suppression of the chamber of peers, reform of the electoral franchise, and finally a declaration of war against Austria.

Guglielmo Pepe claimed this programme as his own in the narrative he published later, but Pepe should always be taken with a pinch of salt. Arriving at the height of a ministerial crisis, he saw himself as the saviour of his country. After being welcomed by his brother Flores-tano, who had remained a lieutenant-general on active service, he was received at Court. 'Mid-day was not yet passed, when the King sent Major Nunziante in one of the royal carriages to convey me to his palace. The patriots by whom I was surrounded, both young and old, urged my speedy departure, saying I was surely come for the public good, and they attributed the King's eagerness to see me, to a deter-mination to listen no longer to his courtiers: yet these same patriots besought me not to drive in the King's carriage with Nunziante by my side, as he was especially obnoxious to all the liberal party. I was obliged, therefore, to take another officer with me, and to request Nunziante to follow us in Florestano's carriage. Yet, as we passed along the streets, there were those who cried, "Yesterday condemned to decapitation, to-day invited and courted."

'Since I had quitted Naples, many improvements had been made in the royal habitation. On entering the room allocated to the officers on duty, I was saluted as a person of high position, and immediately intro-duced to the King. He retained no trace of the boy of ten years old whose beauty I had then admired; with added years he had become colossal, and his countenance did not indicate tenderness of heart. Yet his manner to me was only too gracious; he invited me to sit down on a magnificent sofa, while he took a light cane chair for himself. "Sire," I said, "this is my place, the other belongs to your Majesty." He began by inquiring after Florestano's health, and this inquiry he never failed to repeat in all my subsequent visits; after asking whether my voyage had been prosperous, he talked of France. I told him that when first the French republic was proclaimed no one believed it, but soon after I had convinced myself, and I remained convinced, that a throne would not speedily be re-established in France. We discoursed of the embarrassment in which the Emperor of Austria, the King of Prussia, and other German princes found themselves placed. I said, "Sire, an example is offered to princes, as useful as it is easy to follow, in the person of the King of the Belgians, who has conducted himself in such a manner that his people unanimously entreated him not to abandon them."

'Having conversed some time on the political condition of other states, without saying a word of his own, he pressed me to return again the following day. . . .

'I was again summoned to the King, and the most singular conversation ensued. I said to him, "Sire, my maxim has ever been that a man's first duty is to his country, and that it supersedes all other duties. It results from this conviction, that I feel myself obliged to say nothing to the King, of which I am not thoroughly persuaded myself." —He answered, "I am perfectly convinced that whatever you say either to me or to others is your real opinion, and that you may more firmly believe what I say, I will add that I have read your Memoirs."

'I was not prepared for this; nevertheless I replied, "I will tell you then, Sire, that the wishes of the most exalted and patriotic are, that you should reign with a constitution on a broad basis, and that my own opinion accords with this. In the commencement of the current year, if your Majesty had only granted liberal institutions, I myself, though I should not have returned to my beloved country unless it had been free, should have warmly applauded such political ameliorations, and have prayed that they might continue. But now that France is a republic, that all the European States are responding by a revolutionary movement, neither simple institutions, nor even the constitution already given, will satisfy. The people are like their princes—the more they obtain, the more they desire. In effect, it is easier to restrain the wishes of a people by granting them at once all they ask, than by granting them little by little with a bad grace."

'The King added nothing to my observations, and to say the truth, he did not add fresh reasons to my arguments, to prove the profound conviction of his mind, as his father was in the habit of doing. I talked much of the National Guard, both in Naples and the rest of the kingdom, endeavouring to demonstrate that the strength of the country, the security of the government, and the internal tranquillity of the State, in great measure depended on them.'

Pepe's brother thought he had been too outspoken, but Bozzelli soon came to inform him that the ministry was dissolved, and proposed that he should form a cabinet, offering him the Presidency of the Council and the double posts of Minister of War and Marine. But Saliceti advised him to insist on conditions stated in his programme which the King could not accept. Ferdinand replied with great forbearance: 'His Majesty cannot alter the constitution sworn to by himself and by all. It behoves the lawful authorities, i.e. the King and the Chambers, to develop and fecundate the constitution given on January 29th, without changing its essence. Therefore the programme proposed cannot be accepted.

'The advice which his Majesty receives from all quarters, confirms the idea that he would fail in his duty towards his country by altering the constitution already granted.'

The King was logical, for it was absurd to demand reform of the Constitution before it had been given a chance to start working. He realized that Saliceti was at the bottom of all this. 'His Majesty,' wrote Lord Napier, 'manifested a great aversion to the colleagues of General Pepe, and especially M. Saliceti, though of General Pepe himself he always spoke in terms of esteem. On this subject I took the liberty of remarking that M. Saliceti had certainly not behaved in such a manner as to deserve His Majesty's reliance, but it was now a question of a balance of disadvantages and that M. Saliceti, a needy and enterprising man, might be less noxious in the Cabinet than out of doors, and that, if employed, his popularity would soon evaporate, and along with that, his power of doing mischief.' But the King remained unconvinced. When a deputation went to ask him to appoint Saliceti he replied: 'It is the Constitution which gives me the faculty of forming my own ministry. The nation chooses its deputies; I choose my ministers; and I do not want this Saliceti.' According to the ingenuous Pepe: 'There is no doubt that the King, to avoid greater calamities, had determined to trust the direction of affairs entirely to me, and that he was dissuaded from this by his courtiers, and by Bozzelli.'

XI

A NEW ministry was scraped together on April 3 under the
presidency of Carlo Troya, a moderate liberal and a learned
historian of the Middle Ages, whose venerable appearance was
accentuated by gout, forming a curious contrast with his wild colleagues, most of whom were advanced radicals. In 1850 he told Nassau
William Senior: 'My ministry was the unlucky result of several
coincidences. In March 1848, General Pepe, then supposed to be the
most popular man in Naples, demanded in the name of the people
absolute power for the Chamber of Deputies to revise the Constitution, the abolition of the House of Peers, universal suffrage, and the
surrender of St Elmo and the other fortresses to the National Guards.
The Bozzelli ministry, which had drawn up the Constitution, would
not defend their own work, and resigned. The King had heard that I
had said in conversation that the Constitution ought not to be altered
until its working had been tried. He knew that I was an intimate friend
of Balbo's, then Prime Minister in Piedmont, he knew that we were
both of us historians, and I believe that these things suggested to him
the idea of calling on me to form a government.

'I was then, as I am now, confined to my chair by gout. I knew few
people, and thought of nothing but my history. I saw, however, that

the post was dangerous, and I thought it my duty not to shrink. We stemmed the popular torrent.'

In fact Carlo Troya was little more than a distinguished figurehead. Far from stemming the popular torrent, his ministry was swept away by it. Though Saliceti had been excluded, he continued to agitate in the wings until part of his programme was carried into effect. The Bozzelli ministry had fallen not because they were reluctant to fight Austria, but because they had failed in Sicily. Saliceti and Pepe demanded speedy departure of troops of the line for Lombardy. Princess Belgiojoso had organized the first contingent to leave Naples on March 30, as if to contradict Musset's lines about her:

> *'Elle est morte et n'a point vécu.*
> *Elle faisait semblant de vivre.*
> *De ses mains est tombé le livre*
> *Dans lequel elle n'a rien lu.'*

Perhaps even then she was living vicariously. To enter into the spirit of this 'epic gesture' the Princess's own words should be quoted. 'I was in Naples when the revolution broke out in Milan. I could not resist an overwhelming desire to rejoin my fellow citizens, and chartered a steamer to take me to Genoa. As soon as this became known, I realized the full extent of the keen sympathy which the Lombard cause had kindled at Naples. Volunteers of every class came to implore me to take them with me to Lombardy. In the forty-eight hours preceding my departure my house was never empty; ten thousand Neapolitans wished to follow me; but my steamer could not carry more than two hundred. I consented therefore to take two hundred volunteers, and at once the small column was complete. A whole population thus suddenly roused from a long lethargy, stimulated by the only thought of war and self-sacrifice, had seldom been seen before. Among the volunteers who asked to follow me to Lombardy, some belonged to the first families of Naples; having furtively abandoned the paternal roof they wished to follow me, bringing only a few pence with them; the others, modest employees, gave up the jobs which afforded them a living in exchange for the life of the camp without any regret. Several officers risked being punished as deserters to bear arms against the Austrian; several fathers of families left their wives and children; and one youth whose marriage, long yearned for, was to have been celebrated the day after that fixed for my departure, deferred his dearest duties to defend the fatherland.

'I shall never forget that moment. The sky was superb. We were to embark at five in the afternoon. When I reached the steamer, the sea was covered with little boats which had come to wish us a good voyage. Among the many ships anchored in the port, ours could easily be distinguished by the continual flashing of arms on the upper deck. My volunteers were awaiting me. Within the short time that we were busy with final preparations, we were again besieged by innumerable demands: from all the boats surrounding our steamer voices implored us to write one more name on our list which was already complete. Unfortunately we could only refuse those pressing petitions; and when our steamer left the shore a single cry arose from a hundred thousand throats; all of them left us with these words of farewell: *We shall follow you!*'

According to Lord Napier 184 volunteers embarked; others have whittled the number down to 120 or less. On the following day, March 31, Lord Napier wrote: 'The Neapolitan Government furnished arms and great coats and defrayed the expenses of the vessel. Princess Belgiojoso provided food. She also honoured the expedition with her presence as well as her patronage and enjoyed the acclamations of her satellites in a prominent position on the poop.

'Without the exhortations and the contributions of Princess Belgiojoso it seems doubtful whether Naples would have furnished even this diminutive quota to the battle of Italian Independence. . . . They went under the orders of Mr Giardini and Mr Balzo, retired officers of the Neapolitan army, were organized in two companies, and numbered in their ranks a poet of some fame, Castellano, who is expected to commemorate the triumphs of the war.

'The concourse of spectators was not very great and there was no imposing enthusiasm, and the lower orders of the city maintained an ignorant indifference on the occasion.'

Some writers expressed surprise that the King did nothing to hinder this expedition, since war had not been declared. But he was glad to get rid of such unruly subjects. Most of them had been conspicuous in the recent demonstrations, which the Belgiojoso had been fanning ever since her arrival in February. Ferdinand regarded her as an eccentric nuisance: others saw her as a feminine Jason followed by

Argonauts, and as a naval Joan of Arc. She was a strenuous romantic, whose features had struck Heine as belonging to the poetical domain of dreams. Musset had fallen in love with this alabaster amazon, but she had scorned his advances. For a titled lady still young and alluring to embark with a horde of zealots on a steamer called *Virgil* seemed a fantastically original enterprise to most of her contemporaries, whose attitude, even outside England, was Early Victorian.

The Neapolitan volunteers entered Milan on April 6, preceded by the flamboyant Princess in an open carriage. She waved a tricoloured banner and wore a plumed hat in Calabrian fashion like her followers, who responded to the acclamations of the Milanese by tearing the plumes from their headgear and distributing them amid cries of: *Viva l'Italia! Viva Pio Nono!* Count Casati, the president of the provisional government, was less enthusiastic. 'Princess Belgiojoso has arrived with a troop of 150 adventurers,' he wrote to a friend. 'I fear she has given me a bad present. However I had to go through with the business of haranguing them.' The Princess herself wrote: 'My two hundred volunteers were, after the Piedmontese soldiers, the first Italians who had come to Lombardy to take part in what was then called the *Crusade* and the *Holy War*. The presence of the first Neapolitan volunteers in Milan seemed to guarantee that the war against Austria would become an Italian instead of a Lombardo-Piedmontese war. The consecutive departure of four other Neapolitan legions soon added to the feeling of confidence which the arrival of these first volunteers had already inspired. Some of our governors refused to share this feeling, however. As I was somewhat responsible for the fate of the young men who had followed me from Naples to Milan, I tried more than once to interest the provisional government on their behalf, and I butted too often against an ill-will which was only too apparent. For instance I happened to present my Neapolitan volunteers as the vanguard of an army of a hundred thousand men composed of all the youth of Italy, which would not hesitate to obey the slightest summons. "God preserve us from such aid!" they exclaimed. I thought it useless to prolong the discussion.'

A second batch of volunteers left Naples for Genoa on April 3 when the new cabinet was formed. Others followed. 'Of the serious war with Austria we shall think later,' said the King, who was obliged to feign sympathy with the aggressive party. Cavour had announced that the supreme moment had struck for the Sardinian monarchy, and Charles Albert had declared war on March 24. But Ferdinand had no enthusiasm for the Sardinian monarchy, whose ambitions he distrusted. From Austria he had little to fear, whereas a triumphant King of North Italy might threaten his own independence. The government of Turin had sent Count Rignon as a special envoy to plead for his active collaboration. His demands for military and naval assistance were categorical, but he hemmed and hawed about the Italian league. That could be settled when the war was over, he said. Thanks to the up-heaval in Austria, it could not last long. Ferdinand was quite ready to join an Italian league and even send an army if his Sicilian rights were recognized, hence his wavering attitude towards the campaign in the north. Pepe assured him that he would reconquer Sicily on the plains of Lombardy. Very well then, let him try. Personally, he had a weak-ness for the blunt old fellow despite his politics. Although Pepe was to rail at 'the base subterfuges employed by the King and his courtiers, by superior officers and generals, to oppose the preparations for entering on the campaign', Ferdinand was not insincere when he sent the veteran fire-eater on what he considered a fool's errand.

The Troya ministry was improvised under the ægis of Bellona, and on April 7 war against Austria was declared. The King stated in a proclamation that he considered the Italian league as an actuality and the Congress of Rome as a certainty; an armed expedition was already northward bound; the fate of the fatherland would be decided on the plains of Lombardy, and it behoved every prince and people of the peninsula to co-operate in the struggle; although pressed by other special needs which engaged a good part of his army, he was resolved to do his share. He ended it with an appeal to the people of the Two Sicilies for unity: let them silence all selfish passions and rally round their King! The reference to rebellious Sicily was clear.

After a long conference with Ferdinand on April 4 Lord Minto realized that he would never agree to Sicilian secession. Reporting this to Palmerston, he said it would be necessary to choose another sovereign if the island were to remain a monarchy. At the same time he expressed his fervent hope to Mariano Stabile, the Minister for Foreign Affairs in Palermo, that Sicily would avoid the calamity of a republican government. Stabile read this letter at an informal meeting of members of Parliament on the morning of April 13. One member asked whether the deposition of Ferdinand II might be declared. The majority, including Ruggero Settimo, assented. On the same afternoon the Parliament voted that Ferdinand and his dynasty had forfeited all right to the throne and Settimo announced: 'The throne of Sicily is vacant.' Sicily would be ruled by a constitutional government, and would offer the Crown to an Italian Prince selected by the representatives of the people. The House of Peers also voted in favour of this decree, and its president, the Duke of Serradifalco, perorated: 'This great act makes Sicily free: let us show Europe that we are worthy of our freedom!'

Again Ferdinand protested, but his hands were tied by the Troya ministry which had made him promise to send forty thousand troops to the north. Since he had been deposed by the Sicilians his army seemed more than ever to be necessary at home. Many liberals thought the same. The most intelligent of these, Luigi Blanch, published several articles against Pepe's expedition. He pointed out the folly of entering a war in the north when the kingdom was so vulnerable in the south, 'without any treaty, or compensation, or guarantees, without even stipulating that one side should not make a separate peace, whence the possibility of being left alone in a conflict whose advantages were all in favour of Piedmont. . . . Stripped of her army, Naples would be powerless to keep order, since the national guard provided no adequate protection. . . . If there was ever any need for more troops, it was certainly at this moment.' His strategic arguments were equally cogent, and they influenced several members of the cabinet. This divergence of opinion among the liberals allowed the King to procrastinate.

Pepe, who had a one-track mind, was beside himself, and in reading his version of these events one cannot but feel that Ferdinand was giving him tit for tat. 'The King was desirous,' he wrote, 'that I should admire the qualifications of his soldiers, as well as his own ability in commanding them. I was scarcely arrived in Naples, and not yet in possession of a military uniform, when he requested me to accompany him in my civilian dress. Accordingly I repaired to the palace in my morning costume, and was conducted by the King to a very small cabinet, where I was seated opposite him, without knowing the motive. I felt we were descending, and I then perceived that we were in a machine constructed to descend and ascend, in order to avoid the fatigue of mounting the lofty stairs.

'When we arrived beyond the Maddalena Bridge we mounted our horses, and the King made two regiments of dragoons and lancers manoeuvre. He commanded remarkably well, and his commands were executed with the greatest exactitude. I paid him most well-merited compliments; but I perceived that he considered this elementary part of the science of war as its most sublime point. In the moments of repose there was but little dignity in the conduct of the King towards his soldiers, who dunned him with petitions. Hence there was a want of discipline, and of that noble dignity which rules the multitude on all great occasions.

'On re-entering the carriage, we drove through a new and beautiful street, which leads to the Studi. On the way, I observed to the King the multitude of mendicants, who, naked even to indecency, persistingly demanded alms. He replied to my observation, that it was the fault of the Minister of the Interior. . . .

'We soon arrived at the quarters of the 12th of the line, the greater number of whom were Sicilians. Scarcely had the drums beat when, in an instant, the soldiers, while running, took their knapsacks and placed themselves in order of battle. The King commanded the manoeuvre, and everything was performed to perfection. There was no flattery in my warm congratulations nor in telling him that I had never seen troops move better on the drilling-ground, and that, though the English might excel them in precision, they were certainly inferior in agility. This exercise was scarcely terminated when a crowd of soldiers, subaltern officers, and women, presented themselves to the King, each loudly supplicating for some favour; and he appeared pleased with this. . . . A woman presented herself, saying, "Majesty, I am the wife of Sergeant ——. We have two children, maidens, but *real* maidens; you have promised to give them husbands; I beseech you not to forget the promise, to avoid the sin to which they are exposed, the virtuous young girls!" The King replied, "I will not forget my promise!" . . .

'On returning to the royal palace the King would not permit me to alight, but desired Prince Ischitella to accompany me home.

'In the midst of so much gracious affability the King, through the medium of his Minister of War, and the head of his military staff,

225

continued to refuse all that was most necessary for the equipment of the troops under my charge, and to retard their departure. He employed the latter officer, as in the time of his absolute power, nor could I ever convince him, that his orders should be communicated through the responsible Minister of War. I did not fail to tell him, that I should only obey the orders of the King when thus conveyed to me.

'The next day I went to the King, with the intention of trying if it were possible to move that heart which Heaven seemed to have created in a moment of anger with mankind.

'I said to him, "Sire, having married an Austrian princess, it is to be expected that you should be averse to making war against that power;" and he replied, "You are mistaken; I have always detested Austria." '

Pepe recommended that the King should take command of his army in person, with Pepe as head of his staff. The Sicilians would return to their allegiance; if not, Pepe would go there himself and compel them to do so without spilling a drop of blood. He counselled generosity, and the evacuation of the citadel of Messina: the Sicilians were a grateful people. He wound up: 'You, Sire, who have the military profession so much at heart, who from your earliest years have occupied yourself with the training of your troops, do not let the opportunity escape of gathering the fruits of your labours. You may from the Isonzo, or even from Vienna itself, dictate to Austria the surrender of all the strongholds in which her troops have taken refuge. You will decide the destiny of the Pope, of the King of Sardinia: your glory will live as long as Italy.'

The King, who had had his bellyful of Sicilian gratitude, thought Pepe was talking through his hat. The proposal to evacuate his last stronghold on the island struck him as particularly inept. General del Giudice, the Minister of War, considered that the King's presence in Naples was indispensable, and that it would be *infra dig.* for him to enter the field as a satellite of Piedmont. The Pope had made strenuous efforts to promote an Italian league, but Charles Albert lost interest in it as soon as he declared war. The government of Turin refused to send delegates to Rome, as Naples had done, and proposed a congress in the north of Italy, which was to arrange the terms of a military alliance, alleging that while the war continued nothing else was worth discussing. This fact is glossed over by partisan historians. The league might have staved off many a disaster. Finally, after agonies of indecision, the Pope pronounced his shattering allocution of April 29. 'We assert clearly and openly,' he declared, 'that war with Austria is far from our thoughts, seeing that We, however unworthy, are the Vicar of Him who is the Author of peace and the Essence of love.' He denied having given the Papal troops any other commission than that of defending the States of the Church. Pio Nono had bravely torpedoed his own popularity, which had been boosted by a conspiracy of misunderstanding. If the patriots were infuriated by what they called the fatal allocution, King Ferdinand welcomed it as manna in the desert.

Exasperated by the King's delaying tactics, General Pepe had fallen ill in the meantime. There is pathos as well as comedy in his account of these days. The King dared not break his promise, but he did his best to evade it. Personally, he was all graciousness to Pepe: 'The King was so obliging as to send me one of his own riding horses, with a complete caparison both for parade and common service. . . . With me, to succour Venice, to be masters of the Adriatic, to enrich ourselves with the treasures of Trieste, and to leave that avaricious city without even a fishing-boat, were settled ideas. I therefore demanded that seven battalions should be embarked in six magnificent steam frigates, and that with these troops I should disembark in the Lagoon. The King opposed this plan, saying that I would thus place myself in a *cul-de-sac*. I persevered; the minister was on my side, and what I demanded was decided on. Unhappily, in consequence of the agitated life I was leading, never having a minute's repose, I was attacked with a violent fever, which lasted six days. The King took advantage of this accident to oppose the embarkation of the troops; but being afraid of public opinion, he made the council meet in my house, and wished Florestano to preside. . . . It would be tedious to detail all the arguments used against the expedition by sea. Though confined to my bed, I should perhaps have been more successful in inducing them to follow my opinion if I had employed intimidation rather than argument; but I was apprehensive, in the first place, that the brigade which was to follow me by land, being *without* me, would never pass the Po; and I . . . was not mistaken. Secondly, the Vice-Admiral Cosa assured me, that with seven battalions on board the frigates would be unable to work, and that consequently the Austrian vessels might engage with positive advantage. Thus it was decided that the troops under my charge should go by land; and even in this I was thwarted by the Papal government, who demanded that they should proceed by single battalions, and only one squadron a day. They would thus have reached the Po with a delay which would have been ludicrous to the population on the road.

'At last the brigade, composed of 17,000 men of all arms, started; they were to be followed by 24,000 more, and it was determined that I should embark at Ancona on board the steam corvette *Stromboli*. Before my departure I received the following letter from the Minister of War, in which he tells me, on the part of His Majesty, that when I reach the Po, I must wait for further orders before crossing it. I placed the letter in my private portfolio, with the firm intention of considering it as *not received*. It must be evident to every one that the intention of the King was not to satisfy the noble desire of the nation in sending an army into Lombardy, but that he studied the means of preventing it from joining the campaign. . . . If I had made known the contents of this letter to the public, or even to the ministry, the King would inevitably have been assassinated.'

Thus while the King raised obstacles on one side Pepe had no intention of obeying his orders when he sailed for Ancona on May 4. After so many years of exile he was a stranger to the army, which remained devoted to Ferdinand. Most of his officers shared the King's aversion to the northern campaign; the generals appointed to accompany him made specious excuses and complained of bad health. 'The following month,' he wrote bitterly, 'when the war with Sicily was in question, they all begged to be employed!'

The Troya ministry, so bellicose abroad, was flabby at home and refused to quell local disorders. It drifted along from one situation to another through sheer incapacity to do anything else, distrusting the King, who distrusted it in return. The doctrinaires and radicals of which it was composed, Troya, Dragonetti, Ferretti, Conforti, Imbriani, Scialoja and Ruggiero, with all their brains and talent for intrigue, failed to understand the real condition of the country or the character of the people, who did not understand the cause for which they were asked to fight. As Giuseppe Paladino wrote, 'neither the war, nor nationalism, nor independence were popular in the south'. War meant heavier taxation, and the departure of family breadwinners. Lord Napier, sympathetically inclined towards the new régime, was forced to admit on April 15: 'In the meantime the internal administration of the provinces has gone to wreck. The land tax is unpaid despite the protestations and seductions offered by the Minister of Finance. The laws remain unexecuted and the police and municipal authorities are powerless. The old system has been completely shattered and none has been constructed to supply its place.'

The press spared nobody: the journalists used their newly found freedom to wallow in an orgy of vituperation. According to Napier many had confidence in the acumen of the Finance Minister Count Ferretti, who had 'the perilous fame of being able to discover and elicit money from sources where another would search and draw in vain'. Soon Napier was complaining of an ordinance 'by which the exportation of specie and bullion from the peninsular portion of the kingdom is forbidden. . . . This regulation, if effectual, would be productive of great inconvenience to the mercantile interests. . . . It is to be presumed, however, that illicit methods will be generally employed in carrying money out of the country'. Ferretti failed to cope with the growing anarchy. One day when he had to attend a Council meeting he told the crowd of applicants in his office that he had no time to see them. The national guard on duty at the door expostulated with him and said: 'Before being the King's minister you are the minister of the people. You should not go to the palace without receiving the citizens who expect to see you. Stay here.' Ferretti had to yield. On another occasion a woman who handed him a petition was armed with a pistol in case he rejected it.

Money was required for the northern expedition, and Ferretti resorted to a loan of three million ducats, two millions of which were to be forced on the public, the rest was to be 'voluntary'. Settembrini relates that he contributed the third of his salary and took this offer in writing to Ferretti, but he could not get near him owing to the siege of pestering claimants. He felt sorry for the harassed minister and handed it to one of his subordinates. 'Poor Ferretti had it printed, and congratulated me: I thought I was doing my duty, but I remained an exception, as no other offer was made. Everybody asked to be reimbursed for damages they had suffered, to be rewarded for merits acquired in the revolution, for the breath they had expended in shouting. And their manner of asking was furious, crazy and obscene. . . .

All the ministers were plagued with petulant and arrogant demands from men who seemed to be drunk, and wanted to be heard by force, claiming everything by force, for they believed that liberty was a banquet at which each had a right to sit down to a hearty feed. They climbed every staircase and shouted in every house: it was a hideous anarchy; and there wasn't a sensible man of any opinion who did not yearn for a strong government, instead of these lawyer-ministers who never stopped blathering about legality and liberty and who only had faith in their blather. After letting everything go to ruin they became panicky and handed in their resignations, as did Ferretti, Imbriani, and Ruggiero.' Settembrini thus confirms the assertions of De Sivo and the pro-Bourbon historians. 'The Ministry of the Interior,' he wrote, 'framed an electoral law by which even a scoundrel could be elected deputy. "What sort of a law is this?" I asked a friend. "It will give us men of our own colour," he replied. "You always speak of colour, never of flavour," I retorted. The elections took place on April 18, and turned out better than I had expected, as on the whole respectable men were chosen. The first of May was settled for the opening of Parliament, then this was deferred till the fifteenth.' Lord Napier also wrote: 'The popular choice is said to have fallen on persons of moderate opinions and of respectable and eminent reputation. The lower orders have manifested no interest whatever in the proceedings.'

The lower orders, who were poor, felt that the Constitution had made them even poorer. Don Michele Viscusi's explanations were all very beguiling, but after so many fine promises there was more hunger and unemployment than before. Trade was stagnant: the spectacular festivities in which the people delighted had almost ceased; the theatres were empty; dances and musical entertainments had lost their attraction, whereas politics had become a general obsession. The shops were deserted: everybody was saving for an emergency, and there was little money in circulation. Yet millions were being squandered on armaments, pensions and salaries to the swelling army of new bureaucrats while taxes were unpaid and nothing came in from Sicily. Though newspapers had increased by the dozen about two hundred printers rioted on April 25. The national guard was sent to find out what they wanted. More pay and less work, they replied. Attempts were made to placate them but a pistol went off, the guard opened fire, and the printers were scattered in panic. This led to the resignation of the

Prince of Strongoli, commander of the guard, who stated in an indignant order of the day that their duty was not to repress their fellow citizens. Gabriele Pepe, another veteran of 1820 but no relation of the fiery Guglielmo, took over the command of the 'nationals', as they were called. This Pepe won immortality for wounding the French poet Lamartine in a duel because of his remark that Italy was the land of the dead. The national guard now included three categories: the former civic guard in their old green uniforms which they were still allowed to wear, the spick and span 'progressives' in light blue, and the auxiliaries with only brass badges to distinguish them from other civilians. The first were regarded as crusty conservatives by the second, and both tended to despise the latter, most of whom were revolutionaries of one kind or another, conceited and officious, anxious to emulate their Parisian namesakes.

Besides the printers, tailors, bricklayers and cloth manufacturers rioted for better conditions, while the ministry was all intent on the campaign for the redemption of North Italy. A student arrested for distributing seditious posters was set free thanks to a demonstration under the police headquarters on April 28. When the Ministry of Justice appointed new magistrates there was another demonstration by disappointed applicants. The patrols sent out to keep order were hooted and jeered at. There was much grumbling against the chamber of peers, fifty of whom had been selected by the King; there were louder demands for a constituent assembly. Deputies began to arrive from the provinces with bands of brigand-like henchmen, bearded Calabrians with daggers, pistols and blunderbusses, while the ancient monastery of San Lorenzo, where the municipal magistrates used to hold their sessions, was being prepared for the opening of Parliament on May 15.

The appearance of a French squadron under Admiral Baudin started a rumour that republican France would support her Neapolitan sympathizers. Several hundred radicals went to welcome the French ships, and a deputation 'in the name of the people' declaimed florid speeches and odes to liberty on board the flagship *Friedland*. In spite of a luke-warm reception officers of the national guard followed suit, and they made the utmost of the fact that they had heard the *Marseillaise*. Seditious proclamations were scattered through the provinces; one entitled 'Of the supreme magistrature of the kingdom', attributed to

Saliceti, summoned all people to join 'a sacred legion of redemption' in order to promote the Constitution of 1820 until a constituent assembly had sanctioned it. Dire threats were fulminated against opponents; tempting rewards were promised to adherents. Sodano, the secretary of the Progress Club, distributed this with the injunction: 'Run to Naples on May 15th, to water the withered plant of liberty with your blood!' Hundreds of impressionable students rushed to the capital, all eager for a patriotic fray.

'The mine was loaded with gunpowder,' wrote Massari in his *Casi di Napoli*, 'it only needed a spark to set it on fire, and this spark was the question of the oath'—to be administered at the opening of Parliament. The deputies assembled for preliminary discussion in the communal palace of Monteoliveto on May 13. Archdeacon Cagnazzi, a grizzled veteran who specialized in political economy, was elected president, but as he was very deaf and his voice was inaudible, Doctor Vincenzo Lanza, a well-known physician and professor of pathology at the university, was elected vice-president. The ministry had published the inauguration ceremony programme: the deputies were required to take an oath of allegiance to the King and the Constitution. Objections were raised to this for various reasons, but chiefly because there was no mention of their rights to change the Constitution. A slight alteration of words, backed by common sense and goodwill, and everything could have been settled without fuss. But it soon became obvious that the deputies aspired to the powers of a constituent assembly; from now on their aim was to cancel the oath altogether.

The republican faction sowed distrust of the Troya ministry as well as of the King. The official programme was rejected: it was moved that a deputation be sent to the cabinet to discuss a different formula. Meantime the henchmen of the radical deputies were spreading alarm and despondency. Outside the assembly building they shouted: 'Deputies, the King is betraying the nation; he is plotting against you. Take courage, we are on your side!' One deputy called Zuppetta jumped up on a balcony and bellowed: 'Citizens, the deputies need no encouragement. Zuppetta gives you his word of honour that we shall die before allowing the King to betray our constitutional rights!' The majority, however, seemed to think that some sort of oath was necessary, but that the King should swear to it rather than themselves: why should their future activities be shackled? Four deputies proceeded to

Arrival of first Neapolitan railway at Portici, by S. Fergola. Museum of S. Martino

Troya's house and one used truculent language about the forces at their disposal: the French squadron in the bay would be certain to assist them. Merely to end the dispute the ministry assented, but they had overlooked two important details: first, that the assembly had not yet acquired a legal status, secondly, that in claiming to reform a Constitution to which the King had already sworn they were creating a combustible situation. Even if they were acting in good faith it was foolish to waste time quibbling in such an emergency. Certainly it looked as if they wished to push matters to extremes.

The King pointed out that the deputies had no right to decide to change the Constitution before Parliament was opened. He agreed to modify the oath by adding that the chamber had the faculty to develop (*svolgere*) the Constitution, but the rest of it was to stand. Raffaele Conforti, the Minister of the Interior, brought this decision to the deputies and implored them to think of Italy and the war of national independence. But the vice-president Lanza replied: 'The chamber will provide for the war better than the ministry does.' The deputies unanimously refused the King's offer, and in the heated discussion that followed Zuppetta moved that the Parliament, 'considering that the royal refusal to sanction a constitutional act puts the country in danger, declares the form of oath proposed by the King inacceptable, and regards his refusal as an infraction of constitutional law; hence the Parliament should remain in session as the sole mandate of the nation.'

After many painstaking attempts to reach a compromise the King, with the utmost moderation, decided that the opening of Parliament should take place without any form of oath whatever. But these debates dragged on for some twenty hours, and the storm they churned up had spread beyond the assembly. At one moment Giovanni La Cecilia and Pietro Mileti with a handful of followers had rushed dramatically into the hall to announce that the royal troops were marching to attack the chamber. La Cecilia was a captain of the national guard who had returned from exile to step into the Ministry of the Interior, thanks to the King's pardon, after a career that was only consistent in conspiracy; Pietro Mileti was a Calabrian fencing-master and professional agitator: both hoped to hasten a catastrophe. Abatemarco, the prefect of police, was able to refute their allegation since he had personally delivered the King's order to General Labrano, commander of the city garrison, that no soldier was to leave barracks.

La Cecilia contradicted him flat and told him he had been duped. Abatemarco turned to the assembly and said: 'Gentlemen, please wait until I have proved this to be false.' Mileti stood flourishing a clumsy musket while Abatemarco left the building to investigate. The court-yard was crammed with national guards playing with their firearms as if they were new toys, but no regular troops were visible. General Labrano assured him that the King's order had been obeyed. But already there were signs of rebellion in the streets. Barricades were being erected along the Toledo.

'These barricades were the first preparations for the funeral of liberty,' wrote General Guglielmo Pepe. 'Positive data are wanting as to their first authors, which proves that they could not have been persons of note.' The evidence points towards La Cecilia and Mileti, combined with the republican deputies and their provincial henchmen, who were most conspicuous in the ensuing struggle. They had long been itching to imitate the Parisian pioneers. Those who remonstrated with them were branded as cowards and traitors, beginning with Gabriele Pepe, commander of the national guard. Mattresses were dragged on to street balconies, doors were bolted and barred; there was a babel of shouting and hammering, digging, slamming of shutters, accompanied by drums and bugles: booths, church confessionals, chairs and stools, carts, tables, shop-signs were piled together with earth, paving stones, tiles and mortar on top of them. Several deputies ran to implore the people to pull down the barricades, but they were not listened to. The Prince of San Giacomo was forced to abandon his splendid carriage and many other proud family coaches were reduced to shambles.

The King had agreed to suppress the oath of allegiance, but he foresaw the end of his reign if he allowed himself to be blackmailed by barricades. The Princes of Ischitella and San Giacomo urged him to send troops to demolish them, but he was determined to avoid bloodshed if possible. Hence the troops were confined to barracks while the barricades increased, and it was rumoured that thousands of armed rebels were marching on the capital from Salerno. The King summoned Colonel Piccolellis of the national guard and said: 'I have discarded the oath and withdrawn the troops, yet they are still building barricades. What more do they want?' The colonel did not know what to answer, except that his efforts to restore calm had failed.

Another colonel, Letizia, and the mayor Antonio Noya, asked for a few soldiers to accompany them, but the King repeated: 'No soldiers, no uniforms! The citizens themselves must do the job.' The mayor and the colonel went off again and exhausted every argument. The barricaders kept on shouting: 'These are our safeguards against betrayal.' When this was reported to the King, he still refused to order the troops out. 'There is greater courage in command than in obedience,' he said, and sent word to the assembly that the opening of Parliament depended on the removal of the barricades. It was already long past midnight. All the royal family spent a sleepless night in the King's study. A ship was anchored in the bay in case they should have to escape.

Before morning Dr Lanza, the vice-president of the assembly, issued a proclamation thanking 'the glorious and intrepid national guard and the generous population for the dignified and virile attitude they had assumed to protect the representatives of the nation.' Since the purpose of the chamber had been achieved, they were invited to remove the barricades and all signs of enmity so that it could proceed to open Parliament. But the mischief-makers declared it was all a lie: the King had conceded nothing, and if he had, it was only to get rid of the barricades. None of the streets should be cleared until the forts had been delivered to the national guard and the regular troops had been sent at least thirty miles from the capital. This had been proposed by the deputy Ricciardi. Others had proposed that the King should abdicate.

The accounts of that memorable May 15 are various and contradictory. Most of the liberal historians blame the King for the bloodshed and accuse him of premeditated perfidy. Actors and spectators wrote under the emotional strain of the moment, but even from these, from Settembrini, the Prince of Ischitella, Count Gennaro Marulli, and the letters of Alfonso di Casanova, it is apparent that the strenuous minority and their provincial confederates had usurped the powers of government owing to the ministry's weakness. A wave of hysteria had spread from the chamber of deputies to the street, and the King, who had done everything except use force to ward off disaster, was at last compelled to take action. Seeing that all printed and personal appeals from Gabriele Pepe and the deputies had proved futile, and that the barricades were still standing on the morning of the 15th, he ordered the troops out. Altogether there were seventeen large and sixty-two small barricades throughout the city.

Settembrini relates that he rose at dawn and went out with his gun. In front of the Angri palace on the Toledo he met Giovanni La Cecilia swaggering with a Turkish sabre and puffing at a cigar. 'What's this?' he asked him. 'Can't you see? It's the revolution,' he replied. 'What revolution?' La Cecilia strutted off without answering. 'Perhaps he thought me foolish,' wrote Settembrini, who went on to look at the larger barricades and their motley gangs of defenders, some in national guard uniform and others in black with Calabrian peaked hats, all chattering as wildly as the deputies. After a while he met Gabriele Pepe and asked him: 'General, why doesn't the national guard obey the orders of the chamber?' 'I have spoken to these gentlemen,' he replied, 'and they refuse to listen to me. Try and tell them yourself!' 'What am I, compared with you, General?' Whereupon a young man he knew approached with a fanatical gleam in his eye and spluttered: 'Whoever speaks of removing the barricades is a traitor and I shall shoot him.' And he pointed his gun at Pepe, who jerked it deftly upwards as if it were an insect, saying: 'Don't be silly,' and walked away with his back turned. Settembrini seized the young man's arm and said: 'Do you realize whom you have been threatening with your gun? Have you ever heard of Gabriele Pepe? He is a gallant soldier whose chest is covered with scars and who has defended the honour of Italy against the Frenchman Lamartine when he insulted us. He is a great and wise citizen, a man of unique virtue, before whom you and I should both kneel.' The young man turned pale and said: 'To-day we have all gone mad.'

Soon after 11 a.m. the firing began. Two shots rang out near the royal palace. One of the royal guards was killed, another fell wounded. There was a loud clapping of hands, and Mileti shouted: 'Now we're in for it, brothers. At last we can fight for ourselves and the fatherland.' Without waiting for orders the troops camping on the square started firing at the rebels, who fired back to renewed applause from neighbouring balconies. It took half an hour to destroy the first and most solid barricade, whose defenders withdrew into the adjacent Cirella palace to discharge their weapons from padded windows. The inmates, who had felt so safe behind their mattresses, were very indignant when it was their turn to be slaughtered. The palace had seemed impregnable. Firing on the troops had been such fun while it lasted. This was not playing the game. Then the fort of Sant' Elmo thundered thrice, but only with powder, and hoisted the red flag, a signal for the garrison to take up arms. General Roberti, the commander of the fort, had refused to obey orders, preferring to lose his post, as Guglielmo Pepe wrote, 'rather than commit an infamous fratricide'; Major Zanetti obeyed in his stead. 'What are you doing?' the general asked him. 'My duty,' answered the major. But it was the general who won the plaudits of the historians. The red banner was not hoisted a moment too soon. The King, who had been watching the castle anxiously in fear of betrayal, heaved a sigh of relief. 'The first shots gave him back all his resolution,' wrote a Swiss officer in a report of these events. After three months of agonizing doubt the King's self-confidence had suddenly returned. When his startled ministers mustered courage to see him during a lull that morning, he asked: 'Are you satisfied now that you have thrown the country into civil war?' 'It may still be remedied,' they replied, 'if Your Majesty deigns to order a cease fire.' But it was the King's turn to say: 'Too late.' According to some he snapped: 'Mind your own business!' and added in Latin: 'For you too the day of justice is at hand.' Be that as it may, they confessed their impotence and resigned *en bloc*.

Guglielmo Pepe wrote indignantly: 'The diplomatic corps all repaired to the King's palace, even including Lord Napier, who on the 29th of January had shown himself so favourable to the cause of liberty. Not one of these diplomatists said a syllable to persuade the King to put a stop to the inhuman slaughter, and give orders for the troops to return to their quarters.' But the cause of liberty had degenerated into licence and anarchy. The ministry and the deputies had shown too clearly that they were unfit for responsible government. Was it a mere coincidence that this revolt had broken out soon after 17,000 of the best Neapolitan troops had left the kingdom?

The diplomatic corps had had considerable difficulty in reaching the royal palace on foot. The Spanish ambassador, acting as their spokesman, offered the King sympathy and moral support, and the King, thanking him with his hand on his heart called Heaven to witness that all this was happening in spite of himself. 'God only knows what I suffer!' he exclaimed. This was visible in his features, for he looked haggard and worn and his hair had turned quite grey. Nobody would have suspected that he was only thirty-eight. He paced up and down the room with elephantine tread. 'From time to time Ferdinand stopped and said to those who were about him, or to such of the corps of foreign diplomatists as kept arriving—"Gentlemen, I did not expect this! I have not deserved this of my people! I have granted the Constitution, and I intend faithfully to maintain it! I have granted everything—I have done everything to avoid bloodshed; and now they blockade me and my family in my own house." When the troops moved, and the firing began at the great barricade at the end of the Toledo, scarcely two hundred yards from the palace, he was still more agitated, though evidently not by personal fear, for which there was not, during the whole day, the slightest ground. To a general officer who came up for instructions, he said, in the hearing of hundreds— "Spare my misguided people! Make prisoners! Do not kill! Make prisoners!" A little later, when the signal-guns were first beginning to roar in the streets, a superior officer came in and asked permission to take military possession of that great pile of building . . . containing the War and Finance offices, and nearly all the public offices of the state (Palazzo San Giacomo, on Piazza Municipio), "With that building well filled with troops," said the officer, "I promise Your Majesty that we will soon reduce this canaille (*canaglia*) to reason." The King stepped up to him, and putting his hand on his shoulder, said, "Be calm, sir, and do not call the people *canaglia*! They are Neapolitans— they are my countrymen and subjects! They are misguided by a few bad men; but they are still my people!" And when the officer was taking his departure with the necessary order Ferdinand called him back and again said, "Be calm! If you allow yourself to be transported with passion there will be great slaughter, and this I would by all means avoid! Take prisoners, but do not kill! There are many now in the streets who by to-morrow will repent of their error!" '[1]

A cheerful sun shone on scenes of hideous carnage. Almost every Neapolitan family had some relative involved in the conflict. Apparently the radicals had imagined that the Swiss, being republicans, would mutiny; some of them had fraternized with the national guards, whose first battalion was quartered in Via Santa Brigida, not far from the royal palace. Here the most solid barricade had been erected, and every window had a mattress with at least one gun behind it. When

[1] Charles MacFarlane, *A Glance at Revolutionized Italy*. London, 1849.

two companies of Swiss grenadiers and fusiliers marched up the street, loud voices cheered them but warned them not to advance. 'Switzers, go back!' But Captain de Muralt leapt on to the barricade. 'Halt, Captain, or you're a dead man!' shouted someone behind the mountain of obstructions. De Muralt, who had distinguished himself for valour in the French expedition to Constantine, raised his sword and rallied his company: '*En avant!*' 'So you're determined to die?' a voice yelled while a shot rang out. De Muralt was wounded in a hand: three fingers were blown away. 'It is nothing,' he called, 'forward!' There was a hail of bullets from all the upper balconies. This time De Muralt was wounded in the shoulder-blade. 'It is nothing, comrades. Forward!' he repeated. 'You really want to die!' barked the same voice from the barricade—reputedly that of a Sicilian doctor called Mollica. De Muralt fell face downwards, shot in the forehead. Many other assailants were killed and wounded before the barricade of Santa Brigida was demolished. The Swiss fought with greater ferocity in consequence. Few lives were spared in the houses from which they had received such lethal fire. The reprisals were merciless. The horrors of that day have certainly not defied description, since descriptions of them abound. They are too wearisome to bear repetition, but *cela n'empêche pas*. There is even a set of artless water-colours illustrating a few salient episodes: these were painted by Dr Quadri, an eccentric eye-surgeon, and published by Professor Gino Doria with an amusing commentary.

To see such a conflict steadily and see it whole was beyond the capacity of any individual chronicler, but Settembrini's account best conveys its tragic futility. 'To-day we are all mad,' his young friend had remarked, but he, too, could not resist joining the lunatics. Before the Montemiletto palace he heard his name called out: 'Where are you going? Come in here; further on there is danger.' It was Filippo Cappelli of Reggio, who clutched his arm and said: 'We shall fight from the houses: this has been decided, everybody is doing the same. Don't you see that there isn't a soul on the street?' So Settembrini accompanied him. Upstairs he found Errico Sannia, a mummer from the Fiorentini theatre in the uniform of a national guard, with several he did not know. He looked out from a balcony: a blue sky, brilliant sunshine, the Toledo was deserted, the barricades were without defenders, a cannon thundered from the royal palace, and from all the neighbouring houses rose a shout: 'Death to the Bourbon!' He remarked to Cappelli: 'They answer the cannon with shouting.' 'But also with fire.' 'What's the use of it, and what are those barricades? They are obstacles made by boys: a cannon will shatter them. It was stupid to put them up, especially in the broadest and longest street. Masaniello also fought from barricaded streets, but he saw that they were too narrow for cannon and cavalry. We have built barricades where there is ample space for walking, just to imitate the French.' 'You are right, but here we are, and we must do our duty.' 'We'll do our duty, we'll even obey a few fools and madmen. God prevent us from going to our ruin.'

Their conversation was punctuated with explosions.

'The Prince of Montemiletto had kindly sent us refreshments and while we were taking them we heard: *Viv' o rre*—"Long live the King!"—that terrible cry of the populace after plunder, the cry of '99. The Swiss soldiers were coming up Via San Giacomo, and from the Lieto palace opposite there were several gunshots. Cannon fired in reply, shattering a corner of the building, and a dense fusillade followed. We then saw the Swiss, whose cannon had burst open the great entrance, rush furiously in. At this moment the Prince appeared with a dazed expression and said to us: "Gentlemen, you see the Lieto palace; further resistance is useless. If you fire we shall all be slaughtered, and the house will be sacked and burnt down. I beg you not for my sake but for that of my wife who has long been ill, and is now suffering from serious convulsions. Resistance at present is futile: save yourselves for better times." The sight of the Lieto palace, the incessant firing, the raucous shouts of the rabble, persuaded us to stay where we were. The Prince led us to a secret part of the house and, dressed in the uniform of a royal chamberlain, had his front door opened wide and presented himself to the soldiers. He told them that there were no national guards within, and he was believed and treated with respect. He was also thanked for the wine which he had distributed. . . .'

Another eye-witness, Federico Persico, described the Swiss bursting into the Lieto palace, from whose windows they had been decimated. Edmondo Morbillo, a brave and handsome young nephew of the notorious police commissioner, and the deputy Enrico Castellano, had been shooting from the balconies with other national guards. When the front door collapsed Morbillo took refuge on an inside platform of a well, but the planks gave way and he was drowned. Castellano climbed down a rope into a deserted side-street and escaped, lacerating his hands in the process: they were bandaged when Persico went to see him several days later. According to Persico these young intellectuals could not resist shooting at the foreign mercenaries 'who differed from us in language, religion, and customs, yet who were paid with our money and were ready to shoot us if necessary.' That the Neapolitans, even when they were political opponents, helped each other against the Swiss is illustrated by one of Dr Quadri's water-colours. Captain Felicetti, adjutant of the royal guard, saw a platoon of Swiss soldiers marching off a prisoner to execution, and recognized him as the relation of a friend. He rebuked them for maltreating an unarmed citizen who had not resisted them in any way and showed no signs of belonging to the national guard. The Swiss replied that they were sure he was a national guard from the port district who had fired on their comrades. They proceeded to search him in Felicetti's presence and found dozens of cartridges as well as the brass badge hidden in his hat. But Felicetti would not give in; he insisted on their consigning the prisoner to himself. The Swiss were amenable to persuasion, and Captain Felicetti sent the prisoner safely home.

One of the last heavy barricades stood before the fine sixteenth-century Gravina palace near Monteoliveto.[1] This belonged to the radical deputy Giuseppe Ricciardi and served as the headquarters of the rebellious opposition. It was defended by volleys of musketry from the upper storey windows, so that when the Swiss and royal guards under Major Alessandro Nunziante were able to penetrate the courtyard they were in a vindictive mood. All the inmates caught with muskets hot in their hands were slaughtered and over fifty were arrested, though many escaped through secret passages or climbed over walls at the back as the troops entered in front. The roof caught fire—some said because the inmates had been burning seditious publications, others because the lazzaroni had thrown a firebrand into one of the attics—and the flames destroyed the whole top floor before the troops were able to extinguish them. The smoke drifted into the hall where the deputies were sitting, some still hopeful, but most of them too bewildered to decide what to do next. Zuppetta dramatically appeared with a collection of bullets, still red-hot, which he flung

---

[1] Built *circa* 1540 by an unknown architect, it was used as the Post Office before 1860 and is now the seat of the University Faculty of Architecture.

before them saying: 'Behold the King's generous gifts to his people!' Some fancied that the French had landed and that the King had fled. Others proposed a provisional government to be called the Committee of Public Safety. The chamber was declared to be in permanent session, and published a statement accordingly. The national guard was to come under the Committee of Public Safety which was to report continuously to the Chamber about the progress of operations and issue decrees. The Committee, composed of five deputies, set to work by informing the ministry of these decisions and appealing to Admiral Baudin to mediate, but he refused. It also sent a peremptory message to General Labrano, commander of the garrison, 'demanding why the conflict between the troops and citizens had started, and insisting that all violence should cease immediately.' The General replied that the troops had taken up arms in self-defence after serious provocation, but that he was most anxious to co-operate with the Chamber in order to end this catastrophe. The Committee then sent him two deputies to negotiate an armistice, but owing to the blockades and the street-fighting none of these envoys returned.

Most of the deputies lingered on in the hall of Monteoliveto until an officer presented himself in the King's name and ordered them to dissolve. It was seven o'clock in the evening. They were quietly escorted to their houses by gendarmes, except the round dozen who sought asylum on French ships. Saliceti fled to Rome. The flight of these deputies seemed a spontaneous confession of guilt. Before they dispersed a protest was written by Pasquale Mancini and smuggled out by Stefano Romeo for future publication, after being signed by sixty-six deputies. According to this protest to the nation, to Italy, and to the whole of civilized Europe, the Chamber had been attacked 'with unheard of infamy by the violence of royal arms, and in the inviolable persons of the sovereign representatives of the nation . . . and declared that it had only adjourned because constrained by brute force; but, far from abandoning its solemn duties, it had dissolved momentarily to meet again wherever and whenever it could do so, in order to take those measures which are demanded by the rights of the people,' etc. etc. Many of the deputies whose names appeared on this document were to deny having signed it. Several swore that they had never heard of it.

Outside Monteoliveto the struggle also went on till evening, when the troops laid down their arms and bivouacked along the Toledo and on various public squares. About six hundred prisoners had been taken to three frigates in the bay for their own safety: they were soon pardoned and released. The most prominent rebels had scuttled; those who remained went into hiding, shaved their long whiskers and disguised themselves as royalists. As soon as it was possible to protect property against plunder this was done, but it had been impossible to prevent pillage in the heat of attack, and the houses of prominent radicals fell a natural prey to what Pepe called 'the dregs of the populace.' With so much else to do, the police could not keep an eye on all the roving bands of lazzaroni in quest of loot.

'That night was steeped in anguish,' wrote Settembrini, who had crept home to his wife and children through dark deserted streets. 'Not a light appeared in the city, not a voice was heard: it seemed a tomb. It was the silence of dread. The shouts of *Viva il Re* still rang in my ears and I thought: "How many must have been killed! And what of tomorrow? The populace is unbridled: they will attack private houses and slaughter all their inmates. And all on account of a few boobies who wanted the barricades, not indeed to fight but to frighten an angry man who had soldiers and cannon and the soul of a Bourbon; and they expected to drive him away with shouts and threats. They have given him what he lacked, the consciousness of his strength. He feared us: now he despises us, because he has seen that we are quarrelsome, weak and cowardly. They wanted to ape the French and thought they would make Ferdinand run like Louis-Philippe. . . . But an enemy cannot be chased away with shouting: arms and men and strategy should have been prepared. . . . A hundred men properly led would have fought and won. What did Palermo do, or Milan? What has Naples done? Barricades! bloody childishness. Not Naples, but a few drunken lunatics have ruined everything. And all on account of an oath as to whether the Constitution should be altered or not. Oh lawyers, oh *paglietti*!—(Neapolitan nickname from the black straw hats they used to wear)—you deserve slavery. What will tomorrow bring?" '

According to the official *Journal of the Two Sicilies*, about one hundred and thirty people were killed, but this is too conservative an estimate. A Swiss officer calculated that there were more than 1900 victims on both sides. There were many more wounded, especially at the barricades and in the houses attacked by the Swiss, but a large number of these were treated by private doctors in great secrecy. There is no truth in the legend that the King turned to the lazzaroni and said: 'Naples is yours!' Undoubtedly the lazzaroni, who loved their King almost as much as San Gennaro, took this patriotic perquisite for granted and helped themselves. The Swiss were also accused of pillage. This has been refuted by the respectable Colonel de Riedmatten, who made a systematic inspection of his regiment and only discovered a stolen watch, for which the culprit was punished with a flogging.

When Major Nunziante reported to the King that all resistance was over, he is said to have embraced the Queen and exclaimed: 'Let us go at once and thank the Holy Virgin of the Carmine. I shall give tokens of my gratitude to all those who fought for me.' He had gained far more than he had lost on this tragic day. Since January 29 he had granted concession after concession; in spite of his private reservations he had given the liberals their chance, and what had they done with it? Owing to the mess they had made, a steady tide of opinion had turned in his favour. More and more of his subjects agreed that it would be better to restore his absolute authority. For an autocrat with an innate conviction of his divine right he had shown remarkable moderation until he was actually threatened with civil war.

It was absurd to pretend, as his opponents did, that he and a *camarilla* of Court reactionaries had deliberately provoked the insurrection in order to drown the Constitution in blood and recall the troops from the north. The deputies and the national guard were the chief culprits. But even if it had been converted into a victory for the King, that day contained the virus of defeat, and the downfall of his dynasty can be traced to its repercussions. Unfortunately it helped to emphasize his less amiable qualities and to narrow his political views: he never entirely recovered from the shock. Charles de Mazade,[1] a keen-eyed contemporary, wrote: 'Within a few hours he had made an important discovery: he had seen that his army was loyal and that this revolution, looked full in the face, was not so formidable as others supposed. May 15th was more than a Neapolitan day, for it had a European significance and threw light on a dark situation. Till then the revolution had seemed irresistible, striding from capital to capital

[1] *Op. cit.*

244

amid the collapse of governments and vacillations of dazed opinion. On the same day, at the same time, in Naples and in Paris, it was suddenly stopped by a mysterious force. This was the beginning of all contemporary reactions, soon as unlimited and violent as the revolution itself; and it was from Naples that the signal was sent. A virile defence was necessary, and Ferdinand won European prestige by his vigorous initiative. He contributed towards breaking the formidable spell of revolution. With his pride and love of power he must have derived a secret satisfaction from his recovered sense of freedom.'

XII

Loyalists rewarded—National guard disbanded—Martial law—Flight of deputies—Insurrection in Calabria—The Neapolitan troops recalled from North Italy—Sicilian expedition to Calabria—The crown of Sicily offered to the Duke of Genoa—Opening of Parliament at Naples—Extinction of Calabrian revolt—A rejected address: Parliament prorogued—Filangieri's expedition to Sicily—Bombardment and surrender of Messina—French and English intervention.

THE King had regained full power, and intended to keep it. No more compromise with the radicals after the mad excesses and dissensions of the last three months, culminating in the catastrophe of May 15. Ferdinand had been the first of Italian sovereigns to grant a Constitution, but this had been attributed to cowardice and the radicals had imagined that they could strip him of all his rights. The experiment having failed, he was proud of being the first to dam the revolutionary flood.

On the same day a new cabinet was formed, which published the following proclamation: 'An act of flagrant illegality occurred in this capital on the night of May 14/15: in order to foster unmerited distrust of the royal government, barricades were erected in the middle of public streets with the criminal aim of subverting order and causing bloodshed among the citizens. It is deplorable that part of the national guard, which should have protected the safety and tranquillity of families, not only took part in this regrettable tumult but itself launched an attack against the royal militia, which seeing its comrades suddenly fall under fratricidal fire, resorted to the sacred right of self-defence, and impelled by a just but irrepressible indignation retaliated against force with force. After several hours of lamentable strife most of those who tried to overthrow the State were defeated and dispersed. Calm

246

has already been restored and the most vigorous measures have been taken to investigate the true origin of so criminal an attempt, discover its authors, invoke the justice of the law upon their heads, and publish all the facts in detail. Respectable citizens may rest assured that a stricter vigilance will be kept by the royal government so that no disorder of the same kind will be repeated in future or new obstacles be opposed illegally to the maintenace and full exercise of those liberties which the Constitution has solemnly established and which His Majesty is firmly resolved to protect in all their inviolable integrity. . . .'

The reference to the Constitution is noteworthy. Had it been abolished that morning nobody would have been surprised. Popular feeling was against it. Early on May 16 a fanatical mob marched through the streets with white banners and images of the Madonna. 'Down with the Constitution!' they shouted, 'Long live the King!' They came to a halt before the royal palace and called for their beloved sovereign, who thanked them with affectionate words and gestures from his balcony, but he let them know that the Constitution was still valid. In the afternoon he reviewed various regiments inside and outside the city and went as far as Portici to visit the wounded there. He was received with frantic acclamations. Among the cheers many voices urged him to abolish the Constitution. On his return to the palace he summoned all his generals, thanked them for their loyal support and asked them to convey his gratitude to the troops. After paying tribute to the fallen he promised to reward those who had distinguished themselves for gallantry.

A few days later these rewards were granted with so lavish a hand that the liberals were outraged. Lord Napier wrote: 'Distinctions were conferred on the officers and ranks, and double pay for a month was issued to all. For this the King himself is principally responsible. Prince Cariati, an honourable soldier, opposed it in Council, for he thought with justice that all traces of such an unhappy civil conflict should be effaced, and that had the army even performed its distressing duty with all the clemency possible in such a struggle, it ought still never to have borne the insignia of a triumph. But the army, both Swiss and Neapolitan, were guilty of great excesses of rapacity and cruelty, and although these may have been exaggerated by common rumour they were certainly such as to merit severe investigation and punishment, and the very officers were not exempt from imputations of conniving at these abuses, and consequently the King in conferring honours and emoluments and in a manner absurdly lavish and indiscriminate, seemed certainly to identify himself with the acts of his agents whom he ought rather to have disavowed and brought to justice.' It must be remembered that Lord Napier belonged to the opposition. The King, like most of his subjects, felt relieved from a ghastly incubus.

The national guard was disarmed and disbanded; martial law was declared; and the opening of parliament was postponed till the first of July. The press was muzzled provisionally: in any case most of the subversive editors had fled or gone into hiding. Among lighter newspapers the *Omnibus* continued publication. 'On May 15th,' it wrote a few days later, 'between blood and terror, we had another lesson about the tendencies of our populace. The great reformers were enlightened as to its glorious possibilities and could therefore realize what to expect in future! When the national guards fired on the troops from the barricades the populace was seen to side with them because a short while previously they had paid them to build these obstructions. As soon as the troops gained the upper hand the populace began to stone the national guards. When the latter were thrown into confusion the populace followed the troops, assaulted private houses, sacked them and shattered their contents, then secretly made off with the booty to their dens. . . .' A few 'generous actions' of the populace were also recorded. The porters of one district, for instance, fell upon the looters with clubs.

The most radical and republican deputies fled with their bands of armed henchmen to their native provinces, especially to Calabria, where they started an insurrection. On May 18 a 'committee of safety' was formed at Cosenza, and on May 19 another was formed at Catanzaro. The Palermo parliament ordered three days' mourning for the events of May 15 as well as public prayers in all the churches, and published a decree offering asylum to all those 'persecuted by Neapolitan tyranny.' In spite of much talk about rearmament their initial success had made the Sicilians too complacent. When a deputy proposed on May 22 that the chamber should take vigorous steps to defend the country, the president replied that Sicily was always prepared to repel any attack. One expedition of volunteers had left for Lombardy; another was ready to aid the Neapolitan people in their struggle against Ferdinand.

Whatever Ferdinand's feelings about Charles Albert, the civil war gave him sufficient reason to recall his troops from the north, which he did on May 18. He is still abused for this. Settembrini wrote that 'to recall the troops from the war of independence was a base, stupid, infamous and cowardly betrayal which resulted in great disasters for Italy, and another ten years of servitude and sorrow. . . . King Ferdinand betrayed Italy thinking he would save his crown: twelve years later the whole of Italy descended on his kingdom and expelled the Bourbons. All human faults and follies contain the causes of the punishment which must overtake them sooner or later.' But Settembrini was wise after the event. It is by no means certain that, as Pepe wrote, 'the co-operation of his army during all the month of June would have infallibly decided the liberation of Italy from foreign yoke.' Even Lord Napier considered the recall of the troops from Lombardy as an act of sound discretion. 'There never can be peace or alliance between the popular faction and the King of Naples,' he wrote, meaning by popular faction those who were detested by the people. 'They may spare him while he can be useful to their aims . . . they will ever nourish a secret or a declared determination to cast him down. Nothing that he can do will ever appease their enmity.' Prophetic words!

Ferdinand was essentially practical, and the safety of his own kingdom came first. Why should he make sacrifices for the ambitious Charles Albert while Sicily and Calabria were in revolt? Characteristically General Guglielmo Pepe, who was then in Bologna, decided to disobey the King's order. On the same day he received it, May 22, he informed the Minister of War at Turin that notwithstanding his instructions he was ready to cross the Po and place his forces at the disposal of Charles Albert.

Pepe had been given the alternative of returning with his army, or else resigning its command to General Statella. The Neapolitan volunteers might, if they desired it, join the Papal forces under General Durando. Knowing that the troops were devoted to the King, Pepe at first resigned to Statella, who promptly ordered the different corps to go home. 'In the meantime,' wrote Pepe, 'news of the orders from Naples spread along the Italian shore, and it was said that my life was in great peril. When a multitude of officers came running to defend me, I asked them if they would also have assisted me in preventing the troops from returning, which not only diminished the numbers of the defenders of Italy, but sent fresh aid to despotism in Naples against the liberals who had risen in favour of Neapolitan liberty.

'The brave among the national guard put their hands on their swords, saying, "This is for you, Italian General!" and I, grasping my own sword, added, "This is for Italy as long as I live!" . . . Without losing an instant, I wrote and declared to Lieutenant-General Statella that he must regard the letter I sent him, ceding to him the command of the troops, *as not received*—that I had resolved to resume the command. Statella not only resigned the command-in-chief, which I had conferred on him, but . . . declared that it did not suit him to serve any longer.'

To King Ferdinand and Ischitella, the Minister of War, Pepe wrote that he would neither send nor lead the troops back to Naples, since this would be fatal to Italian independence, and would dishonour them for ever. 'Will it be believed,' he added naively, 'that for a long time neither the King nor the Minister answered my letters, though they blamed my conduct and repeated to those around them the orders which had been sent to me.' We are faced with two irreconcilable points of view. 'I showed a king,' wrote Pepe, 'that the love of country can make the bread of exile sweeter than the highest favours.' And, in an order of the day exhorting his army to cross the Po: 'A general-in-chief has the right of modifying, on his own responsibility, the orders he receives from his Government; above all, when these modifications have in view the national honour and the King's interest.' Naturally the King considered himself the best judge of his own honour and interest. To him love of country meant love of Naples. Piedmont was as foreign as Austria, though each in turn had provided him with a spouse.

When Pepe told his troops that they would be fighting in a noble cause, they invariably added, 'and for our King!' It was scarcely surprising therefore that the majority preferred to obey the latter, whose cause they considered theirs. 'It was not prudent for me to send troops which had not yet broken discipline against such a numerous rebellion,' sighed Pepe. A Bolognese patriot tried to persuade the populous cities on the highway to Ancona to let their national guards attack the returning Neapolitans during the night, 'but their artillery inspired too much fear in these communities.' There were several acute cases of divided loyalty, however, among officers who wavered between obedience to the King or to their ideal of Italian patriotism. Brigadier Lahalle was so distracted that he shot himself. Only two battalions, a small force of artillery, and some volunteers, accompanied Pepe to Venice.

Conditions in Calabria were favourable to anarchy. A rusty feudalism still survived though nominally it had been abolished, and in many districts there was chronic poverty and unemployment. The people were pugnacious individualists. The aristocracy had ceased to be patriarchal: most of them had drifted to the capital while their rapacious agents supplanted them in wealth and influence. With the best of intentions the King alone could not cure the economic diseases of this backward region, which required more drastic reforms than the patchwork measures of a paternal protectionism, such as control of prices, reduction of taxes, and public works to relieve unemployment. But the King was harshly criticized by the rising bourgeoisie who fancied that they could do better, for themselves at any rate. These were temperamentally attuned to the writings of Mazzini and of their own Benedetto Musolino, a rich republican of Pizzo who had founded the 'Sons of Young Italy' sect. To a minor extent they were also influenced by the socialist theories of Saint-Simon and Fourier, but they remained Carbonari at heart with a penchant for conspiracy and secret societies.

The Calabrian deputies who had been largely responsible for the barricades at Naples, still regarded themselves as the legal representatives of the people. After their sudden dispersal they made Cosenza their headquarters. Here a new 'Committee of Public Health' was organized on June 3 under the quixotic Giuseppe Ricciardi. 'On one point,' wrote Ferdinando Petrucelli, 'there was general agreement: the proscription of the Bourbon dynasty.' Regional historians have lingered over the details of this insurrection with more passion than sense of proportion. 'The Sicilian expedition to Calabria,' wrote Beltrani-Scalia,[1] 'is an event of such importance that it cannot be left without special mention. Naturally, every writer who has described its adventures has given his narrative a different political hue, so that there have been many errors and exaggerations, which make it very difficult to

[1] Martino Beltrani-Scalia, *Rivoluzione di Sicilia*. Rome, 1932.

reconstruct the truth. It will suffice to note, for instance, that while Poerio says the expedition consisted of 2000 men with eight cannon, the latter are reduced to seven and even six by others; and the number of combatants is whittled down to barely 500 by Ricciardi, to 380 by Pier Silvestro Leopardi, to 300 by the Bourbonist Rossi.'

Ricciardi assured the Sicilians that the irregular forces in Calabria were more than a match for the royal army, and the Sicilians were inclined to believe him. Whatever they pretended, they could never feel absolutely free while the citadel of Messina remained under Ferdinand's control. All their attempts to capture it had failed: the royal fleet continued to supply it with victuals and ammunition, and the garrison was incorruptible. Their present aim was to occupy Reggio and the opposite coast, and blockade the citadel with their batteries. Ricciardi's was more ambitious: he hoped to emulate the triumphs of Cardinal Ruffo and march on Naples with the banner of Italy. Ignazio Ribotti, who was put in charge of the Sicilian force after a picaresque career in Portugal, France, the Papal States and Spain, was a citizen of Nice like Garibaldi; he was a comparative stranger to Sicily and he knew even less about Calabria, which dealt him a rude shock. On June 12 his expedition sailed from Milazzo on two steamers, the *Lily of the Waves* and the *Vesuvius*, but at the last moment there were many desertions. On the 13th they caught sight of a Neapolitan steamer and made a hasty landing at Stromboli to avoid capture. Here another large batch of volunteers insisted on going home. Ribotti sent them back on the *Lily of the Waves*, and embarked on the *Vesuvius* with about six hundred men, almost half the original force.

They landed at Paola on June 14. Musolino and other Calabrian leaders were suspicious of their intentions from the start. Even Ribotti's subordinate Colonel Longo criticized their 'lack of energy and audacity'. General Ferdinando Nunziante had landed at Pizzo on June 6 with 2000 royal troops and occupied Monteleone, the chief town in the district, without any opposition; and on June 10 another 3000 landed at Sapri and marched to Castrovillari, so that the rebels were soon caught between two fires.

Ribotti had scarcely touched ground before he received four different messages from Costabile Carducci, Mileti, Colonel Longo, and La Corte, president of the committee of Paola: one to avoid combat since the royal troops were at Sapri; another urging an attack on Castrovillari; the third urging an attack on Monteleone; and the fourth, on behalf of the central committee begging him to send a division with six cannon to Cosenza and the rest to Campotenese. At the same time one of his officers complained of the insubordination of the Messina and Palermo squadrons, and Musolino complained of 'muddle and scandals' in his camp at Filadelfia, where there were no regular supplies, no lodgings or means of transport, and the soldiers were bored and disgusted. 'Enthusiasm is damped;' he wrote on June 16, 'desertions will soon reduce us to complete disintegration.' Yet Colonel Longo, who was also in Filadelfia, wrote in a more sanguine strain, all eagerness to fight the foe.

From the documents published by Marulli,[1] it would appear that there was verbal rather than physical combat. To keep their spirits up the Cosenza committee continued to spread reports of imaginary victories. Ribotti proceeded with the utmost caution. He had little enough confidence in his own troops, while more and more of the Calabrians deserted as the harvest season approached. There was guerrilla activity through the month of June, but the royal garrisons had been strengthened in all three provinces of Calabria. The finances of the insurgents became desperate. Knowing every inch of their territory the guerrillas had occasional advantages over the Neapolitans, but their forays were usually futile. The natives who depended on the Mongiana arms factory for their livelihood, were exasperated when they destroyed all the machinery, which had been imported from England at great expense. Moderate liberals were alarmed by the increasing violence of peasants against landowners. On June 10, for instance, the vice-mayor of Cellara reported to the Cosenza committee that 'all these inhabitants, except a few men of honour, supposing there to be no more laws or security for the lives and property of citizens, continuously threaten to give way to those excesses which are dangerous to everyone, and to municipal employees in particular.' They seized Church and public property, waving banners and beating drums. These spontaneous anarchists were immune to liberal ideals; many of them had a vague affection for the King, feeling that he would protect them against landlords whose avarice was more apparent than their liberalism.

[1] Gennaro Marulli, *Documenti storici riguardanti l'Insurrezione Calabra.* Naples, 1849.

The Cosenza committee became acutely aware of its isolation. Its propaganda often recoiled like a boomerang, as when towns and villages which had surrendered turned treacherously against the royal troops, who retaliated with regrettable ruthlessness. After occupying Catanzaro, Nicastro and Tiriolo, Nunziante was joined by General Busacca's column from the north which had entered Cosenza on July 7. The republican committee had escaped to Corfu on July 3, but Musolino and Mileti made despairing attempts to galvanize resistance by promising their followers more pay and a new era of remunerative revolution, to begin with the sacking and burning of royalist property. As Nunziante's host drew nearer Mileti was left to shift for himself. Mauro accused Ribotti of corresponding with defeatist citizens in Castrovillari who wished to reach a shameful settlement with the enemy—'a suspicion which, even if unfounded, provokes distrust and discouragement among our men.'

The wretches who had to bear the brunt of it were sick of civil war. Ricciardi, the would-be dictator, wanted them to fight on in the woods of Sila together with the Sicilian volunteers, but Ribotti, albeit a veteran of fiercer battles, had had quite enough. After a dangerous obstacle race in the midst of a frightened and hostile people, the Sicilians embarked on the night of July 6. On the 11th they were captured by the Neapolitan ship *Stromboli* and taken to the fortress of Nisida. The method of their capture infuriated Lord Napier, who wrote on July 17: 'A report having reached me yesterday morning that the *Stromboli* employed Her Majesty's Flag to deceive and surprise the Sicilians, I consequently lost no time in discovering the manner in which that unnecessary artifice had been used. . . . When the *Stromboli* came in sight she had no colours; on approaching the Sicilian brig she hoisted the British Flag. The Sicilians who had no food or water and had suffered the greatest hardships, abandoned themselves to joy, and displayed the Sicilian Ensign which they raised and lowered three times as a salute to their supposed deliverer. On this the *Stromboli* hauled down the British Flag and replaced it by their own, having fired two shots, took possession of the brig. . . .' This led to protests from the Sicilian representatives in London, but nothing came of them.

When the Sicilian expedition was captured on July 11, the Palermo Parliament sat voting for another sovereign. The choice was less easy than it sounded. Since the exclusion of the Bourbons the only eligible Italian princes were the Duke of Genoa, the younger son of Charles Albert, and the even younger son of the Grand Duke of Tuscany. It was proposed that the crown be offered to Ruggero Settimo, but he was too sensible to accept such a burden. Finally the Duke of Genoa was chosen, and an English steamship suitably called H.M.S. *Porcupine* was sent to Genoa with an official delegation to convey the invitation. Ferdinand instantly warned Turin that acceptance would mean war with Naples. And the fortunes of war were turning against Charles Albert. Consequently he thanked the Sicilians for the honour, but informed them that he could neither accept nor refuse the crown for his son without considering the highest interests of Italy. The Duke of Genoa added that he would obey his father. The subject was allowed to hover, and the Sicilians were kept waiting.

It would have been strange if Ferdinand had submitted passively to the insults from Palermo, and this proposal to palm off his crown on the House of Savoy was the last straw. The salvation of Sicily was paramount, but he wished to make sure that neither England nor France would interfere. England, which in this context meant Palmerston, had announced in June that she would recognize the island as an independent State if the throne were accepted by the Duke of Genoa. France preferred the nine-year-old son of the Grand Duke of Tuscany. At the same time both countries were supposed to be mediating between King Ferdinand and the Sicilians. For all his avowed sympathy with the latter Palmerston was unable to impose recognition of the rebel State upon his own government. Ferdinand shrewdly suspected that this sympathy was platonic. Charles Albert's reverses were changing the international situation. England and France would soon lose their Sicilian fervour, but Ferdinand had to walk warily. Napier reported on July 18: 'Count Ludolf has been despatched to Paris and London on a special mission relative to Sicilian affairs. At Paris he will probably endeavour to sew a jealousy of England, insinuating falsely that it is the policy of Great Britain to acquire an undue ascendancy in Sicily. He will also allege that that island is in a state of disorganization and ruin, and that a large party, disgusted with the revolutionary government, thirsts for the restoration of the King. Such at least is the language of the Court Party at Naples.

'At London Count Ludolf will, like Prince Castelcicala, enlarge on the misfortunes under which Sicily groans. His Excellency is said to have positive and contingent instructions. Among the latter I am assured is numbered . . . a complaint against myself and a request for my recall.'

Knowing where Napier's partiality lay, the Minister for Foreign Affairs politely avoided discussing the subject with him. 'With regard to Prince Cariati, with the most loyal intentions possible and the most benevolent disposition, His Excellency has something so easy and debonair in his way of dealing with matters the most momentous, that I have had great difficulty in fixing him, even for a moment, to a serious consideration of the affairs of Sicily, and I believe that several of his colleagues are still in the old delusion that Her Majesty's Government are actuated by some sinister policy and are driving at some selfish interests in that kingdom, and your Lordship can well credit how difficult it would be to do any good with persons so perverted.'

Fearing a repetition of May 15, there was a large exodus from Naples before the opening of Parliament on July 1. But nothing untoward happened on that day. Most of the shops were shut, and the streets were almost empty. Nearly all the same deputies had been re-elected, but there had been fewer voters: the majority had little desire for representative government. The King was not present, and only seventy-four out of a hundred and sixty-four deputies attended: the rest were skulking or had taken to flight. The Duke of Serracapriola read 'an insignificant discourse with some hesitation,' according to Napier. This was the King's speech, expressing sorrow for the calamities of May 15 and hope that the present occasion might lead to a revival of prosperity. 'I have no reason to believe that our peaceful relations with other Powers have changed in any way,' he said, and called God to witness the purity of his intentions: 'nothing else remains but to invoke you and history as my witnesses.'

Perhaps the speech seemed insignificant because it contained no reference to Sicily or the war of independence. As the opening of Parliament had been so quiet more deputies plucked up courage to attend subsequent meetings. Recovering their audacity, they censured the conduct of General Nunziante in Calabria and the treatment of Sicilian prisoners. Lord Napier, writing on August 2, echoed their views: 'The revolt in Calabria has been completely extinguished but an evil has grown up during and after the contest which has produced great prejudice to private interests, and provoked many indignant comments both in the public of Naples and in the Chamber of Deputies. General Nunziante and his confederate officers found it politic to stir up among the lower orders a party hostile to the insurgents and paralysing the rebellion, so that the royal authority was actually restored rather by intrigue and promises than by military force. . . . General Nunziante has exercised an arbitrary power, in dissolving the national guards and putting weapons into the hands of persons devoted to the royal interest . . . the military power is absolutely predominant, and no element of active resistance is at present prepared against a usurpation on the part of the King.' General Nunziante and the army had cause to resent such unfair criticism. The *Military Journal* more correctly described the fifty-six deputies who had censured them as 'a faction which did not represent the nation . . . and because most of them were implicated in the revolt of May 15, as well as in those of Calabria and the Cilento, the army demands their exclusion from the Chamber.'

Waxing bolder, the deputies voted an address in reply to the King's speech which was as tactless as it was ill-timed. A prompt change of ministry and participation in the war of independence were demanded. The events of May 15 had 'fatally interrupted that complete confidence which should bind the King and his people together.' Ferdinand was tacitly blamed for 'the unexpected and rapid dissolution of the Chamber of Deputies,' and for 'the ignorance in which the people had been obstinately maintained.' That the King rejected such an address is scarcely surprising. The army, most of the clergy, the magistrature, the government and the masses were on his side. After two months of filibustering sessions he prorogued Parliament until November 30.

Calabria pacified, more attention could be paid to Sicily. Since Charles Albert's defeat at Custoza on July 24 there was even less chance that the Duke of Genoa would accept the Sicilian throne, yet the islanders never despaired. The published 'Acts of the General Parliament of Sicily, 1848–49' show that they were luxuriating in a curious Cloud Cuckoo Land. How much time and ingenuity were wasted, for instance, on re-baptizing city streets and squares, ancient and modern, whose names were malicious reminders of the Bourbons; or in deciding precisely where a flag sent from Genoa was to be hoisted, or whether the festival of Saint Rosalia was to be celebrated! 'Sicily had thought of many things,' as de Mazade wrote, 'of everything save arming herself, as if she should never be attacked.' Her historians are wont to blame England for this singular oversight. Prince Granatelli and Luigi Scalia, the Sicilian envoys to London, wrote on July 11 to Baron Friddani, their colleague in Paris: 'Lord Palmerston has repeated to us several times that the salute to our flag is an act of recognition, and has promised that gradually we shall be given others more important.' For these innocents Palmerston personified England, and their optimism was encouraged by Lord Minto, Lord John Russell, and other big Whigs whose personal sympathy seemed to act on them like a drug. But neither England nor France was disposed to enter a war for Sicily's sake.

The Neapolitan press had been clamouring for the reconquest of the rebellious island. According to *Il Tempo*, England would not dare to interfere, and France would only tender advice. But still the Palermo Parliament was reluctant to alarm the country. Perhaps it really seemed more important to suppress the Jesuits who, as elsewhere, managed the only good schools which were open to boys of every class. Gioberti's accusations against them were repeated in Parliament with embellishments by Giuseppe La Farina, whose motion to suppress them was easily carried on July 31. Nothing was done to restore even moderate security. Abductions for ransom and robberies with violence were of daily occurrence, and the public usually knew more than the police about them. 'In such a deplorable situation the voice of humanity was silent,' wrote Beltrani-Scalia. Sicily was even then the headquarters of the *mafia*. To paraphrase a recent authority, Signor Salvatore Palazzolo, the *mafia* is a state of mind, a certain attitude towards social relations almost peculiar to Sicily. Then as now there were many unconscious *mafiosi*, who did not belong to the secret society but helped it to flourish by their passive tolerance and a misguided sense of honour.

The Sicilian press was, if possible, even more polemical than the Neapolitan, and at least one editor was publicly assaulted. His newspaper, *L'Occhiale* ('The Eyeglass'), had heaped ridicule on the officers of the new army, two or three of whom seized the editor, stuck an eyeglass made of cucumber-rind on his nose, plastered the offending publication on his back, and dragged him through the streets of Palermo, accompanied by the catcalls of the mob, until some national guards came to his rescue. This was stigmatized in Parliament as an unworthy attempt against the freedom of the press, and led to the resignation of the Minister of the Interior, Marchese Fulco della Cerda.

Regarding the island defences, the President published an official letter to the Minister of War on July 31, expressing complete satisfaction with the coastal fortifications. The *Memoirs* of Torrearsa, *inter alia*, make it plain that the provisional government were blinded by chauvinistic vanity.

The King chose General Filangieri, a brave and experienced soldier and a highly civilized man, to lead the Sicilian expedition, but he felt uneasy about the ambiguous attitudes of England and France. England had promised to recognize the island as an independent State if the throne were accepted by the Duke of Genoa. In spite of the Austrian victories in North Italy the Sicilians still clung to the hope that the Duke would accept King Ferdinand's crown. Though Palmerston had assured the Neapolitan ambassador 'that Her Britannic Majesty's Government would not offer any kind of impediment to the military expedition which the King was preparing for the purpose of restoring peace and order in Sicily,' as soon as this expedition was ready both Lord Napier and M. de Rayneval, the new French minister, addressed long notes to the Prince of Cariati, 'remonstrating against the known intentions of the King to attempt the reconquest of his Sicilian dominions.'

De Rayneval, writing on August 28, pretended to be chiefly concerned with preventing bloodshed. An attempt by force of arms, the success of which was problematical, he asserted, would only make it more difficult to negotiate in future, and the moment was favourable for a settlement. 'On what terms could a union take place? The two extremes are, on the one hand, absolute independence, to which Sicily aspires, and, on the other hand, the fusion of the two crowns with separate administrations. There is between these two extremes a middle term, which is acceptable. For instance, would a son of the King be welcomed in Sicily?' Though an expedition might not fail altogether, it might produce but little effect, he continued. Both France and England were strongly opposed to it on principle and consequently, 'whatever their feelings on the Italian question, it is much to be feared that those feelings will turn to the detriment of the Neapolitan Court, if the expedition takes place. . . . It is more than probable, in fact, that King Ferdinand . . . may lose in a great measure the support which he would at present find in the two governments if, by taking their wishes into consideration, he essayed by peaceful means to do that which he now aims at effecting by the force of arms.'

Napier's briefer note of August 29 admitted that he was not yet in a position to divulge the intentions of his government, but he was convinced it would deeply deplore the effusion of blood which would doubtless accompany the premature renewal of hostilities. He too spoke as if the expedition were doomed to failure.

The King's reply to these 'friendly proposals' was to speed his expedition, which left Naples on August 30. Torrearsa had but recently informed the Palermo Parliament that there was no danger of a Neapolitan invasion, as the English would never allow it. Having had no orders to oppose it, Admiral Parker sent H.M.S. *Porcupine* to Messina and Palermo to warn the Sicilians that an expedition was already on its way. Torrearsa broke the news to a packed Parliament: 'Gentlemen, I do not come to announce a serious misfortune, but to inform my brave fellow-citizens that we shall very soon have to expel that enemy who wishes to overthrow our fatherland.' He added that 20,000 Neapolitans were coming, but it would only be the struggle of a day. The Sicilians would conquer again. There were unanimous cheers for war. Palermo was illuminated as if for peace. High-spirited manifestos were issued by the government and municipality: 'Let every house become a fortress, every man a soldier, every scrap of iron a weapon. Let the cowards come: the whirlwind of our fury will instantly sweep them away.'

Using Reggio as a base, General Filangieri decided to attack Messina, where royal garrisons still held the citadel and the forts of San Salvatore and Don Blasco dominating the city and the straits. On September 1 he sent notice of approaching hostilities to all the foreign consuls in the coastal towns. Before the bombardment, which started on the 3rd, the Sicilian batteries had fired heavily into a Neapolitan steamer grounded under the citadel, which fired in turn upon the batteries and threw some shells into the town. The captain of an English man of war, H.M.S. *Gladiator*, protested to General Pronio, commander of the citadel, against what he called 'this inhuman and unprovoked aggression'. It was a mere portent of what was to follow. General Filangieri's duty was to take the town, and he took it.

It was hardly to be taken without bloodshed. 'The blood of both the belligerent parties had been heating for months, and was as hot as lava.' Owing to the savage defence the bombardment lasted five days.

Paternò, the Sicilian Minister of War, announced: 'Our glory has begun.' But it was the glory of self-immolation. In the meantime one third of Messina was destroyed. *The Times* correspondent, quoting a letter from 'one of the most respectable British subjects in the island,' said that the worst damage was inflicted on the southern section where the citadel and the insurgents' batteries crossed fire. Over a distance of about three miles not twelve houses had escaped destruction. 'The Messinese made a desperate resistance, but of course they could do nothing against so strong a body of disciplined troops. . . . The national guard, with few exceptions, showed more passion than active courage, and abandoned the city without firing a shot. The constant shower of shot and shells would have, however, disheartened braver people even than the Sicilians. The loss of life has been very great, but it is difficult to come to any true statement of the numbers. Filangieri has admitted to a loss of 1,500 to 1,600 men, besides the killed and wounded in the citadel. 400 of the soldiers were sprung by a mine at the Terranova gate. The English vice-consul at Reggio states that 900 wounded were taken over there from the citadel. . . .'

On September 6 an official proclamation announced to the people of Palermo that the Bourbon assassins had been driven out with bayonets; on the same day at Messina Piraino, 'commissioner of the executive government,' appealed to the captains of the English and French men of war to ask Filangieri for a 24 hours' truce. Filangieri demanded the immediate surrender of the city, a condition which nobody dared to accept. On the 7th he ordered the royal fleet to sail back to Reggio, 'to banish any idea of retreat.' On the same afternoon the Sicilian telegraph, which had been removed to a neighbouring hill, sent the news to Palermo: 'All the batteries are held by the enemy. The city is consumed by fire.' Next day Messina was occupied by the royal troops, but many parts of it were still burning, and owing to the quantity of hidden mines and ammunition—a Dominican monastery had sheltered an imposing arsenal—the Neapolitan sappers took two more days to put out the flames.

After the capture of Messina the whole neighbourhood surrendered to Filangieri. Though a council of war decided to resist to the utmost at Milazzo, the local inhabitants and the Sicilian troops who had withdrawn there from Messina refused to obey this decision. 'Without firing a shot,' wrote Filangieri, 'the whole area extending from Messina to Barcelona, and from the south of Messina to Scaletta, became ours. We gained one hundred and fifty cannon, six thousand muskets, two hundred tons of gunpowder, a great many projectiles, sixteen gunboats, and the *Vesuvio*, the strongest of the Sicilian armoured steamships.' The King sent a special messenger to Filangieri with his own grand cordon of Saint Ferdinand in diamonds. 'Tell him,' he said, 'I am proud that it should pass from my breast to his.'

Sicilian historians have accused the Neapolitans of atrocious cruelties, and *vice versa*. Not content with rape, the royal troops were said to have hacked off the bosoms of their victims, and butchered babies and bedridden invalids. The Sicilians, on the other hand, were said to have roasted and eaten the flesh of at least sixty wounded prisoners, and hawked human offal in the streets, bargaining over freshly torn out tongues for cannibal sandwiches, and pinning Neapolitan ears like rosettes to their buttonholes. Filangieri himself wrote that his dead and wounded were 'obscenely mutilated.'

Messina subdued, the rest of Sicily might have soon been recovered and the civil war ended but for the interference of the French and English admirals at this juncture. These insisted upon a suspension of hostilities 'in the name of humanity.'

'The voice of humanity,' wrote Admiral Parker to Lord Napier, 'imperatively requires that some measure should be taken to prevent the renewal of such shocking scenes of devastation in other parts of Sicily. . . . I am induced to hope that Your Excellency, as a last effort, will insist upon the Neapolitan Government commanding an immediate suspension of hostilities, which may spare me the necessity of adopting measures for the support, by armed force, of an armistice . . . until an appeal can be made to the Government of Her Majesty and her allies for the termination of so afflicting a contest.' Admiral Baudin wrote to M. de Rayneval in the same strain, and General Filangieri was forced into unwilling compliance on September 11. The armistice was announced in Palermo as having been imposed on the King of Naples by England and France, and agreed to by the Sicilian government 'without in any way compromising their cause.'

The Times correspondent, who distinguished himself for his impartiality, asked why the two admirals did not prevent the bombardment of Messina in the first place, if the feelings of humanity were so powerful as they alleged. 'Is it not strange that when the great blow had been struck under their eyes . . . they should have interfered to prevent what no doubt would have taken place—the bloodless occupation of all the other towns on the island coast, save Palermo?' Was it not fair, likewise, he continued, to inquire why the Sicilians were allowed to send a hostile expedition to Calabria in June, and did not that attempted invasion of his *terra firma* justify the King's reprisals? Had the Sicilians a right to rebel which was not conceded to Ireland and Lombardy, or were England and Austria at liberty to hang and to shoot, while Naples was to be reduced to passivity? Admiral Baudin had been very eloquent about the necessity of avoiding bloodshed, but how many lives had General Cavaignac sacrificed in repressing the late insurrection at Paris?

These were questions which also occurred to the King and his ministers. Many Neapolitans thought and said that the French and English admirals had only allowed the attack on Messina because they felt sure that General Filangieri would be trounced. The Prince of Cariati protested in vain against this belated interference as contrary to the rights of sovereignty and the laws of nations. Meanwhile, he wrote, 'the submission of the principal cities of the island is now delayed, thanks to the indirect encouragement of the rebels; so that there is the greater reason to complain inasmuch as the calculations of His Majesty's Government were based on the repeated assurances of the Foreign Ministers of France and England that the national forces of their respective nations would observe the strictest neutrality.'

The King refused to accept mediation officially, but he swallowed the pill unofficially, as it were, for fear of antagonizing France and England. This resulted in a situation which became more and more complicated. A whole volume would be required to follow the diplomatic maze of which Naples, Palermo, Paris and London were the intersecting paths, but it would be exceedingly tedious and inconclusive.

On behalf of the two admirals the naval officers at Messina settled lines of demarcation, separated by a neutral ground, which were to be respected by the belligerents. Certain ports were also selected, which were to be open to the vessels of each flag. The Neapolitans held Messina and Milazzo, with the north coast, to Termini, and the coasts of the Faro di Messina as far south as Scaletta; while the line of demarcation for the other side began at Capo Tindaro and extended in nearly a straight line to Taormina. Secret orders were given to the naval commanders to intervene by force, should hostilities be renewed.

Filangieri's expedition was therefore paralysed after his initial victory. The Palermo government was given another chance to recruit its strength, to bring in war supplies, and improve its defences. French and Polish officers arrived to drill, discipline and command the untrained Sicilians.

While the diplomats exchanged equivocating notes Filangieri made strenuous efforts to restore what is called normal life to battered Messina. He announced through the mayor Marchese di Cassibile, who was promptly declared a traitor by Palermo, that the King had forgotten the past errors of his people and had granted the most ample pardon to all except the leaders of rebellion. Messina was to be a free port; those whose property had been damaged were relieved from all taxation; the rest were relieved from half taxation without exception. And as if to chime in a happier age, a huge bronze bell was solemnly restored to the city's most popular church. 'This bell,'—so ran the inscription—'torn from its sacred usage in Santa Maria della Lettera by the rebels of Sicily in the year 1848 in order to make cannon, having come into the hands of the Neapolitan troops during the conquest of Messina, is returned to its ancient church by the generous and pious King Ferdinand II and by his gallant army commanded by Filangieri.'

Conciliation was the watchword in Messina. But the masochistic Sicilians refused to be conciliated. The crown-offerers were still kicking their heels in Turin. An Englishman who met them there, wrote: 'Those gentlemen had now been nearly eight weeks in Piedmont, and had gotten no answer. On their first arrival they waited upon the King in camp, expecting that the crown would be accepted with joy, and that the Duke of Genoa would be forthwith sent to Palermo. . . . Charles Albert, who ought to have dismissed them with a polite negative, would say neither no nor yes. He must have time to deliberate; it was an important decision; his family was not large; he had but two sons; the war was not yet over; the Duke of Genoa was a soldier, and his services were required. In the end he courteously recommended

_Ferdinand II.
King of Naples.
(as he appeared at
Sir Richard Acton's
private Party on
March 1st 1834.)

March 1st 1834.

King of Naples.

Ferdinand II as he appeared at Sir Richard Acton's party, 1834

the crown-offerers to go to Turin, and there wait for an answer. They were still waiting for an answer when General Filangieri took Messina. . . . This offer of the Sicilian crown to a prince of Savoy has caused numerous jealousies and heart-burnings in Italy. The republicans were wroth against the Palermitans for not having availed themselves of so charming an opportunity for proclaiming a republic. Those who were dreaming of the great Italian kingdom . . . were angry that the Palermitans, instead of asking for a king for themselves, had not voted the union and incorporation of their island with the Italic kingdom. "This," said they, "would be union and fusion. Sicily is too small to be a separate kingdom. It ought to be part of *our* kingdom, as Sardinia is." They tried to bring over some of the crown-offerers to this way of thinking; but, although they took them to the Circolo and to the Abbé's (Gioberti's) levées, I believe they met with little success, and that the short reply of the Sicilians to all their arguments was, that they must have a nationality of their own, and that they would be torn to pieces if they told the Palermitans that they were to be united with Piedmont and Genoa and Sardinia. One of Gioberti's disciples said, "If it were not for the *crève-cœur* it gives that bloody tyrant King Ferdinand, I wish these Sicilians had never come here with the offers of their crown. . . . They embarrass our movements; they spoil our plan of unification. Even should Charles Albert consent —which he can never have thought of doing—we would never allow the Duke of Genoa to go away to Sicily. It is not to be expected that we should. If these Sicilians would only open their eyes, they must see that there was never in any quarter the slightest intention of complying with their wishes. But here they stay and stay! However, their pro-longed mission must irritate the Bourbon of Naples, and that is always a consolation to us." '

XIII

CHARLES MACFARLANE, who had spent ten years of his youth in Naples, returned there in August, 1848, and left an unvarnished account of his impressions:

'Although the King was strong in the affections of the popular body, in the steadiness of the Swiss, and in the devotion of his own native troops, and although the anarchic party had not been able to raise their heads since the 15th of May, there were frequent noises and disturbances in the streets, and there was every day some report more or less confidently spread that the revolutionists meant to try again, and that there would be more barricades. The very first night after our arrival we witnessed a scene curious to us, though not at all rare nowadays in Naples. Having had an early dinner and a good deal of exercise after it—we went to supper. The *trattoria* I selected was the Corona di Ferro, well known to all English travellers between the years 1816 and 1827. It was then one of the best houses in the city. I was told it had sadly fallen off, but I went to it for the sake of old recollections and associations. . . . It was a sort of club house for young English artists, young littérateurs, and nondescripts. . . . In those symposia, whereat we were always right merry if we were not always witty, we assembled in a room upstairs; but this evening we sat in the room on the ground floor which has folding doors that open upon the street—the grand street of Toledo. We were sitting quietly at table;

there was nobody in the room except ourselves; it was about ten o'clock—when, all of a sudden, there was a terrible clattering, and screaming, and shouting in the street. Before we could begin to wonder what it meant, the landlady rushed into the room, clutched up the silver forks and spoons, and shrieked to the waiter to close and bar the doors. When this was done she said, "Patriots or Royalists, they are all thieves! whenever there is a *fracasso* (row), somebody is plundered! What a life for honest people! and this is the life we have been leading ever since last January, when the King promised the Constitution!" She and the waiter advised us not to stir until the riot should be over. There was no getting out of the house, for all the doors were barred, and there was no seeing what was going on in the street. We heard a marching of troops, a clattering of arms, and tremendous vociferations; but there was no firing, and the *baruffa* was soon over. It was not until the next day that we learned the cause and the nature of the disturbance, which had terrified a great many besides our hostess of the Iron Crown. An officer stopped at a tobacconist's to buy a cigar. The tobacconist, like many others of his calling, had added to his ordinary trade that of newsvendor, and his counter was covered with the revolutionary papers, satirical broadsides, and very gross caricatures. One of the last gave great offence to the officer, as it held up to ridicule not only King Ferdinand, but the whole Neapolitan army. The man of the sword asked the man of the weed whether he was not ashamed to sell such scandalous trash as that? "How," said a priest of the radical and union-and-independence of Italy party, "have we not the liberty of the press? Are we not a constitutional people? And are not you, a soldier, ashamed of being here when you ought to be with Carlo Alberto fighting against the barbarians? Ah! our King is but a *Coglione*, and our soldiers are but poltroons!" The officer stretched out his arm towards the priest's nose. Somebody (already a crowd had gathered by the open shop-door) struck down the officer's arm, and others threatened him with personal chastisement. Two or three other officers, who chanced to be passing by, stepped up to the rescue of their comrade, and a loud squabble and a confusion ensued. Attracted by the noise a small body of police and a patrol of the Royal Guards came up from the palace, upon which nearly all the rioters took to their heels, running up the narrow streets and lanes on the left hand side of the Toledo. But while the hullabaloo had lasted the tobacconist and newsvendor had been robbed of sundry packets of cigars and some snuff. The patriots swore that the military had committed the theft, and had made the *baruffa* for that sole object. The military said that the priest and his friends had stolen the goods. In all probability some poor vagabonds, who belonged to neither party, had availed themselves of a favourable opportunity and committed the theft; but the accusation and counter-accusation are in keeping with all the rest, and show the madness and unscrupulousness of Italian factions.'

Trade was depressed, as in every part of the Mediterranean at this time. 'The want of employment was beginning to be seriously felt, and although the streets no longer thronged with the ragged, vociferous, merry beggars of former times (who used to tell you that they were dying of hunger with a strength of lung and a jovialness of countenance that made you envy them), we were rather frequently accosted, and more particularly in the dusk of the evening, by decently attired people with woe-begone countenances, and with other indications that begging was to them a new and a painful trade. Some had taken to other professions. Petty larceny and a skilful jerking out of pocket-handkerchiefs were not uncommon things in my time; but burglary or street-robbing was certainly rare. I had been accustomed to go through the streets at all hours of the night . . . without once meeting with a street robber; and as I did, so did many others of my countrymen. Now, I was therefore rather surprised, one night when upon asking the way to a particular street of a very respectable looking man, he held me in talk for some seconds and, fancying that my attention was engaged, made a bold snatch at my front pocket. On relating the circumstance to an old Neapolitan friend, he said, "These things occur nightly; but what will you?—*cosa ne volete*—it is desperation! Since our glorious revolution, which made it necessary to find places for new men, so many have been turned out of their places and into the streets!" '

Since the last opening of Parliament the King seldom appeared in public. This was said to be due to plots against his life, but his health had suffered from the strain of the last few months and there had been a recurrence of his old complaint, which he wished to conceal. Besides, he was in no mood for amusement. Even the Piedigrotta festival was overshadowed by his despondency. As Lord Napier wrote: 'The Feast of the Nativity of the Virgin is peculiarly dear to the people of Naples, and it has been adorned by the presence and the piety of successive kings. Indeed excepting the great national festival of St Januarius there is no holiday which discloses such a blaze of religion. By ancient usage a royal procession goes to the sanctuary of the Madonna of Piedigrotta, on which occasion the troops are drawn out in unusual numbers, and the King with his family pass along the streets in state followed by a train of courtiers in hereditary coaches which for several generations have contained and attested the devotion of the Bourbon Dynasty. The distinguished virtues of the present Sovereign are faith and prudence; and he has exercised the latter by remaining at home since the 16th of May. It was therefore expected that on the present occasion His Majesty's faith would prevail, and induce him to appear in public and pay his services at an altar for which he has always shown the greatest predilection. The public has nevertheless been disappointed, and the King has practised both his qualities by going to the vicinity of the sanctuary by sea. About six o'clock His Majesty embarked at the private stores on board a steam vessel and coasting the Riviera di Chiaja lay to off the Church, and sent his aides-de-camp on shore for the blessing. He then returned to the palace. The royal ensign was hoisted on the forts and the usual salutes were fired.

'The populace to whom the spirit of religion and loyalty without their outward graces is not palatable, can scarcely be satisfied with such invisible acts of worship, and it is not thus that the King will reconquer the wavering affections of the lazzaroni. The intelligence of the reduction of Messina having been reported on the Feast of the Virgin has given His Majesty a greater confidence in his heavenly allies, and when the Duke of Cajanello congratulated him on the happy news, he replied, "*Pasqualino, mia è stata la Madonna!*" '

MacFarlane said the King was almost as much a prisoner as was Louis XVI in the Tuileries after the flight to Varennes. 'He received his ministers daily, but hardly any one else. In the cool of the evening he and his family took air and exercise in a very long balcony at the back of the palace, overlooking the glorious bay, the volcano, the mountains, and the island of Capri. In these narrow and melancholy promenades Ferdinand could be seen from several points of the city. A much frequented coffee-house stood so near that it was thought a rifle-ball fired from it might reach the King in the balcony; and it was rumoured that some of the secret police—men apt to invent more than they discover—had information that some of the barricade men had bound themselves by oath to shoot at the King from that coffee-house. The police shut up the café, and it remained closed. It seemed to me that all this was little and contemptible, and that the King's immuring himself was very impolitic. . . . The only excuse for the King which I heard was this—he did not quit his palace because he apprehended that the people of Santa Lucia and other portions of the ultra-loyal populace, excited by his appearance in the streets, would make a tumult, and fall upon the constitutionalists. By night, voices had frequently been heard shouting near the palace "*Viva il Re! Abbasso la Costituzione!*" By not appearing at the opening of Parliament, Ferdinand contributed to give to that assembly the phantomy, unreal character which it has had in the eyes of the majority of the Neapolitan people.'

The British fleet was still lying off Castellammare, which had greatly improved since MacFarlane's former visit. Instead of the mean house that aspired to the title of *locanda*, there were now a dozen or more comfortable hotels; furnished houses to let to visitors had been trebled; the main street and the quay had been widened and beautified. 'Throughout the town there was an appearance of neatness, comfort, and finish which were only beginning when I was last here. For this result the place had been chiefly indebted to the annually increasing influx of wealthy foreigners; and of this fact the fixed population was fully sensible. The people of Castellammare and the neighbourhood had always been distinguished as very hot royalists: the absence of foreigners and the falling off of their prosperity in this troubled year had made them very anti-constitutional and almost counter-revolutionary. "Who," said they, "have driven away the English lords and the Russian and German princes, and the other foreigners who fed us and enriched us? Who but these revolutionists? We have had no prosperity—no peace since this constitution was made. We do not want the constitution. We want peace and the foreigners back again. Our houses are empty, our horses and asses are unemployed; we have nothing to do!" Though not very pleasantly announced at Naples, the long visit of the English fleet was a God-send to Castellammare, for the officers and men of so considerable a force naturally spent a good deal of money on shore, and many of the ship supplies were purchased in the town. We chanced to be there on a pay-day, and in the course of that day and the three following ones, the best part of 3000*l*. were expended in the town. Our fleet was indeed the only good customer. The Neapolitan nobility and gentry, receiving hardly any rents from their estates, were living quietly and economically, and there were no wealthy foreign visitors.'

At Pompeii the excavations were at a standstill. 'In the good peaceable times,' said an old guide, 'there was never any month, hot or cold, that did not bring us a good number of visitors. Except your officers and sailors, nobody ever comes near us now. If this lasts we must all starve!' The plans to prolong the railroads had had to be shelved with other schemes of development, but the country people looked cheerful and well fed. And the magnificent new road to Sorrento surpassed MacFarlane's expectations: most of it had been cut out of the live rock. 'It required some previous knowledge of the road, and of the strength of its bridges and their good parapets, to avoid a feeling of alarm. . . . It was something like a trial of the nerves to a short-sighted man to see himself whirled along a road which every here and there seemed to terminate on the very edge of a tall cliff, under which were sharp rocks and the deep sea.'

He also noticed a great moral improvement in Neapolitan society. 'Exemplary wives and mothers now abound, and may be said to form the rule, while those of less commendable reputations are only the exception. . . . No doubt the moral tone of the Court since the accession of the present King has had an influence on the right side. His enemies, who have accused him of everything else, have not ventured to charge Ferdinand with dissoluteness or incontinence. He is a strict observer of domestic morals and decencies, an important fact in a country like this, and a great deal to say of any King of Naples. In these respects his Court has been a model, which some of the princes of the continent would have done well to imitate.'

The Queen Mother's death on September 14, was another reason for Ferdinand's aloofness. Her late Majesty, as Lord Napier wrote, 'was deservedly esteemed for her amiable qualities and enjoyed the love of the poor people to whom she distributed great sums in alms'. Almost until the end, despite her corpulency, she had retained the generous appetites of a simple, uninhibited child.

Whatever the benefits of a constitution in other countries Ferdinand could only see the harm it had brought to his own. All his practical schemes of improvement had had to be set aside. Perhaps the most promising of these had been the railway from Naples to Brindisi which would nearly bisect the kingdom, passing through several of its most important provinces and towns. To complete this plan the ancient double harbour of Brindisi was to be cleared of silt and rebuilt. Owing to its position it was bound to attract trade from the Levant, and the railroad would bring overland travellers from India to Naples within a few hours. Thinking of this and other projects which would have enriched the country, he was all the more furious with the liberals.

In Tuscany a so-called democratic ministry was forced upon the gentle Grand Duke Leopold. In Rome the progressive Pope was being made to rue his over-impetuous reforms. The new nationalism threatened to replace Christianity as a religion. The political clubs and the popular press whipped up the passions of the ignorant masses until a revolution seemed inevitable. Agitators pullulated, ranging from the Prince of Canino, Lucien Buonaparte's son, to such priests and friars as Father Gavazzi who preached war against the rich, as well as against the Austrians. It meant nothing to them that the Pope had appealed to the Austrian Emperor to withdraw his troops from Italy; and the defeat of Piedmont had not diminished their bellicose ardour.

Count Pellegrino Rossi was the one statesman who might have averted a revolution, and this was realized when he consented to form a ministry in late September. Having won the Pope's confidence in spite of being a free-thinker who had married a Protestant, he was mistrusted both by clericals and republicans. His first aim was to restore order and revive industry; his policy, like Gioberti's, was to lay the foundation of independence by means of a federation with the Pope as president. He promptly grappled with the abuses which his predecessors had winked at, and whatever he did was denounced by the demagogues as an attack upon liberty. But he refused to be intimidated.

The extremists were all out for his blood and their chance came on November 15 before the opening of Parliament. He paid no attention to the anonymous letters warning him of his danger. As he stepped from his carriage into the palace of the Cancelleria he was greeted with howls of 'Death to Rossi! Down with him!' and surrounded by uplifted daggers. The assassin who dealt the fatal blow by stabbing him in the neck was Luigi Brunetti, a son of Ciceruacchio the rabble-rouser. Not a finger was raised to defend the intrepid minister or to arrest his murderer, who was lauded as a patriot by the benighted mob. A torchlight procession marched to Rossi's house and insulted his widow's grief with blasphemous parodies of the *Miserere*. Next day the Mazzinian Sterbini, who had instigated Rossi's murder and controlled the popular press, planned an armed insurrection when the Pope would not agree to the summoning of a constituent assembly and to a declaration of war upon Austria. Soon bullets were whistling into the Pope's ante-chamber and Monsignor Palma, his private secretary, was shot dead. When a cannon was brought up to his front gate he protested to the diplomatic body assembled in the Quirinal. Deserted by his cabinet, he was forced to compromise with the insurgents. The loyal Swiss Guards were disbanded, and Pius IX became a prisoner with the civic guards as his hostile warders. It was only a year since Metternich had written of him: 'Warm of heart and weak of intellect, he has allowed himself to be taken and ensnared, since assuming the tiara, in a net from which he no longer knows how to disentangle himself, and if matters follow their natural course, he will be driven out of Rome.'

Slavery, martyrdom or escape were the alternatives now offered him. He wisely chose escape. This was planned by Count Spaur, the Bavarian minister, with the aid of his French colleague the Duc d'Harcourt, who read aloud to the Holy Father in his closed library while he was changing into the garb of an ordinary priest and continued reading, to deceive those within earshot, even after he had left the Quirinal with his valet Filippani. A cab conveyed His Holiness to Ariccia in the Alban Hills, where Countess Spaur, her son, and the German Father Liebel awaited him in a large Berlin carriage. The whole party drove to Gaeta, the Pope reciting his breviary with Father Liebel during the afternoon: it was November 24. Next morning they were met outside Gaeta by Arnau, the first secretary of the Spanish legation to the Holy See, and Cardinal Antonelli in disguise. The Pope's identity was to be kept secret until King Ferdinand was informed of his arrival, so the party stayed at a simple inn while Spaur went on to Naples. Spaur and Arnau having exchanged passports, since the former had been entrusted *ad interim* with the affairs of the Austrian legation, old Brigadier Gross, who now commanded the fortress of Gaeta, was puzzled by Arnau's ignorance of German. When the Spaniard pretended that he had lived abroad so long that he had forgotten the language, he viewed the visitors with deep suspicion.

Ferdinand welcomed Count Spaur with a cordiality which scarcely concealed his elation. Pius IX, whose name had so often been shouted as a battle-cry against himself, was now his guest, removed from liberal influence. He quivered with excitement as he read the Pope's letter: 'Sire, The momentary triumph of the enemies of the Holy See and of religion endangering the Chief of the Catholic Church, have forced him, in his own despite, to leave Rome. I know not to what part of the world the Lord's will, to which I submit with all the humility of my soul, will lead my wandering steps; in the meantime I have taken refuge in the States of Your Majesty with a few faithful and devoted persons. I am ignorant of your intentions regarding me, but I think I should inform you, by means of Count de Spaur, the Bavarian minister to the Holy See, that I am ready to leave Neapolitan territory, should my presence in Your Majesty's States become the subject of alarms or political difficulties.'

Difficulties forsooth! He gave orders that two regiments of infantry were to sail immediately for Gaeta, and himself followed the same night with his family and Count Spaur. As soon as he arrived he escorted the Pontiff to the royal palace inside the town, where his family assembled to pay him homage, after which the Neapolitan Court and officers were admitted to a papal audience. To the latter His Holiness said significantly: 'You form part of an army which is a mirror of discipline and loyalty, which has upheld the law with its blood and delivered the kingdom from the scourge of anarchy.'

He praised 'this kingdom which still offers Italy an example of law and order,' and exhorted the Neapolitan ministers 'to assist continually, with alacrity and courage, a pious King who shows so much zeal for his country's welfare.' Italy resembled a sick man with a high fever, turning from side to side, longing for a relief which he failed to find. Only God could remedy such an evil. 'You are at present engaged in preparing new laws, which We hope will benefit these good populations. But We see that this kingdom already abounds in wise laws, and there is only need, with Divine assistance, for their scrupulous execution. Here the times require prudent modifications, not sweeping legislative reforms.'

To his subjects the Pope sent a message that he had been compelled to leave Rome in order to perform his duties without hindrance; he denounced as sacrilegious the violence to which he had been subjected, and appointed a commission to govern in his absence. But Rome had fallen into the hands of extreme republicans, who were clamouring for a constituent assembly. This assembly met on February 5, 1849, and on the 9th proclaimed a republic. The Pope's reply was an appeal to the Catholic powers to vindicate his rights. Their intervention was certain, but owing to the rivalry of France and Austria—and France was now a republic of dubious complexion with Louis Napoleon as President—it would take time to materialize. When Tuscany also proclaimed a constituent assembly the Grand Duke followed the Pope to Gaeta on February 21. The frontier fortress of the Neapolitan kingdom had suddenly become the stronghold of reaction.

After the capture of Messina Ferdinand never doubted that he would recover the whole island. The chances of doing so peacefully were slender, but he wished to conciliate England and France, though he realized that the prolonged armistice helped the rebels to re-arm. Questions about it had been raised in the English Parliament. Messrs Hood and Co, ironfounders, having undertaken to supply fifteen pieces of cannon to the Sicilian Government, and being unable to do so in the time specified, had applied to the Secretary of Ordnance to be allowed to receive back from the stores of that department the ordnance required, on the understanding that they should be replaced. The Secretary consulted with Lord Palmerston, since 'the Board had reason to believe that the Sicilian Government specified by Messrs Hood meant the island of Sicily, which had declared its independence of the kingdom of the Two Sicilies'. Palmerston replied that he saw no objection to a compliance with Messrs Hood's request, if the guns were not immediately wanted for the British service. This might have been called a breach of neutrality. As a subtle afterthought Palmerston wrote to his brother Temple, who returned to Naples on November 27, that 'it was possible the King's government might complain that facility had been given in England to the Sicilian contractor, in which case he was to say that the authority was given *inadvertently*, that Her Majesty's Government regretted what had occurred, and that nothing of the sort should hereafter occur, while the differences between the Sicilians and the King of Naples were unsettled'. Having gingerly admitted an 'inadvertence' and climbed down to a form of apology, he revenged himself by instructing the British consul at Messina 'to collect the details of the Neapolitan atrocities' as choice morsels to 'put into the mouth of the Queen in her speech in Parliament'. Greville observed:[1] 'The mention in the Queen's Speech of the "King of Naples", instead of the King of the Two Sicilies, is now said to have been a mere inadvertence, but I have no doubt it was . . . put in by him intentionally and with a significant purpose.' Palmerston's vendetta against Ferdinand was almost Sicilian in its tenacity.

Ferdinand managed to keep his temper. He received Temple graciously, 'and expressed himself with calmness and moderation upon the subject of discussion'. But he could not agree that it was indispensable to separate the army of Sicily from that of Naples. He might give the island a separate Constitution, but he considered one army essential for the security of both kingdoms. Given time, he thought even France and England would weary of Sicilian obstinacy.

La Farina, who had succeeded Paternò as Minister of War in Palermo, found that in spite of patriotic appeals the Sicilian troops were insufficient. The national and the municipal guard encroached on the regular army, and these undisciplined formations lacked a dynamic leader. La Farina invited the already renowned Garibaldi to take command of the army, but Garibaldi stopped at Leghorn on the way, where he was drawn by the stronger magnet of Central Italy. Sicily seemed too remote. La Farina then turned to General Antonini, a fervent Mazzinian who had lost one arm fighting the Austrians at Vicenza and was ready to lose another in defence of Sicily.

Antonini received a flattering ovation on his arrival at Palermo, where he was appointed a field marshal and Inspector-General, but his language was too blunt for the rhetorical Sicilians and as a battle-scarred veteran he disliked taking orders from a cocky young upstart. He insisted on a series of immediate reforms, which were quite unpracticable. How could an army of 30,000 be raised at this eleventh hour? On January 20, 1849 he resigned in an open letter to the Sicilian people, accusing the government of unpardonable indolence and ineptitude for their neglect of the island's defences during the past year. Mieroslawsky remained, however, a Pole who had taken prominent part in several insurrections. Antonini had recommended him in

[1] *The Greville Diary.* Edited by Philip Whitwell Wilson. London, 1929.

the first place and La Farina had conferred on him the rank of general. Baron Friddani and Michele Amari, the Sicilian agents in Paris, proposed General Trobriand, who had won a reputation in the Napoleonic wars, as a substitute for Antonini, but he soon fell out with Mieroslawsky and resigned more quietly than his predecessor.

With few exceptions the foreign volunteers were mere adventurers. As the natives were allergic to conscription La Farina tried to recruit soldiers in France and Switzerland, but his efforts were frustrated by personal rivalries, dread of republican propaganda, lack of funds and the rapacity of agents who dunned him for more and more money. Even the purchase of two ships in England, guaranteed by Messrs Willcox and Allen of the Peninsular and Oriental Steamship Company, proved abortive. Only one of these reached Sicily before the end of the revolution. According to Beltrani-Scalia, the multiplication of taxes and forced loans aggravated the general discontent, so that the majority failed to appreciate the advantages of a liberty which had degenerated into anarchy, and of an independence whose cost was so exorbitant.

Gradually the Sicilian commissioners in London and Paris became aware that the two great powers which had given them most encouragement were beginning to back out of an embarrassing situation. One of these commissioners, Luigi Scalia, confided to his diary such jottings as this: 'Everything went wrong to-day: Palmerston out: Willcox and Cottrall (bankers) also; came home to find Lord John Russell puts off the interview we were to have had with him. I try to read: even Dante seems insipid. Bad news from Sicily too.' 'Dined at Lord Minto's; he said, "The rising in Ireland has done a great deal of harm to the Sicilian cause; it has frightened the timid. Until July and even until August the English Government were determined to help you." Met at dinner Lord Fortescue; warmly in favour of Sicily. He has a son who was, and possibly still is, in Sicily. Lord FitzWilliam is also favourable, and Lord Ellenborough has almost decided to speak in our favour (in the House of Lords). Lady Melgunde, most amiable and pretty, and most sympathetic for the sad story of Sicily.' 'Went to the Haymarket Theatre to try and distract my thoughts but it was impossible!'

Evidently London society felt deeper sympathy for the troubles of the distant island, seen through a haze of classical romance, than for those of nearer Erin, where over half a million had died of famine and pestilence. But between sentiment and action there was an awkward gap. Scalia's jottings had all the pathos of his trustful ingenuousness. His niece Tina Whitaker wrote that 'he would only dine at houses where the cause of his dearly loved island could be advanced or aided;' but he exaggerated the value of that aid. Lord Palmerston had invited him to stay at Broadlands, but for all his dislike of 'Bomba' he had become distressingly cautious. His brother Temple reported on December 30, 1848: 'Since the arrival of the Pope at Gaeta the King of Naples, who had previously confined himself within the walls of his palace, has passed the greater part of his time in that town where he has fitted up an apartment and resides with the Queen and the royal children. The army is now the principal object of His Majesty's care and it is to be increased to 110,000 men, which is nearly double its previous amount, a great portion of which will be raised by conscription and the rest by voluntary enlistment.'

After six months of fruitless negotiations Ferdinand was resolved to end the Sicilian armistice, which had been wholly to his enemies' advantage. On February 28, 1849, Filangieri informed the English and French ministers of the King's ultimatum: he granted the Sicilians a separate Parliament and administration, a viceroy, and a general amnesty to all except forty-four who were exempted by name. These conditions were amplified in a long proclamation to the Sicilians, declaring that he wished to forget their political offences and urging them to return to their private occupations, heedless of those who were seeking to delude them. Considering all their Acts of Parliament since the revolution as of no effect, he granted a Statute based on the Constitution of 1812.

Both Temple and de Rayneval thought these terms sufficiently satisfactory to exert themselves in favour of their acceptance. They even accompanied Admirals Parker and Baudin to Palermo when the Prince of Butera, acting as Minister for Foreign Affairs, refused to lay the ultimatum before the Parliament whose Acts it had annulled. The two admirals took umbrage when Butera asked them if they had come as mediators or merely to impose the King's ultimatum on the island. They replied that their mission was to prevent more bloodshed and obtain a lasting peace. On March 7 the Palermo Parliament called every man between eighteen and thirty years old to arms. On March 15 Admiral Parker wrote to Temple: 'Every occurrence has induced the impression that the Ministers were actuated by a predominating desire to gain time, and eight days have elapsed without our being able to obtain any written document that can lead us to suppose there is a disposition to accept the terms of which we have been the bearers.' When the two admirals gave formal notice of the cessation of the armistice, both Temple and de Rayneval rushed to Palermo to make a last effort to save the peace. But the Sicilians wanted war. The King's terms were rejected by acclamation, and the humanitarian admirals were roundly abused for their pains. The combined fleets left Palermo at the end of March, Admiral Parker having sent steamships to the chief coastal towns for the protection of British life and property.

'I never saw such excitement,' wrote an Englishman from Palermo a week before the armistice ended. 'As we went through the streets, thousands in every direction waved hats and handkerchiefs, crying out, "*Guerra, guerra, ed ora!*" It was as exciting as a bull-fight, and the numbers joining in the cries much larger. They were well armed with percussion guns, and were busy landing cannon at the mole. They have thrown up several batteries in different places, though not worth much. Many labourers had been working in the trenches, and ladies had set the example, the Duchess of Monteleone having used her spade and basket.' The English consul Goodwin reported that six or eight thousand persons of all ranks had marched through the streets with hoe, hammer and basket on their shoulders, to work at the trenches outside the city.

The Piedmontese army was defeated at Novara on March 23 and Charles Albert abdicated. The Sicilians who had chosen his son as a sovereign could expect no help from that quarter: they realized with a shock that they had to shift for themselves. Old Ruggero Settimo was proclaimed 'father of his country'; the national guard was rallied; and the university students were formed into a legion under La Farina: at first it was proposed that boys of thirteen should join it, but some-one having pointed out that war was not a lark, the age of admission was raised to sixteen. Amid flowery speeches Mieroslawsky marched towards Messina, while about twelve thousand Neapolitans landed at Riposto on April 3 and advanced on Catania.

Filangieri's victory was assured when he occupied Catania on April 7: soon Augusta, Syracuse and Noto surrendered. Mieroslawsky was wounded, and the demoralized Sicilians retreated to Palermo without a commander. General Filangieri received innumerable deputations bearing olive branches, protesting their devotion to the legitimate sovereign. The Palermo government tried to conceal the facts; the press continued to spread fantastic lies, but the horde of ragged fugitives, including stragglers from the foreign legion, were a sufficient contradiction of their claims. A strong party led by Baron Riso and the national guard was opposed to further resistance, but the warmongers could still play havoc with the ignorant mob. La Farina tried to persuade Ruggero Settimo to become dictator, and several historians think he might have saved Sicilian independence. But he was old and tired; although a genuine patriot he had never been a revolutionary leader. Admiral Baudin's offer to mediate on April 14 was accepted by a parliamentary majority; the ministry resigned; and the King sent word from Gaeta that he wished the municipality of Palermo to take over provisional government. On the 28th Settimo sailed on H.M.S. *Bulldog* for Malta, his party having failed to dam the current of compromise. By this time the King was reviewing his troops at Fondi. He had assembled between five and six thousand men to help restore the Pope. Some nine thousand French troops under General Oudinot had landed at Civitavecchia with the same purpose.

Before surrendering the Palermitans wanted a general amnesty, and Filangieri sent Colonel Nunziante to obtain one from the King. There were ominous disturbances during the interval. On May 2 Captain Dundas reported to Temple: 'Within the last 48 hours there has been a decided attempt on the part of all the disorderly people in the neighbourhood to get up once again the cry of "Guerra!" ... The mob are in possession of the forts and have been helping themselves to arms, and in short there is the most complete anarchy. ... It appears to me that the town is completely at the mercy of the mob who are all armed, and the only surprising thing is that hitherto there has been no outrage. ... I have not the least doubt that the National Guards are quite inclined for peace, with the bulk of the inhabitants, but as in most other cases of the same kind the desperate characters domineer. ...' Those who could not escape on foreign ships fled to the country, while the royal troops were closing in on the city. On May 9 Captain Pelham of H.M.S. *Odin* wrote to Temple: 'This morning all is quiet ... and I have heard that the King has granted a general amnesty, but that people being in spirits will perhaps not be satisfied. I since hear that the *capi* and authors of the revolution are not included in general amnesty but that all the liberated convicts, murderers, robbers, etc, are freely pardoned! Who are the *capi* and instigators of the revolution? They must mention names or no one will be secure.... P.S. Amnesty excludes only those who *architettarono* the revolution. Riso is going about town distributing the proclamations and crying—Peace and Pardon. Nobody believes him and say it is a trick because Filangieri wants provisions.'

But it was no trick. Only forty-three prominent leaders of the revolution were excluded from the amnesty. The Sicilian bands which attacked the Neapolitan outposts near Palermo on May 8, 9 and 10, were easily repulsed, and the national guard restored order in the city. On May 15 the royal troops marched quietly into Palermo and occupied the neighbouring forts. The King expressed his gratitude to Filangieri by conferring on him the title of Duke of Taormina—he was already Prince of Satriano—together with a revenue of 12,000 ducats. But he soon became known as 'King Charles', a nickname unpleasing to the ear of King Ferdinand. He combined tact with a firmness which won the grudging admiration of most Sicilians. His decree ordering the death penalty for those who refused to surrender their weapons was considered inhuman, but it helped him to obtain complete disarmament. Nassau William Senior, who met him in January 1851, wrote: 'He is sixty-five, large, with an agreeable countenance and a charming manner and address. If I were to be a slave I should not wish for a pleasanter master. "His first object," he said, "on assuming the government, was to produce security." This he has effected. All Sicily is now as safe as France.'

In London the Sicilian commissioner Luigi Scalia entered in his diary on June 13: 'We had an appointment to see Palmerston. I went with Granatelli and Amari. We were kept waiting for more than an hour. At last, at my suggestion, we sent a message, and were then received. Palmerston seemed very much embarrassed and said, "There are certain misfortunes for which there is no help. You must wish for better days; there is no more hope now." ... Palmerston ended by saying, "France has betrayed you, and England has abandoned you!" To this we replied, "England must prevent the excess of reaction. England desires to see the establishment of Liberal Governments without the tyranny of Russia or the licence of a Republic." But

Palmerston answered, "I did not fail to counsel you to come to an agreement (with Naples). Now all is over!" '

The King and most of his ministers remained convinced that Lord Palmerston, Lord Minto, Lord Napier, Mr Temple, Admiral Parker, in short all the English authorities, had conspired to wrest Sicily from Naples. 'If that were not so,' said Prince Comitini to Nassau William Senior, 'why did Palmerston send a fleet to Naples, and refuse to say what were its instructions? Why was the invitation to the Duke of Genoa sent in an English steamer? Why was the Sicilian flag saluted? Why was Filangieri stopped short after he had taken Messina, when a week more would have made him master of Sicily?' Senior replied that he could not acquit Lord Palmerston, and the British authorities in general, of having believed much too easily in the ability of the Sicilians to resist the Neapolitans. If the Sicilians had resisted Ferdinand with the spirit and resolution which the Spaniards opposed to Bonaparte, 18,000 men, of whom two-thirds were Neapolitans, would never have subdued the country. This single error accounted for the rest of Lord Palmerston's conduct.

'Some one had blunder'd.'

XIV

ACCORDING to an old proverb, 'Where the Pope is, there is Rome,' and the beautiful city-fortress of Gaeta was for nine months the provisional capital of Roman Catholicism. Papal blessings were showered on visiting pilgrims, and were commemorated in at least one picture by Ferdinand II's protégé Francesco Verfloet. After dwelling on the wonderful technical elaboration of this artist, especially in the delineation of architectural subjects, Lord Napier wrote: 'Equal pains have been equally misapplied in the representation of the Pope's Benediction delivered in the Fortress of Gaeta. Here the fugitive Pontiff, the zealous Ferdinand, the whole of the Royal Family, the Cardinals, the Court, and a number of personages, diplomatic and military, are inserted, with a revolting formality. The ramparts, the cannon, the steam-vessels of war, share the blessing, and ensure the safety of the spiritual father.' But it is this formality which gives the picture its historical and topographical interest.

Gaeta was an oasis all the more edifying after the blasphemous saturnalia of the Roman republicans. Its whole atmosphere was saturated with bygone holiness. Saint Louis of Toulouse had lived as a friar in the church of San Francesco after giving up his right of succession to the throne of Naples to his younger brother Robert the Wise. Above the *Montagna Spaccata*, the mountain split by that earthquake which shook the world on the day of Crucifixion, rose the sanctuary of the Holy Trinity, where Pio Nono prayed aloud 'as in an ecstasy' soon after his arrival, offering himself as a sacrifice for world peace and invoking blessings on Ferdinand and his faithful subjects—a prayer which Ferdinand was to repeat verbatim at a meeting of the astonished local clergy. From this church a staircase led to a chapel suspended on a rock between two precipices. Far down below the sea rolled into a huge cavern.

Between conferences with cold-blooded, cynical diplomats it was a consolation to visit such venerable shrines as that on Mount Civita, which crowns the valley of Itri, where the oak groves were regarded as sacred even by brigands. The sanctuary contained an image of the Blessed Virgin attributed to Saint Luke. According to tradition it had been transferred here in 717 when Leo the Isaurian, Emperor of Byzantium, founded the sect of Iconoclasts. Two Basilian monks saved it from profanation, but they were caught by the imperial police, shut up in a chest with the holy image and hurled into the sea. The chest floated to Messina, where none but the Bishop could open it. The two monks stepped out none the worse for their long voyage in so cramped a compartment and related their miraculous experience. But the treasure vanished unaccountably. While the Messinese were lamenting its loss the people of remote Itri were all rejoicing. A farmer who had been searching three days for his ox, discovered it kneeling under an oak on Mount Civita. The exasperated yeoman belaboured the beast, but it remained motionless staring up into the branches. Since his blows were ineffective his eyes followed the dumb animal's rapt gaze. On beholding the radiant image he too knelt down and adored. Soon all the neighbourhood came crowding to the spot. When the news reached Messina, a party went over to investigate the facts. Sorely bewildered they returned to tell their fellow-citizens what they had seen. Suspecting that the image had left them owing to their sins, they started an annual pilgrimage to Mount Civita. A chapel was built round the image in the oak, whose trunk was encased within a marble altar. Since then the chapel had grown prodigiously, enriched by scores of miracles.

These excursions blended the natural with the supernatural at a time when Pius IX was concerned with defining the dogma of the Immaculate Conception. His encyclical asking the Bishops for advice on the subject was issued from Gaeta on February 2, 1849.

Filled with crusading fervour, Ferdinand could hardly wait to march into the Papal States. Unfortunately the Pope's more powerful allies were unable to co-operate. Since the defeat of Piedmont at Novara on March 23 Austria was free to intervene but France was anxious to prevent this. The Prince President Louis Napoleon was courting the clericals to divest himself of a republican constitution. Nothing was settled at the conference of ambassadors at Gaeta, but behind the scenes France and Austria—hostile in public for reasons of internal policy—reached a private agreement about French intervention.

The difficulty was to obtain the approval of the French Chamber, which was soothed with an assurance that the government wished to safeguard the influence of France and lend its support to liberal institutions. General Oudinot was appointed to command the expedition. Before sailing he told his troops that they were to protect the Romans against all tyranny or dictation, whether from foreign interference or domestic faction: he did not mention the Pope.

The troops, about nine thousand, landed at Civitavecchia without opposition on April 25, shouting '*Vivent les deux républiques!*' Hoping for a bloodless compromise with the Roman triumvirs, Oudinot informed them that if Rome were abandoned by France they would soon succumb to an Austrian invasion. The first triumvir Mazzini, whose aim was to annihilate the Papacy, swept this consideration aside. He was determined to resist. Thanks to Garibaldi and his legionaries, he was able to do so. Professor G. M. Trevelyan has glorified these events in his *Garibaldi's Defence of the Roman Republic*. When General Oudinot attempted to capture Rome by surprise he was repulsed with a loss of three hundred killed and as many prisoners. He had to withdraw and wait for reinforcements.

In the meantime Ferdinand had entered a separate campaign with a force of nine thousand Neapolitans, crossing the frontier on April 28. He set up his headquarters at Albano on May 4. The triumvirs launched a furious proclamation against him, and one of them exclaimed: 'We have plucked and eaten the cock, we shall now devour the macaroni!' Hoping that the French had been chastened by their drubbing, Ferdinand sent a liaison officer to discuss co-operation with Oudinot. At first he appeared willing to collaborate, but the situation was transformed by the arrival of Ferdinand de Lesseps who had been sent from Paris to negotiate with Mazzini. General Oudinot was forbidden to act in concert with the Neapolitan forces, and de Lesseps arranged a truce with the triumvirs. Meantime the Roman forces were rapidly increasing. As Professor Trevelyan pointed out in eloquent paragraphs[1] great was the lure of the red shirt, which acted like a charm.

Ferdinand became conscious of his isolation: he might yet have to face the combined attacks of the sister-republics. On May 17 he decided to leave the Papal States. He sent Oudinot a letter of dignified reproach before retiring from Albano in the direction of Velletri. Garibaldi and the Roman General Roselli chose this moment to take advantage of the French truce so that it should appear as if they had chased the Neapolitans out of the republic. They followed the royal army by forced marches with Garibaldi and his guerrillas dashing about in front and Roselli advancing more cumbrously behind. If their purpose was to cut off Ferdinand's retreat, they failed. In spite of republican propaganda the Neapolitans were far from demoralized: even Professor Trevelyan admitted that they had 'pushed forward too rashly into the heart of the Garibaldian position'. They attacked the guerrillas, harrying their flank with a vigour which sent many of them sprawling in all directions. Garibaldi was almost killed in one encounter, and the affair was exaggerated by both sides into an important victory. On the Neapolitan side there were twenty-two killed and sixty wounded; on the other the losses were probably greater. Velletri was quietly evacuated during the night, and no more was seen of the enemy, who had been recalled to Rome.

The Pope was shocked by the French armistice and his first impulse was to issue a solemn protest. Esterhazy, the Austrian ambassador, restrained him: he pointed out that a rupture with France would be disastrous at this moment, when the Catholic party was gaining power. The conference of Gaeta continued, and the Pope held firm against French pressure to grant the Romans liberal institutions. De Lesseps was recalled to Paris after signing a treaty with the triumvirs on his own responsibility, by which the French army was to protect Rome against Austria and Naples while remaining outside the city. Oudinot having received reinforcements, resumed hostilities on June 3. Ferdinand again offered to co-operate with him, and again his offer was rejected, as France wished to gain full credit for restoring the Pope. A desperate struggle against the besiegers was prolonged

[1] *Op. cit.*, p. 152.

until June 30 when the walls of Rome were breached. In spite of Mazzini's protests, the constituent assembly declared that further defence had become impossible. The French troops entered Rome on July 3, and General Oudinot sent his chief of staff Colonel Niel to Gaeta to lay the keys of the city at the Pope's feet, and to announce his victory to King Ferdinand. Letting bygones be bygones, the King gave him a courteous reception, and when Oudinot visited Gaeta they discussed the campaign most amicably together. To the disgust of Prince Ischitella, he was asked to convey the order of San Gennaro to the French commander. Ferdinand replied to his expostulations: 'Well, France wanted all the glory of conquering the new-born republic . . . and I wish to reward her success, because it has brought her back into the European party of order. She will cease interfering with our work of reconstruction.'

The Pope sent a message of rejoicing to his subjects, but he did not return until April 1850. The delay was to silence French clamour for liberal concessions. Three Cardinals, the so-called Red Triumvirs, were appointed to govern during his absence. Instead of going to Rome he went to Naples.

While the bells of all the churches were ringing, a flotilla escorted his launch to the steamship *Tancredi*, whose captain and crew knelt down to receive him. The artillery of the fort fired a parting salute of 101 guns. This was the first time a Pope travelled on a steamship, and Pius sent thousands of blessings to the crowds which had gathered on shore. The air was crystalline: Procida, Miseno, Baia, Pozzuoli, Nisida, Posillipo, floated between turquoise sky and sapphire sea, orange groves, vineyards and shimmering beaches sharp as in a miniature, gradually unfolding into the stupendous Vesuvian panorama, so often described, surpassing all description. H.M.S. *Prince Regent* was the first in the bay to salute the Pope's arrival; the forts and men of war repeated the royal salvo. The palace of Portici was placed at his disposal, and remained his residence till the following April.

Ferdinand was exultant: with the recovery of Sicily, the collapse of the Roman Republic, followed by the restoration of the Pope and the Grand Duke of Tuscany to their thrones, the good old days of patriarchal government seemed to have returned. Parliament, after being prorogued a second time, had been convoked on February 1, 1849. Again the deputies were in open conflict with the government,

287

which had collected taxes independently. To save its dignity the assembly had introduced a bill providing the government with the temporary power of imposing taxes and voted an address to the King demanding the dismissal of ministers whose anti-constitutional behaviour made them unworthy of his confidence, and whose continuance in office fomented discord between the Crown and the country. The King rejected this address, and the ministers abstained from subsequent meetings where laws were passed without their sanction. On March 13 Parliament was finally dissolved and the 'constitutional comedy' was over.

But the subterranean forces were still at work. Many moderates as well as ultra-radicals had joined the secret Society of Italian Unity, whose aim was 'to liberate Italy from the internal tyranny of princes and from every foreign power, reunite her and make her strong and independent'. This highly organized sect—not to be confused with Mazzini's 'Young Italy' which it resembled—had been founded by Silvio Spaventa, who specialized in propaganda among the troops. Its members lived dangerously, watched by the irritated and none too scrupulous police. They had expected Garibaldi's legion to invade the kingdom. When this hope was dashed the more sober members withdrew, leaving the field to extremists, who formed a committee of action. One after another of their leaders were arrested. Profoundly frustrated, they printed a manifesto urging citizens to keep away from the Piedigrotta festival on September 8: 'Honest and upright citizens! Contempt is now added to insult, betrayal and perjury. A few hundreds of blackguards dressed in civilian clothes, suborned on purpose by the real party of disorder, will make a demonstration in favour of that Bourbon under whose sword so many thousands of innocent victims have barbarously perished. To-day they will joyfully trample on this ground still reeking with the blood of innocent citizens. A faction will rejoice while myriads are weeping in fetters and cruel torment.

'People, will you tolerate this insult? By God, you might make him pay dear for it even in spite of a hundred thousand bayonets! The day of wrath approaches, and the vengeance of the people is the vengeance of God. The troops are not against you, except the starveling Swiss, who will be destroyed by your fury.

'People, to-day neither fatherland, nor justice, nor honour, summons you to take part in a ridiculous demonstration and an unrighteous festival. You should go far away into the remotest streets and show that you are proud of your rights. . . . Death to perjurors! death to the Jesuits!'

But the people welcomed a return to 'the good old days'. Twenty-five thousand troops marched past the King, who was greeted with overwhelming acclamation. Undaunted, the committee of action persevered. Knowing that the Pope was to bless the population from the royal palace on September 16, they printed more manifestos, one of which ran: 'People, the voice of reaction incites you by every means to go and receive the Vicar of Christ's blessing; but the Pope is merely a tool of the Bourbon, who is exploiting him for his secret and perverse designs, to whitewash his iniquity, legalize his treachery and perjury, and absolve him from his many crimes! Pius IX is a prisoner!' etc. One conspirator suggested letting some snakes loose among the crowd to provoke a panic, but the local chemists could only provide him with dead ones. An explosive was chosen as a substitute. Even if it failed to reach the Pope or the King, it should wound several spectators—serve them right for attending—and, with luck, start a general stampede.

Nobody paid any attention to the manifestos, and the explosive burst prematurely, causing some dismay but no material damage. The culprit was more dazed than anyone else when, slightly scorched and smoking, he took to his heels. His name was Salvator Faucitano, a municipal contractor who had been egged on with promise of better pay by Francesco Giordano, a rising engineer. Thanks to friends in the British legation Giordano managed to escape but Faucitano was arrested. The ceremony proceeded without interruption. The city garrison in serried ranks surrounded the palace square, the centre of which was filled with religious congregations, children's schools and a vast crowd yearning to see the Pope and share his blessing. All eyes were strained towards the balcony hung with tapestry and velvet and surmounted by a dais of gold brocade. At midday the thunder of guns was followed by a flourish of trumpets, and a hundred thousand people fell on their knees as the serene and stately white figure advanced to the balcony, surrounded by the King and royal family. Even Protestants had to admit that nobody could bless more beautifully.

This was not an anti-Constitutional demonstration, as the King's enemies alleged. Before sailing from Gaeta Ferdinand had remarked:

'To-day the throne of Charles III has been placed on a pedestal of granite.' He had never been prone to rhetoric. By inviting the Supreme Pontiff to bless his subjects from the royal palace he hoped to consolidate his position as a monarch by divine right.

All except the liberal minority felt that the constitutional experiment had failed. Temple, who steadily echoed the minority, wrote that 'the most violent members of the reactionary party are men who under the French occupation from 1806 to 1815 had filled high offices, had been dismissed from them in 1815 and were supposed to be rather of liberal mind'. In August 1849, the Cariati-Bozzelli ministry was succeeded by that of Giustino Fortunato, a believer in enlightened despotism whom Settembrini described as a 'ferocious and insatiable hyena'. In fact he was an urbane and flexible survival of the Murat régime, like his colleagues Ischitella and Carascosa, and Filangieri in Sicily. The liberals held him responsible for the popular petitions which poured in during the next six months from all over the kingdom imploring Ferdinand to abolish the Constitution. If so he deserves credit for an ingenious idea.

According to R. De Cesare,[1] Fortunato's formula was destroyed in 1860, when it would have been hard to reconcile with the national plebiscite. De Cesare printed a sample which he said he obtained from the nephew of a mayor who had refused to sign it. The document ends: 'May it please Your Majesty to withdraw the concession extorted by violence and perfidy with the violation of the most sacred duties and prepared with the most sacrilegious and iniquitous sectarian aims. Let the people return under the sole power of your paternal sceptre; and we and our children shall bless, with the restored might of absolute monarchy, the sacred name of our good magnanimous King Ferdinand II.'

De Cesare has been copied by Mazziotti and others, who alleged that police agents were indefatigable in their endeavours to oblige all persons in authority to sign this petition, and that whole communes and municipalities were suborned with promises of grants for public works, railway concessions, remission of local taxes, or financial remuneration. But as even Mazziotti admitted,[2] the country was tired of upheavals, which had been fomented by a small section of the

---

[1] *La Fine di un Regno*, Vol. I, pp. 11, 12.

[2] Matteo Mazziotti, *La reazione borbonica nel Regno di Napoli*. Rome, 1912.

educated classes. The masses stood aloof, unconcerned with questions outside their orbit. Ferdinand was good enough for them, and they shared his craving for a quiet life. Though Fortunato had started the ball rolling there is no reason to suppose that others did not join spontaneously in the game. Formal deputations arrived in the capital from every province with petitions signed by hundreds of thousands: had the peasantry been included they would have been signed by millions. Of course there were howls from the liberal press. Yet there was some sense in the Bourbonist retort, as quoted by De Sivo: a few hundreds had shouted for the Constitution in 1848 and they had had a right to do so, whereas now that nearly all the municipalities in the kingdom were demanding its repeal they had no right to do so.

The Constitution was suspended rather than suppressed. Gradually Ferdinand got rid of those who had been closely connected with it and the subject was tabooed. The white flag with the Bourbon lilies replaced the exotic tricolour; the Jesuits returned to their old homes and resumed their excellent teaching; and the official journal dropped its 'Constitutional' prefix.

Having triumphed over his enemies, Ferdinand wished to cancel all memories of 1848. But the past refused to be buried. Gaetano Peccheneda, a former Freemason and a creature of Saliceti under the French occupation, had become director of police, and he gained a sinister influence over the King by keeping his dread of conspiracy alive. The political trials which dragged on for the next few years were to prove more harmful to Ferdinand than all the conspiracies and insurrections of his reign put together. His enemies were to find an unexpected ally in that master of moral indignation Mr Gladstone, who happened to be in Naples at the time.

The trial which Gladstone attended was that of the Italian Unity Society whose existence has been proved beyond a doubt though all its members lied in self-defence. And he only believed the defence. Faucitano's arrest after the ill-timed explosion of his hand grenade had led to further arrests and revelations. To unravel the long threads of this tangled skein was a labour of at least fourteen months, and the investigations were complicated by intrigues and perjuries, denunciations, confessions and retractions, in which truth and falsehood were mixed in varying degrees. Any government would have prosecuted a secret sect which threatened its very existence and encouraged political assassination with such proclamations as the following: 'Only you, brothers, only you lag behind. It is true that you have this Bourbon tiger who tears your limbs and drinks your blood, this hypocrite, this scoundrel, this most villainous Ferdinand. But are you not Italians? Have you not a dagger? Will none of you give his life for twenty-four millions of brothers? A single man, a single dagger-thrust would give Italy freedom, and would change the face of Europe.'

Some may admire the bold idealists who risked writing and printing such appeals; but they are best admired from a comfortable distance. Faucitano's explosion had seemed a portent of fresh barricades. Naturally the judges felt called upon to safeguard public order. Navarra, the president of the criminal court, reminded them that 'the magistrate's duty was to clear the country of noxious weeds'.

Even before Faucitano's arrest the police had received several denunciations worthy of note. The first of these had been sent in by Luigi Iervolino, a former non-commissioned officer, on April 23, 1849. He stated that he had been forced by poverty to apply to Carlo Poerio (an ex-minister in Carlo Troya's cabinet) for a job, and to obtain one more easily he had asked to join the sect of Unitarians, Poerio had agreed and sent him to Nicola Nisco (against whom the police already had a dossier of political accusations), who had introduced him to a certain D'Ambrosio for initiation; whereupon Iervolino had become the confidential agent of Poerio and his cronies, especially of Nisco and Settembrini. He had spread propaganda and distributed a proclamation exhorting citizens not to pay taxes, smoke, play lotto, or do anything to increase the public revenue. Owing to his zeal and efficiency he had been promoted in the sect, of which he denounced other members. Many of his statements were corroborated by other sources. Apparently he did not realize that he should have revealed the sect twenty-four hours after it had come to his knowledge, but the police were ready to excuse the omission if he continued to disclose the activities of fellow-sectarians. He reported conversations he had heard in the houses of Poerio and Settembrini about Garibaldi's invasion, with plausible details.

Somebody warned Poerio that Iervolino was a spy, but not before Settembrini had asked him to distribute a seditious proclamation. This led to Settembrini's arrest. Of course he denied any connection with the sect, or that he had written any proclamation, or contributed

292

to any newspaper. He had always been strictly moderate. Had he not refused an important post in the Ministry of Education, or even to become a deputy, on account of his hatred of disorder? He admitted knowing Poerio but denied acquaintance with Iervolino or the other man who was alleged to have helped him distribute proclamations, which he suggested had been forged maliciously by the police. He answered the commissioner's enquiries with such ability and aplomb that he expected a speedy release: nothing could ever quench his optimism.

Piqued by these denials, Iervolino proceeded to rattle off more circumstantial details. He gave a minute description of Settembrini's house and the people he had met there.

Carlo Poerio's was the most distinguished name which cropped up in many of the accusations. He had been born into the Opposition, for his father, a famous advocate, had been exiled twice; his uncle had fought in the Sardinian army; his cousin had been wounded fighting the Austrians in 1848; and his brother Alessandro, a learned poet and philologist, had joined General Pepe's expedition and died in the defence of Venice. After three terms of imprisonment he had served in Troya's cabinet but he had only played a secondary rôle, perhaps because he preferred conspiring behind the scenes. Though he was warned to escape he decided to brazen it out. Arrested in July 1849, he too denied belonging to the sect. He had recommended Iervolino for the post of usher to the president of the chamber of deputies, but knew nothing about D'Ambrosio who had initiated him into the sect. After pointing out that a letter supposedly addressed to him by Luigi Dragonetti was a clumsy forgery, he dictated the following statement: 'Mr Commissioner, I am profoundly amazed that on such flimsy grounds the authorities intend to involve me in a political trial for sectarianism. I pride myself on belonging to the sect of honest men. My monarchical-constitutional sentiments are known to all, and in the councils of the King as in the legislative assemblies both as a public and as a private man I have always upheld them courageously, openly and loyally. Nothing will make me swerve from my duties both as a respectful subject of the August Sovereign, who has granted us the Constitution, and as a citizen devoted to my country. If these noble sentiments of mine are the real cause of my misfortunes, I shall not therefore repudiate my principles and shall bear my present misfortunes with calm resignation and perfect faith in the future. The charge brought against me is evidently false and libellous, and can only derive from party spirit, which exploits every means of attaining its ends. However, I wish to face my accuser to show that he is impudently lying, since I am at present unable to refute a vague accusation lacking any proof. I still have faith in human justice, though we live in times of immoderate passions. Even if this were to fail me, I should always have the approval of my conscience and calmly rely on the justice of God.'

Poerio maintained this dignified attitude throughout his trial, regardless of all the mud that was thrown at him. He failed to see that the immoderate passions had been unleashed by his own party. Nobody can deny that the writings of Settembrini were highly inflammatory. The magistrate and journalist Michele Pironti, who was arrested in August, had vied with him in violence as editor of *L'Independente*, a paper with vague socialist tendencies. Its programme was thus announced in the first number, December 4, 1848: 'This journal is written for that numerous part of society which eats the bread of sorrow, which is hardened by grief and fatigue, which suffers and hopes and calls itself the People.' Pironti denied the charges against him except that he had helped Patella, the revolutionary parish priest of Agropoli, to escape from the kingdom, the police having seized a letter which Patella had written to him on that occasion.

Specimens of the subversive literature propagated during the last year, together with the rules and diplomas of the Unity sect and a cache of arms, had been detected near the printing shop of Gaetano Romeo, who merely admitted having printed the stuff, and blurted out the names of those who had given him commissions. He had heard the society discussed and Poerio, Settembrini and the young Duke Proto had been mentioned as its leaders. Proto, the wittiest of the three, had already absconded. Romeo's revelations led to more arrests without improving his own predicament. According to Luciano Margherita, who gave a complete account of the Unity sect's activities, Pironti became its leader after Settembrini's arrest and when he was taken into custody an association of 'Stabbers' (*Pugnalatori*) was organized to kill Longobardi and Peccheneda of the police as well as Navarra of the criminal court. Consequently Navarra expressed scruples about sitting on the bench, but the court overruled them.

The public prosecution of the forty-two accused lasted from June 1, 1850, until the end of January 1851, and some of the cleverest Neapolitan advocates defended the prisoners, who seized this chance to blacken the government and enlist world sympathy for their cause. Most of them were accomplished publicists and propagandists, and they played to their audience with consummate art, aware that it contained an élite of foreign diplomats. William Temple was always an ostentatious attendant. At first he sat among his colleagues, but when he complained that he could not hear well enough the president Navarra allowed him to sit near the Public Prosecutor so that, as a police official said, 'he seemed to be one of the magistrates.' Not content with this privilege, Temple obtained permission to sit in the anteroom where the Grand Court made its decisions, interrupting when he failed to understand. That he was Palmerston's brother made him more conspicuous. The prisoners regarded him as their protector and invariably exchanged greetings with him, for he had helped many of their friends to escape. George Fagan, the first attaché who usually accompanied him, was on intimate terms with Poerio and often spoke to him in court. He was a son of the Irish painter-consul during Bentinck's dictatorship, and had been born and brought up in Palermo with a bias against the Bourbons. According to Settembrini he acted as guardian angel to the political prisoners and hoped that his constant presence in court would intimidate the judges. Their recording angel was William Ewart Gladstone.

The result of Gladstone's Neapolitan holiday is notorious. If Lord Nelson had been the champion of the Bourbons, the Conservative member for Oxford was to be their powerful assailant. Thanks to his *Letters to Lord Aberdeen*, the description of Ferdinand II's government as the 'negation of God' has become proverbial.

'In the autumn of 1850,' wrote Lord Morley in his standard biography, 'with the object of benefiting the eyesight of one of their daughters, the Gladstones made a journey to southern Italy, and an eventful journey it proved. For Italy it was, that now first drew Mr Gladstone by the native ardour of his humanity, unconsciously and involuntarily, into that great stream of liberalism which was destined to carry him so far. . . . He went to Naples with no purposes of political propagandism. . . .' But *c'était plus fort que lui.* The political trials were the topic of the town. Temple, Fagan, and Giacomo Lacaita, legal adviser to the British embassy, 'opened his eyes to the condition of things' and told him hideous tales of Bourbon tyranny, of the atrocious state of the prisons, and the barbarous treatment of their unfortunate inmates. His moral indignation thoroughly roused, he wished to see these horrors for himself. But, as Solomon remarked: 'The eye is not satisfied with seeing.' Gladstone wished to make others share his astigmatic vision. We know not if Naples benefited his daughter's eyesight: certain it is that it beclouded Gladstone's. Forgetful of the horrors at home so vividly described by Dickens and Mayhew, or haply unaware of their existence, since his opus on *The State in its Relation with the Church* had engrossed his attention hitherto, he attended a few trials, visited two prisons, and made copious notes of what he heard rather than what he saw. No obstacles were put in his path or in that of his friend Nassau William Senior, whose published *Journals* illuminate the background of Gladstone's *Letters to Lord Aberdeen.*

Senior was a Master in Chancery as well as a respected professor of political economy, whose life was chiefly spent among politicians. His curious principle of 'the last hour'—in connection with the Ten Hours Act of 1848—disconcerted many an earnest reformer, for it seemed to prove that it was only in the last hour of running a factory that any profit could be made, hence industry was doomed if the hours of labour were reduced to ten. Small wonder that his economic theories have joined the limbo of intellectual lumber. But the itinerant professor still shines as a reporter. His endeavour was always to draw out the thoughts of others, as his daughter said, and the embittered liberals he met in Naples were eager to be drawn. The first of these was Carlo Troya, who had led the constitutional government: 'He is a fine-looking old man, but confined to his chair by gout. A priest was with him during my visit, so that he talked reservedly. "Naples," he said, "is no longer a part of Europe. We are cut off from information as to all that is passing in the rest of the world, Italy included, except what we collect from your newspapers. So few persons read English that the government lets them in." ' A few days later, without the priest, he talked very freely, explaining that he owed his safety to his crippled state, and to his having a brother and a brother-in-law in the actual cabinet; most of his former colleagues were exiled or under arrest; and he proceeded to regale his listener with a lurid account of

Queen Maria Theresa, second wife of Ferdinand II

Neapolitan prisons which was the very substance of Gladstone's famous *Letters*. 'Among the exiles, and, to a certain degree among the prisoners,' he added, 'may be reckoned the King, for he has taken refuge within the palace walls of Caserta, and ventures to Naples only from time to time to attend some ceremony when he can be surrounded by 40,000 troops. He does not shed blood, and therefore thinks himself the most merciful sovereign in Europe, while thousands have died, and thousands are slowly dying, in his prisons. No passion is so cruel as fear.' Tocqueville, whom Senior took to see Troya, must have thought of these words when he wrote: 'I am ready to believe that the King of Naples is naturally mild and kindly, but he is afraid, and the worst of all tyrannies is the tyranny of cowards.'

Gladstone, Senior and Tocqueville were to a certain extent privileged guests, but one is struck by the freedom of their intercourse with those who were supposed to be under strict surveillance. One is equally struck by their credulity and their ignorance of the Neapolitan character. The thousands of State prisoners perishing in loathsome dungeons were taken on trust. And yet, strangely enough: 'Troya soon forgot the present in the past, and spent half an hour proving to us the identity of the Daci, the Getæ, the Gothi, and the Normans—a fact which we had no wish to contest. "How happy," said Tocqueville, as we left him, "a man must be who in these times can interest himself in Dacians and Goths."' There we get a fleeting glimpse of Neapolitan character, but the insight of a psychologist is lacking.

Senior's impressions of the city and people betray his own bleak temperament: 'Charles Greville calls the Toledo the liveliest street in the world. I think it the most hateful place that I ever had the misfortune to traverse. Filthy carriages, full of filthy people, threaten every instant to crush you. Filthy pedestrians, whose contact is loathsome, elbow you at every turn; the air is full of dust and stink; horrible beggars swarm round you. The houses are so high, and it is so narrow, that no sun ever reaches you; and of this narrow space, half is occupied by vendors of fish, old clothes, baskets, bread, and the refuse of a chandler's shop; and as it is at least a mile long, you cannot struggle through in less than half an hour. It is the principal road to the interior of the town. If the hackney-coaches were endurable one would never walk through it: but they are not to be entered with safety, as we found by woeful experience, so that from time to time it must be encountered.'

So much for the Toledo. And now for a walk along the Villa Reale, Mergellina, and up the Vomero hill. Though mid-December it was almost unpleasantly hot. 'The disgusting population of Naples was all abroad—basking, quarrelling, gambling, and begging over the whole road. In cold countries the debased classes keep at home; here they live in the streets; and as the dwellings of the rich and poor intermingle, the same house, which in its first and second floors is a palace, having often its cellars turned into dens of misery and vice, you never are free from the sight, or, indeed from the contact, of loathsome degradation. I never saw so hateful a people; they look as wicked as they are squalid and unhealthy. I see why they were decimated by cholera.' The music of humanity, still or sad, merry or strident, was evidently disagreeable to this well-bred Early Victorian. After a ride into the country he remarked: 'Naples without Neapolitans is perfection.'

Senior and Gladstone moved in the same society and shared the same burden of national prejudices. But for all his bias Senior recorded the views of the other side occasionally. The King was a frequent subject of conversation. 'He is not,' said a lady, 'a man of much literature. But he has seen and thought a good deal. He is admirable in private life, and full of good intentions and kindness as a public man. His task is not an easy one. The people whom he has to govern are children not knowing what they want, and never wanting the same thing two days running. His ministers are not much better, and he is surrounded by a hostile diplomacy.'

Most of his associates were friends of Poerio if not enemies of the King. What did he know of the private history of Carlo Troya, of Manna the ex-Minister of Commerce, of General Sabatelli? The latter was a disappointed aspirant for the embassy in Vienna, smarting because the post had been given to the Sicilian Prince of Petrulla. In his rage he wrote to Schwarzenberg that Petrulla had been involved in a scandalous law-suit, when it had been proved that he had stolen money and diamonds from Marchesa Cavalcante, the lady he had been wooing. He had also been associated with brigands and highwaymen and forged bills of exchange. Temple had remarked about Petrulla's mission to Vienna: 'I hope the decorations he is taking (for

Schwarzenberg) are not in diamonds!' Sabatelli's intrigues against the appointment of the Prince of Carini to the embassy in London led to his downfall. When Senior met him at Lord Holland's he was in the King's good graces, which added a certain pungency to his remarks. 'All Neapolitans are suspicious;' he said, 'no one trusts his neighbour or even his friend, or ought to do so, but the King is even more suspicious than his subjects are. When you talk to him, he never listens to your arguments. He is only trying to guess what may be your motive for endeavouring to deceive him, for that you *are* deceiving him he has no doubt. The only history that he has studied is the history of his grandfather and his father. Each of them was governed by his Prime Minister and his wife. He has resolved to be governed by nobody, and is constantly asserting his free will by some unaccountable caprice. Then he has the utmost confidence in his own talents and judgement, and ascribes any difference from his opinion to your folly or to your dishonesty. His knowledge, too, of European politics is limited and vague. He fancies that Naples is as important a part of Europe as it is of Italy, and believes that backed by Austria he is a match for the whole world. Your diplomacy will, therefore, do nothing with him. The worst thing that can happen to his subjects on this side of the Faro or on the other is, that you should plead their cause.' And the man who spoke thus of his sovereign aspired to represent him abroad! Surely the King's suspicions were not unfounded.

Manna, who was Sabatelli's son-in-law, told Senior that 'the two important prisoners, to punish whom the whole trial is got up, are Poerio and a man of letters named Settembrini.' And Troya said he disbelieved 'the existence of the supposed secret society of which Poerio is charged with being a member.... Poerio is guilty of having been a deputy, a minister, and then a member of the *côté gauche*. These are the real crimes for which the Procuratore Generale demands that he be sentenced to thirty years' imprisonment in irons: and they are sufficient.'

From such sources as these Gladstone derived his conviction that attachment to the Constitution was regarded and punished as a crime, and that there was only one conspiracy—against men 'the most virtuous, upright, intelligent, distinguished, and refined of the whole community'. The trial of the forty-two was all a tyrannical fraud:

Poerio, 'a refined and accomplished gentleman, a copious and eloquent speaker, a respectable and blameless character,' would have been highly honoured in England or any other civilized country. Whether he had been disloyal did not concern him: he took it for granted that all the evidence was perjured. Naples was barbarous, the King a monster. And Gladstone shuddered at the thought that he might have had to suffer the same fate had he been born in Naples.

It is improbable that he understood what he heard of the trial. Many of the accused had retracted their original statements, alleging that they did not know the people whose names they had mentioned, that the cross-examiner had dictated their replies; others declared that their statements had been falsified, that they had been prompted and terrorized by the police, that they could not remember or had been too bewildered to know what they had said; others, that they had been tortured and maltreated. Faucitano denied having caused the explosion and alleged that he had been kept on black bread and water for nine days, threatened with corporal punishment, and forced to drink a lot of wine on an empty stomach before confessing. When the crown witnesses were called there were loud protests and frequent interruptions from the accused and their advocates. The Public Prosecutor pronounced his 'Conclusions' on December 4, 6 and 7, and the speeches for the defence lasted through December and January. The court retired to deliberate on January 31, and it was not until the next afternoon that it returned to give verdict and sentence.

Only Agresti, Settembrini and Faucitano were condemned to death, but they were reprieved by Ferdinand in spite of the strong feeling in official circles that they deserved capital punishment. Two others were sentenced to life imprisonment, the rest to terms ranging from thirty years to two weeks. Poerio, Pironti and Romeo were sentenced to twenty-four years in irons. Eight were acquitted. 'A graduation of penalties,' wrote De Sivo, 'which shows the scrupulousness of the judges and the laws.' Ferdinand's horror of bloodshed enabled his worst enemies to strike again, with greater subtlety.

In one sense it was true that Poerio and Settembrini were the most important prisoners, for both had chosen the martyr's rôle and played it heroically to the end. Poerio had the personal magnetism and forensic skill, but Settembrini had the literary talent which can be a formidable weapon in the hands of a determined martyr. He contrived to smuggle his written self-defence out of gaol and have it printed: he accused the police of building an elaborate castle of lies, and insisted that he was the victim of the King's personal vengeance, that his crime was only a crime because the Constitution, sworn to by Ferdinand, had been destroyed.

A student of psychology might draw an interesting parallel between the characters of the professor and the monarch he abhorred. Both were remarkably stubborn and single-minded, with a tendency to over-simplify their judgements of men and things. In his *Protest of the People* Settembrini had portrayed Ferdinand II as the evil genius of his country, the living embodiment of all its misfortunes. Had Ferdinand replied with a *Protest of the King of the Two Sicilies*, he would have doubtless damned Settembrini as a most dangerous mischief-maker and disturber of the public peace. But the latter enjoyed the last word, for he lived to write his *Memoirs*—now available to the young in a 'school edition'. And in the meantime Mr Gladstone let off his anti-Bomba bombs.

XV

VERY quietly but not very accurately Mr Gladstone continued to collect his startling information, haunted by the idea
that but for the grace of God he might have been in Carlo
Poerio's shoes. He had heard Poerio's defence in a 'prostitute court'
and talked to him in the Vicaria and in the fortress of Nisida, 'scenes
fitter for hell than earth,' as he described them. No prisons were
comfortable, even in England, at this date, but Neapolitan gaolers
were probably kinder than their colleagues elsewhere and a sort of
rough humanity made up for insanitary conditions. The thousands
arrested every year for debt in England were treated with disproportionate harshness. In Naples treason was considered a more heinous
crime, but a certain respect mingled with compassion was shown
towards the educated classes who had gambled with the law and lost.
Evidently Gladstone had not visited prisons before, so the shock was
both novel and intense. For here the convicts were chained two by two
as in other parts of Italy, and as in France, Spain and Portugal. The
penalty was an antiquated one, but he had been told that it had been
abolished and revived only recently for the special benefit of Poerio
and his companions by the Count of Aquila, the King's brother. This
was untrue, though Temple reported the same to Palmerston, adding
significantly: 'It is to be hoped that some change will speedily take
place in this treatment which is hardly in accordance with the present
state of European civilization.' Poerio told Gladstone he feared that
his own case had been made worse by Temple's intervention; not that

he blamed him or considered it officious. He had adopted the motto, 'to suffer is to do'.

'I was particularly desirous,' wrote Gladstone in a private memorandum, 'to have Poerio's opinion on the expediency of making some effort in England to draw general attention to these horrors. . . . I said to him that in my view only two modes could be thought of—the first, amicable remonstrance through the cabinets, the second public notoriety and shame. That had Lord Aberdeen been in power the first might have been practicable, but that with Lord Palmerston it would not, because of his position relatively to the other cabinets (Yes, he said, Lord Palmerston was *isolato*), not because he would be wanting in the will. Matters standing thus, I saw no way open but that of exposure; and might that possibly exasperate the Neapolitan government, and increase their severity? His reply was, "As to us, never mind; we can hardly be worse off than we are. But think of our country, for which we are most willing to be sacrificed. Exposure will do it good. The present government of Naples rely on the English Conservative party. . . . Let there be a voice from that party showing that whatever government be in power in England, no support will be given to such proceedings as these. It will do much to break them down. It will also strengthen the hands of a better and less obdurate class about the court. Even there all are not alike. I know it from observation. These ministers are the extremest of extremes. There are others who would willingly see more moderate means adopted." On such grounds as these (I do not quote words) he strongly recommended me to *act*.'

When Gladstone returned to London at the end of February 1851, he could speak of little else. He induced Lord Aberdeen, who had no sympathy whatever for the revolutionaries of 1848 but who was essentially humane, to write to Prince Schwarzenberg, now the Austrian Chancellor, and ask him to use his influence with Ferdinand to alleviate the plight of political prisoners, especially of Poerio. Schwarzenberg's reply was slow and unsatisfactory: 'he reminded Lord Aberdeen that a political offender may be the worst of all offenders, and argued that the rigour exercised by England herself in the Ionian Islands, in Ceylon, in respect of Irishmen, and in the recent case of Ernest Jones, showed how careful she should be in taking up abroad the cause of bad men posing as martyrs in the holy cause of liberty.'

What if one of Ferdinand II's ministers, we might add, were to take up the cudgels for Smith O'Brien M.P. and the young Irelanders?

Seeing that nothing was likely to be achieved by private remonstrance, Gladstone published his two long *Letters to Lord Aberdeen* at the beginning of July. He had rehearsed their contents and tested their dramatic effect in many a conversation, and he had been gratified to observe that they had excited the liveliest interest. The international sensation they created was even more gratifying. A second edition was required almost before the first was in print, and the pamphlet was translated into many languages.

Palmerston was exultant, for this was an unsolicited vindication of his foreign policy. He instantly had copies despatched to British representatives all over Europe, with instructions to present one to each government. In the House of Commons he declared that Mr Gladstone had done himself great honour. 'Instead of seeking amusements, diving into volcanoes and exploring excavated cities, he had visited prisons, descended into dungeons, examined cases of the victims of illegality and injustice, and had then sought to rouse the public opinion of Europe. It was because he concurred in this opinion that he had circulated the pamphlet, in the hope that the European Courts might use their influence.'

Italian exiles and the disciples of Mazzini were equally enthusiastic. The Conservative member for Oxford became a hero of international liberalism, including the Paris Reds. But several sagacious men like Guizot expressed polite misgivings. The alternative in Italy, said Guizot, was the King of Naples on one side, Mazzini on the other; and between the two of them he did not hesitate.

Schwarzenberg had sent duplicates of his correspondence with Aberdeen to General Martini, the Austrian ambassador in Naples, together with a copy of Gladstone's first letter, urging him to inform Fortunato and show the documents to the King if Fortunato agreed. Had the Austrian Chancellor been invited to interfere officially he would have declined, but he said that the question assumed a different aspect because it had been raised by two such distinguished Conservatives as Lord Aberdeen and Mr Gladstone. 'We should fail in the duty imposed on us by the intimacy of our relations with Naples, if we did not enlighten them about the step taken by Lord Aberdeen, by means of which he has succeeded in preventing his friend from launching immediately, as was his intention, a public accusation against the Neapolitan government. By doing everything in our power to avoid such a scandal we hope that our motives will not be misunderstood.'

Castelcicala, the Neapolitan ambassador in London, had already warned Fortunato about Gladstone's intentions without any result. Even when he heard of Aberdeen's letter to Schwarzenberg, Fortunato did nothing. Either he attached no importance to the matter or he was afraid of the King's anger. The subject was never mentioned to Ferdinand until the storm broke. Castelcicala was reprimanded and recalled. Before leaving London he asked Palmerston somewhat ingenuously to distribute fifteen copies of a formal reply from his government to Gladstone's letters, a reply both mild and moderate, point by point. Palmerston retorted with an insulting diatribe, prophesying violent revolution unless his government hastened to redress the wrongs to which their attention had been drawn, and refusing to touch a pamphlet 'consisting of a flimsy tissue of bare assertions and reckless denials, mixed up with coarse ribaldry and commonplace abuse.'

There was no danger of revolution so long as King Ferdinand stood at the helm with a large and faithful army. Having been baited by Palmerston for so many years—an exorbitant indemnity was now being claimed for damages to English property in Sicily during the rebellion—the King regarded this as just another proof of English hostility. He failed to realize that Gladstone had contributed a powerful piece of propaganda to the cause of Italian unity, all the more powerful because its source was so respectable. The trial of the insurgents on May 15, 1848, went on and on. Political offenders were removed to remoter fortresses. Ferdinand was so vexed with Castelcicala that he refused to see him, but when he discovered that both Fortunato and his own private secretary Corsi had kept him in the dark he dismissed them without more ado. Fortunato had been invited to a royal hunt on the next day, January 19, 1852. An hour after midnight he was wakened by a messenger with an urgent despatch. Imagining that the hunt had been deferred, he was taken aback to read a decree of dismissal. 'He's a true Tiberius in sextodecimo,' the old minister exclaimed. At the meet next morning the King looked round with a twinkle in his eye and said to the Duke of Sangro: 'Where's the father of the hunt? Perhaps his valet forgot to call him. Let's leave a carriage for him to catch up with us.' The carriage waited in vain.

Ferdinand was not sorry to brush off this last link with the veteran liberals. Henceforth he reigned as undisputed autocrat, for his ministers were little more than submissive clerks. Ferdinando Troya, who had been minister of ecclesiastical affairs and public instruction, the 'reactionary' brother of constitutionalist Carlo, succeeded Fortunato as president of the council, and Luigi Carafa di Traetto became 'director' of foreign affairs, a post described as provisional, which he held till 1860. Two officers of mediocre capacity were appointed the King's secretaries. He preferred 'directors' to ministers because he paid them less and felt that they were more manageable. Likewise he preferred sending mere chargés d'affaires to foreign Courts. He sent his orders to each department separately—in some instances without consulting the minister at the head of it, or informing him previously of his intentions. The kingdom grew more and more isolated. Ferdinand's invariable reply to foreign criticism was that he knew his own people best and what régime suited them. The Bourbons of Naples, as he put it, were not wood to make tops of.

An attempt by Baldasseroni, the Tuscan Prime Minister, to draw Ferdinand into a league of conservative Italian States failed dismally. The Grand Duke Leopold II had been restored to Tuscany by a popular vote, but there too the Constitution had fallen into abeyance, wrecked by the so-called democrats, Montanelli, Guerrazzi and their clique. When the Count of Trapani married his own niece, the Grand Duke's daughter Maria Isabella in 1850, the Florentine press had attacked the marriage viciously on political grounds; and Baldasseroni had annoyed Ferdinand by advising the Grand Duke to retain the Constitution after his flight to Gaeta. Among Ferdinand's counter-proposals to Baldasseroni were: the exclusion of Austria from the league and a declaration of return to absolutism. But the conservatives of Rome, Florence, Parma and Modena considered Austrian adherence necessary. 'What could we four corpses do without Austria, but with Naples in her stead?' exclaimed the Modenese Malaguzzi. 'Certainly the latter will not revive us.' Without Austria, said Baldasseroni, Italy would become the prey of France and suffer from chronic revolutionary strife.

Ferdinand feared that an Italian league under Austrian patronage would unite France and England against it. Situated, as he was fond of saying, 'between holy water and salt water,' he based his foreign policy on Anglo-French rivalry in the Mediterranean and hoped to gain Louis Napoleon's support against Palmerston. The *coup d'état* of December 1851, showed that the French were equally tired of party strife and that they too longed for peace and security. Several months before the Prince President became Emperor, Ferdinand was prepared for that event. Antonini, his envoy in Paris, had already received his credentials to the new sovereign with a blank left for the prospective title, so that he was the first to recognize the new French Empire, a gesture which Napoleon III was to bear in mind. When over 10,000 French political prisoners were transported to Cayenne and Algeria, many for life, no Gladstone arose to denounce their trial and conviction. Yet sixty-six deputies were condemned to perpetual exile, eighteen for a lesser period, and nearly one hundred thousand suspected insurgents were arrested shortly after the *coup d'état*, on the orders of officials as zealous as those in Naples.

Temple continued to send his brother detailed reports of the political trials as if nothing else were happening in Naples. In April 1851, Lord Napier resumed his duties as secretary to the British legation, which had become a stronghold of anti-Bourbonism. According to Temple, the Italian Unity sect was an invention of the police, and the King's party had been the chief promoters of the barricades on May 15 'for the purpose of bringing on a crisis which might lead to the overthrow of the Constitution.' He railed at the quarantine regulations owing to an outbreak of yellow fever at Rio de Janeiro: 'There seems to be every disposition on the part of this Government to separate this country as much as possible from the rest of Europe, by throwing every difficulty in the way of all communications with them. In this it would seem to take the Chinese Government for its model.' The internal state of Sicily, of course, was 'far from satisfactory'. Everything Temple could think of was grievously wrong with both Sicilies and he gloated, like Gladstone, on the catalogue of woes with which his friends supplied him. It is scarcely surprising that the King was irked by this querulous busybody, who reported on April 3, 1851: 'It seems that the King of Naples decidedly disapproves of any of his subjects either sending goods to the Great Exhibition . . . in London this year, or of their visiting England themselves during the approaching summer. . . .

'Persons who have expressed a desire of visiting London during the Exhibition have been dissuaded from applying for passports, as it has been hinted to them that if they went there they might not be allowed to return.

'The idea of the Government seems to be that the Exhibition will afford a pretext for the assembling of all the violent Republicans in Europe, and the Neapolitans by mixing in such society would run great risk of having their minds tainted with revolutionary doctrines.

'What danger would be incurred by the goods which might have been sent for exhibition does not appear to be quite so evident.'

Ferdinand's lack of interest in the Great Exhibition is comprehensible. Neapolitan trade had suffered from the upheavals of 1848. All his attempts to develop and improve it had been frustrated by Poerio and his clique, who had given more thought to fighting the Austrians in Lombardy. Many a sensible scheme had had to be shelved, such as the railway from Naples to Brindisi and the rebuilding of that ancient double harbour, which should attract considerable trade from the Levant. Now Ferdinand was chiefly concerned with the reconstruction of his battered kingdom, with building new docks, roads and railways.

While Palmerston was fulminating against Ferdinand and piling on indemnities for the merchants in Sicily, the fine old city of Melfi in the province of Basilicata was devastated by an earthquake worse than any that had occurred since 1805. 'The morning of the 14th of August was very sultry, and a leaden atmosphere prevailed. It was remarked that an unusual silence appeared to extend over the animal world. The hum of insects ceased, the feathered tribes were mute, not a breath of wind moved the arid vegetation. About half-past two o'clock the town of Melfi rocked for about six seconds, and nearly every building fell in. . . . The awful event occurred at a time when most of the inhabitants of a better condition were at dinner; and the result is, that out of the whole population only a few peasants labouring in the fields escaped. More than 700 dead bodies have already been dug out of the ruins, and it is supposed that not less than 800 are yet entombed. A college accommodating 65 boys and their teachers is no longer traceable. But the melancholy event does not end here. The adjoining village of

Ascoli has also suffered, 32 houses having fallen in, and the church being levelled with the ground. More than 200 persons perished there. Another small town, Barile, has actually disappeared; and a lake has arisen from the bowels of the earth, the waters being warm and brackish.'[1] Even in the open country carts drawn by oxen were suddenly swallowed up. Whole families wandered about stupefied, some searching among the ruins, women weeping, children crying for their parents, and a great many buried alive.

Although his youngest son Joseph, Count of Lucera, was fatally ill —the child died at the end of the month—the King set off to superintend the relief work in early September. He reached Melfi on horseback under a heavy rainfall and went at once to inspect the ruins by torchlight. After a sleepless night in a ramshackle hut, he held a public audience early the next morning, visited the hospitals and toured the entire neighbourhood, distributing alms and comfort, praise and blame, with that spontaneous warm sincerity which endeared him to his unsophisticated subjects. The prisoners who had been released during the earthquake, had helped to rescue those who had been trapped under falling masonry. Ferdinand pardoned these, but he dismissed the intendant of the province, who had been accused of withholding the workmen's wages and misapplying the charitable funds entrusted to him for distribution among the sufferers. A relief committee was set up under the local bishop, and the King returned the following year to inspect the new buildings and roads he had planned.

Though always ready to go where he felt he was needed, Ferdinand was reluctant to return to Sicily. Filangieri had done much to restore order and relative prosperity to that anarchic island. A grizzled old warrior, austere in his personal habits, he thought, like the late Lord Curzon, that his position required a certain air of pomp. He gave magnificent balls and receptions in the royal palace, where his handsome daughters acted as hostesses. Through his wife, born a Moncada di Paternò, he was related to half the Sicilian aristocracy, who despite their aversion to Neapolitans availed themselves greedily of his lavish invitations. The fact that he had an admirable Parisian *chef* also helped to rally the rank and fashion of Palermo round so distinguished a representative of the old régime. It was a long time since they had

<hr>

[1] From the *Athenæum Journal*, September 13, 1851.

been regaled with such sumptuous banquets. Full dress uniform was *de rigueur*, and there was far more glitter than in the royal palace of Naples. The *Journal of Sicily* continued to publish florid addresses of loyalty to the King from the various municipalities, and Filangieri was anxious for him to come over and propitiate the island in person. He told Senior[1] that he did not believe in the hatred which our Blue-book described as existing against the King. 'The Sicilians,' he said, 'hate the Neapolitans and, so far as they identify him with Neapolitan rule, hate the King, but they have no personal dislike to him. They know him, indeed, only by acts of individual kindness. Wherever he has been he has done good; he has made roads and bridges and relieved individual distress.' Unfortunately it was not in Ferdinand's nature to forget an injury. When he finally decided to visit the island he avoided Palermo, thinking this would teach it a lesson: it was rather a mistake.

To strengthen his army was his constant care since 1848. 'The army,' reported Temple in February 1852, 'has been increased to nearly three times its usual number, and greatly exceeds the force required for the maintenance of internal tranquillity, and it absorbs a large portion of the national revenue, which might be more advantageously applied to more useful purposes. The only troops upon which reliance can be placed in times of danger are the Swiss, and their numbers have been increased to about one third above their usual complement. They receive better pay and better clothing than the Neapolitan troops.' Though stout and scant of breath, Ferdinand felt rejuvenated among his officers. Perhaps they were the only men with whom he felt thoroughly at ease. He had decided to hold manœuvres on a grand scale in Calabria, combined with a tour of inspection, in October 1852.

Except in a single case where his host was rewarded with a title, Ferdinand refused to accept private hospitality. The Calabrian gentry, as rare travellers have testified, were hospitably inclined. 'As there are no inns in that province except on the coach-road which skirts the western coast,' wrote Lear, 'the traveller depends entirely on introductions to some family in each town he visits.' The few inns were squalid: 'the numbers of formidable vermin were so great and distressing in the sleeping apartments, that we could not contemplate

[1] Nassau William Senior, *op. cit*, Vol. II, p. 64.

the animated beds without a shudder. . . .' But the passage of a stranger in these parts was so unusual that it roused embarrassing curiosity, and as Lear confessed: 'The greatest penance of this roving life is the state of exhaustion and weariness in which you arrive at your evening abode; and as you feel very properly obliged to play the polite for a certain time to your entertainers, the wrestling between a sense of duty and an oppressive inclination to sleep is most painful. The good people, too, persist in delaying supper (in order that they may provide a good one) till you are reduced (ere it comes) to a state of torture and despair, in the protracted struggle between hunger, Morpheus, and civility.'

The King's own cook preceded him in a van with a complete kitchen service. When he could not stay with the local intendant he would spend the night in some religious house. Often he seemed to take a perverse pleasure in stopping at places ill-prepared to receive him, perhaps because they gave him an insight into lives remote from his own. At a Capuchin monastery he was much amused by a Brother Anthony who dispensed medical recipes although he never washed, and who was reputed to work miracles. This friar shared his cell with a pet dormouse. On showing it to the royal guest he remarked that the people should be as devoted to His Majesty as the rodent was to himself.

Triumphal arches with such inscriptions as 'Long live Ferdinand II, the most clement of monarchs!' and

> *'You are great, you are pious, our Father and King,*
> *Your fame and your glory will ne'er cease to ring!'* —

flags, fireworks, chiming church-bells, illuminations and acclamations punctuated his strenuous progress. He only allowed himself a few hours' sleep before rushing on as if propelled by an engine. Public and private audiences began the day, when favours, subsidies and pardons were speedily distributed. Gracious and brusque in turn, he was apt to be caustic with those whose loyalty he doubted. When the judges of the criminal court of Cosenza came to pay him their respects, he glared at their president Corapi and said: 'I am dissatisfied with you.' The court had recently acquitted a certain Morelli, who had been accused of subversive activities. Corapi bowed in silence, retired to doff his robes, and returned in a frock coat to tender his resignation. This was accepted, but his dignity had impressed the King, and he was granted a pension equivalent to his whole salary. To those who appealed on behalf of relations involved in a political trial Ferdinand said gruffly: 'Let justice take its course.' Temple was rebuffed with a similar reply when he tried 'to ascertain how far the King feels inclined to attend to the suggestion, that the time has arrived for showing more clemency to political offenders—which had been offered to him not only by Her Majesty's Government, but from the Governments of Russia and France.' During an interview at Easter—'The King assured me that he was much gratified by the friendly sentiments expressed towards him by my Government . . . that he was convinced that the suggestions offered by it were dictated by the most friendly motives— He stated that we must not judge of the Neapolitan people by those of other Nations—He did not know whether prisoners were chained or not, but that was a matter dependent upon the law, with which he could not interfere.—That the prisoners of Montefusco (whither Poerio, Pironti and Nisco had been transferred) . . . are removed to the apartments which were formerly occupied by the governor. He mentioned these persons in terms of some bitterness, but added that they were however "men". His Majesty was very gracious . . . but did not give me much reason to hope that any immediate change of system is in contemplation.' With regard to political offenders he remained consistent until his dying day.

Neapolitans are notoriously unpunctual, but Ferdinand had a habit of arriving long before he was expected. Having calculated the hour of his arrival the authorities of Catanzaro had arranged to assemble in the intendant's house at 2 p.m., which allowed them ample time for their midday meal and a refreshing nap. The King turned up at twelve-thirty to find the city deserted. He drove straight to the Cathedral: it was closed, and the Bishop was taking his siesta. This seemed suspicious: he feared some sinister plot. One of his carriage horses stumbled on the cobbles, which increased his irritation. At the intendant's house there was no guard of honour, only a few savage-looking urban militia dressed like brigands. Where was the intendant? Suddenly roused from slumber, that distracted functionary had rushed to the Cathedral, buttoning himself up on the way. Failing to find the King there, he returned all out of breath.

Catanzaro bestirred itself frantically. The magistrates ran to the public attorney's to don their robes and grabbed each other's in the scramble, and there was another mad chase to the bolted Cathedral and thence to the intendant's residence.

'At last I find somebody who will show me to my room,' exclaimed Ferdinand on perceiving the intendant's wife, flustered and dishevelled at the top of the stairs. 'Who are you?' he added, seeing a bearded young dandy beside her. Hearing that this was the receiver-general Musitano, of whom he had not had favourable reports, he said: 'Go at once and get that beard removed. You have no business here.' Just as his grandfather had connected whiskers with Jacobins, Ferdinand regarded beards as badges of liberalism, especially when worn like a fringe.

A few hours of uneasy silence followed the storm. While the King retired behind closed doors it was rumoured that he would leave immediately. His first impulse was to drive on to Pizzo. The intendant, the local commandant, and the captain of gendarmerie were all demoted; others were only spared the same fate when it was explained that their lapse had been due to a misunderstanding: he had been expected three hours later. But like his great-uncle Charles IV of Spain, he kept his own time and fancied that others should keep it by a sort of telepathy. Yielding to the tearful entreaties of the intendant's wife, he spent the night at Catanzaro. That lady had also appealed to his brother the Count of Trapani, who replied: 'I am very sorry, Madam, but I can do nothing for you. His Majesty has chosen me to accompany him in preference to the other princes because I am the only one not to bother him with recommendations.'

Before sunset Ferdinand inspected the new road to Cotrone and attended Benediction before dining with his suite. He talked of returning to Naples from Pizzo, but he was always changing his mind. In spite of his vaunted severity, he pardoned forty-two prisoners for political and other offences. The audience he held next day was typical. The deputation from Cotrone came first on the list, but when it was announced by the majordomo the King shouted: 'No, sir. The deputation from Pizzo!' Though smaller than Cotrone, the 'most faithful' city of Pizzo was still to be distinguished for its capture of Murat. Its deputation included Don Gaetano Alcalà, a son of the Duke of Infantado's agent, who was warned by a friend while waiting in an ante-room to remove his small goatee. A razor and a mirror were produced, and he shaved just before he was summoned. He found the King standing in the middle of the hall with the Hereditary Prince on his right and Trapani on his left. Invited to honour Pizzo with a visit the King replied amiably: 'I am sorry for the inconvenience you had in coming all this way, and equally sorry for the greater inconvenience we shall cause your city, since we have decided to embark from there to Naples.' Alcalà regretted the sacrifice of his goatee. Baron Barracco invited the King to Cotrone on behalf of that city's deputation, which had travelled forty miles on horseback as the coach-road was not yet completed. Ferdinand said he would gladly grant their wishes on a future occasion and thanked them for their pains. After more formalities he visited the hospital and college where the youngest pupil recited an ode to him and a chorus sang a welcoming hymn. He chucked the precocious cherub under the chin and thanked the rector and teachers effusively. As it was raining he insisted on seeing everything in the school. The teacher of natural history showed him a collection of shells, one of which, his own discovery, he had christened *Rotopea borbonica*. The King kept his composure, but when an adjoining field was pointed out to him as the botanical garden he remarked with a smile: 'You had better plant some lettuce.'

Another beard caused trouble at Marcellinara. The King had heard many complaints of the tyranny and injustice of the rich Calabrian landlords, many of whom were liberals in politics. When he saw the hirsute Baron Sanseverino he snapped at him: 'Owing to your behaviour you great Calabrian proprietors are driving the people towards Communism. This will lead to your own undoing, not to ours. Go away and remove that beard.' At first he ordered his arrest, but later sent him to Catanzaro, where he remained under police supervision for more than a year.

To celebrate the Queen's saint's day—she was expecting another child—a mass review was held at Tiriolo and many more political prisoners were pardoned. Ferdinand commuted the death sentences of Silvio Spaventa, Barbarisi and Dardano to life imprisonment; Scialoia and Leopardi were to be banished; and the sentences passed on others were reduced. The decree spoke of the King's 'inexhaustible clemency,' but Temple thought it far too niggardly. On October 28 he reported: 'During the King's visit to the Calabrian provinces His Majesty commuted the sentence of death pronounced by the Grand Court of Cosenza upon one prisoner to thirty years of irons. He reduced the term of imprisonment in irons of 23 persons from 25 to 18 years, and the punishment of 10 other persons has also been diminished and two have been pardoned. In addition to these acts of clemency His Majesty has ordered that the penal prosecutions for political offenders instituted against 720 persons at Cosenza, and of 1170 persons at Catanzaro shall be abolished, from which it appears that in addition to all those who had been tried by the Courts of Cosenza and Catanzaro for political offences there were 1890 persons either in prison or obliged to lie concealed in consequence of orders having been issued for their arrest.

It is said that these measures of severity were adopted by the Intendente Signor Mazza from an excess of zeal rather than from any specific orders emanating from the police or the Government. If so, it is very fortunate for the inhabitants that His Majesty visited that part of his dominions, and it is to be hoped that he may be induced to extend his tour to the other provinces of his kingdom where a similar state of things may exist, and convince himself that Mr Gladstone's statements upon the subject were not so much exaggerated as his Ministers endeavoured to impress upon the world.'

Sometimes Ferdinand's obstinacy led to his own discomfiture as when, against advice, he insisted on taking an impossible road to Mongiana. 'I may break, but I do not bend,' he said. The result was that his carriage sank into a sandy riverbed. He shouted to his postilions to whip up the horses, which reared and kicked with only damage to the vehicle. He was forced to spend the night at Pizzo in a somewhat cantankerous mood. Though spacious lodgings had been prepared for him, he chose to stay at a poky little monastery next to the church of Saint Francis of Paola. The Father Superior had said to him: 'I know that Your Majesty has honoured other monasteries on your journey, and hope you will not disdain to honour this humble house of our great Calabrian saint.' But he was taken aback when the King replied: 'With the greatest pleasure.' All the luggage had been forwarded to his original destination, which added to the confusion. The royal *chef* lost patience when told that neither coal nor water was available. 'So you invite the King to stay when you haven't any water!' Dinner was served on rough tables in a dark corridor as there was no refectory. Several of his suite had to sleep on the draughty floor.

Next day the party set forth in lighter carriages, the King in a small phaeton with his son beside him and the valet Galizia behind. Towards midday Ferdinand asked Galizia what he had brought for breakfast. He produced two chickens, but alas, had forgotten the bread. 'Never mind,' said the bluff monarch, and ordered an officer to procure two 'ration loaves'. Noticing that his son only ate the chicken, he asked: 'What's the matter? aren't you taking any bread?' The Prince complained that it was tough and stale. 'Eat it and be truly thankful,' said the King. 'This is what the soldiers eat, better fellows than we.'

Two busy days were spent at Mongiana, the big arms factory. Ambitious plans were discussed for its development. The King hoped to make it the most important Mediterranean arsenal, a potent contribution to national independence.

There were more audiences and inspections in Monteleone and other towns. At Bagnara the King chose to put up at a primitive inn. The innkeeper's wife offered him her finest linen, but he told her: 'That isn't what you give your other clients. No, no, I want your ordinary stuff. You must treat me the same as the others.' When she changed the sheets he said: 'That's what I like. These are the best days of my life.' Until 1860 the proud innkeeper used to show visitors the humble room the King had slept in.

At last Filangieri prevailed on him to cross over to Sicily. On October 23 he sailed to Messina, where he was acclaimed with such frenzied festivities that even he was flabbergasted. Sicilian chauvinists have tried to belittle this enthusiastic reception, but the facts have been recorded by eye-witnesses.[1] Cheers rent the sky as he climbed into an open carriage upholstered in yellow damask, and it was hard to prevent the crowd from detaching the horses and dragging it through the streets. A petty official called Grosso clung to it bellowing 'Long live the hero of the Two Sicilies!' so repeatedly that the King asked who the man was. 'What a blockhead!' he remarked. When told that he was now 'a blockhead by royal decree', Grosso laughed with delight and bellowed all the louder.

In Messina, whose population was estimated at 60,000 and whose trade was more considerable than that of any other port in Sicily, everything was done on a grander scale than in Calabria, from the chanting of the *Te Deum* in the Cathedral to the gala performance in the theatre entitled 'The Public Prayer', a musical allegory which ended with the descent of two small genii from Heaven with a golden

[1] See *Memorie Storiche ovvero Messina nel 23 e 25 ottobre 1852*. Messina, 1852.

streamer inscribed 'Long live Ferdinand II' and a chorus of boys and girls singing his praises. Thousands of leaflets were scattered among the audience: 'The gratitude of the people is the triumph of sovereignty'—'Who is more grateful to the august Ferdinand II than the people of Messina?'—'Having restored peace and order, Sire, we beseech you to grant one more favour: your august presence!'—'Our prayers have been answered. Long live the Trajan of the Two Sicilies!' etc., etc. Ferdinand was also called the new Titus and the image of God on earth: '*Giusto, benigno e pio/Immagine di Dio!*' If all this was as insincere as some have alleged, it was an effective substitute for sincerity: the mask had become the face. Ferdinand, whose sincerity has also been doubted, took it graciously in his stride: when he did not crack jokes he betrayed his emotion, and doffed his cap to the people again and again.

Catania vied in celebration with Messina. More harbour works and hospitals were inspected, more deputations were interviewed, but Ferdinand was able to relax in the spacious monastery of San Niccolò. He remembered many of the monks by name and repeated his usual greeting to clergy: 'I kiss your hands.' After Mass, during which it was noticed he often kissed the saints' images in his missal, his eyes moist with tears, he wished to hear the famous organ. As it was said to be the finest in the world John Galt's description is worthy of quotation. 'The effect of the sonata which is performed in order to show the whole genius of the instrument, may be compared to the course of a river from the fountain-head to the sea. It begins with a sweet little trilling movement, like the sound of waters trickling in a far remote pastoral upland. The breadth of harmony increases, and the mind is excited to activity, while the introduction of a delightful echo suggests the images of a rapid stream, and bands of huntsmen, with horns and hounds, coursing the banks. Continuing still to rise and spread, the music takes a more regular character, and fills the imagination with the notion of a Thames, covered with moving vessels, flowing through a multitudinous city. Occasional military movements gradually open all the fountains of the instrument; and the full tide, deepening and rolling on, terminates in a finale so vast, so various, so extraordinary an effusion of harmony, that it can be compared only to the great expanse of the ocean agitated by a tempest, and the astonishing turbulence of a Trafalgarian battle.'

But relaxation was rare. Ferdinand left Catania at midnight and during the seven hours of his return journey by carriage to Messina he never closed an eye. To the deputations which met him along the road his benevolence was abounding. At Messina he only rested four hours before hearing Mass and receiving more deputations. Among others he saw Marchese, who was popular in spite of being a tax-collector. 'I remember your father,' he said. 'There was a real gentleman! What can I do for you?'—'Your Majesty should repair an injustice, the tax on windows.'—'I didn't put it on. You put it on yourselves.'—'Right, Your Majesty, but the poor man's hut with one or two windows pays as much as Your Majesty's palace. Moreover the payment of the land-tax is heavily in arrears. How am I to collect it? Must I sell the pallets of the poor?' The King told him to come back later with a written petition, and in due course houses with no more than three windows were exempt from taxation and arrears payments were condoned.

The Duke of Calabria attended his first ball that night, but he appeared more embarrassed than amused, whereas the Count of Trapani whirled round like a top with the prettiest of the ladies and enjoyed himself immensely. 'Messina will ever be dear to my heart,' said Ferdinand before he left it.

The festivities went on after his departure; extravagant odes and declarations of homage continued to pour in so copiously that Filangieri had to send a circular to intendants to limit their output. Shocked chauvinists have attempted to dismiss all this as mere mob servility. But an impartial French observer, Odilon Barrot, was so genuinely impressed that he wrote: 'A sublime spectacle! this is the most dazzling reconciliation of a legitimate sovereign with his people!' And on the whole the King's tour was a success. Without any conscious effort to court popularity, uncompromisingly true to himself and his sense of duty, he had charged through the Calabrian provinces, and on to Messina and Catania, like a benignant bull. Those who were gored were a minority of corrupt officials, local bullies and demagogues. The majority were heartened by his obvious determination to help them and their communes. The countless audiences, the considerable subsidies he had granted, the pardons and reprieves, the penal prosecutions he had quashed, above all his personal interest, left pleasant memories in out-of-the-way places. Ferdinand had received 28,000 petitions in less than a month. His preference for the Count of Trapani who 'did not bother him with recommendations' is therefore understandable. Though he never overcame an innate distrust of his Calabrian and Sicilian subjects, it was possibly some consolation to be described by them as 'the image of God on earth' so soon after Gladstone had described his government as the negation of God.

XVI

FOR the next seven years Naples was a haven of peace and growing prosperity. Unfortunately peace and police went together in awkward harness, as Ferdinand was determined to prevent disorders at any cost, and prosperity was checked by bad harvests, phylloxera, more earthquakes and a cholera epidemic.

Lord Palmerston doggedly pursued his vendetta against 'King Bomba', whose contempt for foreign critics infuriated him all the more. If he understood his own people, he misunderstood his age. He failed to realize the power of the press over world opinion. No censorship could cope with the hostile literature smuggled into the country. Banned books and newspapers came to have the exciting charm of forbidden fruit: had they been allowed they could not have done more mischief. An enlightened press in Naples might have foiled foreign propaganda, but owing to stupid censorship the local newspapers were stale, flat and uninteresting. The small but influential reading public snatched at any publication from abroad.

Since 1848 the police had become a government within the government. The chiefs were fanatical royalists with more cunning than culture. Peccheneda, who was considered a monster, had started his career under the Corsican Saliceti during the French occupation. Manna, who had been minister of commerce during the constitutional régime, told Senior[1] in 1850: 'People begin to regret Del Carretto.

[1] *Op. cit.*, Vol. II, p. 26.

In his time there was tyranny, but there was some motive for it. If you were arrested you could guess why: you had probably said something offensive to the Government, or offensive to a Minister, or offensive to a Minister's servant, or you had refused to comply with some intimation of the wishes of the police. Now people are put in prison and let out again without any assignable cause. Del Carretto's police, too, did something for the convenience of the town. The streets were tolerably clean, the beggars were forced either to support themselves or to inhabit the great poorhouse, the streets were thoroughfares instead of markets.'

As prefect of police Peccheneda commanded an army of inspectors, detectives and spies whose excess of zeal alienated sympathy from the government, but they undoubtedly helped to crush conspiracy. The plotters hibernated until the dismissal of Peccheneda's successor Mazza, who was only appointed a director 'exercising the same power as if he were minister, but with lower rank and less salary,' in accordance with the King's new policy.

Temple reported on November 6, 1852: 'Great hopes had been entertained that after the death of M. Peccheneda and the King's visit to Calabria, a change in the present system of rigour would be adopted, but this expectation has been greatly damped by the late appointment of the present Director of the Police, which has caused considerable uneasiness and dissatisfaction even to the most devoted adherents of absolute monarchy. Monsieur Mazza, although said to be less venal than his predecessor, having a large private income, is considered to be a most violent and active partisan of the reactionary policy, a proof of which is the number of persons against whom he had caused penal proceedings to be taken, which were abolished by the King during his late visit to Calabria; and indeed the measures adopted by him during the time he was Intendente were so much disapproved of by the late General Nunziante, military commander of the district, a devoted royalist and personally attached to the King, that the latter was induced to resign his command, and his death which ensued not long after that resignation was attributed in great measure to the mortification he suffered in consequence of having been prevented from carrying out the amnesty, which he had promised to grant in the King's name, by the opposition of Monsieur Mazza.'

Temple had his knife into Mazza from the start, and he was to be the ultimate cause of his disgrace. But at least Mazza's tyranny proved beneficial during the cholera epidemic of 1854. Alarming rumours were nipped in the bud and those who spread them were prosecuted; so were the usual sharks and profiteers. Prices were controlled; butchers reluctant to serve the public were threatened with a thrashing; both meat and lemons were made available to the poor; the chemists who denied them medicine were arrested and those who closed their shops were forced to open them; grave-diggers were organized and punished for dereliction of duty. Arbitrary measures; but even the liberals had to admit that there had been some good in them.

While many fled to the country, including Murena, the Minister of the Interior, the Cardinal Archbishop Riario Sforza set a noble example, bringing the Sacrament to the dying and distributing money, medicine, food and linen among the poor in the most densely populated districts, where the plague was rampant in its most gruesome shapes, the dead and the dying huddled in hopeless misery. To the desperate in dark alleys he brought comfort and hope, and a great number of those he visited recovered. The King, in spite of his extreme horror of infection, spent much time encouraging the sick in hospitals and elsewhere. When a crowd gathered round him shouting, 'Sire, we are being poisoned,' he answered: 'Well, I've come along to be poisoned with you and keep you company!' Considering the prevalent ignorance of hygiene and that some 14,000 caught the disease, it is scarcely surprising that 7016 died of it in Naples. The Sicilian coastal towns were also infected in spite of every precaution, but the epidemic decreased during the autumn and vanished in the winter.

Sicily had seldom been so well governed, but Filangieri was constantly thwarted by Giovanni Cassisi, the Minister for Sicilian Affairs at Naples, whom he had recommended for that office. In Messina Cassisi had been a friendly collaborator, but in Naples he became the Lieutenant-General's worst enemy. His personal vindictiveness extended to Palermo, where he had once been involved in a scandal, so that Filangieri's schemes to improve that city met with obstruction. The struggle became acute when Filangieri planned a network of twenty-one new roads to be built within six months, covering 625 miles and including eight suspension bridges. Remembering the sulphur imbroglio, Ferdinand would not authorize a contract with the French firm proposed by Filangieri, who was asked to find Sicilian contractors instead, whereupon Cassisi insinuated that these were a screen for the French and that Filangieri would reap illicit profit; so the contract was shelved. Lest it should be said that he did not want the roads to be built, Cassisi proposed a different contractor for each province. From time to time Filangieri went over to explain his views to the King, who received him with cordial assurances of agreement on principle. But the Lieutenant-General, a man of action, was baffled by the slanders and intrigues of the wily Sicilian. Tired and disgusted, he went to Ischia for the restorative baths until the King accepted his resignation in October 1854. For the next five months his post remained vacant. It took a great deal of persuasion to induce Prince Castelcicala to accept it. At sixty-four he was too old, he protested (Filangieri was seventy), besides, his health was wretched—he had been wounded in the head at Waterloo and the wound had never healed: he had to wear a silver plate over it (Filangieri had been permanently lamed in battle). Then his wife died, and he had to go into mourning. The King and Cassisi overruled his protests: to Palermo he went in May 1855.

From now on Cassisi had his own way. He removed most of the officials who had served under Filangieri except Maniscalco, the indispensable chief of police. Though Filangieri's most ambitious schemes fell through, some 480 miles of new road were built; the docks of Palermo, Messina, Trapani and Girgenti were enlarged; Milazzo, being Cassisi's birthplace, was endowed with a new harbour; and Sicily was connected with Naples by electric telegraph, which was extended throughout the island. Moreover the budget was balanced and the public funds rose steadily.

Though Ferdinand had been the first to recognize Napoleon III as Emperor, he had cause to fear the return of a Bonaparte who had been a Carbonaro. He had always admired Czar Nicholas I, and he could scarcely conceal his partiality for Russia when the Crimean War broke out. But Austria agreed with Prussia to maintain an armed neutrality, and Ferdinand had no choice except to follow suit. Since France and England were allies his position became increasingly difficult, but in spite of their harassing tactics he stood his ground.

Napoleon III had the parvenu's prestige complex, so that trifling incidents were apt to lead to explosions. A tremendous fuss was created because two French officers were detained by quarantine regulations. One of these, Baron Du Casse, a staff captain and aide-de-camp to Prince Jerome Bonaparte, had written a biography of Joseph Bonaparte in ten volumes and it was feared that he intended to spread Muratist propaganda; the other was the Duc Lesparre, a lieutenant-colonel and aide-de-camp to the French Minister of War. Maupas, the French minister in Naples, applied for an exception to be made in their favour, as they were to attend the autumn manœuvres. The King ordered the Board of Health to consider their case, but the decision was negative. As another steamer was returning to Marseilles shortly after their arrival, they seized this opportunity to embark. In Paris they complained bitterly of their rude reception, and the French government 'saw in this act a wish to offend'.

Maupas was ordered to leave the capital without waiting for any explanation. Lowther, the British chargé d'affaires reported on November 10: 'I have this day seen a person closely connected with the Court who informed me that it was the intention of the King and of the Neapolitan Government to prevent the affair of the departure of M. de Maupas . . . from becoming serious. . . . I understand that His Majesty is very much annoyed at what has taken place, that he considers that all was done which could be done on this occasion, His Majesty having twice ordered the Board of Health to assemble to reconsider the case and to make an exception if possible in favour of the two French officers. Had any offence to France been intended, he would not have taken even this step. My informant told me that it was His Majesty's opinion that the French Government had been too hasty, that offence had been taken where no offence was meant. . . . He seemed also to wish me to understand that the Neapolitan Government felt that that of France had some motive (*arrière-pensée*) in getting up this quarrel.' The general opinion in the diplomatic body, added Lowther, was that the French Government had put themselves in the wrong: 'At the same time . . . great blame is to be attached to the Board of Health (which could have made an exception in the circumstances) and that His Majesty whose power is absolute could have given permission for these gentlemen to land had he wished to have done. I should state that the greatest difficulty always exists in transacting any business with this Government. No one is considered responsible, and it is with considerable trouble and much loss of time that answers can be obtained to the numerous complaints which are being daily made against the agents of the Government, and the present occasion has been made great use of for expressing disapprobation of the administration in general.'

Maupas returned after a month's absence and diplomatic relations with France were resumed, thanks to Antonini, Ferdinand's ambassador in Paris, who was a clever diplomat of the old school. Sometimes his deafness caused misunderstandings, as when he returned from Naples and the Emperor asked him: 'How's the King?' 'Perfectly dreadful,' he replied, thinking he meant the sea voyage. The Emperor had to laugh. But Antonini's ear-trumpet often served as a diplomatic resource. When relations with France were strained, anticipating a scene with the Emperor, he put the trumpet in his pocket. After Napoleon's tirade he answered: 'I beg your pardon, Sire, I forgot my ear-trumpet and could not hear a word of Your Majesty's speech.' The Emperor could only pretend to be amused.

Maupas continued to pester Ferdinand. Could the French use Brindisi as a temporary base for their fleet? Could they use Messina as a depot for French steamships plying between Marseilles and the Dardanelles? The King answered no; determined to be neutral. Maupas then said he was very anxious that the Neapolitan Government should reserve until later any formal declaration on the subject, 'as even a declaration of neutrality might have an influence upon the course which would be pursued by Russia'.

Then Baron Brenier arrived on a mission which kept his colleagues guessing. 'Up to the present time,' wrote Lowther on February 14, 1854, 'the purpose of M. Brenier's mission has not transpired, but the feeling at Court seems to be that he is engaged in making general observations on the state of this country rather than on any other particular object. I should add that M. Brenier was received with marked attention by every member of the royal family at the state ball which His Majesty gave last evening.' This marked attention had little significance, since Ferdinand had taken an intense dislike to him. During his audience with the King Brenier had introduced Tuscany into the conversation, remarking pointedly that it was time for sovereigns to become more liberal and conciliate their subjects by granting them consultative assemblies if not constitutions. Experience had shown, said Ferdinand in reply, that constitutions were not suited to southern peoples and consultative assemblies were only the thin end of the wedge. Personally he did not need to conciliate his subjects, with whom he was on the best of terms. Brenier went on to plead for the political prisoners, and especially for the release of Ribotti, who had led the Sicilian expedition to Calabria in 1848 but who was a Sardinian subject. Ferdinand retorted that Ribotti had been caught red-handed, and that in sparing his life he had done enough for him. In short Brenier's mission was not a success. The King described him to the Austrian ambassador as 'another Minto'.

Relations with France did not improve when Ferdinand forbade the export of sulphur, and of a thousand cattle which a French trader had acquired for the army in the Crimea. Further annoyance was caused by quarantine regulations when the cholera was raging. Lowther had been asked to purchase three thousand quarters of wheat for the British troops in Malta. On July 7 he wrote: 'I have thought it advisable first to make enquiries as to whether any corn factor would undertake this commission without the permission of the Government, well knowing that the application, if made, would certainly be refused, and the fact of my making such application would only serve to induce this Government to take steps preventing the clandestine exportation of grain.' Owing to Austrian intervention this permission was given, but a request to buy cattle for Malta was refused.

When Sardinia supported the Western allies in January 1855 Ferdinand's position became even more difficult. Palmerston inveighed against him in London and Temple returned to heckle him in Naples. His friendly neutrality towards Russia was violently attacked in the *Morning Post* and other newspapers. Temple and his half-Sicilian attaché George Fagan, who often used disguise in collecting information and only avoided arrest by his diplomatic immunity, kept up a guerrilla warfare with the Neapolitan police. Despatch after despatch went to London with the gravest allegations against police tyranny, and Palmerston embellished them in the House of Commons. A characteristic sample is dated June 28, 1855: 'I enclose the accompanying papers consisting of a copy and translation of a circular letter which was framed by the Government and transmitted by the Intendente of each province to their sub-Intendente for their information and guidance, giving them rules for the superintendance and treatment of such persons as may be suspected of disaffection towards the Government. A copy of this paper was communicated to me confidentially, and I transmit it to your Lordship as affording some means of judging of the internal state of the country and the manner in which it is governed.

'Besides those persons who wear a beard or a soft hat considered to be the outward signs of being a member or a partisan of the *Unità Italiana*, all persons are liable to be treated as disaffected and to be imprisoned for any length of time, at the mere will of the police and of their agents, both in the capital and in the provinces.

'Latterly many persons have been arrested, and upon the friends of one of them who was an old and inoffensive man, having represented to the Minister of Police that he was wholly innocent of any offence, they were given to understand that the police were aware of that, but that it is necessary for the Government to make demonstrations of its power.

'The consequence of this state of things is that people feel no confidence in the Government, in the Courts of Law, or in one another, each man feeling that his neighbour may be a spy, either out of enmity to him, or desirous of obtaining the favour of the police.

'All business therefore is greatly obstructed, as any attempt to enforce the performance of a contract by a person supported by the police would be vain, and might lead to the imprisonment and ruin of the individual making the attempt, who would be denounced as a liberal.

'But little hope exists at present of any change occurring in the system of Government, as it was established by the King in 1849, as he himself is reported to have said to the Prince of Bavaria, and his ministers have been selected as the persons best suited for carrying it out, being chosen for their unquestioning obedience to orders rather than for the possession of any moral qualities or mental attainments. Indeed upon one occasion when a Minister represented to the King that it would be desirable to remove an Intendente whose ignorance rendered him wholly incompetent to fulfil his official duties, he was told he was there to obey orders and not to give advice.'

A trivial incident led to the removal of Mazza, the director of police. There was a rule forbidding entrance except on business to the manager's box in any theatre, and on seeing his *bête noire* Fagan in the manager's box of the Fondo theatre Mazza ordered him to leave it. According to some, Fagan was unaware of the rule; according to others, he had quizzed Mazza with his eye-glass and made provocative gestures. If he had intended to bait him in public, he succeeded. It is evident that Mazza lost his temper. Temple's version, in a telegraphic despatch of August 16, was slightly different: 'The Director of Police Mazza has warned Neapolitans not to associate with the British Legation, and having seen Fagan in the box of the Duke of Satriano, the superintendent of theatres sent to tell the Duke that he would be severely punished if Fagan were admitted there again. I shall demand satisfaction for this affront and will report by next packet.' At the same time the French were demanding satisfaction because the governor of Messina had refused to hoist the flag on the citadel on August 15, Napoleon III's birthday; but the Mazza incident had louder and longer repercussions. His indignation rising, Temple wrote on August 18: 'If Mr Mazza continues to hold his present situation, no real improvement can be expected to be introduced into the internal administration of this country, nor any security afforded to the British Legation against the repetition of similar affronts.'

The director of foreign affairs Carafa sent Temple an evasive reply, assuring him that the British legation would always be treated with the regard due to its position. Mazza was not mentioned. A joint note from the British and French envoys was then handed to De Marsilio, the King's representative, and Temple reported on August 25: 'We stated to M. Marsilio that it was not from any wish on the part of our Governments to dictate to a Sovereign Power the course it should pursue, that the communication was made, but that the proceedings of the Neapolitan Government towards persons of all classes were of so cruel, arbitrary and unjust a character as to be considered by them to be at variance with the dictates of humanity and the civilization of the age, and calculated to create the very danger which they were intended to avert; that our Governments had a right therefore to remonstrate against conduct which tended to discredit monarchical institutions.' (All the Neapolitan acts, prohibition of export of grain, etc.) 'afforded undoubted proofs of the desire of the Government to favour as far as circumstances will allow the interests of Russia and to thwart those of the Allies.'

De Marsilio stated in reply that cruel as it might seem the policy of repression 'had been attended with complete success as the country was perfectly tranquil'; that the ban on the export of grain was domes-

The opening of the Naples dock, 1852, by S. Fergola

tic and 'had no reference to political objects'; that while the King desired to maintain the best understanding with England and France he could not but consider the articles which had lately appeared in their journals, and the speeches lately delivered in the English Parliament on the affairs of Italy, as showing an unfriendly feeling towards him. ... (The *Times* had proposed a punitive expedition to Naples as soon as affairs in the East had been settled. Since Commodore Perry had dealt summarily with the Japanese *Shoguns* it was intolerable to have 'another Japan' within easy distance of Malta and Marseilles.) Temple concluded that the King had no intention of changing his policy or 'listening to any advice however valuable which may tend to stop him in a course which must ultimately lead to the most disastrous circumstances.' And Carafa seemed patiently determined to misunderstand the ground of his complaint: Mazza's treatment of Fagan. On September 8 Temple informed him that the matter was out of his hands, adding confidentially that nothing would satisfy his government but Mazza's removal.

A week later, when the Austrian minister warned the King that the English would send a naval squadron to enforce compliance, Mazza had been dismissed. Still Temple was not satisfied, since Mazza's chief enemies at Court, Prince Ischitella, Minister of War, and the Duke of San Cesario, Master of the Horse, had also been dismissed. He suspected that Mazza wielded more power than ever, and that the subordinate police authorities continued to be entirely under his orders. Nor were his doubts dispelled when the King sent him a message that Mazza was no longer connected with the police, and that 'His Majesty had some reasons of his own' for his dismissal. Carafa told him that after the King's definite assurances he could not return to the subject: did Temple doubt His Majesty's good faith? Of course not, said Temple: he was merely dissatisfied with the wording of the decree.

These daily pinpricks made Ferdinand more stubborn. The appointment of Baron Brenier to replace De La Cour as French minister seemed a calculated affront. Austria's cringing attitude towards the allies disgusted him. He warned Martini, the Austrian ambassador, that the Crimean War had revived all the hopes of those who loved disorder. The Mazzinians would exploit Muratism, Sicilian autonomy, anything that served their purpose. Hitherto the moral and material force of the Neapolitan government had been able to restrain it. But now England and France were trying to undermine that force so that it could no longer repress the revolutionary hydra which had hidden roots in the kingdom. Austria had every reason to be concerned with the preservation of peace and order, especially in Italy, yet she allowed violent attacks in the press against the Neapolitan government, as if to make common cause with those who disliked the actual state of Italy. But who would be the greater sufferer in the end?

Ferdinand's patience had been strained to the utmost. He was not disposed to yield another inch. After so many years of tension and appeasement, his reaction to the Congress of Paris in 1856, however unwise, was all too human. Peace had been signed on March 27 and the Congress was about to adjourn when Cavour seized the chance he had long been waiting for. He had paved the way with many a secret interview and with an impressive memorandum to Napoleon III 'On the means by which the reconstruction of Italy might be effected.' At an extraordinary session on April 8 the French Foreign Minister and plenipotentiary Count Walewski raised the Italian question, denouncing Papal misrule and the 'intolerable despotism' of the Neapolitan administration. Lord Clarendon vehemently supported him in a speech worthy of Mr Gladstone, and threatened Naples that the consequences would be serious if the advice of united Europe were neglected. There could be no peace without justice: the King should grant an amnesty and open his prisons.

Cavour sounded mild after this philippic: he exposed the arrogant dominion of Austria as the chief cause of Italy's misfortunes. But under his bland exterior Cavour was indeed 'the lion of the Conference'. It was thanks to him that, as he said, the Italian question had become for the future a European question. 'Two facts will remain,' he added, 'which are not without some importance. First, the stigma branded on the conduct of the King of Naples by France and England in the face of united Europe; and second, England's condemnation of the Papal Government in terms as precise and energetic as the most zealous Italian patriot could have desired.' But King Ferdinand and the Pope were condemned without a hearing, for neither was represented at the Congress. Clarendon had been well warmed up for his diatribe by Cavour. There was no British ambassador in Rome at this time and Temple, the minister in Naples, was Palmerston's brother, *c'est tout dire*.

When Temple and Brenier presented their official notes on May 19 and 21 demanding an ample amnesty and the reform of Neapolitan judicature, Carafa told them that the King did not recognize the right of any foreign power to interfere with the internal government of his country, whose tranquillity he guaranteed. An extensive amnesty had been prepared, but the action of the Congress had delayed this. Temple, who could hardly believe his ears, called at the Foreign Office on June 20 'to ascertain what the real intentions of the King were upon the subject.' On June 22 he reported: 'The King had instructed him (Carafa) to express his appreciation of the friendly feelings which animated our Governments in making the communication, but as he had the best means of knowing the internal state of his own dominions he must be allowed to act according to his own judgement; that his conduct from the beginning of his reign had afforded sufficient proofs of the clemency of his disposition, but he considered that the present moment was not opportune for granting an amnesty according to the suggestion of our Governments, that the minds of the disaffected had been much excited by late events and that any concession made while this excitement continued would only tend to embolden the revolutionary party, raise their hopes, and endanger the tranquillity of the country....

'I told him that I deeply regretted the decision which the King had come to, for I considered it very possible that the Governments of England and France would consider the answer as evasive and unsatisfactory. I observed to him that the Government had nothing now to fear from the revolutionary party who were few in number, without leaders, and without any common plan of action. That a perseverance in the present system would render the feeling of discontent general throughout all classes, and that much more dangerous consequences might be expected to arise from impairing the friendly feelings which existed between Western Powers and Naples than could be apprehended from an act of clemency on the part of His Majesty which would tend to strengthen those feelings, and at the same time regain for his Government the confidence of his subjects.'

The King's retort was logical. Even if he were to grant an amnesty and other concessions of his own free will, he would appear to be yielding to foreign threats. His resulting loss of authority and prestige was bound to provoke those disturbances which England and France seemed so anxious to prevent. And Ferdinand saw quite clearly that their ally Sardinia (Piedmont) stood behind them on tiptoe, agog for more trouble at Naples. He could discern more dimly the designs of the French dictator, who had drastically curtailed constitutional liberty at home. Might he not seize this excuse to support the dynastic claims of his Murat cousins? If the Neapolitan government had nothing to fear from the leaders of the revolutionary party, it was because they were either in prison or in exile.

Ferdinand might have replied with ruder, more specific arguments and comparisons. Thousands of Poles had been exiled by the Russians. Why had not Lord Clarendon asked for them to be amnestied too? As it was, his firm refusal was taken as an insult. '*Nôtre dignité exige une réparation*,' said Walewski. The question remained: what sort of reparation? Once again England and France could not see eye to eye. Palmerston blustered about three line-of-battle ships to anchor opposite the royal palace, half an hour for a boat to take a letter ashore, an hour for the reply, and half an hour for the boat to return with it, and if the fleet brought off Bomba's political prisoners, so much the better. Greville confided to his diary in September[1]: 'The quarrel with the King of Naples appears to be coming to a crisis, and though it will not produce any serious consequences now, the precedent of interference we are establishing may have very important ones at some future time, and though philanthropy may make us rejoice at some coercion being applied to put an end to such a cruel and oppressive government as that of King Bomba, it may be doubted whether it would not be sounder policy to abstain from interference with what only indirectly and remotely concerns us.'

Both England and France decided to break off diplomatic relations with Naples and threatened a naval demonstration in the bay. The Russian and Austrian ministers attempted to mediate and urged the King to make concessions before it was too late, but they could not induce him to change his mind. He waited calmly on events, which did not move so fast as they do now. Temple expired in the meantime and Petre, the chargé d'affaires at the British legation, inherited his partisan pessimism. He had to confess that there was 'little likelihood of any disturbance, for the present at least, of the tranquillity of this

[1] *The Greville Diary.* Edited by Philip Whitwell Wilson, Vol. II, p. 386. London, 1927.

capital. Signor Bianchini who, as Minister of Police, seems to stand out in honourable relief from among those of whom he is the nominal head, has wisely discountenanced and suppressed those riotous demonstrations of loyalty by the dregs of the population, which the police have been frequently accused of originating for the purpose of decoying the unwary into demonstrations of an opposite character.' Even so his despatches became gloomier and gloomier.

The political trials went on, as if in a spirit of bravado. Don José Buschental arrived from the Argentine with a proposal to found a colony of political prisoners on the banks of the Uruguay or the Parana, which struck the King as an excellent solution. But this was not the same as an amnesty. Carafa estimated that five or six hundred prisoners would accept, and Buschental was surprised at the smallness of the number. The allies were not to be fobbed off with such alternatives. Brenier and Petre were far more nervous than the King, as if the whole of Naples would explode before they had time to pack their bags. 'I regret to say,' wrote Petre on September 22, 'that even now, when the danger of persistence is more imminent and must be palpable even to His Majesty's mind, I can see no likelihood of the King being swayed by more prudent counsels. Unfortunately, the principles which he has imbibed from an education in which all the lessons of history have been carefully suppressed, and from the study of family annals too fruitful in pernicious example, have implanted in the King's mind an almost fanatical belief that his governing policy is not amenable to human criticism and that it can only be changed or modified at his spontaneous will and pleasure. If compelled therefore to act at variance with this belief, His Majesty would look upon himself as virtually dethroned, and thus the worst consequence of resistance to the demands of the Western Powers would be forestalled. . . .

'Those who are supposed to be acquainted with the character of the King state it as their opinion that at the first appearance of coercion His Majesty would at once quit the country with his family, and leave the guardianship of his throne to the fidelity of the army, and to the devotion of the lazzaroni.

'The loyalty of this latter class of His Majesty's subjects is coupled with the lust of plunder, which at the first moment of anarchy or confusion they would hardly fail to gratify at the expense of the lives and property of their fellow citizens.'

The masses who were devoted to the King were still lumped together contemptuously as 'lazzaroni' by the democratic diplomats, embarrassed by the fact of Ferdinand's popularity. Mr Gladstone's thesis on the negation of God erected into a system of government had to be maintained in the teeth of steady progress and rising prosperity. The French ambassador Rayneval had candidly reported from Rome that 'an appearance of prosperity strikes the eyes of the least observant. Gaiety of the most expansive kind is to be traced on the faces of all. It may be asked whether this can be the people whose miseries excite to such a degree the commiseration of Europe?' This was even more true of Naples, where living was cheap and poverty was less tragic than in colder climates, and where what many foreigners fancied necessary was found not to be necessary at all. But Petre took his cue from the frustrated liberals. On October 16, as zero hour approached he reported: 'The eager anxiety with which the arrival of the allied squadrons in the bay of Naples is looked for by those who are disposed to hail their advent as the forerunner of political enfranchisement continues undiminished. Nothing however would seem to warrant a suggestion that the effervescence of public feeling will lead to collision or breach of the peace of this capital.

'A casual observer might indeed fail to detect under the sparkling surface of Neapolitan life the dark current of discontent and misery that flows beneath, and the apparent placidity and meek endurance with which the yoke of government is borne are quoted by its defenders as proofs that the mass of the people are content and desire no change.

'M. Carafa himself a few days ago in the course of a conversation appealed to my sense of justice to testify to this fact from what had come under my own observation. I replied that if such were really the case the moment was singularly opportune for initiating measures of clemency and reform, but the assertion, I added, tallied ill with what had previously been alleged by the Neapolitan Government as a cogent reason for their not complying with the wishes of the Allied Powers, viz. that the adoption of the policy suggested by them might jeopardize the safety of the throne and the interests of social order.'

The French and British notes were presented to Carafa on October 21: since their advice, approved by the whole of Europe, had been rejected, it behoved their dignity to withdraw their representatives.

Brenier and Petre left the kingdom a week later, amid cheers from groups of bold liberals along the Toledo. No naval demonstration followed their departure. The prospect of a Muratist coup which would strengthen France's position in the Mediterranean on one side, the fear of a British occupation of Sicily on the other, caused the allies to renounce this expedition. Napoleon III would not fail to back his cousin, as he admitted to Baron von Hübner, the Austrian ambassador in Paris; and Petre's liberal cronies had told him that Muratism, 'gilt with the military prestige of France, and representing the triumph and glorification of military rule, was likely to make rapid strides in the Neapolitan army.'

This tame fizzling out of the Paris Congress fireworks disappointed Cavour. Ferdinand had no regrets. He had stood up for his rights and asserted his independence.

XVII

WHILE Ferdinand's government was under cross fire from England and France, he was leading a peaceful life in the bosom of his large family. Queen Maria Theresa bore him eleven children, two of whom died in infancy. There was a close community of interests between this devoted pair, for the Queen was as pious as she was prolific; and though she could never roll her r's she spoke fluent Neapolitan with a Teutonic accent. Both shunned Court ceremony and preferred Caserta to the capital. They divided the summer months between Gaeta, Ischia and the Quisisana palace above Castellammare, where the simplicity of their existence resembled that of any prosperous merchant.

In the capital they were obliged to exhibit themselves and entertain on a grand scale. The court balls were spectacular, and the costumes worn at one of these in 1853 may be admired in an illustrated album. The King, more prim and proper than his grandfather, was equally fussy about fancy dress. Thus when Giovanni del Balzo appeared as a Calabrian brigand he was ordered to retire and make himself respectable. When he returned to apologize a few days later the King said: 'Remember, brigands should not enter the royal palace even in disguise.' Though he disliked ceremony he took it seriously. He set so high a value on his orders of knighthood that he seldom conferred them. They were all the more appreciated in consequence. The Order of San Gennaro was usually inherited, but application had to be made for it by the recent holder's heir. In one case a tardy application came from a gentleman with a passion for horses who stank of the stables and was none too clean. The King agreed that he was entitled to it, adding: 'The Order of the Bath would suit him better. Unfortunately it is not mine to bestow.'

The Court almanacs show few changes in the officials of the royal household, who served as gentlemen of the chamber *con esercizio* or *di entrata* or as 'majordomos of the week': the former were also called 'gold keys' from their badge of office, inscribed V.R.S. (*Vitæ Regis Securitas*) to denote that they could enter any room in the palace. Nearly all these posts were honorary, except the adjutants general who held the first rank at Court functions under the superintendence of the chief majordomo, the Prince of Bisignano, whose wife was chief lady-in-waiting to the Queen. In spite of the long list of sesquipedalian titled ladies-in-waiting in the almanac very few were required to be on duty. The Queen was said to be unreasonably jealous of them and would keep them waiting for hours in an ante-room, only to be dismissed with a curt message of thanks. It is scarcely surprising that she was unpopular.

Amid the architectural splendours of Caserta the Victorian homeliness of the King's family life seemed oddly out of place. Linen was hung up to dry in marble halls; the children romped with the servants and played crude practical jokes on their tutors and governesses; the Queen sat over her sewing near the cradle of her latest infant, while the King rocked another babe in his arms and distributed lollipops. De Cesare and others have left many anecdotes showing the despot in this amiable light. When the mayor of Naples, Don Antonio Carafa, brought him a specimen loaf of the bread being baked for the poor during the cholera epidemic, he found His Majesty dandling one of his youngest scions. The lively tot made several attempts to grab the loaf and set up a howl when it failed. 'Don Antò, do give him a slice,' said the King, 'or he will never allow us to talk.' He carried on the family tradition of scattering facetious nicknames: the French were dubbed hairdressers, the English dried codfish sellers, the Russians tallow-eaters, etc. Not even his children were spared, for the Hereditary Prince was called *Lasagna* or *Lasa* for short, either because he was partial to that variety of macaroni or because of his long pale face. The 'Son of the Saint' was more like a shy seminarist than a prince, and it was rumoured that his contempt for material things had been fostered by his confessor in league with his stepmother, who hoped he would abdicate in favour of her offspring. He had been taught Latin and French, canon and civil law, but he was most familiar with the lives of the saints. Above all he adored the young mother he had never seen, who

> *'Oftener upon her knees than on her feet*
> *Died every day she lived.'*

One of the first ceremonies for her beatification had taken place in Santa Chiara on January 31, 1853, the seventeenth anniversary of her death, when her coffin was opened in the presence of the Cardinal Archbishop, the Apostolic Nuncio, three famous surgeons and two Court ladies who had witnessed the Queen's last moments. There was general amazement when the corpse was found to be intact and the limbs still flexible. The skin was well preserved, the nose had retained its natural shape, the lips were half parted, the teeth firm and white, the hair like that of a live woman; only the eyes were sunken and the body was emaciated. Whereas gangrene had set in at the time of her death a fragrant odour was now perceptible. After a minute examination an official report was written on parchment and placed in an urn at the foot of the coffin, which was sealed with twelve seals and laid in a marble tomb. Crowds from all over the kingdom came hither to burn candles.

If the Hereditary Prince had any aversion to women it was because he idealized his mother at the expense of the rest of her sex. When hundreds invoked her intercession and miracles were attributed to her, comparisons were not only odious; they were absurd. Her halo accompanied him and lit up his loneliness. He could not love his Austrian step-mother, who naturally preferred her own children and paid little attention to the son of her embarrassing predecessor. But Francis was too meek to cause friction. The King was fond of his *Lasa*: perhaps pity and awe blended with his affection for the strange silent youth with whom he had so little in common. His other children were more recognizably chips of the old block. In the afternoon he would take them out for a drive, and the plump monarch whipping up his well-groomed English horses was one of the spectacles of Caserta or wherever he happened to be.

The soulful Swedish novelist Fredrika Bremer saw him at Ischia and wrote[1]: 'We have occasionally in our rambles met the King, sometimes with the Queen, sometimes with the royal children. The King himself drives the little carriage with its pair of handsome horses. He looks like a well-conditioned butcher; the countenance not ugly, rather the contrary, but quite too fat. He looks around him with a restless, hasty glance. The Queen's countenance is still youthful and agreeable, but with a something so sad in her expression, that one can see plainly that the cheerful sun of Italy does not shine for her. She is said not to have a happy disposition. She dresses in the most simple style, and her mode of salutation is graceful. . . . The princes and princesses are handsome children, and there are a great number of them.' On another occasion, however, the members of the royal family struck Miss Bremer as 'unusually plain in person—all with large, pale countenances, without any marked feature. The King, notwithstanding his stoutness, is the best-looking of his race, except the Count of Syracuse. . . . The Crown Prince has a long, gloomy countenance, particularly unpleasing. It is said that he has been hitherto a great bigot, but it is hoped that a favourable change may be produced by his marriage. . . . Two little princes are handsome children, with a resemblance to their august papa.'

Sometimes the simplicity of the Queen's domestic arrangements seemed excessive even to her husband, whose tastes were far from sophisticated. 'Teté,' he was heard to exclaim (an abbreviated form of Tetella, as he called his consort), 'bit by bit we'll end up with having to wait on ourselves at the dinner-table!' Macaroni was Ferdinand's staple diet, apart from which he had a relish for fried codfish, despite its British connotations, and all sorts of *pizza*, mozzarella cheese, vermicelli with tomato sauce, stewed eels, and onions both fried and raw. The latter he chewed almost daily, crushing the pungent bulb between thumb and forefinger since a knife would spoil the savour. For a man of his vast bulk he was abstemious.

When there was not a military parade a brisk family drive was his usual relaxation after the long hours he spent at his desk, for he wished to be informed of everything that was happening in the kingdom. Whatever his state of health his curiosity was unflagging. Bishops

[1] Fredrika Bremer, *Two years in Switzerland and Italy*, translated by Mary Hewitt. London, 1861.

339

and diplomats, metropolitan and provincial officials corresponded directly with the royal secretariat. Most of his instructions were verbal, but many were issued in brief autograph letters on sheets of ordinary paper. His calligraphy was clear and self-confident; his style blunt and idiomatic. *L'état c'est moi* was the keynote of his correspondence. Though devoid of literary merit his letters prove his extraordinary industry and attention to detail.

Audiences absorbed the rest of his time. Tuesdays were usually reserved for the military: he made little distinction between different ranks and took a personal interest in their problems. To each he listened patiently with an impassive countenance, jotting down memoranda and popping questions. He held petitions in his right hand and folded them in token of dismissal. Any reference to 1848 would irritate him, otherwise he was apt to be jocular. Civilians were received on Fridays. An official noted their names and asked the purpose of their visit: when there was a large crowd precedence was given to those whose business seemed most urgent. It was calculated that the King saw between 150 and 200 persons on days of public audience. Sundays were devoted to prayer and the family circle: he attended Mass daily and recited the rosary every evening with his consort and children. On Mondays he presided over the Council of Ministers, and on Wednesdays he consulted with its members individually. Thus he was certainly the busiest man in his kingdom.

Ferdinand had little help from his brothers. The Prince of Capua continued to wander in exile with his morganatic wife, whose insistence on being recognized as a royal princess had prevented any reconciliation. Other causes had aggravated his position, such as his appeals to Lord Palmerston, who had exploited a family fracas in time of tension, and his intrigues with Neapolitan refugees, who flattered him as 'the living symbol of Ferdinand's despotism' and as a worthy successor to the throne. In 1848 he had aspired to the crown of Sicily. Feckless and extravagant, he fell an easy prey to money-lenders, adventurers and parasites. When Palmerston got bored with him he was taken up by the government of Turin. It was Victor Emmanuel II who recognized his wife as Princess of Capua: to Ferdinand II she was merely known as 'la Smith'.

The Prince led a harassed existence, in perpetual flight from his creditors. Viel-Castel[1] describes him as cutting an eccentric figure at a ball given in the Tuileries by Napoleon III in 1853: 'He was promenading his Penelope. . . . This Prince is stout, vulgar, and usually rigged up like a rustic charlatan. He is adorned with a long and dirty grey beard, and his hair is also long, dirty and grey.' At any rate he made a pleasant impression on a cockney costermonger, who told Henry Mayhew:[2] 'When I served the Prince of Naples, not far from here (I presume that he alluded to the Prince of Capua), I did better and times was better. . . . He was a good customer, and was wery fond of peaches. I used to sell them to him at 12s. the plasket when they was new. The plasket held a dozen and cost me 6s. at Covent-garden—more sometimes; but I didn't charge him more when they did. His footman was a black man, and a ignorant man quite, and his house-keeper was a Englishwoman. He was the Prince o' Naples, was my customer; but I don't know what he was like, for I never saw him. I've heard that he was the brother of the King of Naples. . . . I never heard whether the Prince was the King's older brother or his younger. I wish he may turn out his older if there's any property coming to him, as the oldest has the first turn; at least so I've heard—first come, first served.' The costermonger said he liked to talk about him, 'he was such a customer when he lived near here.' But he was always moving, from Malta to Marseilles, from Geneva to Aix-les-Bains. One suspects that the burly bearded Prince, who was 'wery fond of peaches', suffered secretly from his exile and regretted his youthful folly; one also suspects that he was henpecked by Penelope, who bore him a son and a daughter. Though he survived Ferdinand his last hopes were dashed by the events of 1860.

Ferdinand's second brother, Leopold, the Count of Syracuse, made no bones about his liberal opinions ever since he was Lieutenant of Sicily, yet Ferdinand retained a warm affection for him. Some said that his liberalism was a screen for his licentiousness and compared him with Philippe Égalité, but his sincerity has been proved by his private correspondence.[3] Luckily he left Naples before the storms of

[1] *Mémoires du Comte Horace de Viel-Castel sur le Règne de Napoléon III*, *Tome I*, p. 168. Paris, 1942.

[2] *Mayhew's London*, edited by Peter Quennell. Selections from 'London Labour and the London Poor', by Henry Mayhew (1851). London, 1951.

[3] See Benedetto Croce: *Varietà di Storia Letteraria e Civile. Serie Seconda*, pp. 239, 249. Bari, 1949.

1848 and returned after four years' absence in 1850. He was convinced, as he wrote, that a Constitution would 'save the whole family from the ruin that threatens us'. Most of his letters harped on this theme: for an epicurean he was profoundly pessimistic.

Evidently Ferdinand regarded him as a lovable black sheep. He had never carried indiscretion so far as to marry beneath him, which may explain why he was petted and pardoned while Charles remained an indigent remittance-man. When he had a paralytic stroke in 1854 the King rushed to his bedside. 'Popò!' he cried in deep distress, but the Prince could not reply; he could not even recognize him. Finally the King hung a holy relic round his neck, saying: 'Popò, the Madonna will be merciful.' Two weeks later he was out of danger, and though he posed as an agnostic he never removed the amulet as long as he lived. After his recovery he flung himself into the social whirl with devil-may-care zest.

The Marquise de Sassenay,[1] who was in Naples at this time, described him as a genial Mæcenas surrounded by blind and one-eyed musicians. 'The Count of Syracuse,' she wrote, 'gave nocturnal parties in the ruins of Pompeii and had comedies performed in the amphitheatre illuminated by torches. Once the entertainment began with the famous Thalberg at the piano. He entertained like a *grand seigneur*, and organized such exquisite receptions at Naples and in his Sorrento villa that invitations were much sought after. One day he invited us to an oyster dinner on Lake Fusaro and the bivalves were served in twenty-two different ways. He was very generous, maybe too generous, and was often harried by creditors. To flatter the Queen he sculpted Virgins and Saints for her, and thus obtained the favour of their Majesties, who paid his debts. However, he occasionally had rows with his royal brother. He cared little for etiquette and yielded with ill grace to the custom of men kissing a prince's hand. Neapolitans who were aware of this merely brushed his hand with their lips and hastily withdrew. Unlike the King, the Prince was rather dissolute. I had an occasion to prove this one day while riding in his carriage, for we passed another in which sat a vulgar woman who was his mistress. I had only glimpsed her occasionally and recognized her too late. When the Prince smiled I must have given him a questioning glance, for he remarked: *"Ce n'est pas une femme comme il faut, mais comme il en*

[1] Marquise de Sassenay, *Souvenirs de Naples 1854–1869*. Paris, 1927.

faut." (Which might be rendered: 'She's not in society, but necessary to society.') "One should certainly choose something prettier," I retorted. "The lesson is a good one," he said with a burst of laughter. Thanks to him, I was able to visit various monasteries absolutely forbidden to women, as princes of the royal family were privileged to bring feminine visitors.' Champagne was served to the guests at La Cava, but no monks attended the repast. The Count of Syracuse had a wager with her father-in-law to drive a four-in-hand through the narrow streets of Pompeii, which he won in a pony-chaise with four small horses.

The Marquise sums him up as a sprightly hedonist in the midst of a dull and dreary Court. In fact he had a separate Court of artists, writers and musicians, who followed him from his palace on the Chiaia to his villa at Sorrento, where he made the eyes of Fredrika Bremer goggle.[1] It was during a display of fireworks on the evening of the Ascension of the Virgin. 'He was seated, with the gentlemen of his Court, before a café on the principal street, and flung thence dozens of cigars among the people: one box after another was emptied in this manner. This soon assembled a crowd of young and old men, who fought for the cigars, and pressed ever nearer upon the Prince, who himself snatched the caps of several from their heads, and threw them away among the crowd, in order to free himself from them; till at length the gentlemen of his Court were obliged to use their canes actively for the same purpose. This scene was renewed several times. A stand with all kinds of confectionery and cakes stood at no great distance, on the opposite side of the street, and this the crowd obtained leave to plunder by a sign from the Prince; so madly, however, did they rush upon their prey that again the canes of the gentlemen were put in motion before order could be re-established. But it seemed to amuse the Prince. A large, powerful man, with a very handsome countenance, he is particularly popular in Sorrento for his kindness and liberality. Both he and his brothers, the Counts of Aquila and Trapani, are said to be real Turks with regard to women, and the sympathies of the popular Prince for the people have in them nothing either elevating or ennobling to the same.'

A solemn statue of Giambattista Vico in the Villa Nazionale bears witness to the serious side of the Prince's character. He tried to express

[1] *Op. cit.*, pp. 333, 334.

his political aspirations in a sculptured group representing 'Naples and Piedmont holding hands over the altar of the common fatherland and Italy crowning them.'

Having married one princess of Savoy he wished the Heir Apparent to marry another, purely on political grounds, for his own marriage had been a failure. To suggest this idea to the King he invited the whole Court to a special performance in his private theatre. The poetic drama composed for the occasion by the liberal Duke Proto, more famous in later years for his mordant epigrams, was entitled 'Alda, the Star of Mantua', with the Duchess Ravaschieri, Filangieri's daughter, in the title-rôle supported by a cast of distinguished amateurs. The verse was turgid but the allusion clear when Alda turned to the Duke of Mantua and declaimed a stanza urging him not to choose a bride from among his foes, 'since from the north no fruitful zephyr blows, but choose the flower of Italy, the rose.'

There was great excitement among the audience, and Laura Acton, then Princess of Camporeale, shouted to the leading actress from the wings: 'Courage, Theresa, for our country's sake!' Many glanced at the Heir Apparent, but he looked demurely downwards with an air of unconcern. He was immune to the thrill which had electrified the rest of the audience. Yet his mother had been a Piedmontese princess. In those days, as when his uncle Syracuse had married the Prince of Carignano's sister, the House of Savoy had been 'reactionary': now it claimed to represent the ideal of a united Italy. Ferdinand saw this as inflated dynastic ambition. Oddly enough, so did Mazzini. Victor Emmanuel's daughter Clotilde, the rose alluded to in the play, was to be sacrificed for Italy to Napoleon III's disreputable middle-aged cousin 'Plon-Plon'. Had she married the pious young Duke of Calabria she would have been less unhappy, and she might have saved the dynasty. But Ferdinand's prejudice against Savoy was indomitable. He appeared to enjoy the performance of 'Alda' more than his son, but he was heard to exclaim, as if he had been scratched: 'See what the Duchess has done to me this evening!'

The charms of Neapolitan society during the last decade of Ferdinand's reign have been described with such intricate detail by De Cesare in *La Fine di un Regno* that all students should read it as a corrective to the histories of Nisco and other liberals, who were obsessed with the prisons, police and political exiles and wrote as if

Naples were nothing but a sprawling den of misery and corruption. De Cesare stands out from his colleagues for relative impartiality. Travel books of the same period had reached saturation point and their monotony is overwhelming, for as some of their authors admitted, they approached Naples with a stock of ready-made impressions, and looked about them to have these confirmed, so that anything agreeing with them was noted and recorded, while the rest was unheeded and forgotten. Thus with the so-called lazzaroni. As the sharp-eyed American Hillard[1] remarked in 1853: 'The traveller who comes here from the north, when he sees a man in a ragged garb, on a sunny day, sleeping under the shelter of a wall, sets it down in his note-book as an unexampled phenomenon, exults in having caught a lazzarone, and very likely flowers out into a dissertation upon the subject. But men, in warm weather, may be seen sleeping in the open air in Rome and Florence, not to say Paris and Vienna, and it is thought no strange thing. The truth is that the whole race of lazzaroni, as a class characteristic of and peculiar to Naples, has nearly disappeared. . . . In other respects, too, the peculiarities of Naples are growing less and less marked, and those racy traits of life and character which so much impressed the travellers of an early period, are fast disappearing from observation.'

Since Gladstone's *Letters to Lord Aberdeen*, however, a guilty feeling mingled with enjoyment. The foreign travellers who continued to flock to Naples felt they ought to spice their visit with some of the horrors they had read about. Even *The Times* had become sensational on the subject. Yet one and all, however reluctantly, were forced to acknowledge that Naples was full of life, movement, and gaiety. Herman Melville, fighting off a nervous breakdown, seems to have been elated by the contrast between 'burning mountains—the monstrousness of the remorselessness of Nature—' and the carefree capital. In his 1856–1857 journal, not intended for publication, he remarked:[2] 'Now, one would think if any *modern* city were here built and etc, they would be sober in view of these things. But no. Gayest city in the world. No equipages flash like these; no beauties so haughty. No cavaliers so proud, no palaces so sumptuous . . . Apt representation of

---

[1] George Stillman Hillard, *Six months in Italy*. Boston, 1853.

[2] Herman Melville, *Journal of a Visit to Europe and the Levant*. Edited by Howard C. Horsford. Princeton, 1955.

that heedlessness, benignly ordained, of man which prevents him one
generation from learning from a past—"Let us eat, drink and be merry,
for tomorrow we die." Such seems the lesson learned by the Neapolitans from their scenery.—The beauty of the place, in connection with
its perilousness.—Skaters on ice.' Of the Strada di Toledo he remarked surprisingly: 'Could hardly tell it from Broadway. Thought
I was there.' Melville's curious poem 'Naples in the Time of Bomba'
begins with an episode jotted down in his journal as: '*Tumblers in
narrow street*. Blocked way. Balconies with women. Cloth on ground.
They gave way, after natural reluctance. Turned round and gave me
the most grateful and graceful bow. Handkerchiefs waved from balconies, good humoured cries, etc—Felt prouder than an Emperor.
Shabby old hack, but good fellow, driver.' He concludes that in
spite of—

> '*Those shocking stories bruited wide,*
> *In England which I left but late,*
> *Touching dire tyranny in Naples—*
> *True freedom is to be care-free!*
> *And care-free seem the people here*
> *A truce indeed they seem to keep*
> *Gay truce to care and all her brood.*'

Victorian moralists blamed the very climate they had come to
bask in, apart from 'King Bomba', for what they chose to consider the
degradation, the lack of decency in habits and ways of living, of the
Neapolitan people. 'Their fine climate is their curse,' wrote one of these
pedagogues.[1] 'Many of the wants and desires which with us are the
greatest stimulants to industry, and to all the virtues that spring from
industry, are of little importance here in the catalogue of human grati-
fications. Life may be enjoyed without them; and therefore the industry
is wanting, along with the motives.'

Among the more perceptive travellers Fredrika Bremer was certainly the most sincere. She wrote with an anti-Catholic bias, but she
tried to be fair, as the following passage proves:[2] 'I have so often heard
speak of "the frightfully miserable condition of the Neapolitan population", that I took a little carriage, and expressly commanding the

[1] Samuel Laing, *Notes of a Traveller*. London, 1842.
[2] *Op. cit.*, pp. 366, 367.

driver to take me to the very worst quarters both of the city and the suburbs, found to my surprise considerably less misery than I expected. I saw everywhere the people at work, and in the very poorest dwellings —the doors of which generally stood open—comfortable beds, and clean linen; sometimes the families were at their meals when everything looked nice and orderly. The city overflows with articles of food, especially vegetables and fruit. Immense pumpkins with golden-yellow insides, masses of tomatoes, bright peperoni, figs in ornamented pyramids with yellow and red flowers between the rows, oranges, pears, plums, apples, walnuts, and many more, fill the fruit-stands, tables, or benches, and are carried about in large baskets upon asses. One sees most people occupied in eating. Of noise and crowding there is always enough, especially in the narrower streets. . . . The greater number of the more indigent population seem to be well-dressed and industrious. It is true that one now and then sees, even in the Toledo—the principal trading street in Naples—women and children lying near some house, or before some gate, with countenances that indicate wretchedness and savage anger; and in other places men and women who exhibit diseased or imperfect limbs, and call upon the passers-by, who generally pay no attention at all—and indeed it is asserted that these lying or sitting figures get up at night and become dangerous to the wealthy foot-passengers; but on the whole I have not seen in Naples more misery than in London, Paris, or New York. The beggars are more unabashed, that is all; and one sees them most numerously in the great squares and the wealthy parts of the city.'

Fredrika Bremer was a self-conscious professional author: it is rather from the unprofessional and unself-conscious Marquise de Sassenay, writing for the amusement of her grandchildren, that we get an idiosyncratic *pot-pourri* of the cosmopolitan Naples at this time. The Marquise went there for her husband's health and spent the summer at Castellammare, then the fashionable but still rustic resort of the foreign embassies. Here her daughter was born. 'A simple village midwife came to assist me. This seemed to me quite natural. According to local custom I was put into a provisional bed, brought from I know not where and swarming with bugs. . . . As the midwife could not talk to me—we did not understand each other's language— she spent her time invoking all the saints in Heaven, muttering

"*Santissima Maria, San Giuseppe,*" etc. When I looked up at her she stopped to say: "*Tutto va bene, poco a poco.*" She wished to reassure me that all was well, but as I only understood the meaning of *poco* I got desperate, thinking she meant that all was going too slowly. My child was born without impediments, whereupon I was moved into a bed free from bugs and had to fast for nine days. I cried from hunger but my Cerberus was inflexible. A nurse was found in Naples who came all dressed up like a shrine: she wore a skirt of blue satin with broad gold bands, an apron of white muslin trimmed with lace, a jaunty cap, and sparkling earrings, a figure from comic opera, but an excellent nurse. The Bishop of Castellammare arrived in great pomp to baptise the infant. After nine days I was declared to be well. Two days later I presided over a large dinner to celebrate the child's birth. On the thirteenth day I took a long donkey ride, and as I am still alive and well and have been a great-grandmother for twenty years, this proves that there was some virtue in the primitive method of nursing.'

The Marquise repeated current gossip about the royal family and their frugality, which struck her as sordid; but she was charmed by the easy-going friendliness of society. 'Instead of waiting for us to be introduced, they came to visit us first, saying: "We are at home, and it is for us to do the honours."' But foreigners enjoyed many privileges, of which they took ample advantage. 'Like the churches and convents, a foreigner's house was inviolable: a criminal hiding there could not be arrested. I can give an instance of this from personal experience. My Italian cook had disguised himself as a policeman to kidnap a married woman. It was impossible to arrest him for this misdeed, for he never left my house and continued to give me perfect food as the tradesmen brought all he required. But when I had to entertain some friends newly arrived from France, I suggested sending someone to Naples to do the shopping, fearing I should not find all the extras I required at Castellammare. "I prefer to go myself," he answered, "and I shall take good care to avoid being recognized." I admit I felt none too sure of this. Instead of disguising himself, my cook picked a quarrel with the *carabiniere* at the station and I was soon informed that he was under arrest. Very annoyed, I went to see the sub-prefect and implored him to restore my cook, if only for twenty-four hours. "Impossible," he replied, "he is about to be prosecuted for seduction, of which he is guilty. We could not arrest him in your house, but now

348

that we have him he cannot be released and the trial must follow its course." I persisted, explaining to this amiable functionary what an embarrassment it would cause me. Anxious to be helpful, he continued: "I am willing to lend you the prisoner if you guarantee that he returns to prison tomorrow evening." I could not promise that, but I proposed to go bail for him. The sub-prefect refused, but in his eagerness to oblige me he offered to restore my cook accompanied by a gendarme. I agreed, and returned home with the culprit and his guardian, delighted and amused by this original dénouement. I then obtained authorization to keep my prisoner till the end of his trial. Instead of going back to prison he stayed in my house with his jailor, who never left him and guarded the door while I gave him my orders. The gendarme was most obliging: he peeled the vegetables and made himself useful to his prisoner, who did his best to attend to his wants. When the trial was over and the gendarme bade me farewell, he said: "I'm in despair. What a pity! I had such excellent meals. I have never been so happy as in Your Ladyship's house." The cook was sentenced to three months exile, and as his place of exile was two or three kilometres from my villa he remained in my service.'

Eventually the Marquise moved into the villa which the Margravine of Anspach had occupied at Posillipo, whose magic had not yet been marred by too many blocks of buildings. 'Fortunately for the natives,' she wrote, 'living was cheap. The quarantine in which the kingdom was kept and the prohibition to export in a country which had three harvests a year, made existence easy. . . . Only luxury was expensive, but the hot climate and the simplicity of the inhabitants induced them to wear few clothes. The Neapolitan only feared sunstroke: stark naked, his sole idea was to cover his head with a woollen cap. . . . With five in the family we kept a good table and spent on the average fifteen francs a day for copious, even sumptuous meals, yet the cook made his market profit. A *rotolo* of meat (somewhat less than 2lb.) cost six *sous*. Everything else, wages and forage, etc., in the same proportion. I had five horses, two coachmen and a stableman who boarded out, and five thousand francs a year covered all my expenses, including the wages of three servants whom we did not feed. Throughout Naples a cab drive cost one *carlino* (about fourpence) and the drive from my house to Naples, about four kilometres, cost two *carlini*. Only beggars walked. Everybody kept a carriage: rather than go without a Neapolitan would stint himself of all home comfort. There were so many carriages along the broad Chiaia that one had to go at a walking pace: they stopped frequently for conversation, to make appointments and organize a dance or picnic. Before the drive it was customary to go shopping. A woman never left her carriage to enter a shop, and I often wondered if this custom had been introduced by jealous husbands. You stopped in front of the shop and the articles required were brought out for your selection. Dressmakers always came to your house for fittings.'

'Pass down the Toledo, the finest two-mile street on the Continent, and you will get an idea of the amount of mercantile business in sundry departments,' wrote J. G. Francis.[1] 'Gloves are a prodigious staple: at every third or fourth door dangles a mimic hand, and there is no fit like that of the Naples kid at a shilling the pair. . . . Next to these the "*belle arti*" shops astonish one by their multitude. . . . Casts and models from the Museum, lamps, tazze, patere, terra-cotta heads, lava and coral ornaments, with drawers of sparkling fossils from Vesuvius, perhaps the prettiest item of the lot. In this rainbow-tinted climate every one sketches and paints, but they don't all paint well. Besides the countless daubs in oils and splashes in water colours, mostly copied one from another, here is that monstrous invention the "gouache" caricaturing the inimitable face of nature in a style only fit to paper a bedroom.'

These were the halcyon days of the Posillipo school of painting and of popular Neapolitan song, which became identified with the Piedigrotta festival since 1835 when Raffaele Sacco made so resounding a hit with *Te voglio bene assai*. All Naples sang this sweetly sentimental ballad, so that an anonymous versifier wrote in mock protest:

> *Good-bye fair Naples, I must fly.*
> *And if you ask the reason, why*
> *This flight so suddenly inspired?*
> *It is because I'm sick and tired*
> *Of* Te voglio bene assai!

From now on every year could be distinguished by the song or group of songs which had roused a furore at the Piedigrotta: *Cocchiere d'affitto* was the champion of 1836, *Luisella* of 1845, *Li capille de*

[1] J. G. Francis, *Notes from a journal kept in Italy and Sicily*. London, 1847.

Carolina of 1850. *Santa Lucia*, which soon became world famous, was written by Enrico Cossovich, a Dalmatian sailor who settled in Naples, and set to music by Teodoro Cottrau in 1849. Many a finer song has been written since then, but the dewy freshness of that early period has vanished. Salvatore Di Giacomo, the first great conscious artist in Neapolitan dialect poetry, whose stanzas live apart from the music composed for them, complained that in his prime, the turn of the century, Neapolitan songs were influenced by the French: now they are modelled on the transatlantic juke-box product. Di Giacomo's was the golden age. His humble predecessors were content with facile and obvious themes and rhymes, mere skeletons which the singer and his guitar clothed in flesh and blood. The joys and sorrows of a love that is never too deep or poignant, a duel between bold pursuer and bashful pursued, full of passionate glances and malicious double meanings, invocations to a jet-eyed Carmela on her balcony, to sun, moon, stars and sea—such were the common themes of the great majority. The soft bloom of the eighteenth century was still upon them.

Fredrika Bremer was haunted by *Santa Lucia*. 'The bright side of the natural and popular life of Naples is expressed in the words and music of this song,' she wrote, and printed the words in the hope that it might soon have a worthy translator. The wandering troubadours who came in the evenings with their guitars had neither pure nor beautiful voices in her opinion, but they were often strong and always full of expression; and they sang her favourite barcarolle with a passion which made the heart beat faster.

Among other typical street-scenes of this period she described a young girl on the Chiaia who took her stand under a tree and began to sing as she thumped her tambourine to a lively rhythm. 'Immediately a circle of girls was formed round her, together with children better or worse clad. Two ragged girls began to dance with castanets; two others followed their example, well-dressed and handsome, who struck the castanets extremely well, and danced well also. Many joined in the same way, the castanets passing from one pair to another. Nursemaids came up, placed their little ones in other women's arms, and went in for a dance for a moment; then resumed their infants, kissed them, and looked on while the others danced. The tambourine, like the castanets, went from hand to hand: they who beat the former sometimes sang a monotonous, unmelodious, but rhythmical song. At length the dancers amounted to above a dozen young women, who evidently were all dancing for their own hearts' joy, whilst older and younger sailors stood smoking at some distance, without in the slightest degree disturbing the girls, whose dance—a kind of tarantella —they seemed to watch with pleasure, but as an everyday affair.'

The carriages careering along the Chiaia three or four abreast in the late afternoon; the tarantella dancers with their tambourines and castanets; the towering cliffs and terraces hung with gardens in the background; Capri crouching on the twinkling waterline; the fishermen's boats and nets and naked urchins groping for mussels among the rocks of Mergellina, or disporting themselves like dolphins, diving into the sea for the *carlini* flung in by foreigners; the umbrageous alleys of the Villa Reale where fresh breezes tried in vain to stir the fig-leaves of the statues; the tattered and teeming traffic along the Molo, story-tellers, puppet-players, vendors of all wares, sailors, mendicant friars, groups of tousled laughing women, millions of oranges from Sorrento being unloaded, silks and sulphurous wines from Sicily; the carnival hubbub around Castel Capuano; the rows of wooden stalls along the shore of Santa Lucia, each displaying a fantastic variety of those edible jewels called *frutti di mare*, arranged most decoratively to whet the appetite among festoons of lemons, towards evening lit by flickering lanterns; the menacing mountain beyond with its crimson flames; and at night long necklaces of yellow diamonds against the blue-black velvet of the bay: all these were facets of the visual and audible charivari of Naples which could not be obscured by a few prisons, and it would be false to insist with Gladstone on a dungeon's eye view of the great southern metropolis.

XVIII

EXIT Mazza, enter Mazzini! Since Ferdinand had had to part with his ruthless chief of police the sectarians were emboldened to creep out of their coverts and conspire in broad daylight. Bianchini, who had replaced Mazza, was reputed to be the only progressive man in the government; he was also acting Minister of the Interior and the author of a popular work on political economy entitled *Del ben vivere sociale.* Fredrika Bremer was introduced to him by the Swiss banker Meuricoffre, and thus described her interview:[1] 'Entering a large room, we found a great number of persons assembled, gendarmes, women and men, some ill and others better dressed; and amidst this throng now stood and now moved about a tall thin gentleman in plain clothes, with grey hair, pale countenance, and handsome features, the expression of which was insignificant, whilst his demeanour was animated. He seemed to speak with every person, receiving the while or returning great sheaves of papers. His quick grey eye soon perceived me and my friend, on which he called to a servant, who conducted us through the crowd into a vestibule, and thence to the minister's private room. After a few minutes he came.

' "Have I then the honour of seeing His Excellency Bianchini?" I asked, rising at the same time.

' "Yes, madam," he replied; "I am that Bianchini of whom so much notice has been taken in Europe! My work has been translated into

[1] *Op. cit.*, pp. 361, 362.

many different languages, and in Belgium they have established a professor's chair for the sole purpose of enunciating my doctrines. I have received for that work decorations from fourteen crowned heads. All my predecessors have deceived themselves—all have treated science as the highest popular good; one-sided this, and imperfect. I alone have treated it in its completeness, and have given it a sure basis; I am the first who has comprehended the question in its whole breadth; the first," etc., etc., etc.

'Thus continued the speaker, whilst I sat amazed, in silent wonder, at this naïve self-glorification. When at length he gave me the opportunity of saying anything, I inquired about his system.

' "No system," he replied with vivacity; "but I have made it evident that neither happiness nor wealth can be enduring to a nation if it do not rest upon order, etc., a moral basis; if the intelligence, the will, and morals of a people are not of an elevated character, so as to give a safe guidance to the material development, as well as the chief direction to life. My doctrine, therefore, is for all people and for all forms of government, even for the republican—only not for the red republican, because that, indeed, has no moral law."

'I expressed my satisfaction in his views, and asked by what means he conceived that so high a moral standpoint could be attained to with the people.

'He energetically avowed himself to be an advocate of modern progression; of "free trade, free communication, railways", etc.

' "And freedom of the press?" I inquired.

' "In a certain degree," he replied, "there must be the censorship—but this ought to be rational, mild, paternal!"

' "And—a free constitution?" I asked.

'But to this question he either would not listen or not reply, and instead returned to his great work and its great new idea, of the moral foundation being the chief means of a nation's temporal well-being.

'I know not when I have seen a man so naively captivated by himself. But under a form of government so despotic as that of Naples it is nevertheless an excellent thing when a minister with two such important portfolios has good desires and, to a certain degree, liberal tendencies. At the same time, these cannot effect much under the present King. He alone is the ruling power in more than a common degree, and will continue to be so. . . .'

The benevolent Bianchini, while dreaming about *Il ben vivere sociale*, apparently failed to notice that the intelligence and morality of his police were not of an elevated character: at any rate they were outwitted again and again by the agents of Mazzini. In November 1856 the Mazzinian Baron Bentivegna, who had been a deputy in the Sicilian Parliament during the revolution, started the ball rolling with an insurrection in the province of Palermo. After breaking open the prison of Mezzoiuso, whose inmates eagerly joined his fraternity, he convinced the neighbouring districts that an English army had landed at Palermo, disarmed the urban guards, and proposed to overturn the government with some two hundred henchmen. When a disciplined force was sent against him his band dispersed and he went into hiding. Another Mazzinian called Spinuzza led a similar revolt at Cefalù, where the tricolour was hoisted; the local archives and portraits of the King were destroyed, but the ringleaders were soon seized, sentenced by court martial, and executed—Bentivegna in December and Spinuzza in the following March.

These abortive risings seemed more significant in the light of Agesilao Milano's murderous attack on the King. At the annual review in honour of the Immaculate Conception on December 8 a private soldier named Milano stepped out of the ranks during the march past and aimed a violent bayonet thrust at Ferdinand on horseback. This would have been fatal had not the pistol-case at the saddle turned the weapon aside, which glancing off inflicted a slight wound. Before Milano could make his second lunge Major Latour galloped up and knocked him down: he was hustled away. Few had noticed what had really happened. The King remained perfectly calm. To his brother-in-law Don Carlos, Count of Montemolino, who rushed to his aid, he whispered: 'Stand back and keep silent!' His admirable presence of mind probably saved the country from civil war. The commander of the Swiss regiments confirmed Nisco's statement[1] that if the attempt had been noticed by many it would have been imputed to a military plot, and the Swiss would have been ordered by their officers to fire on the Neapolitan troops. Perhaps this was what Milano had hoped for, as the army was known to be loyal.

The King sat on his horse until the review was over; then he was quickly driven back to the palace and his private physician was sum-

[1] *Op. cit.*, pp. 446, 447.

moned. Fearing that the bayonet might have been poisoned, the Queen knelt down and sucked the wound herself. Fortunately it did not seem serious, but as the King was over-excited the doctor prescribed a sedative. In the afternoon he drove out with his family through the most crowded streets to show that he was unhurt.

The idealistic assassin was a twenty-six-year-old Calabrian of Albanian origin who had been intoxicated by smatterings of Roman history and Mazzini, and who saw the King as a combination of Nero and Caligula in consequence. He had fought under Ribotti in the Calabrian revolt of 1848 and had threatened to murder Ferdinand during his tour in 1852, but owing to his indiscretion he was locked up. So guileless did he appear that he was soon released. Having won the confidence of a royalist military contractor, he was admitted into the regular army in spite of his turbulent past. Either the Argus-eyed police were myopic or else they were caught napping. In his case the tribunals damned as ferocious by Gladstone were peculiarly lenient, for Milano had never wavered from his purpose. During the next six months his conduct was irreproachable. Clandestine news of the King's negotiations with the Argentine to deport political prisoners spurred him to take action. During his court-martial he indignantly repudiated the plea of insanity advanced by his advocate and insisted that his plan had been long premeditated. He was sentenced to death and hanged on December 13. When he heard the verdict he is said to have exclaimed: 'My God, I die like a thief for Italian liberty.' His sympathisers made a martyr of him: he was praised in passionate odes, commemorated at meetings, and canonized by the liberal press in Turin and elsewhere, above all by the political refugees. Few stopped to consider the wanton carnage that might have followed his gesture. A medal was struck in his honour; in 1860 Garibaldi assigned a pension to his mother and sisters.

There was a spontaneous outburst of affection for Ferdinand all over the kingdom. Triduums of thanksgiving and Te Deums in every church, illuminations, festivities, magniloquent addresses, deputations which travelled from remote provinces in the depth of winter to congratulate the King on his escape, cantatas and sermons about the miraculous intercession of the Blessed Virgin, a pastoral letter from the Cardinal Archbishop, diplomatic envoys from the various Courts of Europe: judging from these Ferdinand was truly beloved. The commune of San Benedetto Ullano, Milano's birthplace, expressing horror at the sacrilege and jubilation at the miracle, disowned any connection with a 'monster of execrable memory' and implored the clemency of a sovereign so merciful and pious, the delight of all his subjects.

Ferdinand received the deputations and diplomats with the utmost affability, but his nerves had been shaken and he suffered from frequent nightmares. He dreamt that men with iron pikes dug up Milano's coffin and carried it down to the docks for transportation, passing in front of the palace. Next day he informed the police, and they inspected the cemetery, but no body-snatching had occurred. A new church was built in honour of the Immaculate Conception on the Secondigliano road, not far from the site of the thwarted assassination, and a home for cripples was founded at Capodichino in memory of the King's escape.

The throne had been drawing closer to the altar since the Council of Bishops at Caserta earlier in the year: after Milano's attempt Ferdinand's piety increased. The clergy recovered many of their lost privileges, such as secret trials for penal offenders and the expiation of sentences in religious houses. Bishops were entrusted with censorship of the press; they also became the inspectors of public and private schools. Detachments of soldiers were sent to take part in religious processions; dozens of churches and belfries were repaired: edification was combined with jollification.

Arrests and expulsions from the army followed the Milano incident, but the police failed to discover any accomplices. His associates Falcone and Nocito were helped to escape by the correspondent of *The Times*. Within less than a month two other incidents intensified the King's alarm. On December 17 a powder magazine in the arsenal near the royal palace exploded, causing many casualties and breaking every window and street lamp in the vicinity. 'I have stated above that the calamity was attributed to accident,' wrote the British consul Gallwey on December 21, 'however, there are strong suspicions that such was not the case, as a soldier, on the night of the 18th, was observed by the sentinel on guard at the powder magazine in the Castel Nuovo, actually digging a mine or passage under the magazine, and suspecting the man's intentions knocked him down with his musket. It is most fortunate that this execrable deed was stopped in time, because the magazine in question is the principal deposit of gunpowder in the capital, and from it the various castles and forts at Naples are supplied; most likely four-fifths of the town would have been blown up. I am informed that two soldiers of the artillery have been arrested and are now under a court martial, suspected of having been instrumental in the explosion of the 16th (*sic*).'

Two weeks later, on January 4, 1857, the steam frigate *Carlo Terzo*, which was to carry a great quantity of arms and ammunition to Palermo, blew up with a terrific explosion at 11 p.m., causing the death of most of her crew. H.M.S. *Malacca*, also lying in Naples Roads, went to her assistance, but what was left of her prow soon keeled over and sank to the bottom. The accident was attributed to a sailor's attempt to pilfer the powder magazine: surprised by a guard he had left his candle there. But the hidden hand of Mazzini was suspected with greater probability.

Two such powerful explosions at such short intervals in the same area were scarcely due to coincidence. They shook Ferdinand's faith in his army. His sense of reality had always been keener than his imagination, but now he had to grapple with shadowy fancies and suspicions which he tried to laugh off in vain. Sometimes he thought he was being slowly poisoned by Milano's bayonet in spite of his doctor's denial. But poison of a more insidious kind had begun to pervade his system, a creeping cancerous dread. At the age of forty-seven he looked sixty, old and grey—if not full of sleep. He slept even less than usual, and had to rouse himself from fits of languor during the daytime. He took refuge in ambitious schemes of road building and land reclamation as well as in works of charity. He spent more time at Caserta than in Naples: for once he would not attend the gala performance at the San Carlo for his birthday on January 12, and the Court ball which was to have been given the same month was deferred.

Popular rumour blamed a gentleman who was reputed to possess the evil eye. The Duke of Ascoli had submitted a list of guests for the King's approval, cancelling the names of those who had died or whose loyalty was dubious, and substituting others. Before pronouncing one name, that of the Duke of Ventignano, he clutched the coral horn dangling from his waistcoat. Ferdinand remarked: 'You know the prejudice against him. I do not believe in it, but I am sure the ball will not take place.' The Duke was sent an invitation; the attempted regicide occurred shortly after and the ball was postponed. The subsequent explosions deferred it indefinitely, and the *jettatore's* notoriety was enhanced. A few shells, still loaded, were then found among some old iron going to be smelted and retrieved in the nick of time. 'A frightful state of things,' wrote the British consul, adding that he would be glad of a ship of war to protect British subjects. Security measures were doubled by the police. As the King had been warned to 'beware of the gas', the gas was shut off from the palace and other royal buildings, and oil lamps were substituted.

After long and laborious negotiations the convention for a colony of political prisoners in the Argentine was signed on January 13, 1857. Each colonist was to be allotted a fair share of fertile land and a sufficient sum for preliminary expenses. The Argentine Republic stipulated that the prisoners were to provide a written statement that they were willing to emigrate, and government officials were sent to persuade them that emigration would end their woes. At Procida over thirty consented, but the influence of Poerio and other leaders dissuaded many who had favoured the idea at first. 'Why so much trouble and expense,' exclaimed Poerio, 'to make us die in America or on the voyage? Let us rather die in prison!' And of course the liberal press raised an outcry about Bomba's 'white slave traffic'. As a result of these clamorous protests the Argentine Republic would not ratify the convention.

In February the Queen gave birth to her youngest son Gennaro, who received the title of Count of Caltagirone, and that Sicilian city sent a deputation to express its gratitude and offer the infant a miraculous relic of its patron Saint James the Great. The liberals took advantage of the celebrations to play a practical joke on the King. A clever imitation of a royal decree was posted all over the capital announcing that since Providence had blessed him with progeny His Majesty would grant a full amnesty to all political prisoners in accordance with the friendly advice of the French and English governments; that he would restore the Constitution of 1848, to which he had sworn on the Gospel; that the Hereditary Prince was appointed Vicar-General; and that the Chambers should be convoked immediately. The birth of another prince as well as the printing, paper and style of the edict made it seem authentic. There was some cheering amid general bewilderment, until the police were ordered to destroy it. As the order came from Caserta, the public had had leisure to discuss it. Again the police were hoodwinked. Ferdinand had to laugh, but he was not amused.

All these incidents encouraged the indefatigable Mazzinians. In February 1857 Mazzini's chief agent in Naples Giuseppe Fanelli informed his leader in London and his colleagues in Genoa that the kingdom was ripe for revolution: a mere spark from outside would suffice, preferably an armed expedition. Carlo Pisacane replied eagerly from Genoa that he could count on his full support, but Fanelli should draw up a plan. Which was the best route; where should the expedition land? Fanelli proposed that it should stop at Ponza to release the political prisoners and proceed with these to land somewhere south of Naples. Having proposed this, his enthusiasm waned as Pisacane's waxed: he became querulous: the whole thing should be delayed. On March 31 Pisacane fumed back at him: 'Your thermometer marked several degrees below zero, whereas the previous day I had received a letter from Mazzini which seemed to have the temperature of boiling water. I would rather boil than freeze. . . .' The expedition was to sail at the end of April or early in May and no nonsense. 'Do you think I'm God Almighty?' wailed Fanelli. The organization was not yet ready: the arms and money were lacking; and he pleaded for a month's adjournment.

Mazzini backed Pisacane in characteristic style: 'We individuals, whatever we do, cannot create the insurrection of a people: we can only create the occasion for it. Either the people act, and all is well, or do not act, and we are not responsible except to God and our conscience. Our only duty is scrupulously to study the right opportunity. To seize it, and with a bold movement offer the initiative to the nation, is revolutionary genius. For me, for us, the moment has arrived.' Mazzini was still in London. Fanelli wrote from Naples on April 16: 'We have no connections on the island of Ponza.' He would require at least six weeks to establish contacts. 'How hard is the plight of a man whose soul boils beyond the limit,' he exclaimed, 'yet who is duty-bound to utter words of ice!' The 'definite' date was shifted to May 25, and then to June 10, and as usual with Mazzini's enterprises the expedition had become an open secret. The intendants of the coastal provinces of Sicily were already on the alert, and the intendant of Salerno was warned to be prepared for a landing near that city.

Prince Charles of Capua

The Duchess of Berry as a girl

Mazzini arrived furtively in Genoa on May 11 to organize contemporary risings there and at Leghorn. Every night he discussed developments with Pisacane, whose fanaticism only equalled his own, a born rebel against authority and tradition, and fundamentally a complete autocrat. The red-haired young journalist Miss Jessie White, darling of all conspirators and correspondent of *The Daily News*, urged Garibaldi to co-operate but he had had premonitory experience of Pisacane at Rome in 1848. Garibaldi answered that if he could foresee the slightest chance of success he would not hesitate to lead the expedition, but he could not foresee it at present: 'I shall not bid the Italians, "Arise!" in order to make the rabble laugh.' Never daunted, Jessie White went on to arrange a meeting between Garibaldi and Pisacane at Turin, but Garibaldi was unmoved by Pisacane's eloquence.

The Mazzinians feared that the Murattists might steal a march on them with the support of the French government. On June 12 Pisacane went to Naples in disguise, after ten years' absence, to discuss final arrangements with Fanelli and the Neapolitan committee and galvanize them into general agreement. His eyes flashed, his voice commanded and threatened the laggards. Which of them would assume the responsibility for inertness? Why not grab this excellent chance to save the people from oppression? They were awaiting the clarion call. Milano's self-sacrifice and other fine deeds showed that they should not be abandoned at this juncture, etc. Fanelli took heart again, but not for long: by the time Pisacane had returned to Genoa he was cursing the moment he got mixed up in this mad business. Having flouted the Neapolitan police and visited his old home with impunity, Pisacane felt optimistic. Jessie White wrote that he returned radiant and transfigured. 'We shall win,' he told her, 'a spark will suffice . . . The revolution is in the hearts of all the cultured classes: Naples will go up in flames. Murattism only exists in the head of Napoleon and his Piedmontese clique. The army will be with us; the people with the winning side.'

Pisacane was to command the expedition with two Calabrians as his lieutenants, Baron Giovanni Nicotera, still under thirty, who had joined Mazzini's 'Young Italy' at the age of nineteen and had fought against the Neapolitan army near Rome, and Giovanbattista Falcone, aged twenty-three, who had been a school friend of Agesilao Milano.

They were to leave Genoa as ordinary passengers on the postal steamer *Cagliari* on June 25, preceded by Rosolino Pilo with a few boats carrying arms and ammunition which were to meet them at a certain point en route. Pisacane mustered the twenty-five members of the expedition before departing and gave each a dagger, a pistol and a red cap with his final instructions. He asked Jessie White to look after his companion Enrichetta Di Lorenzo (who had deserted a husband and three children for his sake and for whom he had deserted the Neapolitan army in 1847), and the daughter she had borne him, as well as his private papers and 'Political Testament'.

The latter provides some clue to his mentality and contains such statements as: 'I believe that only Socialism is the not distant future of Italy and perhaps of Europe. . . . I am convinced that railways, telegraphs, the improvement of industry, trading facilities, machinery, etc., by a fatal economic law, so long as the product is distributed by means of competition will increase this product, but will always accumulate it in the hands of a minority and impoverish the masses. Hence this vaunted progress, by increasing the sufferings of the people, will drive them to a terrible revolution which, by suddenly changing all the social orders, will redound to the profit of a minority. . . . With such principles I should consider that I had failed in a sacred duty if, seeing the chance of striking a blow at a certain point, place, and appropriate period, I had not exhausted every effort to make it succeed. . . . The flash of Milano's bayonet was a more effective piece of propaganda than a thousand volumes written by doctrinaires. . . . The propaganda of ideas is a chimera . . .; the education of the people is an absurdity. Ideas result from facts, not facts from ideas . . .; if I do not succeed, I deeply despise the ignoble herd that condemns me, and set little value on its applause in case of success.' His contempt for 'the ignoble herd' and for popular education came strangely from a professed Socialist.

Twelve members of the expedition signed a parting message 'To our brothers of Italy' for future publication, explaining the motives of their enterprise: 'Our conscience tells us: so long as twenty millions of Italians are slaves we have no right to be free unless we devote our lives to the emancipation of all. Our small fatherland of Genoa and Piedmont is not sufficient! . . . Therefore we depart. . . . We are compelled by a selfish and cowardly government to fly through the darkness like smugglers. . . . The ordeal is difficult: the foe we intend to attack is strong . . . the province in which we hope to plant the Italian banner is inhabited by good but ignorant people who will probably be made to believe that we are bandits or pirates come for plunder. Perhaps we shall be received like the Bandiera brothers. So be it! Poor people, we have only our lives to give to Italy and we offer them with all our hearts. . . .'

About an hour after the steamer *Cagliari* sailed from Genoa the captain was seized and a naval comrade familiar with the route took over his command. To exculpate himself the captain requested a memorandum of this transaction, which Pisacane wrote and twenty-one of his partisans duly signed. It ended thus: 'Despising the calumnies of the common herd, strong with the justice of our cause and the vigour of our spirits, we declare ourselves the initiators of the Italian revolution. If the country does not respond to our appeal, without cursing her we shall know how to die like resolute men, following the noble phalanx of Italian martyrs. . . .'

For some reason which he could not explain Rosolino Pilo's boats failed to meet the *Cagliari* as arranged. The steamer cruised back and forth in every direction at a low speed with headlights blazing, while Pisacane wondered whether to proceed or wait or return to Genoa. In the meantime a cargo of guns destined for Tunis was discovered in the hold, so they sailed on to Ponza. Here the plan succeeded beyond all expectation. They surprised the small garrison and, helped by the crowd of exiles (who were free to circulate from dawn to sunset), they released the eight hundred prisoners in the fort, collected more arms and ammunition, destroyed a barrack and police station with all the archives, while the terrified inhabitants barricaded themselves in their houses or fled into the fields. Most of the convicts celebrated their release with an orgy of looting. These rather than Pisacane had become masters of the island. Many of them believed that the *Cagliari* party were an advance patrol of the revolutionary forces on the mainland. All of them wished to embark, but space was limited. Eventually 323 were taken, including soldiers, political and common prisoners, and exiles: the rest had to be satisfied with a promise that the ship would come back for them. Owing to the confusion of embarkation and the need of refuelling the whole of June 27 was spent at Ponza. Towards midnight when the anchor was being hauled, a mysterious boat was

seen scudding away in the darkness. A launch was lowered to inter-
cept it, and Nicotera toppled overboard in his excitement. While he
was being rescued the boat was lost sight of. It contained the parish
priest, who had decided to report on these happenings to Gaeta where
the King was in residence. More time could not be wasted. The ship
sailed on to Sapri.

Pisacane had been educated at the Nunziatella military college which
Ferdinand I had founded in 1787. He was a soldier by vocation and
had written several essays on military topics. Delighted to put his
theories to practice, he assumed the rank of general, conferring that of
colonel on Nicotera and of major on Falcone, and appointing a council
of war with a military code of his own. In the first flush of success he
felt sure that his three hundred would soon be trebled and quadrupled.
While dividing them into companies he forgot the quality of the troops
at his disposal, most of whom had been convicted of theft or homicide.
Nicotera and Falcone were less sanguine about their dependability.
Why not drop them somewhere along the coast and let them shift for
themselves? But Pisacane could not believe that having obtained freedom they would disappoint their deliverer. He took it for granted that
they hated the Bourbon dynasty. He would soon inspire them with
his own ideals.

The landing at Sapri passed off quietly, all too quietly, on Sunday
evening, June 28. Nobody had come to meet them at the little white
house as had been prearranged with the Neapolitan committee:
Fanelli had not even sent a messenger. The challenge 'Italy of the
Italians!' was shouted without any response. After the hectic scramble
of disembarking, the silence was disconcerting. The beach was
deserted except for two telegraph employees, who were promptly
arrested. Sapri had a population of about two thousand fishermen and
peasants, and was situated inland between two hills. Before marching
there Pisacane tried to invigorate his men with a speech: 'Sons, we
were twenty-one individuals to liberate you from the island; now you
must liberate the kingdom. . . .' The small squad of urban guards fired
a few perfunctory shots and took to their heels. Most of the inhabitants
had fled, the doors of their houses were bolted, the windows shuttered.
It was easy to 'occupy' such a place and destroy the royal insignia,
but this was not the welcome they had been led to expect. A rich landowner who had been recommended to Pisacane as a patriot likely to

assist him in every way was visibly startled at his approach: he made it quite plain that he wished to be left in peace. Pisacane indignantly commandeered his insufficient store of bread and firearms. He had been sadly misinformed.

Next morning he marched on to the village of Torraca where the whole population was celebrating the feast of Saint Peter. Some of the peasants called 'Viva Murat!' and fraternized with the rebels. Pisacane's proclamation was read to the crowd: 'Citizens, it is time to end the unbridled tyranny of Ferdinand II. For you it is enough to wish it. He is universally detested. The army is with us. The capital awaits the signal from the provinces to settle the question at a single blow. For us the government of Ferdinand has ceased to exist: another step and the triumph will be ours. Let us unite and hasten towards our hopeful brothers. . . .'

The audience gaped in blank apathy. Word had already got round that there had been looting in the district. Nobody volunteered to join the expedition. At Casalnuovo, half-way to Padula, Pisacane's optimism revived. He seemed to be expected. A revolt had started: the rebels had routed the police and occupied their barracks; the royal arms were shattered, the telegraph was destroyed, the seditious proclamations were cheered. Yet none of these riotous peasants would join the crusade. Pisacane could only suppose that they had been antagonized by the rapacity of his recruits. To set an example, a man who had robbed a poor woman was tried by the 'council of war' and condemned to be shot. At Padula, instead of the five hundred volunteers he had counted on he found hostile indifference.

The royal troops were advancing, but Pisacane still imagined they would mutiny and join the three hundred liberators. It was the other way round: two-thirds of his men flung their arms away and either ran towards the enemy or in other directions to hide: thirty-five were shot like dogs in a blind alley. Thanks to Colonel Ghio, whom the King had allowed to replace Pisacane's brother, the hundred who stuck to their leader were able to get away. Misled by a young peasant, they wandered over rough mountain paths until they dropped with hunger and fatigue. Next day they staggered on to Sanza, where the villagers were supposed to be hospitable. They could hear the church bells ringing. The parish priest warned the people that a horde of brigands was coming to rob, murder and ravish, and a price was on their heads.

Armed with clubs, sickles, and whatever came to hand, even women and boys rushed to attack their liberators. Pisacane fell wounded, and still the peasants advanced with savage cries. He had the strength to shoot himself before they made mincemeat of him. Falcone and another stabbed himself; Nicotera was left for dead; the rest were killed or wounded. The survivors were sent to Salerno for trial: seven were sentenced to death and reprieved by the King, three were sentenced to life imprisonment, and the rest to twenty-five years in irons. On the other hand rewards, promotions and honours were distributed even among those who had done little to earn them. The parish priest of Sanza complained that he and his flock deserved a larger share for the glory of their self-sacrifice, though none of them had been hurt in the conflict.

The liberals felt that Pisacane had discredited their cause, and most of the political prisoners agreed with Settembrini, who wrote to his wife: 'I am deeply grieved and curse those villains who send gallant young men to die, to be massacred, under pretence of liberty. . . . Poor country, lacerated in a thousand ways by fools and scoundrels. . . . How much blood, how many sufferings and tears for these rash ventures!' To Silvio Spaventa it seemed that 'the fruit of ten years of persecution' had been wasted, and only the government had gained. But three years later Pisacane was lauded as the precursor of Garibaldi's expedition. Every Italian schoolboy was taught Mercantini's song about 'The Gleaner of Sapri':

> *They were three hundred, they were young and strong,*
> *And they are dead and gone!'*

In fact there were no gleaners on that desolate beach. The women they encountered at Sanza were frenzied harpies: one of them prodded the wounded Nicotera in the head with a pitch-fork. But the gentle gleaner of the song was doubtless intended for a symbol of Italy.

After Pisacane's landing at Sapri the captain of the *Cagliari* was free to sail to Salerno to report on what had occurred: instead he steered for Ponza to fetch the rest of the convicts. About twelve miles west of Capri, half-way between Sapri and Ponza, the Sardinian flag was hoisted when two Neapolitan frigates hove into sight, but he could not avoid capture. The passengers and crew were arrested, and there were many conflicting statements during the following trial. The captain maintained that he had intended to return to Naples, but the evidence was against him. If his crew had been Pisacane's reluctant prisoners, why had they taken part in the Ponza affair? Why had he anchored off Sapri most of the night? Why had he then proceeded in the direction of Ponza? Some of the captives alleged that he had distributed arms and wished them good luck; and that the discovery of the cargo of guns had not been fortuitous. Moreover the crew included two English engineers named Park and Watt who had explanatory letters from Miss Jessie White proving their knowledge of the conspiracy. They had entered into the spirit of the adventure and given it their active support. Thanks to these Sir James Hudson, the British minister in Turin, was able to butt into the diplomatic controversy that ensued, since the *Cagliari* had been declared a lawful prize.

To most objective people it appeared a plain case of filibustering, but not to Cavour, who instantly demanded that the ship be restored to her owners of the Rubattino Company, and the release of her captain and crew. Backed by Hudson, he insisted that she was protected by the Sardinian flag and had been boarded illegally in waters beyond the limits of Neapolitan jurisdiction.

The tedious controversy was complicated by a change of government in England. In February 1858 Lord Derby's Tory ministry succeeded Palmerston, who had fallen as a result of the Orsini outrage. When Cavour appealed for British assistance 'in a question of common interest to all sea Powers', it appeared that Hudson had overreached himself in promising that assistance, and that the secretary of the British legation in Turin had made a mistake in transcribing an official note. An interrogative had been turned into an affirmative sentence, and Hudson had signed this without reading it. The mistake was not detected till three months later. To Cavour the excuse seemed lame, for it could not be denied that Lord Clarendon had encouraged his truculence towards Naples. But Lord Malmesbury had replaced Lord Clarendon at the Foreign Office, whose sympathy was diverted towards Austria and away from France. Austria attempted to isolate Piedmont and reconcile England with Naples, succeeding to the extent that Ferdinand ordered the release of Park and Watt. Malmesbury expressed his appreciation and a *rapprochement* seemed likely.

On the other hand Ferdinand remained deaf to Sardinia's claims. But Cavour was ably served by Marchese d'Azeglio, his ambassador in London. Public opinion in England had been anti-Bourbonist since

Gladstone's letters, whereas Piedmont had been a gallant ally in the Crimean War. Marchese d'Azeglio appealed to public opinion in a declaration of Sardinia's rights and determination to defend them with firmness and energy: having agreed on principle Great Britain should surely act in concert with Sardinia. The press was sympathetic. Accused of flabbiness and tergiversation, Lord Malmesbury behaved accordingly. On May 25, 1858 he sent two threatening notes to Naples, in the first, alleging the innocence of the two English engineers, and demanding an indemnity of £3000 sterling to be paid to them within ten days; in the second, declaring the capture of the *Cagliari* and the imprisonment of her crew a violation of maritime law, and urging the Neapolitan government to satisfy Sardinia's just demands, supported by England. Should the government of the Two Sicilies reject them, Great Britain and Sardinia would seek the arbitration of a friendly power in the hope of avoiding evils which might become very serious. Sardinia sent a similar ultimatum.

Malmesbury's tergiversation is further proved by a letter from Count Bernstorff to Carafa, dated June 1, 1858: 'Lord Malmesbury told me in strict confidence that there is a means, which seems to him quite simple, of enabling the Neapolitan government to refute victoriously all Sardinia's claims for an indemnity, and that he could not understand why it had not been adopted some time since. Why had not the Neapolitan government made a counter-claim from Sardinia? Why not tell the government of Turin: The ship which flew the Sardinian flag and which you have taken under your protection, has landed armed rebels on my coasts; these have killed my officers and men and set buildings on fire. To subdue them I have been put to considerable cost. For all this you owe me compensation: you should assign pensions to the widows and orphans of the victims, and compensate me for the expenses incurred by the civil war started on my territory. If you think that you also have a right to an indemnity for the crew and owners of the captured vessel, we shall see which of the two parties is the most indebted. Lord Malmesbury has assured me that after Sardinia had taken the *Cagliari* under her protection she could not decline responsibility for the acts of her crew and proprietors.'

Had Ferdinand taken this broad hint and sent Bernstorff a telegram asking him to settle the indemnity for the two engineers at once, he might have prevented joint action between England and Sardinia, but he did nothing about it, convinced that the aggression had been manifestly on the other side and that the Genoese police had connived at Pisacane's expedition. Seeing his rights flouted by the respectable Lord Malmesbury, he replied on June 8 that he had never thought himself strong enough to oppose Great Britain; and since she had espoused the cause of the *Cagliari* further argument was futile. He had deposited the £3000 demanded with the banker Pook, and would entrust the vessel with her captain and crew to Lord Lyons, the British minister in Florence. It was a dignified surrender of right to might.

The fate of Pisacane's expedition seemed to have eliminated the Murattist menace, and to have discredited Mazzini's tactics. 'The question,' said Mazzini in defence of his efforts, 'was not between the Republic and Royalty, but between action and inertness.' In this case action served as an admonition that nothing serious could be accomplished without the support of Piedmont, and Garibaldi took note.

In the case of Orsini's outrage in January the unexpected happened. At first Napoleon III's reaction was more severe than Ferdinand II's after Milano's attempt. France was divided into five military commands; a general became Minister of the Interior; and a Bill known as the Law against Suspects was passed, whereby two thousand people were arrested and some four hundred were deported. Since no Frenchmen had been involved, these measures seemed somewhat arbitrary. But Napoleon relaxed after Orsini's execution: he wished to show how badly the assassin had blundered. The secret meeting with Cavour at Plombières followed in July, and war against Austria was planned for the spring of 1859. The Pope and the King of Naples would present serious difficulties, said Napoleon. Cavour replied that both would be easy to deal with: the Pope might be allowed to retain the Patrimony of St Peter if he gave up the Romagna; as for the King of Naples, a chance revolution would send him toppling. Napoleon could not conceal his wish to give Ferdinand's throne to his cousin Murat, but it was agreed that the Two Sicilies should be left alone for the time being. Ferdinand's goodwill mission to congratulate the Emperor on his lucky escape from the bombs had been superfluous.

XIX

The Duke of Calabria's betrothal to Maria Sophia of Bavaria—The last royal marriage by proxy—Ferdinand's journey to meet the bride—His fever and nightmares at Ariano—Deterioration at Lecce—Change of plans—Maria Sophia arrives at Bari—A melancholy nuptial blessing— Ferdinand's sufferings—Family bereavements—Vain remedies—The King's return to Caserta—Landing of political prisoners at Queenstown— France and Piedmont declare war against Austria—A passport to the next world—Ferdinand dictates his Will and dies.

ENGLAND and France had tried to wrest from Ferdinand what his pride and principles forbade him to concede: he had borne the breach with equanimity. He had tried to concentrate on self-sufficiency in industry and agriculture, keeping taxes down, improving roads, telegraphic communications and public works in general. The finances of the kingdom were flourishing in spite of such catastrophic set-backs as the earthquakes of 1857–8, when vast areas of Basilicata were destroyed and more than ten thousand lives were lost. Even De Cesare admits[1] that there were abundant signs of 'new economic life and industrial awakening'.

To cultivate his garden behind a high Chinese wall had become the limit of Ferdinand's aspirations. He was merely following the quietist, municipal policy of his ancestor Charles III. Those of his more restless subjects who hankered after novelty—'the politically articulate forces of the country', as they were often described—were exiled or in captivity. But, as Metternich said, 'it is useless to close the gates against ideas: they overleap them'. The ideas were leaping like gazelles over the gates which Ferdinand had closed. Though autonomist sentiment remained strong in the Two Sicilies, the Piedmontese and Mazzinian

Op. cit., Vol. I, p. 225.

currents were gaining momentum. Thanks largely to Cavour, an Italian kingdom under the constitutional sceptre of Victor Emmanuel seemed to many liberals the most desirable solution. 'We want an Italy mistress of herself and of her own destinies;' as La Farina put it, 'no Austrian domination and Lorraine, Este, Bourbon principalities, vassals of Austria.' Ferdinand, who had never been the vassal of any foreign power, was misrepresented in such propaganda.

'Friends of all, foes of none, independent. . . . To renounce this wise policy would be to betray the interests of the country and compromise it without further hope. . . . Divine mercy, in which the King puts blind and implicit trust, will come to the aid of the royal government. . . .' In these words Carafa had echoed Ferdinand's dogma to Carini, his minister in London. But it is difficult to find friends and even more to keep them if you insist on isolation, hence Ferdinand was described as an ogre in the foreign press. The foreign diplomats at Naples were bored, for there was seldom anything new to report. Turin provided all the political thrills. Nobody could tell what had happened at Plombières, but sensational results were expected. The activity of Gropello, the Sardinian minister in Naples, was striking in contrast with the passivity of his colleagues. 'He seeks all occasions to make propaganda and win proselytes for the ambitious and visionary policy of the Count of Cavour,' wrote the Austrian minister in July 1858. Cavour displayed more skill in sowing the seeds of war than had ever been displayed in preserving peace, as a Frenchman remarked.

While Cavour was negotiating with Napoleon III for war, Ferdinand was negotiating with the Bavarian Court for a daughter-in-law. Not many Catholic princesses were available; and it is improbable that Francis, the heir presumptive, was consulted when Maria Sophia, a daughter of Duke Maximilian of Bavaria and a younger sister of the Empress Elizabeth of Austria, was chosen for his bride. The official demand was made in Munich by the King's plenipotentiary Count Ludolf in December 1858, and the engagement was announced in Naples on January 4, 1859.

The bride and groom had only seen each other's portraits. That of Francis in a miniature medallion framed in diamonds had been carried on a white velvet cushion during the engagement ceremony, and a lady-in-waiting had clasped it round the bride's neck. Though buttoned into a hussar's uniform the figure was neither martial nor dashing: the long head and disproportionate high brow, sad eyes and awkward nose conveyed an impression of lymphatic weakness. It was not an inspiring picture—no young girl's dream of knighthood. The Princess, on the other hand, was sweetly seventeen in a Keepsake Annual style, if not as tall and magnificent as her sister Elizabeth of Austria. She too had been brought up to an open-air life of unusual freedom, accustomed to riding and roaming the Bavarian Alps, so that her charm was that of a wild flower rather than of a hot-house orchid.

The marriage was celebrated at Munich on January 8, 1859, with King Maximilian of Bavaria's brother Prince Luitpold representing the Duke of Calabria. It was a memorable ceremony, for the bride was the last royal personage to be married by proxy. Prince Luitpold entered the royal chapel at 7.30 p.m., accompanied by Count Ludolf and his secretary. Princess Maria Sophia and her parents followed: the bride in brocade and foaming lace with orange-blossom and a long white velvet train, a coronet over her veil. A loud cannon announced the arrival of the King and Queen, the latter in crimson velvet embroidered with gold. After the deed conferring proxy on Prince Luitpold was read aloud in Italian and German, the Archbishop of Munich blessed the wedding rings and delivered a brief homily about her good fortune and the importance of the career awaiting her. She listened with becoming emotion, and received the nuptial blessing to the chiming of Munich bells and salvos of artillery. The choir then sang a glorious *Te Deum*.

Farewell festivities filled the next few days, culminating in a splendid State ball. On January 13 Maria Sophia took leave of the sovereigns, and the station was crowded with those who had come to see her off. 'God be with you and grant you long life. Do not forget us!' they cried. Waving an exquisite hand she called out: 'Adieu!' Her brother Prince Ludwig with a small Bavarian suite accompanied her to Vienna, where her sister the Empress gave her a fervent welcome. She was to sail to Manfredonia from Trieste, but the voyage was delayed by news of King Ferdinand's illness.

Against his physician's advice Ferdinand had insisted on travelling through Puglia in the depth of winter to meet the bride. He was excessively obese for his age and easily prone to exhaustion. Doctor Ramaglia urged him to wait until the weather improved. Perhaps his tone was too peremptory, for it was said that the King snapped at him: 'How much did you get for giving me this advice?' Opposition of any kind made him stubborn. He suspected some ulterior motive and that settled it: off he went. Since the journey had been kept secret no preparations for it were made until the last moment.

The royal party set forth in six carriages on January 8: the King and Queen were accompanied by their sons the Counts of Trani and Caserta as well as by the bridegroom. The weather was arctic; everybody was wrapped in furs and heavy overcoats. Nobody looked cheerful except the King, who laughed and cracked jokes with a rather forced hilarity until he caught sight of two Capuchin friars. These he regarded as unlucky omens. He crossed himself on leaving the palace, and the others did likewise. The first halt was at the shrine of Saint Filomena at Mugnano where they were greeted by a military band. The Bishop of Nola blessed them, and the Princes offered their amethyst shirt buttons for a reliquary to contain the Virgin Martyr's blood. But the cold increased steadily: soon it began to snow. Occasionally the King left his carriage to walk, and as he was puffing at one of his favourite Neapolitan cigars a postilion boldly asked him for the stub. Ferdinand gave him an entire cigar thinking that would please him better, but the man accepted it grudgingly and put it in his pocket after hesitating as to whether he should light it. The King chuckled and said: 'So you wanted to smoke mine, eh? Take it.' Such trivial incidents, recorded by De Cesare and others, endeared Ferdinand to his subjects in a manner difficult for moderns to conceive. Twelve years previously his carriage had capsized on the slope of Monteforte and he had built a new road there. In memory of the danger he had then escaped he asked the Queen and Princes to recite the rosary with him.

The whole of Avellino turned out to welcome them in the snow. After a hot drink, Ferdinand had to meet the local authorities who were introduced to him by the intendant with a flourish of adjectives. Showing slight impatience the King asked what there was for dinner. The local speciality was a large type of macaroni called *pacchere*, which in dialect meant a smacking. When this delicacy was promised he remarked to one of the ladies: 'That's a fine sort of welcome, eh Madam?'

It was still snowing next morning with a northerly gale, but Ferdinand ignored those who urged him to wait. 'Look what a lovely surprise I have ordered for you,' he said to the Austrian-born Princess of Scaletta. 'Doesn't this snow make you think you are in Vienna?' As usual he had received many petitions and distributed alms on a munificent scale, including such practical items as dowries, beds, clothes and provisions. He offered a cigar to the intendant, who kept it under a glass dome as long as he lived.

After Avellino the weather got worse. The horses stumbled, and the King had to trudge at least a mile leaning on the arm of one of his sturdy guards. Even so he was determined to go on to Foggia. The peasants had sprinkled gravel on the slippery highway, but the storm grew so violent that Ferdinand reluctantly agreed to spend the night at Ariano. Bishop Michele Caputo, with whom he proposed to stay, had not been prepared for his reception and fainted from shock at the news. The travellers were worn out. The Queen was half numb, having had to walk in her light satin shoes, and the King seemed petrified. The Bishop's palace had not been heated, and the charcoal braziers made little difference.

That night at Ariano was to give rise to sinister legends. No doubt the King had caught a chill, which combined with fatigue and indigestion to bring on a fever with nightmares. Nisco and others have related that his valet Galizia heard a strange noise in the King's bedroom and went in to find him brandishing a pistol against an imaginary assassin. Ferdinand felt sure that a door had opened in the wall and that he had seen the malefactor escape. An immediate search yielded no results. The King ordered his servants to say nothing about it, but he could not sleep another wink. Galizia remained convinced that the Bishop had plotted the King's death: later it was rumoured that he had tried to poison him, and the Bishop bragged about this after 1860 to ingratiate himself with the new régime. Everybody was struck by the King's ghastly pallor at Mass next morning. Shivering in his heavy cloak, his temples throbbing from insomnia, he started out for Foggia, where instead of resting he showed himself to the applauding crowd and sat down to confer with his ministers, signing several decrees in connection with his son's marriage and a special amnesty commuting the life sentences of political prisoners to deportation to America, of which more anon.

He went on to Andria after another miserable night, stopping to visit the agricultural colony of San Ferdinando which he had founded twenty years since for the families which had been transferred there from the malarial saltmarshes of Barletta. The demonstrations in his honour were touchingly naïve. At Massafra, where he had to change horses before Taranto, the good people shouted in chorus: 'A favour, Your Majesty, a favour!' 'What do you want?' he asked. 'Just a sight of Your Majesty', they replied. In spite of intense fatigue he rushed on from place to place with alert critical eye, his temper flaring out when the gendarmes beat back the crowd with their rifle-butts. 'You don't know your jobs', he shouted. At Taranto he ordered the commander of the cavalry squadron to be arrested, having noticed that the horses were spavined or knocked up; and he grumbled about the slow progress of the harbour works. Even on the night journey to Lecce deputations came to meet him along the road. He entered Lecce soon after dawn on January 14, preceded by four gendarmes with flaming torches and followed by half a dozen with drawn swords, while all the bells of the city were pealing. The festoons of lights glimmered like opalescent gossamer on the rococo palaces in the early morning. Already four bands of musicians were playing aubades and anthems in the public squares and Saint Oronzo seemed to be conducting them from his high column.

On stepping from his carriage Ferdinand excused himself for disturbing so many people at this early hour; pulling up his breeches, he remarked to one of the guards of honour: 'It's devilish cold, guard.' 'But it has not chilled the ardour of the citizens who wished to welcome Your Majesty', came the neat retort. Ferdinand smiled and repeated this with gusto at the subsequent reception. The intendant's palace had been redecorated by a Neapolitan upholsterer whom he was glad to recognize: '*Nè, Antuò, ccà te truove?*' The local aristocracy had lent additional furniture, but no fires had been lighted in the chimneys. The King drank a cup of soup and lay down on the camp-bed that always accompanied him on his travels. But he was soon back at work, discussing the affairs of the province with his ministers; then all attended Mass and an official reception, followed by private audiences. At two p.m. the royal party visited the Cathedral, where the Bishop blessed them after a sermon and the *Te Deum*. A convent school was then inspected and poems were recited by the pupils: it was a strenuous afternoon, for there was another reception during which the King remained standing.

A gala performance of *Il Trovatore* had been arranged for that evening. When asked if he would honour the theatre with his presence, Ferdinand assented. Having heard that the popular comedian De Biase was in town, he remarked: 'A fig for the *Trovatore*! I want to hear Don Checco and enjoy myself.' A new show had to be improvised at the last minute, to the amazement of those who had come to hear Verdi's opera. The boxes were crammed, illuminated with wax candles, and the stuffy hall was only ventilated by icy draughts from the stage. The King's massive torso bulged out of his box, and the Queen looked crushed beside him. Ever and anon, as was his wont, he rose to pull up his breeches. Each time this happened, presuming he was about to retire, the audience rose with him in unison. At the end of the first act he decided to leave: he was still shivering in his cloak, and he was thoroughly exhausted. Yet he felt obliged to attend the banquet and watch the display of fireworks in his honour. He did not retire till ten o'clock, intending to proceed to Bari next morning. During the night he was feverish, and an acute pain in his groin prevented him from sleeping.

At dawn the Queen summoned the intendant and asked him for a good doctor. 'We have two, Your Majesty, d'Arpe and Leone,' he replied, 'the former is more famous and experienced but he is a liberal; the latter is a man of order.' 'Call the latter', said the Queen. When he came he was not admitted to the King's bedroom. The Queen merely described the symptoms, on the strength of which she demanded a diagnosis. The doctor supposed that the King's illness had been caused by the cold and discomfort of his journey, and prescribed a complete rest. However, the King received more visitors throughout the day, and towards evening he was aching in every limb. The Queen was deeply worried.

After another feverish night Ferdinand insisted on being bled. Marotta, the best phlebotomist in Lecce, was summoned: he rushed to early Mass before the ordeal. Even in bed the King was an awe-inspiring sight: his formidable girth alone imposed respect. The phlebotomist quaked before royalty in the flesh: he was almost as pale as the patient. 'Bleed His Majesty just as you bleed me', said the intendant to give him courage. The King asked if he had brought a new lancet, and since it was not new he told him to wash it carefully, while anointing his own forehead with the oil of the lamps burning before the holy pictures around him. The three Princes entered and kissed their father's hand, saying: 'Good morning, Papa, how are you feeling to-day?' Then they stood stiffly in a row opposite their father, who held out his arm to Marotta over a basin of hot water. When the blackish blood oozed out Marotta exclaimed: 'Good health, Your Majesty!' and plunged the King's hand into the hot water. After several minutes he drew it out and the King asked: 'How much blood have you drawn?' 'The usual ten ounces, Your Majesty.' 'Thanks, you have given me health. May the Lord give you health in return, my son!'

The Duke of Calabria offered some taffeta to bandage the wound; and the phlebotomist made his bow and awaited further orders: he was told to return a few days later. Eventually he claimed a royal pension for this service.

The King was not a whit relieved: far from it. Severe coughing and vomiting continued, and Doctor Leone thought he was suffering from 'pulmonary congestion with gastric complications'. The frightened Queen telegraphed to Naples for the Court physician Ramaglia. Day after day she sat sewing beside the King's bed, and an altar arranged for daily Masses in the room during his illness. The Princes also came in for their regular meals. Ferdinand wanted them to behave as if there was nothing the matter, so they went for long drives in the neighbourhood, inspecting schools and orphanages, where the Duke of Calabria's extreme modesty was admired by the teachers if not by the pupils.

A week later the King's fever abated, but it was decided that the Duchess of Calabria should sail to Bari instead of Manfredonia in the beginning of February. On January 25 Doctor Ramaglia was in favour of continuing the journey though Ferdinand was very weak, and the royal party proceeded to Brindisi where the usual ceremonies could not be avoided. In the presbytery of the Cathedral Ferdinand was much upset by the presence of a completely bald man. What business had he there? he enquired. Either from fear of the evil eye, which was occasionally connected with baldness, or on account of some sinister presentiment, he gave instant orders to have the egg-head removed. Both the Queen and the Archbishop tried to coax him to eat at the banquet prepared for him, but he had no appetite. To oblige them he eventually chose an oyster, saying: 'I'll eat this because it is a genuine product of Brindisi.' It was noticed, however, that he cut it in half and only swallowed a section.

More bands and processions with banners met him in Bari. The horses were detached from the royal carriage and it was dragged through the streets in triumph. Ferdinand told the Bishop that he was half dead. He paused for breath at every step as he tottered up the stairs of the palace. Though he could hardly stand he appeared at the balcony and waved to the cheering mob. Then he was helped to bed, so ill that he never recovered. The festivities went on without him, and Bari was crowded as never before. There was not enough accommodation for so many Court officials accompanied by their families and servants: some had to stop at Foggia, others returned to Naples.

On February 3, a sunny springlike day, the bride's approach was announced by repeated cannon fire at ten in the morning. The Queen as well as the Duke of Calabria climbed on board the frigate which had brought her from Trieste, and there was a rapid exchange of greetings and embraces. The Duke clasped both his bride's hands and kissed her forehead: they spoke to each other in faltering French, she a little pale from the sea voyage, he abashed by the beauty of his Bavarian bride. She had so many questions to ask which he could not answer. The Queen spoke her language and took charge of the situation: not only had she been instrumental in arranging the match, but she had sent Nina Rizzo, one of her most trusted maids, to wait on her as a confidential intermediary and rehearse her for her future rôle. But the King's illness had deepened the Queen's habitual gloom, and her smile of welcome lacked warmth in consequence. Beside the graceful Duchess with sparkling eyes she seemed a demure and dowdy governess, and she took to behaving like one. The crowds of spectators gave loud vent to their enthusiasm and cheered the Duchess long after she had entered the palace.

Haggard and emaciated, propped on pillows, Ferdinand sat up with a strained effort at self-mastery to receive her. It was a disappointment and mortification as intense as his physical torment for him to meet her in these dreary circumstances. He broke down when he embraced her, sobbing as he hugged her close to him, as if to seek solace in her fragrant youth. He apologized for having kept her waiting in Vienna and discussed her recent experiences. She was touched to tears by this spontaneous flood of tenderness and there was an instant bond of sympathy between them. The Queen then led her to her apartments where she had to dress for the nuptial blessing. An altar had been installed in the large drawing-room of the palace. While the distinguished congregation were agog for a glimpse of the bride and groom there was a gust of muffled laughter. The Count of Caserta had attached a ludicrous paper tail to the uniform of one pompous functionary, which was deftly removed by a colleague before the victim had noticed it. After celebrating Mass the Bishop preached a flowery sermon and blessed the married pair. The Pope had sent his blessing by telegraph.

Serenades and illuminations lent enchantment to the evening, and Maria Sophia was introduced to the savoury dishes of the country at a large official banquet. She had not had a moment's relaxation since her arrival: ever and anon she was asked to show herself to the people. In her light white crinoline at the balcony, with a coronet of orange-blossoms on her braided auburn hair, she was the very picture of a radiant bride. Such unusual beauty did not have to act a rôle, for it fed the dreams of all beholders, who took it for granted that she must be happy. The bride and groom went to wish the King good night, and he embraced and blessed them again before they retired. The Count of Caserta was punished for his prank, 'worthy of a lazzarone', with confinement to his room for three days, reduced to one day owing to his mother's intercession.

According to De Cesare, the paramount chronicler of these events, Francis fidgeted in an ante-room until Nina Rizzo announced that Maria Sophia had gone to bed. The Duke appeared strangely bewildered and spent the time saying his prayers until his bride fell fast asleep. Then he crept into a corner of the bed with the utmost care not to disturb her. And this happened every night during their stay at Bari; which might help to explain Maria Sophia's craving for distraction as well as her furtive tears. But according to her niece, Countess Marie Larisch, whose Ouida-esque memoirs are more amusing than reliable[1] but whose family gossip was not wholly without foundation, a grotesque *contretemps* on the wedding night disgusted Maria Sophia with her husband. Writing half a century later, Countess Larisch refers to Francis as if he were already the King: 'The young bride was duly put to bed, with much ceremony, by her ladies-in-waiting,

[1] *My Past*, by the Countess Marie Larisch. London, 1913.

379

and after King Francis had joined her, the bedroom doors were locked and the keys were taken away by a high official. Unfortunately the King had over-eaten himself at the State banquet, and in consequence was violently ill nearly the whole night. As there were no bells in the bed-chamber, the unpleasant state of things which confronted the officials next morning when they unlocked the doors may be well imagined.'

No doubt the Empress Elizabeth had given her younger sister some worldly advice and warned her not to expect an ideal husband, but the reality was depressing all the same. With the best of intentions poor Francis must have struck her as dull. He tried sincerely to please her and gradually his efforts were rewarded with a semblance of affection. At first the divergence of their tastes and habits was glaring; and the contrast between her open-air life at Possenhofen on the Starnberg lake and the cramped airless hospital atmosphere of this provincial palace in Bari was melancholy and macabre, dominated by the King's mysterious illness and the Queen's anxiety, while solemn doctors and priests came and went muttering ominously and shaking their grizzled heads. But Maria Sophia was a cheerful extrovert by nature, determined not to succumb to despondency. Ferdinand wished to conceal the gravity of his condition; and it was part of her duty to appear gay and unconcerned in public. Hers was a girlish glamour of royalty rarely witnessed in Bari; at the theatre in her diamonds and lace she was the cynosure instead of the stage performance.

Francis, still under his stepmother's thumb, would not allow Maria Sophia to ride, and as this was her favourite exercise it caused a rift between them: she would bide her time. An amazon could not be caged. Having little else to do she joined the younger Princes on their excursions in the vicinity and shared in their childish games. The Count of Caserta was still a romping schoolboy at eighteen, prolific in practical jokes of the apple-pie bed variety. They went fishing along the coast and Maria Sophia attempted to fry their catch with calamitous results: several table-cloths and napkins were burnt and the fish were reduced to cinders amid boisterous laughter. Such frivolities helped to disperse the pervading gloom. The Queen, over-indulgent towards her own obstreperous brood, resented Maria Sophia's vivacity and thought she should spend most of her time in prayer and acts of contrition. But she nagged at her in vain. No daughter of the Wittelsbach family could be whittled down to pattern.

Long hours at the King's bedside had frayed the Queen's nerves, for she seldom left his room. His sufferings were interminable, and the doctors were as helpless as the patient. Their knowledge of medicine appears to have been mediæval: no anaesthetics were available, and every movement renewed his agony. Fever, prostration, wasting away of the flesh, were aggravated by an abscess in the thigh which required a prompt operation, but nobody dared suggest it for fear of increasing his alarm. All shrank from so tremendous a responsibility. Linseed poultices and resolvents brought no relief whatever. After bleedings and blisterings and nauseating concoctions he began to lose faith in doctors and their prescriptions. In his worst paroxysms he prayed fervently and invoked the Madonna and saints. His bedroom became a sanctuary of reputedly miraculous relics. Sometimes he gasped: '*Me l'hanno jettata!*—' ('They have put the evil eye on me!'). He reviewed the detailed incidents of his journey to Bari, the Capuchins, the bald pate at Brindisi, Bishop Caputo and the trap-door in the wall; he suspected that Milano's bayonet thrust had injected him with poison, and there is just a possibility that it started a streptococcus infection.

Besides the Austrian Archdukes William and Rainier and the Archduchess Maria, the Grand Duke Leopold of Tuscany, Ferdinand's genial cousin and brother-in-law, had come to Naples for the wedding, but the young Archduchess Anne, his eldest son's wife, died of consumption on February 10, and the bereaved family returned sadly to Florence without seeing the King or his heir. Shortly after this the Count of Aquila's daughter expired and Leopold of Tuscany's daughter who had married Luitpold of Bavaria fell desperately ill, deepening the fog of gloom that had settled on the Court.

In spite of the false optimism of official reports, rumours of the King's real condition had spread to Naples. The Count of Syracuse went to Bari to discover the truth, and was visibly alarmed by the change in his brother's appearance. It was suspected that the Austrian Archdukes were trying to inveigle Ferdinand into an offensive and defensive alliance, and that the Count of Syracuse had gone to frustrate their plans. Victor Emmanuel's *grido di dolore* (cry of anguish) speech on the opening of Parliament at Turin had, as the British minister Sir James Hudson declared, fallen like a rocket on the treaties of 1815; the Franco-Sardinian alliance had been cemented by the marriage of dissolute Prince Napoleon, the son of Jerome Bonaparte, and Victor Emmanuel's sixteen-year-old daughter Princess Clotilde, a veritable lamb led to the sacrifice. Everybody was in a fever of apprehension, especially Cavour, since Napoleon III had warned him that unless Austria attacked, Sardinia must expect no help from France. Diplomacy was straining to prevent the war that Cavour was invoking with all his heart and soul. But no fever could assuage Ferdinand's fixed neutrality.

Worrying about the children he had left behind at Caserta, the King dreaded having to spend the whole winter at Bari yet he also dreaded the prospect of moving. One of his physicians, Longo, believed that only an operation could save him, but the timid Ramaglia, who being in constant attendance was overpowered by the personality of his patient, demurred. As Longo's frankness had appealed to Ferdinand, the Duke of Calabria urged him to explain the advantages of an operation to his father, and he promised to do so. In the meantime he would try a mercurial solution. Doctors Ramaglia and Leone, supported by the Queen, had much ado to persuade Ferdinand to be moved into a lighter, more spacious apartment facing south. Four burly sailors carried him, and in crossing the vestibule where there was a marble statue of himself he exclaimed: 'Behold two statues!' But his new room only upset him. He complained that there was altogether too much light and air and ordered them to carry him back. On passing the same statue he waved a languid hand at it and said mournfully: 'Goodbye, Ferdinand II!'

The mercurial solution had been useless, and when Dr Longo broached the subject of a slight operation the King was horrified. 'Your Majesty,' said the doctor, 'in this predicament your misfortune is to be King. If you were some wretched commoner in a public hospital, you might have been cured by now.' 'Do as you please with me,' replied Ferdinand wearily, and the operation was decided on. At first a surgeon was to be summoned from Naples, but the Queen feared this would spread general alarm and asked if there was a skilled surgeon in the town. Longo recommended one, but there was another hitch. The Queen and Ramaglia thought it better for the King to leave Bari, whereas he preferred to stay, knowing that his enemies would rejoice at his condition. He was eventually persuaded by Father Ludovico of Casoria, who exhorted him to leave as a duty to God and his subjects. On March 7 he was carried on board the *Fulminante*. 'This is the tomb's ante-chamber', he muttered. The royal family followed his curtained stretcher in mourning for other relations, but it seemed the King's funeral procession. Yet he asked the intendant and mayor to thank the authorities and citizens of Bari on his behalf. 'If I was unable to attend the festivities in person,' he added, 'my heart was always there.'

Aloft on a gun-carriage sat the young Duchess feasting hungry eyes on the sea and inhaling the salt air ecstatically. After her cramped and musty quarters in the intendant's palace this was delicious freedom. Long hours she sat there musing, watching the legendary coast, the distant volcano, envying the sea-birds swooping and crying, thankful that at least her honeymoon was over, for the future could not be more lugubrious. Brave though she was by nature, it had required strength to keep up her spirits when she was so conscious of being alone among such very strange strangers. Her husband hovered near her like a lost marionette, offering her chocolates and chaste little caresses. She scarcely noticed him. The splendid sparkling sea claimed all her attention. Raffaele and Vincenzo Criscuolo, father and son, two bred-in-the-bone sailors from Santa Lucia, waited on the King devotedly and forced him to smile at their simple jokes and homely sayings. They had become part of his family, and stayed with him till the end.

After a sea voyage of fifty hours to Resina a special train conveyed the King to Caserta. He raised the curtain of his litter to greet old friends and servants, and they were appalled at the transformation, the cadaverous face and hollow tragic eyes. When he embraced his children they wept and shuddered at the sight. One of the Princesses fainted and the seven-year-old Count of Bari ran like a frightened hare through the enormous palace and lost his way so that it took more than an hour to find him.

The surgeons already assembled at Caserta agreed that it was necessary to operate at once. Trinchera, the oldest and most famous of these, seems to have been the clumsiest, for he inflicted needless pain by miscalculating the point of incision. Ferdinand had to rest several days while this wound was being medicated. A second incision was made when quantities of pus were expelled from the femur. This afforded some temporary relief, but five days later a purulent infection began to spread all over the body, causing various tumours and congestion of the lungs. It is a wonder that the patient survived. The accounts of his prolonged agony are harrowing, and his enemies gloated on them with vindictive relish. 'I have entered into all this painful detail,' wrote one, 'to show how severe was the affliction which he, who had caused so much misery to others, was at last called to pass through in his own person.' It was compared to that which laid King Herod low. But he retained a firm grasp of power, continuing to discuss State affairs with his ministers and sign edicts between his groans.

The news from outside brought no comfort. The sixty-six political prisoners who had embarked for America, including Poerio, Settembrini and Silvio Spaventa, had landed at Queenstown in Ireland instead of New York. Having been transferred to an American ship at Lisbon, Settembrini's son Raffaele had joined the crew in disguise and had successfully intimidated the captain. 'In setting foot on this free soil,' wrote Poerio to Gladstone on March 12, 'the first need of my heart was to seek news of you.' He did not write in vain. Within a few days a subscription of £10,000 sterling was raised for the refugees, who were received with sympathy and applause wherever they went, while Mazzini did his utmost to exploit the situation. Most of them dribbled back to Italy in April and settled in Turin or Genoa with a conviction that 'deliverance from Bomba' was close at hand. Panizzi, the principal librarian of the British Museum since 1856, looked after the distribution of funds, for which he got little credit. Not even Poerio was spared the malicious insinuations of his less famous fellow-exiles. For a person who had endured such hardships and privations he struck Lord Malmesbury as inordinately plump.

Cavour hoped that Ferdinand would die of rage, but his indignation seems to have acted as a febrifuge. From his sick-bed at Caserta he was trying to follow Cavour's elaborate chess-game. Russia had proposed a congress of the powers, and it looked as if Napoleon were shrinking from the prospect of war. Ferdinand was utterly sceptical of the congress and resolved to remain aloof. As he told the Austrian minister Martini, he did not recognize the right of any power to call an independent State to the bar. When Cavour was on the verge of despair the military party in Vienna played his game for him. On April 23 Austria delivered her rash ultimatum at Turin requiring disarmament within three days. The Sardinian reply was a categorical refusal, and Napoleon informed Vienna that he should regard her invasion of Piedmont as a hostile act. Three days later the Austrian army under the command of General Giulay crossed the Ticino. Cavour was exultant. Victor Emmanuel and Napoleon issued stirring proclamations, while the Austrians lost their initial advantage by hesitant leadership. On April 27, two days before the Austrian invasion, Tuscany got rid of her Grand Duke who had wished to remain neutral. He left the country without any fuss, and a provisional government offered the dictatorship to Victor Emmanuel, who declined it. Carlo Buoncompagni, however, his minister in Florence, was appointed 'commissioner extraordinary for the war of independence', and he was soon succeeded by Baron Ricasoli, who was all for a kingdom of Italy under Victor Emmanuel.

Ferdinand had been given up as a hopeless case by the doctors. Among these Lanza, who had recently returned from exile, suggested ironically that he be nourished with woman's milk. Another colleague, Rosati, could not help laughing at this, which prompted Lanza to add: 'The King will die after contemplating his own corpse: there is no further remedy.' Alluding to the royal amnesty which had enabled him to come home, this amiable doctor remarked to his cronies: 'The King gave me a passport to return to Naples and I have given him one for the next world'. The gravity of Ferdinand's condition could no longer be concealed from the people. On April 12 he believed he might die at any moment and wished to receive the Blessed Sacrament. All his family except his youngest children were present at this solemn ceremony. At the cost of great effort he contrived to sit up in bed, a skeleton of his former self: he was resolved to die with dignity. To each of his brothers he made some request: he entrusted his fleet to Aquila, his army to Trapani. He made Generals Filangieri and Ischitella promise to assist and advise his heir. All the theatres were closed on that day. Yet he survived, and his brain remained extraordinarily lucid.

Throughout his horrible illness the Queen seldom left his sickroom: she knelt praying beside him, she watched by him at night in an armchair or sofa, ever at his beck and call, and she tried to prevent distressing news from reaching him. She was therefore embarrassed when the Hereditary Prince came in and said: 'Uncle Popò has been driven out, Papa.' 'Which Uncle Popò?' (The Grand Duke of Tuscany and the Count of Syracuse were both so called.) 'The Tuscan.' But Francis could tell him nothing more, so the King sent for Carafa, who stammered through the latest despatches with a harassed air. 'The booby!' exclaimed Ferdinand. 'Having gone at this time, he is not fit to return.' Francis, who had hitherto been kept in the dark about his father's policy, was now given an eleventh hour briefing about government. Ferdinand's memory was keenly retentive until he died: one by one he mentioned all the names of those who could be trusted, scrupulously distinguishing between the true and false friends of the dynasty. He warned him never to make any compromise with the revolution or take sides with Austria or Piedmont: he should wait patiently on events, regarding the Papal States as an outer bulwark. He advised him to change the ministry but not the character of the government. Above all he adjured him to maintain his zeal for the Faith and consult Cardinal Cosenza on religious matters.

When Victor Emmanuel went to Genoa to meet his ally the Emperor of the French on May 13, 'it was roses, roses all the way', as Thayer wrote.[1] But it was rue for Ferdinand, whose plight was so desperate that he dictated his will to his heir in the presence of the Queen, the Counts of Trani and Caserta, and Monsignor Gallo, and signed it with a tremulous hand. On the 20th the pain in his left lung became excruciating: he was unable to expectorate, yet the brain was still clear and he expressed himself with precision. At mid-day he received Extreme Unction from Monsignor Gallo surrounded by his weeping family, each of whom he embraced and blessed, with a supreme effort to appear serene. Though his voice was very feeble he gathered strength for a last speech of farewell. He said he could die without remorse since he had always tried to do his duty as a Christian and a sovereign. The crown of Italy had been offered to him but he would not accept it: had he done so he would suffer remorse for injuring the rights of other sovereigns, and especially of the Pope. He thanked God for having enlightened him; he was leaving the kingdom as he had inherited it from his ancestors. . . .

It was a struggle to squeeze the sentences from his throat. He was gasping for breath, and the sweat stung his glaring eyes. To quieten him the doctors begged the Princes to leave the room. The Queen

[1] Thayer, *Cavour*, Vol. II, p. 13.

came and went in a state of frantic agitation; the Hereditary Prince stood sobbing in a corner.

Ferdinand's final agony started near mid-day on May 22. Monsignor Gallo recited prayers while the royal family and household knelt weeping round the bed. At one moment the King opened his eyes and said: 'Why do you weep? I will not forget you.' Turning to the Queen, he added: 'I shall pray for you, for our children, for the Pope, for our subjects, friends, enemies and sinners.' He could speak no more. With one hand on the Crucifix of his confessor and another clutching the Queen, he expired shortly after one o'clock.

These last four months had seemed like four long years to those who had sat and stood and prayed beside the slowly disintegrating King, and they were utterly worn out and emptied of emotion. To many it was as if the kingdom had disintegrated with Ferdinand II, whose formidable will-power had kept the Two Sicilies together for twenty-nine years. It was hard to realize that he was only forty-nine. The Queen could not bear the thought of his being embalmed, but there was no alternative since his corpse had to be exposed to the public. His Spanish brother-in-law, Don Sebastian, commissioned the painter Domenico Caldara to depict his emaciated features in their final calm, and it is somewhat curious that the Queen ordered twelve copies of this ghastly record for distribution among various courtiers. Was it not better to remember him in the prime of life?

XX

OVERPOWERED by his father and stepmother, who could ill conceal her dislike of this offspring of her saintly predecessor,[1] Francis had taken refuge in a stiff protective reserve. To many his expression looked wooden. His speech was hesitant and slow. He had none of his father's Neapolitan geniality and facile flow of words. He remained 'the Son of the Saint', a young man of lofty but limited principles, with a contempt for the world and the flesh and an almost mystical veneration for his father, whose autocratic spirit, looming beside that of his ethereal mother, haunted and paralysed his future movements. His reserve was a barrier to popularity: it was interpreted as stupidity by enemies of the dynasty. But he was not stupid: he was dazed by his new dignity, for which he realized that he was unprepared. To whom should he listen? It was as if everybody were chattering at the same time, proffering contradictory advice. The widowed Queen represented Austria and reaction; his uncle the Count of Syracuse was pleading for an alliance with Victor Emmanuel, while another uncle, the Count of Aquila, had begun to pose as a liberal, and the Count of Trapani stood betwixt and between. The foreign diplomats only added to the King's confusion. The Court was a labyrinth of intrigue.

The deepest intriguer was the widowed Queen. Ferdinand had been

---

[1] Her affectionately phrased letters to him written in later years seem to disprove this, but we suspect that the phraseology was conventional.

everything to her: she had even been jealous of his affection for the children. During the last months of his decline she had become the dominating partner. It was bitter indeed for so masterful a matron to resign her position to a light-hearted girl of eighteen.

Maria Sophia soon showed that she had a will of her own. Gaiety can be a most effective weapon. She laughed at the absurd meanness and bigotry of the Austrian prude and went out of her way to shock her. As Maria Theresa had been consistently disagreeable to her ever since her arrival it was only tit for tat. She surrounded herself with pet dogs and talkative parrots and, heedless of her stepmother-in-law's protests, went galloping through the woods with only one or two escorts. Once out of mourning, she changed her dress frequently during the day and took to wearing elaborate jewellery. Nina Rizzo, the maid whom Maria Theresa had selected for her special guidance, a widow from Marseilles with several children, became her fawning confidante and pandered to her caprices. This was another bitter pill for the Queen Dowager, whose intrigues had not been successful. Even before her husband's death she had plotted to get Francis set aside in favour of her own eldest son, the Count of Trani.

Neither the ultra-royalists nor the liberals had much confidence in the new King, whose ineptitude they exaggerated. The ultra-royalists argued that since Ferdinand II had repudiated his father's system in 1831 to the extent of appearing a liberal, Francis might be tempted to do likewise in an emergency. They feared the influence of his uncles Syracuse and Aquila. Little or nothing was known of Trani, except that he was bound to obey his mother, and continue the policy of Ferdinand. He was reputed to be able and enterprising: in fact he was ignorant and conceited. Demonstrations in his favour had broken out at Foggia in May, but they were soon smothered and buried in silence. When Filangieri offered Francis the written proofs of his stepmother's conspiracy he refused to look at them. 'She was my father's wife,' he said. The Queen Dowager pretended it was merely a plot to divide the royal family and showed her hatred of Filangieri by slamming the door in his face.

In this factious atmosphere Francis II succeeded to a throne that was none too steady. Ideological hostilities were sharpened and complicated by the war in the north. Foreign envoys with conflicting missions arrived hot on each other's heels. First came the Austrian

Baron Hübner on May 31 to warn Francis not to listen to Franco-Sardinian proposals, to confirm his neutrality, and make no concession to liberal demands. The Baron was able to reassure Vienna on all these points. A suave and accomplished diplomat, his *Memoirs* glitter beside those of his luckier colleagues. 'I cannot permit myself,' he told Francis, 'to give you advice, but if you wish to remain neutral, you should not open a tribunal here.' The King asked him if the Empress Elizabeth resembled his wife. 'Yes indeed,' answered Hübner, 'but in comparison with her sister the Queen has a completely southern expression, as if she had been predestined for Italy since her birth.' 'Not for Italy,' replied the King with a smile, 'but for Naples and Sicily, for the kingdom of the Two Sicilies. I do not know Italy.'

On Ferdinand's death, Lord Malmesbury required Henry Elliot to congratulate Francis II on his accession and to resume diplomatic relations with Naples: he arrived on June 4. His mission was not intended to last more than a few weeks, but as soon as Lord Palmerston became Prime Minister and Lord John Russell Foreign Secretary, Elliot was appointed permanent minister there. 'When I left England in May 1859,' he wrote,[1] 'the war of France and Sardinia against Austria had just begun, and Lord Malmesbury's feelings were so strongly on the side of the latter that he was afraid lest the young Sovereign of the Two Sicilies might be induced to throw in his lot with the Liberal party, which was calling for an alliance with Victor Emmanuel, and his very last words to me were an injunction to use every endeavour to dissuade the Neapolitan Government from joining the allies. If there had ever been a chance of their doing so it was past before I reached Naples, so that I was not called upon to act upon instructions which it would have been very repugnant to me to execute, though there is little doubt that if King Francis had then frankly and fairly adopted the course so much dreaded by Lord Malmesbury he would have averted the fall of his dynasty. Lord Palmerston and Lord John, with a much truer appreciation of the movement for constitutional reform that was going on throughout Italy, and of the discontent prevailing in the south, clearly perceived that a persistence in his father's system of government must before long lead to the loss of his throne, and I was not backward in following their instructions to

[1] Sir Henry G. Elliot, *Some Revolutions and Other Diplomatic Experiences.* London, 1922, p. 5.

do all in my power to impress upon the King and his Ministers that a refusal to satisfy the just expectations of the people would be followed by their ruin.' Lord John Russell, as we know, had been consorting with Poerio and Settembrini, whose opinions he took to represent the just expectations of the Neapolitan people; and Lord Palmerston was an inveterate enemy of the Bourbons.

The most difficult mission was that of the Piedmontese envoy Count Salmour, who was instructed by Cavour to negotiate an alliance against Austria, and urge an amnesty and political reforms, leading to a revival of the lapsed Constitution. The Franco-Sardinian victories would have lent more ballast to his arguments if his English and French colleagues with similar aims had not pulled in different directions. Salmour was received graciously by the King but he could extract nothing from him except a politely expressed hope that his relations with the Sardinian Court would become more intimate. He got no further with Filangieri, who struck him as excessively false, 'a colossal egoist, old and worn out,' incapable of appreciating any generous idea.

Filangieri had been appointed President of the Council and Minister for War soon after the news of the battle of Magenta (June 4), which had provoked jubilant demonstrations outside the palace of the pro-Piedmontese Count of Syracuse. Both the French and Sardinian legations had been brilliantly illuminated; the Austrian minister had protested; and the King summoned the veteran general who, far from unwilling to serve (as his daughter pretended), was an ambitious candidate for premiership.

Baron Brenier, the French envoy, did not arrive until June 21, three days before the allies won the battle of Solferino, which was followed by the separate armistice of the French and Austrian Emperors at Villafranca and Cavour's outraged resignation on July 12. Like most Italian patriots, Cavour considered the armistice an act of treachery, but Solferino had been an expensive holocaust. As Napoleon III's aide-de-camp General Fleury wrote: 'It's a victory, to be sure. But what tears, what blood! If it were to begin again, I feel certain the Emperor could not stand it.' It was all very well for Cavour to sneer: 'He was tired; he was bored; he was hot.' Napoleon III had not enough troops to attack the fortresses of the Quadrilateral, and now Prussia might attack him on the Rhine. The mobilization of Prussia was the determining factor. Furthermore he drew a sharp distinction between Italian independence and unification, which he regarded as contrary to French interests. His ambition for a French dynasty in Florence had been frustrated: all Central Italy had rallied to Piedmont, and the Pope was in danger of being overwhelmed. In order to dam the unitarian flood he urged extensive reforms on Francis II and Pius IX, reforms which would align their political institutions with those of Piedmont. His next aim was to promote an Italian Confederation over which the Pope would preside nominally but France in actual fact. England now stepped into the breach, and Palmerston, once more in office, became a loud champion of Italian nationalism. He wanted 'a strong Italy, able to hold her own against Austria and France alike.' Thus while Elliot and Brenier were pressing for similar reforms in Naples their paths were divergent.

According to Elliot:[1] 'No clue to what France was driving at could be obtained from the attitude of my French colleague, which was perplexing and continually changing, for at one moment he went out of his way to advertise himself as supporting the Liberal party, and at the next he was seen to be hand and glove with the Palace reactionaries; but it was not in the nature of the man to remain quiet, and as he was entirely ignorant of his Emperor's real designs he kept dancing first on one leg and then on the other, according to what he supposed them at the moment to be, with the result that in the end both he and his Government were regarded with an equal distrust by all parties.

'The Emperor Napoleon always loved a tortuous mode of proceeding, and it was his habit on critical occasions to employ, in addition to his accredited Ministers, unavowed agents, to whom, unknown to his Minister for Foreign Affairs, he conveyed his more secret views; and the language held at Turin by these agents was frequently so much at variance with that which Baron Brenier was directed by Count Thouvenel to hold at Naples that it was scarcely surprising that he should be perplexed.'

According to Brenier, Elliot's attitude was equally devious and perplexing. On December 5, 1859, he wrote to Walewski: 'For some time the British Minister has laid much stress in conversation on the fact that not only does he not insist on the necessity of a Constitution

[1] *Op. cit.*, p. 23.

Francis II as Duke of Calabria

for Naples, but that the kingdom has no need of a Constitution or of new institutions, and that it had better "get along as well as possible with what it has". This new attitude and language of the British Minister gives the Neapolitan Government still greater confidence. I cannot believe that moderation has inspired Mr Elliot, but rather the desire to put himself on different ground from that where he supposes the Emperor's Minister to stand. Six months ago Mr Elliot was shouting, as it were, for a Constitution. Perhaps he found out that Prince Filangieri, Mr Cumbo and the Emperor's Minister had come to an agreement on a project which might have had some chances of success without certain defections. He has changed his tone and now pronounces himself in favour of a *statu quo* which causes him neither indignation nor remorse.'[1]

No less perplexing and devious was the behaviour of General Filangieri, Prince of Satriano and Duke of Taormina. His prestige was considerable with its aura of Napoleonic romance and chivalry refurbished by his successful reconquest and governorship of Sicily. His person was handsome and distinguished, the very type of aristocratic soldier with a French education, and he was respected at home and abroad. Trevelyan described him as 'by far the greatest subject in the kingdom', and nearly all historians agree with De Sivo that he could have saved the dynasty. At first it looked as if he wished to do so. 'Prince Filangieri,' wrote Elliot on June 7, 'is keen in his desire immediately to put an end to the innumerable abuses which prevail in the administration, but he is not in favour of calling the Constitution into operation at the present moment. He conceives that in the struggle now going on in the north of Italy a strict neutrality is the proper policy for Naples, and he is convinced that a meeting of the Chambers would almost inevitably be followed by a vote in favour of an immediate alliance with Sardinia for the expulsion of the "stranger" from Italian soil.'

Perhaps, at seventy-five, Filangieri felt too old to embark on the sweeping programme that was necessary. He loved power, and had he been as great as his prestige he would have wielded it to better purpose. 'So far we have had a King who was minister;' it was said, 'now we have a minister who is King!' But instead of using his age

[1] Costanzo Maraldi, *Documenti Francesi sulla caduta del Regno Meridionale*, pp. 95, 96. Naples, 1935.

and experience to manage Francis, who was fifty-two years his junior and modest to a fault, he repeatedly threatened to resign when he was thwarted. He aimed at a golden mean and hoped to please everybody. Whatever his intentions his advice proved fatal.

Several decrees of political amnesty were promulgated on June 16, 1859. As a result over 190 notorious conspirators came rushing home to spread propaganda on behalf of Cavour, Mazzini or Murat and organize revolution in the capital and provinces. Another decree abolished the list of so-called *attendibili*, those political suspects who were supposed to be under police surveillance. Unfortunately this was counteracted by Francesco Casella, the chief of police, who sent a secret circular to his subordinates advising them to consult the list if necessary. Elliot was among the first to discover this from his liberal cronies, and he gave it wide publicity. Though Casella was dismissed, his folly served as excellent fuel to the King's enemies. Francis himself had been ignorant of Casella's little trick. On June 21, when Elliot congratulated him on his 'recent humane measures', 'the King replied that he was glad to have been able to make a beginning, and that he had an especial pleasure in putting an end to the system of maintaining a list of "*attendibili*", which he designated in the strongest language as an atrocious and unjustifiable invention. . . . That the King is sincere in believing that he has removed the whole class from the ban under which they had been placed, I cannot entertain a doubt, but he will before long discover how effectually he can be thwarted in his best measures by the almost omnipotent Police which has been created by the late Sovereign.' Events were to prove that the omnipotence of the police was over-estimated. Agesilao Milano had been one of the *attendibili*, yet he had been able to join the army and aim a blow at the King, and the authors of subsequent outrages had never been identified. The most dangerous traitors were still at large; many were snug in government offices.

The royal family had moved to Capodimonte during the period of deepest mourning, and on the surface they lived in tranquil harmony. The King's half-brothers began to enjoy a new sense of freedom: already the eldest were discussing separate establishments and plans for foreign travel. Francis let them do as they liked so long as they were not rowdy. The disconsolate Queen Dowager schemed away in the background, more cautiously since Filangieri had come to power.

Maria Sophia could indulge her love of open air exercise without fear of criticism, and her closer intimacy with Francis put an end to certain indiscreet speculations. In her company Francis had begun to taste the pleasure of living. Thanks to Nina Rizzo, who had confided to Father Borrelli the King's confessor that his marriage had not been consummated, the worthy priest had overcome his morbid embarrassment. And the young Queen's heart warmed towards the gentle mate who could refuse her nothing though his piety was a bore. He had inherited a strain of fatalism from his mother, together with a dread of sin and indifference to worldly vanities. He could never abandon himself to the beauty of his wife without a pang of guilt. But he admired her radiant vitality even more than her physical charms, and she soon showed that she had courage.

Towards midnight on July 7 the peaceful slumber of Capodimonte was shattered by a beating of drums, wild guttural vociferations, random shots, and the tramping of hundreds of feet, louder and ever louder. At first it was supposed that they were regiments coming to protect the royal family owing to some sudden turmoil in the city, as there were only twenty-four guards at Capodimonte. The outer gates were barred in the nick of time. While Admiral Del Re, the Duke of Sangro and Colonel Schumacher went to see what was happening, it was rumoured that all the Swiss regiments had revolted and intended to capture the royal family. Fancying that they were Neapolitan troops, the Queen Dowager said that the loyal Swiss should be sent for. On hearing the truth she wakened her sleeping children and made preparations for flight. Francis had an acute premonition of coming trouble. He knew that Piedmontese agents had been at work. Perhaps they had started a revolution in the army. According to Salmour this had been a perfect opportunity for it: 'The Queen Dowager swooned; the King also fainted and spent several hours with his doctor and confessor.' But Salmour is not to be trusted: his agents had been partly responsible. While many of the women had hysterics, Maria Sophia stood calmly on her balcony until the noise died down. Though the Swiss Colonel Schumacher repeatedly asked the rebels what they wanted, it was difficult to hear or make himself heard amid the pandemonium. After shouting themselves hoarse they were somewhat appeased when he assured them that the King would consider their requests. He advised them to await the royal decision on the

Campo di Marte, or 'Field of Mars', where important military reviews were held.

Among various accounts of this incident, the least familiar and perhaps the most graphic was written by a Swiss soldier who took part in it.[1] 'It was rumoured that Switzerland would take serious measures to prevent recruiting on her frontier. The agreements between the Neapolitan government and various cantons were to lapse without option of renewal; that with Berne was abrogated. The soldiers discovered this. . . . On the morning of July 7, 1859, a fatigue party going to the army bakehouse heard members of the fourth regiment complain that their colonel had taken the crest of Berne off their banner and replaced it with the Bourbon lilies. We had drunk the smelly water of Santa Lucia just under our commissariat, and had sauntered together talking of our country, friends, enemies and hopes. We had shaken hands, promising mutual aid and support. The day passed quietly. That evening after roll-call each went up slowly to his dormitory with a chunk of bread in his cap, together with a clove of garlic or a little onion for his supper. From the distance a vague noise ascended towards us. We thought it must be one of those religious processions before which the people prostrated themselves. The drums at the Capuan Gate were summoning the guard.

'I was standing on the balcony of the sergeant-major's room, and in the semi-darkness of the vaults below I could see the guard running; then I heard gun-shots, a flash, and a man tottered heavily forward, upsetting several stacks of the guns for sentries on duty. The firing continued without interruption. The great door closed with a bang, and I could hear the double turn of the key creaking in the rusty lock which a gun-shot burst open. The soldiers began running through the dormitories, which were like vast ant-heaps dispersed by a footfall, and the sergeants shouted "To Arms", and each had a scuffle at the arms-rack for his rifle. Many stumbled on their way down the stairs to the courtyard. . . .

'From the gallery connecting the quarters of the first with the second company I peered down thirty feet. The infantry of our regiment were scampering over corpses: the guard-sergeant, an old scoundrel, was stretched on the ground face downward, a bullet

[1] Auguste Meylan, *Souvenirs d'un Soldat Suisse au Service de Naples de 1857 à 1859*. Geneva, 1868.

having pierced his skull through the crown of his cap. Night had fallen, and there was utter confusion. Two young men left the guard-room holding our two banners. Only then I realized everything, but how many did not understand and fired their guns without knowing why. In the streets outside there was panic: shops were shut, people barricaded their doors, and the lazzaroni ran about yelling: "The Swiss are killing each other!" Women crossed themselves and knelt before the Madonna del Carmine: memories of May 15 were still green. The fusillade went on with redoubled intensity; cartridge cases littered the flagstones of the court. . . . The soldiers were shouting "Long live Switzerland! Long live the King!" and the officers tried to pacify them. Those of our company did their duty bravely and tried to rally their men. In vain, for the men left their ranks to join those of the Carmine who were carrying the banners. All the rest of the company followed the mass and in a moment we were in the nar-row lanes leading to San Giovanni a Carbonara, the barracks of the third regiment. There the same scene was repeated: though the gates were fastened we scaled the walls, pushing and scrambling, running under fire into the central yard. There again the two banners were removed, drums beat the attack, and the whole troop, followed by a few from the third regiment, went charging up the Via Foria, passing the Bourbon Museum. The sentries of the museum took cover behind their boxes, the guard stood mute under arms. The slope of San Potito was soon climbed, and here the struggle became more intense. The heavy doors were bolted; a few shots reverberated; an officer and a drummer were killed. The officer of the guard, a young man of eigh-teen, defended himself valiantly, but a gunshot nailed him to the wall.

'The general alarm resounded everywhere. From the windows of the fourth regimental barracks a steady fire greeted those who wished to enter. There too the banners were seized, and eventually carried off by our men. The drum-major, at the head of his drummers, made them beat the Swiss march, and all shouted together: "Hurrah, hurrah! the soldiers of the Jura are coming, hurrah!" An infantry corporal collapsed beside me with a bullet in his kidneys: unable to rise, he dragged himself after us in a vain attempt to follow. I could hear his desperate cry grow fainter in the distance. He was finished off by the soldiers of the fourth regiment who left their barracks firing at our last ranks.

'It was ten p.m. and the whole city was hushed. The ships in the port were gathering steam, prepared for every eventuality. Government officials thought there was a general tumult. Messengers on horseback galloped to and fro. The gunners saddled their horses and got their cannon ready. Our troop, between nine hundred and a thousand strong, took the road to Capodimonte, where Francis II was residing. The first ranks, a confused medley of all the Swiss regiments, were led by corporals and a few sergeants. There were sappers in broad white aprons and black caps, infantrymen, grenadiers with white epaulettes, buglers in white jackets with yellow stripes at the collar. All of them marched at the double and halted before the high railings of the palace, where torches flickered on garlands of wistaria and climbing jasmine. The palace beyond was suddenly lighted by liveried footmen; the serried ranks of soldiers, their rifles still hot on their shoulders, were massed in shadow. From rank to rank the rumour spread that the King had rejected our claims: we were to return to barracks and our demands would receive consideration if they were found to be legitimate. This reply angered us all the more and we bellowed: "No! Justice, we want Justice! To the Campo di Marte!"

'Half an hour later we were in the thick grass of that open field where we had so often manœuvred for days on end. The stars were particularly bright, and the Milky Way shone like a river in the sky. Thought returned with relaxation, and I wondered how this would finish. Thinking of the men killed, of this revolt against an iron discipline, and the banners carried off, I seemed to see the whole army cry for vengeance. The moon lit up the vast plain surrounded by trees, and one could hear the white owls in the coppice: they fluttered about almost touching our stacks of arms. Each unbuckled his knapsack and lay down in the dew-drenched grass.

'Along the road there was a tavern which we used to haunt: it was known as Pulcinella's since episodes from his career—he was the chief character in all Neapolitan farces—were depicted on the walls. Many of the soldiers ran there and called for drink, declaring that the King would pay for everything and pay well. The tavern-keeper, a true Neapolitan, recommended himself to all the saints and refused credit. Platoon fire stretched him dead. When I heard of this, the result of our struggle did not seem doubtful. Why stain our glorious mutiny with this dastardly deed? Those who had committed it would surely be the first to suffer. When the topers had drunk their fill they joined us and lay down, their heads on their knapsacks, and gradually silence reigned on the Field of Mars.

'Under the trees in the distance one could just discern a faint black mass drawing nearer and spreading in a silent ribbon. Was it an illusion? During insomnia a thousand ideas and tangled images dance before one's eyes. Pictures of the peaceful life at home passed before me and then, when I remembered the harm that had been done, I felt a shock which prevented me from sleeping. On either side of me my comrades slept the sleep of those untroubled by the future. . . . The cicadas were chirping again, and under the trees far away I could still see that black and silent mass approaching. Then I fell fast asleep.

'It was two-thirty or three in the morning when I was wakened by drums beating the réveille. Soaked in the abundant dew which is a substitute for rain in this climate, we all rose rubbing our foreheads, as if to clear our minds. The Field of Mars, in all its expanse, was occupied by troops. Facing us, near the toll-house, we recognized the horses of the senior officers of the fourth regiment. The artillery section was a little further off. On our right the thirteenth battalion of light infantry was deployed like a winding serpent, then the cavalry and orderlies of the eleventh Neapolitan line regiment. Each of us shouldered his knapsack and wiped his dripping gun. We shook hands all round. Near me Bérard, nicknamed the Glutton, was singing lustily. Suddenly he embraced me and exclaimed: "This is the great day!" And he went on singing. . . .

'The sun rose and the dew slowly evaporated in floating mist. The air was very still. An unusual sound among the first ranks warned us that something was happening. We were encircled and we were being summoned to surrender. The Germans yelled back: "*Lieber sterben!*" ("Rather die!") Then a cannon rent the air; the smoke of powder mounted in a spiral. We closed ranks and our guns were loaded in record time. There was a brief lull. Our Brigadier-General Riedmatten appeared in the distance, surrounded by his staff. He gave his orders and the firing began: artillery thundered, and the splinters of machine-guns raised clods of earth and brushwood which spattered us like rain. The din was such that you would have said a squadron of heavy cavalry was passing. The fusillade began to right and left of us. We

399

could understand no more: pressed back and further back, we were firing rapidly the while. Two hundred of our men detached themselves and charged towards the cannon. Every shot felled them: the ground was covered with corpses, the firing slowed down, and we borrowed each other's cartridges. Our supply was drawing to an end; we had not enough powder, yet the firing was redoubled. We glanced at each other: the catastrophe was near. My gun scorched my fingers, my cartridge pouch was empty, while all the troops converged. Then the rout began: knapsacks were flung away and rifles strewed the ground in heaps. From seven to eight hundred men fled from the plain without looking back; the wounded fell heavily forward, their strength exhausted.

'It was nearly six in the morning. Only the six banners, two of which were broken, several hundreds of rifles and shoulder-straps and corpses remained as death had struck them. . . . The fourth regiment debouched into the field, capturing those who attempted to escape. They had seized the flags we had taken from them the day before, and these men who had asked for our help and support had just been mowing us down. In the distance one could see a troop entering the copsewood, still firing at random. Five of us, including myself, were running for all we were worth, never stopping at the toll-house, at full speed along the wide dusty road. The peasants, who knew nothing about all this, gaped at us in terror. Before the female lunatic asylum I stopped for breath while my comrades went on running. The door opened and I was let in. Here I was given a wash and a cordial to drink while they cleaned the stains of mud and blood on my uniform. I stayed nearly an hour with these good lunatics in a dreadful state of anxiety. When I wished to leave a kind wardress embraced me and said: "I have a son in the army." I returned to the city without being noticed. As I looked fairly clean nobody imagined I had come from the Campo di Marte. I reached the barracks just when our regimental march was being played, escorting the company with our two captured banners. The dormitories were almost empty. . . .'

General Alessandro Nunziante, who had recently been appointed adjutant-general by the King, commanded the troops who mowed down the mutineers. His excess of zeal on this occasion had a sinister significance in the light of his subsequent conversion to Victor Emmanuel. The rebels had dispersed after the first shots, yet he continued to order fire. About eighty were killed and over two hundred fell wounded; the rest were rounded up and disarmed.

The Swiss regiments were among the best in the Neapolitan army and had given abundant proofs of loyalty. For this very reason the liberals and political exiles had long been scheming to get rid of them. Leopardi, the Neapolitan chargé d'affaires in Turin during the constitutional interregnum in 1848, had stirred the resentment of the Swiss Federal Government with sensational allegations about Swiss atrocities on May 15, and the sore had been rubbed periodically during the next decade until the Federal Council decided to abrogate their convention with Naples in 1859. The removal of the cantonal crest from the banners had been a mere pretext: the men had been told that they would forfeit their nationality by remaining in the King's service.

Filangieri had offered to resign on July 5 and retired to his villa near Sorrento, yet he was back in Naples on the night of the mutiny. He promptly advised the King to disband his Swiss regiments, though this time they had proved their loyalty in action against their compatriots. Gold napoleons had been found in the pockets of prisoners and casualties, and Filangieri maintained that all of them had been corrupted by foreign agents: many of them, moreover, would wish to avenge their slaughtered comrades and further bloodshed was inevitable if they remained. Francis proposed that Filangieri, Lanza and himself should each lead a regiment to Caserta, Nocera and Nola until their excitement cooled, but Filangieri retorted that the Swiss 'were more worthy of Garibaldi than of forming part of his honourable and faithful army,' and played upon his dread of revolution. Francis was far from convinced, but Filangieri's military prestige was so great that he yielded regretfully to his arguments.

'My father's most ardent desire,' wrote Filangieri's daughter,[1] 'I might add, his last enduring ideal and hope at that time, was to restore its ancient decorum to the Neapolitan army. This hope . . . which he had faith in realizing, so filled his heart and mind that he could not share the timorous regrets of the Court and certain members of the government on account of the Swiss defection. . . . My father urged the King to take the only practicable course in dealing with that element of order transformed into disorder, which was to disband

[1] Teresa Filangieri Fieschi Ravaschieri, *Il Generale Carlo Filangieri*. Milan, 1902.

the whole Swiss legion, releasing it from all engagements past, present and future, and this was done accordingly. Their discharge, however, was not imposed but voluntary, since every Swiss soldier was offered the choice between leaving with the nice little sum of seventy ducats (equivalent to £11–7–6d gold, with the ducat at 3/3d) or remaining unconditionally under the Bourbon banner and obeying our military code. Nearly everybody chose discharge with the gratuity, whence a new decree dissolving the convention for the second Swiss regiment was followed on the same day by another decree releasing the other regiments from all their pledges.'

The clinking coins and nostalgia for their native mountains were tempting inducements. Filangieri and Nunziante were applauded for liquidating these valuable veterans at such expense when, as De Sivo remarked, they should have been paid to remain and their numbers should have been doubled. The army was weakened by their departure and the revolutionaries were correspondingly strengthened. When the Swiss regiments were finally embarked for Marseilles, the Piedmontese minister to Naples Gropello wrote to Cavour on August 19, 1859: 'I believe this event will have almost the same importance for Naples in the long run as the total and complete expulsion of the foreigner from Italy.' He considered that 'without the Swiss regiments which were admirably disciplined and directed, the Neapolitan army was in a wretched plight, without martial spirit or intelligent leadership.'

Francis unbosomed himself on the subject to Brenier, who wrote to Walewski on August 16, 1859:[1] 'The King seemed deeply pained by the defection of these troops so long regarded as a model of loyalty and firm bulwark of the throne. "After all," he added, "it is only one division less and we have enough troops with the remainder: our macaroni-eaters (the nickname for Neapolitan troops) will suffice. They are good soldiers, rather slow to adapt themselves to military discipline but easy to lead and, thank Heaven, more loyal than the Swiss who suddenly let themselves be won over by the machinations of revolutionaries and by Piedmontese money. I will say nothing of the King of Piedmont, for he is too good a kinsman to play me such a trick, but Cavour, the emigrants and Rattazzi are very capable of doing so and I have positive proof that the Swiss soldiers were suborned. Those who had not been gained by bribery were persuaded

[1] Costanzo Maraldi, *op. cit.*, pp. 59–68.

by other forms of corruption, and the mission of M. Latour (the Swiss envoy) brought the crisis to fruition. I thought myself entitled to refuse them the pension allowed them by my father's decree, but Prince Filangieri considered it expedient and politic to wind up this affair with an act of generosity and avoid the trouble which might arise from armed resistance, and I have yielded to his opinion, but not without deep regret and disgust. Had the Swiss regiments revolted in the open country I should have acted differently . . . but I was unwilling to risk bloodshed in the city and aggravate the general crisis, which is serious enough. . . . Consequently I preferred to pay off the Swiss as mercenaries and no longer treat them as soldiers. It will cost us dear, from five to six hundred thousand ducats for the present and perhaps two million ducats altogether. Our finances are in good order although we are not rich. . . . I must admit I had never foreseen such an expense: it is inconceivable how rapidly the gangrene has spread." '

Brenier replied that he was less surprised than the King, that he thought it impossible to depend on the loyalty of mercenaries and keep them immune from revolutionary contagion. He was surprised that the actual crisis had not occurred sooner. He advised Francis 'to restore that confidence to the Neapolitan troops which they had shared in an unequal manner with the Swiss, and to seek in the very heart of the country that irresistible force which consolidates as well as founds dynasties—the suffrage of all.' Francis might obtain it by granting concessions which had long been overdue. An unreliable army, a liberal but not anti-dynastic public opinion, and no more Swiss regiments: such was the actual predicament. . . . The time for a régime of repression was past and buried with the late King. Since the Swiss had gone the police were the only relic of that régime, and their despotism was an outrage to the King's person and to the beginning of his reign. It was essential that this despotism should end. Brenier felt certain that even the ultras would be satisfied if the King gave the country certain reforms; he would not say a Constitution since he knew that the word was repugnant to His Majesty. . . .

'Ah, a Constitution, that is just what Mr Elliot advises me. Is that your idea too? The word Constitution may denote something very flexible.'

Brenier went on to describe the advantages of the French type of Constitution until he noticed that the King was glaring at him with a defiant expression and that the subject had evidently become obnoxious. When he stopped talking the King rose to open a window with a magnificent view. 'See how beautiful it is,' he remarked, 'and how sad at the same time to think that the defection of the Swiss should spoil the delight of ruling so fine a country! Yonder at Naples, Maddaloni and Nocera they are now being told of their discharge. . . . I should like to keep a few of them, if only a hundred veterans, in memory of that old tradition of loyalty on which our dynasty rested. They are not as depraved as some people imagine, and if Piedmont and cantonal radicalism had not contaminated them these regiments would have remained. The bad elements would have gone and we should have kept the good, replacing the tainted ones with fresh recruits.'

The King's attitude and expression betrayed his inward distress: he scrutinized the horizon as if it were a crystal ball. 'Come,' he continued, 'I must telegraph to find out what they are doing over there. Having suddenly succeeded to the crown so little prepared to receive this heavy burden, in circumstances which my father could not have foreseen, I am alone to direct everything. Prince Filangieri, whom I love and shall trust as long as he lives, supports me with his rich experience. Though he is amazingly vigorous and energetic, I cannot believe he will not succumb to fatigue. As for me, I was beginning to feel tired and came to Castellammare for a rest, to ponder calmly on all the subjects we have been discussing and find the inspiration I am seeking, which I pray God for every day. So far I could only follow one course, that which my father has left me, love my country and protect it against the odious people who want to upset everything. After the affair of the Swiss has been settled we shall see: perhaps there will be trouble in Sicily which is being disturbed by so many emissaries! Well, we shall see. . . . I'll do my best with my poor Neapolitan soldiers, and then God's will be done!'

While Elliot, the self-appointed spokesman of the liberals, considered that the King's intelligence was 'naturally of a low order', Brenier was impressed by its infinite superiority to the tendentious reports he had heard of it. Elliot had noted that 'an entire want of sympathy or feeling for others was visible in a cold manner, unlike everything you would wish to see in a young man of twenty-three', and illustrated this with an improbable anecdote. Brenier wrote: 'everything in his person shows that all affectionate and gentle sentiments are as absent from his heart as from his system of government'. While the King, as he admitted, took his hand with the utmost cordiality, Brenier read into his features 'cunning, dissimulation, duplicity and absolutism'. Filangieri, the faithful old minister, had warned him that 'aridity of soul, cold and inaccessible obstinacy, were his chief characteristics', and Brenier wondered how these could be reconciled with his piety, which seemed sincere. Spanish history, he mused, offered similar contrasts between the practice of Christian and kingly duties: perhaps religious and political fanaticism sprang from the same source. Filangieri attributed the King's *sécheresse de cœur* to 'a physical defect which separated him from the rest of humanity, but in spite of the details revealed to me I cannot believe that the sterility of his temperament is the cause of his aridity of soul'. How shocked poor Francis would have been by these inter-diplomatic ruminations!

Some light relief was necessary after so much heavy weather, and Francis found it in his wife's society. She was a child and he was a child—when they fancied they were in private. But there was no real privacy for princes. Father Ferretti, a friend of the King's confessor whose rooms adjoined the royal apartments, was irresistibly tempted to peep through the keyhole when he heard carillons of feminine laughter. Behold the King dressed up in a crinoline, pirouetting around the Queen like a gawky sylph, while Her Majesty was convulsed with merriment. The peeping priest revealed this unexpected vision in strict confidence to a friend, not with malice but merely to prove the King's innocent good nature. Happily those were the days before Freudian interpretations. Perhaps the King's 'aridity' was reserved for public occasions in general and for bores in particular.

XXI

FORMAL celebrations for the succession of Francis II did not
begin till July 24, when the first phase of mourning for Ferdinand
was over. The young King and Queen drove in state to the
Cathedral while thunderous guns saluted them from the forts and
ships of war.

The atrabilious Elliot reported characteristically: 'The reception of
Their Majesties on their progress was, I am informed, respectful, but
not enthusiastic.' Elliot's informant was mistaken, for then even more
than now the people of Naples enjoyed a pageant, and this one appealed to their smouldering national pride. Here was the son of their
sweetest and youngest Saint Maria Cristina—the Pope had pronounced her venerable but she had already been beatified by the
people—proceeding to the shrine of their oldest and most venerable
Saint Januarius beside his radiant Bavarian Queen, for a glimpse of
whose smile vast crowds had assembled from all over the capital,
pushing and scrambling and craning their necks, hoisting their babes
and sucklings in spontaneous glee. Maria Sophia did not disappoint
them. While Francis looked pale and aloof, she blushed and sparkled
with the desire to gratify these dear demonstrative subjects who felt
duly rewarded and bellowed their admiration. Some rise to the
occasion, but she made the occasion rise to her, a star before the era of
cinematography. From the diamonds in her auburn hair to her satin
shoes her glamour was genuine. And when she stepped out of the

royal coach and entered the Cathedral she moved with inimitable grace and dignity. Though the head of Saint Januarius was exposed on the altar the blood in the phials liquefied. This had not been known to happen before, and was regarded as a happy augury.

Next day, as Elliot reported, 'Their Majesties held a Court and received the Corps Diplomatique and the gentlemen of the country, and it excited much comment that on a solemn occasion of this kind His Majesty's uncle the Count of Syracuse should have considered it right to absent himself with the design apparently of publicly exhibiting the coldness of the relations between the King and himself.' Court receptions on this scale had not been held for several years, and were as much appreciated by Neapolitan tailors, dressmakers and other tradesmen as by the high dignitaries who took part in them, though many a costume had been laid in camphor. The Queen saved the function from being too solemn, for when the long file of magistrates in black robes and 'Don Basilio' hats marched in with all the pomp they could muster, so strange a contrast to the glittering uniforms and crinolines, she could not help laughing, and her silvery laughter was infectious. The ceremony ended amid general gaiety which Elliot failed to notice, perhaps because he was determined to be dour. The gala evening at the San Carlo which followed revived the past splendours of that social institution. The typical costumes of the different provinces were represented in a magnified tarantella, after a somewhat insipid 'Inaugural Dance' set to music by old Mercadante, the Nestor of Neapolitan composers. The boxes were bowers of roses, and the illuminations were such as to gladden an audience which could never be surfeited with dazzling light no matter what wrinkles and blemishes it might betray.

Elliot remarked that the King was living in a fool's paradise. He ridiculed the opinion of Count Buol, the Austrian Foreign Minister, that 'there was really neither general discontent nor any kind of misgovernment likely to lead to it . . . everything was perfect in this model monarchy'. Count Buol was out of touch with the opposition. Yet Elliot must have realized that the King was nervous about Garibaldi, who was reported even then to have organized an expedition against Naples, for he wrote on August 1: 'In reply to my enquiries he (Filangieri) assured me that there was every reason to suppose the information to be correct, and that General Garibaldi had already taken up some of the steamers which are to convey his force . . . Prince Satriano did not conceal his apprehension that if the landing of so large a force as the expedition is expected to consist of, is successfully effected, the consequences may be extremely serious.' Calabria was vulnerable owing to its long coast line. At this moment, said Filangieri, he could not collect there above 1300 bayonets to oppose the enemy's landing. His own knowledge enabled him to affirm that the very first effect of the appearance of an invading force would be the separation of Sicily. Would the British fleet, he asked, allow such a thing to take place without interfering to stop the proceedings of a band of free-booters? Elliot could not promise any intervention. He reminded Filangieri of the frequent warnings given by Her Majesty's Government 'on the system of government pursued here'. Hence he should not be surprised 'if they decline to take any active measures in defend-ing the Neapolitan government from the consequences of their obstinate rejection of their warnings and advice'.

Brenier pooh-poohed these alarms and blamed the Neapolitan police for a mere *canard*. Like Cavour later on, the Piedmontese minister Dabormida declared again and again that Garibaldi would never embark on such an attempt with the aid of his government. The French minister in Turin believed him, and when Brenier quoted his despatches to Filangieri the latter expostulated against the childishness of such credulity, adding that he had positive proofs of Piedmontese connivance. If anarchy gained ground in Naples, Sicily *ipso facto* would fall under British patronage. Brenier retorted that the best weapon to annihilate Garibaldi and *écraser l'infâme*, as Voltaire said of a very different foe, was to grant a Constitution. He was more out-spoken than Elliot, imagining that this was what his master wanted, though Walewski was to disclaim any responsibility for it 'as emanat-ing from the Emperor's will'. Owing to his French sympathies Filangieri was inclined to favour a moderate form of Constitution, but he thought it prudent not to advertise the fact. He was a braver general than politician. Aware of the King's blind spot, for 'Constitu-tion-Revolution' had been dinned into his ears since infancy, Filan-gieri wished neither to jolt him nor to be jolted. He already had a draft prepared by his friend Giovanni Manna, whom Elliot described as 'one of the most upright and sincere of the Constitutional party'.

'The project is of so moderate a nature,' wrote Elliot on September

2, 'that it can hardly be expected to satisfy such of the liberal party as think that the transition from absolute despotism to perfect freedom should be made in one step, but it is hoped that the consent of the Crown and the support of an important part of the nobility may be obtained for a system based as I understand . . . upon a representative body controlled by a Senate named for life by the Sovereign and alone possessing the right of initiative.

'I enquired what it was proposed to do in regard to Sicily and was informed that it was intended that the island and the kingdom should have totally distinct local administration, but that the subjects common to both should be discussed in the above-named assemblies which would sit alternately at Naples and Palermo.

'The difficulties of arranging one representative body for the two countries are not denied, but those in the way of a total separation have been considered still greater, and it was not difficult to perceive that one of the chief reasons which prevented the latter idea from being entertained was the condition that it would meet with strenuous opposition from the French Government, on account of the influence which it would be likely to give Great Britain in Sicily . . . The resemblance borne by the project in preparation to the system prevailing in France is too close to escape observation.' He added that this information had been communicated to him under the promise of the strictest secrecy.

According to Filangieri's *Memoirs*, he submitted the draft to Francis on September 4. Francis would not deign to peruse it or show it to his other ministers. 'The King's cool reception of my proposal,' wrote Filangieri, 'was accompanied by a few embarrassed words, which made me suspect there was truth in the common report that the late King on his deathbed had made him promise not to change the form of government adopted after the events of 1848–1849.' Since Filangieri had been enjoined not to mention this awkward interview, Brenier imagined that he had done nothing about it. Eventually he felt sure that Filangieri was playing a double game: 'he presents himself to us as the partisan of reform whilst he persuades the King to persevere in a course of resistance and repression'.

In any case Filangieri offered to resign, but the King would not accept his resignation. Instead he was granted a long leave of absence during which General Carascosa and Marshal Garofalo would act as his deputies at the council and ministry of war. Elliot, who went to visit him at Sorrento, reported: 'I was received with his usual cordiality, and was soon convinced though he is undoubtedly unwell and suffering severely from his old wound, that, as he himself declares his malady is more of the spirit than of the body. He begged that our conversation might be considered strictly private and confidential and as passing between General Filangieri and Mr Elliot, and not as between the Ministers of two different Sovereigns, and then went on to say that he absolutely despaired of effecting any good, and that, as he had told me from the first he was determined not to remain at the nominal head of affairs unless he saw that he could do it with advantage.

'He considers the King as firmly wedded to the principle of despotic government in its most despotic form, that he was convinced that there was no hope of weaning His Majesty from it. "He is prepared," continued the Prince, "to stand by his system at all hazards and to the last extremity, and rather than give in upon it he will allow himself to be driven first from Naples to Gaeta, and then from Gaeta to England."

'The dangers of the King's position he said were undoubtedly great, but they may still be avoided. The re-establishment of the Constitution sworn to by the late King is not advisable, for it went too far for a first measure of the kind, but a return to a Constitution sufficiently liberal to rally round it the great mass of the Constitutional party has become a necessity. But even that could not be accomplished without means being taken to avoid two dangers which he foresaw, first the defection of the army, and secondly the separation from Sicily. If the King were grudgingly to grant a Constitution, the army would probably say that it had been imposed upon His Majesty and as they had sworn to obey him as absolute Sovereign they would disband themselves rather than serve a Constitution. This danger could be averted by the King giving the Constitution with good will, by his speaking to the troops, and by his publicly showing himself determined to adhere to it. . . .

'(The Prince's remarks were) made in the strongest and most emphatic language. He did full justice to many good qualities which he said the King possessed, and which made him estimable as a man, while as a Sovereign his ideas are such as to cause despair. . . .'

Filangieri remained an absentee Prime Minister with all the emoluments of office. Considering his feelings as expressed to Elliot such conduct is difficult to account for. A true statesman never despairs: he prepares for the future. In any case despair calls for desperate remedies. Central Italy was being rapidly 'Piedmontized' in the teeth of Napoleon III. Parma, Modena and the Romagna now formed the single province of Emilia under Farini's dictatorship, for the era of regional dictators had begun, and Garibaldi with an army was threatening the Papal frontier and fomenting unrest in the Papal provinces. In Naples twelve thousand copies of a clandestine pro-Piedmontese newspaper were being distributed in spite of the 'omnipotent' police, who suspected that the inflammatory press was lodged in the Piedmontese legation. Twelve thousand Neapolitan troops under General Pianell were sent to guard the Abruzzo frontier against a Garibaldian invasion, but this menace subsided in November when the Piedmontese and their partisans realized the political folly of 'raising a European question round the Pope'. That could be done later, when the Central Italian question had been settled without antagonizing France.

The Peace of Zurich signed by the recent belligerents on November 10 differed little from that of Villafranca and envisaged an Italian confederation, which was to be discussed at a future Congress. But the proposed Congress never took place. If Piedmont were to annex Central Italy, thought Napoleon III, why should not France annex Nice and Savoy? And this was a matter for private negotiation. Realizing that all Europe would rise against him if he disclosed his real aims in public, he sabotaged the Congress at the last moment with a semi-official pamphlet, attacking the Pope's temporal power. The gist of *Le Pape et le Congrès* is: 'the less the territory of the Papal States, the greater their ruler. Thus Pius IX would be truly inspired were he of his own free will to cut away his rebellious provinces and henceforth confine himself to the city of the Holy Apostles'. Naturally the Pope could not agree. He denounced the pamphlet as 'a conspicuous monument of hypocrisy and a disgraceful tissue of contradictions'. And he prophesied that the sword of God in the hands of men was ready to strike down Napoleon III. Persuaded by Victor Emmanuel, Garibaldi resigned his command on November 16, *reculant pour mieux sauter*.

That Francis II was far from living in a fool's or any other paradise may be seen from Brenier's and Elliot's despatches. 'The idea that seems especially to predominate in his mind,' as Elliot wrote in September 1859, 'is apparently an excessive dread of the aggressive policy of Piedmont, which he considers likely by degrees to incorporate the whole peninsula.' Events were to prove that his dread was not excessive. At the end of September Napoleon III sent General Roguet on a special mission to induce Francis to grant a Constitution, but he remained obdurate. Filangieri entertained the French general, whose father had been his colonel in the days of the first Napoleon, and repeated his conversation in a long hortatory letter to the King on October 2: 'If this important but youthful Sovereign understood his position in relation to Italy and the rest of Europe,' said Roguet, 'and became convinced of the necessity of giving his kingdom monarchical and constitutional institutions as in France, not only should he count on the firm support of the Emperor Napoleon but, come what may, he would play a leading rôle in Italy.' 'What do you think would happen if the King decided not to change the laws and institutions of the Two Sicilies?' Filangieri inquired. Without a moment's hesitation Roguet replied: 'In that case I could only foresee misfortune for your King and country.'

The King wrote promptly to Filangieri: 'I have read your letter of yesterday with attention, and feel more convinced than ever that the ruin of this poor country is the pernicious contact and influence of foreigners.'

General Roguet informed Napoleon III that Francis was extremely conscientious, that he 'showed energy, a certain purity of heart, and a desire for good'. In his opinion the King could only be saved from the Italian movement by throwing himself into the arms of France. But Napoleon III had precipitated that movement. The revolts in Parma, Modena, Tuscany, the Romagna and elsewhere had followed his appeal from Milan before the campaign: 'Italians! Unite yourselves in a single purpose, the emancipation of your country. Fly to arms under the banner of King Victor Emmanuel. . . . To-morrow you shall be free citizens of a great country.' Then, when the movement veered beyond control, he had recoiled in dismay. His half-baked idea of an Italian Confederation under the presidency of the Pope had only caused general resentment, and it is hardly surprising that Francis was distrustful. Beside his official policy, as M. Maurice Paléologue wrote, the Emperor pursued several private policies with a swarm of Italian agents. 'Decisions he made in the morning, he reversed in the evening;

that which he declared to one, he denied to another.' Perhaps only Cavour could fathom his mental processes.

To the growing indignation of Brenier and Elliot, the acting Minister for Foreign Affairs Carafa continued to rebuff their combined admonitions. Brenier desired more forceful measures, but Elliot considered that there were 'numerous and obvious objections in the way of a resort to pressure, or to threats of any kind'. Carafa's favourite argument was that the country was peaceful and contented without political exigencies or even ideas, and therefore required no change whatever; that it was inopportune and premature to make concessions which were misunderstood by the masses, and only desired by thoughtless chatterboxes.

Naples needed peace like the rest of Europe, and most citizens were relieved that peace was restored between France and Austria. They hoped to develop their local industries, to which the King gave a fresh impetus by his enthusiasm for public works. He set up a commission to enlarge the port of the capital, build a modern dock, and improve communications. The railway was to be prolonged as far as the frontier: lines were to run to Brindisi and Lecce, through Basilicata to Reggio, through Abruzzo to the Tronto. Other railways were planned for Sicily, and new lighthouses were to be erected along the coasts. Provincial councils were to be increased; customs duties and tolls were reduced. Of course Brenier and Elliot derided such reforms as trivial. Again there happened to be a grain shortage, and the government bought corn from abroad and sold the local produce at a loss in Sicily and the mainland, for which it was cursed by the new economists, those merchant-hoarders who saw their profits vanish and complained, as De Sivo wrote, of the tyranny of a government which provided bread cheap for the people.

De Sivo was a voice in the wilderness of liberal historians and a spokesman of the quiet majority when he wrote:[1] 'Naples had fewer soldiers than France, fewer ships than England, less liberty than America, fewer fine arts perhaps than Rome, less polish than Paris; but these alone do not bring felicity. Yet of all these things it possessed such a total that in relation to its territory and conditions it was second to none. Commerce, arts and letters, morality, religion, security, creature comforts, industry, science, civil liberties it possessed

[1] Giacinto De Sivo, *Storia delle Due Sicilie*, Vol. II, p. 3. Trieste, 1868.

in abundance. There was pleasant living at slight expense, full of recreations and enjoyments; and those who were not involved in subversive sects had the utmost civil freedom and could do whatever they liked. Altogether the kingdom was the happiest in the world; and most of the foreigners who came there waxed rich and stayed on. The population increased by a quarter in forty years. . . . The statistics of crime were low, homicide was rare, paupers were few, hunger was almost unknown; religious and private, communal and government charity provided; no paper currency, but all silver and gold, few taxes, few restrictions, with little you could enjoy everything. Work was easy, the cost was light, there were many popular holidays, respect for social superiors, justice, protection, security for all, and order always.'

On the surface Naples seemed to have returned to normal, with about half a million inhabitants and barely five thousand troops in the various barracks. The last of the Piedigrotta festivals on a majestic scale was celebrated on September 8, 1859. All the bells in the city pealed frantically on that morning when the sacred and profane were blended with traditional exuberance, and there was a vast pilgrimage towards the Queen of Neapolitan Madonnas. In the afternoon 47 battalions, 33 squadrons and 64 pieces of artillery took part in the parade before the royal palace, and such a variety of scintillating uniforms was not to be seen there again, royal guards in scarlet with bearskin caps, Calabrians in green, cuirassiers in gleaming armour, hussars in white jackets, dusky Sicilians and sturdy mariners, who lined the whole way to the church at Piedigrotta. Bands played on the square and accompanied the march with tunes grave and gay. A flotilla with a forest of little flags was moored at Mergellina. Naval guns answered those of the five castles as the royal procession advanced very slowly beside the sea: first a squadron of the guard of nobles mounted on their own fine steeds, then halberdiers from the castle garrisons on foot, then a lumbering rococo ceremonial coach quite empty with footmen behind it, followed by eight carriages with six horses to each containing court chamberlains emblazoned with insignia, then the King and Queen in a high carriage drawn by eight thoroughbreds, the King stiff with regalia, the Queen Titania-like with a diamond tiara. Two companies of bodyguards followed, and twelve more carriages containing the King's brothers, uncles and suite with another squadron of guards wound up the procession. Each carriage stopped at the church, and it was dusk when all returned after their orisons.

Thousands came in from the country for this annual event, and the gaudy costumes of the peasantry in festive mood, as well as the red-capped fishermen and street urchins in improvised fancy dress and vendors of refreshments, added colour and noise to a scene peculiarly animated even for Naples. Drums, trumpets, tambourines and fire-crackers heightened the Babel of shrill and raucous voices. The taverns adorned with trellises of foliage did a roaring trade, but there was little drunkenness as in northern cities, though censorious foreigners pretended to be shocked 'to behold a whole people, and a people professing Christianity, thus giving themselves up to all manner of ungodliness and gross indulgence'. Towards evening the street urchins ran about with paper lanterns on sticks, and there was much dancing and singing and fun in the Posillipo grotto. The garden of the Villa was open to all and many spent the night there, with considerable damage to the flower-beds. It was essentially a popular festival, a September Saturnalia. Shorn of its official pageantry it languished until it was artificially revived as a festival of Neapolitan song towards 1880, when *Funiculì, Funiculà* spread its fame to the ends of the earth.

Grandiose court receptions and religious festivals, lavish performances of opera and ballet at the San Carlo, where the ballerina Boschetti raised a furore in Taglioni's 'Rita' and in 'Loretta the Diviner', of which one critic wrote that it seemed as if her brains were in her toes; rollicking farces and spicy skits at the San Carlino; rhetorical melodramas by Scribe and his emulators at the Fiorentini theatre; crowded cafés where the wits assembled to bandy sparkling epigrams such as those of the young Duke Proto and Marchese di Caccavone, rendezvous of liberal-radicals where the wildest rumours were more prevalent than authentic news and hoaxes were perpetrated from sheer excess of fantasy,—Parthenope was as spectacular as of old but all the livelier for the political excitement which affected everybody more or less. The Count of Syracuse aired his sympathy for Piedmont with impunity, but he was surrounded by a more vulnerable clique of artistic rebels. The most buoyant enjoyed flouting authority; the most brazen got themselves arrested and enjoyed a fleeting fame. If their pocket-books were well lined they were treated with deference, and most of them could afford a little bribery and corruption. For many a year they would be able to dine out on their prison experiences, which were usually more entertaining than those related by Gladstone. There was no cause for serious alarm, since Elliot and Brenier were standing by to protect them. These amiable ministers made the most of any political arrest: in fact they did little else. Theodore Cottrau, whose music shop not far from the royal palace was a notorious centre of subversive propaganda, was never bothered by the police because he was a friend of Brenier. Clandestine newspapers were printed and distributed with a freedom unheard of in genuine police states, and the liberal 'Committee of Order' continued to plot the downfall of the Bourbons undisturbed.

The Sicilians had already forgotten the pangs of their past revolution and were chafing again more volubly under Bourbon rule, as they have chafed before and since. Prince Castelcicala was a mild and phlegmatic governor: according to him the island was as happy as it was peaceful, with no danger of disaffection. But this outward serenity was largely due to Salvatore Maniscalco, the ruthlessly efficient director of police who had risen to power as Filangieri's right-hand man and remained indispensable. Born on a boat between Palermo and Messina, he was considered Messinese though his family was Palermitan: he knew the psychology of his people and so thoroughly organized the police that even his enemies admitted that Sicily had never enjoyed such safety. In appearance he was not a typical Sicilian, for he was a short fair man with blue eyes who listened more than he talked, and whose emotions were masked by an ironical smile. His private life was rigidly respectable, and Filangieri was godfather to the eldest of his six children. So successful had he been in crushing conspiracy during the last decade that he had become a living legend. He knew that he was hated as a pillar of Bourbonism, but he was fearless. He had a friend in every commune who kept him minutely informed, and he took a personal interest in details. His virtues were those of a dutiful if narrow Conservative who believed that Sicily required public safety, low taxes and cheap living; and that the alternative was anarchy and chaos.

Nearly all foreign observers wrote of the Sicilian people's chronic hostility to the Bourbons, but this was more true of Palermo than Messina. The masses were potential anarchists; the intellectuals wanted autonomy and fancied that this could be achieved gratis by the altruistic efforts of Garibaldi and the Piedmontese. Most of them could not bear to join the army. Thanks to the indefatigable partisans of Mazzini a desire for unity with Italy had been growing. The two Sicilian exiles Francesco Crispi and Rosolino Pilo were among Mazzini's most strenuous agents, and the Modenese Fabrizi manipulated the wires of conspiracy from Malta, where the British authorities winked amicably at his cache of arms and ammunition. Another Sicilian exile, Giuseppe La Farina, was secretary of the National Society, whose aim was 'to put the great principle of Italian independence and unity under the House of Savoy before every other political form'. As an ex-Mazzinian who had become an intimate of Cavour he was able to draw many adherents. The victories of Magenta and Solferino could not fail to rouse enthusiasm in Palermo. On June 24, 1859, the 'Nobles' Club' was so brightly illuminated that Maniscalco for once lost his self-control. He raided the club in a most undignified manner, put out the lights, closed the premises, and arrested several of its younger members. The culprits were soon released but they set a new fashion: other exalted young idlers seized a chance to infuse patriotic meaning into their hitherto meaningless existence and piped up for a period in prison. Garibaldi was implored to deliver them from tyranny. He replied on September 29 that he would come with pleasure when everything was ready for him. First 'a more intimate communication with them and stronger connections' were desirable: no foolish risk as in the Pisacane fiasco. If they could not manage a successful rising, let them unite and strengthen themselves. His answer raised their hopes.

Francesco Crispi arrived in August, disguised as a tourist from the Argentine with a false passport acquired from Mazzini, to amalgamate the conspirators of Palermo and Messina. He promised that Garibaldi would not fail them, and that Mazzini would lend his passionate support, as an earnest of which he presented his Palermitan cronies with precise models of Orsini's bombs. His suggestion was that they should hurl replicas of these among the troops when they were being reviewed on October 4, the King's Saint's day. Maniscalco prevented this by arresting a few conspirators, portrayed as innocent victims by Elliot and his clique. A revolt led by young Campo at Bagheria near Palermo was promptly subdued, and Campo fled to Genoa to return next year with Garibaldi. The King's written comment on Castelcicala's report of this rising was: 'We always prefer prevention to repression.'

The conspirators proceeded to hire an assassin to murder their chief impediment. On Sunday November 27 Maniscalco was stabbed in the back at the entrance of the Cathedral where he had gone to Mass with his wife and two small sons. It was raining, the streets were deserted, and it was easy for the thug to escape through the narrow lanes near by: only his false beard was found. Maniscalco recovered to receive the congratulations of the conspirators as well as of the King, who increased his salary and sent him the Grand Cross of Francis I. The assassin was to claim and receive a pension from Garibaldi.

In October a Mrs Mary Esperance Schwartz, travelling with a Foreign Office passport, had called on the British vice-consul Rickards in Messina and shown him a letter from Garibaldi: 'You will proceed to Messina, call upon Mr Joseph Rickards . . . ascertain from him who are the members of the Revolutionary Committee, communicate with them, ascertain whether they possess the means, and are ready to begin and carry on the Revolution and to place themselves in correspondence with me.' But the wary vice-consul refused to oblige her, and the disappointed lady returned to Leghorn. Rickards was also asked to forward several letters from Leghorn to a merchant in Messina. Thinking that an illicit correspondence was indicated, he ventured to open them. 'The contents,' he informed Elliot, 'surpassed my preconceived opinions. It appears the writer of those letters is an agent of a noted Italian General plotting with the Revolutionary Committee in Sicily the overthrow of the present Government. The landing of armed men in the island is proposed and the Committee are desired to send a formal requisition to that effect. The writer urges the strong necessity of first assassinating the Director of Police at Palermo . . . allusion is made to the lady (Mrs Schwartz) sent to Messina some time ago and whose mission, the writer adds, failed in consequence of Mr J. R. declining to have anything to do with her.' Maniscalco was not wholly unprepared, for as Elliot reported on December 6, 'a week previous to his attempted assassination he had written to say that he knew that agents of Mazzini had arrived in Sicily with that object, and that he trusted the King would provide for his wife and children if he should fall a victim'.

All this provoked greater police vigilance and tension between the government and the governed. Palermitans of high rank like Princess Niscemi hid political suspects in their palaces; the opulent Baron Riso gave frequent balls on the first floor of his mansion in the central Toledo, for dancing masqueraded the meetings of conspirators on the floor above, 'men in evening dress slipping upstairs between a gay valse or contre-danse to help in the making of bombs for the coming revolution'.[1] These balls hoodwinked the police. Plotting had become the mania of every class: it was evidently exhilarating for the plotters, who revelled in risk and secrecy and thrilling escapes, but it made for monotonous reading *à la longue*.

'We very much doubt,' wrote Nicomede Bianchi, 'if Francis II and his counsellors, whatever policy they chose to pursue, could have succeeded in steering clear of revolution.' Ferdinand II might have succeeded, but Francis lacked the qualities of leadership and Filangieri, for all his prestige and experience, failed him by fading away into semi-retirement. Surrounded by crab-like bureaucrats who dreaded any kind of change, the King stood pathetically alone, stunned into immobility by the swarm of events, each with a poisonous sting in its tail. It looked as if he were awaiting supernatural intervention. A man of prayer, he kept up a placid façade.

The New Year festivities of 1860 were deceptively gay, and there was little hint of the approaching metamorphosis. Both the King and Queen received a warm ovation at the San Carlo, and the homage of their subjects seemed quite sincere. To celebrate the King's twenty-fourth birthday a fine new frigate was launched at Castellammare: she was christened the *Borbone*. Who could have guessed that within a few months the same ship would be rechristened the *Garibaldi* and would bombard Neapolitan troops?

The new Piedmontese envoy Marchese di Villamarina arrived towards the end of January to persuade Francis that Victor Emmanuel had not the slightest intention of upsetting his kingdom. 'While engaged in the enterprise of national independence the House of Savoy had no ambition or desire to dominate over Italy. The liberation of the peninsula from the Austrian yoke would benefit Naples as well as Piedmont. Far from threatening the royal dynasty of Naples, the Piedmontese government sincerely wished to see it strengthened by the content of the population, and by removing those foreign influences that stood in the way of their independence. There could be no greater security for Italian independence than a good understanding between

[1] Tina Whitaker, *Sicily and England*, London, 1907.

419

the two largest Italian States. . . .'[1] According to Brenier, Villamarina added that Victor Emmanuel would make every effort to stop the progress of annexationist ideas beyond the Legations, but that events were moving so rapidly that the Piedmontese Government could no longer be responsible for their consequences unless timely concessions were made.[2]

King Francis was not persuaded, and who can blame him? Only three months later Victor Emmanuel was reported to have said 'that he would be at Naples before the end of the year', and Sir James Hudson, the British minister at Turin, commented: 'I quite believe that he is capable of saying so, because when he received a sword of honour from the Romans, he said "*anderemo al fondo*", and because also he is in the habit of blurting out just what happens to be present to his mind at the moment.'[3]

The King's uncle Syracuse advertised his political sympathies by driving about in public with Villamarina, who immediately became the patron of the Neapolitan liberals. While insisting on his friendly intentions he pretended to be afraid of a Neapolitan attack, as if the troops guarding the frontier were likely to invade the Romagna. Actually Napoleon III wished Francis to occupy the Marches and send substitutes for the French forces still in Rome. Since his annexation of Nice and Savoy was assured he hoped to restrain further Piedmontese expansion. On March 11 a plebiscite in the central States of Emilia and Tuscany declared for union with Piedmont; on March 24 Cavour signed the treaty ceding Nice and Savoy to France, subject also to a plebiscite, after which he remarked to the French agent: 'Now we are fellow conspirators, aren't we?' But they were conspirators with a difference, and certainly Cavour was the sharper of the two. He had returned to power on January 20, announcing that his policy would be 'Italian to the extreme bounds of possibility'. This was to be the year of his triumph.

Francis could only see snares on every side. Though Brenier tried to make him believe that Napoleon III would guarantee any troops he sent into the Papal States from Piedmontese aggression, it was clear

[1] Nicomede Bianchi, *Storia della Diplomazia Europea in Italia*, Vol. 8, p. 275.
[2] Maraldi, *op. cit.*, p. 105.
[3] G. M. Trevelyan, *Garibaldi and the Making of Italy*, pp. 305, 306. London, 1911.

that he would never fly in the face of his fellow conspirator. The liberals wanted a Neapolitan force to replace the French in Rome as this should weaken the military defence of the kingdom, while Francis feared that his soldiers would be corrupted and demoralized by revolutionary agents.

Cavour threatened to recall Villamarina if a single Neapolitan soldier crossed the frontier. That settled the matter as far as Francis was concerned. 'I need to defend myself,' he told Brenier on March 7, 'against Piedmontese intrigues and secret agitations in my kingdom, especially in Sicily.' Hence the political arrests for which Brenier and Elliot had taken him to task. 'In Sicily,' he said, 'since the arrival of a certain Benso related to Cavour, the agitation has increased considerably, the word of command has been given, and they are working for annexation; in Naples the movement exists but it is weaker. However, when I saw an *august* personage, no, I am mistaken, he is not *august* but of high rank (the Count of Syracuse), taking ostensible part in these Piedmontese intrigues and encouraging them with his voice, I had to do something. Believe me, the King of Naples is not the happiest of mortals: you should be sorry for him, his situation is very difficult. The King of Naples had to check this movement, but he did not do so alone: he wished to assemble his council and obtain the written opinion of his ministers. With a few variants they formulated this conclusion: "It behoves the Ministers of Police in Sicily and in Naples to do their duty conforming to the law." Persons notorious for their bad intentions have therefore been arrested, and the King cannot intervene in a measure judged necessary to the tranquillity of his kingdom and perhaps to his own safety.'

Both Brenier and Elliot objected that this method of keeping order did not appear to conform to the law, and that the circumstances did not seem serious enough to warrant such exceptional measures, especially considering the names and positions of most of the people arrested.

The King retorted: 'You do not know everything; the facts have been concealed from you. What do you expect the King to do when his Minister of Police puts before his eyes the proofs of a permanent conspiracy against his authority and his dynasty? He must allow the ministers who are responsible to act.'

Unfortunately the ministers were not entirely responsible, said

Brenier. In a constitutional country they would be, but in Naples the King was saddled with the burden, and it was he that suffered from the discontent produced by his ministers. Brenier offered to protect him from the effects of this discontent. Whereas the late King had been able to indulge in ruthless repression with impunity, times had changed: people were less docile, less prone to submit to arbitrary methods. As he had remarked before, very little would suffice to satisfy the country, which was attached to the principles of monarchy. Why then proceed with arbitrary measures which created enemies where none had previously existed?

'First of all I must make my authority felt since they refuse to recognize it', the King told him. 'It is possible that my Minister of Police has behaved somewhat roughly but that is his nature and I did not choose him in any case. Had there been any hope of these gentlemen repenting they might have been admonished, but it would have been quite useless.'

Brenier said he thought the King's authority lost more than it gained from the methods of his Police Minister; his very best friends deplored this state of affairs. Having given this minister absolute powers His Majesty should suppress them and perhaps him, cancel the instructions authorizing him to act despotically, and publish an amnesty followed by reforms.

Francis repeated that the most urgent necessity was to restrain those who wished to create disorder and frighten those who were plotting against the dynasty.[1]

The Neapolitan government's show of force and resolution would deserve no reproach if it were justified by imminent danger, explained Brenier to Thouvenel. What made it inexcusable in his eyes was that it happened to be a mere parade of vigour addressed indirectly to the Princes of the royal family who wanted to stir up a little *fronde* against the King. Yet he observed in the same letter that a spark would suffice to kindle a revolution in Sicily, while the Neapolitans 'were expecting, as usual, a signal from abroad'.

Elliot's report of his interview with the King, dated March 8, is an interesting appendix to Brenier's: 'I represented that a Sovereign must either secure the love and confidence of his subjects or rule them by fear and intimidation, "by which last system," interrupted the King,

[1] Maraldi, *op. cit.*, pp. 111–116.

"he will not go on very long." I agreed with His Majesty and added that I begged he would not be offended with my plain speaking if I told him openly that during the last few days he had lost immensely of his hold over the affections of his subjects.

'I told him that it was everywhere known that he worked indefatigably at public business, and that credit was given him for entertaining a sincere desire for the welfare of his people, but that it was now universally believed that he had put himself absolutely into the hands of the Director of Police, who had induced His Majesty to enter upon a system which was already alienating from him the affection of his subjects, and which would forfeit for him the sympathy of every government in Europe.

'The King listened to me without apparent impatience and said he was quite willing to admit the truth of most of the arguments which I had used, and that nothing could be more repugnant to his own feelings than the adoption of measures "à la Turc", as he designated those against which I had been raising my voice.

'That a Sovereign, however, was placed in the cruel position of having to decide whether it was best to resort to means which can only be defended upon the ground of necessity or to leave events to take their course till some act shall have been committed which would justify him in the eyes of all the world in the adoption of the most rigorous measures of repression.

'In this latter case, though he might have the satisfaction of knowing that he would not be blamed by the world, would his conscience be free from the reproach of not having prevented disorder and consequent suffering by the application of a timely severity, even though it might not be sanctioned by the ordinary law?

'The arrests and banishments which had taken place, he had only consented to on the unanimous advice of his Council and upon the conviction that the circumstances were such as to call imperiously for them.

'When the water, he said, comes up to a man's neck he was justified in taking measures to escape from drowning which would not be allowable if the water had only reached his knees,—and in this case he considered that the water had reached his neck; but His Majesty did not inform me of the precise nature of the danger which he apprehended.'

423

Between the background intrigues of his family and those of the Piedmontese party, between his suspicions of Napoleon III, his fears of British aims in Sicily, and the advancing tide of unitarian ideas, swollen by that class which owed its wealth to the Bourbons' destruction of feudalism, Francis was indeed not the happiest of mortals. The propaganda against his dynasty was whetted by mockery, and it was easy enough to disparage this unprepossessing young man. His great-grandfather had been nicknamed *Nasone* (Big Nose), his father *Bomba*, and he was dubbed with the diminutive *Bombino* and alternatively *Franceschiello*, which sounded both pathetic and absurd.

Francis II and Maria Sophia
at Gaeta

XXII

THE resignation of General Filangieri, the absentee Prime Minister, was finally accepted on March 16, 1860, and an even older man, the octogenarian Prince of Cassaro, was prevailed upon to form a new ministry. A mild liberal of greater integrity than parts, Cassaro had vegetated in rural retirement during the last twenty years, ever since he had incurred blame for British leanings in the sulphur fracas. Having long lost touch with younger generations, he could only appoint fellow veterans who despite their noble intentions, lacked the requisite stamina to support the distracted young King with a dynamic programme. General Winspeare, the new Minister of War, was a tottering patriarch of eighty-two. But the King's ministers were not his only counsellors. A circle of reactionary diehards, nicknamed 'the strategists' by Filangieri, surrounded the embittered Queen Dowager and waged guerrilla warfare against any suggested change. The most dogged of these, Alessandro Nunziante, whose whole family owed its rise of fortune to the Bourbons, was to desert the sinking ship, but others, like the Duke of Sangro, remained loyal to the end, steadfast despite their intellectual limitations. Cassaro's cabinet was never strong enough to counterbalance this Court camarilla.

Napoleon III continued to urge Francis to invade Papal territory and occupy Rome, adding vague promises of protection against foreign aggression, but Francis was convinced that any intervention providing Piedmont with a *casus belli* would be calamitous at this juncture. Besides, he had little reason to trust a Bonaparte. As Elliot observed: 'The persons here who would gladly see the present dynasty make way for a French Prince have long been hoping anxiously that the King might be induced to take up a position which, by bringing him into collision with Sardinia, could precipitate his ruin; it is therefore calculated to give rise to very grave reflections.' In spite of French manœuvres and intrigues there was no question of Naples forming an offensive alliance with the Pope and Austria: this was merely a Cavourian pretext.

On March 30 Cavour wrote to Villamarina, his minister at Naples: 'Evidently events of great importance are preparing in the south of Italy. . . . You know that I do not desire to push the Neapolitan question to a premature crisis. On the contrary, I think it would be to our interest if the present state of things continued for some years longer. But . . . I believe that we shall soon be forced to form a plan which I would like to have had more time to mature.' Villamarina showed this letter to Elliot, who remarked that it 'appears to imply that the ambition of Sardinia or of Count Cavour is by no means permanently satisfied by the late acquisitions to the kingdom of Victor Emmanuel'. To Cavour Villamarina answered that King Francis had the army on his side and that the government was still very strong 'for the purpose of keeping down the people'.

At the same time Maniscalco, the efficient Police Minister in Palermo, warned Francis that there was a recrudescence of revolutionary fever on the island. The agents of Mazzini and Cavour had long been proselytizing the Sicilians. 'What are you waiting for?' Mazzini challenged them on March 2. 'Dare, and you will be followed. But dare in the name of National Unity . . . Garibaldi is bound to come to your assistance.' A month later the revolutionary committee of Palermo dared. The opulent Baron Riso on one side and the plumber Francesco Riso on the other were the leaders of the famous revolt which broke out at the Gancia convent on April 4 and cleared the way for Garibaldi's coming.

The Baron provided his plumber namesake with bombs and other weapons, but Maniscalco having got wind of the plot as usual, there was a brisk exchange of shots between Riso's gang and the police patrols. The rebels took refuge in the convent, where they were captured together with their monkish confederates. Other parties of insurgents were intercepted and at first it looked as if the plot had miscarried, for the people failed to rise simultaneously. General Salzano, the military governor, declared a state of siege in Palermo and ordered the citizens to surrender their arms. While the revolt was quelled in the capital it flickered throughout the vicinity. Small bands of peasants, brigands and desperadoes, known as the *squadre*, continued to fire spasmodically night after night in the suburbs, as if to keep the people's nerves on edge. On April 7 six prominent members of the revolutionary committee, including Baron Riso, were arrested and locked up in the fortress of Castellammare: each was allowed ninety ducats a month to alleviate the discomforts which only proved temporary yet conferred a histrionic halo of martyrdom. Well-organized mass demonstrations followed, with cheers for Victor Emmanuel soaring from the centre of the city. As a deterrent, thirteen of the rebels caught with arms at the Gancia convent were sentenced to be shot, an act which inflamed the liberal press all over Europe against the hapless Francis. Skirmishes with various *squadre* near Palermo continued till April 18 when they were severely routed at Carini, a small town about eighteen miles from the capital. But Mazzini's Sicilian colleague Rosolino Pilo had landed near Messina on April 10 to kindle the dying embers of the insurrection. In village after village on the way to Palermo he preached the gospel of National Unity and announced Garibaldi's coming as a certainty before Garibaldi himself had made up his mind. The effect was electrifying. Under Pilo's fervid leadership the *squadre* remustered and camped on the hither side of Monreale above the capital, watching and waiting for the advent of their Messiah.

False reports of successes against the royal troops had reached Messina, whence vice-consul Rickards wrote on April 8 that political agitation had become alarming. 'Thousands of people of all classes assembled in Strada Ferdinanda, and a collision with the troops appeared inevitable; it was however resolved to maintain order, not to interfere with the soldiers, and to massacre the police that patrolled the street if not immediately recalled. . . . In the meantime rumours were spread that in case of a rebellion the General would bombard the town and the soldiers pillage the houses; the pacific portion of the inhabitants, as if seized with panic, rushed into the country, carrying their moveables, etc., with them.' Whereupon Commander Marryat, H.M.S. *Intrepid*, M. Boulard, the French vice-consul, and Rickards went to the Governor, who emphatically denied the rumour. The forts, if attacked, would only fire on the attackers. Next day there was another mass gathering on the Strada Ferdinanda. Strong patrols ordered the mob to disperse in vain, and at 6.30 p.m. 'fired volleys of musketry in every direction' for about fifteen minutes, but Rickards was unable to ascertain the number of casualties. British travellers could not leave for the Continent and business was paralysed. Though the custom-house had reopened, wrote Rickards on April 11, 'it is scarcely safe to be moving about out of doors in the midst of an infatuated mass of raw recruits, few of whom have ever had a musket in their hands before this day week. So much for happiness and contentment in Sicily.'

Elliot reported from Naples on April 12 that the members of the government whom he had questioned professed such entire ignorance of what was happening in the island as to render it hopeless to expect information from that quarter. Perhaps this was because the King had 'been taught to believe that Her Majesty's Government occasionally turn a longing eye to Sicily'. Reinforcements were being despatched. 'There can be no doubt,' he added, 'that even though the outbreak may have apparently been crushed, the universal and deep-seated discontent has ripened into a disposition to revolt which renders the situation highly critical.'

On April 3, the day before the outbreak in Palermo, the Count of Syracuse had sent his royal nephew a letter which was widely circulated in manuscript as well as in the clandestine press. 'The principle of Italian nationality,' proclaimed the King's uncle, 'having remained for centuries in the field of ideas, has now descended vigorously into that of action. To disregard this fact would be delirious blindness when we see others in Europe powerfully promoting it, others accepting it, and others enduring it as an extreme necessity of the times.' France and England, to neutralize each other, would upset the country and the throne; Austria could never recover her lost preponderance. There was only one outlet: to follow a national policy, form an alliance with Piedmont, and abandon that municipal isolation which exposed Naples not only to galling foreign pressure but even worse, to internal discord.

This letter was probably written by the Count's secretary Giuseppe Fiorelli, who slipped across the frontier and was forbidden to return. Though it created a sensation at home and abroad, it had no effect on Francis. Carafa told Elliot that he did not complain of the Count expressing his opinions to the King, but that a prince of the royal family should thus publicly announce himself as the leader of his opponents was a proceeding which he thought no one could approve. According to Elliot, the Count expected to receive his passport from the Director of Police at a moment's notice. 'I cannot however find that this expectation is based upon any good ground, and the Government will probably consider that His Royal Highness, who is married to a sister of the Prince of Savoy-Carignano, might be more dangerous if he were to establish himself in Piedmont as the Chief of the Neapolitan Emigration than he will be if he continues to reside at Naples.'

A meeting of Neapolitan exiles was held at Turin on April 7 under the aegis of Poerio and La Farina, and all save four voted for the union of the Two Sicilies with Piedmont. The National Society raised a subscription to aid the Sicilian insurrection, and the Neapolitan exiles also sent Cavour a printed address of solidarity with Victor Emmanuel. Cavour had already thought of sending General Ribotti, who had led a brigade of Sicilian rebels in 1848, with an expedition to the island. While the Piedmontese War Minister, General Fanti, was negotiating with Ribotti on his behalf Victor Emmanuel was 'holding out the hand of friendship', as some historians express it, to his 'dear Cousin' of Naples. This offer of cordial alliance, approved by Cavour, was in fact but a thinly disguised ultimatum which he must have imagined that Francis would reject. It has often been regarded as a proof of Victor Emmanuel's sincerity, and as such is worth quoting once more. Its plausibility should be weighed against the writer's knowledge of Garibaldi's preparations: 'Italy can be divided into two powerful States of the North and the South which, if they adopt the same national policy, may uphold the great idea of our times—National Independence. But in order to realize this conception, it is, I think, necessary that your Majesty abandon the course you have held hitherto. The principle of dualism, if it is well established and honestly pursued, can still be accepted by Italians. But if you allow some months to pass without attending to my friendly suggestion, your Majesty will perhaps experience the bitterness of the terrible words—*too late.*'

At the same time Elliot, who shared the Unitarian sympathies of Sir James Hudson, the British minister at Turin, was discussing the Sicilian rising with Carafa. 'I said that it was very possible,' he reported on April 16, 'that the revolutionary committees of Genoa or Leghorn might be mixed up in the present movement, but unless he was in possession of very strong evidence I should hesitate to believe that the Sardinian Government were trying to excite revolution.' (They were too busy consolidating their recent gains for 'fresh complications'; whereas the revolutionary committees of exiles from Naples and Sicily were burning for the opportunity of being revenged upon the government from whose summary acts they were suffering.) 'M. Carafa solemnly affirmed that he was in possession of ample proof that the Sardinian Government were directly, and the French Government indirectly, the instigators of the present movement.' According to the French press the movement had been instigated by the British. Napoleon III said that if England occupied any part of the island there would be war, and France would annex Belgium.

In spite of Villamarina's denials both Elliot and Brenier were aware that Garibaldi's expedition was being organized with the unofficial backing of King Victor Emmanuel. There had been several premature reports of its departure during the last fortnight, so that when the news of the embarkation of the Thousand reached Naples on May 6 it was less astounding than to the rest of Europe. Elliot wrote on May 9: 'If General Garibaldi should succeed in effecting a landing with any considerable body of followers and with a supply of arms . . . the insurrection will again break out with a vigour which the universal exasperation may render extremely formidable to the Royal Cause.'

The Thousand and One Nights Tales of Garibaldi and his Thousand have been told and retold: how they gathered in a suburb of Genoa, seized the two steamers *Piemonte* and *Lombardo*, and set out on May 5 to conquer Sicily. And the Genoese authorities, subjects of King Victor Emmanuel, who had not declared war on his 'dear Cousin' of Naples, had witnessed their preparations and let them go. Thanks to what Berenson called G. M. Trevelyan's '*chanson de geste* about the paladin Garibold', English readers are almost as familiar as Italian with these exploits.

The Sicilian insurrection could not have been renewed with any success but for the arrival of the adventurous paladin, legendary even during his lifetime. D'Azeglio said he had the brains of an ox, but he was an inspired leader of irregulars. Apart from the hero-worship he battened on, his bravery and personal magnetism raised him above the other demigods of the Risorgimento. He was the popular figurehead of the movement launched by Mazzini and managed by Cavour, but he was as impulsive and capricious as a *prima donna*. Here was romance personified. His appeal to the Victorian imagination was equivalent to that of a grand opera buccaneer or Scandinavian Viking, fighting as he pleased and when he pleased for the exhilaration of fighting, except that an independent and united Italy was the object of his life. The Thousand conjured memories of the Argonauts. They were drawn chiefly from North Italy, for the most part students and members of the legal and medical professions.

By contrast Francis II seemed sadly prosaic. Hostile propaganda portrayed him as the fatuous heir and ape of the dreadful ogre 'Bomba'. He possessed no magnetism, and if he had any heroic qualities they were invisible. To most foreign observers both he and his dynasty appeared to be doomed. His lovely young Queen was pitied and admired, but all her Bavarian charm and high spirits could not counteract the glamour of the bearded *Condottiere* in the scarlet shirt. Heroics were to win the day—coupled with unscrupulous statesmanship. 'If we had done for ourselves the things which we are doing for Italy,we should be great rogues', as Cavour remarked in private conversation.

Only on May 1 Carafa as the King's mouthpiece had aired his views on Sicily to Brenier. He believed that the malcontents would never be satisfied until their independence was proclaimed: they would revolt against any power that was not exclusively Sicilian. The annexationist idea had become the rage, but it was the ephemeral result of a national effervescence whose sole aim was to divide the Two Sicilies. The islanders were so vain and volatile, so attached to monarchical forms and aristocratic memories, that if the King were to cross over as he had intended to before the insurrection, if he were to hold a Court and public receptions, royalty would soon recover its former prestige and influence on popular sentiment. The King was planning to reside in Palermo for two months in the year and appoint one of the royal princes Viceroy, but the choice was extremely embarrassing. The

Count of Syracuse had become impossible; the Count of Aquila was not sufficiently reliable; the King's younger brother Count Trani was unsuitable for other reasons (of inordinate ambition); the King's other brothers were far too young; his uncle the Count of Trapani lacked the ability: hence this important question was practically insoluble. The King would probably go to Palermo as soon as the excitement caused by recent events had died down. Carafa felt sure that this voyage would convert the disaffected. But it was already too late.

The Neapolitan cruisers which were to guard the island against invasion proved as unequal to their task as the Neapolitan generals. Everything was to favour Garibaldi and foil the unfortunate Francis. Assured by some Englishmen who had sailed from Marsala that there were no Neapolitan ships in the port, he steered straight for that destination, which owed its development to the colony of English wine merchants, established since the days of Nelson. The Englishmen lived behind lofty walls, hoisting the Union Jack in time of crisis. Only recently a punitive force under General Letizia had restored order in the town after the destruction of the Bourbon arms, but it had just been recalled to Palermo: thus the coast was left clear for Garibaldi's landing. 'This was,' as Trevelyan wrote,[1] 'the first of the series of fatal military mistakes by which the Governor Castelcicala and his successors succeeded in losing the island to an armament ludicrously inferior to their own.'

General Letizia having disarmed the British colony, two warships from the squadron at Palermo had been detailed for their protection, H.M.S. *Argus* and *Intrepid*, which arrived at Marsala three hours before the *Piemonte* and *Lombardo* steamed in between one-thirty and two p.m. The *Piemonte*, Garibaldi's ship, anchored inside the mole among a flotilla of English merchant vessels, while the *Lombardo* grounded on shallows near the lighthouse. By dint of threats and cajolery hundreds of little boats helped the Thousand to disembark. As an English eye-witness wrote to *The Times*, May 25, 1860: 'The landing was effected in gallant style, and with most extraordinary celerity and order.'

By the time the Neapolitan ship *Stromboli* steamed up all the passengers of the *Piemonte* had disembarked, but there were still a considerable number on board the grounded *Lombardo*, which might have

[1] *Garibaldi and the Thousand*, p. 232.

been sunk. The captain of the *Stromboli* finding the *Argus* and *Intrepid* beside the Piedmontese steamers, concluded that they were supporting the invaders: from a distance the red uniforms of the Garibaldini appeared to be English. More English than Neapolitan warships had been cruising round the island, and suspicions of their hostile intentions seemed now to be confirmed. Yet no war had been declared, and Captain Acton of the *Stromboli*, a great nephew of the powerful minister Sir John, was painfully perplexed. There can be no doubt that the presence of the *Argus* and *Intrepid* partially paralysed the Neapolitan commander; and Garibaldi was to appreciate this fact in his *Memoirs*. Captain Winnington-Ingram, of the *Argus*, has left an account as artless as it is convincing of this pregnant incident:

'May 11th—Anchored off Marsala in 9 fathoms and about two miles distant from the town. *Intrepid* (Commander Marryat) anchors inshore of us. About 11 a.m. I landed with Commander Marryat, and we both called on our Consul, Mr Cousins, and Mr Harvey (manager of Mr Woodhouse's wine establishment), to obtain information respecting the present political state of the country around Marsala so that Commander Marryat might convey the latest news that evening to our Admiral at Malta. Whilst conversing with Mr Edwards (Mr Harvey's assistant) two Sardinian merchant steamers were reported to be coming in from seaward full of armed men. They steamed round the *Intrepid*, and then pushed on for the Mole. One of them got safely into the inner harbour, but the other grounded at its entrance. Shore boats came off to the latter vessel, and she commenced disembarking a number of red-shirted men, and landing them near the lighthouse at the end of the Mole. A Neapolitan war steamer and a sailing frigate were in sight to the eastward. The former, with signals flying, was rapidly closing with the Sardinian. It was a critical moment, and we asked each other's opinion as to whether she should open fire upon that vessel before the men were clear of her, for, if so, we might witness a fearful slaughter under our very eyes, and at the same time stand a good chance of being ourselves struck by a ricochet shot. A doubt seemed to occupy the mind of the Neapolitan commander, for he brought his vessel to a standstill close to the *Intrepid*, and hailed that sloop to inquire if those were English soldiers landing. He of course received a reply in the negative, but was told that there were English officers ashore as well as the commanders of both English ships. Upon this, he requested that a message be sent to recall those officers, as he was about to open fire upon the parties landing from the steamers. In the meantime, the Sardinians were putting ashore men, stores and ammunition as fast as possible. The gunner of the *Intrepid* now joined us, bearing the Neapolitan commander's message, on which we despatched him at once to the town to warn our officers, and at the same time requested Vice-Consul Cousins to cause the British flag to be hoisted on all houses and wine stores appertaining to Englishmen in and around Marsala. Presently, a boat was seen to quit the Neapolitan war steamer and pull towards the grounded Sardinian. She had not, however, reached more than half way to the vessel, when a panic appeared to seize those in her, and a retreat was hastily made to their ship, which now opened fire upon the Mole with her heavy guns. Commander Marryat, Mr Cousins and myself embarked at once in a gig of the *Argus*, and proceeded on board the Neapolitan to beg her captain to direct his shot and shell clear of the British wine establishments. To our surprise we found that officer to bear the name of a fine old English Roman Catholic family, and to be complete master of our language. He is now (1883) Admiral Acton and Italian Minister of Marine. He seemed much impressed with the responsibility of his situation, but promised not to injure British property, pointing out to us that his guns were laid for the Mole only, and along which the red shirts were seen making their way for the town as fast as encumbrances would permit them. We now left him, and were pulling for the *Intrepid*, when the Neapolitan sailing frigate came bearing down upon our boat, and her officers hailed and waved to us to pull faster. Hardly had they done so when a veritable storm of shot and missiles of all kinds, delivered from her broadside guns, passed over our heads, but fell short of the Mole. One of her shot, however, entered Mr Woodhouse's wine establishment, and nearly killed Mrs Harvey, the manager's wife. The next vessel to arrive upon the scene was the *Capri*, a hired armed steamer in the service of the King of Naples. She commenced firing but we could not trace the course of her shot. An officer from her went on board the *Intrepid*, with the cool request that one of the latter's boats should go to the Sardinian steamers and demand their surrender. He received a very decided negative reply. I now returned to the *Argus* and shifted her anchorage nearer the wine-stores for their better protection. The Sardinian steamers being completely deserted, the Neapolitans sent in armed boats to take possession of them. They succeeded in bringing out the one that had entered the inner harbour, but scuttled the other that had grounded at its entrance. The Neapolitan steamers continued, during this operation, to fire heavily at parties dragging guns and ammunition into the town, but we only saw one man knocked over. The patriots stood fire splendidly, and appeared to be altogether a fine body of men. Hostilities ceased at sunset.'[1]

Hostilities had not ceased: they had scarcely begun. Prompted by Francesco Crispi, who had become Garibaldi's political organizer, the municipal council of Marsala signed a statement that the Bourbon dynasty had ceased to reign in Sicily, and offered the dictatorship on behalf of Victor Emmanuel to the patriot from Nice, who accepted it without demur. The islanders were well disposed, but disappointingly few of them showed the fighting spirit he had expected. The Dictator's first decree proclaiming a general conscription for Sicily was still-born. The disestablished dynasty had known better. The *squadre* increased, however, owing to adroit propaganda: irregular irregulars and volunteers, they would not feel cramped by dismal discipline.

It was the northerners who bore the brunt of conflict against the regular troops at Calatafimi. Most of the generals who opposed Garibaldi were in their dotage and behaved accordingly. Sicily was held by some 23,000 Neapolitan troops, yet Castelcicala wired frantically to Naples for more as soon as he heard of Garibaldi's landing. When these arrived they joined the main force at Palermo instead of chasing the invaders. General Landi, antique at seventy, puffed and panted after his battalion in a heavy carriage, taking six days to cover thirty miles. Though he was strengthened by two extra battalions, he loitered nervously at Calatafimi, a town of eight thousand inhabitants on a slope between two hills near the ruins of Segesta, exhausting his soldiers with futile marches about the rugged countryside to impress the foe, while Garibaldi was resting his Thousand at Salemi, eight miles further south, and proclaiming himself Dictator again with suitable pomp. From now on the balcony played as important a rôle in his wooing of the population as in *Romeo and Juliet*. Following his example, dictators and balconies were to become almost inseparable.

Garibaldi's mood was very different from that of the doddering Landi. Fortified by a cup of coffee at about three o'clock in the morn-

[1] Rear-Admiral H. F. Winnington-Ingram, *Hearts of Oak*. London, 1889.

ing of May 15, such was his elation before going to battle that, as Trevelyan felicitously phrased it, he 'sang like a lover going to meet his mistress'. It were invidious to compete with Trevelyan's lyrical description of this battle, in which the Neapolitans fought bravely against their fanatical assailants. At one moment even the intrepid Bixio thought of retreating. 'Here we make Italy or die', said Garibaldi. Then the Neapolitans, who seemed on the verge of victory, ran out of ammunition, and instead of supporting and encouraging their resistance Landi bewildered them with orders to retreat, thereby challenging the Garibaldini to charge them with might and main. Their retreat proved a cumulative defeat in the sense that it led to a rapid series of disasters. Landi gave up the struggle, and found specious excuses for his incompetence while dragging his demoralized army back to Palermo. Garibaldi's first victory on this mythopoetic island was decisive in its results. A fortnight later, on May 27, he was established in the heart of Palermo.

The Neapolitans felt they had been basely betrayed by General Landi. King Francis was equally ill-served by most of his generals, who thought more of their emoluments than their duties. His protest against Piedmont through diplomatic channels for what Brenier called 'this act of indiscreet dexterity' fell on deaf and indifferent ears. 'One can already perceive a secret connivance between the Sicilian insurgents and the British navy, with Sicily lost and the throne threatened in consequence', wrote the French envoy, but the connivance, which Elliot denied, had been fortuitous, just another stroke of luck. The large number of English ships in Sicilian waters—lately they seemed to have increased—struck the suspicious Frenchman as 'a token of the protectorate, at least moral, which England would like to impose on the settlement of this serious affair'.

On May 14 the King had summoned that reputed *deus ex machina* Filangieri from the uplands of Sorrento to a stuffy Council of State, and pleaded with him to make one last effort to save Sicily for the throne. The proud veteran persisted in his refusal on the score of his age and infirmities, but he made it clear that the present crisis was due to the rejection of his advice. And he now proceeded to give the worst advice possible by recommending as his *alter ego* General Lanza, a septuagenarian Sicilian who had once been his Chief of Staff, when he had created much amusement by falling from his horse in farcical style on a spectacular state occasion. Furthermore Filangieri proposed a plan which only helped to addle this *alter ego's* far from lucid intellect. This was to evacuate Palermo while keeping a garrison in the contiguous fortress of Castellamare, and concentrate the bulk of his troops at Messina and Girgenti, marching back to the capital when the tide had turned in his favour. The King and the majority of the Council wished to hold Palermo at all costs, and from there send forces to attack the invaders. Lanza vacillated between these plans. His conciliatory proclamation promising moral and material reforms and a free pardon in the King's name to all those misguided subjects who made a prompt act of submission met with no response. He was instantly affected by the panicky atmosphere of Palermo, and his reports to the King were calculated to induce the utmost alarm and despondency. On May 18 the King sent General Nunziante to urge him to take the offensive against Garibaldi, but he preferred to wait passively in the capital. As a sop he sent 3000 troops under the Swiss Colonel Von Mechel and Major Bosco, both gallant commanders, to strengthen the garrison of Monreale. These fell upon the foe with vigour, and they might have done for him had not Garibaldi outwitted them with a clever stratagem, by making them suppose that he was retreating to Corleone and the interior of the island. While Von Mechel was led astray by a detachment of Garibaldini, the main body had given him the slip under cover of darkness and doubled back towards the capital, where Lanza had been lulled into false security.

Three British naval officers who had driven along the coast from Palermo to Misilmeri on May 26 were amazed to hear that Garibaldi was dining in a neighbouring vineyard, and were thrilled when the general sent a messenger inviting them to visit his headquarters. The suavest of ambassadors could not have charmed them more than this red-shirted warrior chief with the beautiful beard who spoke their own language and said such nice things about England. He offered them fresh strawberries and said he hoped to meet their Admiral very soon; he had particularly enjoyed 'the splendid effect produced by the royal salutes from all the ships of war in honour of Her Majesty's birthday'. The young Englishmen drank his health and that of Italy. Two American officers also paid him a visit, and one presented him with a revolver. Then came *The Times* correspondent Colonel Eber, who happened to be Hungarian, bringing detailed information about the

Neapolitan defences. Thanks to his correct estimate Garibaldi decided to force an entrance into Palermo by the Termini gate which was the least strongly guarded.

Lanza's behaviour during this crucial period remains inexplicable though many Sicilians are prone to fits of lethargy. Time and again he received warning of the enemy's approach, but he appeared to be convinced that the 'filibusters' were retiring in bedraggled rout from Corleone. Scouts told him of the red-shirts advancing from Gibilrossa; the Police Minister Maniscalco and several trustworthy officers urged him to take extra precautions, as a rising had been arranged by the liberals for the morrow. He had but one parrot answer: '*Bombarderò*—I will bombard!'

On May 27, true to his public announcement, Garibaldi galloped up to the so-called Termini gate, which was really a high barricade, and as soon as it was demolished by Bixio's company he rode through the rubble down the street that now bears his name. He rode on to the Fiera Vecchia, or 'old market', where the revolution had started in 1848. From this strategic centre the 160,000 inhabitants were roused to the support of their invaders, while Lanza, who had ample forces to check the rising, did nothing but bombard the city from land and sea, bringing execration upon the name of his gentle sovereign. The invaders were the only ones to benefit from this barbarous policy, if policy it could be called. Captain Tommaso Cava of the Neapolitan General Staff, wrote in his spirited vindication of the army to which he belonged:[1] 'After two hours of bombardment, and several more of plunder and arson, General Lanza thought he had done enough, and became almost entirely inactive, while Garibaldi occupied all the points which he most required. On May 28, the next day, under the futile pretext of collecting and shipping his own wounded to Naples, Lanza asked Garibaldi for an armistice of twenty-four hours. He availed himself of the presence of an English Admiral in those waters to make this request, but as the Admiral replied that he could not intervene in negotiations between the Neapolitan General and Garibaldi and that he should treat with him directly for the armistice desired, Lanza retorted with affected dignity that a Commander-in-Chief of the King of the Two Sicilies could never so demean himself as to confer with a chief of brigands. On May 29, however, only

[1] *Difesa Nazionale Napolitana*, p. 87. Naples, 1863.

twenty-four hours later, Generals Letizia and Chrétien on behalf of General Lanza arranged with Garibaldi, dressed as a Piedmontese General on the English Admiral's flag-ship, an armistice which was to last until the dawn of May 31.'

Except for the royal palace and its purlieus, and the remoter Mint and Castellamare fortress, the capital had fallen to the rebels by mid-day on May 27. The royal troops outside the walls were cut off from the palace, where Lanza had foolishly concentrated 18,000 men, who were also cut off from supplies and communication with the fleet except by semaphore. The population kept up a pandemonium of bell-ringing and the rustic *squadre* could not help wasting precious ammuni-tion for the sheer delight of making plenty of noise. The women were ready with boiling water and every kind of missile to hurl at the Neapolitans, as in 1848. Effective barricades were set up in all the main streets under the guidance of a special committee, and the street fighting continued for three days with growing intensity until the royal palace was threatened.

When Lanza crawled down from his perch to negotiate with 'His Excellency General Garibaldi', the latter could well afford to stop firing since he was practically without ammunition. The difficulty was to conceal his tremendous relief from the Neapolitan officers who brought him Lanza's abject petition, sent in spite of the knowledge that Von Mechel's and Bosco's regiments had returned from Corleone and that he could have ordered a combined attack with these valuable reinforcements. To their rage and mortification, Von Mechel and Bosco were ordered to observe the treaty he was about to arrange. This was another heavy blow to the royal cause.

At the conference on board H.M.S. *Hannibal* on May 30 Admiral Mundy treated Lanza's delegates and Garibaldi with equal courtesy, though his partiality for the latter was obvious. He had been deeply shocked by the recent bombardment, which he called 'an eternal disgrace to a civilized government'. The Neapolitans had expected to draw up terms for an armistice with the English Admiral alone, and they objected to Garibaldi's presence as well as that of the French, American and Piedmontese commanding officers. But Mundy insisted that they must confer on equal terms: he was only there to protect British subjects and property and had no authority to act as mediator. After a peppery meeting an armistice until noon next day was signed, and Garibaldi gained an opportunity to procure the ammunition so desperately needed. More barricades were built to isolate Von Mechel, and the city was illuminated as if for victory.

At a council of war in the palace that evening Lanza seemed disposed to attack when the truce expired, but despairing reports induced him instead to ask Garibaldi for another three days' continuance of the armistice. Nothing loath, the Dictator consented, with the stipulation that he should appropriate the royal Mint, which contained over five millions of ducats. Whereupon General Letizia and Colonel Buonopane were sent to Naples to report on the armistice to the King and receive his instructions.

What Cavour himself had described on May 12 in a letter to Nigra as 'a crazy escapade' had been crowned with fabulous success. The whole of Europe was astounded. It was David and Goliath all over again, and the sympathy and admiration of the liberal majority went out to David and his sling, to Garibaldi's Thousand against the twenty-three thousand Neapolitans—for the contribution of the Sicilian people was almost overlooked. A Neapolitan maliciously remarked that not only was the leader of the insurrection a foreigner, meaning not a Sicilian, but that all his ablest officers were foreigners too; that in fact the Sicilians had the great merit of keeping quiet and allowing themselves to be liberated, but that here their merit began and ended. Yet the Sicilian people on the one side and Neapolitan ineptitude on the other had made that victory possible. All shades of public opinion, however confused, were blended in dislike of the old régime, with the vociferous intellectuals in the vanguard. Both in Naples and Sicily the notion of annexation and a single Italian kingdom had developed suddenly, as Elliot observed, but the uneducated masses knew little or nothing about this ideal: they hoped for a better chance to earn a decent living. In Sicily they also hoped to avenge their grievances and settle family feuds, and could therefore be roused more easily from their Oriental torpor. Garibaldi's triumph in Palermo seemed the direct interposition of Providence.

Foiled by the folly of his generals, King Francis hoped to be saved by the efforts of diplomacy. It is an extraordinary tribute to Filangieri's enduring prestige that in spite of his disastrous advice he still commanded an attention that was almost superstitious. At a Council of State on May 30 he urged Francis to make a personal appeal to Napoleon

III to guarantee the autonomy of his kingdom. After a tempestuous debate his proposal was approved; and at a subsequent meeting on June 1 there was a unanimous vote for French mediation; in the meantime a Constitution was to be prepared. 'I put myself into the Emperor's hands', said the King with resignation, since England refused to intervene and the other powers would do nothing.

'M. Carafa spoke with despondency of the prospect of affairs,' reported Elliot, 'and said almost with bitterness that the Neapolitan Government had from all sides received assurance of the good wishes of the other Powers but that not one seemed disposed to stretch out a helping hand in the hour of danger.' When Carafa introduced the subject of an appeal to the Courts of Europe at an assembly of the heads of all the foreign missions in Naples, Elliot felt it his duty to protest. 'We (the French, Spanish and British ministers) were said to have intimated our belief that our respective Governments would not "admit" of any changes in the Dynasty or disposition of the Kingdom of Naples.... No such intimation nor anything resembling or approaching to it had ever passed my lips.' Elliot had merely said that the British Government wished well for the stability and prosperity of Naples, which was a very different matter. As for Sicily, he found nobody, however attached to the royal cause, who believed that the King's authority would again be re-established in the island upon its former footing.

His own solutions to this question were: '1. The constitution of Sicily into an independent kingdom under the same sovereign as the kingdom of Naples. 2. The erection of Sicily into an independent kingdom under a sovereign chosen from the royal family of Naples. 3. The erection of Sicily into an independent kingdom under any sovereign of their choice. 4. The annexation of the island to Sardinia.' He considered it too late for the first three, 'and the enthusiasm which Garibaldi has excited renders it almost certain that the annexation will be pronounced by acclamation, if events are permitted to take their natural course. That the annexation of Sicily will be followed by a revolution in Naples is a conjecture that may safely be made.' And the annexation of Naples was bound to result. Were the Great Powers, he demanded, prepared to assent to the formation of a single great Italian State? If so, why interfere?

General Letizia and Colonel Buonopane arrived from Palermo in the midst of these discussions. Their pessimistic account of the whole population in revolt and of the army, so cut off from the possibility of receiving either supplies or assistance that their capture by Garibaldi appeared inevitable, made the King decide to capitulate. The greatest horror of the bombardment of his subjects had been expressed by England and France, and he had no desire to exacerbate it. 'For my part,' wrote Elliot, 'I remarked that whatever horror the measure must inspire, Garibaldi had no interest in its discontinuance, for he must be well aware that every shell fired on the town from a Neapolitan gun diminished the chance of the two countries being again re-united.' The generals on the spot had suspended hostilities, and the responsibility was theirs.

XXIII

D IPLOMACY could not keep pace with the whirl of events. On June 6 General Letizia and Colonel Buonopane signed a capitulation with Garibaldi whereby some 20,000 Neapolitan troops were to evacuate Palermo. These were marched to provisional quarters in the suburbs and shipped back to Naples whenever sufficient transport could be found for them between June 8 and 19. Though they were to depart with 'the honours of war,' with their equipment, stores, artillery, horses and baggage, while the Dictator took over the forts, barracks and military establishments after an exchange of prisoners, not a few of them wept for shame as they filed off in a seemingly endless column before grinning groups of their red-shirted victors. They could not understand their humiliating defeat: had they not been betrayed by their commanders?

Old General Lanza looked as self-satisfied as if he had won a campaign. At a final parade, like a flamboyant mockery of militarism, one miserable soldier stepped from the ranks and shouted to the General in hoarse resentment: 'Look, Your Excellency! Just see how many we are! Must we really leave like this?' 'Be off, you drunken sot!' the General replied. He had been composing a long letter of self-pitying justification to the King, enumerating his bygone services, of which the less said the better. He blamed Von Mechel for letting Garibaldi slip through his fingers, but failed to mention the 18,000 troops he had kept pent up in the royal palace with nothing to do. He spoke of the useless bombardment—useless indeed without any synchronizing attack. He stated untruly that Von Mechel had arrived after the armistice, and blamed Letizia and Buonopane for having prolonged it, but he had signed the armistice himself and surrendered the Mint with five millions of ducats (equivalent to twenty-two millions of *lire* pre-war value). He said he was poisoned with grief and regret and longed for death, but he did not attempt to die fighting for his king and country. He accused Letizia and Buonopane of appearing on the scene at the last moment to deprive him of the credit for the capitulation. Yes, he would die of sorrow, he concluded; but he was to marry again, in spite of his advanced age, and survive the disaster another five years. He sailed back to Naples with his staff on June 20, but by the King's orders he had to land at Ischia, where a council of generals was to inquire into his conduct. The avalanche of calamities for which he was largely responsible saved him from a court-martial.

While the Neapolitan troops ebbed from Palermo fresh reinforcements arrived almost daily for Garibaldi. More than 20,000 volunteers embarked from Genoa and Leghorn within the next three months. The tricolour flag was flown from the Castellamare fort, soon demolished with pickaxe and spade by the local population. Baron Riso and his fellow hostages were released and carried like heroes through the capital, while the Dictator settled in the royal palace.

Admiral Mundy and the other foreign witnesses of the evacuation, were full of enthusiasm for Garibaldi. That so many had been defeated by so few seemed to prove that the Lord was on the side of the few. Even those who had disapproved of the invasion as an act of piracy contrary to the law of nations were converted to this belief, hypnotized by the hirsute image of the buccaneer of destiny.

If diplomacy trailed slowly behind events, it was usually in favour of the *fait accompli*, as poor Francis was soon to discover. 'When the King of Naples needs France, he will be able to count on me,' Napoleon III had told the Neapolitan envoy Antonini, whose sovereign had been the first to recognize the new Emperor of the French.

Antonini was bold enough to remind him of that promise, but the Emperor shrugged his shoulders. The King of Naples referred to then was dead and gone; his heir was of a very different kidney. Why rake up the past? Too much had happened since 1852.

The French Foreign Minister Thouvenel reflected his Emperor's change of attitude with malicious embellishments in his dispatches to Brenier. The Emperor, he wrote, was reluctant to accept a mediation which was offered him *in extremis*. The Neapolitan Government had got itself into one of those dilemmas which foreign counsel could not remedy. It was as difficult to persuade a sovereign to order his troops to lay down their arms and pay a huge subsidy to the rebels, as to urge him to transform one of his capitals into a heap of ruins. 'Between dishonour and barbarity it is not for us to choose. The option belongs by right to those who have placed themselves in this dismal alternative. . . .' Owing to the divergent opinions of the Powers a combined mediation was impracticable. A French mediation might not be accepted in Palermo and would probably provoke British countermeasures when it was essential to act in harmony with England if a conflict was to be avoided. This was not merely a matter of local insurrection: the adverse party to the King of Naples was the idea of Italian Unity. 'Even if we do not favour this idea, are we to combat it openly? How would this rôle suit us, and if we assumed it would not England find support in Turin and popular sentiment?' Such a policy would contradict that which the Emperor had followed in 1859, and would lead to an alliance with Austria. That Italy was about to make a dangerous use of the independence she owed to France was unhappily notorious, but was this a good reason to turn against her and refute his own actions?

Imagining that Piedmontese annexation of Sicily could neither please France nor England, the King was hoping to gain time. He understood the danger threatening him, wrote Brenier, but he thought it behoved his dignity not to admit it. He would leave the terms of mediation to the Emperor. These were telegraphed by Thouvenel on June 5: Sicilian Home Rule under a prince of the royal family of Naples, a Constitution for Palermo and Naples, and an alliance with Piedmont.

After seeing the King on June 7 Brenier felt sure that he would reject these terms, and that rather than lose Sicily he would try to recover it by force. The royal army would be concentrated at Messina, which would become the pivot of military operations as in 1848. If he agreed to the first item, said the King, England would soon seize the island, and how would France like that? The second item was acceptable if the union of the Two Sicilies could be maintained, but the third was impossible. The aggrandizement of Piedmont had not been recognized by the Powers, not even by France. Why should it be imposed on him? 'In the midst of this crisis which might be fatal to his dynasty the King remains calm. Sometimes he affects manners more than juvenile and a complete detachment from the Crown. He seems uninterested in retaining a power no longer based on the immutable foundations of the past, and only to perform his duty as a sovereign to satisfy his conscience, lest it be said that he surrendered without combat. He is in any case prepared for catastrophes. "There are so many sovereigns wandering about Europe that I'll go and keep them company," he remarked to M. Carafa. He does not even hide from certain members of the diplomatic corps that he thinks his reign will soon be over.'

At the same time Carafa told Elliot that the Neapolitan Government would gladly accept British mediation 'upon almost any terms which should seem to offer a security for the continental dominions of the King,' to which Elliot retorted that Great Britain had no intention to interfere over Sicily. 'His Excellency replied that the King would lose his throne rather than consent to negotiate with Garibaldi on the independence of Sicily, but that the case would be widely different if His Majesty was negotiating with other Powers. I said that this sounded to me rather like a suggestion that His Majesty's honour would be saved by an appearance of having given way before the superior force of a Great Power, and was therefore not likely to find favour with Her Majesty's Government.'

Cavaliere de Martino's mission to Paris with an urgent autograph letter from the King to the Emperor deprived him of his last illusions. 'Let us hear what lies the two Neapolitan envoys will be telling the Emperor,' snapped Thouvenel audibly before De Martino and Antonini were received by Napoleon III, whose reply could be summed up in the words 'Too late.' He deplored recent events in Sicily and regretted that his 'disinterested advice' had been neglected, but France was in a quandary. The case of Naples differed from that of Rome, which was occupied by French troops and complicated by the

446

religious question. If Rome were attacked he would have to defend the Pope. But words could not check a revolution. The Italians were shrewd: they realized that having shed the blood of his soldiers for their national cause, he would never turn his guns against it. In consequence Tuscany had been annexed against his wishes and interests. The same might happen to Sicily.

The Neapolitan envoys argued that Napoleon's interests resembled theirs; that Sicily was in danger of becoming a British protectorate. But Napoleon was unmoved. Alliance with Piedmont, he insisted, was their only chance. 'Cavour is practical; he is aware of the risk of revolution. . . . He would like to move slowly and surely, whereas the revolution is leaping into the unknown. It is in Turin that you will have to act.' This was a mere repetition of his original proposals. He added for their benefit, however, that he would be delighted if the King could manage to defeat Garibaldi. In vain the Neapolitans pleaded that if the principle of non-intervention was to be maintained, Piedmont should be prevented from aiding and abetting the revolution, the source of which flowed directly from Turin.

The busy Brenier had been nagging at the King all this while to grant a Constitution, and Elliot complained of 'the extreme mystery, to use no harsher word, which he thought it necessary to observe here.' According to the British envoy the government was in a state of almost hopeless impotence. 'At a time when every hour is of importance and when every day lost adds to the amount of sacrifice which will ultimately have to be made, there is not a sign of one step having been made to avert the catastrophe which the Court and the Government as well as the public believe to be approaching. . . . I asked (Carafa) whether in the event of France and England declining to come forward at all, I was to understand that the King was prepared to sit down and to allow himself passively to be swallowed up in the flood which we are told is approaching without making an effort to save himself. . . .'

Like Hamlet (as interpreted by Coleridge), Francis II had a 'lovely, pure and most moral nature, without the strength of nerve which forms a hero.' He was a Neapolitan version of the moody Dane, sunk in the silence of his fatalistic reflections. A hero would have led his army against Garibaldi. Francis relied on prayer, above and below.

In spite of the plethora of contrary evidence, he persisted in treating

447

Filangieri as his potential saviour. After Filangieri, he counted on his father's younger henchman General Alessandro Nunziante, who had already agreed to command an expedition against 'the filibusters'. He now sent Nunziante to the retired veteran with an urgent appeal to return to the helm of State. 'Too late!' quoth the wily old raven of Sorrento, 'much as I should like to repeat the miracle of Lazarus, I am only a wretched mortal.' Such was the effect of these words on Nunziante that he promptly began to trim his sail to the wind blowing from Piedmont. The veteran ex-viceroy, consciously or unconsciously, from ill-health or pique or general depression, had sown the seed of treachery in the most reactionary of Bourbon courtiers.

His last interview with the King was worthy of Pulcinella in an extempore Neapolitan farce. When Francis steamed across the bay in his yacht to make a final appeal to the soldier-statesman, he tottered hastily into bed fully dressed and with the languor of a very sick man received his royal visitor. Their conversation, which lasted more than an hour, has never been recorded. If Francis did not beg him to save Sicily for the throne in person, as some supposed, it is certain that he asked him to lead a constitutional government, and that Filangieri uttered the last of his long series of refusals, mitigated by some scraps of advice about the choice of ministers. But the veteran could scarcely conceal that he had abandoned hope. He was to leave Naples in August; and he did not return until Francis had left it too.

The King's appeals to Filangieri and Napoleon III had only borne bitter fruit, and there was nothing for it but to grant a Constitution. A Council of Ministers and members of the royal family met at Portici on June 21, and after a discussion of Napoleon's reply to the King, resolved to adopt his proposals. The majority voted for a Constitution, a general amnesty, a total change of ministry, an Italian alliance with Piedmont, and an Italian flag, red, white and green with the arms of the ruling dynasty in the centre. Filangieri was absent; so was the King, prostrated by anxiety and nightmare premonitions. Earlier in the month Odo Russell, the British representative in Rome, had written scoffingly to his anti-Bourbonist uncle Lord John: 'The other day the young King of Naples was seized with such a panic that he telegraphed five times in twenty-four hours for the Pope's blessing. Cardinal Antonelli, through whom the application had to be made, telegraphed the three last blessings without reference to his Holiness, saying that he was duly authorized to do so. The Convents are awfully scandalized at this proceeding.' Believers are less apt to smile at the King's natural request, exaggerated for the sake of a good story. One of the three who voted in Council against any concession was old General Carascosa, who said: 'I think the Constitution will be the quickest way to dethrone the dynasty.' This dictum was repeated to Francis and aggravated his doubts. His stepmother urged him to resist; his young wife, on the other hand, who knew little about politics but felt instinctively that the Queen Dowager must be wrong, was in favour of the experiment, while his uncle the Count of Aquila supported Brenier in pressing for this modern panacea, 'almost calling His Majesty out of bed,' as Elliot wrote in dudgeon at the 'undue desire for interference by the French Government.'

The King acquiesced in principle, but he required the Pope's sanction. Pius IX realized that concessions would have to be made, but objected to an alliance with Piedmont. Napoleon had made this last proposal to prevent the aggrandizement of Victor Emmanuel at the expense of Francis II, but it was grateful neither to Naples nor Turin. His conscience somewhat appeased, on June 25 Francis signed the Sovereign Act which revived the Constitution of 1848, embodied a general amnesty for political crimes committed previously, and the formation of a new ministry under Antonio Spinelli, who was both respected at Court, where he had close connections, and outside it, where he was considered a moderate liberal of impeccable integrity.

After telegraphing the news of the King's acceptance, Brenier wrote to Thouvenel on June 23: 'I have barely half an hour to give you a few details of my interview with the King. I found him vastly changed, nervous, overwhelmed with suffering and humiliation, but apparently quite sincerely disposed to enter largely into a new course of political conduct. His Majesty had sent me word by the Count of Aquila that he wished to see me to apprise me of his political programme. He told me at once that it was the Emperor's, except for one modification. There was not to be a *separation* under a *branch* of the family, but a separate Constitution with a Prince of the family as viceroy. The Constitution for Naples would more closely resemble Piedmontese institutions. As the word *alliance* with Piedmont seemed repugnant to the King I proposed to substitute a *concerted agreement* about common interests in Italy. The change of flag has been very afflicting, and the King seemed tortured on the rack while explaining the causes which had influenced his decision. He thinks it will be very unpopular with the army.

'"Poor soldiers," he said, "they are devoted and very indignant. They want to avenge their honour! Oh that Palermo, what a disgrace! Yes, I shall avenge my honour as a Neapolitan soldier, and even if I have to march against Venetia, I wish to recover my military honour. Austria has willed it: I shall fight against her for my honour." I assure you it was pathetic to see this young sovereign succumb to a concentrated despair, with tears in his eyes and his features contracted with pain and moral grief. "You were right to advise me to go to Palermo," he said, "for I should have succeeded in defeating the revolution or else been killed by a gun-shot. If the good Lord spares me I will not die without repairing this dishonour."'

On the eve of publishing the Sovereign Act Francis asked his intimate counsellor Father Borrelli: 'The Queen and her circle want me to give the Constitution. What do you think about it?' The priest answered that it would have been wiser to grant nothing, because the Constitution would only hasten the revolution. Francis nodded and pondered, then added: 'I cannot follow your ideas, although I think them very right.' 'Remember this day, Your Majesty, the 24th of June and the feast of Saint John the Baptist,' retorted Father Borrelli, 'perhaps the last day that I kiss the hand of the King of Naples.'

There is a remote possibility that a Constitution granted soon after the accession of Francis might have saved the dynasty. Granted after the fall of Palermo, it threw a spotlight on the King's despair. The parallel with Louis XVI of France was patent. The great majority of his loyal subjects were bewildered if not appalled. The well-drilled liberal and revolutionary committees had broadcast instructions to receive the announcement in contemptuous silence, and all shades of opinion were tinged with suspicion and distrust. Few citizens even read the proclamation. The ensuing calm was more ominous than hypocritical applause. In the afternoon of that day many shops were closed; the merchants hid their wares; whole families moved into the country; and many wrote 'French or English domicile' on their front doors.

Within an hour, as De Sivo put it, a few lines of print upset the peace and security of many years. In the provinces the Act was regarded with deeper consternation, as a harbinger of anarchy and a betrayal of religion. The annexationists were furious, for an alliance with Piedmont would overturn their brimming apple-cart. Carlo Poerio and the other Neapolitan exiles in Turin raised a reverberating hullabaloo. 'The Neapolitan Government,' thundered Poerio to a rapturous North Italian Chamber, 'has the tradition of perjury handed down from father to son. That is why it now offers to swear to the Constitution, because it is clear that in order to be perjured it is necessary first to swear. I trust that the Ministers of Victor Emmanuel will not stretch out their hands to the greatest enemy of Italian independence.' On the same day, June 29, Cavour telegraphed to Villamarina: 'Take care to render impossible an agreement between the King of Naples and the national party. We must not let Italy believe that by complaisance or weakness we are ready to fraternize with the King of Naples.'

Such counsel was superfluous. Villamarina was the pilot of the annexationist movement in Naples. Since he enjoyed all the privileges of diplomatic immunity, his legation had become the assembly shop of conspirators and Piedmontese agents, and the central post-office of seditious correspondence. Under the new Constitution many a Neapolitan exile rushed home with ample subsidies to launch anti dynastic newspapers, pamphlets and propaganda. While Piedmont was officially and technically on friendly terms with Francis II, Cavour was straining every nerve to stir up revolution in his kingdom. He would pretend to give sympathetic consideration to the proposed alliance with Naples since it had been offered under French auspices and by French advice which he could not afford to reject with scorn.

No cordial ovation greeted the King and Queen when they drove through the capital in an open carriage. Though guns from the ships in the bay saluted the tricolour hoisted on the forts, though the public buildings were brightly illuminated, there was no public rejoicing. Only the King's enemies rejoiced in their hearts. The whole city was unnaturally calm until the evening of June 27 when riots broke out with sudden violence.

The new prefect of police Liborio Romano had made a pact with the formidable secret league of criminals known as the *camorra*, and this was their way of celebrating it. Hitherto persecuted and deported to various islands, the camorrists had many old scores to settle with the police. The annexationists had been lavish with free drinks in the taverns, especially in that of the harpy Marianna de Crescenzo, known as 'la Sangiovannara', which belched forth a mixed rabble of cut-throats, vagabonds, street-urchins and prostitutes into the Toledo. This mob marched with tricoloured banners and cockades, pistols and knives, lazzaroni of a more truculent progressive species, the new proletarian patriots, shouting raucous cheers for Garibaldi and Victor Emmanuel. The police who tried to control them were overpowered. Two police inspectors were murdered; others were badly wounded; their offices were sacked and destroyed.

It was already dark when the French minister drove towards the Toledo in a cheerful frame of mind owing to his success as the leading promoter of the Constitution. Undismayed by the bellowing crowd—did he not deserve the plaudits denied to the royal pair?—he ordered his coachman to whip up the horses when he was assaulted by a ruffian or two who had jumped from behind his carriage. One blow knocked his hat off, another cut open his forehead and partially stunned him. The coachman was also belaboured, but the assailants dispersed before they could be identified.

The King immediately sent two of his chamberlains to express his regrets and condolence, and the Count of Aquila spent half the night with the battered ambassador, whose wound was not serious. A deputation of elders from every quarter of the city presented him with a florid address of sympathy, attributing the offence to royalist re-actionaries. Brenier replied that he was 'convinced of the respect of the Neapolitans for the representative of a sovereign who had wrought wonders for the welfare of Italy.' According to Elliot's report: 'He is himself under the impression that he owes his head wound to the police or the Sanfedisti and royal lazzaroni, and this view is likewise en-couraged by the liberals who do not wish the odium of the outrage to fall upon their party, but there are various circumstances calculated to make us receive this belief with hesitation. Baron Brenier was on his way to call on the Marquis de Villamarina, and was but a short way behind the Minister's carriage who was being made the subject of an ovation . . . and behind him again was another liberal or annexationist mob shouting for Victor Emmanuel and Garibaldi, so that to have supposed Baron Brenier to have been assaulted by the Sanfedisti we must believe them to have penetrated into the stronghold of their opponents and to have been at the time between two different bands of them, who would not have let them come out with impunity. . . . Others say that he was wounded because he hesitated when called upon to shout "Viva Vittorio Emanuele" and this is supported by the fact that several of the liberal bands boasted of having extorted this cry from the French Minister.'

Brenier was by no means satisfied with the verbal excuses he had received, and continued to grumble long after the incident though a scapegoat was found in Giovanni Manetta, an outspoken royalist who owned a smart bathing establishment. Manetta and several other 'notorious reactionaries' were kept in prison without trial for many months before they were released as innocent. Since riots continued on the morrow, fomented by the paid agents of Villamarina and those who wished to sabotage the Constitution, the ministry proclaimed a state of siege until a national guard and a new police force were organized. Liborio Romano restored a semblance of order with the aid of his friends in the *camorra*, by distributing key positions among its most influential adepts. Owing to this compromise with the chieftains of corruption who had ramifications all over the kingdom the prefect of police achieved a popularity unknown to any of his predecessors.

The new ministry was a consortium of malleable mediocrities. Even Liborio Romano, who was soon promoted Minister of the Interior, was little more than an inflated provincial, a sly sexagenarian manipulator of creatures as slippery as himself. His treachery has since been proved beyond a doubt. As he had been conspiring against the dynasty all his life, his promotion was extraordinary; it is more extraordinary that his colleagues Spinelli, the Prince of Torella and De Martino, who had some pretence to dignity, should have consented to be the partners of such a double dealer, but he had wormed his way into the Count of Aquila's graces and the Count was hoping to dethrone his nephew. Dr Trevelyan avers that they were honest men, desirous of working the Constitution and saving the dynasty, but these aims had become incompatible since the fall of Palermo. By making a clean sweep of authentic royalists in public service they hastened the *débâcle*. Ferdinand II's maxim 'Constitution-Revolution' was justified with a vengeance. The King's true friends were estranged;

his enemies were encouraged. Liborio Romano's lame defence in his *Memoirs*, was that he regarded the dynasty as doomed, but wished to save the country from anarchy and civil war. By calling in the *camorra* he paved the way for anarchy and such corruption as had never been known under the old régime, since the camorrists thrived on contraband, clandestine lotto and all manner of extortion. The most disorderly elements now postured in picturesque uniforms as the tutors of law and order. It took more than half a century to extirpate this cancer from Neapolitan society.

Rumour had it that when Giuseppe Ferrigni refused the post of Minister of Finance in the Constitutional government on the plea that the King was dying, the Prime Minister Spinelli retorted: 'But we, like merciful doctors, are trying to keep him alive.' The method of treatment was drastic. The doctors urged their patient to sign a decree reviving the ill-fated Constitution of 1848 on July 1, convoked the electoral colleges for August 19 and Parliament on September 10. The state of siege was raised on July 2, and the political amnesty became operative on July 3, so that all the conspirators were now free to conspire in broad daylight under the indulgent eye of Don Liborio, as Romano was commonly called. A benefit performance in aid of the poorer prisoners and exiles was given at the San Carlo, and the King contributed two thousand ducats from his private purse while the other Princes contributed eight hundred. This was turning the other cheek with a magnanimity which was neither appreciated nor understood. The mushroom crop of new newspapers ridiculed the King's intentions: he was lampooned as the petty tyrant Bombino, alias Franceschiello, the puppet of a camarilla presided over by the wicked Austrian Queen Dowager, whereas Cavour, Mazzini, Garibaldi and Victor Emmanuel were glorified at his expense and their pictures were displayed in shop windows. If only he had possessed an ounce of tyranny! But he was a gentleman surrounded by cads. His excessively punctilious sense of honour was his own undoing. He still had an army of about 100,000 men whose loyalty, like a deep well in a desert, awaited the tap of a dowser's rod to gush forth and drown his foes. But no dowser was anywhere near, and the well was in danger of sinking deeper underground.

An unfortunate symptom of this latent loyalty was the explosion of exasperated grenadiers on July 15. These had been provoked by the insulting demonstrations of Don Liborio's camorrists. 'All that is certain,' wrote Elliot in his usual vein, 'is that a number of soldiers ran down the most public streets forcing people to cry "*Viva il Re*", and though the people when invited in that way would have cried "*Viva il Diavolo*" their compliance did not save them from being slashed and cut. Conyngham was at a window in the Toledo, and saw them pass under his feet, acting literally as if they were mad or drunk, which they probably were, having been primed beforehand, for they went cutting indiscriminately at carriages, lamp-posts, or anything that refused to shout for the King. Our consul, Bonham, found himself in the middle of it before he knew where he was, and was surrounded and made to show his loyalty like the rest, which he did without being invited twice, but, not having taken off his hat at the mention of the sacred name of royalty, it was knocked off by a neat cut from a sword. Of course, I have asked for satisfaction. The Prussian Minister, Perponcher, who had only arrived three days before, was close behind Bonham, and would have been treated in the same way if an officer had not given him a convoy. The officers behaved well throughout, and did what they could—to the extent, it is said, of running some of the men through the body. . . .'

Next day the King visited several barracks and admonished the soldiers that since he had given the Constitution he was determined to uphold it and see that it was respected by all. The simple-minded men were puzzled if not offended: could their poor young sovereign not tell his friends from his enemies? Remembering the rages of the late King Ferdinand, bless his soul in Heaven, as well as his personal interest in their affairs, they regretted him all the more bitterly. For his sake they would try to defend his son in spite of himself. Francis signed propitiatory proclamations, praising the citizens for having kept calm, and exhorting his army and marine to be 'champions of justice, humanity, discipline, and love of the fatherland,' but similar outbreaks had occurred elsewhere, at Capua and Caserta. At Gaeta the garrison would only shout 'Long live the King!' when the Constitution was read to them, instead of cheering the latter thrice in obedience to instructions. The government suspected that all this was due to the machinations of Court reactionaries. As a result General Pianell became Minister of War instead of General Ritucci, and Liborio Romano became Minister of the Interior and of Police instead of Federico Del Re. The plan to reconquer Sicily was dropped. Supported by Generals Nunziante and Pianell, the council of ministers voted for an armistice and diplomatic action—at a period when diplomacy was dominated by Cavour. Nunziante had already decided to desert; Pianell's behaviour was more ambiguous and his order of the day on stepping into office was a farrago of contradictory rhetoric. A muddle-headed defeatist, he thought it impossible to reconquer Sicily and attributed its loss to the demoralization of the army. 'Put your trust in your commanders,' he urged the troops, 'and in that passive obedience which is the foundation of every disciplined army!' But it was the commanders who had been demoralized in the first place, the wretched Landi and Lanza in Sicily, followed by Nunziante and Pianell in Naples.

Since the fall of Palermo Cavour had been able to adopt a bolder policy. 'The macaroni are not yet cooked,' as he wrote to Nigra on June 25, 'but as for the oranges which are already on our table, we are fully determined to eat them.' More steamers, financed by Victor Emmanuel, sailed to Sicily from Genoa with volunteers, and Admiral Persano was instructed to help Garibaldi surreptitiously. But whereas Cavour was eager to devour the oranges at once Garibaldi preferred to wait until the macaroni were cooked. The political situation in Palarmo was complicated by these rival appetites. Garibaldi feared that after the dessert course Cavour would prevent him from crossing to Naples and thence proceeding to Rome. La Farina, whom Cavour had sent over to obtain immediate annexation, was expelled by the Dictator on July 7. His report on the chaotic condition of the island was scathing: he described 'the camarilla round Garibaldi which has the reality of power' as 'a horde of savage drunkards.' Cavour concluded that Garibaldi was 'carried away by the intoxication of success.' If so, he carried others with him including the reluctant Cavour, who was forced to re-adjust his spectacles after the victory at Milazzo on July 20.

That victory was made decisive by General Pianell and the ministry at Naples, who feared that Garibaldi's defeat would wreck the Constitution. General Clary, who had at least prevented the rebel *squadre* from seizing Catania, had been ordered to retire to Messina with his 15,000 men. Apparently he was demoralized by the granting of the Constitution. From that moment he began to exaggerate the strength

Queen Maria Sophia, by A. Riedel

of the enemy: like Generals Landi and Lanza he demanded more money and reinforcements when the King prompted him to take the offensive, since 'even a small victory would raise the morale of the troops.'

It was futile to compromise between offensive and defensive plans, but this was what happened. The King wanted a counter-attack in Sicily; his War Minister wanted—or so he declared—to organize the defence of the mainland. General Clary shilly-shallied between them. In mid-July a partial offensive was launched by Colonel Bosco, the bravest of his officers, who was sent to protect the threatened garrison of Milazzo and occupy strategic positions in the neighbourhood, but he was warned not to fight unless the Garibaldians attacked him. A pitched battle was inevitable in spite of these equivocal instructions. There was desperate fighting on both sides among the high cane-brakes and sharp cactus hedges under a pitiless sun on July 20. At first victory favoured the Neapolitans; only towards evening did it revert to their opponents. If the Neapolitan fleet had protected Milazzo, Garibaldi could not have occupied that town. But the Neapolitan fleet was only represented by one frigate, the *Veloce*, which had deserted to Garibaldi, and was now bombarding the royal cavalry on the beach with all her shot and shell. Her commander Amilcare Anguissola had initiated a long series of desertions by sailing into Palermo instead of convoying a royal troop-ship to Reggio. Garibaldi harangued the crew and baptized her the *Tukory*, after his Hungarian lieutenant who had been killed on entering Palermo. Forty-one of the crew joined his banner; the remaining 138 opted for loyalty to the King.

When Colonel Bosco appealed to General Clary for reinforcements he said he lacked sufficient transport. In the meantime Pianell had ordered him to remain on the defensive, and Bosco was severely censured for resuming hostilities. Owing to scarcity of food and water, lack of rudimentary hygiene, general discouragement after defeat and incipient mutiny, the castle of Milazzo was none too easy to defend. General Clary, whose 15,000 men were chafing under inactivity at Messina, had an impulse to relieve Bosco on July 22 and signalled that he was sending three regiments to Milazzo, but the order was countermanded a few hours later. Even General Pianell in Naples felt he should do something to rescue the reckless colonel, but he was saved the trouble by mutiny in the marine. Instead of the expedition

Bosco had hoped for, empty transports arrived to remove him and his men. Admiral Persano feared that these ships had come to bombard the Garibaldians, and he embraced the Dictator effusively when he heard of their peaceful mission. From the *Fulminante*, flying a flag of truce at the foremast, Colonel Anzani landed to negotiate the terms of capitulation. The garrison were to leave with their arms and half the mules; all the cannon, ammunition and what was left went to the victors. Messina surrendered without bloodshed on July 28, when Clary signed an abject treaty with Medici, of which the chief terms were cessation of hostilities for an indeterminate period and the occupation of the city by the Garibaldians. The Neapolitans were to keep the citadel, but as they were not allowed to fire a shot its guns were purely ornamental. The Constitutional government had abandoned Sicily. Garibaldi, on the crest of the Sicilian wave, prepared to cross the Straits of Messina.

'Admiral Mundy told me yesterday,' wrote Elliot on the day of Clary's capitulation, 'that he had received from the Sardinian Admiral, Persano, a hint that Garibaldi was just going to start for the Continent, so that, if not stopped by the King's mandate, we shall have stirring events before long.'

The story of Victor Emmanuel's mandate is well known: how Garibaldi received two letters from his sovereign on July 27, the first, for European consumption, expressing disapproval of his Sicilian expedition and advising him 'to renounce the idea of crossing to the mainland . . . provided the King of Naples pledges himself to evacuate the island and leave the Sicilians free to decide their own future;' the second, for private consumption, giving him permission to disobey the former. Mr D. Mack Smith has cast doubt on this,[1] pointing out that several versions of the King's official letter and of Garibaldi's reply exist, whereas the King's second letter did not come to light till 1909 and 'the evidence suggests it was not delivered.' It is probable that Count Litta, who brought it in person, assured Garibaldi of the King's wholehearted sympathy, and that his word was quite sufficient.

Victor Emmanuel had more in common with Garibaldi than with Cavour: they were both rough diamonds with a love of bold adventure. Cavour's daring was of a more subtle order, masked by Machiavellian diplomacy: his real intentions were never easy to fathom.

[1] *Cavour and Garibaldi 1860*, pp. 125, 126.

While play-acting with Manna and Winspeare, the Neapolitan envoys who had gone to Turin to discuss an alliance, putting them off with terms which King Francis could never accept and putting them on with attentions purely polite, he was endeavouring to provoke a 'spontaneous' rising in Naples before the Dictator arrived. On July 20 Farini, his Minister of the Interior, told the credulous Neapolitans that a Bourbon victory over Garibaldi would be 'the salvation of Italy', adding rudely, 'if only I had twenty thousand of our troops, I should have courage enough to throw Garibaldi and his army into the sea.' But after the victory at Milazzo Cavour spurned Francis's envoys. To Nigra he wrote: 'The Neapolitan Government, at the first movement of Garibaldi outside Palermo, are seized with a panic terror and hasten to declare their readiness to evacuate the fortresses which they still occupy, without waiting for them to be invested or besieged! This act of arrant cowardice which we had neither demanded nor recommended, renders the position of the King of Naples much more difficult vis-à-vis ourselves and vis-à-vis Garibaldi.' He fervently congratulated the Dictator on his victory and at the same time sent secret orders to Admiral Persano to delay his crossing of the Straits 'by indirect methods as long as possible.'

Villamarina reported that Naples was ripe for revolt and that the régime was disintegrating. Before the end of July Liborio Romano had been suborned to set up a provisional government. Nunziante and several other Neapolitan generals were eager to collaborate provided they retained their military rank. Nisco, Bonghi, Pisanelli and an enterprising élite of exiles and secret agents encouraged the optimism of Villamarina, who reported on July 23 that he expected a spontaneous rebellion to break out within a few days. For all the zeal of Cavour's emissaries, the Neapolitans reacted in a manner mainly theatrical. They gesticulated, they speechified, they cheered Victor Emmanuel, but they did not revolt. The prosperous middle classes had no desire for a civil war, while the poorer people were still attached to the royal family: unity and annexation meant nothing to the masses. At most there was a vague fancy for novelty, a childish wish to set eyes on the hero who was said to have shaken the bullets off his cloak as if they were so many peas, the magnetic Messiah of Marsala who had put whole armies to rout. Some hoped for loot as in the good old days. Cavour's propaganda was most effective in the King's own family. The Count of Syracuse had long been a candid collaborator, and for a while the King's other uncles Trapani and Aquila played his game.

Whether Cavour wished to prevent Garibaldi from crossing to the mainland or not, Napoleon III was anxious to stop him if England agreed to join in a naval blockade. After a dramatic pause, about which the historians differ—some say at Cavour's urgent appeal, while others deny this though the statesman was a super-chameleon—Lord John Russell refused Napoleon's invitation to co-operate with the French fleet. Faithful to his policy of non-intervention, he informed the French ambassador 'that the force of Garibaldi was not in itself sufficient to overthrow the Neapolitan monarchy. If the navy, army, and people of Naples were attached to the King, Garibaldi would be defeated; if, on the contrary, they were disposed to welcome Garibaldi, our interference would be an intervention in the internal affairs of the Neapolitan kingdom.'

When De Martino expressed his regret that Britain would not join France in preventing Garibaldi from extending his operations to the continent, Elliot replied 'that Her Majesty's Government had advocated the doctrine that the affairs of Italy should be decided by the Italians themselves . . . that it was, moreover, a matter of notoriety that the country had become almost unanimously anti-dynastic, and if Her Majesty's Naval Forces were used to prevent the passage of Garibaldi to the mainland they would be acting contrary to the wishes of nearly the whole Nation.' Those wishes were only known to Elliot through the liberal camarilla he consorted with, and indeed this appeared to represent the nation in the press, for the Bourbonists had been silenced.

Francis II had to fend for himself, surrounded by traitors. The royal palace was infected with panic. The Queen Dowager removed her younger children to Gaeta, and there was a general exodus of ex-ministers and functionaries who had been forced into retirement. It was an unusually torrid summer. 'I wish the public had been so considerate as to have chosen another time of year for their revolutionary proceedings,' wrote Elliot, 'for to me it is very inconvenient and annoying to have to run in and out between Naples and Castellammare (then a fashionable summer resort), as the railroad in the dog-days is not amusing, and I find that during the last week I spent exactly twenty-four hours on the road. I have established a good sailing-boat and, if not kept in town till the breeze dies away, I sail back from town, and thus, instead of an odious roasting, spend a couple of very agreeable hours, finishing off with a swim to give one an appetite for dinner. . . .' Not everyone could enjoy the diplomat's amenities. The Queen splashed about like a mermaid in the bay, more venturesome than her ladies-in-waiting, one of whom in her virginal innocence feared that sea-bathing might get her with child.

The King tried to keep up a cheerful front though he was grieved by the desertion of so many he had trusted. General Nunziante's conduct was even more distressing than that of Anguissola, who had handed over the ship *Veloce* to Garibaldi. Besides resigning, he returned all his decorations because they had been given him by a government 'which confuses honest, loyal and upright men with those who only deserve contempt'; while his wife returned her brevet of lady-in-waiting to the Queen. In a parting message to the troops he had commanded, Nunziante exhorted them to join those he had but recently called filibusters. Instructing Admiral Persano to convey the *Maria Adelaide* from Palermo to Naples, Cavour wrote on July 30: 'In appearance you will remain at the disposal of the Princess of Syracuse (Filiberta of Savoy-Carignano, the Count of Syracuse's wife) but in fact you must co-operate with a rising in Naples, without Garibaldi's intervention. The principal actors will be the Minister of the Interior Liborio Romano and General Nunziante. You will be put in contact with them by Baron Nisco. . . . I think I can rely on them because the Minister is an old unitarian liberal, honest and proved, and the General has given us enough proof to have him hanged if necessary. . . .'

Disaffection in the navy was worse than in the army. Even before the loss of Milazzo sixteen senior officers conveyed to Admiral Mundy their determination to quit the service if he would promise them an asylum on board his ships, intimating that their example would be followed by the whole navy. Admiral Mundy of course refused. At the end of July Antonio Ciccone, one of the exiles returning to Naples, wrote buoyantly to Bertrando Spaventa: 'At Civitavecchia we found five officers who had left their posts in Naples and were on their way to Piedmont via Marseilles to cross over to Sicily. Another twenty were prepared to do likewise and I think they have done so.

If things continue as at present the army will be without officers. Here I have found wonders: the immense majority is for annexation. There is a dynastic party but it dare not show itself, either from fear or from shame. In the army the chiefs are for the nation, but they are beginning to get rid of them. . . . The soldier is for reaction, not through affection to the dynasty but on account of the promised pillage. All speak of Garibaldi, and there is a song which ends: "Garibaldi is our King".' Others wrote in the same strain. The government was cracking up. But the army—that was the difficulty, 'the soldiers rather than the officers.' The Neapolitan army was still intact: it might yet inflict a defeat upon Garibaldi.

XXIV

THE romantic figure of the conqueror of Sicily, the hirsute hero of the flaming shirt and flowing poncho, loomed like a rising sun across the Straits of Messina, and the legend of his invincibility struck awe in people with a strong instinct for hagiolatry. Very soon the new Cæsar would return to the peninsula. If the Neapolitans did not want his brand of liberty, he would make them want it, by Jupiter! He was nationalism, liberalism and romanticism incarnate, three in one. Apart from his legend, he was known to be a simple and temperate man who was content to wash his own shirt and sleep on straw, which was endearing.

Francis II was also simple and temperate, but his stiff courtesy failed to charm and his effigy was wooden in comparison with the glamorous Dictator: at twenty-four he looked neither young nor old, neither a visionary nor a man of action. Modestly and unconsciously, he stood for aristocratic individualism, moral dignity and an easy-going tradition which had served Naples well in spite of abuses which existed everywhere else at that time. He had been brought up to think that liberty derived from Christianity, not from any political or economical abstraction; that the moral reform of the individual came before the material reform of society. He was generally accused of obscurantist immobility, of not keeping step with the times, but in fact he was seldom allowed to stand still. Pushed hither and thither by extremists of the right and left and by moderates of the centre, it is scarcely surprising that his purposes wavered when those he had trusted failed him. In the single year since his succession to the throne he had not been given a chance to achieve equilibrium. Though he was quite as Italian as Victor Emmanuel of Savoy, now in French possession, he was dubbed a foreigner by the foreign press. Naples had assimilated his ancestors long ago. During the last century his dynasty had become identified with his people, and he failed to see why these should wish to be annexed to a kingdom in the remote north-west of the peninsula. They had even less in common with the Piedmontese than he had. But this was the Romantic Age, and Garibaldi seemed to have all those attributes of high romance in which Francis II was so sadly deficient.

Alexandre Dumas *père*, the most celebrated of living novelists, was among the first to appreciate this, He was cruising in the Mediterranean on board his small yacht *Emma*, whose crew included a pretty midshipwoman in a dapper jacket and trousers, when he heard of Garibaldi's landing at Marsala. Aged sixty yet bursting with boyish vitality, he steered straight for Sicily 'to see historical romance in the living reality', as Trevelyan said. He reached Milazzo in time for Garibaldi's victory and penned the first glowing account of it. From this moment, wrote Maxime Du Camp,[1] 'Dumas became Garibaldi's ambassador. He had about fifty thousand francs in reserve for his travel expenses: he proceeded to spend these on rifles which he forwarded to Messina; he went to Turin to see Cavour, to Genoa to stimulate the recruiting committees, to Naples, where he had an interview with Liborio Romano, the Minister of the Interior . . . to Salerno, where he was welcomed by the pealing of bells; everywhere he brought the watchword, he conversed with prominent leaders and endeavoured to prepare the way for Italian unity.' No doubt he imagined his influence far greater than it was.

This exuberant Hercules, as described by his friend Du Camp, was a prodigious talker. 'He was an instrument of permanent sonority; it sufficed to touch it to hear it; after ten or eleven hours of conversation —and what conversation!—he was as nimble as when he had started.' But he was an even more prodigious writer, and his writings, which exerted a fascination on thousands of readers, rendered an immense

[1] *Souvenirs Littéraires*, Vol. II, p. 179. Paris, 1892.

service to Garibaldi. He bore the Bourbons of Naples a personal grudge, as he believed that his father had been poisoned by them. (General Dumas had been taken prisoner under Ferdinand I in 1799 and had died several years later, so the poison must have been slow to work.) The super-romancer's literary campaign against the Bourbon dynasty was all the stronger owing to this conviction, but his *Mémoires de Garibaldi, Les Garibaldiens* and his copious articles in *L'Indipendente* have hardly received their due from historians of the Risorgimento.

A galaxy of other famous writers lent their pens to the Italian cause, but few lent their human presence; and the presence of Dumas in the flesh was divinely appropriate. Though he could not help interweaving fantasy with fact, he best conveys the swift tempo of Garibaldi's exploits and the spontaneous exaltations of his followers. His account of his first meeting with the hero in Turin is characteristic: 'As was always the case with him, Garibaldi's door was open to all visitors, without even an orderly in the antechamber, without even a valet to announce the caller. Consequently I was forced to announce myself. I entered. He was standing enveloped in his poncho. Colonel Türr, my friend of a dozen years, and Colonel Carrasso were seated.

'On entering I glanced at the clock. "General," I asked, "what time is it?"

' "Eleven o'clock", Garibaldi answered, somewhat astonished that an unknown person should enter his room to ask him the time.

' "What is the day of the month?" I continued.

' "Wednesday, the fourth of January", replied Garibaldi, more and more astonished.

' "Well, General, listen carefully to what I predict for you to-day, this fourth of January (1860), at eleven o'clock in the morning. Within a year you will be Dictator. Now let me embrace you."

' "You are Alexandre Dumas", said he, as he stretched out his arms to me.'

Garibaldi and Dumas both had the faculty of creating astonishment and this was a salient facet of their attraction. Francis II never dreamt of astonishing anyone and he was utterly devoid of histrionic talent. In the meantime there were various causes for the panic which was spreading through the capital. 'Among these,' reported Elliot on August 15, 'may be named the short-sighted intrigues of the re-actionists, and the rapidly increasing activity of the Republican or

Mazzinian party, the dread of whom is becoming so great that many who a short time ago were anxiously looking forward to the arrival of Garibaldi now anticipate with fear the moment of his coming, as likely to be . . . a period of anarchy and confusion. . . . Reasoning men begin to ask themselves whether Garibaldi will have the power to restrain the element of anarchy which will accompany him from Sicily.'

The press published lists of candidates for Parliament, selected chiefly from the recent exiles and political prisoners who most shrilly professed unitarian and anti-dynastic opinions, but the assembly of electoral colleges was postponed till August 19 and again till September 30 because, according to the royal decree, 'the disturbances in Sicily and Calabria were unfavourable to an impartial election'. Everybody knew that Garibaldi was waiting to cross the Straits, and the prevailing tension on both sides has been described by many observers. The reactionaries feared the liberals and *vice versa*; the Cavourian unitarians feared the Garibaldians and Mazzinians and *vice versa*; the new national guard and police force mustered by Liborio Romano feared the regular army; the middle feared the lower classes, and, as **De Cesare** wrote, 'the government feared everybody, without being feared by a soul'.

Liborio Romano took elaborate precautions against being murdered: driving in a closed carriage into the city from his villa at Posillipo, he would change his costume before taking another carriage to the back door of a certain bank where he could sleep in safety, guarded by the caretaker, no doubt a member of the camorra. He was involved in so many intrigues that he must have been rather muddled: first the insurrection on behalf of Cavour to forestall Garibaldi, then the formation of a provisional government and an appeal to Admiral Persano to land the Piedmontese troops waiting on board ships in the harbour, as well as sundry negotiations for the reception of Garibaldi, who seemed most likely to win the race, while Romano remained officially the minister and spokesman of King Francis.

The Neapolitans refused to oblige with a convenient insurrection. On August 16 Cavour vented his exasperation in a letter to Ricasoli: 'We have given Naples everything necessary for a revolution, arms, money, soldiers, men of counsel and men of action. If after all this the kingdom turns out to be so rotten as to be incapable of action, I do not know what to do; and we must resign ourselves to the triumph either of Garibaldi or of the reactionaries.'

Even on August 6 Elliot envisaged the possibility of the King going to Gaeta, and expressed his reluctance to follow him: 'though I am accredited to the King I see no reason why I should be tied to his tail, so as to make a political demonstration of adherence to him.' He proposed to stay on at Naples, with the *Intrepid* gunboat at his disposal, which would carry him back and forward once or twice a week to see the Minister for Foreign Affairs if necessary. Thus again he would avoid an odious roasting, and finish off the day with a swim to give him an appetite for dinner. . . .

Though a devout unitarian like his colleague Hudson in Turin, Elliot was shocked by the last proceeding of the Count of Syracuse, who had told *The Times* correspondent that he had sent King Victor Emmanuel his adhesion to the annexation, and that it had been accepted. 'Till within the last fortnight "our own correspondent" has had a sort of idea that the Count of Syracuse might be erected into a King in due time; but latterly he has become convinced that, if the present King goes, his whole kith and kin must go with him, and he was astounded by this declaration, and asked what His Royal Highness meant by giving his adhesion to the annexation and whether he had become a Sardinian subject. He said Yes, that he was now a Sardinian subject, and would soon be the only Bourbon Prince who could live in Italy; and, on being further questioned, said that the King here did not yet know it, but would do so the following day. What followed was very amusing. "Our own correspondent" telegraphed his news to *The Times*, not mentioning how he heard it; but his telegram, as he might have guessed, was not forwarded, and he was summoned first to see the Minister of the Interior and then the Minister for Foreign Affairs, who assured him that the thing was not true.

'Wreford, the correspondent, is quite a truthful man, and there can be no doubt that the Prince told him what he says; but it seems to be no less certain that neither the Government nor the King knew of this royal desertion till they learnt it from the telegram of the newspaper correspondent. . . .

'There is one piece of advice I should be uncommonly tempted to give, and that is that the King should pack off every single member of his family—man, woman and child—except his wife. The Count of

Syracuse has thrown him off; Aquila is plotting against him, for himself or for France; Trapani is intriguing as hard as he can for reaction and divine right, of which Trani seems to be looked to as the future champion; while the Count of Caserta, the next brother, is said to have more brains and devil than any of them, and has been bred up by the same old mother, who certainly has done enough to entitle her to pass the rest of her days in tranquillity in foreign lands. . . .

'A very amusing effect of the Count of Syracuse's vagary has been to send his latterly ultra-liberal brother Aquila slap back to reaction. The latter meant to have started himself as the Liberal one of the family, and now his brother has taken the wind so completely out of his sails that he is driven to try something else. Was there ever such a set?'

Elliot observed with approval that the King's private chancellery had been abolished, and that telegraphic communication was to come under the control of Liborio Romano, thereby ending 'one of the great means of reactionist intrigue'. Besides, the provincial authorities had had their cyphers changed, so that no private correspondence could be carried on with the Princes or royal household, which had been 'well cleaned out' by Don Liborio the *camorrista*. A unique case of a Minister of the Interior relegating his King to the interior of his palace and all but locking him up in one of the closets.

Francis II was unfortunate in those uncles who flaunted their feathers at this time of crisis. Compared with the arch-conspirator they had patronized, they were callow novices, but they provided some light relief to a sombre story.

His eldest uncle, the Prince of Capua, was still wandering forlornly between Geneva, Spa and Aix-les-Bains with his morganatic English spouse and adolescent offspring, a son and a daughter. Ferdinand II had bequeathed him 20,000 ducats, but this was slight compensation for more than twenty years of enforced exile. Francis II ordered that all sums due to him were to be restored as well as the estates which had been sequestrated. These were considerable, but the order had come too late. All the Prince's inheritance was to be confiscated by Garibaldi and declared national property. King Victor Emmanuel offered him an allowance, but he was advised to reject this lest it should prejudice his claims to his patrimony. After the Prince's death in 1862, Victor Emmanuel recognized his widow's title as Princess of Capua and granted her an apanage with the residence of Villa Marlia, near Lucca.

Her children died young, and the recognition for which she had yearned and schemed so indomitably came too late to console a widow worn out with the struggle to escape sleuth-hound creditors while keeping up appearances.

The King's second uncle, the Count of Syracuse, was compared with Philippe Égalité, but his liberal sympathies were overshadowed by a more evident enthusiasm for ladies of easy virtue. His Piedmontese wife, a sour-tempered bigot who had never inspired his affection, served as so much grist to Cavour's mill, for he sent a warship to Naples under the pretence of protecting her. The ship was full of *bersaglieri* who were paraded all over the city, fraternizing with the Neapolitan troops and trying to debauch them: 'the most active revolutionary agents that could be sent', wrote Elliot, 'and Admiral Persano appears to be as unscrupulous an officer as an unscrupulous master could wish to employ.'

Lavishly generous, an easy prey to plausible parasites and charlatans, the Count of Syracuse was constantly in debt. Cavour helped him out with various sums of money, as he might be useful in case of a rising—that rising he hoped would break out before Garibaldi's arrival. Baron Nisco had suggested that he might be appointed Regent. But Syracuse was not taken seriously in Naples. Though he hob-nobbed with Villamarina, Admiral Persano and other Piedmontese, and made himself conspicuous at a memorial service for Guglielmo Pepe which was more of a public manifestation against the Bourbon dynasty, he had no real influence. At forty-seven he was still a plump playboy with a provocative beard which he flaunted as a badge of liberalism. 'What a pity there must be a lunatic in every family!' his royal nephew had exclaimed. 'Lunatics at least have their lucid moments, but idiots never', was uncle Syracuse's comment. He was fond of repeating: 'It was predestined that the dynasty of Charles III should end with an imbecile.'

The King's third uncle, the Count of Aquila, made an eleventh-hour attempt to rescue the dynasty, but he was foiled by his former cronies. Hand in glove with Baron Brenier, he had urged Francis to grant the Constitution. He had also befriended Liborio Romano and recommended him for the ministry, thinking he had discovered a serviceable tool, whereas he was used by his protégé as a step-ladder to be kicked away as soon as he had climbed into office. When he realized his blunder he tried secretly to form a loyalist government under the Prince of Ischitella, Pietro Ulloa, and his martial brother General Girolamo Ulloa, who had gallantly defended Venice against the Austrians and commanded the Tuscan forces; put Naples under martial law; reorganize the national guard and the police; and expel all foreigners holding Piedmontese passports.

Embittered against the Piedmontese and incensed because Ricasoli had promoted Garibaldi over his head, General Ulloa had returned to Naples at Aquila's summons to salvage the autonomy of the Two Sicilies. Had he been given the supreme command of the army in Calabria, he might well have succeeded, but Colonel Bosco and several other officers of the old guard protested so vigorously against the appointment of a former subordinate of General Pepe (although their superior in the art of war) that the inept General Vial was appointed in his stead. The Count of Aquila was mortified, but the *coup d'état* he was said to have plotted has not been proved. As he was one of the very few to advise the King to strike out boldly, change a ministry riddled with traitors, and impose martial law, Liborio Romano had every reason to get rid of him, and his account of Aquila's abortive *coup d'état*, repeated by Elliot, Nisco and others, has won general credence. Elliot's version is that Aquila was simultaneously urging reactionary counsel upon the King and the government, and negotiating with the extreme liberal and republican party. 'The explanation of this apparently contradictory course seems to be that he was aware that any reactionary movement on the part of the government would probably be followed by an immediate demonstration on the part of the liberals, which was expected to result in the expulsion of the King. When that object had been effected it was intended that the army and the republicans should join together,—the former imagining the Count to be working in the interest of the dynasty, and the support of the latter being secured by a distribution of arms which had taken place among them, and by the promise of an appeal to universal suffrage, under which H.R.H. flattered himself that he would be elected Vicar of the Empire.'

The only evidence Don Liborio could produce against the Count was probably concocted by himself. His police seized several cases containing uniforms and weapons identical with those of the national guard. These were said to have been imported from Marseilles as 'hardware', and addressed to H.R.H. According to Don Liborio, they were to equip a gang of ruffians who were to provoke a rumpus with the real national guard, murder a few ministers and outstanding liberals (including himself), and proclaim Aquila regent, or saviour of the dynasty. Elliot added that the police also confiscated 'a less dangerous, but perhaps not less important, consignment consisting of a case of portraits of H.R.H. waving his hat in the air in the apparent act of encouraging his followers'.

Don Liborio rushed to the King and reported his uncle's plot in the most lurid colours. As an old protégé of the Count's he could tell him quite enough to make his hair stand on end. The King merely replied with gentle irony that Aquila might aspire to the empire of Brazil—referring to his Brazilian wife, Princess Januaria of Braganza. Not satisfied with this retort, Don Liborio rushed on to frighten Spinelli and his colleagues, who decided at a Council meeting that the Count must be banished. After some demur the King's consent was extorted: his uncle was to be sent on an improvised mission to England, nominally to purchase frigates for the royal navy. He was prevented from seeing the King and was even threatened with imprisonment before he agreed to sail at midnight on August 14. The Constitutional-ists who had declaimed against the tyranny of Ferdinand II proved equally tyrannical when they exiled this Prince without a fair trial. 'Thus free institutions were saved,' wrote Don Liborio, 'and the effusion of much bloodshed among the citizens was spared.' He was given a frantic ovation by the unitarians. Half Calabria was already in the hands of revolutionary committees, and sedition was spreading through Basilicata. The peasants were led by rich feudal landlords who hoped for greater power and independence under a distant régime in Turin. Personal ambitions and mediæval blood-feuds were strangely blended with the rhetorical fervour of the new liberalism. The national guard were ready to support the invaders. Don Liborio had taken care to disarm the old royalist militia.

Garibaldi was still waiting, his eyes riveted on the Calabrian coast. On either side of the Straits of Messina the suspense became unbearable. In Naples at the sound of gunfire a priest fainted below the altar and there was a stampede of the faithful in church; young women mis-carried; frayed nerves were ignited by any explosion of unfamiliar noise. On August 15, the day after Aquila's departure, Elliot reported:

'We had our first alarm at Castellammare the night before last. I was just going to bed, about a quarter to twelve, when a sharp fire of musketry began down at the harbour. . . . After this firing had gone on some little time, some additional excitement was produced by the cannon beginning also to fire; but although this was taking place very close to us, we could neither see it nor succeed in getting any correct information as to what was going on, and by one o'clock or soon after everything got quiet, and it was clear that the attempt, whatever it was, had failed. . . . It turned out that it had been a most dashing attempt to cut out and carry off a Neapolitan two-decker which is lying close to the arsenal, preparing for sea. A steamer, supposed to be the *Veloce*, whose captain deserted with her to Garibaldi a few weeks ago, came quietly in without showing lights and brought up close to the arsenal, answering, when hailed, that she was a Frenchman; almost immediately after they lowered boats and tried to cut the hawsers of the ship which lay close by; but the people were baffled by finding her moored with a very heavy chain, and then they tried to carry her by boarding, whereupon the firing commenced from both sides, and ended by the aggressors being beaten off, there being on the ship one man killed and four wounded, one of the latter being the Captain Acton who had commanded the *Stromboli* at Marsala when Garibaldi landed, and who has been not more than a week since acquitted by the Court of Inquiry of having favoured the landing.

'The strange steamer at first lay so much in a line with the French ship *Eylau* that the Neapolitans did not dare to fire cannon at her, and even some of the musket balls fell on board the Frenchman, and when she retired she slipped between her and the *Renown*, so as to make it impossible for many shots to be fired at her, though as it was some balls went near both ships. It certainly was a wonderfully plucky proceeding, but they must have counted on treachery on the part of the Neapolitans, or they never could have tried such a wild scheme. . . .'

The capture of this two-decker, the *Monarca*, had been plotted by her own captain Giovanni Vacca with the Piedmontese Admiral Persano; Acton was only second in command. Vacca subsequently took refuge on board the Piedmontese flagship *Maria Adelaide*, where he was joined by many fellow-officers—another warning that Francis could no longer count on his navy. Though the attempt failed, it served as a reminder that Garibaldi might make a surprise landing at

Naples as at Marsala. Rumours that he had already landed filled the air.

As a military feat Garibaldi's crossing of the Straits from Giardini, below Taormina, on August 18/19 has received ample measure of praise from the historians. News of the landing near Melito reached Naples by telegraph, but in spite of the 16,000 troops scattered between Reggio and Monteleone, where General Vial had established his headquarters, nobody moved to the defence of Reggio when Garibaldi attacked it two days later. The garrison of this key city had not been increased, and its commander General Gallotti was to distinguish himself by an even prompter readiness to admit defeat than the royal generals had evinced in Sicily. Colonel Dusmet, the most energetic officer on the spot, was detailed to guard the Cathedral Square while the entrances to the town were entrusted to the questionable national guard. Dusmet and his youthful son were fatally wounded in the fiercest encounter that followed the invasion. Except the castle, where Gallotti sat tight with his garrison, all Reggio fell to Garibaldi on August 21. General Briganti approached with 2000 men but retreated after a desultory exchange of shots upon hearing that the Garibaldians were as thick as flies. Though the members of the garrison were eager to attack the invaders they were not permitted to: General Gallotti flatly refused to join the relieving force. The same story was repeated *ad nauseam*: the troops who showed spirit were seldom if ever encouraged by their commanders. The castle, which might have held out a month, was surrendered within twenty-four hours, together with thirty-four cannon, five hundred rifles, copious provisions and ammunition, horses and mules.

Garibaldi was now master of both shores on the Straits. In his *Memoirs* he paid tribute to 'the tacit collaboration of the Bourbon navy, which might have delayed our advance towards the capital. Our steamers freely transported the Army of the South (no longer called the Thousand) all along the Neapolitan coast without hindrance. This could not have been done with a wholly hostile navy.' In several instances the crews were more loyal than their officers. Indignant because they had not been ordered to attack the renegade ship *Veloce*, the crew of the *Ettore Fieramosca* locked up their captain and officers in the bilge. At the subsequent court martial the captain and officers were acquitted while the sailors were punished because, as De Sivo wrote, 'in those days whoever took the part of his king and country was counted a rebel'.

After the capture of Reggio Garibaldi was reputed to be unconquerable as well as invulnerable. The Neapolitan generals were utterly disconcerted by his guerrilla tactics, so novel to men with little enough experience of ordinary warfare, and a superstitious dread pervaded the simple soldiers, who could not understand the apparent enthusiasm of the Calabrians for their enemies, an enthusiasm spiced with the pleasures of private revenge. But thousands of the soldiers disbanded in Calabria owing to the treachery and weakness of their commanders were to fight bravely later on the Volturno and Garigliano, and even follow the King to Gaeta. The massacre of General Briganti by his own troops after his surrender at Villa San Giovanni was but an isolated symptom of the smouldering fury and frustration of these loyal men who were forced to witness the sudden degradation of all they held dear. To cries of 'Traitor!' and 'Say Long Live the King!' his body was riddled with bullets and torn to pieces in the main street of Mileto. Such an incident was not calculated to cheer his brother generals, who surrendered one after the other until the dispersal of the Neapolitan army in Calabria was complete. The rest of Garibaldi's campaign until he entered Naples was a military promenade.

In the meantime Admiral Persano assured Cavour that Don Liborio was helping his cause 'so far as he was allowed to by his very delicate position' as the King's sworn minister. On August 20 when he knew that Garibaldi had landed, Don Liborio helped his cause more brazenly by presenting Francis with a long memorandum. After summarizing the political situation at home and abroad and dwelling on the dissolution of the navy and the collapse of discipline in the army, he advised the King to leave the country for a while, placing the regency in the hands of a virtuous minister who deserved universal trust (denoting himself), since a return of the mutual confidence between the people and their sovereign had become not only difficult but impossible. Even supposing that the royal army proved victorious it would be a melancholy triumph, worse than defeat, won at the cost of general devastation and torrents of blood—a triumph that would rouse the indignation of all Europe and create an abyss between the King and the people whom God had entrusted to his paternal heart. The document concluded: 'Let Your Majesty on departing address the people with true and magnanimous words, which shall bear witness to your noble decision to avert the horrors of civil war. Your Majesty will then invoke the judgement of Europe, and await from time and the Almighty the triumph of right. We give this counsel with the sincerity of a good conscience (the conscience of Don Liborio!) and it is the only counsel we can give. We are certain that you will accept it; should you unhappily reject it, we will have to resign the high office entrusted to us, feeling that we have not deserved the confidence of our King.'

The King's answer to this preposterous missive should have been Don Liborio's arrest, but he chose to ignore it. Of course Don Liborio had no intention of resigning: that wily sexagenarian was wallowing in a seventh heaven of unadulterated treachery. Bliss was it then for traitors to be alive! He was preparing to switch his allegiance from Cavour to Garibaldi and bask in the latter's aura. Surreptitiously on the night of August 23 he visited Alexandre Dumas on board the gay yacht *Emma*, and asked him to urge the Dictator to speed his arrival. Naïvely impressed by his nocturnal visitor's reputation as the most influential person in Naples, Dumas wrote without more ado: 'Liborio is at your disposition, together with at least two of his fellow-ministers, at the first attempt at reaction on the King's part. At this first attempt, which will free him from his oath of allegiance, Liborio Romano offers to leave Naples with two of his colleagues, to present himself to you, to proclaim the deposition of the King and to recognize you as Dictator.' His messenger, who reached Garibaldi at Soveria on August 30, was sent post-haste to tell Liborio to stand at the ready for a popular rising yet keep it on ice, as it were, until he entered the capital. Garibaldi followed hot on the messenger's heels, lest Cavour should forestall him and end his dictatorship.

Liborio had the impertinence to inform the King that he had called on Dumas as an intermediary, in order to dissuade Garibaldi from his enterprise by offering him a tempting bribe.

'It might be useful,' Cavour had telegraphed Persano, 'to get the Count of Syracuse to write a letter to the King his nephew. . . .' Uncle Syracuse needed no prompting. After Garibaldi's landing he had held a banquet for the officers of the Piedmontese fleet and drunk many a toast to Italian Unity. On the 24th he sent Francis a letter which received the widest publicity. It had been carefully composed by his secretary Fiorelli and submitted to Persano's scrutiny five days before it appeared under the Prince's signature. As a document of dramatic interest it is worthy of translation: 'Sire, when I raised my voice to avert the perils which threatened our House, I was unheeded; see to it now, when I predict even greater misfortunes, that I may find access to your heart, and not be rejected by irresponsible and more pernicious counsel. The changed conditions of Italy, and the sentiment of national unity which has grown gigantically during the few months following the fall of Palermo, have deprived Your Majesty's Government of the strength which upholds States, and rendered impossible an alliance with Piedmont. The populations of Upper Italy, horrified by the reports of the Sicilian massacres, repulsed the Neapolitan ambassadors, and we were grievously abandoned to the fortunes of war, alone, without allies, a prey to the resentment of the multitudes that arise in all parts of Italy demanding the extermination of our House, which has become the target of universal reprobation. Moreover the civil war, which now invades the continental provinces, will overwhelm the dynasty in the complete ruin which the iniquitous craft of perverse counsellors has long since prepared for the descendants of Charles III of Bourbon. The blood of citizens, uselessly shed, will again inundate the thousand cities of the kingdom, and you who were the hope and centre of the people's affection will be regarded with horror as the sole cause of a fratricidal war.

'Sire, while there is yet time save our House from the curses of all Italy! Follow the noble example of our royal relative in Parma, who released her subjects from their allegiance and made them arbiters of their own destiny as soon as civil war broke out (i.e. war between Piedmont and Austria). Europe and your people will credit you for your sublime sacrifice, and you will be able to lift your head confidently before God, who will reward the magnanimous action of Your Majesty. Strengthened by misfortune, your heart will expand to the noble aspirations of the Fatherland, and you will bless the day when you generously sacrificed yourself for the greatness of Italy.

'With these words, Sire, I fulfil the sacred duty imposed by my experience, and I pray God that He enlighten you and make you worthy of His blessings. From Your Majesty's most affectionate uncle Leopold, Count of Syracuse.'

'Whatever one thinks, this letter does high honour to the Patriot

476

Prince', wrote Admiral Persano. It does him less honour when one realizes that he had received substantial sums of money from Cavour and had been promised the regency or viceroyalty of Naples with Tuscany as a possible alternative. However true that the whole condition of Italy was changing rapidly, and that the ideal of national unity had gained many converts since the fall of Palermo, it was hardly charitable of the King's 'most affectionate uncle' to push his tottering throne in so public a manner. Insofar as it hurt the King and damaged his cause even more, it produced the desired effect. Syracuse had befouled his own nest most successfully. Others besides Elliot exclaimed: Was there ever such a set!

'If I were not responsible for the Crown to my people and family,' said Francis, 'I should have cast away this burden some time ago.' Within a short year he had seen enough of human treachery and ingratitude to disgust him for a lifetime. He was to see even more within the next few days. He had lost confidence in most of his advisers, and was beginning to lose confidence in himself. Only an extreme sense of duty and an assurance that his own conscience was clear buoyed him up against despair. His more fortunate ancestors had been able to dispel their gloom with hunting and healthy exercise, but the pale 'son of the Saint' had no such outlet. His wife was too young to understand the complex tragedy of his predicament: her capacity to enjoy life was undimmed by forebodings. She could see the absurd side of everything and laugh it off. Perhaps her laughter was a tonic in these dreary days when his whole world was sliding away from him.

It is difficult to sympathize with the weak, however decent, and few sympathized with Francis. The Pope's nickname for him, 'the little Job', was singularly apt. The advice of his would-be comforters was hopelessly contradictory. The least martial of men, Francis thought seriously of leading his army against Garibaldi, or at any rate of encouraging his troops by his presence in the field. The Queen and his half-brothers, the so-called Palace party, were all in favour of this: though his appearance was not inspiring, his royal blood still exerted a mystical prestige. The son of their good Ferdinand and of the pious Maria Cristina meant more than the paladin from Nice to the common soldier. But his generals distrusted the army and each other. The truculent Bosco, recently promoted a general, pointed out that if the King left Naples the revolution plotted by the agents of Cavour and

Mazzini was bound to break out: he would then find himself between two fires. Ought he not rather to stay and defend the capital? Don Liborio, the Count of Syracuse, Alessandro Nunziante, Admiral Persano and Villamarina were all trying to make the King leave by hook or by crook. If he left Naples, he could entrench himself at Gaeta until the time was propitious for a successful counter-attack. Brenier advised him to strengthen his position behind a defensive line running through Salerno, Avellino and Ariano, reminding him of his great ancestor Louis XIV's dictum: *'lorsqu'il s'agit de défendre une couronne, il faut plutôt que l'abandonner perdre la vie.'* Simultaneously Brenier was insisting on what he called suitable reparation for his public battering two months previously, though the King had done everything possible to placate him. He claimed the grand cross of Saint Ferdinand for Thouvenel, a sum of three millions and a half of francs for the French who had suffered by the bombardment of Palermo, and the royal palace of Chiatamone for the residence of the French minister. Moreover he demanded these trifles within twenty-four hours; otherwise he threatened to take down his arms and apply for his passport. Even Thouvenel considered them exorbitant, and Brenier, to his chagrin, was soon recalled.

The Duke of Caianiello was sent on a special mission to Napoleon III on August 29 to convey the King's regret for the outrage but the Emperor, more satisfied than his envoy with the reparations already accepted, thought it useless to receive him. Caianiello was much upset by what he justly considered an affront to his master. Thanks to the good offices of Canofari, the Neapolitan minister in Paris, he obtained an audience on September 4. Napoleon remarked suavely that this was no time to demand reparations and increase the embarrassments of his Court, which was already overloaded with them. After reading the King's letter he assured him of his desire to help; that Thouvenel had done his best through diplomatic channels. Caianiello discussed the 'neutralization' of the capital to save it from destruction, but as Napoleon said, events were moving too fast for diplomatic action: any French *démarche* in favour of Naples would rouse English suspicions that he might wish to preserve its autonomy for a member of his own family—and he was anxious to avoid trouble with his ally. Let the King, he concluded, lead his faithful troops to battle and keep the royal flag flying as long as possible!

Don Liborio's conduct at the State Council of August 29 makes one doubt the authenticity of his memorandum. Perhaps it was a device to hoodwink the historians. In this dubious document he had warned the King of the futility of resistance or reliance on his army; he had also threatened to resign if his advice were rejected; yet in Council he supported his colleagues in favour of resistance. The question was whether the King should go south to Salerno, for which the War Minister Pianell drew up a defensive plan, or retire north behind the Volturno, where the population was stubbornly loyal and the towns of Capua and Gaeta were strongly fortified. Pianell's plan fell through after the incredible disintegration of Ghio's forces at Soveria, where ten thousand men handed over their rifles and cannon to Garibaldi and scattered in all directions. Another expedition to Calabria seemed futile even if it were feasible, with the three provinces and Basilicata in revolt. Garibaldi's Englishman, the eccentric Peard, often mistaken for the Dictator though he was taller and adorned with a longer beard, was availing himself of this error to spread spurious panic-making reports, among others, that Garibaldi was close to Salerno. As a result of this bluff the royal troops in that city were ordered to retreat to Nocera on September 5, so that Peard, still impersonating the Dictator, could enter Salerno in triumph the very next morning. Here Evelyn Ashley, Lord Palmerston's private secretary, turned up to share the excitement and don the red shirt. The Dictator and his staff arrived the same evening.

Francis II cultivated an air of deliberate detachment: he appeared inscrutably calm while his generals wrangled and spat venom at each other. With each he seemed to agree but took no action, while the news got worse, suspicions blossomed into calumny, dread into panic, cowardice into desertion (disguised as a new form of patriotism). Prince Ischitella, who saw him every day, urged him alternately to lead the troops in the field and hold the capital. The King's mind was already made up, but he kept his thoughts to himself.

In Puglia there had been various outbreaks in the King's favour, especially at Matera, Bari, Bovino and Ariano, where the national guard had been assaulted and anti-royalist landlords had been frightened away. In Naples too the liberals were alarmed by a loyalist proclamation, which was construed as the watchword of a *coup d'état* by Don Liborio—for his own glorification. This 'Appeal for Public

Safety from the Neapolitan people to their King Francis II' placarded about the city on August 30, implored him to pack off the ministry, expel the foreigners conspiring against the throne, disarm the citizens, and substitute a loyal police for that which Don Liborio had organized. The latter discovered that a French legitimist priest called Hercules De Sauclières had been responsible for its distribution, if not for its composition, and propounded a theory that he was an agent of the Count of Trapani, another of the King's uncles. Don Liborio and General Pianell burst into the royal palace dramatically late at night to brag of the terrible plot they had nipped in the bud. 'You are brighter at discovering royalist plots than sectarian ones', said the King sarcastically. Don Liborio exaggerated this incident in his *Memoirs*, which are as little to be trusted as their author. The case against De Sauclières and the printers of the proclamation was quashed by Garibaldi's amnesty of September 11, 1860.

The only minister who retained his optimism was Don Liborio: all his weak-kneed colleagues were worried. Cavour's numerous agents were still trying to anticipate Garibaldi with a revolution of their own, to win over the royal navy (in which they succeeded), to control the Neapolitan forts, and prevent the royal army's disintegration. Many senior officers like Nunziante were secretly employed by Cavour to keep their units intact for future use, not only against Austria, but possibly against Garibaldi. The Cavourian Committee of Order and the Garibaldian Committee of Action were at daggers drawn. Though the King had assured all the commanders of the national guard that not a gun should be fired in the capital unless there was provocation, and the 'neutralization' of Naples had been announced in a circular to foreign governments, malicious rumours were rife that the forts were ready to rake the city with fire.

Pianell acknowledged his impotence by resigning, and the other ministers followed his example on September 3. Francis asked them to stay at their posts until he could replace them, but Garibaldi was within a few days' march. Neither Ischitella nor Pietro Ulloa, whom the King applied to in this emergency, could form an interim cabinet. Ulloa argued that the sole solution had become military: after a victory it would be easy enough to muster a new ministry. Better jog along for the present with Spinelli and Don Liborio, whose removal might lead to anarchy and bloodshed. Peard's mendacious telegrams forced the King to declare his intention of retiring to Gaeta 'to defend his legitimate rights'. A council of war was hastily summoned. The veteran General Carascosa tried to persuade Francis to remain in the capital. 'If Your Majesty sets foot outside Naples you will never return', he croaked. But Francis had promised to spare his capital the horrors of war, and the majority agreed that the best line of defence lay to the north between Capua and Gaeta. Small garrisons were to hold the Neapolitan fortresses, and the national guard were to keep order during the King's absence. On September 5 Francis announced his decision to the ministers, the commanders of the national guard and the mayor, thanking them for their efficiency and asking them to persevere during his absence which could not last long. He reminded them that he had kept his promise to save the city from damage. His speech was more embarrassed than usual, and it was obvious that he was deeply moved. According to De Cesare,[1] the source of all subsequent accounts of these last days, Francis stammered: 'your Joe (Don Peppino) . . . and our Joe is at the gates.' He commissioned Spinelli to compose a farewell proclamation to his subjects, while De Martino was to draft a protest to 'the European powers. Liborio Romano claimed to have written the former, but the style is too clean: De Cesare asserts more credibly that its author was the prefect Bardari.

In public Francis appeared imperturbable, but it must have cost him an effort. On his last drive through Naples in an open carriage with the Queen it was noticed that the royal couple were chatting and smiling as if nothing were the matter. They were greeted respectfully, but nobody raised a cheer. Nobody realized the poignancy of the situation. Outside the royal pharmacy near the palace some workmen were already removing the Bourbon lilies. The chemist, though no liberal, was anxious to be on the safe side. Francis drew Maria Sophia's attention to the scene and both burst out laughing. They were determined not to show that they were suffering from emotional strain. After that placid drive they had little relaxation. There was more business to be transacted: decrees to be signed until the last moment, and a thousand and one preparations for departure. But the palace was empty of the usual cohort of courtiers. Only the most loyal remained, and these could not hide their sorrow.

Elliot reported on September 5 that the King's resolution to leave

[1] *La Fine di un Regno*, Vol. II, p. 368. Città di Castello, 1900.

gave every prospect of a peaceful transition, which was 'the one thing that people have latterly been anxious about. . . . It is impossible to describe the loathsome exhibition that has been made, during all these late times of excitement, of meanness, cowardice, ingratitude, and every other low quality. The men that lived at Court, and fattened upon the Court, have been the first to rat, or at least to run away, leaving their "poor young King", as they always called him, to shift for himself, after having themselves done all that was possible to get him into his present mess by encouraging him to resist all change in the system under which they alone prospered. And the Liberals have not shown to any better advantage; the only appearance of vigour they have exhibited being a determination to illuminate the town in honour of the King's departure, which they will no doubt boast of as a vast act of courage.'

Did Francis really expect to return to Naples? Outwardly he behaved as if he did, and in the rôle of his cheerful and undaunted consort Maria Sophia was of the greatest moral support. According to Brenier[1] the King had no further illusion about his fate and that of his dynasty, and all his final arrangements had had but one aim: 'to show a spirit of resolution and save the Crown, as much as possible, from the humiliation inflicted on himself.' Even those preparing his downfall were affected by his cool composure, for they could not trust themselves to behave with such dignity.

[1] Maraldi, *op. cit.*, p. 160.

XXV

T HE last King and Queen of Naples left their capital for the last time very quietly, without any pomp, just as if they were leaving for a well-earned holiday. The morning of September 6 had all the diaphanous splendour and luminosity of lingering summer on the Mediterranean—another proof of nature's indifference to human vicissitudes—and early birds had already seen the King's part- ing address placarded about the sun-steeped city. In a period clotted with bombast its simple restraint was poignant. All the same, it read like an epitaph: 'Among the duties of Kings, those in time of adversity are the grandest and most solemn, and I intend to fulfil them with resignation free from weakness, in a serene and hopeful spirit, as befits the descendant of so many sovereigns. Once again, therefore, I address the people of this metropolis which I am about to leave with deep regret.

'An unjust war contrary to the rights of nations has invaded my dominions, although I was at peace with all the European Powers.

'The changed system of government and my adherence to great national and Italian principles have availed naught against it; rather the necessity of defending the integrity of the State has provoked inci- dents which I have always deplored. Wherefore I solemnly protest against this unjustifiable hostility, on which present and future ages will pronounce severe judgement.'

He went on to specify that the diplomats accredited to his Court were cognizant that he wished to spare his subjects the ravages of war and save their lives and property, the churches, monuments, public buildings, art collections, and all that belonged to the patrimony of the city's civilization and greatness and belonged equally to future generations, above transient passions. Alas, how little was this noble wish respected, how little has man advanced since it was expressed!

But the war was drawing nearer: together with part of his army he was going where he could best defend his rights. The rest of his troops would watch over the security and inviolability of the capital together with the national guard.

The valedictory ended: 'As a descendant of a dynasty which has reigned over these continental regions for at least 126 years after saving them from the miseries of prolonged viceregal government, my affections remain here. I am a Neapolitan; and cannot bid farewell to my beloved people, my compatriots, without bitter grief.

'Whatever be my destiny, I shall always cherish for them a lasting and affectionate remembrance. I recommend to them peace and concord and the observance of their duties as citizens. Let not an excessive attachment to my Crown become a source of turbulence. If the chances of the present war should lead me back among you, or if on some future day which it may please Divine Providence to determine, I recover the throne of my ancestors, more splendid owing to the free institutions with which I have endowed it, what I most fervently pray for is to find my people united, strong and happy.'

So far no severe judgement has been pronounced against Garibaldi's invasion, but it is interesting to note that Sir Henry Elliot, a stubborn adversary of Francis II, criticized the manners of Napoleon III and Victor Emmanuel in terms quite indignant for a supporter of Italian unity. 'We should have to go back a long way,' he wrote, 'to find such a course of deliberate underhand work as has been carried on by our Imperial ally and our pet Constitutional King. If the latter would even now behave like a gentleman and go to war with Naples I would forgive him, for it would be the greatest benefit he could confer upon Italy, as he might conquer this country and place it at once under a regular Government; but the deliberate encouragement of a revolution which neither he nor anyone else can be sure of guiding . . . while professing friendship to his victim all the time, is as discreditable as anything ever done by a Bourbon.' Even in this myrmidon of Lord Palmerston the English love of fair play panted for expression. Great statesman though he was, Cavour had sent fair play to Coventry. In that respect he created a sorry precedent, whereas Garibaldi was merely following his star.

The King's parting address was read with more consternation than relief. The frowning forts were still garrisoned and any light-headed loyalist might set a match to the powder-keg. The embrasures in the castle of Sant' Elmo were said to have been altered to allow the guns to be depressed, the better to enable them to rake the crowded streets. 'The Son of the Saint' in their midst might yet ward off calamity by intercession with his mother in Heaven: he was a man of prayer, a devotee of San Gennaro. The newcomers were reputed to be godless. . . . A proclamation from the prefect of police exhorted the citizens to keep calm and not 'rashly compromise the glorious destiny now dawning' over their country, but the Neapolitans had never been distinguished for that particular trait. Don Liborio still controlled the dregs of the population by means of the *camorra*, to whom great rewards were promised, but fear of the unknown controlled the vast majority.

Besides General Nunziante, Mariano d'Ayala had done his utmost to wean the army from its allegiance; he had published numerous articles and made eloquent speeches, assuring his former comrades of the Nunziatella that each would find a cosy commission in the army of Victor Emmanuel, with his rights of seniority respected, etc. 'The Neapolitan soldiers,' he wrote, 'have confirmed their traditional valour even in this most desolate war; and now it behoves all, if not them alone, to save the fatherland. The Neapolitan officers and men will bring the treasures of their tactical and strategic knowledge, their discipline, their bearing, the beauty and decorum of their uniforms, their arms, their horses, their batteries; and they will be most worthy of the august and respected title of Italian soldiers.' He preached in vain. Most of the army marched out of Naples to Capua, refusing to desert their King in time of danger.

Several baggage vans also left the palace, but the King only took a small fraction of his personal property, including very few objects of intrinsic value. The vast royal collections of gold and silver plate were left behind and turned over to Garibaldi by the officials to whom they had been entrusted. Nor did the King withdraw his holdings from the banks, which amounted to some eleven millions of ducats. By his special orders none of the valuable paintings and furniture belonging to the Crown were removed with a few exceptions, which proved his religious piety rather than his artistic taste. Apart from a favourite Madonna known variously as the 'Colonna Raphael' and the 'Madonna of the Nuns of Sant' Antonio',[1] these consisted of family portraits, a mediocre bust of Pius IX, sixty-six reliquaries, a life-size figure in wax of Saint Jasonia which had been in his private chapel, and an assortment of holy images and what the French neatly classify as *bondieuseries*.

The faithful Captain Vincenzo Criscuolo begged the King to disregard Don Liborio and those who tried to induce him to sail away furtively, under a foreign flag. Admiral Persano had ordered the Piedmontese ships anchored off Santa Lucia to take up positions opposite the military port, and almost block the narrow channel. Persano's aim was to prevent the fleet from following Francis, and it looked as if he would prevent the King's departure. But Captain Criscuolo of the steamer *Messaggero* had received orders to sail for Gaeta at six the same evening, and he was determined to carry them out in spite of trouble with individual members of the crew, chiefly with fractious firemen. The *Messaggero* was a modest vessel of 160 horse-power and four guns but still the King's own, and he would sail under his own flag.

Like curs with tails between their legs the constitutional ministers went to take leave of the young monarch they had served so ill. It was merely their duty, however unpleasant, as Spinelli reminded them. Francis received them with a good-natured courtesy they had done nothing to deserve. According to De Cesare's familiar account, one of them wept crocodile tears. If their consciences pricked them, which is doubtful, they could not help being impressed with the significance of the occasion. For each in turn the King had a few

---

[1] This was eventually presented to Bermudez de Castro, who bequeathed it to Francis II. For many years it was lent to the South Kensington Museum. After the King's death it was bought by Martin Colnaghi, from whom it was acquired by Pierpont Morgan, who in 1915 deposited it on loan at the Metropolitan Museum, New York. For this information I am indebted to Mr John Pope-Hennessy.

gracious words, but his 'Thank you, thank you!' sounded sarcastic when one of them condescended to congratulate him on sparing Naples the horrors of civil war. His words to Don Liborio have been variously interpreted. He is said to have remarked: 'Look out for your head, Don Libò.' To which ambiguous warning—he might have been alluding to peril from Piedmont—the wily patron of the *camorra* is said to have retorted characteristically: 'Sire, I will do my best to keep it on my shoulders as long as possible.' 'The end of a dynasty!' wrote the acting Finance Minister Giacchi to his wife shortly after. 'Tomorrow we shall resign our powers to Garibaldi, pure and without stain. . . . As for me, I have had the great good fortune to save the country and this is the highest title of nobility for my family.' Such presumption is illuminating, as if, but for his efforts, the mild and pious Francis would have allowed his beloved birthplace to become a heap of ruins.

Even more illuminating is Don Liborio's telegram to Garibaldi next day: 'To the invincible General Garibaldi, Dictator of the Two Sicilies from Liborio Romano, Minister of the Interior and Police: Naples awaits your arrival with the keenest impatience to salute you as the redeemer of Italy, and to place in your hands the power of the State and her own destinies. . . . I await your further orders and am, with boundless respect for you, invincible Dictator, Liborio Romano.'

Except the English, French and Piedmontese envoys, all the foreign diplomats who received the King's protest went privately to bid him farewell. Besides those who were to accompany their sovereigns to Gaeta, hardly twenty Court officials were present for the final hand-kissing, a dismal parody of so many bygone ceremonies. Only one of the leading courtiers, Marchese Imperiale, the chief equerry, had the courage to attend. So moved was the King that he said: 'I shall never forget your loyalty to my person, but I wish to give you a token of this.' Offering him the grand cross of the Order of Saint Ferdinand, he added: 'Very seldom has the motto of this Order been so apt as in your case: *fidei et merito*.' All the royal servants were there: at least they realized what they were losing, and many burst into tears. To comfort them, the Queen said: 'We shall soon be back.' Did she really believe it? At any rate she behaved as if she did, and left most of her wardrobe behind. She held her head high as she walked arm in arm with her husband down to the dock, in a simple travelling dress and a straw hat decked with flowers. Francis wore uniform as usual. They were followed by a restricted *élite* of incorruptibles. Foremost among the ladies who refused to leave the Queen was the aged Duchess of San Cesario who, as Maria Sophia wrote later, proved 'a second mother' to her: '*Dans les circonstances les plus critiques et aux jours de dangers et de désastres vous avez été près de moi quittant tout ce qui vous était cher pour nous suivre et nous donnant chaque jour des preuves de votre fidélité et de votre dévouement. Le temps passe, mais mes souvenirs restent et la vieille amitié que j'ai pour vous est à l'épreuve du temps et de la distance. Ces sentiments sont aussi ceux du Roi qui me charge de vous le dire.*'

Before sailing Captain Criscuolo signalled to the Neapolitan warships in the roads to accompany the sovereigns to Gaeta, but Persano had been lavish with Piedmontese largesse. The crews had been told that the King would send them to Trieste. Hence the vessels remained at anchor. Off Procida, the *Messaggero* met a squadron of four steam-frigates which also disobeyed the royal commands. (The next day they passed over to the Piedmontese navy, but many of their crews were to join the King at Gaeta.) The sea was as smooth as an artificial reservoir; the sky glittered with stars: all seemed serene, yet the voyagers on board the lonely little ship were thoroughly dejected.

Both Francis and Maria Sophia had been put to a severe test for so young and inexperienced a couple, and they had smiled through it with stoical composure. Like actors who had played exigent rôles to the best of their ability before a hostile audience, now that they were left to themselves behind the scenes they were exhausted. Physically and mentally younger than her husband, Maria Sophia could brush the past behind her without undue regret. Naples had been an extraordinary revelation to her and she had been as entertained by it as a child at a pantomime, but she had also seen much of misery, treachery and ingratitude: the charm of its picturesque strangeness had worn off, and a change was not wholly unwelcome. She possessed more pluck than the princes among whom her lot was cast, and she could still regard the world as a place of brightness. Conscious of her beauty and splendid constitution, she was impatient to live a more heroic life. Gaeta would give her that opportunity. For Francis it was different. He had known no other country, and he was haunted by the host of images of familiar people and things he was being torn from with a bitter sense of foreboding. The note of change struck him like a painful

The Chapel of San Gennaro, by Giacinto Gigante

discord. The unfamiliar did not appeal to him, and he dreaded the prospect of exile. He was aware that he was no hero: he had no aggressive instincts. But an indomitable sense of duty would come to his aid.

No refreshments were served on the *Messaggero*, for none had any appetite for food. Eventually the Queen retired to a small deck-cabin and fell asleep. The King paced the deck alone, his head bowed under the stress of tormenting thoughts, and when the Captain went to inquire if he was resting Francis said to him with a sigh: 'Vincenzino, I believe the whole navy has betrayed me, and that none of the ships we signalled to will follow us to Gaeta.' Criscuolo tried to soothe his anxiety, though quite aware that this was dismally true, but the King interjected: 'The Neapolitans would not judge me fairly by my works. I am conscious of having always done my duty. As for them, they will only be left their eyes to weep with.' The embarrassed sailor continued to comfort him with kindly platitudes. 'I don't know why remorse does not kill all those who betrayed me,' Francis exclaimed. 'Only God can reward your fidelity, dear Vincenzino. As for me, I shall never forget you.' Then he asked where the Queen had retired. Finding her fast asleep in the deckhouse, he was reluctant to waken her though a chilly night breeze was blowing. Very gently and tenderly, he covered her with his cloak. At six o'clock next morning they reached Gaeta, and the Princes who had preceded them with the Queen Dowager climbed on board to pay their respects, followed by the local authorities. Old Father Borrelli sobbed as he kissed the King's hand. 'I remember well what you told me at Portici, Father, on the 24th of June,' said Francis. 'If Your Majesty has not been a great king on earth, you will be a great saint in Heaven,' the priest retorted. His prediction had been correct, for the belated Constitution had flooded Naples with the King's enemies when he required all the power at his disposal to build a dam against the avalanche descending from Piedmont.

Garibaldi's entry to Naples by special train on September 7 has been described by dozens of friendly authorities—with less emphasis on the train journey than on the mob's ovation, which reached a pitch of hysteria surprising to those unfamiliar with the vagaries of the Neapolitan populace, intensified in this case by the *camorra*. Count Ricciardi drove the whole length of the Toledo waving a tricoloured flag and shouting: 'Garibaldi arrives at midday. Everybody to the station!'—until he lost his voice and another patriot took over. Don Liborio and the national guard had to sweat out an hour and a half on the station platform in scorching heat before the train unloaded the liberator. The mob soon swamped the guard and swept Don Liborio far away from Garibaldi's carriage, where he had struggled to sit and flaunt his happy partnership: his welcoming address was drowned in the prevailing pandemonium. Already the venerable camorrist was stung with the presage of his own decline.

The King's orders were strictly obeyed. Not a single shot was fired at the Dictator, who stood up in his carriage with folded arms and flashing eyes amid the shrieking throng, advancing at a snail's pace towards the Foresteria, the annexe of the royal palace where the King used to entertain his guests. Here Mariano d'Ayala greeted him with another harangue and pressed on his hairy cheek 'the kiss of five hundred thousand Neapolitans' before he had a chance to orate from the balcony on behalf of all Italians and humanity, thanking the multitude assembled on the palace square, who were passing from the yoke of tyranny to the rank of a free nation, for the sublime act they were accomplishing to-day. Since he had tactfully expressed his desire to visit the shrine of San Gennaro as soon as he arrived, he proceeded to the Cathedral, where his fighting Franciscan friar Pantaleo celebrated a *Te Deum* of doubtful orthodoxy and the relics of the Patron Saint were shown him by the quaking canons. Fra Pantaleo, a Sicilian version of Friar Tuck, leapt into a pulpit in vestments bristling with weapons and delivered an impromptu sermon, the gist of which was that God first delivered the Law to Moses, then sent an improved version of it by His son Christ the Redeemer, and now fulfilled it in its final perfection by means of the new Redeemer Garibaldi.

The superb Palazzo d'Angri had been requisitioned for Garibaldi's Neapolitan headquarters, and a period of public delirium commenced which had less to do with 'joy at liberation from tyranny' than with a simple desire to make merry, as in the past, for the Piedigrotta festival on September 8. The Dictator had promised to be punctually at Naples for this occasion. The Bourbons had always celebrated it with regal pageantry. Though it was raining cats and dogs, Garibaldi drove to the sanctuary with Don Liborio, and after a little speech in favour of Christianity, he was half suffocated by the embraces of men and women who were delighted to discover that he was not an atheist after all. 'Don Peppe', as they dubbed him, had made an excellent impression by reserving his first visit for San Gennaro and his second for the Madonna of Piedigrotta. Nevertheless the national guard, and the crowds who had assembled out of idle curiosity, were soaked to the skin, and some could not help thinking that Heaven was weeping for the absent 'Franceschiello'. There may be a subtle joy, as Baudelaire remarked, in deserting an old cause in order to find out what one will feel in serving a new one. The merrymakers had not yet found out what they felt. For the time being they were intoxicated with novelty and relieved to have escaped from civil war. But after the hangover they would have welcomed Francis II with equal fervour. Garibaldi was a heady potion. Only ten days later Elliot was reporting that many of the Neapolitans 'would give their ears to get rid of him and are quite astonished to find that he did not come here in order to be their very humble servant'.

Garibaldi's first decree following his entry presented the Neapolitan fleet *en bloc* to King Victor Emmanuel, an act often praised for its generosity, but in fact Admiral Persano had already won over most of the officers. Piedmont thereby gained, as Mr Mack Smith has pointed out,[1] 'a more substantial navy than she already possessed, in which there were five ships able to outgun any of her own'. He also showed his goodwill to Piedmont by requesting the Bersaglieri in the bay to garrison the city. His thoughts were directed towards Rome, and he was planning to march forward and proclaim the King of Italy on the Capitol. But in this direction at least Cavour, encouraged secretly by Napoleon III with his *'Faites vite!'*, was able to forestall him. Four days after Garibaldi's arrival in Naples the Piedmontese invaded Papal Umbria and the Marches, and on September 18 General Lamoricière's brave little motley force of Papal volunteers was routed by General Cialdini's 17,000 troops at Castelfidardo before they had a chance to reach their destination at Ancona. Ten days later Ancona had to surrender, after a heavy bombardment by Admiral Persano's fleet, and two more provinces belonged to King Victor Emmanuel. The brief and successful campaign had been aided by Napoleon's tacit connivance while his own forces under General Goyon were still protecting Rome, so that the Pope and General Lamoricière, misled by his

[1] *Cavour and Garibaldi*, p. 211.

ambassador De Gramont who seems to have been kept in the dark, had relied on French intervention.

At first Garibaldi was pleasantly surprised. He felt optimistic about defeating or 'converting' the rest of the Neapolitan army, since it had crumbled with such facility hitherto. It never occurred to him that there was a hard core of loyalty to King Francis among the rank and file. After September 6 there was a steady concentration of royal troops behind the Volturno river, where the population was devoted to the King. Nearly all the disbanded corps came of their own free will, many from distant provinces of Puglia, Calabria and the Abruzzi, and as Cava wrote,[1] 'it was moving to see how those soldiers barefooted, in rags, worn out by their long journey to avoid the places occupied by Garibaldini, were heartened as soon as they had joined their comrades. Shouting *Viva il Re!* they asked for rifles even before asking for bread, of which they had greater need. "But why did you come here instead of going to your homes?" they were questioned. "Because it is our duty," they replied.'

Naturally there was much confusion before this army of some 40,000 soldiers could be reorganized, but all were eager to prove that it was not for lack of courage that they had succumbed to the revolutionary rollers. The King often went to Capua to embolden his men, who showed a very different spirit now that they were rid of the defeatist ministry and most of their treacherous officers, though at Capua too there were a few falterers and deserters, such as the feeble governor General Pinedo who fled to Naples from his responsibilities. Provisions and ammunition were collected; the defences of Capua were strengthened; and mutual confidence between the soldiers and their officers was restored. While a new ministry was formed under General Casella at Gaeta, General Ritucci was put in command of the army which occupied Capua and its neighbourhood. Strategically Francis was in a strong position both for offence and defence, with Naples only eighteen miles from Capua across level country, and he launched a hopeful appeal: 'Soldiers, it is time that the voice of your King should be heard in your ranks, the voice of the King who grew up with you, who has lavished all his care upon you, and who now comes to share your lot. Those who, by letting themselves be deceived and seduced, have plunged the realm in mourning, are no longer among

[1] *Difesa Nazionale Napoletana*, p. 13 note.

us. . . . I appeal to your honour and loyalty, that we may wipe out the disgrace of cowardice and treachery by glorious deeds. We are still sufficiently numerous to annihilate an enemy which employs the weapons of deceit and corruption. . . . Will you permit your Sovereign to abandon the Throne, and leave you to eternal infamy? No! At this supreme moment let us rally round the flag to defend our rights, our honour, and the fair name of Neapolitans, which has been discredited.'

General Ritucci was an estimable person, but he was lamentably cautious when he should have been bold. Most of this critical September was wasted in delaying defensive tactics while it was possible to launch a vigorous counter-offensive. Garibaldi, on his side, was too shrewd to attack Capua after a series of royal sorties in which his volunteers were invariably worsted. During a brief visit to Palermo to curb Sicilian impatience for annexation to Piedmont, his reckless Hungarian subordinate Türr captured the small hill-town of Caiazzo on September 19, but his casualties in a reconnaissance against Capua had been so severe that he was forced to retreat from the walls, pursued by the Neapolitan General Rossaroll who, though nominally retired at the age of seventy-five, rode forth and charged the enemy until he fell wounded. The King's half-brothers, the Counts of Trani and Caserta, fought with equal valour. Had the advantage gained been followed up, the consequences might have been disastrous for the Garibaldians, stunned by their first heavy reverse.

The Neapolitans soon showed that they had recovered their morale. Caiazzo was stormed and recaptured on September 21 with even heavier losses among the red-shirts. The royalists were flushed with confidence, but General Ritucci remained far too cautious to risk a big attack and advance on the capital as the King kept urging him to do. Another precious week was wasted: while Garibaldi improved his communications the royal army was weakened by division into separate forces, one of which was under the Swiss Von Mechel, more daring than intelligent, who repeated the mistakes he had made in Sicily, behaving as if he were quite independent, and scorning liaison with his commander-in-chief. A golden opportunity for a combined assault on Garibaldi's troops at Maddaloni and Santa Maria was missed, while Garibaldi reorganized his volunteers and stiffened them with Piedmontese detachments, drawing fresh supplies from Naples. Disappointed by Ritucci, Francis tried to find a more enterprising substitute, but the French generals to whom he applied would only come on condition they obtained the Emperor's consent, an oblique formula of refusal.

The crisis came on October 1 in a series of battles known collectively as the Battle of the Volturno. At last Ritucci decided to break through Garibaldi's line and open up the road to Naples. The assault took place before dawn and led to the fiercest fighting in the whole campaign. Helped by thick fog, some royalist columns penetrated the Garibaldian line between Sant' Angelo and Santa Maria while others surprised and routed the defenders of San Tammaro, who fled to Naples and spread such a panic that D'Ayala, the commander of the national guard, had much ado to smother alarms and prevent a counter-revolution. Garibaldi rushed from his headquarters at Caserta (how fallen from its ancient splendour!) to the battle area, where the King and his brothers encouraged the loyalists to excel themselves.

On his way to Sant' Angelo by carriage Garibaldi had a narrow escape. His coachman was killed outright and a member of his staff was fatally wounded, but the Dictator was able to jump out and walk to Sant' Angelo. This was a prelude to a long day's carnage in which he drove back the Neapolitans with desperate bayonet charges and repeated the word 'victory' like a magic spell before any sign of victory was apparent. Towards two o'clock in the afternoon the Garibaldians seemed to be routed, but Garibaldi proved a better strategist than his foes. The Neapolitans were scattered over too wide a front, whereas he could bring up fresh reserves from Caserta by railway. And according to his *Memoirs* it was the reserves who saved the situation after three o'clock when the Neapolitans showed symptoms of exhaustion. 'Had these been repelled by an enemy force, the result of that day would at least have been indecisive. Which proves that the dispositions of the Bourbon generals were none too bad.' There were heroic episodes on both sides, but those of the Neapolitans have been played down by most historians. Trevelyan[1] has left the clearest account of that day of doom for the Bourbons of Naples, 'the last of Garibaldi's great feats of war'. Eventually the Dictator telegraphed the message to Naples: 'Victory all along the line.' But his elation was marred by the loss of many champions, especially that of Pilade Bronzetti who,

[1] *Garibaldi and the Making of Italy*, pp. 238–256.

with 280 comrades, held out against a vastly superior force in the mediæval ruin of Castel Morrone for four hours, a delay which 'very probably saved Garibaldi from destruction'.

A group of English sailors on leave from H.M.S. *Hannibal*, smitten with Garibaldimania like all ranks from Admiral Mundy down, played a small part in the conflict by helping to man some captured guns, which did not—*pace* Dr Trevelyan—appear in the light of benevolent neutrality to loyal Neapolitans.

Instead of a triumphant return to his capital, it was a dreary return to Capua for the King. He knew that his prospects had been blighted, though General Ritucci regarded the issue 'more as a missed attempt than as a lost battle'. On the morrow some two thousand royal troops entered the town of Caserta, but Garibaldi brought in several companies of Piedmontese Bersaglieri by train who cleared them out after a sharp struggle, and Bixio's force delivered the finishing stroke. In spite of Garibaldi's brilliant defensive strategy his dearest aim had been frustrated, for he could not advance on Rome while Francis still had an army to march into Naples. His volunteers had held firm, but they were obviously unfitted to capture Capua alone. A military stalemate continued for the next three weeks while an acute political contest over the question of annexation developed round the Dictator. Should the people be consulted by plebiscite, or should they have an assembly of elected representatives? Cavour insisted on the former, and it was only after many tempestuous debates, mass demonstrations, and petitions with thousands of signatures that Garibaldi yielded to what he reluctantly interpreted as the desire of the Neapolitan people.

If only to justify a Piedmontese invasion without any declaration of war a plausible plebiscite would have to be held in Naples. As Cavour expressed it to the Chamber of Deputies in Turin on October 2: 'Garibaldi's expedition sailed in the name of Victor Emmanuel. . . . The King and Parliament cannot allow provinces recently emancipated to remain for long in the uncertainty of provisional government. . . . Not that he (Victor Emmanuel) means in any sense to *dispose* of the peoples of southern Italy by his sovereign decree; but he has a duty incumbent on him to give them a chance of emerging from provisional government by the free manifestation of their wishes. . . .' Winspeare, the envoy of Francis II at Turin, was duly informed by Cavour that having abandoned his capital Francis had virtually abdicated; the civil war and absence of a stable government there endangered public order, and Victor Emmanuel had been implored to put an end to the prevailing anarchy. Winspeare replied that a Piedmontese occupation was contrary to every civilized law: preceding events, the kinship and amity between the two monarchs made it outrageous—a scandal to modern history. The protests of King Francis and his military exertions at Capua were an answer to the strange postulate of his assumed abdication.

The mixed members of Garibaldi's provisional government were relishing their first taste of power at the expense of the liberated people. Judging from the reports of Elliot and Aymé d'Aquin, who had replaced Brenier and could not be suspected of pro-Bourbon sentiments, the interregnum until Victor Emmanuel's arrival was a cacophonous crescendo of anarchy which would have been farcical had it not entailed so much suffering. The poor complained that there was no work, that food had become prohibitively dear, that their horses and donkeys were requisitioned and not paid for, the cabs and hackney coaches carried off to the camp for the wounded, etc. 'It was not to be expected,' wrote Elliot on October 10, 'that a great revolution could take place without great evils; and in truth the state of the country is as bad as possible, and all the old abuses are continued and sometimes exaggerated by the new officials, who imprison and flog on suspicion or slight proof of political misdemeanours, while crime is left totally unpunished.' Police there was next to none, while there was 'a decided disposition to annex property belonging to other people,'—in particular 'about £2,000,000 standing in the name of various members of the Royal Family in the Great Book, which in all countries has been held sacred even by revolutionary Governments, and this will disgust many people.' Aymé d'Aquin reported that the new governors of the provinces made the most deplorable use of their omnipotence. 'Some of them behave not as agents of a free government but as veritable tyrants. For instance the governor of Chieti in the Abruzzi, Clemente de Cesaris, inflicts the penalty of flogging as in the worst days of absolutism.'[1] To the despair of his real admirers, noted Elliot, Garibaldi unfortunately considered himself a great administrator, and issued decrees, of which some were good, but others as monstrous as anything that was issued by the kings his predecessors.

[1] Maraldi, *op. cit.*, p. 188.

'The resistance of the King's troops at Capua,' Elliot had written on September 27, 'will put the Sardinians in an awkward position, but it will not do for them to hesitate now, and notwithstanding all their protestations of a wish to be friends with Francis II, nothing remains for them but to come and give him the *coup de grâce*, and to take absolute possession of the kingdom, which is fast getting as anxious to be out of Garibaldi's hands as it was a few weeks ago to get into them. . . .' 'Capua is in a very feverish country, and the malaria will soon begin to play Old Harry among them (the volunteers) so, as I said before, they must have the Sardinians to get them out of their difficulties; but what excuse is to be found for invading the country and knocking on the head the young King, who with 40,000 or 50,000 men is still holding his ground? However, excuse or no excuse, they must now go on, for if Victor Emmanuel stops to look behind him we shall soon see him become a pillar of salt.' It was high time for Victor Emmanuel to take possession of the kingdom, he proceeded, 'for ugly things are doing here which very much lower one's opinion of Garibaldi. A new Ministry was formed yesterday, and the man who is made Minister of Marine is Anguissola who, while he commanded the *Veloce*, deliberately ran it into Palermo and gave it up to Garibaldi. His (the Dictator's) reconciliation with Mazzini is true, and he seems openly to adhere to the doctrine of the dagger, for in last night's *Gazette* appeared a decree, signed by Garibaldi, announcing that the memory of Agesilao Milano, who tried to assassinate the King, was "sacred to the country on whose altars he had sacrificed himself with incomparable heroism, while freeing her from the tyrant who was oppressing her." '

The squall arising over an appointment bestowed on Alexandre Dumas provides a comic intermezzo. According to the censorious Elliot: 'No small disgust has been created by the nomination of Alexandre Dumas as the Director of the Museum and of Pompeii, etc, and people fully expect that, with such a blackguard there, some of the greatest treasures will soon be missing. The said Alexandre Dumas is lodged at one of the royal palaces, drinking the King's wines and feasting at the public expense with the choice company that he is in the habit of keeping about him, among which there is a very charming midshipwoman who does duty in the yacht in a dapper jacket and trousers. . . .'

According to Maxime Du Camp the post was purely honorary: Dumas had asked for it as his sole reward for his generous services to the Italian cause in order to continue the excavations at Pompeii, which had been recently neglected by the fallen government. He had taken up this scheme with his usual enthusiasm. 'You will see, you will see what we'll discover!' he told Du Camp. 'We'll bring the whole of antiquity to light with pickaxes.' His table was piled with plans of Pompeii which he surveyed with quasi-paternal pride. 'He wanted to write to Paris for the immediate dispatch of scholars, archæologists, artists who should assist him in his labours, direct the digging, classify and identify the objects. There was no longer any question of Capua, which still held firm and threatened to hold for a long time, or of Gaeta, where troops were being reassembled, or of the French fleet which was ill-disposed if not hostile, or of Lamoricière who was strenuously equipping his men; he could only think about Pompeii, the house of Diomedes, the theatre and the veterans' barracks. *Hic jacet felicitas*, he said to me with his jovial laugh, repeating the inscription engraved on one of the houses of the sleeping city. . . . We were no longer to deliver peoples, we were to deliver ruins; and we wasted no illusions. Dumas wished to write straight off to Victor Emmanuel to ask him to supply a company of sappers for the excavations. He had reckoned without his host, to wit the people of Naples, who objected to the appointment of a foreigner to a post without salary, who asked if the régime of privilege was to be revived, who considered that the intrusion of Alexandre Dumas among the ashes of Pompeii was a scandal, and who murmured: *Fuori straniero!* Dumas was quite aware of this, but we had been warned and were on our guard.

'Among the populace of the Santa Lucia district where all the riots of Naples are hatched we had a few friends who were not chary of information when this might concern us and who were amply repaid for it. From one of these men named Gambardella we heard that in the palace of the Foresteria, which served as our headquarters, a manifestation was being rigged up to demand Alexandre Dumas's expulsion. Its exact day and hour were indicated to us. I received prompt instructions from General Türr and duly went along to Dumas's abode with two senior officers who had been forewarned. The guard of Castelnuovo, not far from the little Chiatamone palace, had been entrusted to a Hungarian company, commanded by a captain we could rely on. It was evening; Dumas was still at table, surrounded by a few of those habitual guests who never failed him. He was in excellent form, laughing heartily at the stories he was telling. A noise came from outside, distant and vague, like the sound of waves over shingle. As it came nearer he pricked up his ears and said: "So there is a manifestation this evening. Against whom? against what? What do they want next? haven't they got their *Italia una?*" When the clamour became more distinct: "Out with Dumas! Throw him into the sea!" the two colonels and I went outside and stood before the door of Chiatamone; the Hungarian company was massed in the first courtyard of Castelnuovo; the sentinels had been doubled; the captain—who is actually a brigadier-general—was leaning against the door with folded arms. The manifestation advanced, preceded by a big drum and tinkling bells and a flag with the Italian colours: it consisted of about three hundred brawlers bellowing with all their lungs without knowing why: it was by no means formidable, for it sufficed a few words and blows to disperse it. The sight of the soldiers lined up in the street was enough to put it to rout; the whole incident scarcely lasted five minutes. When I went back into the palace I found Dumas sitting with his head between his hands. I tapped him on the shoulder; he looked up at me with tearful eyes and said: "I was accustomed to the ingratitude of France but I did not expect that of Italy." . . . Count X, who was one of the colonels accompanying me, remarked: "It is always same rabble as in the time of Masaniello." Dumas shrugged his shoulders and replied: "Pooh! the Neapolitans are just like other people; to expect a nation not to be ungrateful is to ask wolves to be herbivorous. It is we who are ingenuous to take so much trouble for the creatures. When I calculate what the unity of Italy has brought me and will bring me, it is really not worth reproaching myself: work lost and money spent; there must be something wrong with the character of those who wish to turn me out on that account." '

The incident rankled although a banquet was held in his honour and he received a permit to shoot in the park of Capodimonte. It was well known that Dr Bertani and other Garibaldians were dipping their fingers freely into the public purse. Aymé d'Aquin wrote to Thouvenel on September 29: 'The valet of M. Alexandre Dumas has received 45,000 francs for revolvers distributed among the Neapolitan population, though he had already been paid for them by their purchasers. It is said that his master demands 500,000 ducats for his share.'[1] Perhaps the novelist was suffering for his valet's misdemeanours.

Luckily for Italy, said the Neapolitan newspaper *Il Pungolo*, when Garibaldi's friends tried to turn him into a Cromwell, he remained a Garibaldi. So he invited King Victor Emmanuel to march into his new dominions. The plebiscite was held on October 21, and Naples declared for annexation to the kingdom of Italy; Sicily did likewise. As the voting was open, the minority of negative voters displayed considerable courage. A great many had little or no idea of what they were voting for, and even a large proportion of the educated classes, as Elliot judged, 'would prefer that Naples should remain a separate kingdom.' But desire for peace and dread of revolution, coupled with a gambler's instinct and a lust for novelty, settled the matter to Cavour's satisfaction. Several intelligent witnesses remarked on the dearth of positive annexationist opinions, but as Marc Monnier pointed out this was the first time the common people had ever been consulted about their destinies: 'It was well worth seeing them yesterday, these barefoot ragamuffins who had become citizens, clutching their voting cards which they were unable to read. They gathered together in groups, led by a band with flags waving, singing Garibaldi's hymn and shouting in chorus "*Sì, Sì*"....'

Seven thousand Piedmontese troops were already in Naples when Victor Emmanuel and his army entered the kingdom on October 15. But even when the plebiscite became a *fait accompli* Victor Emmanuel would not enter the capital until he had won a victory over Francis II. On October 26 Garibaldi and Victor Emmanuel met near Caianello, and there are too many eloquent descriptions of that encounter for us to compete with them. It is not clear whether the Dictator galloped up to the King or *vice versa*, but apparently Garibaldi reined up his horse and shouted: 'I hail the first King of Italy!' Victor Emmanuel answered tersely: 'Thank you,' and the two clasped hands. They rode on together, followed by their respective staffs, revolutionary red-shirts and conservative uniforms. Was this, as some averred, the proudest moment of Garibaldi's life? He seemed to have submerged any feeling of personal ambition. Subsequently his friends noticed the melancholy sweetness of his expression. The favour he had asked of the King, that his volunteers might have the honour of fighting in the front line

[1] Maraldi, *op. cit.*, p. 182.

on the Garigliano river, had been denied. 'Your troops are tired; mine are fresh,' said Victor Emmanuel. 'It is my turn now.'

Francis II was thus beleaguered by two hostile armies. Although, to Garibaldi's mortification, his red-shirts were allotted to the rear, some of them were to guard the lines for the Piedmontese siege batteries, for while General Della Rocca was to bombard Capua the rest of the newcomers were to attack Gaeta and the Neapolitans on the Garigliano.

The heavy bombardment of Capua began on November 1 and lasted all night, which entitled Victor Emmanuel to share Ferdinand II's nickname of King Bomba. The city was soon wrapt in a pall of smoke, for many of the buildings caught fire, and the civilian population suffered worse than the garrison. Deputations of women and clergy protested to the aged Cardinal Archbishop Cosenza, who wrote to the governor De Cornè that 'as father of the flock entrusted to him by God he entreated him to spare the city, under any condition whatever, from further destruction, and that he would assume responsibility for the consequences to God and the King.' At a military council several officers pointed out that the fortifications were still intact, the morale of the soldiers high and their honour far from satisfied; and that a longer defence might benefit the forces on the Garigliano. But the prelate's appeal prevailed. The bombardment continued even after the white flag was raised at five in the morning of November 2. Capua capitulated, and its garrison of about 9,000 men were transported to Genoa as prisoners of war. The officers were allowed two francs a day, for which they had to wait in a queue for hours like paupers in shabby clothes, while former comrades who had deserted to the foe swaggered past them in resplendent uniforms. But at least, as De Sivo remarked, their conscience was clear.

XXVI

SINCE the loss of Capua the dominion of Francis II was limited to the fortress of Gaeta and its dependent village of Mola, the citadel of Messina and the impregnable mountain stronghold of Civitella del Tronto in the Abruzzi: a few solid rocks and sandy beaches; but he still had a faithful army of about forty thousand men. Heaven might intervene: Francis never lost hope. The hesitant and equivocal Napoleon III might yet support him under the influence of the Empress Eugénie, who expressed her warm sympathy in letters to Maria Sophia; Austria, Russia and Prussia had declared unmitigated disapproval of Victor Emmanuel's proceedings, and they might do even more. Cavour felt apprehensive of an Austrian attack. Whereupon the British Foreign Minister Lord John Russell stepped forward with his famous dispatch to Sir James Hudson, dated October 27 and published early in November.

'Her Majesty's Government,' wrote Lord John, 'can see no sufficient ground for the severe censure with which Austria, France, Prussia, and Russia have visited the acts of the King of Sardinia. Her Majesty's Government will turn their eyes rather to the gratifying prospect of a people building up the edifice of their liberties and consolidating the work of their independence.' Hudson reported to his chief that when Cavour read it, 'he shouted, rubbed his hands, jumped up, sat down again, then began to think, and when he looked up tears were standing in his eyes. Behind your dispatch he saw the Italy of his dreams, the Italy of his hopes, the Italy of his policy.' And from Naples Elliot wrote: 'Villamarina's first exclamation was that it was worth more than 100,000 men, and King Victor Emmanuel appears to have spoken to Admiral Mundy in terms almost as strong.' King Francis may be pardoned for not sharing this enthusiasm. His eyes could only see the destruction of Neapolitan independence and the reduction of his kingdom to a bailiwick of Piedmont.

On November 7 Victor Emmanuel entered Naples side by side with Garibaldi under a torrential downpour. The mood of both coincided with the weather, and the rain caused blue rivulets to drip from Victor Emmanuel's dyed hair and beard onto his dapper uniform. The triumphal arches and allegorical decorations in honour of the occasion were ruined. Umbrellas filled the streets like a procession of giant mushrooms, and the ships at anchor in the bay were tossed about like toys. Gazing at the scene from the windows of the Foresteria Alexandre Dumas and Maxime Du Camp noticed that the Garibaldians had vanished: not a single red shirt was visible. The Piedmontese army and the Sicilian national guard lined the royal palace square, and Dumas remarked that they would gobble the chestnuts without burning their fingers at the fire: 'Assuredly kings are as ungrateful as peoples. One should do good in an abstract manner and never think of any reward: it is the only way to avoid disappointment and to possess one's soul in peace.'

Garibaldi had not wished to take part in a celebration from which his volunteers were excluded. He had other reasons for resentment, but General Cialdini, whom he liked, persuaded him to put in an appearance. Victor Emmanuel was to have reviewed his troops at Caserta; they had all been drawn up in front of the palace and had been kept waiting in vain. 'No apology or explanation was sent, or has ever since been offered. Further to point the moral, Victor Emmanuel did not even write an order-of-the-day thanking the men who had won for him the crown of the Two Sicilies.'[1] Moreover Garibaldi

[1] Trevelyan, *Garibaldi and the Making of Italy*, p, 278,

detested General Fanti, the commander-in-chief of the Piedmontese army, as well as Farini, who had been chosen by Cavour as Lieutenant-General for the Neapolitan Provinces. But the old magic still worked, and there was more cheering for Garibaldi than for the King.

On November 8 Victor Emmanuel was invested with the sovereignty of Naples and Sicily in the throne-room of Francis II, while his courtiers and those of Garibaldi glowered at each other in hostile groups. Garibaldi resigned his Dictatorship and refused all the titles, honours and rewards offered him in exchange for adding to his master's crown 'a new and more brilliant jewel'. His requests to stay on another year as Lieutenant-General instead of his enemy Farini, and to incorporate all his officers with the same rank in the regular army, were also refused by the King; and on November 9 he left for his lonely island of Caprera. In a farewell message to his volunteers he urged them to rally round Victor Emmanuel, beside whom all rivalry and rancour should cease, and to be ready to follow him again in March 1861, or February if need be, to 'give the final shock, the finishing blow to the tottering edifice of tyranny.' But his own bitterness against Cavour, Farini and Fanti continued to rankle, and he could not help saying to Admiral Persano that he had been treated like an orange whose juice had been squeezed to the last drop and whose peel had been thrown into a corner. Before leaving he went on board H.M.S. *Hannibal* to thank Admiral Mundy for his 'sincere proofs of friendship in all kinds of circumstances', and the ship's officers and crew were as intensely moved as the Admiral by 'the look of intense love' on his face. He was far more of a hero to the English than to the Piedmontese.

On the day of Garibaldi's departure Elliot wrote that he carried with him 'the personal respect and admiration even of those most opposed to his projects and loudest in their denunciation of the lawlessness of his enterprise, for although the corruption which has prevailed in every branch of the administration during his Dictatorship has far surpassed anything that was known even in the corrupt times which preceded it, he himself has to the last remained free from a suspicion of having shared in the plunder. . . . A general feeling prevails that he has not received at the hands of King Victor Emmanuel the consideration that his great services seemed to entitle him to. . . . I understand however that His Majesty has expressed his sense of his services in the handsome language and would willingly have conferred

upon him the highest honours in the gift of the Crown; but nevertheless his Ministers and advisers cannot entirely be acquitted of a want
of consideration or generosity, and there is no doubt that having
bestowed two kingdoms upon his Sovereign, General Garibaldi's last
days at Naples have been embittered by the sense of neglect and
ingratitude.'

In an open letter to Garibaldi beseeching him not to abandon the
South, Alexandre Dumas remarked on the wretched plight of the
Neapolitans: 'more mendicants than ever, no work, tranquillity
disturbed, disunion evident, civil discord between fellow-citizens,
knives drawn against bayonets, etc.' In spite of the plebiscite, and
perhaps as a result of it, party politics had begun their dislocating
influence. Never had there been such a welter of corruption—'a
general scramble for good things,' as Elliot described it, 'such as I
do not suppose was ever witnessed in any other country.' There were
thousands of applicants for the governorships of the fifteen provinces,
and there were above 2,500 who considered they had a perfect right
to be made Cabinet Ministers. 'Having been in prison for any cause
whatever during the Bourbon reign,' continued Elliot, 'is a claim
considered irresistible by the candidates, and has constantly been the
only qualification required in the filling up of the places; but these
gentry now come to the Ministers and back up their demands by
exhibiting the muzzle of a pistol to induce them to acknowledge their
merits—so that now the Minister of the Interior has literally got a
guard of Piedmontese soldiers to protect him from the danger he ran
from these noble aspirants for public service.'

The Lieutenant-General Farini hoped to remedy this state of
affairs and 'set up an honest and strong rule at Naples,' but his first
impressions were pessimistic. As he wrote to Cavour: 'the country
here is not Italy but Africa, and the bedouin are the flower of civic
virtue when compared to these people.' Many a self-righteous norther-
ner has aired similar prejudices, but it was scarcely promising for the
newly annexed to be governed by aliens who harboured such opinions,
which were even shared by some of the natives returned from exile. In
parliament at Turin the federalist Giuseppe Ferrari had sharply
criticized this 'racial contempt', pointing out that the legal system of
the Two Sicilies had been excellent, 'and better than any other at
present existing in Italy.' But he had spoken to deaf ears.

While Farini saw the Neapolitans as barbarians who cared little for liberty, Maxime Du Camp[1] considered that they had rather more than was good for them. 'There is much to be done,' he wrote, 'but there are many obstacles to surmount, and the greatest will be the fantastic liberty which these people have enjoyed until now. . . . Never has a tribe of savages had a material liberty equal to that which dishonours the southern Italians. It will suffice to scour Naples to be convinced of this. If the capital is thus, imagine what the provincial towns must be. From a physical point of view the police are not merely tolerant, they are accomplices: they do not repress, they encourage. Half the population sleeps in the streets, wallows under porches, makes alcoves of sentry boxes, mattresses of pavements, and pillows of stones. . . . Mendicity is more than tolerated: it is a regular profession. This disgusting liberty of sleeping in public, of mendicity and excrement, is the only liberty the people of the Two Sicilies could enjoy; and they enjoy it to the extent of most outrageous abuse.'

Before long Naples was ringing with cheers for Francis II and the white flag of the Bourbons was hoisted in the market-place. There were numerous arrests, but the cheers were repeated louder and louder in the provinces. Farini was alarmed by the symptoms of a counter-revolution: he concluded that 'there were less than a hundred believers in national unity among seven million inhabitants.' Victor Emmanuel was pained to discover that he was viewed as a conqueror rather than as a liberator. Above all the peasant class, which formed the vast majority, was disillusioned, for it derived no benefit from the dissolution of the monasteries and enclosure of common lands and had fared better under the old régime. The country landlords had become more tyrannical and the tax-collectors more rapacious. Lord John Russell was informed by his nephew that there was 'very strong feeling' for the exiled Francis among the lower orders.

Like old King *Nasone* of blessed memory, Victor Emmanuel spent most of his time shooting on his magnificent new estates, but unlike that merry monarch he made no effort to be amiable on his rare appearances in the capital. Perhaps he could not conceal his private opinion that the Neapolitans were *canaille*. His language was coarse but incomprehensible to his new subjects, and though he might look digni-

[1] *Expédition des Deux-Siciles*, p. 343, Paris, 1881. First printed in the *Revue des Deux-Mondes*, 1861.

fied it was known that his amours were not. The last Bourbon kings had been free and familiar with high and low but rigidly uxorious: Victor Emmanuel with his overbearing manner and roving eye was compared unfavourably with good King Ferdinand and his gentle son. In a very short time his prestige became deflated. The sooner he went away the better, said Lacaita, and Cavour agreed with him. 'That inconsiderate young man, Francis II, seems bent on remaining at Gaeta in order to vex and annoy his royal brother,' as Elliot had written: in spite of all previous calculations there was no immediate prospect of driving him out. Somewhat mortified by this *contretemps*, Victor Emmanuel had to return to Turin for the opening of Parliament.

While the Neapolitan intellectuals were discussing whether Francis II would resist or surrender and such ethical problems as whether he was right or wrong, Du Camp, a Garibaldian, recorded his own inward thoughts: 'As a man he is absolutely wrong to prolong a resistance which cannot save him in any case. As a king he is right, not because it guarantees his honour, but because he puts kings-by-the-grace-of-God under an obligation to declare themselves and succour him, under penalty of leaving the principles by which they reign to the hazards of revolution. Governments which derive from the same origin are responsible to each other: under pain of death they owe each other assistance and protection in time of emergency. The French republic of 1848 perished and had to perish because she failed to help the other republics founded soon after herself, by virtue of the same rights invoked. If the absolute kings of Europe do not save this member of their family who is fighting for their common principle, they will be lost sooner or later: the day will come when they will also be deserted. Turning towards those who called him brother, the falling Francis II will say: "*Hodie mihi, cras tibi!* I was not only royalty, I was a principle which has been further weakened by my fall. Beware, for soon it will not have enough strength to support you, who fearing to diminish yourselves, did not dare to come and throw your weight in the balance.'

Honour was paramount, but Francis did expect support from a few fellow-sovereigns. His hopes were raised by Napoleon III, who ordered the French fleet to prevent Admiral Persano's bombardment of Gaeta. Elliot, who disapproved of this interference since it allowed the Neapolitan garrison to receive supplies, presumed that the young

Queen had thrown her blandishments round Admiral Le Barbier de Tinan, 'who is a shaky old gentleman, and that this is one of the reasons he encourages them to stay.' Lord Palmerston was so indignant about it that he had a violent quarrel with the French ambassador Persigny and applied for his recall. Apart from his feud with the Bourbon dynasty, he believed every word he was told by the Piedmontese envoy, no matter how preposterous. Lord Malmesbury noted later in November[1]: 'Lady Tankerville called and told me she went to see Lady Palmerston this morning. While she was there Lord Palmerston came in in a furious passion with the Emperor of the French for preventing the bombardment of Gaeta, and saying the atrocities committed by Francis II were dreadful; that he had ordered people's eyes to be put out, their noses cut off, etc, and that it was necessary to put an end to this state of things. Lady Tankerville expressed her disbelief of the story; at which Lord Palmerston got more angry and said it was official and therefore must be true.'

Had there been a slight tincture of cruelty in Francis's composition he might have been more successful. But he remained the true 'Son of the Saint', invariably courteous, chivalrous, kind and self-controlled, trusting in the goodness and sincerity of others, even of his enemies, punctiliously respectful of forms and etiquette. Never doubting the justice of his cause, he lost it through excess of virtue. He was a perfect gentleman, and most of those who followed him to Gaeta were gentlemen of sounder principles than intellectual talents, loyal patricians who had never cared to thrust themselves forward among the crowd of self-seeking courtiers in time of peace and prosperity. Unfortunately the spirit of aggressiveness was predominantly on the other side. The cautious Bourbon generals were no match for Cialdini, who had captured the village of Mola di Gaeta (now Formia) soon after the fall of Capua so that his advanced outposts were within less than two miles of the fortress. But the Bourbon garrison was heroic, and during the three long months of a pitiless siege a young heroine was ever ready to inspire them with her glowing presence and determination to share their fate, the Queen who smiled so bravely under a hail of bullets, who rode up to the batteries at all hours to cheer the gunners, and who never failed to comfort the wounded and the sick, without

---

[1] *Memoirs of an Ex-Minister, an autobiography by the Right Hon. the Earl of Malmesbury, G.C.B.* London, 1885.

shrinking from sights and sounds that would shatter other sensitive nerves. She had decided to remain with her husband until the climax. The radical press of Europe still ridiculed his effeteness, but he proved his essential nobility now that he was left to defend his last ramparts against a ruthless assailant.

The spiritual bond uniting this pathetic young couple in adversity is more memorable than the military campaign of these three months. Sieges are even more wearisome to read about than to experience, and this was no exception. The victims were doomed from the start: they had lost their capital and most of their navy; their army was dwindling rapidly, since some 17,000 troops had escaped into Papal territory and been disarmed there had been more desertions; Colonel Pianell, the General's brother, had surrendered with his whole battalion to the Piedmontese. The plebiscite had become a *fait accompli*, and England was firmly opposed to any sort of intervention: her remonstrances with Napoleon III were to lead to the withdrawal of his squadron from Gaeta. After November 12 the remnant of the Neapolitan army shut up in the fortress amounted to 934 officers and twelve thousand men.[1] Their guns were antiquated compared with those of the assailants, 18,000 strong, and they were overcrowded in too cramped a space with insufficient supplies, but as their conditions got worse their courage grew. There were 14,000 inhabitants including the population of the Borgo suburb within the besieged area, who depended on military rations when they had exhausted their own meagre stock. Two or three French steamers had been chartered to bring stores from Civitavecchia, but their service was neither regular nor certain, as it was not always safe for them to land. The two hospitals and field ambulance became inadequate when a typhoid epidemic started.

Besides Francis and Maria Sophia, the Queen Dowager and her numerous family, including the Counts of Trani, Caserta, Girgenti, Bari and Caltagirone, together with the Princesses Maria Annunziata, Maria Immacolata, Maria Grazia and Maria Luigia, and the Count and Countess of Trapani, were crammed into the modest royal palace. There were twenty-two Court dignitaries with somewhat empty titles, for Vice-Admiral Del Re was Minister of a non-existent Marine and Marchese Ulloa Minister of a sadly diminished Interior; and there

---

[1] These figures are quoted from the Italian War Ministry publication: *L'Assedio di Gaeta e gli Avvenimenti Militari del 1860–1 nell'Italia Meridionale.* Rome, 1926.

were seven members of the diplomatic corps who had followed the King reluctantly from Naples.

The military details of the siege have been copiously chronicled with overpowering dullness, and even Charles Garnier's account of it leaves much to be desired.[1] But the French observer, though somewhat dry, succeeds in communicating the cumulative boredom and agony of its development, and his is the most readable of contemporary descriptions that have come to light.

Boredom sets in early. 'Cafés must be closed at two o'clock after nightfall, i.e. at seven p.m., by order of the Governor. This strikes me as unintelligent: it might be expedient in a town where cafés are political resorts as they were in France in 1848–9, but here there is nothing of the kind. Gaeta has no theatre—*salons* do not exist—nobody could even dream of entertainments. How are we to spend the long winter evenings? In France at least we have the ingle-nook, or what we have given the charming name *foyer*. But the *foyer* is unknown in Italy.' Garnier's impatience with the King's religious scruples and the spinsterish prudence of his staff breaks out now and then, as when the King forbade firing at a church where several enemy officers had settled and Vice-Admiral Del Re would not let a French volunteer venture out in a storm to capture a Piedmontese corvette. 'This corvette was isolated: the repeated thunderclaps during three or four hours and the deep darkness only shot by lightning would have covered the attack, even if the other Piedmontese ships anchored before Mola happened to be on the watch. The King was doubtful of its success. Finally yielding to M. de Salvy's demonstrative arguments, His Majesty said: "Very well, go ahead and arrange it with the Minister of Marine." But Vice-Admiral Del Re raised so many objections that the French officer retired discouraged. By now the King might have gained an extra corvette if M. de Salvy had been permitted to tempt fortune. They are so little used to *coups de main*!'

Local residents were allowed to wander among the batteries, so that it was quite easy for three Piedmontese officers disguised as Frenchmen to inspect them at leisure 'with all the desirable facilities. . . . They were shown with extreme politeness everything they wished to see.' On their way out they were recognized by some genuine French officers, but apparently they managed to slip away. By Novem-

[1] *Journal du Siège de Gaëte.* Bruxelles, 1861.

ber 18 many of the guns had not been mounted on their carriages. 'They should have put everything in a state of defence long ago. The work at the batteries proceeds slowly: a larger number of workmen might be employed considering the strength of the garrison.' After a fortnight the bored diplomats contrived in most diplomatic style to leave the austerities of Gaeta for the fleshpots of Rome.

'A note from the Minister of Foreign Affairs to the representatives of the Powers thanks them for showing their devotion to the royal cause and to the person of His Majesty by coming to reside at Gaeta. His Majesty expresses his gratitude not only to the ministers but also to the governments they represent. Not wishing, however, to expose them to the consequences of a bombardment, the King invites them to go to Rome where they will be considered as still residing near his royal person.[1] Honours are also conferred on the diplomatic corps. The nuncio, Monsignor Gianelli, Count Szecheny the Austrian minister, Prince Wolkonsky the Russian minister, and Count Per-poncher, the Prussian minister, are awarded the grand cordon of the Order of Saint Januarius. . . . Count de Loss, the Saxon minister, has the grand cordon of Saint George, and Cavaliere Frescobaldi, the Grand Duke of Tuscany's chargé d'affaires, that of Francis I.

Now let us lift the veil off this official world. Their Excellencies could find little amusement at Gaeta: they could not even dine at Mola. Their gaze turned longingly towards Rome, and they thought of applying for the King's sanction to retire there. It was a delicate matter, and they discussed their tactics in private session. The representatives of the three great northern Powers were the most anxious to leave, and one of them intimated to the King's *entourage* that they would be gratified if His Majesty were to guess and grant their wishes. At first the King was vexed, but with his usual good nature he gave his consent, and even went so far as to decorate them. But the diplomats were not at all satisfied with simple authorization. Rightly fearing that their governments would reprimand them and that their courage might be liable to suspicion, they begged His Majesty to give them a formal invitation instead. Again His Majesty consented. . . . The Spanish minister, Bermudez de Castro, Marquis of Lerma, has behaved more chivalrously than his colleagues. Not only has he stood aloof from these petty manœuvres, but he has announced that he will never

[1] Gaeta is ninety miles distant from Rome and forty-seven from Naples.

leave the King and will run the same risks . . . remembering that he comes from the land of the Cid. He was not included in the distribution of honours for the simple reason that he had been decorated a long time since.'

Optimism was restored by the arrival of General Bosco, released from his six months parole after the battle of Milazzo. At least he was aggressive. Garnier wrote on November 19: 'He joins the King while the others forsake him. This is an event in Gaeta. Had Bosco been at Capua on the morrow of the battle of Caiazzo the royal army would have crossed the distance separating it from Naples in a single stage. Some of the senior officers were jealous of him because his conduct was a sharp criticism of their own, but the soldiers trust him. After the triumph of the revolution in Sicily he retained his prestige even in the opposite camp, and the fair sex pronounced his name with a tender inflexion. . . .' He was a burly swashbuckler with a huge handlebar moustache. Though he led a couple of brisk sorties, he did not succeed in improving the situation. His bark was far worse than his bite.

On November 20 the Queen Dowager left for Rome with seven of her younger offspring, but nothing could induce Maria Sophia to leave. 'Without children it is easier for her to devote herself to her domestic duties. Glory be to strong women who have enough character and intelligence not to dissuade their beloved mates from the path of honour!' The Archbishop of Gaeta sailed away on a Prussian steamer with the diplomatic corps. 'He is a man of advanced age,' wrote Garnier, 'which may justify to a certain extent his desertion of his flock. What is less comprehensible is that in spite of the scarcity of victuals His Lordship has never dreamt of granting the faithful permission to eat meat on days of abstinence.'

The food shortage was noticeable quite early. 'The spirit of foresight has never distinguished Neapolitan administrators,' remarked Garnier. Potatoes were scarce; rice could only be found at intervals; macaroni appeared like a meteorological phenomenon; fish was exceedingly rare; occasionally a hoard of beans might be discovered; dried figs and raisins had become a princely delicacy; carobs were more common—'horrible fruit which resemble the rind of chick-peas' —but the chestnuts which used to be roasted at every street-corner had vanished. Local inns only prepared food for those who brought their own provisions, but an exception was made for Garnier and a few foreign volunteers. 'Heavens, what an inn! What cooking!' exclaimed the long-suffering Frenchman, who was much struck by the King's abstemiousness. Eventually a soup of bad rice, a plate of beans and cheese became his regular diet. Owing to lack of starch it was impossible to wear a decent shirt. As for hygiene, it was lucky that few were aware of it: the researches of Lister and Pasteur were still in an experimental stage, and microbes were free to multiply in barracks and hospitals.

The King made a gallant attempt to smile when he reviewed his garrison on a wet November afternoon, but Garnier had to admit that he looked harassed: 'misfortune has given him a precocious maturity'. His courtesy to the enemy on all occasions must have exasperated his friends, especially when four Piedmontese ships with cargoes of grain and coal were driven into Gaeta by foul weather. Instead of seizing them he let them go, with a warning that if other merchant vessels flying the Piedmontese flag appeared in the harbour 'they would be subjected to the laws of war, lest his royal magnanimity be interpreted as weakness.' On December 8 General Cialdini, requiring a respite to complete his preparations for a renewed offensive, notified the governor of Gaeta that he had received an order to suspend fire for three days. Brigadier Marulli, on behalf of General Ritucci who was ill, replied that the fortress would also cease fire as an act of courtesy, if General Cialdini gave his word of honour not to undertake any siege works until the three days expired. Cialdini sent no reply, yet the King gave orders not to fire until the enemy started again. A royal proclamation to his subjects repeated that he had chosen to leave his beloved capital rather than expose it to the horrors of a bombardment like those of Capua and Ancona. 'Traitors, suborned by an alien foe, sat beside faithful servants in my council: in the sincerity of my heart I could not believe in betrayal. After so many vicissitudes I was too distressed to punish them and open an era of persecution: hence the treachery of a few, combined with my clemency, facilitated the invasion, which was carried out by means of adventurers who paralysed the loyalty of my peoples and the valour of my soldiers.'

While the shelling of Gaeta went on day after day Cavour sent Count Vimercati to Paris with a personal letter to Napoleon III protesting against the intervention of the French squadron. After considerable delay the Emperor replied that if Victor Emmanuel agreed to an eight days armistice he would advise Francis to abandon the struggle and in case of refusal would withdraw his fleet. The shelling became more intense with the new year, and on January 7 the royal residence was hit. 'One shell,' wrote Garnier, 'entered the room of Colonel Pisacane above the Queen's dressing chamber. The Colonel was absent: of course he will leave it to the rats—if it suits them. The King wanted to stop up the hole with a table. "Pardon me, Sire," said General Tabacchi, "but what use will that table be?" "To prevent the rain from coming in," replied His Majesty. Generals and ministers surrounded him and implored him on their knees to take shelter in the casemate opposite the palace, under the sea batteries. The King yielded, but I strongly suspect that it is only to protect the Queen whom he adores. . . . I must add that the palace is no longer habitable, for all the window-panes are shattered. The Marquis of Lerma told me a charming remark of the Queen's. They were standing near a window when a bullet exploded and broke the panes. "Well, Madam," said the Spanish minister, "you wanted to see the bullets at close range: you have been served to your heart's content." The Queen replied with her bewitching smile: "All the same, I should have liked a little wound!"

'The casemate to which their Majesties have retired is fairly large, but all the ministers except the Minister of War, and all the branches of administration are installed there. It is sub-divided into a quantity of cells which barely contain a bed, a chair and a table. These are separated by planks and screens. The windows are boarded and lamps are kept burning in most of them. A narrow space like a corridor is packed with members of the general staff, who are busy with orderlies, messengers and clerks continually coming and going, and lackeys without livery lounging languidly, just as they did in luxurious ante-chambers.'

Under pressure from Piedmont and England, Napoleon III had decided to recall his fleet, but to soften the blow he proposed an armistice. On January 8 Victor Emmanuel ordered Cialdini to suspend hostilities from January 9 until the 19, when the French squadron was to depart. Cialdini took advantage of the next twenty-four hours to launch a concentrated attack on the fortress with all his batteries, if only to show the French that Gaeta was 'doomed to fall by virtue of

Italian cannon.' The fortress replied with equal intensity. Cialdini wired Cavour the same evening that the French Admiral had been deeply impressed, and that the demonstration had been most effective. It was certainly effective in showing the strength of the fortress and the courage of its defenders. According to Garnier: 'The sailors serving the guns climbed on to the castle rampart when the cannonade was at its height and began to dance in a ring. The enemy took aim at them, but they were not even scratched. Tired of dancing, they sat down to a card-game. If only the officers of the Neapolitan marine had had the mettle of those brave fellows! The massive oaken beams in front of their Majesties' casemate were smashed to smithereens. . . .' He concluded that the damage might have been much worse. General Bosco had tried to organize an expedition to Calabria, but there was no longer any question of that. The foreign diplomats returned from Rome before the armistice expired to congratulate the King on his birthday. 'This proves that their Excellencies are not devoid of gallantry, but perhaps His Majesty would have preferred their presence during his ordeal to the politest of compliments.'

In reply to Napoleon III's letter urging him to capitulate Francis wrote that his cause was also the cause of other sovereigns, of the rights of nations, and of the independence of peoples: 'I am the victim of my inexperience, of the cunning, injustice and aggression of an ambitious Power. I have lost my kingdom, but I have not lost my faith in the protection of God and the justice of man. My rights are to-day my sole inheritance, and in their defence I am prepared to be buried, if needs be, beneath the smoking ruins of Gaeta. . . . I have made every effort to persuade H.M. the Queen to leave, but was forced to yield to her tender entreaties and generous resolution. She wishes to share my fate, and devote herself to the care of the sick and wounded in the hospitals. . . .'

Hideous wounds and ghastly illnesses failed to daunt Maria Sophia, who spent most of her time between hospitals and batteries, equally regardless of shot and shell. Yet there was nothing masculine about her appearance: men spattered with blood and mud gazed at her with almost religious adoration and kissed the hem of her skirt with feverish lips. The sight of her graceful figure stepping lightly through the stench of airless wards thrilled the poor wretches lying on straw pallets with an ecstasy of joy: her eyes gave more than sympathy, her smile brought more than comfort. D'Annunzio described her glance as 'intoxicating as the waving of banners', and indeed she seemed to promise victory. More than her gentle inexpressive husband she was the living symbol of their ideal. The men would do anything for her. They felt instinctively that she was their best friend. One who realized that he was about to die begged a hospital nun to call her late at night, but was told that she was sleeping and needed rest as she was completely worn out. Her maid, however, knowing her eagerness to satisfy the wounded, woke her up; and she hurried off to see the dying man. Almost in a whisper the soldier gasped out: 'I have a wife at home, and should like to leave her the little money I have managed to save, but it will never reach her unless Your Majesty takes charge of it.' With tears in her eyes the Queen promised to oblige him and thanked him for this token of his trust. And there were many other touching instances of the same intimate trust.

Before the armistice expired General Cialdini offered terms for what he considered 'an honourable and advantageous capitulation'. These were firmly rejected, and Cialdini could not help exclaiming: 'If they were not Italians, I should be proud to fight against such men!' Gaeta was still overcrowded, and it would be even more difficult to obtain provisions after the departure of the French ships. Three hundred fever patients were evacuated to Terracina. Members of the garrison who wished to leave might do so, but only three officers and 130 invalid soldiers availed themselves of the opportunity. Other troops had been embarked on French ships and landed at various points on the coast. Some went into the mountains and others into Papal territory to join bands of loyalists and continue the struggle behind the Piedmontese lines.

On January 18 Admiral de Tinan went to take leave of the King and Queen and remarked in courtly style that he was jealous of his officers, most of whom had received portraits of their Majesties, whereas he had been forgotten. The King promptly gave him two signed photographs. This delicate attention had been the Queen's idea; the King would scarcely have thought of it. The admiral was visibly affected when he took leave of the sisters of charity at the hospital. He asked them not only to pray for the King and Queen but also for France, who had great need of their prayers. And he presented them with a precious milch cow and various supplies for the sick.

The French squadron sailed from Gaeta on the 19th before sunset. The admiral saluted the royal flag and the Santa Maria battery saluted the French flag in return. Three Spanish ships also sailed with the Prussian corvette *Ida*, which had conveyed the diplomatic corps to Gaeta during the armistice. 'This is truly a day of desertions,' wrote Garnier. 'The ambassadors have gone, except those of Austria, Bavaria, Saxony and the nuncio. Needless to say the Spanish one is immovable.... Owing to the blockade which would stop communication with the diplomatic corps if it retired to Rome, and considering that he needs official witnesses vis-à-vis the rest of Europe, the King asked these gentlemen to remain. Their Excellencies were surprised and disconcerted: upon their arrival they had encouraged His Majesty to persevere to the bitter end. Suddenly they changed their language, arguing that his honour had been saved, etc, and went off to deliberate their reply. Once outside the royal casemate, they expressed the utmost repugnance to staying on. Meanwhile they received a note repeating His Majesty's request in writing. The diplomatic corps then split into two camps: one composed of diplomats accredited solely to the Court of the Two Sicilies; the other of those who were also accredited to the Holy See. For the latter the pretext of departure was ready to hand and they hastened to assert it: the King could hardly object. As for the other section, the nuncio and the Bavarian minister decided to stay and the Saxon was cajoled to do likewise, but the Russian declared that he was summoned to Rome on special business, and that he could make himself more useful to the King there, while the Prussian chargé d'affaires said that nothing would induce him to remain. Finally the Austrian minister, Count Szecheny, having been reprimanded by his government for leaving Gaeta on the previous occasion, had to make a virtue of necessity: from this rock he gazes despondently towards Rome.'

The French fleet having sailed, Admiral Persano was free to bombard Gaeta to his heart's content, and he sent word to that effect on January 20. A royal commission calculated that the fortress could hold out another two months: even so the prospect was grim. While Persano manœuvred the fourteen ships of his fleet before the fortress, Francis was cheered by another address from his officers renewing their allegiance and declaring their resolve 'to meet either the joys of triumph or the death of the brave with the proud and dignified serenity befitting soldiers.' The combined bombardment from land and sea began with a flourish on the 22nd: during eight hours the Piedmontese land batteries hurled about 18,000 projectiles against the fortress, which responded with 10,679, while bands played cheerful music. About twenty were killed and a hundred wounded on the Neapolitan side. Amid the tremendous volley of shells and bullets Maria Sophia could not be kept indoors. Garnier relates: 'The Queen was longing to climb up to the Ferdinand battery, but the King would not let her. She appealed to General Schumaker, who became her advocate and finally obtained permission under his own responsibility. Maria Sophia was welcomed by the gunners with the most ardent manifestations of love. The Piedmontese greeted her in their own fashion. While her gracious Majesty watched the combat and exposed herself with that valour of which all Europe speaks, a Piedmontese shell falling into the sea at the foot of the rampart made the water splash in a boiling cascade which threw three or four little silvery fish onto the esplanade of the battery, at the very feet of Her Majesty. In front of another battery a plunging shell brought up a huge fish of the kind called *spinola* here. In spite of the firing, a sailor named Falconiere climbed over the parapet and brought back the product of this singular fishery. The *spinola* was offered to the King, who deigned to accept it and served it to his entire Court. . . . At the hospital of Saint Catherine, which was hit by four bombs and where one man had his arm amputated, the patients tried to rise with the arrival of each projectile and shouted: "Long live our King!" '

Was this episode of the big fish and the little fish intended as a parable, a heavenly hint that Francis could only benefit from a big offensive? The garrison fought gloriously, but it was a magnificent flash in a battered and rusty pan. On January 25 an epidemic of typhoid broke out: over 800 soldiers were prostrated by it the next day. The hospitals were crammed; the nurses overworked; soon medical resources were paralysed. Hunger followed, for provisions were fast running out. Though the soldiers were undernourished—most of them had been without meat during the last three months—their morale was splendid. While typhoid was spreading Garnier noted on January 30: 'The sailors have kept their gaiety amid the sad trials to which we are condemned: they celebrate carnival in their own fashion. Though remote from the balls of the San Carlo theatre, they improvised masquerades. I saw them dance hectic tarantellas in grotesque costumes to the tambourine. Then they sang a popular ditty accompanied by farcical pantomime inviting Victor Emmanuel to run back to Turin, ending with the refrain: "Long live little Francis, our King!" A bomb whistled towards the festive group, and the tambourine player held it out like a plate, as if to catch manna from the sky, while his comrades clapped their hands. Further off a wounded man was being carried to hospital on a stretcher. The sailors glanced at it as if to say: "It will be our turn to-morrow!"—and finished their couplet and dance with more cheers for the King.'

Six generals collapsed with typhoid, including Casella, the Minister for War, and Ritucci, the governor of the fortress. Ferrari, who had been the King's tutor, the Duke of Sangro, his aide-de-camp, in every sense 'a noble of Nature's own creating', and Monsignor Eicholzer, the Queen's confessor, succumbed in turn to the fever. Was this not another parable, a sign of heavenly wrath? The Piedmontese had suffered many casualties, but they were at least well fed and free from the epidemic. And they had made excellent use of the armistice: their guns had increased in power and precision.

Both enemy fire and typhoid continued with greater intensity. A series of devastating explosions began on February 4 when several important powder magazines were hit, causing heavy loss of life, destroying large stores of ammunition, wrecking adjacent buildings, and burying hundreds of sappers and civilians under the rubble. The defences round the drawbridge leading to the land gate were so shattered that communication with that quarter was cut off. The Neapolitan batteries replied heroically, but one after another was silenced. General Traversa, the indefatigable commander of engineers, was killed with Colonel de Sangro. To prevent the breach from being repaired Admiral Persano shelled the ruins during the night from gunboats, including the *Monarca*, which had formerly belonged to the King, while the Count of Caserta encouraged a band of volunteers to rescue those who had been buried alive. But this became impossible under constant fire: too many had been crushed and pinioned under masses of débris. There was no talk of surrender, but the governor Ritucci appealed to Cialdini for a truce of 48 hours to extract the dead and wounded. Cialdini agreed on condition that the damage caused by the explosion was not repaired, but the bombardment was resumed on the 9th with greater vigour. Generals Ritucci, Bosco and Polizzi were in favour of capitulation, but General Riedmatten pointed out that the fortress was still in a position to resist. Cialdini had offered to transport the sick to Naples, knowing that this would prove that the hours of Gaeta were numbered.

Appalled by the spreading massacre and destruction, Francis decided to negotiate on the 11th. 'Gaeta is lost. No illusions', wrote Garnier. 'Yesterday evening General Cialdini was asked for a fortnight's truce to discuss terms of surrender. . . . The Piedmontese general declared his readiness to negotiate but he refuses to grant an armistice and suspend hostilities. Firing has continued steadily since yesterday: this morning it was more vigorous than before. . . . The sick lack essential supplies and most of those whose limbs have been amputated die. There are over a thousand wounded and typhoid cases in the hospitals.' The few Neapolitan batteries still standing thundered away fitfully: the last cannon was fired by a sixteen-year-old boy called Rossi. 'Their heroism is useless. . . . However, each fulfils his duty. They fight only to die. They die simply, obscurely: the names of the victims will be mostly forgotten but their conscience is satisfied.'

Owing to frequent interruptions the negotiations in the Piedmontese camp at Mola lasted three days, amid the roar of artillery and rattle of musketry. General Ritucci had protested that it was usual to grant an armistice and avoid further bloodshed; he disclaimed any responsibility for this. Cialdini retorted angrily that he would not have an armistice because he was convinced it was only 'a new stratagem to gain time and delay the final assault': his language was so insulting that General Ritucci resigned and General Milon took his place. On the third day of negotiations a shell struck the magazine of the Transylvania battery, containing 36,000 pounds of powder. The damage was terrific: fifty-six soldiers and two officers were killed. But the firing continued until 6.15 p.m. on February 13, when the capitulation was signed and approved by Generals Milon and Cialdini. All the troops of the garrison were to leave with the honours of war, but they were to be treated as prisoners until the fortresses of Messina and Civitella del Tronto surrendered, after which the Neapolitans were to be disbanded, and the foreign volunteers sent back to their countries.

War had never been officially declared on Francis by his royal cousin of Piedmont, and he took no part in the negotiations for surrender. Napoleon III had had the grace to leave the corvette *La Mouette* at his disposal after the recall of his squadron, and it was on this modest vessel that the last King of the Two Sicilies sailed into permanent exile on February 14, 1861. His parting proclamation to the garrison of Gaeta was more eloquent in its unaffected simplicity than most proclamations. It ended: 'Thanks to you, the honour of the army of the Two Sicilies has been saved: thanks to you, your Sovereign can still lift his head with pride, while in the exile where he will await the justice of Heaven the remembrance of the heroic loyalty of his soldiers will afford the sweetest consolation in his misfortunes. . . .

'Generals, Officers and Soldiers, I thank you all and shake your hands with affection and gratitude. I shall not bid you good-bye, but *au revoir*. Keep your loyalty intact, as I shall ever cherish my gratitude and affection.'

Eloquent too, as that of an eye-witness without literary pretension, was Garnier's account of the departure of the King and Queen: 'At 8 a.m. the Piedmontese vanguard took possession of the land batteries and climbed the height of Orlando's Tower. . . . The Neapolitan troops were drawn up in a line from the King's casemate to the sea gate, less than 300 paces. Their Majesties left the casemate to board the *Mouette*, the King as a simple officer with sword and spurs, the Queen in a little hat with a green feather. A band played the national anthem. . . . I followed the procession from a short distance. It was a scene of august simplicity, solemnity and sadness. Ragged and exhausted soldiers presented arms to their Sovereigns for the last time, tears rolling down their cheeks. The expression of general woe was more striking as they advanced towards the sea gate. They hastened to kiss the King's hand. There was sobbing in the streets. The cruelly tried population . . . forgot their own misfortunes to bewail those of their princes. The King, now very emaciated, was ghastly pale: one could read his emotions on his features. I could not see the Queen's face . . . I looked away. As soon as they passed the sea gate a loud chorus of "Long live the King!" from the people and the garrison saluted the man portrayed as a dreadful tyrant.

'The party was received with royal honours on the *Mouette* by officers and sailors in full uniform, the sailors on the yards. The royal flag flew from the mainmast. A hundred passengers, ambassadors, ministers, several generals and officers, the servants of the royal family, and half a dozen French officers climbed on board: some of the latter, treated as the King's aides-de-camp, thus escaped Cialdini who had uttered coarse threats against them. . . . I too had the honour of being taken as a passenger. The Sardinian squadron advanced to the middle of the roadstead in order to enjoy its triumph and watch the departure of the exiles from closer range. The King and Queen gazed coldly at Persano's fleet while the *Mouette* stood in the roads for over an hour. As soon as all the passengers were on board the royal flag was lowered, and only the French flag protected the vanquished sovereigns. When the steamer started the port battery saluted the King with twenty-one guns: a large flag hoisted on the bastion was slowly raked thrice, and was then removed from the rampart. The remains of the garrison mustered on the esplanade of the battery cheered the King until the *Mouette* had rounded the headland. . . .

'During the short passage to Terracina the King and his brothers, the Counts of Trani and Caserta, showed an admirable serenity and deigned to converse with each of us. For a long time the King had lingered alone at the stern, leaning on the gunwale and contemplating the cliffs of Gaeta. While the French were dining in the saloon he appeared on the threshold and said with gracious affability: '*Bon appétit.*" We rose but he slipped away. . . . The exiles retire provisionally to Rome: only the Vicar of Jesus Christ seems to me worthy of offering them a shelter.'

Many individual acts of heroism and self-sacrifice during the three months' siege have never been recorded. Anecdotes may be gleaned from the musty pages of De Sivo, from the naïve military chaplain Father Buttà and a few obscure memoirs, but most of them were handed down orally from father to son and forgotten, drowned by the fanfare of Garibaldian trumpets which thrill us in Verdi's operas even now. *Væ victis!*

Moralizing historians were to wallow in the downfall of a dynasty which had been described so often as perjured and contemptible, and as 'the negation of God'. Yet this dynasty had always found brave defenders during the 126 years of its reign, and none were braver than those who fought on the Volturno and Garigliano and finally at Gaeta.

Men do not fight so tenaciously without a cause. The garrison which held the last bulwark of the Bourbons with little hope of victory were not only martyrs to military honour; they were not only concerned with redeeming lost prestige; they were fighting for a King they loved with all his faults, for a Queen who embodied an ideal of womanhood, and for an independence whose loss their passive compatriots were all too soon to deplore. Only six months later Massimo d'Azeglio, the former Prime Minister of Piedmont, described the state of the south as follows: 'At Naples we overthrew a sovereign in order to set up a government based on universal suffrage. And yet we still to-day need sixty battalions of soldiers to hold the people down, or even more, since these are not enough; whereas in other provinces of Italy nothing of the sort is necessary. One must therefore conclude that there was some mistake about the plebiscite. We must ask the Neapolitans once again whether they want the Piedmontese or no.'

Those who moralize about retribution should also ponder the fate of Napoleon III ten years after the fall of Gaeta; and of the great-grandson of Victor Emmanuel, eighty-four years since. The monarchies to which Francis II had appealed in his agony were all to collapse amid bloody hecatombs, except England and Belgium. The Problem of the South—'la Questione Meridionale'—arose after 1860. Hitherto the south had gravitated towards a single centre, Naples: now it was forced to gravitate towards Turin, and a civil war resembling that in Ireland was the result. However, it is not our task to judge, but to record, and the history of the Bourbons of Naples ends at Gaeta.

XXVII

FRANCIS II and Maria Sophia were to survive themselves and each other. It has been told that before sailing for Terracina on the *Mouette* the King embraced the last soldier he met on shore and said: 'Kiss all your comrades who love me and tell them that we shall meet again within a year's time.' Whatever his private meditations he behaved as if he were certain to recover his kingdom. Pope Pius IX invited the royal exiles to stay at the Quirinal with all their suite and handsomely returned the hospitality he had received from Ferdinand II thirteen years ago. But he had not the resources of Louis XIV of France and could not afford to harbour another James II indefinitely. Fortunately Francis owned the Farnese palace and other property in Rome, but it had fallen into neglect since the time of Ferdinand I who had moved all its treasures to Naples, the precious marbles, bronzes, manuscripts and rare furniture which had recently been appropriated by the Piedmontese. Only the superb frescoes and sculpted ceilings remained. Now the bare apartments were hastily restored with more view to convenience than to æsthetic considerations, with stout doors for privacy and glass panels against draughts. In early summer the King left the Quirinal for the Alban hills and settled in the Farnese palace on his return: this was to be his residence until 1870 and the seat of his shadow cabinet, or government *in partibus*. Surrounded by Neapolitans who were determined to be faithful to him whatever happened, he saw his last hopes of reconquest evaporate.

At first the Piedmontese domination seemed ephemeral, and the diplomats of those countries which had not sanctioned the *fait accompli* treated Francis as the legitimate sovereign of the Two Sicilies. His halls were full of prelates and ministers who almost believed themselves at Capodimonte. Though he instinctively recoiled from cruelty, he was persuaded to subsidize brigandage as a weapon of counter-revolution, for he regarded the Piedmontese as the real brigands. Eccentric adventurers, Carlists and French legitimists helped to rally bands of ex-Bourbon soldiers, deserters and fugitives from conscription who waged sporadic guerilla warfare against the new régime, especially in the Neapolitan provinces. Owing to ruthless repression, and to the concentration of 120,000 regular troops in the south, this minor civil war flickered out after 1865. Francis continued to protest as each power in turn recognized the new kingdom of Italy and more and more foreign diplomats withdrew from the Farnese palace. His protests were ignored.

Pietro Ulloa, the virtual Prime Minister of his shadow cabinet, has left a detailed description of the odd characters who formed the royal *entourage* during this Roman decade.[1] It was a cantankerous little world of crystallized ultras who believed blindly in the divine right of kings, and of pernickety constitutionalists who bickered less about how to reconquer the kingdom than about how to govern it when it had been reconquered. That they were to be its future governors they took for granted, in spite of the diseases of old age and a galloping death rate. There were indomitable applicants for rewards, honours and employment, ranging from senile generals to seedy pamphleteers, nearly all at daggers drawn. There were monks and brigands, ex-magistrates, spies and policemen. This undignified menagerie did nothing to enhance the King's prestige, which had risen during the siege of Gaeta. It was said that he had been a mere child when he left Naples, but that he had become a king, a man, and a soldier when he left Gaeta. He was still child-like, however, in his judgement of human beings, always ready to trust them and see their better side. Of those who injured and disappointed him—and they were the majority—he never came to feel like Blake:

> '*Thy friendship oft has made my heart to ache:*
> *Do be my enemy—for friendship's sake.*'

[1] Pietro C. Ulloa, *Un Re in Esilio*, edited by Gino Doria. Bari, 1928.

Except in very few cases, Maria Sophia frankly preferred horses and dogs.

Francis was harassed above all by the members of his own family, by his bigoted, scheming step-mother, his disgruntled uncle Trapani, his spendthrift swashbuckling half-brothers. The Queen Dowager made another attempt to reassert her old authority and interfere with the younger Queen's amusements. This led to unpleasant scenes with the Duchess of San Cesario, Maria Sophia's devoted lady-in-waiting, who told her: 'As long as I am with Her Majesty nobody will have any reason to complain or right to criticize her.' The Dowager chose to forget that Maria Sophia had become 'The Heroine of Gaeta' whose picture had been published all over Europe, whose prowess had become legendary, who had been showered with gifts and pæans of praise from unknown admirers, receiving a golden laurel wreath from a bevy of German princesses and a sword of honour from the ladies of Paris. Her courage had shone like a dazzling meteor in the deepening twilight of the dynasty, and this was particularly mortifying to the older woman. Not that Maria Sophia cared: she flaunted her independence more and more.

Louise Colet, one of those illiberal liberal dames of letters who scribbled copiously about United Italy at this time,[1] noted the obvious incompatibility of temperament between the Bavarian amazon and her mate: 'The King was wearing a general's uniform with the ribbon of Saint Januarius: he had the hesitating, grotesque appearance of Thomas Diafoirus (in Molière's *Malade imaginaire*): his vulgar head, with a protuberant nose like that of his ancestor *Nasone*, was topped with a three-cornered hat adorned with a tuft of white feathers. He seemed very young, but it was a sickly youth, as if aged prematurely, sanctimonious and wan. The Queen formed a striking contrast owing to her elegance and beauty. A Spanish mantilla raised gracefully over head so that one could see her fine hair through the black network of lace floated over a black velvet gown which set off her slender figure. Her fresh features smiled from this coquettish frame; her eyes, the gentlest and liveliest in the world, had long lashes to temper their brilliance; the delicacy of her complexion enhanced the charm of her face; her smiling rosy lips made one forget the imperfect teeth. Her whole gracious person revealed sprightliness and resolution: she leaned on her husband's arm as on that of a Court chamberlain. One could guess her

[1] *L'Italie des italiens.* Paris, 1864.

indifference and disdain for this uncouth creature. Romantic dreams hovered over her pretty forehead: the heart of her adventurous ancestor King Lewis of Bavaria beat within her bosom. Dynastic expedience had linked these two beings, but it was easy to foresee their severance since then. The King seemed impervious to so many charms, and she was visibly not in love with this monkish stripling. Fêted in Rome by the French legitimists and the dignitaries of the Papal Court, she appeared very active and gay during the first months of her exile; cargoes of French millinery arrived for her every week. She vied with the Empress Eugénie in the taste and fantasy of her clothes. One evening, after the Easter celebrations, she exhibited herself at the theatre in a crimson dress which suited her to perfection. It was jokingly said that she had donned Garibaldian attire in the hope of rallying young Italy to her cause.'

This was the conventional picture caricatured by the Unitarians, eager to pull the royal couple down from the pedestals raised by Gaeta. Hostile demonstrations were organized when they went driving on the Pincio. Once when they attended a performance at the Argentina theatre, a ballerina removed all the lilies from a bouquet and ostentatiously tore them to pieces. This incident put an end to one of Maria Sophia's few distractions in public.[1] Old Bermudez de Castro helped her to while away the dull Roman evenings with quixotic conversation, but even the courtly homage of this faithful crony who had shared the bombardment of Gaeta became a subject for scandal. The Queen Dowager complained that he came too often and stayed too late: his morals were by no means irreproachable, and these regular *tête-à-têtes* with Maria Sophia might be misinterpreted; besides, they were derogatory to the King's dignity. Naturally Francis paid no attention and Maria Sophia made a point of asking him to stay on. Tongues continued to wag until even the Pope thought it advisable to exert a little pressure. He suggested that the King of Bavaria should intervene, which he did on his visit to Rome. But Maximilian met with such stubborn resistance that the Pope had recourse to Queen Isabella of Spain. Bermudez de Castro was finally recalled.

[1] To discredit the heroine of Gaeta the anti-Bourbonist 'Committee of Action' propagated photographs representing the Queen in obscene poses. Two shady photographers confessed that they had substituted Maria Sophia's head for that of their naked model. Copies were sent to Francis II and other sovereigns.

Unlike her husband, Maria Sophia was not religious, and she was certainly not resigned to the boredom of exile in Rome. This boredom was alleviated by the arrival of her sister Matilda, who married the Count of Trani, her half-brother-in-law—another unhappy marriage. Matilda shared her propensity for riding and country life, but even the companionship of a congenial sister is no substitute for the joys of matrimony. She could not help comparing her demure and clumsy husband with other men she met, most of whom were more prepossessing in one way or another, and her craving for mutual ecstasy was frustrated. Condemned to frustration and inaction, she became nervous and irritable. Like all the Wittelsbach sisters, she detested cats as intensely as she doted on other animals. As the garden of the Farnese palace was infested with these felines she went out with her gun and destroyed them by the dozen. She had always been an excellent shot.

While scandal-mongers associated her name with old Bermudez de Castro, perhaps on account of his conceited bragging, it is probable that she had a love affair with a Belgian officer at this time. Rome did not agree with her, and she hankered after her native land, but according to her niece Countess Larisch[1] there was a more intimate reason for her departure in 1862. She looked ill, and she was said to be suffering from a pulmonary ailment: 'in reality she retired to the Ursulines' convent in Augsburg to give birth to a love child', whom Countess Larisch alleged to have met in Paris in 1877. Francis, left alone at the mercy of fanatical day-dreamers and backbiting intriguers struggling for influence, gave way to complete despair. 'Oh, how much better off we were at Gaeta!' he exclaimed to Ulloa. Only then had he been able to forget his own unhappiness amid the cataclysm. In a shy, inexpressive fashion he was devoted to Maria Sophia. A stoic hitherto, he broke down and talked of abdication, to the horror of his ever-hopeful entourage. With his wife's desertion—and he must have divined the reason for it—his cup of misery was overflowing. The loss of his kingdom, the cruel knowledge that he was unloved, if not despised, by his wife, apart from the other members of his family, the perpetual poisonous calumnies of the press; above all, the torment of his own character, his profound self-distrust and sense of his own inadequacy, of being cast for a rôle quite beyond his abilities, paralysed the

[1] *Secrets of a Royal House,* by Marie Louise, Countess Larisch von Wallersee-Wittelsbach. London, 1934.

little energy that remained in him. He was more isolated than ever, trapped behind the tragedy of his destiny as behind iron bars, expiating the original sin of having been born. He had lost everything but his mystical faith in the Crucified. The present was sombre enough; the future was too fearful to contemplate: the ruin of his country, for which he felt responsible, and the barren wilderness of his solitary exile. Ulloa has drawn a memorable picture of him lying supine, fully dressed, on his austere little bed in the Farnese palace, and groaning: 'The Pope was right when he called me "the little Job"!'

Fortunately Maria Sophia was persuaded to return next year, thanks to the combined efforts of King Maximilian, the Apostolic Nuncio in Munich, the Prince of S. Antimo and the devoted old Duchess of San Cesario. She was welcomed as warmly as the returning prodigal. But the incessant intrigues among ultras and constitutionalists clogged the atmosphere of the Farnese palace: they became increasingly academic and detached from reality. Occasionally a ceremonious reception, as when the King of Bavaria paid them a visit, revived the illusion of a restoration to the throne of the Two Sicilies, but when the royal guests departed the stony silence of the huge halls and frescoed galleries became almost menacing, reminding them that in reality they were temporary refugees in the Eternal City. Victor Emmanuel removed his capital from Turin to Florence in 1865, when France agreed to recall her troops from Rome within two years. 'Of course you will eventually go to Rome,' said the French Foreign Minister, 'but a decent interval must elapse to relieve us from responsibility.' The outbreak of the Prussian-Austrian war in 1866 enabled Victor Emmanuel to join with Prussia and, in spite of crushing defeats at Custozza and Lissa, liberate Venetia from Austrian domination. By the end of the same year the French evacuated Rome, though many of them elected to remain in the Papal service.

The Queen Dowager Maria Theresa died of cholera which she caught while nursing her stricken children, one of whom also succumbed in August 1867. Her death at least brought Francis and Maria Sophia closer together, for she had always made mischief between them. The puritans, as the Neapolitan reactionaries were called, had lost their chief oracle and patroness; the Count of Trapani was but a feeble substitute. Her enemies had been wont to compare her with her ancestor Maria Carolina, but she had none of the latter's intellectual tastes: all her virtues had been domestic. She had even nursed Francis through smallpox when nobody else dared go near him. Owing to the extreme narrowness of her political views she had been unduly maligned.

Garibaldi seized the opportunity of the French evacuation to march on Rome, but this time luck failed him. Yielding to the importunities of the Empress Eugénie, Napoleon III sent an expedition to Civitavecchia, and on November 3 the red-shirts were routed at Mentana. A French garrison remained in Rome for the next three years, until the outbreak of the Franco-Prussian war in 1870.

Gradually Maria Sophia came to realize that she was not the only sufferer from a dynastic marriage. After so many years she could not fail to be moved by Francis's firm devotion, by his unselfishness and patience with her caprices. In 1868 a happy prospect brought a little colour into his pallid cheeks. Without any mystery the Queen was expecting a baby. 'All have contributed towards this harmony so ardently desired,' wrote Ulloa, 'especially the Queen's mother and the Empress of Austria. . . . It is a real triumph for the Duchess of San Cesario, who has infused all the warmth and affection of a mother into their reconciliation. The Queen's embarrassment is full of charm. But how cruel it is to observe the vexation of other members of the family!'

On Christmas eve, 1869, after ten years of matrimony, a little daughter was born. The Princess was christened Maria Cristina Luisa Pia after her paternal and maternal grandparents and the Pope, who acted as her godfather. On December 30 Ulloa recorded: 'Yesterday the ceremony of the baptism was magnificent, surpassing our expectations and amazing the Roman Court. Besides the dispossessed Princes and their families, Prince Hohenlohe, brother of the King of Roumania, and the Duke and Duchess of Alençon (a sister of Maria Sophia) were present. The Austrian and Bavarian legations were also there to represent the Empress, who acts as godmother. But what made the celebration splendid was the concourse of over two hundred gentlemen who had come expressly from Naples, and fifty-two ladies, only three of whom reside in Rome. My eyes were fixed on the Duke of Alençon, who must have thought of his grandfather's exile and realized that he had never been fêted in such a manner in adversity. Even so the King did not wish Neapolitan residents in Rome to be invited, because the halls of Palazzo Farnese were not capable of containing them.

Riancey (one of the leaders of the French Legitimist party under the Empire) . . . seemed astounded by the enormous gathering and pleased by the cheerful and animated bustle of Neapolitans. I passed them all in review for his benefit, mentioning their historic and illustrious lineage. When I exclaimed: "Oh, if it had only been a Prince!" he reminded me that when a Princess, later to become Duchess of Parma, was born before the Duke of Bordeaux, the Parisians said: "It is the rose that precedes the lily!" '

This rose soon withered, and no lily was to follow. The infant Princess only lived three months. For a whole week Maria Sophia had sat by her cradle without undressing or going to bed, and after the child's death in the evening she clung to the little corpse all night in a frenzy of despair. The Marquise de Sassenay has related that the French sculptor Prosper d'Epinay was to have done a portrait of the child. 'One night he was suddenly wakened and told that Francis II wanted him to come at once. He hurried to the Farnese palace, where he found the King in tears. "My child has just died," he said, "the Queen and I both wish you to make a cast of her face." Never having practised this special art, d'Epinay went off to find one of the men he usually employed for such work. He could find nobody. Much upset but anxious to grant the King's wish, he decided to run home and collect the necessary material for making the cast himself. On returning to the Farnese palace he was ushered into a large room dimly lighted. Its only piece of furniture was the cradle in which the dead Princess was lying. The Queen was weeping and praying on her knees, and the King knelt beside her. D'Epinay approached the royal couple and knowing how painful the process was to witness, he begged Francis to retire and escort the Queen from the room during the operation. The King then whispered to his wife, who made a gesture of refusal. D'Epinay insisted that he could not perform his task in the presence of their Majesties, who then decided to withdraw. Alone, the artist applied the plaster and waited for it to dry before removing it; but in his flutter he had forgotten to smear oil over the dead child's face previously, so that when he wished to remove the plaster he failed. D'Epinay then had a moment of panic, and setting himself astride the cradle to increase his efforts he struggled to make the mask yield.

While intent on this tragic task he thought of the parents' anguish if the face of their child were disfigured by the operation. Mercifully their Majesties were spared this affliction, for eventually the mask yielded and the features remained intact.' The Princess was buried in the church of Santo Spirito dei Napoletani behind the Farnese palace.

This calamity made Rome odious to Maria Sophia. Now she could only think of leaving it. 'The child was a powerful link between the King and Queen,' wrote Ulloa, 'and since it has been broken their former coolness may return with all its consequences. I fear that the first of these will be a hasty departure for Germany, leaving the King alone for eight months and damping our spirits and hopes. Comedies always accompany tragedies, however. I am told that yesterday there was an altercation between Cardinal Monaco and Monsignor Gallo about the question as to whether the child was to lie with her feet towards the high altar or towards the atrium. Gallo upheld the last opinion, as a privilege of the Neapolitan royal family. And thus the small corpse was laid.'

Francis maintained an impassive calm, but it was noticed that he wandered restlessly in and out of the Queen's apartment. She had already begun to pack, and as if she had been seized with a sudden aversion for her Neapolitan retinue she refused to see them. In the meantime a commission of bishops was held for the beatification of the King's mother and its members were anxious to inform him that her saintly virtues had been clearly made manifest, supposing that this would help to console him for the death of his daughter. But he was still in deepest mourning and he, too, decided to leave Rome. He left the Farnese palace on April 21, never to return. In the same year, thanks to the German attack on France all the French troops were withdrawn from Roman territory and Victor Emmanuel was free to conquer the Holy City, which was annexed to Italy by plebiscite on October 2.

As long as the Queen's parents were alive Francis and Maria Sophia spent the summer in Bavaria; the rest of the year they lived quietly in Paris, where the frivolous Countess Larisch visited them in the spring of 1877. 'The deposed royal couple,' she wrote, 'had grown to regard each other with a kindly, if somewhat resigned, tolerance. When I arrived in Paris, chaperoned by Mademoiselle Bertha, I did not expect Aunt Maria and the King to meet me, as it was very late at night.

Nevertheless the royal couple awaited me at the station. Uncle Francis was extremely friendly, and Aunt Maria her usual beloved self. I felt immediately at home as soon as we drove up to an old-fashioned but cosy dwelling; its very simplicity was impressive. Despite the late hour a *souper* was served, and I could see how time had healed old wounds. Aunt and Uncle had grown very much attached to each other, after almost two decades of married life. Always ailing, the ex-King was on a very strict diet, and every bite of food he consumed was watched by Aunt Maria. If ever Uncle Francis ordered a dish not on his diet list, the ex-Queen, like any good wife, would admonish him, putting her hand on his arm: "*Assez, cher ami! Je t'en prie!*" And the King would desist, a bit regretfully . . . like any other husband. After all the curious young girl's ideas I had entertained about these two, this little domestic scene touched me greatly.'

A sufferer from diabetes, Francis II died at Arco in the Trentino, which then belonged to Austria, in 1894. But: 'the King is dead, long live the King!' His half-brother Alfonso, Count of Caserta, was next in succession and published a proclamation asserting his rights to the throne of the Two Sicilies.

'Admirable in his conduct, both as a man and as a husband,' had been the minister Ulloa's verdict on Francis II: he did not add 'as a King'. The gentle dignity of his character had won universal respect. He had forgotten and forgiven his enemies, but his letters to Neapolitan loyalists, steeped in melancholy and resignation, betray his distaste for the contemporary scene: every year, as he wrote: 'surpassed the year preceding it in sorrow and falsehood'. Until his death he continued to protest that he was Neapolitan in heart and soul, and to express a hungry interest in all the news that reached him from his former kingdom. He felt thoroughly convinced that the Neapolitan people had remained loyal to him. In December 1893, he wrote to his old friend the former ambassador Ludolf: 'May God will that from this period of dark confusion, towards which we are approaching, another very different period will emerge, of reparation and rectification of wrongs suffered, granting all of us strength to bear the former and make the best use of the latter.' And a few weeks before he died: 'You tell me that patience makes a martyr of man: I sincerely hope so for the sake of my soul, but I do not count much on it, considering our fragility and that of the human factors on which we depend.' His gloom was also due to ill-health, and his wife's abundant vitality failed to overcome it. She could not be blamed for escaping from him now and then, for such gloom is apt to be contagious. He wished to be buried near his infant daughter in Rome—a desire that was not fulfilled until 1938.

Maria Sophia, who happened to be in Paris when Francis died, rushed to Arco for the funeral ceremony, which was attended by innumerable Austrian and Bavarian royalties and lasted five hours. The Archbishop of Trent officiated, and the drums of an Austrian regiment rolled in honour of the departed monarch while guns boomed in the distance like the echoes of those at Gaeta. All the old incorruptibles, led by the knights of San Gennaro, held a memorial service in Naples: the long list of their resonant names and titles may be disinterred from their legitimist newspaper, the *Vero Guelfo*.

Maria Sophia returned to France and settled in Neuilly-sur-Seine. Though her husband had long been a walking shadow—he seemed to have been an invalid ever since she could remember—she was still addicted to life. Tall, slim, erect, she refused to become a pitiable relic of a vanished dynasty. She never pitied herself. She continued to ride every day: like her sister Elizabeth she looked magnificent on horseback, and her fine stables of race-horses and thoroughbreds were the last extravagance she was able to indulge. She desired nothing from the past and had long ceased to count on the future. The more she had known of human society, the more she admired her horses. Having renounced happiness long ago, she seemed to be content: she made the present moment satisfy her.

Age spiritualized her beauty. Distinguished novelists attempted to portray her: Alphonse Daudet in *Les rois en exil*, and Marcel Proust in *La Prisonnière*, the sixth volume of *A la recherche du temps perdu*: both paid tribute to her charm and heroic mould, yet she eluded them. She was too 'horsy', too much a creature of the open air, to harmonize with Proust's orchids, even if Charlus was the son of a Bavarian duchess. One of the few private houses she frequented in Paris was that of Baron Adolphe de Rothschild, whose father had been head of the Naples Bank, a staunch friend who would have no dealings with the usurpers. There she was still treated as a Queen, with the privilege of selecting the guests. But the future blighted her family like the characters of an Elizabethan melodrama: dreadfully one after another was destroyed—her cousin King Ludwig drowned, her sister the Duchesse d'Alençon (who had been engaged to Ludwig) burnt alive at a charity bazaar, her nephew the Crown Prince Rudolph shot at Meyerling, and her favourite sister the Empress Elizabeth murdered at Geneva. During the first world war she was driven from Paris where she had lived for forty-four years. She returned to her native Bavaria, a fugitive with a commanding air, unbowed by her many misfortunes: she was still to be seen on horseback in her late seventies. Her nephews and nieces were a solace in her old age, and they marvelled at her energy: the fire of Gaeta still flickered in her piercing eyes. Suddenly, quietly, she died in Munich in 1925. She had seen her husband's gloomy predictions verified. The Russian and Austrian empires had crumbled and collapsed, and a new clean-shaven Dictator had marched on Rome. 'His was the idealism of Mazzini,' wrote an English admirer, the historian Sir J. A. R. Marriott,[1] 'combined with the practical statesmanship of Cavour and the heroic temper of Garibaldi.' Or so it seemed to many at the time. Ironically, the first important Fascist Congress was held at Naples in 1922. The liberal Nemesis overtaking Bourbon tyranny had been overtaken by an anti-liberal Nemesis, which made the Bourbon tyrants look like gentle lambs.

[1] *The Makers of Modern Italy, Napoleon—Mussolini.* Oxford, 1931.

Genealogical Table

FRANCIS I, KING OF THE TWO SICILIES

(1777–1830), son of Ferdinand I and IV, King of the Two Sicilies and Maria Carolina, Archduchess of Austria. Married (1) Maria Clementina, Archduchess of Austria, in 1797; (2) Maria Isabella, Infanta of Spain, in 1802.

From his first marriage:

(a) *Carolina Ferdinanda Luisa* (1798–1879), who married (1) Charles-Ferdinand de Bourbon-Artois, Duc de Berry, in 1816, murdered in 1820; (2) Count Lucchesi Palli, Duca della Grazia.

From his second marriage:

(b) *Luisa Carlotta* (1804–1844), who married Francis of Paola, Infante of Spain, in 1819.

(c) *Maria Cristina* (1806–1878), who married (1) Ferdinand VII, King of Spain, in 1829, deceased in 1833; (2) Fernando Munoz, Duke of Rianzares (1810–1873).

(d) *Ferdinand II, King of the Two Sicilies*, to follow.

(e) *Charles, Prince of Capua* (1811–1862), who married Penelope Smyth in 1836 and lived in exile.

(f) *Leopold, Count of Syracuse* (1813–1860), who married Maria Vittoria Luigia Filiberta, Princess of Savoy-Carignano (1814–1874), in 1837.

(g) *Maria Antonia* (1814–1898), who married Leopold II, Grand Duke of Tuscany, in 1833.

(h) *Anthony, Count of Lecce* (1816–1843), unmarried.

(i) *Maria Amalia* (1818–1857), who married Sebastian Gabriel, Infante of Spain, in 1832.

(j) *Maria Carolina Ferdinanda* (1820–1861), who married Don Carlos VI of Spain in 1850.

(k) *Teresa Cristina Maria* (1822–1899), who married Don Pedro II, Emperor of Brazil, in 1843.

(l) *Lewis Charles Maria, Count of Aquila* (1824–1897), who married Princess Januaria of Braganza (1821–1901).

(m) *Francis, Count of Trapani* (1827–1892), who married Maria Isabella, Princess of Tuscany (1834–1901) in 1850.

FERDINAND II, KING OF THE TWO SICILIES

(1810–1859). Married (1) Maria Cristina of Savoy (1812–1836), in 1832; (2) Maria Theresa, Archduchess of Austria (1816–1867), in 1837.

From his first marriage:

(a) *Francis II, King of the Two Sicilies* (1836–1894), who married Maria Sophia, Duchess of Bavaria (1841–1925), in 1859, without posterity.

From his second marriage:

(b) *Lewis, Count of Trani* (1838–1886), who married Matilda, Princess of Bavaria, in 1861.

(c) *Albert, Count of Castrogiovanni* (1839–1844).

(d) *Alphonsus, Count of Caserta* (1841–1934), to follow.

(e) *Maria Annunziata* (1843–1871), who married Charles Salvator of Tuscany.

(f) *Gaetano, Count of Girgenti* (1846–1871), who married Maria Isabella de Bourbon (1851–1931), in 1868, without posterity.

(g) *Joseph, Count of Lucera* (1848–1851).

(h) *Maria Pia* (1849–1882), who married Robert, Duke of Parma, in 1869.

(i) *Pasquale, Count of Bari* (1852–1904), who married Blanche de Marconnay, in 1898, without posterity.

(j) *Maria Immacolata Luisa* (1855–1874), who married Henry of Bourbon-Parma, Count of Bardi, in 1873, without posterity.

(k) *Januarius, Count of Caltagirone* (1857–1867).

ALPHONSUS, COUNT OF CASERTA

(1841–1934). Married Maria Antonia (1851–1938), in 1868, daughter of the Count of Trapani (see above). Their issue: (a) Ferdinand, Duke of Calabria (1869–1960), to follow. (b) Charles of Bourbon (1870–1949), who married (1) Maria Mercedes, Princess of Asturias (1880–1904), in 1901; (2) Princess Louise of France, in 1907.

From his first marriage:

(1) *Alphonsus* (1901), who married Princess Alice of Bourbon-Parma. Issue: Theresa (1937); Charles Alphonsus (1938); Inez (1940).

(2) *Ferdinand* (1903).

(3) *Isabella* (1904), who married Count Zamoyski in 1929.

From his second marriage:

(4) *Charles de Bourbon-Orléans* (1908–1936).

(5) *Dolores de Bourbon-Orléans* (1909), who married Prince Joseph Czartoryski, in 1937.

(6) *Marie-Mercedes de Bourbon-Orléans* (1910), who married Don Juan, Count of Barcelona, in 1935.

(7) *Marie de l'Espérance* (1914), who married Prince Gaston d'Orléans-Braganza, in 1944.

(c) *François de Paul de Bourbon-Siciles* (1873–1876).

(d) *Marie-Immaculée de Bourbon-Siciles* (1874), who married George, Prince of Saxony, in 1906.

(e) *Marie-Christine de Bourbon-Siciles* (1877), who married Peter-Ferdinand, Archduke of Austria, in 1900.

(f) *Marie-Pie de Bourbon-Siciles* (1878), who married Louis, Prince d'Orléans-Braganza, in 1908.

(g) *Marie-Joséphine de Bourbon-Siciles* (1880).

(h) *Gennaro de Bourbon-Siciles* (1882–1944), who married Beatrice Bordessa, Countess of Villa-Colli, in 1922.

(i) *Renier de Bourbon-Siciles* (1883), who married Caroline, Countess Zamoyska, in 1923. Issue: (1) Carmen (1924); (2) Ferdinand (1926), who married Chantal de Chevron-Villette in 1949. Issue: Beatrice (1950).

(j) *Philippe de Bourbon-Siciles* (1885–1949), who married Marie-Louise d'Orléans in 1916 (marriage annulled); (2) Odette Labori in 1927. Issue from first marriage: Gaetano (1917), who married Miss Olivia Garrow. Issue: (1) Adrian Philip (1948); (2) Gregory Peter (1950).

(k) *François d'Assise de Bourbon-Siciles* (1888–1914).

(l) *Gabriel de Bourbon-Siciles* (1897), who married (1) Marguerite Princess Czartoryska, in 1927, (*died* 1929); (2) Cécile, Princess Lubomirska, in 1932.

From his first marriage:

(1) *Anthony* (1929).

From his second marriage:

(2) *John* (1933).

(3) *Mary Margaret* (1934).

(4) *Mary Immaculée* (1937).

(5) *Casimir* (1938).

FERDINAND PIUS MARIA, DUKE OF CALABRIA

(1869–1958), who married Mary, Princess of Bavaria (1872), in 1897. Issue:

(a) *Antoinette* (1898–1956).

(b) *Maria Cristina* (1899).

(c) *Roger, Duke of Noto* (1901–1914).

(d) *Barbara* (1902–1927), who married Francis Xavier, Count of Stolberg-Wernigerode, in 1922.

(e) *Lucia* (1908), who married Eugene, Duke of Ancona, Prince of Savoy-Genoa, in 1938.

(f) *Urraca* (1913), who married Manoel Sotomayor y Luna, Vice-President of Equador, in 1948, deceased in 1949.

Select Bibliography

Owing to the limited scope of this volume and the inordinate length of a complete bibliography, it seemed advisable to mention only the most useful and curious books consulted by the author. For the sake of brevity general histories of the Italian *Risorgimento* and the standard works of Bolton King, G.F.H. and Mrs Berkeley, Trevelyan, Cantù, Carrano, etc., have been omitted. The inclusion of manuscripts in the Neapolitan *Archivio di Stato*, such as the *Affari Esteri* files, the diary and correspondence of Francis I, the family letters of Ferdinand II (*Fascio* 762, 769, 775, etc.) which would fill several pages if detailed, and the Ludolf papers in the *Società di Storia Patria*, would serve no purpose for students outside Italy. From the Public Record Office, London, the tomes of F.O. 70/110–321 cover this entire period. Individual articles have been confined chiefly to those in the *Archivio Storico per le Province Napoletane*.

AGOSTINI, MARIO: Della insurrezione del 1847. . . . Gerace, 1884.

ALETTA, NICOLA: Gaeta (a general guide). Gaeta, 1931.

ANDREOTTI, DAVIDE: Storia dei Cosentini. 3 vols., Naples, 1874.

ANNALI CIVILI *del regno di Napoli*, especially vol. XLV. Naples.

ANNUARIO STORICO *del Regno delle Due Sicilie dal principio del governo di Ferdinando II Borbone*. Naples, 1838.

ANON: Pro Domo Mea. Discorso a posteri sulle vicende del Regno di Napoli e di Sicilia dal 7 settembre 1860 sino al 7 settembre 1863. Naples (?), 1863.

Archivio Storico per le Province Napoletane, Nuova Serie. Vol. XII: G. DORIA: La rivoluzione napoletana del 1848 nelle lettere di uno studente. Vol. XXXI: important for Naples in 1848. Vol. XXXIV: articles by G. Coniglio, W. Maturi, P. Pieri. Vol. XXXV: G. Coniglio: Note sulla politica economica di Ferdinando II di Borbone. Vols. XXXVI and XXXVIII: articles by P. Scarano on relations between Naples and Brazil (1815–60). Under imprint of *R. Deputazione Napoletana di Storia Patria*: Alla memoria di Michelangelo Schipa, 1945, contains valuable articles by N. Nicolini, W. Maturi, E. Pontieri, and R. Moscati.

ARCUNO, IRMA: Il Regno delle Due Sicilie nei rapporti con lo Stato Pontificio (1846–1850). Naples, 1933.

—— Vita d'esilio del principe di Capua. Articles in *Samnium*, Anno V (1932) and Anno VIII (1935).

ARDAU, GIUSEPPE: Carlo Pisacane. Milan, 1948.

AROMOLO, GIULIO: L'ultimo Re di Napoli. Naples, 1942.

ATTI della VII adunanza degli scienziati italiani, tenuta in Napoli dal 20 settembre al 5 ottobre 1845. Naples, 1846.

AVARNA DI GUALTIERI, C: Ruggero Settimo nel Risorgimento Siciliano. Bari, 1928.

BARBIERA, RAFFAELE: La principessa Belgioioso. Milan, 1902.

BASTIDE, JULES: La république française et l'Italie en 1848. Brussels, 1858.

BELTRANI-SCALIA, MARTINO: Rivoluzione di Sicilia. 2 vols. Rome, 1932.

BERNARDINI, NICOLA: Ferdinando II a Lecce (14–27 Gennaio 1859). Lecce, 1895.

BIANCHI, NICOMEDE: Storia documentata della diplomazia europea in Italia dall'anno 1814 all'anno 1861. Vols. III–VIII. Turin, 1869.

BIANCHINI, LUDOVICO: Storia della finanza del Regno di Napoli. Palermo, 1839.

BLANCH, LUIGI: Scritti Storici. Vol. II. Bari, 1945.

BLOIS, TEN-COL. GIOVANNI: Narrazione storica . . . del soggiorno nella Real Piazza di Gaeta del Sommo Pontefice Pio IX. Naples, 1854.

BREMER, FREDRIKA: Two years in Switzerland and Italy. 2 vols. London, 1861.

BUTTÀ, GIUSEPPE: Un viaggio di Boccadifalco a Gaeta. Naples, 1882.

Cambridge Modern History, Vols. X, XI.

CAMPO, FRANCESCO: Cenno storico sulla spedizione dei Siciliani in Calabria. Genoa, 1851.

CANTALUPO, BENEDETTO: I principi e gli effetti del sistema governativo delle Due Sicilie dal 1830 al 1848. Naples, 1850.

CAPRIN, GIULIO: L'esule fortunato Antonio Panizzi. Florence, 1945.

CARIGNANI, V. G.: Paolo Versace, la sua vita e le sue missioni. Naples, 1872.

CARRANO, FRANCESCO: Vita di Guglielmo Pepe. Turin, 1857.

CASANOVA, EUGENIO: R. Archivio di Stato di Napoli. Mostra del Risorgimento italiano nelle provincie meridionali. Naples, 1911.

—— Svolgimento dell'idea e dei fasti nazionali nella Calabria ultra I (1816–60). Rome, 1912.

CASTROMEDIANO, SIGISMONDO: Carceri e galere politiche. 2 vols. Lecce, 1895.

CAVA, TOMMASO: Difesa nazionale Napoletana. Naples, 1863.

CHAMBORD, COMTE DE: Voyage en Italie, 1839 à 1840. Paris, 1933.

CIONE, EDMONDO: Napoli romantica, 1830–1848. Milan, 1944.

—— Il Paradiso dei Diavoli. Napoli dal 400 all'800. Milan, 1949.

COGNETTI, BIAGIO: Sui fatti politico-militari della rivoluzione Sicula-Napoletana nel 1860. Naples, 1869.

—— Passato e presente nel Reame delle Due Sicilie. Brussels, 1862.

COLET, LOUISE: L'Italie des Italiens. Paris, 1864.

COLLETTA, CARLO: Tornate della Camera dei Deputati del Parlamento Napoletano. . . . Naples, 1860.

COOPER, J. FENIMORE: Excursions in Italy. 2 vols. London, 1838.

CORSI, MAGGIORE CARLO: Difesa dei soldati Napoletani. Naples, 1860.

CRAVEN, THE HON. KEPPEL: Excursions in the Abruzzi and northern provinces of Naples. 2 vols. London, 1838.

CROCE, BENEDETTO: Uomini e cose della vecchia Italia. 2 vols. Bari, 1927.

—— Storia del Regno di Napoli. Bari, 1931.

—— Varietà di storia letteraria e civile. Bari, 1949.

CURCI, PADRE: Memorie. Florence, 1891.

D'ALOE, STANISLAO: Diario del soggiorno di Pio IX in Napoli. Rome, 1850.

D'AMBROSIO, G.: Relazione della campagna militare fatta . . . negli Stati della Chiesa l'anno '49. Naples, 1852.

D'AYALA, MARIANO: Vita del re di Napoli Ferdinando II Borbone. Naples. 1860.

D'AYALA, MICHELANGELO: Memorie di Mariano D'Ayala e del suo tempo, Rome, 1886.

DE CESARE, D. GUGLIELMO: Vita della Venerabile Serva di Dio Maria Cristina di Savoia Regina delle Due Sicilie. Rome, 1863.

DE CESARE, RAFFAELE: La fine di un Regno. 3 vols. Città di Castello, 1909.

—— Una famiglia di patriotti. Rome, 1889.

—— Antonio Scialoia. Città di Castello, 1893.

DE DALMAS, ALBERT: Le roi de Naples, sa vie, ses actes, sa politique. Paris, 1851.

DE FELISSENT, G.: Il Generale Pianell e il suo tempo. Verona, 1902.

DE GUICHEN: La révolution de Juillet et l'Europe. Paris, 1917.

DE LA GORCE, P.: Histoire de la Seconde République Française. 2 vols. Paris, 1887.

DE LA VARENNE, LOUIS: Le Congrès des Deux Sicilies à Florence. Florence, 1860.

DEL GIUDICE, GIUSEPPE: Carlo Troya. Naples, 1899.

DEL POZZO, MGR.: Cronaca civile e militare. Naples, 1858.

DE NOË, VICOMTE: Trente jours à Messine en 1861. Paris, 1861.

DE SAMUELE CAGNAZZI: La mia vita (1764–1852). Milan, 1944.

DE SIVO, GIACINTO: Storia delle Due Sicilie dal 1847 al 1861. 2 vols. Trieste, 1868.

DE STERLICH, CESARE: Cronica delle Due Sicilie. Naples, 1841.

D'HERVEY SAINT-DENYS, L.: Un Roi. Paris, 1851.

D'IDEVILLE, HENRY: Journal d'un diplomate en Italie. 2 vols. Paris, 1872.

—— Les petits côtés de l'histoire. Paris, 1884.

DI GIACOMO, RENATO: Il Mezzogiorno dinanzi al Terzo Conflitto Mondiale. Bologna, 1948.

DI GIACOMO, SALVATORE: Il quarantotto. Naples, 1903.

—— Luci ed ombre Napoletane. Naples, 1914.

DI LAURO, RAFFAELE: L'assedio e la resa di Gaeta (1860–61). Caserta, 1928.

DITO, ORESTE: La rivoluzione Calabrese del '48. Catanzaro, 1895.

DOCUMENTI Storici riguardanti l'Insurrezione Calabra, preceduti dalla storia degli avvenimenti di Napoli del 15 maggio. Naples, 1849,

DORIA, GINO: La vita e il carteggio di Girolamo Ulloa. Naples, 1930.

—— Le strade di Napoli. Naples, 1943. (See also under Archivio Storico and Pietro C. Ulloa.)

DU CAMP, MAXIME: Expédition des Deux Sicilies. Paris, 1881.

—— Souvenirs Littéraires. Paris, 1892.

DUMAS, ALEXANDRE, (père): Les Garibaldiens. Paris, 1861.

—— Mémoires de Garibaldi. Paris, 1887.

DURELLI, FRANCESCO: Cenno storico di Ferdinando II, re delle due Sicilie. Naples, 1859.

ELLIOT, SIR HENRY G.: Some Revolutions and other Diplomatic Experiences. London, 1922.

FARNERARI, M.: Della monarchia di Napoli e delle sue fortune. Naples, 1876.

FAUCIGNY-LUCINGE, PRINCE DE: Dans l'ombre de l'histoire, souvenirs inédites. . . . Paris, 1951.

FAVA, FRANCESCO: Il moto Calabrese del 1847. Messina, 1906.

FILANGIERI FIESCHI RAVASCHIERI, TERESA: Il Generale Carlo Filangieri. Milan, 1902.

FINOCCHIARO, VINCENZO: La rivoluzione Siciliana del 1848–49 e la spedizione del Generale Filangieri. Catania, 1906.

FORTUNATO, GIUSTINO: Il Mezzogiorno e lo Stato italiano. 2 vols. Bari, 1911.

—— Appunti di Storia Napoletana dell'Ottocento. Bari, 1931.

FRANCI, GIOVANNI DELLI: Campagna d'autunno del 1860. Naples, 1870.

GARIBALDI, GIUSEPPE: Memorie autobiografiche. Florence, 1902.

GARNIER, CHARLES: Journal du siège de Gaëte. Brussels, 1861.

—— Le royaume des deux Siciles. Paris, 1866.

GELL, SIR W.: Reminiscences of Sir Walter Scott's residence in Italy, 1832. London, 1957.

GEMELLI, CARLO: Storia della rivoluzione Siciliana del 1848–49. Bologna, 1867.

GENOINO, ANDREA: Re, cospiratori e ministri nel processo De Mattheis (1822–30). Cava, 1933.

—— Le Sicilie al tempo di Francesco I (1777–1830). Naples, 1934.

—— Profilo del Marchese di Caccavone. Milan, 1924.

GIAMPAOLO, SALVATORE COGNETTI: Le memorie dei miei tempi. Naples, 1874.

Giornale delle due Sicilie.

GLADSTONE, W. E.: Two letters to the Earl of Aberdeen on the State Prosecutions of the Neapolitan Government. London, 1851. (These were refuted in: 'Rassegna degli errori e delle fallacie pubblicate dal Sig. Gladstone.' Naples, 1851; and 'Confutazioni alle lettere del Signor Gladstone.' Lausanne, 1851.)

GONDON, JULES: L'état des choses à Naples et en Italie. Paris, 1855.

—— Situation et affaires du Royaume de Naples. Paris and London, 1857.

GOODWIN, JOHN: Progress of the Two Sicilies under the Spanish Bourbons from the year 1734–35 to 1840. London, 1842.

GREVILLE DIARY, edited by Philip Whitwell Wilson. 2 vols. London, 1927.

GUALTERIO, F. A.: Gli ultimi rivolgimenti italiani. 4 vols. Florence, 1850.

GUARDIONE, FRANCESCO: Il dominio dei Borboni in Sicilia dal 1830 al 1861. ... 2 vols. Turin, 1907.

HALES, E. E. Y.: Pio Nono. London, 1956.

HERZEN, ALEXANDRE: Lettres de France et d'Italie (1847–52). Geneva, 1871.

HILTON, DAVID: Brigandage in South Italy. 2 vols. London, 1854.

HÜBNER, COMTE DE: Neuf ans de souvenirs d'un ambassadeur d'Autriche à Paris 1851–1859. Paris, 1904.

INSOGNA, A.: Francesco Secondo di Napoli, storia del Reame delle Due Sicilie. Naples, 1898.

LACAVA, MICHELE: Cronistoria documentata della rivoluzione in Basilicata del 1860. ... Naples, 1895.

LA CECILIA, GIOVANNI: Memorie storico-politiche dal 1820 al 1876. 4 vols. Rome, 1876–78.

LA FARINA, GIUSEPPE: Istoria documentata della Rivoluzione Siciliana del 1848–9, etc. 2 vols. Milan, 1860.

LA MASA, GIUSEPPE: Documenti sulla Rivoluzione Siciliana del 1848–9 in rapporto all'Italia. 3 vols. Turin, 1850–52.

LA PEGNA, ALBERTO: La Rivoluzione Siciliana del 1848 in alcune lettere inedite di Michele Amari. Naples, 1937.

LEAR, EDWARD: Journals of a landscape painter in Southern Calabria, etc. London, 1852.

LEOPARDI, PIER SILVESTRO: Narrazioni storiche. . . . Turin, 1856.

LIMONCELLI, MATTIA: Napoli nella pittura dell'Ottocento. Milan—Naples, 1952.

LUCARELLI, ANTONIO: Il brigantaggio politico delle Puglie dopo il 1860. Bari, 1946.

MACFARLANE, CHARLES: A Glance at Revolutionized Italy. London, 1849.

—— Neapolitan Government and Gladstone. 1851.

MACK SMITH, DENIS: Cavour and Garibaldi, 1860. Cambridge, 1954.

MALMESBURY, EARL OF: Memoirs of an ex-minister. London, 1884.

MANZI, LUIGI: I prodromi della rivoluzione del 1848 in Aquila e Reggio Calabria. Reggio, 1893.

MARALDI, COSTANZO: Documenti francesi sulla caduta del regno meridionale. Naples, 1935.

MARC-MONNIER: Garibaldi, histoire de la conquête des deux Siciles. Paris, 1861.

—— Histoire du brigandage dans l'Italie méridionale. Paris, 1862.

—— La Camorra. Paris, 1863.

MASSARI, GIUSEPPE: I casi di Napoli dal 29 Gennaio 1848 in poi. Trani, 1895.

MAYER, C. A.: Vita popolare a Napoli nell'età romantica. Transl. by Lidia Croce. Bari, 1948.

MAZADE, CHARLES DE: Le roi Ferdinand II et le Royaume des Deux Siciles. Revue des Deux Mondes, Tome XXII, August 1859.

MAZZIOTTI, MATTEO: Costabile Carducci e i moti del Cilento nel 1848. 2 vols. Rome, 1909.

—— La reazione borbonica nel Regno di Napoli. Rome, 1912.

MELVILLE, HERMAN: Journal of a visit to Europe and the Levant. Princeton, 1955.

MENCACCI, G.: Memorie documentate per la storia della rivoluzione italiana. 4 vols. Rome, 1879–91.

MENDELSSOHN BARTHOLDY, FELIX: Letters from Italy and Switzerland. London, 1870.

METTERNICH: Mémoires. Vol. VII. Paris, 1883.

MEURICOFFRE, OSCAR: Souvenirs. Privately printed. Geneva, n.d.

MEYLAN, AUGUSTE: Récit d'un simple soldat. Geneva, 1868.

MIEROSLAWSKI, LOUIS: Appendice à la relation de la campagne de Sicile en 1849. Paris, 1850.

Ministero della Guerra: L'Assedio di Gaeta e gli avvenimenti militari del 1860–1 nell'Italia Meridionale. Rome, 1926.

MOENS, W. J. C.: English Travellers and Italian Brigands. London, 1866.

MORLEY, JOHN: Life of W. E. Gladstone. London, 1903.

MOSCATI, RUGGERO: Il Regno delle Due Sicilie e l'Austria. Naples, 1937.

—— Appunti e documenti sui rapporti austro-napoletani. Bologna, 1940.

—— Ferdinando II di Borbone nei documenti diplomatici austriaci. Naples, 1947.

MOUNT-EDGCUMBE, EARL OF: Extracts from a Journal kept during the commencement of the Revolution at Palermo in the year 1848. London, 1850.

MUNDY, REAR-ADMIRAL SIR RODNEY: H.M.S. *Hannibal* at Palermo and Naples, 1859–61. London, 1863.

MUSCI, MAURO: Storia civile e militare del regno delle Due Sicilie sotto il governo di Ferdinando II dal 1830 al 1849. Naples, 1855.

—— Storia di cinque mesi del Reame delle Due Sicilie (da gennaio a maggio 1859). Naples, 1859.

MUSOLINO, BENEDETTO: La rivoluzione del 1848 nelle Calabrie. Naples, 1903.

NAPIER, LORD: Notes on modern painting at Naples. London, 1855.

NAVENNE, FERDINAND DE: Rome et le Palais Farnèse pendant les trois derniers siècles. 2 vols. Paris, 1923.

NISCO, NICCOLA: Storia del Reame di Napoli dal 1824 al 1860. Naples, n.d.

NITTI, FRANCESCO SAVERIO: Nord e Sud. Rome, 1900.

PAGANO, GIOVANNI: Storia di Ferdinando II dal 1830 al 1850. 3 vols. Naples, 1853.

PALADINO, GIUSEPPE: Il 15 maggio del 1848 a Napoli. Milan–Rome–Naples, 1921.

—— Il processo per la setta l'Unità Italiana. Florence, 1928.

PALMIERI, GIUSEPPE: Cenno storico-militare dal 1859 al 1861. Naples, 1861.

PARRY, E. JONES: The Spanish Marriages 1841–46. London, 1936.

PEPE, GUGLIELMO: Memorie. 2 vols. Paris, 1847.

—— Narrative of Scenes and Events in Italy from 1847 to 1849. 2 vols. London, 1850.

PERRENS, F. P.: Deux ans de révolution en Italie (1848–9). Paris, 1857.

PERSANO, AMMIRAGLIO C. DI: Diario privato-politico-militare. 1880.

PETRUCELLI, FERDINANDO: La rivoluzione di Napoli nel 1848. Rome, 1912.

—— della Gattina: I moribondi del Palazzo Carignano. Bari, 1913.

PIANELL, GENERALE: Memorie. Florence, 1902.

PIERANTONI, RICCARDO: Storia dei fratelli Bandiera. Milan, 1912.

PINTO, F., MARQUIS DE GIULIANO, PRINCE D'ISCHITELLA: Mémoires et Souvenirs de ma vie. Paris, 1864.

POTOCKA, COMTESSE ANNA: Voyage d'Italie (1826–1827). Paris, 1899.

PROTO, FRANCESCO, DUCA DI MADDALONI: Mozione d'inchiesta. Nice, 1861.

QUANDEL, PIETRO: Giornale della difesa di Gaeta da novembre 1860 a febbraio 1861. Rome, 1863.

QUANDEL-VIAL, LUDOVICO: Una pagina di storia. Giornale degli avvenimenti politici e militari nelle Calabrie dal 23 luglio al 6 settembre 1860. Naples, 1900.

QUARANTA, B.: Del viaggio del Re N.S. per le Puglie in occasione delle faustissime nozze di S.A.R. il Duca di Calabria con S.A.R. Maria Sofia Amalia di Baviera. Naples, 1859.

RACIOPPI, GIACOMO: Moti di Basilicata. Naples, 1867.

RAFFAELE, GIOVANNI: Rivelazioni storiche delle rivoluzioni dal 1848 al '60, Palermo, 1883.

RICCIARDI, GIUSEPPE: Memorie autografe di un ribelle. Paris, 1857.

—— Una pagina del 1848. Naples, 1873.

RITUCCI, COL. GIOSUÈ: Memoria storica dello attacco sostenuto in Velletri. Naples, 1851.

ROMANO, GIUSEPPE: Memorie di Liborio Romano. Naples, 1894.
ROMANO, SALVATORE: Il Soldato Napolitano o di Napoli a Gaeta. Naples, 1869.
ROSSELLI, NELLO: Carlo Pisacane nel Risorgimento italiano. Milan, 1957.
ROSSI, GIOVANNI GIUSEPPE: Storia dei rivolgimenti politici nelle Due Sicilie dal 1847 al 1850. 2 vols. Naples, 1850–52.
ROTONDO, M. L.: Saggio politico su la popolazione e le pubbliche contribuzioni del Regno delle Due Sicilie . . . al di qua del Faro. Naples, 1834.
RUSSO, FERDINANDO: O 'Luciano' d'o Rre. Naples, 1918.
SALZANO, ACHILLE: La Marina Borbonica. Naples, 1924.
SANSONE, ALFONSO: Cospirazione e rivolte di Francesco Bentivegna e compagni. . . . Palermo, 1891.
SANTORO, SORIA: Dei precipui rivolgimenti delle Due Sicilie nel 1848 e 1849. Naples, 1850.
SARDI: La venerabile Maria Cristina di Savoia, regina delle Due Sicilie. Rome, 1895.
SASSENAY, MARQUISE DE: Souvenirs de Naples 1854–1869. Paris, 1927.
SENIOR, N. W.: Journals kept in France and Italy. 2 vols. London, 1871.
SETTEMBRINI, LUIGI: Ricordanze della mia vita. 2 vols. Naples, 1903.
—— Scritti inediti, containing his 'Protesta del popolo delle Due Sicilie'. Naples, 1909.
SILVA, P.: La monarchia di luglio e l'Italia. Turin, 1917.
SPAVENTA, SILVIO: Dal 1848 al 1861. Edited by Benedetto Croce. Bari, 1923.
SPIRIDONE, FRANCO: Storia della rivolta del 1856 in Sicilia. . . . Rome, 1899.
STRUTT, ARTHUR J.: A pedestrian tour in Calabria and Sicily. London, 1842.
TCHIHATCHEF, P. DE: Le royaume d'Italie étudié sur les lieux mêmes. Paris, 1862.
TORRACA, FRANCESCO: Luigi Settembrini. Naples, 1877.
TORREARSA, VINCENZO FARDELLA, MARCHESE DI: Ricordi sulla Rivoluzione Siciliana del 1848–9. Palermo, 1887.
TSCHUDI, CLARA: Maria Sophia, Queen of Naples. London, 1905.
TURIELLO, PASQUALE: Dal 1848 al 1867. Naples, 1897.
ULLOA, PIETRO C.: Il regno di Francesco I, a cura di R. Moscati. Naples, 1933.
—— Un Re in Esilio. Memorie e diario inediti pubblicati con introduzione e note da Gino Doria. Bari, 1928. (This contains a bibliography of Ulloa's writings, of which the following are most instructive):
—— Coup d'œil sur la situation de la Sicile en 1847 . . . (published under the name of O'Raredon). Geneva, 1850.
—— Pensées et souvenirs sur la littérature contemporaine du royaume de Naples. 2 vols. Geneva, 1858.
—— Rivoluzione del Reame di Napoli. Naples, 1860.
—— Delle presenti condizioni del Reame delle Due Sicilie. Rome, 1862.
—— Lettres napolitaines. Rome, 1863.
—— Lettres d'un ministre émigré. Marseilles, 1870.
—— Di Carlo Filangieri nella storia de' nostri tempi. Naples, 1876.
VILLARI, RAFFAELE: Cospirazioni e rivolte. Messina, 1881.
VOCINO, MICHELE: Primati del Regno di Napoli. Naples, 1960.
WHITAKER, TINA: Sicily and England. London, 1907.
WHITEHOUSE, H. R.: Collapse of the Kingdom of Naples. New York, 1899.

WILLIS, N. P.: Pencillings by the Way. London, 1845.
WINNINGTON-INGRAM, REAR-ADMIRAL H. F.: Hearts of Oak. London, 1889.
ZAZO, ALFREDO: La politica estera del Regno delle Due Sicilie nel 1859–60. Naples, 1940.
—— Ricerche e studi storici. 3 vols. full of useful documents. Benevento, 1933; Naples, 1939, 1953.
ZINO, GIUSEPPE: Ricordi degli anni 1848 e 1849. Turin, 1859.

Index

Francis II—*cont.*
481; valedictory message and departure, 483–489; siege and departure from Gaeta, 508–521; exile in Rome, 524–532; death in Arco, 533
Francis IV, Duke of Modena, 87, 94, 161, 411, 412; Princess Beatrice of Modena, 87, 88
Francisco de Paula, Infante of Spain, 14, 15, 33
Franco-Prussian War, 530, 532
Franco-Sardinian alliance, 381, 382
Friddani, Baron Michele, 258, 277
Frosinone, 45
Fusaro, lake, 133, 342

Gaeta, xxiv, 37, 273–280, 283–289, 306, 336, 364, 410, 455, 460, 467, 474, 478–481, 486–502, 507–520, 523, 525, 527, 528, 534, 535.—Mola di, (Formia), 502, 508, 511, 520
Gaetani, Countess, 168, 169
Gaetani, Onorato, Duke of Laurenzana, 111
Gagliati, Marchese, 33, 124
Galizia, 315, 316, 374
Gallo, Mgr Filippo, 386, 387, 532
Gallotti, Antonio, 27, 29, 30
Gallotti, General, 473
Galluppi, Baron, 153
Gallwey, Consul Thomas, 357
Galt, John, 317
Gancia monastery, revolt, 426, 427
Garibaldi, Gen. Giuseppe, 252, 276, 285, 286, 288, 292, 356, 361, 369, 401, 407–411, 416–418, 426–447, 452–480, 484–505, 530, 535
Garibaldi, Mgr, 176
Garigliano, river, 77, 474, 501, 522
Garnier, Charles, 510–522
Garofalo, Marshal, 409
Gavazzi, Fr, 272
Gell, Sir William, 141–145
Genoa, 59–63, 84, 220, 254, 360–363, 369, 384, 386, 417, 430, 444, 456, 464, 501
Genoa, Duke of, 255, 257, 259, 264, 265, 279, 282
George IV, King, 99
Gerace, 182
Ghio, Colonel (later General), 365, 479
Giacchi, Finance Minister, 487
Gibraltar, 154
Gigante, Giacinto, xxii

Gioberti, Vincenzo, 131, 183, 204, 212, 258, 265, 272
Giordano, Francesco, 289
Giordano, Luca, xxiv
Girgenti, 113, 323, 437
Girgenti, Gaetano Maria, Count of, 509
Giulay, General, 385
Gladstone, W. E., xvii, xviii, xix, xxiv, 291, 295–307, 315, 319, 330, 334, 345, 352, 356, 368, 384, 416
Goodwin, Consul John, 110, 140, 141, 151, 209, 210, 279
Goyon, General, 491
Granatelli, Prince, 258, 281
Granatello, 140
Granville, Earl, 125
Gravina, palace, 241
Gregory XVI, Pope, 60, 72, 77, 161, 170
Grenoble, 35, 36
Gretna Green, 93
Greville, Charles, 154, 183, 276, 297, 332
Gropello, G. F. di, 371, 402
Gross, Colonel, 191, 194, 195, 196, 273, 274
Gualtieri, Duke of, 53, 93
Guardi, Francesco, xxii
Guerra, Camillo, 153
Guerrazzi, Francesco Domenico, 306
Guizot, François, 54, 125, 126, 154–158, 161–165, 174, 304

Harcourt, Duke of, 273
Heine, Henry, 80, 81, 222
Henri IV, King of France, 38
Hesse-Philippsthal, General Prince Louis of, 37
Hill, the Hon. William Noel, 6–11, 14, 16, 21–23, 31, 34–37, 39, 41, 42, 46, 49, 51, 53, 54, 58
Hillard, G. S., 345
Hohenlohe, Prince, 530
Holland, Lord, 299
Howells, W. D., xix
Hübner, Baron A. von, 335, 390
Hudson, Sir James, 367, 381, 420, 430, 467, 502, 503
Hunt, Mr and Mrs, murder of, 12, 13

Iervolino, Luigi, 292, 293
Imbriani, P. E., 205, 228, 230
Imperiali, Marchese Michele, 487
Infantado, Duke of, 313